CW00798183

Orchids

of Europe, North Africa and the Middle East

3rd edition
(revised and enlarged)

Pierre Delforge

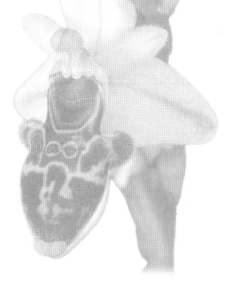

Edited by Simon Harrap

A&C Black • London

Photograph credits

The 1,270 photographs of this guide have been taken by Gérard de Bélair (Annaba, Algeria) 7, Pierre Delforge (Rhode-Saint-Genèse, Belgium) 1,003, Pierre Devillers (Brussels, Belgium) 1, Jean Devillers-Terschùren (Brussels, Belgium) 28, D.M.T. Ettlinger (Great Britain) 3, Wolfram Foelsche (Graz, Austria) 2, Alain Gévaudan (Villeurbanne, France) 6, Peter Gölz (Winterthur, Switzerland) 2, Ernst Gügel (Munich, Germany) 10, Werner Hahn (Koblenz, Germany) 2, Stefan Hertel (Haag, Germany) 11, Jean-Michel Hervouet (Chatou, France) 3, Alexandre Joukoff (Brussels, Belgium) 2, Erich Klein (Eggersdorf, Austria) 2, Einar Kongshaug (Tiller, Norway) 3, Horst Kretzschmar (Bad Hersfeld, Germany) 1, C.A.J. Kreutz (Landgraaf, Netherlands) 122, Jürgen Passin (Langenfeld, Germany) 1, Holger Perner (Geesthacht, Germany) 1, Helmut Presser (Pfünz, Germany) 3, Hans R. Reinhard (Zürich, Switzerland) 2, Jany Renz (Switzerland) 2, Karl Robatsch (Austria) 2, Dietrich Rückbrodt (Lampertheim, Germany) 18, Manfred Schönfelder (Leverkussen, Germany) 5, Kurt Seiser (Vienna, Austria) 1, László J. Szentpéteri (Debrecen, Hungary) 2, Hannelore Spaeth (Germany) 4, Walter Teschner (Velbert, Germany) 1, Daniel Tyteca (Ave-et-Auffe, Belgium) 10, E. Vimba (Riga, Latvia) 1, Jürgen Vollmar (Stukenbrock, Germany) 2, Éric Walravens (Hamois, Belgium) 2, Heinz-Werner Zaiss (Marloffstein, Germany) 4.

Watercolours, drawings and diagrams

Pierre Delforge, Eliza Klopfenstein (Brussels, Belgium), Marc Walravens (Bossut-Gottechain, Belgium).

Editor's Note

Pierre Delforge's *Guide des orchidées d'Europe* is a seminal work that is crammed with data. Such a large volume of information is hard to present in a readable form in any language, and we hope that this English translation is at least as readable as the original French. The opportunity has been taken to correct a few mistakes and to bring the taxonomy and nomenclature up to date. Notably, *Dactylorhiza longifolia* has become *D. baltica*, *Steveniella caucasica* is now *S. satyrioides*, *Himantoglossum* (x) *samariense* now *H.* (x) *montis-tauri* now *H. bolleanum*. The Glossary has been amended to better fit an English-language context and as many localities as possible have been anglicised, but it should be noted that it has not been possible to check all place names and some may remain in their French form.

I would like to thank Tony Holcombe and Tony Leech for their assistance with translation queries.

Simon Harrap, April 2006

Translated from the French by Laurent Penet and Carine Collin.

This English edition published in 2006 by A&C Black Publishers Ltd., 38 Soho Square, London W1D 3HB

Originally published in 2005 in French by Delachaux et Niestlé, Paris
© 1994, 2001, 2005 Delachaux et Niestlé, Paris.
English translation © 2006 A&C Black Publishers Ltd.

The right of Pierre Delforge to be identified as the author of this work has been asserted by him in accordance with the Copyright, Designs and Patents Act 1988

ISBN-10: 0-7136-7525-X
ISBN-13: 978-0-7136-7525-2

A CIP catalogue record for this book is available from the British Library

All rights reserved. No part of this publication may be reproduced or used in any form or by any means – photographic, electronic or mechanical, including photocopying, recording, taping or information storage and retrieval systems – without permission of the publishers.

A&C Black uses paper produced with elemental chlorine-free pulp, harvested from managed sustainable forests.

Printed and bound in Italy by Stige

www.acblack.com

10 9 8 7 6 5 4 3 2 1

Contents

Foreword to the first edition

Orchids are without doubt one of the most beautiful and dynamic successes of recent plant evolution; about one flowering plant species in twelve is an orchid. 19th century horticulturists spent fortunes bringing back large flowering species from exotic forests that were difficult to cultivate. Today, however, orchids are no longer a symbol of a person's wealth, more of a superb and endangered flora and fauna, smothered by the effects of an ever increasing human population.

Europeans have turned more and more towards indigenous species in order to study and protect them and thus try and preserve some of the natural and semi-natural areas still remaining on the ancient continent. Over the last twenty years, the study of European orchids has advanced as much as the other sciences, resulting in three times as many species being known in Europe as in 1970. It is therefore necessary to review our knowledge for the specialist, amateur and general botanist or for the conservationist who wants to make a precise inventory of an interesting habitat that could be protected.

This identification guide aims to be both as complete as possible and to be understandable by all, that is to say to present today's knowledge of species and problems without avoiding complex questions. The classification of European orchids, like that of any other family of organisms, is a science; neither finished nor fixed. Everybody, novice and professional alike, can judge the adopted classification for themselves; the characteristics used for the different species groupings are given.

A work of science is a collective undertaking. I could not have written this book without information, the exchange of ideas and much encouragement from many botanists, both amateur and professional, in Europe and the Middle East, to whom I very grateful but who are too numerous to list here. I should, however, especially like to thank my colleagues in the 'Section Orchidées d'Europe des Naturalistes Belges', with whom I have learnt much during the last 13 years. Thanks especially to the photographers who have allowed the use of rare images, often unique, often accompanied by very valuable suggestions and personal observations. The illustrations would have been far from complete without the work of Madame Eliza Klopfenstein (Brussels), who gave generously of her precious time. Finally, much thanks to Monsieur Pierre Devillers (Institut Royal des Sciences Naturelles de Belgique, Brussels), for having introduced me to modern taxonomy, with particular reference to Europe orchids, and for generously participating in numerous discussions, lectures and field outings during the preparation of this guide.

Rhode-Saint-Genèse, November 1991

Foreword to the third edition

Thirteen years after writing the first edition and four years after the second edition appeared, much has changed. A lot of work has been done on orchids with the publication of very many articles and monographs concerning European orchids, proof of the increasing interest shown in this superb family not only by field botanists, but also, and increasingly so, by geneticists and biochemists. Studying orchids by looking at their molecular composition is a new science with sometimes disconcerting first results, resulting in some important taxonomic modifications of genera; these are, however, often contradictory and may be premature. At the same time classical research has uncovered 150 new species, contested the validity of others already described and induced many minor taxonomic changes.

This third edition, rewritten and enlarged, tries again to offer the amateur naturalist and professional botanist alike, a full and synthetic cross-section of present knowledge, its coherence relying on personal experience of most of the taxa in the guide.

Rhode-Saint-Genèse, December 2004

4

Understanding orchids

Orchids in the plant kingdom

A recently evolved group

Until a few years ago, orchids were considered to be a very recently evolved family. They were thought to have appeared suddenly, their special characteristics clear-cut, in Asia (probably Malaysia) a mere 2 million years ago, as the earliest fossils definitely attributed to this group date from that time. However, the lack of orchid fossils could be due to their way of life: tropical plants grow quickly and have very little chance of being fossilised; nor have those growing on sloping or dry ground. Also, only macrofossils of orchids are known; the minute seeds rot quickly and their pollen, massed together in pollinia and transported by insects, is not scattered over wide areas as with wind-pollinated plants. Thus palynology has revealed nothing for orchids.

The recent discovery, in limestone from the upper Miocene in Germany, of a fossil that was obviously that of an orchid, with both a lip and an inferior ovary, shows that orchids have existed for at least 15 million years and at that time already occurred in Europe, which had a tropical climate. The presence of orchids as early as the Tertiary had already been suggested by botanists who thought that it was impossible for them to spread throughout the world and adapt to such a wide variety of habitats in just 2 million years. Orchids are in effect cosmopolitan; the only areas where they do not occur are true deserts and arctic regions where the soil is constantly frozen. Nevertheless, even if we place the origin of orchids some 20 to 30 million years ago, they are a recently evolved group if compared to the first Monocotyledons (100 million years), the Dicotyledons (150 million years) or the conifers (300 million years).

The systematic position of orchids

The plant kingdom is divided into branches, then sub-branches, classes, orders (suffix: - ales), families (- aceae), and genera that groups similar species. Orchids are a part of the Spermatophyte (or Phanerogammes) branch, plants that reproduce by seed (which distinguishes them from Algae, Fungi, Lichens, Mosses, Ferns...); the seeds result from fertilisation of the ovule, the female organ, by pollen tubes coming from the germination of pollen, the male cells. All Spermatophytes have stems supporting the reproductive organs. Usually the leaves perform the greater part of photosynthesis and the roots provide stability and nutritive functions but have neither leaves nor sexual reproductive organs. Within the Spermatophytes, orchids belong to the Angiosperm branch, plants with a closed ovary containing the ovules (which distinguishes them from the Gymnosperms, plants with the ovules not enclosed in an ovary, such as in the Ginkgos, Conifers, Yews...). There are some 170,000 species of Angiosperms placed in different families and orders grouped into two classes. Orchids are members of the class Monocotyledonae (monocotyledons), plants with a single embryonic seed leaf (cotyledon) at germination, and normally with simple, entire leaves, with parallel veins, and the flower parts inserted in threes (or multiples thereof). They are distinct from class Dicotyledonae (dicotyledons), which have two cotyledons, with branching or fanned veins and 5- or 4-part flowers (e.g. magnolias, aristolochias, buttercups, roses). Within the class Monocotyledonae, orchids are placed in the order Orchideae, distinguished from other orders, Grasses, Sedges, Rushes, and Woodrushes, by their flowers with obvious sepals and petals, as in some other orders within the monocotyledons, such as lilies and irises (Liliaceae, Amaryllidaceae, Iridaceae...).

Orchid anatomy

The flower

(Diagrams of flower parts are also given in the introductions to the genera *Epipactis*, *Serapias*, *Orchis* and *Orphrys*).

Orchids are probably derived from lilies. A comparison between the flower structure of lilies and that of orchids allows an understanding of the similarities that demonstrate their relationship and the derived characters that separate them. Lilies (Fig. 1) have hermaphrodite 3-part flowers, with all floral parts present in multiples of 3, and regular or actinomorphic (star-shaped) because, due to their radial symmetry their flower parts are arranged symmetrically around the flower centre. They also possess a superior ovary inserted into the pedicel at the same level as the perianth and thus visible in its centre. The perianth is composed of 6 tepals arranges in two whorls: the external whorl, the calyx, formed by three sepals, the internal, the corolla, composed of three petals. The tri-locular (3-chambered) ovary is surmounted by a style, which carries, at its tip, 3 fertile stigmas. The pollen is grouped in the anthers situated at the tip of 6 stamens, also arranged into 2 whorls.

In the orchids the 3-part structure is always present, but adaptation of the flower to pollinating insects has brought about differentiation and the reduction of 2 petals in comparison to the 3 sepals; the third petal, the

lip, carries distinctive patterns and is often used as a landing stage by insects; it is specialised and different from the two others. Finally, the sexual structures, with the exception of the ovary, are fused into a column (the gynostegium), which faces the lip. These last two transformations give the orchid flower a bilateral symmetry, with only one axis through which it can be cut to give one half of the flower as the mirror image of the other; it is termed zygomorphic.

In a final important change, the ovary, which has become uni-locular, lies below the perianth and is thus inferior. It contains a large number of minute seeds at maturity. The three sepals forming the calyx have remained rather similar, although the two lateral sepals, symmetrical relative to the flower's axis of bilateral symmetry, have a more or less irregular shape, different to that of the dorsal (or median) sepal, which lies on the axis of the gynostegium. Of the 6 stamens found in lilies, just 3 remain, only 1 of which is fertile, the other 2 persisting only in the form of staminodes, fused into the wall of the stigma cavity and sometimes only detectable as two small coloured patches, the staminodal points. The single fertile stamen has two loculi placed near the tip of the gynostegium, each protecting 1 or 2 pollinia (never more in Europe) constituted of pollen grains assembled in tetrads which are in turn grouped

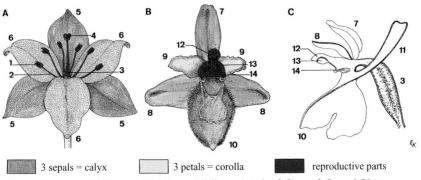

3 sepals = calyx   3 petals = corolla   reproductive parts

Figure 1. Comparison of Liliaceae and Orchidaceae. **A.** Liliaceae. **1.** Anther. **2.** Stamen. **3.** Ovary. **4.** Stigma. **5.** Sepal. **6.** Petal. **B.** Orchidaceae (*Ophrys splendida*). **C.** Longitudinal section through an *Orchis* flower. **7.** Dorsal sepal. **8.** Lateral sepal. **9.** Petal. **10.** Labellum. **11.** Spur. **12.** Gynostegium. **13.** Pollinia. **14.** Stigmatic surface.

into pollen masses sometimes lengthened by a stalk, the caudicle.

The 3 stigma of lilies are still present; 2 remain fertile and are usually fused into a single sticky stigmatic surface; the third (in orchids, the median), is generally transformed into the rostellum, a more or less well developed structure placed between the stigmic surface and the pollinia that prevents self-fertilisation. The tip of the rostellum is normally covered with a sticky substance, contained within 1 or 2 visidia in those species that have pollinia with caudicles, which sticks the pollinia to the pollinating insect's body. The rostellum is sometimes elongated into 1 or 2 bursicles, pouchlike membranes that cover the viscidia and preventing them from drying out.

Among the orchids, the families Apostasiaceae and Cypripediaceae (see Systematic arrangement of European orchids p.31) show an intermediate evolutionary stage between lilies and orchids. The former still have 3 fertile stamens, 3 petals and 3 sepals that are similar, and pollen not gathered together into pollinia. The latter family, represented in Europe by the Lady's-slipper *Cypripedium calceolus*, still has two fertile lateral stamens and granular, sticky pollen not formed into pollinia. Certain degenerate forms of orchids may regress towards a flower structure similar to that of the Aspostasiaceae, for example, *Limodorum abortivum* var. *trabutianum*. If the lip is pointing upwards it is less visible to flying insects and obliges them to settle on it upside-down, head and body facing downwards. It is very likely that mutant plants, in which the lip, turned downwards and more detectable from above, offered a more appropriate landing stage for the insect's weight and have thus been heavily selected by pollinating insects. Most European orchids thus have the lip towards the bottom of the open flower, whereas it is found at the top of a flower in bud; this 180° rotation of the flower, termed resupination, takes place as the bud opens via the twisting of the flower stalk or of the entire ovary if stalkless, sometimes via the whole flower turning (*Liparis, Serapias…*). A few species, however, have their lips turned upwards the top, either because there is no rotation (*Epipogium*), or by a 360° twisting of the ovary (*Malaxis*).

Underground parts

With the exception of 2 genera representing the sub-tribe Liparinae (*Liparis* and *Malaxis*), which can be considered to be epiphytes, all the orchids in Europe are geophytes. Their underground parts comprise various forms of root; roots proper, normally in the form of slender, cylindrical, unbranched filaments, whitish or brownish, an underground stoloniferous stem or a rhizome producing aerial stems, or root-tubers (tuberous roots), organs for storing food that allow the growth of a new plant, but which are not true tubers and certainly not bulbs, albeit that these terms are in common use. In the Liparinae, the food store organ is a pseudobulb, formed by a swelling of the stem.

In European orchids with a very short rhizome or without tubers, the roots arising from the rhizome can be a dense, tangled ball resembling a bird's nest (*Neottia nidus-avis*) or swollen and club-shaped (*Limodorum*); the rhizome can be decorated as in a piece of coral (*Corallorhiza, Epipoguin*). In species with root-tubers, the roots are always placed at its tip. Root-tubers are varied: complete and ovoid (*Orchis, Ophrys*), palmate (*Coeloglossum*, many *Dactylorhiza*), flattened and long-digitate (*Gymnadenia*) or spindle-shaped (many *Platanthera*). There are generally 2 tubers on each plant at flowering time; however, certain species have 3 or more, often attached to the stem by a long underground stalk (*Orchis champagneuxii, Serapias lingua, Ophrys bombyliflora*). Between the roots and aerial parts, there is normally a long underground stem, the neck, covered in whitish, brownish, or sometimes purplish scale-leaves.

Aerial parts

As in most monocotyledons, the stems of European orchids are never branched; they are nearly always erect, more or less circular in section, rarely angular, solid or hollow, hairless or hairy.

The leaves are like those of other monocotyledons, complete, never composite or divided, with parallel longitudinal veins, sometimes with transverse secondary veins forming a visible network (*Goodyera*).

In most of the saprophytic orchids the

leaves, performing no function, have been reduced to scales or a sheath. When the leaves are developed, they may be clustered at the base of the stem in a basal rosette (as in most *Ophrys*) or spaced out along the stem, in which case they can be arranged in a spiral (spirally), in two opposite ranks inserted at the same level (opposite), or alternately at different levels (alternate); the upper cauline leaves can be very small, resembling bracts. In some genera there are only a few leaves, sometimes only two (*Platanthera, Gennaria*) or even just one (*Malaxis, Calypso*).

The inflorescence is often a spike (flowers stalkless) or a raceme (flowers stalked); rarely it comprises a solitary flower (*Cypripedium, Calypso*). The inflorescence can be dense, near lax or lax, often becoming laxer as flowering proceeds. The shape for the inflorescence is variable: cylindrical, conical (*Anacamptis*), ovoid, spiral (*Spiranthes*), unilateral (some *Epipactis*).

Flowers always have bracts, small leaves inserted into the axis of the inflorescence, at the base of the pedicel or ovary; these may be green or coloured as the sepals (*Serapias*), large and leaf-like (*Dactylorhiza, Epipactis*), or reduced to membranous scales (most *Orchis*). Floral characters, very varied, are given in the text describing the genera and species.

The life of orchids

The adaptive strategy of orchids may be judged from their origin and floral characteristics. Evolving relatively recently, they emerged into an environment of animals and plants that was already very diverse with, notably, numerous potential insect pollinators. The aggregation of orchid pollen into heavy pollinia makes carriage by an animal, nearly always an insect, essential, which permits a concomitant specialisation of the lip. In order that pollination leads to effective cross fertilisation, it is not only necessary that the insect carries off the flower's pollinia but also that these are rather quickly deposited onto another flower from a plant of the same species, evidently a complex and infrequent process. From this it follows that the pollination mechanisms must be precise in order that the rare successive visits are to result in fertilisation; on the other hand, this problem is somewhat alleviated by the production of a large number of seeds at each fertilisation. This necessitates the production of small seeds, extremely small in orchids, so much so that they totally lack the food reserves normally present in monocotyledon seeds in order for them to germinate. This last fact has lead to a complex germination mechanism, with the intervention of endophytic fungi and the establishment of symbiosis (a mycorrhiza), an unpredictable process, often aborted and thus accentuating the need of a very large number of seeds to assure the species' survival. Darwin, and Linnaeus before him, had already noted that if all the seeds from a single *Dactylorhiza maculata* germinated as well as those of their descendants, the worlds' surface would be covered by *D. maculata* within 4 generations.

Germination

(Characteristics given in this and following sections concern European orchids.)

Orchid seeds are minute, about 0.5 mm in length and weighing about 10µg (micrograms). They are probably the smallest Monocotyledon seeds; in comparison, rice or wheat seeds are enormous. They comprise a fine, reticulated membrane covering a hardly differentiated, spherical embryo.

In a pollinated flower, when the capsule is mature it splits open to liberate thousands of seeds which are carried by the slightest breeze. Most of these will not germinate, either because they have an abnormality and are not viable, because they are consumed by other organisms or because they fall on habitats where the conditions are unsuitable. Those that end their journey on suitable terrain must, in order to germinate, be invaded by microscopic fungi, the Hyphomycetes, often of the genus

Figure 2. Seed of *Orchis lactea* × 92.
(after LUCKE)

Rhizoctonia, or Deuteromycetes, rarely the Basidiomycetes, living in the soil on roots in the form of a mycelium.

The fungus penetrates the seed and infects the embryo. If it invades the embryo completely, it would destroy it; orchid seeds contain fungicides that appear to confine infection to a portion of the embryo, the other part developing rapidly, mainly by taking sugars produced by the fungus. Thus a symbiosis is initiated, here called a mycorrhiza, beneficial to both partners and lasting for a long time, for example, in *Cypripedium calceolus*, probably the time necessary to form the plantlet. Saprophytic orchids remain dependent on their host for their entire life but in most adult orchids the endophyte's presence is apparently limited to the peripheral zone of the roots.

The invaded embryo is transformed; a small tuber, the protocorm, forms, containing the outline of a plantlet at the base of which adventitious roots form. The young plant straightens and elongates vertically, like a minute asparagus covered with scale-leaves that, on emerging from the soil, become very small green leaves normally arranged in a rosette. Underground, the protocorm becomes a root-tuber and enlarges in species with a root-tuber and elongates in those with a rhizome. Two to 15 years pass between germination and production of the first flower, depending on species and soil conditions.

Annual cycle

All orchids are perennial, capable of living many years and flowering each year if conditions are favourable. They often appear above ground only briefly, flowering and fruiting in a few weeks and then disappearing; most of their life cycle takes place underground (see Fig.3, p.10).

Lifestyle

Ecology

As they have significant food reserves, most European orchids can colonise nutrient-poor soils where competition with other plants, which they tolerate poorly, is reduced. Their relatively early flowering and sometimes brief appearance above ground often allows them to flower and fruit before the remainder of the vegetation is at a maximum. They are therefore, for the most part, favoured by cutting of meadows and summer grazing, and are well-adapted to the stress of dry Mediterranean summers and the fires that sometimes accompany them. Some orchids, with an aerial life of less than 45 days, have established themselves on mountains above the tree-line or in boreal regions. As soon as conditions are unfavourable, following several poor years or the vegetation closing due to recolonisation by trees, the underground parts can persist for a long time, sometimes without producing leaves. For this reason, the felling of a stand of trees or a fire on a maquis can result, in the spring, in the reappearance in open areas of orchids that denser and denser shade kept in a vegetative state underground.

Due to their slow growth, complex germination and symbiotic life style, orchids generally require stable, sometimes climax, conditions (mature beechwood, peat bog…). Traditional pastoral farming practices in Europe over the last few thousand years have considerably extended and stabilised favourable orchid habitats (chalk grasslands, heaths, garrigue, hay meadows…). Agricultural intensification has had a negative effect on these habitats and is very unfavourable for orchids.

Growth

Most European orchids are autotrophic; with green leaves, they manufacture nutrients from soil minerals via their own photosynthesis but, for many, probably also use their mycorrhiza. A few are mycoheterotrophic, feeding on decomposing organic substances [editor's note; mycoheterotrophes acquire nutrients from fungi, which in turn acquire them from the decomposition of organic matter or from other living plants.]; in this situation, considered a further evolutionary step, the radicular system alone is required, the leaves, now unnecessary,

9

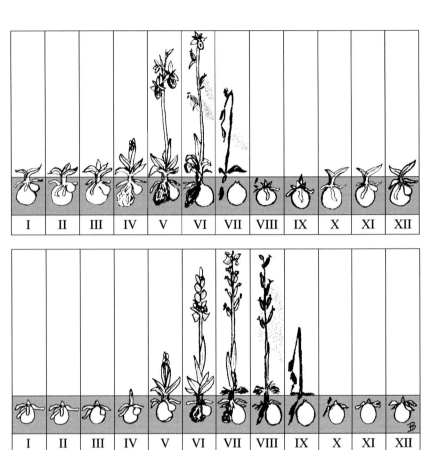

Figure 3. Diagram of the annual cycles of Early Spider orchid *Ophrys sphegodes* (top) and Green-winged orchid *Orchis morio* (bottom) seen at 850 metres altitude in the Vercors (Ga, Isère, France). Each square represents the situation at the start of the month, given in roman numerals. In the *Ophrys*, a small rosette of leaves pushes out of the ground as early as October and is visible all winter, frost often blackens these first leaves. The second tuber starts to develop in November but does not start swelling until April, when the floral spike grows feeding on the over-wintering tuber. The plant is in full flower in May; the second tuber is now almost the size of the first which, now emptied of nutritive substances, crumples. In June seeding is nearly completed, only a single discoloured flower remains on the top of the floral spike; the leaves brown, the winter tuber is exhausted, shrivelled; the second tuber, whitish, full of nutrients is at its maximum size; on the spike, seeds are freed from the capsules. In July, the floral spike browns, dries and collapses; the winter tuber is absorbed and disappears, the second tuber inclines upwards; in August a new plant forms at its summit. The Green-winged Orchid has a similar cycle but the winter tuber, at its maximum size in August, emits a new plant bud that does not emerge until April; the plant stays invisible for 6 or 7 months. Orchids with a rhizome have a similar cycle.

can be reduced, an advantage as the plant needs less energy for growth. A few saprophytic species are totally devoid of chloro-phyll (*Epipogium, Neottia nidus-avis*) whilst others retain a little (*Limodorum, Corallorhiza*). Certain autotrophic species occasionally lack chlorophyll, subsisting on decomposed material by using an apparently very virile mycorrhyzal system. This way of functioning, termed hemi-saprophytism, is sometimes found in *Cephalanthera* and *Epipactis* (see also p.24).

There do not appear to be any truly parasitic orchids in this account. Nonetheless, the *Limidorum* are suspected of parasitissing trees as their very deep roots have sometimes been found intimately attached to tree roots. However, the biology of the genus is poorly known and parasitism has not been established (see p.108).

Vegetative Reproduction

Like many higher plants, orchids have other means of reproducing than their seeds. Root-tuber production during flowering is an excellent means of maintaining a plant. A trauma or freezing of the meristem may promote the appearance of a group of genetically identical plants (clones). Species normally having more than 2 root-tubers (*Serapias lingua, Orchis champagneuxii, Ophrys bombyliflora...*) and those with rhizomes (*Cyprideum, Cephalanthera, Epipactis, Epipogium...*) can produce several identical shoots each year. The supplementary root-tuber is generally attached to the mother plant by a rather long stalk, or the rhizome elongates; these species can form large groups, even a mat, of similar plants, in which the individuals appear to move a little from one year to the next. Orchids with a stolon (*Goodyera repens, Dactylorhiza iberica*) can obviously form similar groups. Lastly, *Malaxis paludosa* has yet another means of dissemination; sometimes, from the tips of its leaves, it produces tiny bulbils, each of which is capable of forming a new plant.

Sexual reproduction in orchids

Most orchid species are adapted to cross fertilisation by complex and precise processes which compensate for the small number of visits by pollinating insects. There are few pollination mechanisms, but a great variety of means of attracting pollinators, sometimes spectacular. As orchid flowers are hermaphrodite, the shortage or complete absence of pollinators is sometimes compensated for, in certain species, by regular self-pollination, sometimes within the floral bud (cleistogamy). Cases of apomixis have also been discovered.

The mechanism of fertilisation

The agglomeration of pollen into pollinia is only an evolutionary advantage if they are fixed securely to the insect that carries them and which, subsequently, can pollinate many flowers with a single pair of pollinia. Apart from *Cypriedium calceolus* and certain species that have evolved towards regular self-pollination, all orchids in the region possess a sticky substance secreted by a modified sterile stigma, the rostellum, contained in one or two glands, the viscidia, which lie at the base of the caudicle in those species with stalked pollinia (sub-family Orchidoideae) or at the tip of the rostellum in those that have unstalked pollinia (all other European orchids). In the first case the visiting insect, brushing against the base of the pollinia, comes into contact with the viscidia which immediately stick firmly to it and the insect's movements in trying to free itself releases the pollinia. In species with bursicles (the Serapiadinae), the initial shock causes the protective membranes to rupture. In species with unstalked pollinia (e.g. the entomogamous *Epipactis*), the insect's contact with the viscidia causes the rupture of the membrane containing the sticky substance which, projected onto the tip of the pollinia, attaches them to the insect.

In both mechaisms, it is so important that the

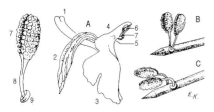

Figure 4. Removal of the pollinia. **A**. Flower of *Orchis mascula*. **1**. Spur. **2**. Ovary. **3**. Lip. **4**. Column. **5**. Stigmatic cavity. **6**. Loculus. **7**. Pollinia. **8**. Caudicle. **9**. Bursicle. **B**. Position of pollinia at moment of removal. **C**. After a short while, the caudicles dry out and rotate the pollinia into a horizontal position.

(After Darwin)

insect is of the correct size that many orchids are only fertilised by a few species of pollinator, even just one, to which they are adapted, other visitors playing no part as pollen carriers due to their inappropriate morphology. In species with unstalked pollinia, the position of the stigmatic surface permits the deposition of pollen when the insect visits other flowers. In the *Serapiadinae*, the presence of a caudicle raises the pollinia away from the stigma. Once out of the loculi, the caudicles dry out and bend forward, bringing the pollinia to a horizontal position, level with the stigma surface (Fig. 4). As this process can take several minutes, it favours cross-fertilisation. Effectively, whilst the caudicles are erect, visiting insects removing the pollinia cannot pollinate that same flower, or any flowers on the same inflorescence visited immediately afterwards, as the caudicles do not usually dry until after the insect has left the inflorescence.

Once the pollinia is placed in contact with a flower's stigma, part of the pollen remains on the sticky stigmatic surface when the pollinating insect departs. Each pollen grain has two nuclei; the larger one allows its germination on the stigma's surface whilst the second divides into 2 sperm nuclei. The germination of a pollen grain leads to the emergence of a very fine pollen tube which penetrates the style and finds the ovule.

The ovule consists of an embryo sack containing 8 nuclei derived from the splitting of the initial diploid megasore mother-cell. One of those nuclei fuses with one of the pollen grain's 2 sperm nuclei. In most monocotyle-

dons, the other 7 nuclei form a single secondary cell that, after fusion with the pollen grain's second sperm nucleus, gives rise to the seed's food reserve, the endosperm. In orchids, this secondary cell degenerates. Fertilisation rapidly provokes ovule maturation, this it turn bringing about swelling of the ovary. The flower withers straight away, whereas without fertilisation it can stay fresh for a long time.

Methods of attracting insects

(A detailed analysis of the ways of attracting insects is given in the pollination chapter for each genus.)

Insect-fertilised orchids attract their pollinators in 3 different ways; offering food to the pollinator, deceiving them or trapping them. In Europe, only *Cypripedium calceolus* traps visitors in its shoe-shaped lip without killing them; all other species have visual or olfactory deceits or offer nutritive substances to the insects.

Food providers

As in all plants, orchids attract phytophagous insects that can eat any part of the plant. These insects are very rarely responsible for cross-pollination. The lack of specificity in such a means of attraction cannot not guarantee the species' survival and can even occasionally result in hybridisation. Certain species have clearly visible nectar with an accompanying strong scent (*Gymnadenia, Anacamptis*, some *Orchis, Platanthera*...); other species produce an abundance of nectar without a marked scent (*Neottia, Coeloglossum*, many *Epipactis*...). Also, all orchids have a sticky stigmatic surface that helps retain dry pollen from the pollinia. This glue, composed of amino-acids and sugars, is regularly consumed by a variety of insects. In certain orchids without nectar that attract pollinators by deceit (many *Dactylorhiza* and *Orchis*), this stigmatic excretion reinforces the deceit, considerably increasing the pollination rate of the species. It is been calculated that *Orchis collina* functions in this way, acting as a food provider for 75% of visits, the other 25% of visitors having been deceived. Bumblebees of the genus *Bombus*, some accomplished robbers, can easily obtain the excretion, even from the floral bud; for them these orchids are excellent food providers.

In some cases, enzymes present in the nectar or in the stigmatic excretion can promote fermentation and apparently feeding insects can become intoxicated with alchohol. The advantage of this peculiarity is explained in various ways; defence against phytophagous insect attack, or an increase in the number of visits by alcoholic pollinators which, due to their intoxication, stay near to the population of orchids, increasing the chances of cross-pollination.

Visual deceits
Many orchid species, like many other higher plants, do not produce nectar and only emit a slight scent. If foraging insects are attracted, it is because they have been deceived by the flowers, which have the appearance of a nectar producing species, similar to the labiates or legumes, with a landing area (the lip), a calyx or tubular corolla (replaced by the spur), and coloured markings that normally lead to nectar (the spots and streaks on the lip). *Dactylorhiza sambucina* and *Orchis mascula* are good examples of this type of deceit, mimicking the flower of a typical nectar-bearing plant. Sometimes the deceit is elaborated by papillae and hairy tufts on the lip that appear to excite the pollinator's sugar-detecting tactile bristles, either on their feet (*Orchis usulata*), or abdomen (eg. *O. militaris*). The flower may also have yellow structures, more or less granular or hairy, that look like pollen: such 'pseudo-pollen' is formed on the parallel ridges of the epichile in the genus *Cephalanthera*, and by a tuft of yellow hairs at the entrance to the hypochile in *Calypso bulbosa*.

Often it appears that a particular nectar providing plant is imitated. Sometimes this is based on a general similarity, such as *Orchis israelitica* (the mimic) imitating a lily, *Bellevalia flexuosa* (the model), or *Orchis pallens* imitating Spring Pea *Lathyrus vernus* (see also p.327). In other cases, the model is simply copied by a few signals, important to the insects, such as *Cephalanthera longifolia* mimicking the Sage-leaved Cistus *Cistus*

Fertlised ovary of *Ophrys spruneri* in the process of ripening; the wilted perianth is visible at the top of the ovary. **Photo A**: Gr, Messinia, 21.IV.1991. P. DELFORGE. Dried spike of *Gymnadenia conopsea* with open capsules and valves (slits). **Photo B**: Be, Namur, 14.IX.1990. P. DELFORGE.

salvifolius, although this resemblance is not obvious to the human eye.

Dependence on mimicry imposes a certain number of constraints on biology and distribution: the mimic must grow alongside its model and thus have the same ecological and climatic requirements; it should also start flowering a little before the model and flower for a long time. The insects' repeated visits to various examples of the model, interspersed with a few visits to the mimic, will only result in its pollination if the pollinia are securely fixed and are not removed during its numerous visits to the model.

Sometimes, the mimic rewards its visitors a little with pseudopollen or excretions from the stigmatic surface; it can then be pollinated, albeit infrequently, in the absence of its model (facultative floral mimicry). Less constrained by its mimicry, it can occupy habitats and even regions where the model is absent.

Another form of visual lure occurs where the flower imitates a hole or nest where the insects come for refuge during bad weather or to shelter from low temperatures during the night. This is the main lure used by the genus *Serapias* and occurs in some *Orchis* species with a hood (*O. papilionacea* and *O. morio*).

Sexual deceits

It is probable that certain olfactory signals are more important than visual ones for insects. It appears that certain orchids emit scents which resemble the pheromones produced by female hymenoptera and used to mark flyways, find certain plants or mark nest entrances. These pheromones can induce pre-copulatory behaviour in males where females are present. *Orchis papilionacea* often appears to be used as a marker by a solitary bee, maybe because its scent resembles the insect's pheromones, a hypothesis that is, however, contested. This has, however, been proven for *Orchis galilaea* and *O. punctulata*.

It is in the genus *Ophrys* that sexual lures are most highly developed, as their flowers produce olfactory and visual imitations of some female Hymenoptera, resulting in the males attempting to copulate with the lip (pseudocopulation). This highly advanced and extraordinary mimicry also exists in *Serapias lingua*, in which the lip's basal callus resembles the female's body; and in certain Australian and South American genera.

Evolution of modes of attraction

The strategy of providing rewards of food by orchids requires a significant input of energy but produces, on average, a high rate of fertilisation; e.g. some 90% of ovaries in *Orchis fragrans* produce seed. However, due to their morphology or size many insects are not effective pollinators. On the other hand, the presence of nectar or other food sources encourages insects to visit several flowers on the same stem, resulting in self-pollination, such that nectar-providing species are often less variable than those that deceive pollinators; *O. fragrans* shows little variation compared to, for example, *Dactylorhiza maculata*.

Although species that use deceits use less energy, as they do not produce nectar, this method produces a lower rate of pollination, compensated for by the large number of seeds in orchids and by the greater number of cross-fertilisations that deceits produce as the pollinating insect, disappointed, generally only visits a single flower on a flower head.

In orchids that mimic plants offering a reward of food, the correlation with the model means that the orchid is visited almost solely by the model's pollinators, which may explain why syntopic orchids that flower at the same time rarely hybridise, despite their potential inter-fertility. Also, geographical variations of the model are selected by pollinators, which brings about the same in the mimic.

The efficiency of a floral deceit, whether sexual or food, depends directly on the pollinator's experience and capacity to learn. The pollinator's naivety is essential for effective pollination of flowers that cheat. Once the pollinator has learnt the nature of the deceit, it no longer visits those flowers. It is therefore necessary that there be few mimics in proportion to the number of models to assure the deceit's success by reducing the rate of learning; dense populations of flowers that cheat have a greatly reduced rate of fertilisation compared to those that are dispersed and low in numbers. It is probable that a certain variability in colour and the absence of scent lengthens the pollinators' learning period in the case of food mimics; however, this rule appears to have many exceptions.

The switch from a plant offering a reward of nectar to one offering no reward, merely a deceit, is not a problem for evolutionary theory.

Male hymenopterans generally emerge earlier than the females and the first stage in the evolution towards a sexual lure probably consists of attracting only males by using one of the plant's scents, some of which, contained in the lip's cuticle, are chemically identical to the pheromones of female bees. Each mutation that makes the flower's cocktail of scents more similar to the pheromones increases the chance of pollination. *Orchis galilaea*, which attracts male *Halictus* spp. without pseudo-copulation occurring is probably at this evolutionary stage. The next stage pushes flowers that mimic nectar-bearing flowers closer and closer to sexual mimics due to the selective pressure of the pollinators choosing the scents emitted by the flower, and subsequently the similarity of the shape and hairiness of the flower are easily explained. The great complexity of sexual lures and great variety of potential pollinators explains the immense radiation of the genus *Ophrys*.

The adaptive strategy of mimicry cannot be considered a co-evolution of between mimic and model or between flower and its pollinator. It is, in effect, a unilateral adaptation of mimicry within the environmental possibilities and constitutes rather parasitism, either of food-providing flowers for which mimicry has no advantage, or of the breeding behaviour of Hymenoptera in the case of sexual lures.

Autogamy and cleistogamy

The low availability of pollinators, due to an often complex mode of attraction, unfavourable weather conditions or establishment in a habitat unfavourable to the insects, can favour in an orchid population mutant individuals that have an inefficient or withering viscidium and at the same time a stigmatic surface more or less inclined towards the anther. This morphology may result in self-pollination, which can occur with the slightest breeze shaking the plant. Regular autogamy in such mutant individuals simultaneously increases their numbers and isolates them; it may be the basis of a speciation event, as seems to have happened in *Epipactis*, for example. Autogamy releases the orchid from its dependence on pollinators and allows it to colonise and remain in habitats with few flying insects: areas at high altitude or latitude, windswept areas, dense woodland with little light. It also offers the possibility of economies in attracting pollinators, e.g. in nectar production.

Saving even more energy, cleistogamy represents a supplementary stage, as self-pollination takes place in the closed floral bud, sometimes meaning the flower does not even need to open. It can also allow a species to completely overcome severe climatic conditions, and certain saprophytic species (*Epipogium, Neottia, Limodorum*) can grow, flower and fruit completely underground in an unfavourable year, and the seeds escaping from the mature pods can germinate as they are immediately invaded by the saprophytic fungus of the mother plant.

In the genus *Orphrys* autogamy is rare, and only regular in *O. apifera*. In this species the caudicles, which are particularly long, dry out a few hours after the flower opens and, contracting, extract the pollinia from their loculi and dangle them in front of the stigmatic cavity. In a dry year or on windy days autogamy can sometimes occur in other species of *Ophrys*.

Apomixis

Certain higher plants can produce seed without the ovules having been fertilised. When apomixis, which is not sexual reproduction, is regular in a species it has the same effects as autogamy; isolation from other taxa and the possibility of colonising areas without the presence of pollinating insects. Apomixis seems to be regular in some of the *Nigritella* orchids, and may be occasional in others, without this having been clearly proven at the moment.

Orchid classification
Systematics

The characters that naturalists believe to be revealing about real affinities between two or several species are those inherited from a common ancestor, all true classification being genealogical...

DARWIN, *On the Origin of Species.*

The complexity of the species concept

Classifying living organisms is a difficult undertaking, based on an accumulation of facts and much that is unknown. Life is ancient; many species have disappeared and we did not witness the birth of those we see around us and that are still evolving. Classifcation, that is to say the study of the diversity of life in order to understand the relationship between organisms, is a scientific discipline only if the evidence on which hypotheses are based can be examined and tested by other researchers and if the operational concepts for systematics are clearly defined, especially when their basis influences the proposed classification.

Most publications on European orchids do not define the species concept on which they are based. And, moreover, they often still use old-fashioned essentialist or taxonomic concepts which implicitly assume that species are units of convenience, applied by man to nature but without a real existence. These systematics do not take into account biological relationships between living organisms; they treat them as objects to be classified arbitrarily, by size or even alphabetical order, which can be justified neither as being objective nor as scientific.

The *biological* definition of a species is a group of organisms that are potentially capable of breeding among themselves but are reproductively isolated from other groups. This definition, undoubtedly more objective than former ones, poses several problems. It can only be tested for sympatric species, not for geographically isolated ones; it does not give a series of operations allowing a species to be identified as such, and further, when applied to plants in which there is no courtship or sexual behaviour, it does not allow for the separation of cryptic species, biologically separated but difficult to distinguish by ordinary means. Also, it cannot be applied to self-pollinated species, where the demonstration of reproductive isolation is impossible, nor to plants that produce numerous fertile hybrids, as so often occurs in orchids.

These difficulties can be avoided if the evolutionary history (phylogenesis) of a species is considered. Indeed, life has only one origin and the observed discontinuities result from speciation events due to the splitting of evolutionary branches. The relationships linking living and extinct organisms are phylogenetic relationships existing between individuals, populations, species and higher taxa. All other relationships, for example genetic or phenotypic, are phenomena correlated with genealogy and thus better understood in a phylogenetic context. An evolving species has a simple ancestry, with its own evolutionary tendencies and its own historical destiny. This definition implies a vertical view of evolution, completely different from the horizontal view of classical biological and taxonomic concepts, but it gives no clear guideline allowing the identification of a lineage and, thus, a species. No other more or less recent species concept (notably phylogenetic, autapomorphic, or the possibility of genealogical diagnosis using genetic similarities) is satisfactory in this respect. A field-friendly species concept for groups of organisms that everybody recognises is probably an inaccessible ideal.

The best classification necessary and sufficient for understanding evolution is still, however, that which covers true phylogenetic relationships between organisms; these past events being unique, there is only one phylogenetic tree that conforms to the natural history of organisms.

The evolutionary process often appears to be gradual; that of speciation can be long and is not yet complete in many cases. Also, the geographical distribution of closely related groups can appear to have a mosaic of haphazardly interconnected characters. For these reasons it is sometimes difficult to define precise species limits, whatever concept is used. In addition, for any species concept, the number of defined species depends on the level of differentiation used by the taxonomist. The level is arbitrary. If a high threshold of differentiation is applied there will be few species with large inter-specific variation (polytypic species); using a low threshold there will be many species, with all visibly different taxa becoming species. Thus, even studies based on traditional taxonomics have given quite different results, largely dependent on the philosophy, often implicit, of the taxonomist.

Another pitfall awaiting the taxonomist is the application of the tools that allow analyses and taxonomic decision-making. The last few years has seen the eruption, in the study of orchids, of chemical, enzyme, molecular and genetic approaches. Each one of these new investigative techniques, the results of which are not always repeatable, provides interesting information that is, however, often contradictory. Moreover, each specialist has a tendency to give weight to the results of his own technique, sometimes to the point where they discredit the study of morphological characters and arrive at a classification based on a single technique; this is best avoided.

Systematics is thus, as in any science, a work in perpetual progress, using several hypotheses to arrive at provisional conclusions, especially nowadays when investigative techniques are evolving rapidly.

The systematics used in this guide

A phylogenetic approach to systematics has been chosen here. Information provided by recent technical advances has been taken into account where results are in agreement. The classification used in the first edition has been maintained, even though many changes, often contradictory, have been published in recent years, even for higher taxonomic ranks. In many genera, lumping or splitting has taken place.

Species are sometimes grouped into subgroups, groups, complexes (an informal category), according to their supposed phylogenetic affinities; the formal category section has sometimes been used. These groupings have been proposed based on phylogenetic systematics and are discussed in a cladistic framework.

Within a species, there may be groups that are not biologically isolated, that may differ in minor morphological details and, sometimes, have a more or less well defined geographic distribution; they are considered as varieties (var.) here, often with their own description. Individuals or groups with more vague limits and ecotypes are sometimes treated as variants (an informal category, equivalent here to the formal rank of form (f.).

Many authors also use the additional rank of subspecies (subsp.). In zoology, this rank is currently precisely defined within the biological species concept and a trinomial name applied. This is not the case in botany, where the subspecies usually supports a morphological species concept. It is, therefore, useless in the understanding of evolutionary relationships, even less so as its formal use often masks them. For these reasons, the subspecies is used less and less by modern taxonomists and is not used here.

Nomenclature

The scientific name

Each individual belongs to a basic group, the species. This, in turn, is part of several taxa arranged in a hierarchy, from the top; kingdom, phylum or division, class, order (suffix; -ales), family (-aceae), sub-family (-oideae), tribe (-eae) and genus. Carl von Linné (1707-1778) proposed naming all living organisms with two words, a generic name and a descriptive adjective, both in Latin. The scientific name, a combination of the two, is attached to a type specimen or sample, preserved in a museum or private collection.

The Linnéan system was slowly adopted but can obviously only function if the same organism is given a unique name and, conversely, that the particular combination of names does not designate 2 or more obviously different organisms. Numerous homonyms and synonyms having been published, scientists got together in 1867 to devise a procedure whereby the correct scientific name of a taxon could be established. The International Code of Botanical Nomenclature (ICBN), revised every 4 years by an international commission, registers the scientific names of plants, excluding cultivated varieties.

Any name published in contradiction with these rules is a nomen illegitimum (nom.illeg.) and is of no value.

Problems of nomenclature

The Nomenclatural Code obviously tries to stabilise and eliminate problems by allowing only one possible combination for a plant at each level. Unfortunately, this ideal has not been attained and nomenclature upheavals, annoying for specialist and amateur alike, remain frequent as long as certain problems remain unsolved. Results from nomenclatural research are not always decisive. Cases without definitive solutions are unfortunately numerous amongst orchids, notably for *Ophrys fuciflora* or *O. holoseric(e)a*, *O. speculum* or *O. ciliate*

(or *O. vernixia*) and also *Dactylorhiza latifolia*, which has been named over the last 50 years, *D. incamata*, *D. majalis* or *D. sambucina*.

Nomenclatural solutions adopted in this guide

The names of orchids used here are obviously the correct scientific names, conforming to the ICBN. In controversial cases, Article 9 in the Preamble to the ICBN has been scrupulously followed. Often neglected in the present race for nomenclatural organisation, it states that 'in the absence of a rule or in doubt, the established use prevails'. Where necessary, nomenclatural uncertainties are indicated in the descriptive text.

Identifying orchids

Looking for orchids

In the multiple forms of plants, European orchids can be quite easily differentiated, by those looking for them, by a unique group of characters. They are ground living plants, herbaceous, upright, always having undivided leaves with parallel veins, an upright stem, with an bunched or spiked florescence, more rarely a single flower; a close look at the flowers shows, in orchids, an inferior ovary, bilateral symmetry, a 3-part structure, in 2 whorls, that with the 3 sepals that are generally the same, and that of 3 petals of which one, the lip, differs from the other two often spectacularly; lastly the male and female

reproductive organs are inserted in a column, the gynosteme. No other Euro-mediterranean plant combines all these features. The broomrapes may sometimes resemble saprophytic orchids, but their flowers have a superior ovary and 4 stamens; the *Lamiacae* (dead-nettles) with bilaterally symmetric flowers with a lip may resemble orchids, but do not have a gynosteme or undivided leaves with parallel veins and have a superior ovary. Once an orchid has been definitely found among other plants it only rests to determine the genus and species.

How to use the descriptions

Region covered by the guide

The region concerned here is demarcated naturally to the north and west by oceans, to the south by the Sahara Desert and to the east by the Urals, the Caspian Sea, the Caucasus and the Iranian and Arabian deserts. It covers the whole of the Western Palearctic, to the west to the Atlantic Islands (Azores, Canaries,

Madeira) and Iceland, to the south the sub-Saharan and Mediterranean parts of the countries of the Maghreb, to the east the Sinai peninsula, Jordan, Syria, Asian Turkey (Anatolia), the transcaspian region (Georgia, Armenia and Azerbaijan), and to the north Scandinavia, Poland, Belarus and European Russia.

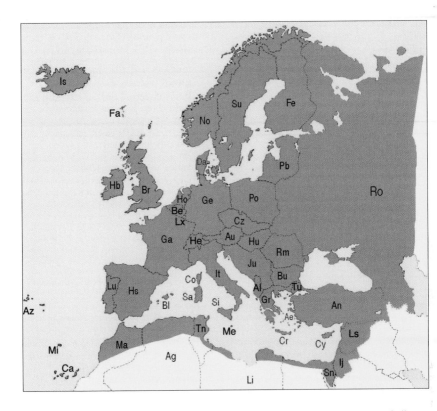

Country abbreviations

The area covered by this guide has been divided into 'territories' or 'countries' (groups of countries, country, large region, archipelago, large island) designated by a two-letter abbreviation based on the Latin name of the concerned area, a system used particularly in *Flora Europaea*. A few changes have been made: that part of the former USSR, according to the 1990 boundaries, that is not entirely covered by this guide, has been given the designation 'Ro', without any distinction of the different floral zones; the Baltic states and the Kaliningrad region are designated 'Pb', the Grand Duchy of Luxembourg by 'Lx'.

?: presence doubtful

†: extinct

? †: probably extinct

Ae: Eastern Aegean archipelago, excluding Astypalea, north to Lesbos

Ag: Algeria

Al: Albania

An: Anatolia (Asian Turkey)

Au: Austria and Liechtenstein

Az: Azores

Be: Belgium

Bl: Balearics

Br: Great Britain, excluding the Channel Islands

Bu: Bulgaria

Ca: Canary Islands

Co: Corsica

Cr: Crete, Karpathos, Kasos and Gavdhos

Cy: Cyprus

Cz: Czechoslovakia (1990 frontiers)

Da: Denmark

Fa: Faroe Islands

Fe: Finland
Ga: France, including the Channel Islands
Ge: Germany
Gr: Greece (without Ae or Cr)
Hb: Ireland
He: Switzerland
Ho: Holland
Hs: Spain and Andorra (without Bl or Ca)
Hu: Hungary
Ij: Israel and Jordan
Is: Iceland
It: Italy
Ju: former Yugoslavia
Li: Libya
Ls: Lebanon and Syria
Lu: Portugal (without Az or Mi)
Lx: Luxembourg
Ma: Morocco
Me: Malta
Mi: Madeira
No: Norway
Pb: Baltic states (Estonia, Latvia, Lithuania and Kaliningrad)
Po: Poland
Rm: Romania
Ro: Russia (former USSR but without Pb)
Sa: Sardinia
Si: Sicily
Sn: Sinai peninsula
Su: Sweden
Tn: Tunisia
Tu: European Turkey with Imroz

Signs, symbols and Latin abbreviations used in the text

◊: see, or refer to.

×: placed in front of a genus name indicates a hybrid genus (nothogenus), in front of the specific name an occaisional hybrid with the rank of species or nothospecies.

∅: diameter.

>: more than.

<: less than.

?: in front of a name or abbreviation indicates that which follows is doubtful.

2n: the diploid number of chromosomes.

asl: above sea level.

auct. (auctorum): of various authors.

auct. non: followed by the author(s) name, indicates a name used by some botanists to designate a plant that does not correspond to the type to which the name was given.

cf. (confere): placed between the generic and specific names, indicates that the plant is temporarily attached to the given species, for want of a better solution.

et al. (et alia): and others; in a bibliographical reference or after a scientific name, replaces the names of co-authors, except the first, if there are more than two.

f. (forma): form.

isonym. (isonymus): superfluous synonym, identical to an already published name.

loc. typ. (locus typicus): the location where the type specimen, to which the taxon description was attached, was collected.

nom. cons. (nomen conservandum): conserved name. In order that strict application of nomenclatural rules, particularly the concept of priority, does not uselessly disrupt nomenclature, family, genus or species names can be conserved with agreement from the general committee of the International Code of Botanical Nomenclature (ICBN).

nom. cons. prop. (nomen conservandum propositum): name proposed for conservation.

nom. illeg., nom. inval. (nomen illegitimum invalidum): an illegitimate or invalid name that does not conform with the International Code of Botanical Nomenclature (ICBN).

nom. nud. (nomen nudum): an invalid name, published without an accompanying description (in Latin) or a reference to a type specimen.

nsubsp. (notho-subspecies): occasional hybrid with subspecies rank.

p.p. (pro parte): in part; placed after a taxon name, indicates that only part of the originally accepted concept is used.

pro hybr. (pro hybrido): indicates that the taxon was described as an occasional hybrid.

sensu: in the sense of; used in conjunction with a name authors have used to refer to different taxa. Example: *Orchis latifolia* L. sensu PUGSLEY refers to *Dactylorhiza incarnata*, sensu Soó refers to *D. majalis*, sensu H. BAUMANN & KÜNKELE refers to *D. sambucina*.

sp. species.

subsp. subspecies

var. (varietas): variety.

vel: or, either …or.

20

Using the keys

This book is a field guide, produced with conservation in mind, and the keys have been produced for use in the field, without the need to take samples, damage or uproot any plant. It can be tempting to try and identify unknown taxa by using the illustrations only. This method can give good results if the identification is corroborated by comparing all of the plant's characteristics with those given in the description. It is, however, prudent to start by using one of the keys; firstly, if necessary, those to the genera, and then those to the groups and species.

The keys are based on two easily observed and opposite characters, whilst avoiding (very much with conservation in mind) the need to examine below-ground structures. Keys are placed as near as possible to the species concerned. For difficult groups several characters are used and, especially in such cases, identification should be based on not one but on several vigorous and healthy plants; the characters indicated in the key being those in the centre of specific variation, reflecting the average in a large population. Identification using a key should therefore, most importantly, be confirmed by the presence in the identified specimens of all the characters given in the description in the text, in which the whole range of normal variation is taken into account.

Using the descriptions

Names

Orchids: Only legitimate scientific names have been used for genera, species and varieties. Most species included here have only been described recently and do not have a vernacular name; they can only be identified using their scientific name. The etymology of the scientific name is given in a separate paragraph.

Author's names: Generally authors names have not been abbreviated, except for a few well known exceptions, LINNÉ (L.), DE CANDOLLE (DC.), MARSCHALL VON BIEBERSTEIN (M.-BIEB.), sometimes also REICHENBACH (RCHB.).

Genus descriptions

1. Etymology.

2. Characteristics. Diagnostic features for genera are given starting with the underground structures and ending with details of the sexual parts of the flower and chromosome number, and including the stem, leaves and inflorescence. These features are not always repeated in the species descriptions and it is therefore useful to memorise them whilst making identifications.

3. Discussion. The number of species in the genus, its distribution and number of species in the guide are given first, followed by a rough phylogenetic reconstruction of the genus to better understand its relationships and presentation. Difficulties that may be encountered in making identifications are explained.

4. Hypochromy. For important genera, an example of hypochromy is illustrated.

5. Pollination. The pollination mechanisms in the genus are explained and illustrated or sometimes, if they are special, described in the species accounts.

6. Hybrids. Interspecific hybrids are illustrated in the genus introduction for the larger genera.

The group descriptions

The presentation of groups is similar to that of the genera but without the paragraphs on 'Diagnostic features' or the 'Discussion'; the latter is often placed at the end of one of the species accounts within the group.

Species descriptions

The species account comprises 4, sometimes 5 sections:

1. Identification section (Etymology, Type, Synonyms or Basionym),

2. Descriptive section (Description and Variability),

3. Ecology section (Flowering and Habitat)

4. Distribution section (Distribution, Countries and Photos) and, sometimes,

5. Supplementary section, 'Note(s)', 'Discussion' or 'Variation'.

The Identification section is sometimes preceded by or contains remarks in cases of important nomenclatural difficulties.

1. Type. The origin of the type specimen and year of description for the species are given. If the specific name is derived from a combination (author's name in parentheses, followed by the author of the combination), this information concerns the basionym. An asterisk (*) indicates that the type is imprecise, lacking or lost; information given in this case concern the lectotype or the neotype.

Synonym(s) or **Basionym.** Only the most common synonyms are given, with eventually the basionym; there is rarely a complete list of synonyms.

2. Description. The species is described taking into account special features given in the introductions to the genus and group. Characters used in the keys are mentioned in the description. This describes the whole plant, then the stem, the leaves and the inflorescence (although part of the inflorescence, the bracts, are described beforehand, just after the cauline leaves, to facilitate comparison). Then there is a description of the whole flower, preferably not one from the tip of the inflorescence, where they are often hardly characteristic, followed by the sepals, petals, lip, column, ovary and finally the chromosome number. The degree of variation in coloration and size is given (the rare extremes in parentheses, to avoid confusion during identification).

Variation. This section underlines particular features in the range of variation and the characters allowing separation from closely allied taxa. Important variants (an informal category) are described briefly, their name given in bold italics and placed between square brackets [*variant*]; where they exist, a legitimate name for them is given in the synonym section.

3. Flowering Season. Months are given in roman numerals. Months given between brackets represent extreme flowering times, possible either in an exceptional year or, in widely distributed species, for plants from the most southernly latitudes and/or growing at low altitudes (early flowering) or the most northerly and/or high altitude (late flowering).

Habitat. Here other ecological information is assembled. 1. Requirements for light: *full sun* (heliophile species of open, grassy habitats, unable to exist in closed habitats except in a poor condition, without flowering or seeding), *mid shade* (photophile species finding optimum conditions on woodland edges, near hedges…) or *shade* (sciaphile species in closed habitats). 2. Soils: substrate pH (acid, neutral or alkaline), sometimes its composition (limestone, siliceous, dolomitic, sandy…). 3. Moisture requirements (dry, moist, damp, wet). Those unfussy species that can adapt to a variety of habitats are qualified as indifferent. The types of habitat where a species can be found are listed simply by reference to the vegetative formation (grassland, meadows, marshes, garrigue, scrub, open woodland, mixed forest…); the citation of phytosociological alliances to characterise habitats is beyond the scope of this guide. With the goal of being concise and simple, *garrigue* is used to describe all low, open, bushy (sub) Mediterranean formations, regardless of region or substrate; likewise, *scrub* is used to describe mid European thicket as much as Mediterranean maquis or pseudo-maquis at altitude. In cases where a species is strictly restricted to a precise habitat type, details of the vegetation type of the habitat are sometimes given. Lastly, the habitat section ends with the species' altitudinal distribution, expressed in metres above sea level (asl).

4. Distribution. For species of limited distribution the range is given precisely. For wide-ranging species it is briefly outlined, indicating to which species formation it belongs (circum-boreal, euro-Siberian, Mediterranean, Atlantic, Caucasian…). The geographical limits of its distribution are then given; within the region considered, indications are given as to relative distribution (widespread, rather widespread, rather local, local, very local) and its abundance where it occurs (abundant, rather abundant, rather rare, rare, very rare); these are not always easy to use, a species can be widespread and abundant in part of its distribution, very rare and local in another, or a population can be numerous one year but not the next; it does however allow an understanding that, within the relatively small population sizes of orchids, certain species are rarer than others.

Countries. The territories or countries are listed (in abbreviated form) where the species has been recorded.

Photos. This section indicates the origins of the photos (territory or country, province or district, canton, nomos, wilaya, vilajet…) as originally written (examples: Viotia and not Béotie; Siracusa and not Syracuse), the date it was taken and photographer's name.

5. Note(s). Supplementary characteristics; life style, pollination mechanism, specific name of the pollinator are given here.

Discussion. Notes on issues regarding the taxon's taxonomy, giving current hypotheses, the validity of the rank adopted here, relationship with other species…

Descriptions of varieties

Noteworthy varieties are described using the same structure as the species accounts.

Aberrant orchids

Colour abnormalities

Many European orchids are purplish or crimson. The anthocyanins, pigments responsible for the colour, are controlled genetically and appear also to be influenced by external factors: mainly the amount of light and acidity of the substrate. The normal range in a population of *Dactylorhiza maculata*, for example, varies from very pale flowers to plants with very dark, heavily marked flowers; in *Orchis morio*, these variations can affect the sepals, the lip and the dark markings separately, increasing the number of possible variations. *O. palustris* and *O. mascula* normally have a large majority of violet or purple plants with a few that are pale pink. These colour variations sometimes appear to be related to distribution: *Anacampis pyramidalis* is, on average, paler in the Mediterranean area, darker in more temperate areas, and redder at altitude in the Alps.

Albinism

A plant can be totally lacking in pigment and thus also in chlorophyll. These individuals, the only ones that are true albinos, are necessarily saprophytic and entirely white or translucent. Rare in the few orchid species normally without chlorophyll, such as *Epipogium aphyllum* or *Neottia nidus-avis*, albinism has only been reported exceptionally in some *Cephalanthera* and *Epipactis*. It can be due to a particularly virulent action by the endophytic fungi, the symbiotic partner.

Hypochromy

Rarely, for similar reasons, in some *Epipactis* the chlorophyll pigments are blocked whilst those of the anthocyanins, responsible for the purplish colouration, are not. These individuals are more or less completely pale violet, leaves included. Relatively frequent, but nonetheless very rare, in *E. purpurata*, this spectacular phenomenon has also been recorded in *E. helleborine* (photo A p.24) and *E. atrorubens*. These plants are often described, wrongly, as being 'chlorotic'. They are not particularly viable and often die early.

Other, not so rare, anomalies can greatly inhibit the influence of anthocyanins, even completely block them. In the latter case, the hypochromtic plant is devoid of both red and blue pigments, and their absence allows the normally masked anthoxanthins and chlorophyll pigments to show through: the leaves have no spots, the flowers are pure white, yellowish or greenish and the pollinia yellow. All orchids that normally have anthocyanins can, exceptionally, produce hypochromatic individuals. They are a little more frequent in regularly self-pollinating species. Hypochromy can affect the flower partially (photo C) or totally (see section on hypochromy in the introductions to the genera *Epipactis, Dactylorhiza, Serapias, Orchis* and *Ophrys*); it is occasionally limited to just part of the lip (photo B).

Hyperchromy

An abnormally high level of anthocyanins is very infrequent. It has been recorded mostly in species of *Orchis* and *Dactylorhiza* in which the perianth segments are almost completely invaded by broad, intensely coloured blotches, often red or purple, leaving only a narrow paler margin (photo A).

Although they have no evolutionary significance, the more spectacular colour abnormalities have sometimes been named as varieties or forms, *alba, albiflora, atrifusca, nivea, purpurea, viridis, virescens...*

Anomalies of shape

Genetic anomalies

As in all living organisms, orchids can be affected by genetic alterations giving rise to monstrous individuals, sometimes termed *lusus*. These abnormalities affect principally the inflorescence and can leave the inexperienced botanist perplexed and give rise to false identifications. So it is best to be aware that an

Epipactis helleborine totally lacking chlorophyll. **Photo A**: Be, Bruxelles, 11.VII.1997. *Ophrys passionis* displaying complete hypochromy on part of the lip. **Photo B**: Ga, Hérault, 20.V.1983. *O. fuciflora* displaying partial hypochromy over the whole flower. **Photo C**: Ga, Isère, 31.V.1981. P. DELFORGE.

inflorescence can be formed solely from bracts or that each of the perianth segments can be missing, deformed, stuck to one of its neighbours or doubled, which is normally not too puzzling (photos B-C).

Anomalies can affect homeotic genes, that is to say genes that control important differentiations, that of the lip for example. In certain cases, this genetic irregularity can produce petals with a lip-like shape or, on the contrary, erase the differentiation of the lip from the other two petals. Sometimes, it is the whole suite of genes that determine the morphological difference of orchids from the Liliaceae that are affected; the sepals are thus analogous to the petals and the flower recovers the radial symmetry of a lily due to the tripling of the column (see photo on following page).

If the lip is not differentiated, the keys become non-functional and identification very difficult; in those species where the lip normally has a spur its absence can be most puzzling and can sometimes even cause doubt that the plant is an orchid at all because the lip lacks the morphology of the family. This anomaly is generally exceptional, except in a few regularly self-pollinating species in which it is so regular as to have been named; this is the case with *Limodorum abortivum* var. *trabutianum* and *Epipactis phyllanthes* var. *degenera* and var. *phyllanthes*.

Acquired anomalies

Anomalies of form can be caused by external factors. If they affect the inflorescence, they only affect one or a few flowers in a season, unlike genetic anomalies that affect all flowers and occur every year. Orchids that grow alongside roads or cultivated areas can sometimes be affected by the use of products that may modify the leaves' or flowers' growth. Parasite attack can produce strange forms, as can the trampling of a young shoot or a late frost that can greatly affect tissue differentiation in the floral bud.

Orchis italica hyperchromatic, (= var. *purpurea*). **Photo A**: Si, Siracusa, 7.IV.1987. *Ophrys tarentina* with lip-like petals. **Photo B**: It, Taranto, 4.IV.1986. *O. fuciflora* with 2 lips. **Photo C**: Ga, Aisne, 10.V.1981. P. DELFORGE.

As can be seen, possible confusion due to anomalies of form are not rare. Orchids are difficult enough to identify and it is better, especially for the beginner, to concentrate on healthy, vigorous, flowering plants.

Hybrids

Hybrids are much commoner in higher plants than in higher animals and are often fertile. Orchids are well known for the ease with which they hybridise and horticulturists have created more than 200,000 cultivated varieties, sometimes by crossing as many as 5 different genera and 20 species to produce one hybrid. Species of *Ophrys, Serapias* and *Dactylorhiza* quite often produce inter-specific hybrids in the wild. Some European orchids sometimes form natural hybrids between species of different genera (inter-generic hybrids). When hybrids are sterile, they remain isolated and occasional; when they are fertile and mix with one or both of the parent species, and the pollinators are not different, hybrids can hybridise amongst themselves and with the parents and create hybrid swarms or hybridogenous populations. In both cases, identification is more difficult and the keys may lead to a dead end or to an obviously incorrect determination.

Occasional hybrids

Looking through a large colony of orchids often results in the discovery of hybrids, aberrant plants but without anomalies, in which the characters correspond to none of the species descriptions.

Before deciding that a plant which defies attempts at identification is a hybrid, it is advisable to eliminate all possibilities within the limits of normal variation in a species, especially an unfamiliar one, as well as anomalies of colour or form. Then, it is better not to concen-

Ophrys ceto with sepaloid petals and radial symmetry. **Photo A**: Ae, Rhodes, 12.IV.1984. × *Dactylodenia* GARAY & SWEET. **Photo B**: *Gymnadenia frivaldii* × *Dactylorhiza cordigera* = × *Dactylodenia illyrica* (JAHN & KÜMPEL) P. DELFORGE. Gr, Kastoria, 16.VI.1990. × *Orchidactylorhiza* SOÓ & SUMMERHAYES. **Photo C**: *Dactylorhiza insularis* × *Orchis mascula* [= × *Orchidactylorhiza atacina* (P. DELFORGE) P. DELFORGE]. Ga, Aude (holotype), 8.VI.1988. P. DELFORGE.

26

trate on an apparently aberrant character, but on a number of characters that for the most part are intermediate between those of the two parent species. Hybridisation can produce new characters, however, for example large size (hybrid vigour). It is therefore important to look at all characters and, once it is thought that the parents have been identified, verify that most of the observed aberrations can be attributed to the influence of one or other of the parents.

Generally, occasional hybrids are uncommon and flower amongst large numbers of the two parents. It may be that only one of the parents is present or even that both are absent if the hybrid is less demanding than its parents and thus able to flower in an otherwise unfavourable year. This is, however, exceptional; when both presumed parents appear to be absent in the near vicinity of the supposed hybrid, great care should be taken in the identification.

Hybridogenous populations

The situation where the number of hybrids exceeds that of the parents and where there are different levels of hybridisation is, without doubt, the most awkward. It is frequent amongst *Dactylorhiza* and *Serapias* species, rarer in *Ophrys* and *Orchis*. In such a colony separation of hybrids from those that are not is subjective and, instead of identifying samples of the parent stock judged to be 'pure', the observer has to be satisfied with noting a hybrid swarm. Trying to identify the species with precision often involves arbitrary decisions if there are not observations over several years and at different times in the season. The identification may need to be confirmed using genetic analyses.

Intergeneric hybrids or nothogenera

There are more than forty inter-generic combinations amongst European orchids. Most are very rare and many are doubtful, especially those between well separated genera that have only been observed once and for which there is no detailed description or reliable iconography. Moreover, the number of nothogenera has been severely reduced by the lumping of genera, e.g. *Nigritella* with *Gymnadenia* so that × *Gymnigritella* becomes *Gymnadenia*. Three intergeneric hybrids are illustrated here (below and photos B-C on the preceding page).

× *Orchiserapias* E.G. Camus. **Photo:** *Serapias apulica* × *Orchis picta* (= × *Orchiserapias ducoroniae* P. Delforge). It, Brindisi (holotype), 30.III.1986. P. Delforge.

Orchid conservation

Plants in danger

Despite there cosmopolitan distribution and great adaptability, orchids, like all wildlife, are suffering from the severe reduction and sometimes total disappearance of their habitats. In Europe, man followed the receding ice sheets northwards in the post-glacial warming. Early farming practices, omnipresent but slow and extensive, influenced the appearance of new habitats and contributed to their diversification. The destruction of natural habitats was compensated by the appearance of new, substitute semi-natural habitats, often favourable to herbaceous plants. The maintenance of these semi-natural habitats depended on man's activities: extensive grazing, transhumance, grazing marginal land and forest, cutting hay, harvesting reeds….

An increasing population, urbanisation, industrialisation, communications development and increasing leisure and tourist activities have, within a century, greatly and rapidly increased man's impact on the landscape. Agricultural mechanisation, the increase in productivity through the massive use of fertilisers and the establishment of productive forestry have caused habitats to become more uniform and reduced diversity. Wetlands are a good example: ecosystems abounding with very specialised life forms have been drained, 'improved', made 'productive', and used for crops. Those few marshes that have escaped destruction often suffer from eutrophication due to the water being contaminated with fertilisers from areas of intensive agriculture.

The recent agricultural revolution has happened far faster than the capacity of orchids to adapt to the changes. Furthermore, it has often left them in too small an area, with populations that are too small, for them to respond effectively even to climate change. Also, orchids, most of which are confined to oligotrophic habitats, have been shown to be especially susceptible to modifications in the substrate, notably those due to nutrient-rich rain, carrying nitrates from intensive stock rearing. Parallel to this, agricultural decline in some areas, coupled with the loss of many traditional rural activities, has meant that many of the remaining semi-natural habitats have slowly disappeared due to spontaneous recolonisation by trees, without these changes restoring diversity to the habitat. To these general causes of the decline of all wildlife, including orchids, in areas of natural and semi-natural habitats in Europe and the Mediterranean can be added specific causes. These are due to the activities of walkers, 'scientists', photographers, horticulturists and gastronomes.

Compared to the massive destruction of natural areas brought about by our industrial society, the picking of a handful of flowers may appear insignificant; this practice is, however, a cause of decline for some species. Forestry and tourist activities have opened up woodlands and mountains to the public; the fashion for off-road vehicles, 4x4s, mountain bikes, quad bikes… has allowed many tracks to be used and allowed access to often remarkable and fragile wild places for a great number of people, transforming them into areas for leisure or sports activities, answering to city-dwellers' whims. Often, picking the prettiest flowers in the area is part of the enjoyment and some rare plants, even those legally protected, suffer as a result. The fantastic Lady's-slipper *Cypripedium calceolus*, for example, picked for many a year and sometimes sold in markets as a cut flower, has completely disappeared from several areas where its habitat has not declined and where it would survive if left to do so by the public. Many *Orchis* and *Dactylorhiza* species with attractive colours suffer from this ignorant practice; an unremarkable bunch of flowers, quickly picked, quickly thrown away.

Other reasons for taking orchids in the wild are of even more concern as they are by experts. A botanical collection may, for the scientist, appear a necessity. Unfortunately it is often a mere alibi for hiding a maniacal desire to collect, especially rife where rare plants are concerned and sometimes prejudicial to their survival. Many sites have been consciously emptied of their rare plants by 'scientists' wanting to complete their collection or, sometimes by a group of students misguided by a naïve botany professor that still insists that the students produce the traditional and unavoidable herbarium during their course. Photographers for whom getting the photo is more important than the plants wellbeing may also contribute to a reduction at endangered sites. Finding a plant in unsuitable conditions, they may transplant it into better light or even taking it back to a hotel room for photographing the plant at ease; if the plant is only in bud, some do not hesitate in transplanting the specimen for latter photography at home, once the flower opens.

Among other threats for orchids, that of the horticulturist can be very important. Increasing a garden collection of specimens from the wild is, in some countries, a continuing tradition. Some amateur gardeners, governed by their passion, do not hesitate in taking protected species, even from reserves. Thus transplanted in a flower-pot or rockery, most orchids will gradually wilt if not in their natural habitat or without their symbiotic partner, thus making the gardener take another specimen from the wild. Professional horticulturists, aware of this market, do not hesitate in including European orchids in their catalogues. They legalise the commerce of these often protected species by stating that they have been cultivated from seed, which is often incorrect. The cultivation of European orchids is still in the experimental, laboratory stage, as most are terrestrial with a symbiotic way of life more complex than that of their epiphytic tropical relatives; traders then often collect vast numbers from the wild, with better results and more economic gain, than trying to produce them. As the price depends on the rarity of the offered specimen, this commerce often endangers the rarer species in some areas. The most important threat to Mediterranean orchids is, however, the culinary use of their tubers. Once often used in Europe and the eastern Mediterranean as an aphrodisiac, tonic or expectorant, the tubers of *Serapiadinae*, especially those that are swollen with starch, which are the very tubers that assure that the plants grow the following season. Still harvested in Turkey, they are dried and made into powder and, under the name of salep, are used in cream desserts and milky drinks that they thicken and add a perfume to.

The tubers are harvested whilst the plants are in flower, by peasants, who dry and con-

fection them, then sold to buyers who pass them on to wholesalers who, in their turn distribute to traders who export the product to neighbouring countries. These activities are very lucrative at each stage of the process, which makes the finding of a substitute product for salep somewhat difficult although probably easy to conceive and produce. The increase in the human population has increased the demand and the number of harvesters, who in 'good' years help to produce 45 tons of salep. As between 1,000 and 4,000 tubers are need to produce 1 kg of salep, it is easy to understand that the pressure put on the orchid populations has become too great and that rare species, such as *Himantoglossum comperianum*, are, in Anatolia, on the edge of extinction. In any case, it is now nearly only possible to find the species in cemeteries, where their harvest is considered to be fatal.

The survival of many of Europe's orchid species depends then, in the short or medium term, on protective measures coupled with a change of attitude.

Possible actions

Threats to European orchids arise, as we have seen, either from an irresponsible attitude of the individual, or economic and social practices that are harmful to wildlife in general. On the personal level, the code of conduct of the orchid enthusiast is formed of obvious rules: reduce to a minimum trampling at a visited site, only take, when absolutely necessary, the smallest possible sample, forget the herbarium, cause as little impact as possible on the surrounding habitat when photographing, in no case consider transplanting and anticipate that all orchid species will be protected, everywhere, respect the rules of any reserve that is visited and, obviously, do not buy any European orchids. Whilst talking to others, an orchid enthusiast concerned with conservation should be careful when asked about exact locations of orchid sites, all the more so if publishing information.

But, above all, orchid protection must be a collective aim. An amateur will quickly feel the need to become a member of a society or club, where they will find published information, aid in identification, technical help, maybe excursions and conservation actions. Many societies have been created exclusively for European orchids and to promote their protection; the basis of their work necessarily means the collecting of data. In centralising their members' observations they produce inventories, atlases, databases, all necessary for pinpointing and determining necessary actions. The fact that many orchid-favourable habitats are semi-natural, and that modern agriculture has abandoned practices for maintaining them, orchid protection often implies site management, either in imitating past agricultural practices, or by re-establishing otherwise perturbed natural cycles. Encouraging members to observe a site regularly, societies acquire a specialised knowledge that allows them not only to adjust and correct reserve management, but in an encouraging recent development, effectively advise forestry service management, those who decide on the management of roadside verges, military sites etc. where the conciliation of their own requirements with the area's potential for nature conservation is more and more common.

Lastly, by alliance with other specialised conservation groups, orchid societies, within more general groups, can make the public aware of the need for nature conservation, and help to ensure its integration into the laws voted by parliaments and policies of politicians. Often, the known and published presence of orchids in threatened habitats arouses public awareness and facilitates decisions in the creation of reserves and protection. And, orchids are excellent bio-indicators, due to their quick reaction to environmental change. Observations in changes in their population can reveal environmental changes. As we have seen, interest in European orchids is becoming organised and initiatives are being taken. Everyone, amateur and professional alike, will find their own pleasure and beneficial occupation. Maybe the present guide will help.

Species accounts

Systematic arrangement of European orchids

Kingdom: Plantae.

Division: Spermatophyta.

Sub-division: Angiosperms.

Class: Monocotylydonae (or Liliopsida).

Order: Orchidales (Orchids *sensu latto*): 1-2(-3) fertile stamens, fused, to varying degrees, with the stigma and style into a single column, ovary inferior containing a large number of seeds without an endosperm. A cosmopolitan order with 3 distinct evolutionary lines, usually treated as sub-families but increasingly considered to be 3 distinct families, the option taken here.

Family I. *Apostasiaceae*: (2-)3 fertile stamens; sepals and petals similar, lip non-differentiated, pollen powdery, not massed into pollenia. 2(-3) genera and c.15 species (South-east Asia, northern Australia). This family has some primitive characters that show its proximity to the order Liliales.

Family II. *Cypripediaceae*: 2 lateral fertile stamens, lip well differentiated, forming a slipper, pollen granular, not massed into pollinia. 4 genera and more than 100 species; (northern hemisphere, but absent Africa). 1 genus in Europe; *Cypripedium*. Other genera: *Paphiopedilum, Phragmipedilum, Selenipedium*.

Family III. *Orchidaceae*: (Orchids *sensu stricto* = Monandrae): 1 single fertile stamen (the median); lip well differentiated; pollen grouped into 2, 4 (-12) pollinia. A cosmopolitan family, with more evolved characters than the previous two families comprising nearly 800 genera, 32,000 species and 200,000 cultivated varieties.

Sub-family A. *Neottioideae*: pollinia without a caudicule, fixed at their top; pollen masses, powdery. Members of this sub-family have simple underground parts and flowers, more primitive characters than the following 2 sub-families.

Tribe 1. *Neottieae*: rostellum without a retinacle, shorter than the anther.

Sub-tribe a. *Limodorinae*: lip divided into a hypochile and an epichile. 4 genera in Europe: *Cephalanthera, Epipactis, Limodorum, Epipogium*.

Sub-tribe b. *Listerinae*: lip not divided into a hypochile and an epichile. 1 genus in Europe: *Neottia*.

Tribe 2. *Chranichideae*: rostellum reaching anther, 1 distinct retinacle.

Sub-tribe a. *Spiranthinae*: roots thick and fleshly. 1 genus in Europe: *Spiranthes*.

Sub-tribe b. *Goodyerinae*: roots thin, fasciculate. 1 genus in Europe: *Goodyera*.

Sub-family B. *Epidendroideae*: pollinia without a caudicule (or with rudimentary caudicules); pollen masses compact and waxy. A huge sub-family, essentially tropical, including notably the exotic genrera V*anilla, Cattleya, Epidendrum, Dendrobium, Vanda, Cymbidium, Oncidium*. Only 5 species in Europe, belonging to 4 genera.

Tribe 1. *Maxillarieae*: 4 pollinia, sympodial plants

Sub-tribe a. *Corallorhizinae*: terrestrial plants. 2 genera in Europe: *Corallorhiza* and *Calypso*.

Tribe 2. *Malaxideae*: 4 pollinia, stem forms a pseudo-bulb.

Sub-tribe a. *Liparinae*: column very short. 2 genera in Europe: *Liparis, Malaxis*

Sub-family C. *Orchidoideae*: pollinia with a caudicule attached to the base.

Tribe 1. *Orchideae*: anther broadly fused to column.

Sub-tribe a. *Gymnadeniinae*: bursicle absent single and/or rudimentary. 10 genera in Europe: *Gennaria, Habenaria, Herminium, Neottianthe, Trausteinera, Chamorchis, Platanthera, Gymnadenia*, and *Coeloglossum* which, with its rudimentary bursicle, is transitional with the following sub-tribe. The European *Gymnadeniinae* are sometimes classified differently, a first sub-tribe regrouping *Gennaria, Herminium* and *Habenaria*, a second including *Platanthera* and a third the remaining genera, to which *Dactylorhiza* is sometimes added.

Sub-tribe b. *Serapiadinae*: 1-2 bursicles enclosing the 1-2 retinacles. 7 genera in Europe: *Dactylorhiza, Serapias, Anacamptis, Orchis, Steveniella, Himantoglossum, Ophrys*.

Systematic list of species

(Taxa preceded with • are briefly described and/or illustrated; they are often considered to be variants.)

Cypripedium
C. calceolus
C. macranthos
C. guttatum

Cephalanthera
C. kotschyana
C. caucasica
C. damasonium
C. longifolia
• —— rosea
C. rubra
C. epipactoides
C. kurdica
C. cucullata

Epipactis

The E. palustris group
E. veratrifolia
E. palustris

The E. atrorubens group
E. microphylla
E. atrorubens
• —— borbasii
• —— triploida
E. cardina
E. kleinii
E. subclausa
E. spiridonovii
E. condensata

The E. tremolsii group
E. turcica
E. lusitanica
• —— duriensis
E. tremolsii
E. latina
E. neerlandica
—— var. renzii

The E. helleborine group
E. helleborine
• —— leutei
• —— minor
—— var. orbicularis
—— var. youngiana
E. dunensis
• —— South Tyne
E. molochina
E. rhodanensis
E. meridionalis
E. schubertiorum
E. voethii
E. nordeniorum
E. pontica
E. heraclea
E. densifolia

The E. purpurata group
E. rechingeri
E. bithynica
E. halacsyi
E. purpurata
E. pollinensis
E. pseudopurpurata
E. distans

The E. leptochila group
E. guegelii
E. campeadorii
E. maestrazgona
E. provincialis
E. leptochila
• —— altensteinia
—— var. neglecta
—— var. peitzii
—— var. dinarica
—— var. futakii
E. komoricensis
E. tallosii
E. aspromontana
E. nauosaensis
E. greuteri
• —— flaminia
—— var. preinensis
E. danubialis
E. olympica
E. degenii
E. placentina
E. muelleri
E. sancta

The E. albensis group
E. albensis
E. mecseckensis
E. fibri
E. confusa
E. bugacensis

The E. phyllanthes group
E. persica
E. troodi
E. cretica
E. exilis
E. fageticola
E. phyllanthes
—— var. olarionensis
—— var. pendula
—— var. vectensis
—— var. degenera

Limodorum
L. abortivum
• —— gracile
• —— rubrum

The E. purpurata group
—— var. trabutianum
• —— brulloi
• —— thracum

Epipogium
E. aphyllum

Neottia
N. nidus-avis
N. ovata
N. cordata

Spiranthes
S. spiralis
S. sinensis
S. aestivalis
S. romanzoffiana

Goodyera
G. macrophylla
G. repens

Corallorhiza
C. trifida

Calypso
C. bulbosa

Liparis
L. loeselii

Malaxis
M. monophyllos
M. paludosa

Gennaria
G. diphylla

Habenaria
H. tridactylites

Herminium
H. monorchis

Neottianthe
N. cucullata

Traunsteinera
T. sphaerica
T. globosa

Chamorchis
C. alpina

Platanthera
P. bifolia
—— var. robusta
—— var. kuenkelei

—— var. atropatenica
P. chlorantha
P. algeriensis
P. holmboei
P. hyperborea
P. oligantha
P. micrantha
P. azorica

Gymnadenia

The G. albida group
G. straminea
G. albida
• —— tricuspis

The G. conopsea group
G. frivaldii
G. conopsea
• —— insulicola
—— var. densiflora
—— var. borealis
G. odoratissima
—— var. pyrenaica

The G. runei group
G. runei

The G. nigra group
G. rhellicani
—— var. robusta
G. gabasiana
G. corneliana
• —— bourneriasii
G. lithopolitanica
G. carpatica
G. nigra
G. austriaca
—— var. gallica
G. widderi
G. archiducis-joannis
G. stiriaca
G. rubra
G. dolomitensis
G. buschmanniae

Coeloglossum
C. viride
• —— islandicum
• —— alpinum
• —— longibracteatum
• —— bracteatum

Dactylorhiza

The D. iberica group
D. iberica

The *D. sambucina* group
D. sambucina
D. insularis
• —— *bartonii*
D. markusi
D. flavescens
D. romana

The *D. incarnata* group
D. ochroleuca
D. incarnata
— — var. *lobelii*
— — var. *brevibracteata*
— — f. *ochrantha*
— — var. *reichenbachii*
— — var. *hyphaematodes*
— — var. *drudei*
— — var. *baumgartneriana*
D. pulchella
D. bohemica
D. coccinea
• —— *dunensis*
D. cruenta
D. osmanica
• —— *anatolica*
D. umbrosa
— — var. *chuhensis*
D. euxina
— — var. *markowitschii*
D. armeniaca

The *D. majalis* group
D. alpestris
D. majalis
D. cordigera
• —— *bosniaca*
• —— *siculorum*
• —— *vermionica*
D. occidentalis
D. ebudensis
D. baltica
D. lapponica
• —— *parvimajalis*

The *D. traunsteineri* group
D. traunsteineri
• —— *deweveri*
• —— *angustata*
• —— *brevifolia*
D. wirtgenii
D. carpatica
D. traunsteinerioides
• —— *francis-drucei*
• —— *eborensis*
D. curvifolia
D. baumanniana
D. smolikana
D. graeca

The *D. praetermissa* group
D. kerryensis
D. purpurella
• —— *pulchella*
D. cambrensis

D. ruthei
D. sphagnicola
• —— *calcifugiens*
D. sennia
D. praetermissa
• —— *integrata*
— — var. *junialis*
D. elata
• —— *munbyana*
• —— *durandii*
• —— *sesquipedalis*
— — var. *brennensis*
— — var. *iberica*
— — var. *ambigua*
• *D. isculana*
D. kalopissii
• —— *macedonica*
D. pindica
D. nieschalkiorum
D. pythagorae
D. urvilleana
D. pontica

The *D. maculata* group
D. saccifera
D. fuchsii
• —— *meyeri*
D. psychrophila
D. hebridensis
D. okellyi
D. foliosa
D. sudetica
D. kolaensis
D. ericetorum
• —— *schurii*
D. islandica
D. savogiensis
D. maculata
• —— *arduennensis*
— — var. *transsilvanica*
— — var. *elodes*
— — var. *rhoumensis*
• —— *podesta*
D. caramulensis
D. battandieri
D. maurusia

Serapias

The *S. parviflora* group
S. nurrica
S. parviflora
• —— *mascaensis*
S. politisii

The *S. vomeracea* group
S. aphroditae
S. bergonii
S. vomeracea
S. perez-chiscanoi
S. levantina
S. feldwegiana
S. patmia
S. orientalis

• —— *cordigerioides*
— — var. *siciliensis*
S. carica
— — var. *monantha*
S. cycladum
S. istriaca
S. apulica
S. ionica
S. neglecta
S. atlantica
S. cordigera
— — var. *cretica*
S. lorenziana
S. cossyrensis

The *S. lingua* group
S. lingua
S. stenopetala
S. olbia
S. gregaria
• —— *argensii*
S. strictiflora
S. elsae

Anacamptis

A. pyramidalis
• —— *urvilleana*
— — var. *brachystachys*
— — var. *tanayensis*
• —— *sanguinea*
— — var. *nivea*

Orchis

The *O. palustris* group
O. robusta
O. palustris
• —— *mediterranea*
• —— *michaelis*
O. elegans
O. pseudolaxiflora
O. laxiflora
O. dinsmorei

The *O. morio* group
O. champagneuxii
• —— *mesomelana*
O. longicornu
O. morio
O. picta
• —— *skorpilii*
O. albanica
O. syriaca
O. boryi
O. israelitica

The *O. papilionacea* group
O. cyrenaica
O. papilionacea
• —— *rubra*
• —— *vexillifera*
— — var. *grandiflora*
— — var. *heroica*
— — var. *alibertis*
— — var. *messenica*

— — var. *bruhnsiana*
O. collina
• —— *leucoglossa*

The *O. coriophora* group
O. coriophora
— — var. *carpetana*
— — var. *martrinii*
• —— *apricorum*
O. fragrans
O. sancta

The *O. mascula* group
O. brancifortii
O. quadripunctata
• *O. (×) sezikiana*
O. anatolica
• —— *taurica*
• —— *kochii*
O. troodi
O. sitiaca
O. spitzelii
• —— *gotlandica*
• —— *asiatica*
• —— *sendtneri*
O. cazorlensis
O. canariensis
O. prisca
O. patens
O. ligustica
O. scopulorum
O. langei
O. pinetorum
O. ichnusae
O. olbiensis
O. laeta
O. tenera
O. mascula
• —— *stabiana*
• —— *wanjkowii*
O. ovalis
O. pallens
O. provincialis
O. pauciflora

The *O. militaris* group
O. anthropophora
O. galilaea
O. simia
O. taubertiana
O. punctulata
• —— *sepulchralis*
O. adenocheila
O. purpurea
• —— *moravica*
• —— *lokiana*
O. caucasica
• —— *aserica*
O. militaris
O. stevenii
O. italica
• —— *longipenis*
• —— *purpurea*

The *O. tridentata* group
O. lactea
• —— *hanrii*
• —— *tenoreana*
• —— *corsica*
O. conica
O. tridentata
O. commutata
O. ustulata
• —— *aestivalis*
O. intacta

Steveniella
S. satyrioides

Himantoglossum

The *H. comperianum* group
H. comperianum

The *H. robertianum* group
H. metlesicsianum
H. robertianum

The *H. hircinum* group
H. formosum
H. affine
• *H.* (×) *samariense*
• *H.* (×) *montis-tauri*
H. caprinum
• —— *calcaratum*
H. adriaticum
H. hircinum

Ophrys

section *Pseudophrys*

The *O. iricolor* group
O. astypalaeica
O. iricolor
O. mesaritica
O. vallesiana
O. eleonorae

The *O. fusca* group
O. lojaconoi
O. forestieri
O. caesiella
O. gazella
O. bilunulata
O. lucifera
O. creticola
O. cressa
O. fusca
O. lupercalis

The *O. funerea* group
O. arnoldii
O. funerea
O. ortuabis
O. zonata
O. hespera
O. gackiae

O. akhdarensis
O. calocaerina
O. perpusilla
O. leucadica
O. creberrima
O. parvula

The *O. attaviria* group
O. thriptiensis
O. attaviria
O. cesmeensis
O. parosica
O. phaseliana
O. sabulosa

The *O. blitopertha* group
O. persephonae
O. blitopertha

The *O. migoutiana* group
O. migoutiana

The *O. obaesa* group
O. fabrella
O. marmorata
• —— *peraiolae*
O. sulcata
O. lucana
O. obaesa
O. pallida

The *O. subfusca* group
O. pectus
O. aspea
O. subfusca
O. lucentina
O. lindia
O. cinereophila
O. laurensis
O. flammeola
O. archimedea
O. battandieri
O. numida
• —— Gargano

The *O. lutea* group
O. melena
O. sicula
• —— *galilaea*
O. phryganae
• —— *corsica*
O. lutea

The *O. atlantica* group
O. atlantica

The *O. mirabilis* group
O. mirabilis

The *O. omegaifera* group
O. dyris
O. algarvensis
O. vasconica
O. fleischmannii
O. omegaifera

O. basilissa
O. israelitica
O. sitiaca

Section *Ophrys*

The O. speculum group
O. speculum
• —— *orientalis*
O. vernixia
O. regis-ferdinandii

The *O. tenthredinifera* group
O. bombyliflora
O. tenthredinifera
—— var. *praecox*
O. villosa
• —— *central Aegean*
• —— *early Cretan*
• —— *very small Ionian*
• —— *rather small Ionian*
O. aprilia
O. neglecta
O. grandiflora
O. ficalhoana
O. tardans
O. normanii

The *O. insectifera* group
O. aymoninii
O. insectifera
• —— *parviflora*
O. subinsectifera

The *O. apifera* group
O. apifera
• —— *friburgensis*
• —— *botteronii*
• —— *trollii*
• —— *bicolor*

The *O. bornmuelleri* group
O. aramaeorum
O. carduchorum
O. bornmuelleri
—— var. *ziyaretiana*
O. levantina
• —— *pseudolevantina*
O. heterochila
O. halia
O. helios
O. episcopalis
O. aeoli
O. andria
O. thesei
O. lyciensis
O. lacaena
O. candica
• —— *minoa*
O. parvimaculata
O. biancae

O. chestermanii
O. annae

The *O. tetraloniae* group
O. conradiae
• —— *sardoa*
O. elatior
O. aegirtica
O. linearis
O. brachyotes
O. santonica
O. vetula
O. medea
O. untchjii
O. dinarica
O. tetraloniae
O. posidonia
O. serotina

The *O. fuciflora* group
O. gracilis
O. calliantha
O. lacaitae
O. oxyrrhynchos
O. celiensis
• —— *cephaloeditana*
O. apulica
O. fuciflora

The *O. scolopax* group
O. sphegifera
O. picta
O. philippi
O. scolopax
O. corbariensis

The *O. oestrifera* group
O. holubyana
O. oestrifera
• —— *bicornis*
• —— *cornuta*
O. rhodostephane
O. sepioides
O. crassicornis
O. leptomera
O. cerastes
• —— *minuscula*
O. cornutula
O. ceto
O. rhodia
O. minutula
O. dodekanensis
O. hygrophila
O. phrygia
O. isaura
O. karadenizensis
O. abchasica
O. lapethica
O. latakiana
O. schulzei

The *O. heldreichii* group
O. zinsmeisteri

O. pharia
O. schlechteriana
O. heldreichii
O. calypsus
— — var. scolopaxoides
— — var. pseudoapulica
• O. "maxima"
O. homeri

The O. umbilicata group
O. attica
O. umbilicata
O. bucephala
O. flavomarginata
O. khuzestanica
O. kotschyi

The O. reinholdii group
O. reinholdii
O. straussii
• —— leucotenia
O. antiochiana
O. cilicica
O. cretica
• —— bicornuta
O. ariadnae

The O. argolica group
O. crabronifera
O. pollinensis
O. morisii
O. biscutella
O. icariensis
O. delphinensis
O. argolica

O. aegaea
O. elegans
O. lucis
O. lesbis
O. climacis
O. lycia

The O. mammosa group
O. ferrum-equinum
• —— labiosa
• —— subtriloba
• —— parnassica
O. gottfriediana
O. spruneri
O. sphaciotica
O. hystera
O. leucophthalma
O. gortynia
O. mammosa
O. alasiatica
O. morio
O. antalyensis
O. amanensis
O. iceliensis
O. hittitica
O. transhyrcana
O. cyclocheila
O. caucasica
O. herae
O. grammica
O. cretensis
O. macedonica
O. helenae
O. epirotica

O. aesculapii
• —— pseudoaranifera
O. hebes
O. negadensis
O. montenegrina

The O. exaltata group
O. cephalonica
O. liburnica
O. incantata
O. archipelagi
O. montis-leonis
O. cilentana
O. classica
O. argentaria
O. tarquinia
O. exaltata
O. panormitana
— — var. praecox
O. arachnitiformis
• —— nicaeensis
• —— specularia

The O. provincialis group
O. argensonensis
O. provincialis
O. quadriloba

The O. sphegodes group
O. massiliensis
O. sphegodes
O. ausonia
O. majellensis
O. brutia

The O. incubacea group
O. incubacea
• —— dianensis
O. passionis
— — var. garganica
O. sipontensis
O. virescens
O. araneola
O. tommasinii
O. illyrica
O. splendida
O. aveyronensis
O. castellana

The O. lunulata group
O. promontorii
O. panattensis
O. lunulata
O. melitensis
O. tarentina

The O. bertolonii group
O. bertolonii
O. aurelia
O. benacensis
O. balearica
O. catalaunica
• —— magniflora
O. saratoi
O. drumana
O. bertoloniiformis
O. explanata
O. flavicans

Artificial key to the genera of European orchids

1	plant with at least 1 fully-developed leaf ... 5		6*	1 leaf, lip white .... *Calypso*
1*	plant with leaves reduced to scales or sheaths and often appearing to lack chlorophyll 2		7	lip divided by a narrow constriction into a hypochile (basal part) and heart- or tongue-shaped epichile (distal part) 8
2	plant entirely violet or green heavily washed violet .... *Limodorum*		7*	plant otherwise 10
2*	colour otherwise 3		8	hypochile concave or cup-shaped, often shining and nectariferous .... *Epipactis*
3	lip pointing upwards, spur thick .. *Epipogium*		8*	hypochile lacking nectar, rolled into a tube and more or less hidden within hood formed by sepals 9
3*	lip pointing downwards, no spur 4			
4	lip unspotted, clearly bi-lobed at tip . *Neottia*			
4*	lip spotted with red, entire .... *Corallorhiza*		9	epichile with parallel longitudinal ridges .... *Cephalanthera*
5	1 large flower, rarely 2 (-3), lip slipper-shaped 6		9*	epichile without ridges .... *Serapias*
5*	more than 2 flowers, lip otherwise 7		10	lip with spur 20
6	more than 2 leaves, lip yellow or purple or extensively blotched purple ..... *Cypripedium*		10*	lip without spur 11

35

11 lip resembling an insect due to its shape and its pattern of hairy and shiny markings
.... *Ophrys*

11* lip otherwise 12

12 plant with only 2 leaves, placed more or less high up on stem 13

12* plant with 1 or more basal leaves 14

13 leaves opposite .... *Neottia*

13* leaves alternate .... *Gennaria*

14 lip three-lobed 15

14* lip entire 16

15 median lobe of lip entire .... *Herminium*

15* median lobe of lip divided, lip resembling a human in shape .... *Orchis anthropophora*

16 sepals and petals forming a hood 17

16* sepals spread 19

17 flowers whitish or coloured, axis of flower spike usually spiralled 18

17* flowers greenish, axis of flower spike not spiralled .... *Chamorchis*

18 leaves net-veined .... *Goodyera*

18* leaves with parallel veins .... *Spiranthes*

19 lip longer than 4mm .... *Liparis*

19* lip shorter than 2.5mm .... *Malaxis*

20 sepals and petals with spatulate tips
.... *Traunsteinera*

20* sepals and petals otherwise 21

21 flowers entirely greenish-yellow, green or brownish-green 22

21* flowers of other colours 25

22 lateral sepals spreading 23

22* sepals and petals forming a hood 24

23 lip long, three-lobed .... *Habenaria*

23* lip oblong, entire .... *Platanthera*

24 lip 5-10mm long .... *Coeloglossum*

24* lip 2.4-4mm long .... *Gymnadenia*

25 lateral sepals erect or spreading 31

25* sepals forming a more or less compact hood
.... 26

26 flowers very small, lip three-lobed, 3-5mm long with linear lateral lobes
.... *Orchis intacta*

26* flower otherwise 27

27 lip strongly three-lobed, central lobe 25-90mm long, forming a more or less twisted ribbon or two filaments ..... *Himantoglossum*

27* lip otherwise 28

28 spur bi-lobed at tip . ... *Steveniella*

28* spur rounded at tip 29

29 2 near-opposite basal leaves . ..... *Neottianthe*

29* leaves more numerous and differently arranged 30

30 at least lower bracts green, leaf-like, longer than ovary 32

30* all bracts membranous, with lower bracts longer or shorter than ovary .... *Orchis*

31 lip entire .... *Dactylorhiza iberica*

31* lip three-lobed, central lobe divided into two secondary lobes .... *Himantoglossum*

32 2 large, opposite basal leaves, flowers whitish to greenish, lip entire, oblong to tongue-shaped, spur longer than ovary
.... *Platanthera*

32* plant otherwise 33

33 flower-spike conical or ovoid, lip three-lobed with two prominent vertical guide-plates at base, spur long and fine
.... *Anacamptis*

33* plant otherwise 34

34 leaves unspotted, flowers numerous and usually small and scented, lip unspotted, almost entire or slightly three-lobed
.... *Gymnadenia*

34* flowers otherwise 35

36 leaves narrow and unspotted, flowers pink to violet but never yellow, spur either held horizontally or pointing upwards (the only reliable character at this stage of a key is unfortunately the shape of tubers, which are entire and ovoid rather than flattened or strongly palmate; please do not dig up the plant but rather consult the species descriptions) .... *Orchis palustris* group

36* plant otherwise .... *Dactylorhiza*

Cypripedium L. 1753

Etymology *Cypri-*: of Venus, born on Cyprus; *pedium: (?pedilon)* slipper. **Characteristics** Rhizomatous geophyte; leaves strongly veined; lateral sepals fused together and held pointing downwards; lip slipper-like, opening partially blocked by column; enlarged staminode concealing stigma, which is 3-lobed and non-glutinous; two fertile lateral anthers; pollen granular and viscous. The genus, whose characters are primitive, is largely circumboreal in distribution and comprises 40 species. Only 3 are found in Europe.

Cypripedium calceolus L.

Etymology *calceolus*: little shoe. **Type*** Ge, Baden-Württemberg (1753).

Description Height 20-60 (-70)cm; stem pubescent; leaves 3-5, oval-lanceolate, large, 12-18cm x 7-9cm, slightly pleated, with prominent veins; bracts leaf-like, longer than flowers; flowers 1-2 (-3), large; sepals and petals crimson-brown; upper sepal lanceolate, erect, 3.5-5cm long; lateral sepals fused, hanging downwards below lip; petals 4-6cm long, narrow, twisted and held horizontally; lip yellow, slipper-shaped (ovoid, bulging, without a spur), covered with viscous hairs inside; margin of opening turned inwards; staminode petaloid, shield-shaped, white spotted red; pollinia 2; ovary long, slightly curved, stalked but not twisted; 2n=20, 22.

Flowering Season V-VII. **Habitat** Mostly mid-shade, on moist, alkaline substrates. Scrub, open to dense woodland and woodland edges, up to 2000m asl.

Distribution Circumboreal, in Europe, Asia and North America. Widespread but rare in boreal and temperate Europe and only found in the montane and subalpine zones in the south of range. **Countries** Au †Be Br Bu Cz Da Fe Ga Ge He Hs Hu It Ju †Lx No Pb Po Rm Ro Su.

Photos Ga, Côte-d'Or, 22.V.2001; He, Graubünden, 6.VII.1987. P. DELFORGE.

Notes Flowers pollinated by bees of the genus *Andrena*. These enter the flower through the opening in the lip and become trapped. They rub themselves against the surface of the stigma as they clamber around inside the slipper but can only escape via one of the two rear exits; in doing so they brush past one of the two anthers and carry away some pollen on their hairy thoraxes. Lady's Slipper, which can be found in populations of several hundred flowering plants, is a spectacular species that has suffered dramatically from picking and the theft of whole plants. Strictly protected.

Cypripedium macranthos
SWARTZ

Etymology *macr-*: large; *anthos*: flower. **Type*** Ro, Siberia (1800). **Synonyms** *C. macranthos* var. *ventricosum* SWARTZ, *C. thunbergii* BLUME, *C. speciosum* ROLFE.

Description As *C. calceolus* but height 15-50cm; leaves 3-4; flowers 1 (exceptionally 2), large, entirely lilac to purple; lip shorter or longer (= *ventricosum*) than sepals; staminode sessile, white with purple spots; 2n=20.

Flowering Season VI-VII. **Habitat**: Mid-shade to shade on acidic to neutral, usually moist, substrates. Broadleaved forests (particularly birch woodland), rarely conifers. Often associated with *C. guttatum*.

Distribution Temperate Europe and Siberia, from Russia in the west to Japan in the east. Rare and local. **Countries** Ro. **Photo** Ro, Siberia, Lake Baikal, 5.V.1996 (cult.). H. PERNER.

Cypripedium guttatum
SWARTZ

Etymology *guttatum:* stained, marked with drops. **Type** Ro, Eastern Siberia (1800). **Synonyms** *C. variegatum* Georgi, *C. orientale* Sprengel.

Description As *C. calceolus* but height 15-35cm; leaves 2, cauline, near alternate; flower 1, small (diameter 3cm), white, largely covered with purple blotches; margin of opening in lip curved outwards; staminode sessile, white with purple dots; 2n=20.

Flowering Season V-VI (-VII). **Habitat** Mid-shade to shade on acidic to neutral, usually moist, substrates. Tundra, mixed and coniferous forests, often associated with *C. macranthos*.

Distribution Circumpolar. In Europe and Asia from White Russia in the west to Japan in the east and south to the Himalayas. In North America occurs in Alaska and northwest Canada. Rare and local. **Countries** Ro. **Photo** Ro. Photo China, Yunnan, 9.VI. 2000. D. RÜCKBRODT.

Key to the genus *Cypripedium*

1   lip yellow .... *C. calceolus*
1* lip purple, pink or white blotched with purple 2

2   lip white blotched with purple, margin of lip opening curved outwards .... *C. guttatum*
2* lip pink to purple, margin of lip opening curved inwards .... *C. macranthos*

Cephalanthera
L.C.M. RICHARD 1817

Etymology *cephal-*: head; *anthera*: anther (a reference to the globular shape of the anthers). **Characteristics** Rhizomatous geophyte; leaves alternate; flowers only partially opening; lip 3-lobed, concave; nectar-less hypochile surrounding column, epichile longitudinal ridged; stigma 3-lobed, lacking a viscidium; pollen powdery; ovary (near-) sessile, twisted; 2n=32, 36, 44. Closely related to *Epipactis* and mainly Eurasian in distribution, comprising at least 15 species; 8 are treated in this guide.

Cephalanthera kotschyana
RENZ & TAUBENHEIM

Etymology Named after Th. Kotschy, Viennese botanist (1813-1866). **Type** An, Adana (1980). **Synonym** *C. damasonium* subsp. *kotschyana* (Renz & Taubenheim) Sundermann.

Description Height 25-60cm; leaves 3-6 (-8), short, flat to slightly keeled, oval-lanceolate, 6-10cm x 2-5cm; lower bract up to 7cm long; inflorescence rather prominent, tall and broad, relatively dense; flowers 5-20, pure white, large, relatively open; sepals elliptic-lanceolate, base narrow, 20-30mm x 7-11mm, lateral sepals sometimes slightly spreading; petals near equal; lip 12-16mm long, almost as broad as long; hypochile white, interior slightly yellowish, concave, lateral lobes surrounding column; epichile concave, broadly heart-shaped, margins slightly scalloped, base yellow, with 3 (-4) longitudinal orange-yellow ridges; ovaries shorter and more erect.

Flowering Season V-VI (-VII).

Habitat Mid-shade to shade, on alkaline to neutral, dry to moist, substrates. Scrub and broad-leaved forests, 400-1800m asl.

Distribution Predominantly eastern Anatolia. Known from *c.* 50 stations dispersed in central and eastern Turkey (Konya, Maras, Tunceli, Erzincan, Bitlis, Hakkari), on the north coast (Samsun, Ordu) and in the south (Adana, Içel). Recently reported from Azerbaijan (Ro). Very local and very rare.

Countries An.

Photos An, Erzincan, 26.V.1990. P. DELFORGE.

Notes The relatively open flowers, as well as their position, suggest a greater tendency towards insect pollination than *C. damasonium*

Cephalanthera caucasica
KRÄNZLIN

Etymology *caucasica*: from the Caucasus. **Type** Ro (1931). **Synonym** *C. damasonium* subsp. *caucasica* (Kränzlin) Sundermann.

Description As *C. kotschyana* but 20-60cm tall; leaves more numerous, 7-9, rather larger, spreading to erect, oval-elliptic, 5-20cm x 4-7cm, longer than their respective internodes; lower bract up to 10cm long; inflorescence denser and often more floriferous; flowers 8-30, slightly smaller, pure white; sepals elliptic-lanceolate, base narrow, 18-24mm x 7-10mm, lateral sepals sometimes near spreading; petals near equal; lip 10-14mm long, almost as broad as long; hypochile white, interior orange-yellow, concave, lateral lobes surrounding column; epichile concave, oboval, margins scalloped, yellowish at base, with 3 (-5) orange-yellow longitudinal ridges that have numerous papillae.

Flowering Season IV-VI. **Habitat** Full sun to shade, on alkaline to neutral, moist to damp substrates. Grassland, scrub and broadleaved forests, up to 1900m asl.

Distribution Southeastern Caucasus and northern Iran. **Countries** Ro. **Photos** Ro, Azerbaïjan, 28.V.2000. C.A.J. KREUTZ.

Key to the genus *Cephalanthera*

1	hypochile with a spur	6
1*	hypochile without spur	2
2	flowers bright pink	*C. rubra*
2*	flowers white or yellowish	3
3	leaves elongated, narrow	*C. longifolia*
3*	leaves oval, rather large	4
4	sepals up to 20mm long	*C. damasonium*
4*	sepals longer than (18-) 20mm	5
5	leaves few, shorter or barely longer than their internode, lower leaves 6-10cm long	*C. kotschyana*
5*	leaves numerous, large, longer than their internode, lower leaves 5-20cm long	*C. caucasica*
6	flowers bright pink	*C. kurdica*
6*	flowers whitish or yellowish	7
7	spur 1-2mm long, sepals 14-20mm long	*C. cucullata*
7*	spur 3-4mm long, sepals 20-36mm long	*C. epipactoides*

Cephalanthera damasonium
(MILLER) DRUCE

Etymology Damasonium: a name given by Pliny to an unidentified plant. **Type*** Ga (1768). **Synonyms** *C. alba* (CRANTZ) SIMONKAI, *C. grandiflora* S.F. GREY, *C. pallens* (S.B. JUNDZILL) L.C.M. RICH.

Description Height 15-60cm; stem rather robust, sinuous, hairless or slightly pubescent at tip; leaves 2-5, short, flat to slightly keeled, oval-lanceolate, 4-7 (-10)cm x 1.8-3.5cm, equal to 1-2.5x their respective internode, longest leaves in middle of stem, rather leathery and near erect or softer and recurved, upper leaf bract-like; bracts leaf-like, lower bract 5cm long, upper bracts longer than ovary; inflorescence lax; flowers (2-) 3-15 (-20), whitish to yellowish, almost closed, erect; sepals, petals and lip connivent, obtuse; sepals oval-lanceolate, 12-20mm x 4-8mm; petals near equal; lip 10-14mm long; hypochile concave, whitish outside, yellowish inside, lateral lobes triangular, white, erect, surrounding the column; epichile kidney-shaped, broader than long, concave, margins scalloped, yellowish at its base, with 3-5 longitudinal orange-yellow ridges, marked with numerous papillae; capsules held vertically erect; 2n=36.

Flowering Season V-VII; relatively sporadic.

Habitat Mid-shade to shade, on calcareous to slightly acidic substrates. Forests, above all chalky beechwoods, pine forests, rarely grassland, up to 1800m asl.

Distribution Europe and Asia in the temperate and sub-Mediterranean zones. Widespread but rarely abundant.

Countries Al An Au Be Bl Br Bu Co Cr Cz Da Ga Ge Gr He Ho Hs Hu It Ju ?Lu Lx Pb Po Rm Ro Sa Si Su Tu.

Photos An, Trabzon, 23.V.1990; Hs, Albacete, 17.VI.1989. P. DELFORGE.

Note Regularly self-pollinating, sometimes even cleistogamous, therefore sets seed more often than other taxa in this group.

Cephalanthera longifolia
(L.) Fritsch

Etymology *longifolia*: with long leaves. **Type***
Su, Öland; Da, Himmerland (1753). **Synonyms**
C. ensifolia (Murray) L.C.M. Richard, *C. xyphophylla* Reichenbach fil., *C. longifolia* var. *rosea* M.L. Perko.

Description Slender, height 15-60 (-70)cm;
stems slightly sinuous, near hairless, very leafy,
often forming clumps; leaves 4-12, erect, 1-3cm
wide, 3-5x as long as their respective internodes,
narrow and lanceolate (sword-shaped), lower
leaves longest, up to 18cm, upper leaves bract-
like; bracts leaf-like, upper bracts very short;
inflorescence near lax; (3-) 8-20 (-35) flowers,
pure white (exceptionally salmon-pink: 'rosea', a
variant without evolutionary significance,
described from Carinthie, Au), half-opening,
scented; sepals, petals and lip acuminate; sepals
oval-lanceolate, 12-18mm x 4-6mm, lateral
sepals slightly spreading; petals near equal,
connivent with upper sepal; lip 7-10mm long;
hypochile whitish, concave, lateral lobes erect,
surrounding column; epichile broader than long,
heart-shaped, concave, white, yellow at tip, 4-7
longitudinal orange-yellow ridges; ovary
elongated, sessile, near hairless; 2n=32.

Flowering Season (III-) IV-VII; rather sporadic.

Habitat Usually mid-shade, on moist, calcareous
or decalcified substrates. Grassy areas, woodland
edges, glades, sparse undergrowth, sometimes
open grassland, up to 2000m asl.

Distribution Europe and Asia in the temperate
and sub-Mediterranean zones, from the Atlantic
to the Himalayas, northwest to Trondheim (No).
Widespread and often abundant, but rarer and
more local towards the northwestern edge of its
range.

Countries Ae Ag Al An Au Be Bl Br Bu Co Cr
Cz Da Fe Ga Ge Gr Hb He Ho Hs Hu Ij It Ju Ls
Lu Lx Ma No Pb Po Rm Ro Sa Si Su Tn Tu.

Photos An, Trabzon, 24.V.1990; Lu, Estrémadura, 3.IV.1990. P. Delforge.

Notes Almost exclusively insect pollinated,
attracting the pollinators of Sage-leaved Cistus
(*Cistus salvifolius*; see p. 14). In the event of
drought, the buds fail to open, becoming brown
and dry and falling from the plant at the slightest
touch, leaving just the stem, bracts and leaves.
Southern populations are usually more
floriferous.

Cephalanthera rubra

(L.) L.C.M. RICHARD

Etymology *rubra*: red. **Type*** Ge, Iéna (1767). **Basionym** *Serapias rubra* L.

Description Height 15-65cm; stem spindly, flexuous, with grey hairs towards tip; leaves 2-8, spreading, 5-14cm x 1-3cm, narrowly oval to lanceolate, acute, longer than their internode, dark green with prominent, sometimes violet veins; bracts leaf-like, upper bracts shorter than flowers; inflorescence lax; flowers (3-) 5-9 (-15), half-opening, light pink to deep crimson-pink; sepals, petals and lip acuminate; sepals oval-lanceolate, 17-25mm x 6-8mm, pubescent on outer surfaces, lateral sepals usually spreading, upper sepal connivent with petals; petals near equal; lip 17-23mm long; hypochile white with fine yellow veins, concave, lateral lobes held erect, surrounding column, sometimes pinkish; epichile elongated, heart-shaped, concave, white with pinkish margins, with 7-15 longitudinal ochre-yellow ridges; column purple; ovary near sessile, linear, pubescent; 2n=44.

Flowering Season V-VII (-VIII); rather sporadic.

Habitat Mid-shade to shade, on calcareous to slightly acidic substrates. Woodland edges, scrubby grassland and forests, particularly chalky beechwoods and oak forests, up to 2000m asl.

Distribution Europe and Asia in the temperate and sub-Mediterranean zones, from the Atlantic to the Caspian Sea. Widespread and sometimes abundant, but very rare at the edge of the range.

Countries Ae Ag Al Au ?Be Bl Br Bu Co ?Cr Cy Cz Da Fe Ga Ge Gr Hb He Ho Hs Hu Ij It Ju Ls Lu Lx Ma No Pb Po Rm Ro Sa Si Su Tn Tu.

Photos It, Rieti, 13.VII. 1989; Gr, Kastoria, 14.VII.1986. P. DELFORGE.

Pollination of *Cephalanthera*

The flowers of the various species of *Cephalanthera* act as a visual lure to attract their pollinators (see p. 14). When an insect of adequate size, mainly bees, visits the flower, the narrow gap between the column and the hypochile forces the insect to rub its thorax against the viscous stigma as it leaves the flower. The anther, which is pressed against the upper surface of the stigma at that time, ejects its pollinia onto the insect's sticky back which will be in position to make contact with the stigma of the next flower visited. This relatively unrefined mechanism (which seems more primitive than in the genus *Epipactis*) and the method of attracting pollinators by deception, without doubt explains why most *Cephalanthera* produce few ripe capsules. Populations are probably maintained and propagated mostly by vegetative means.

Cephalanthera epipactoides
FISCHER & C.A. MEYER

Etymology *-eidês*: similar to; *epipacto*-: [genus] *Epipactis*. **Type** An, Çanakkale (1854). **Synonym** C. cucullata subsp. epipactoides (FISCHER & C.A. MEYER) SUNDERMANN.

Description As *C. kurdica* but robust, (15-) 20-70 (-100)cm tall; leaves 2-4, the largest up to 6cm long; flowers (5-) 10-30 (-50), larger, half-opening, near erect to slightly pendant; buds greenish to yellowish, on opening flowers pure white, yellowish or cream; sepals, petals and lip longer and more acuminate; sepals narrowly lanceolate, 25-36mm x 4-7mm, with fewer papillae on outer surfaces; petals lanceolate, 18-25mm x 5-8mm; lip 15-22mm long, yellowish to whitish with pale yellow veins; hypochile concave with 2 erect, rounded, lateral lobes; epichile narrower and more pointed, narrowly heart-shaped (usually longer than broad), with (6-) 7-9 creamy-white to brownish-yellow ridges; tip of column yellowish; 2n=44.

Flowering Season III-VI (-VII); a little later than *C. kurdica*.

Habitat Mostly mid-shade, on dry to moist, alkaline substrates. Bare ground in open broadleaved woodland and pine forests, more rarely garrigue, scrub and woodland edges, up to 1200m asl.

Distribution Eastern (sub-) Mediterranean, from northern Greece (Thrace) east to Antalya and Ordu (An). Rather local but sometimes abundant where found.

Countries Ae An Gr Tu.

Photos An, Izmir, 11.V.1990; Bolu, 31.V.1990. P. DELFORGE.

Note In *C. epipactoides* and its allies the small number of leaves is compensated for by the number and large size of the leaf-like bracts, which actively participate in photosynthesis.

Discussion *C. epipactoides* is probably a geographic vicariant of *C. kurdica*, with which it comes into contact, notably in the provinces of Antalya and Çorum. Where sympatric, the two species produce few hybrids and maintain their distinctiveness, indicating the efficiency of the isolating mechanisms that separate them. This hypothesis has been recently confirmed by molecular analysis.

Cephalanthera kurdica
BORNMÜLLER

Etymology *kurdica*: from the Kurdish region. **Type** Irak, Esbil (1895). **Synonyms** *C. cucullata* subsp. *kurdica* (BORNMÜLLER) SUNDERMANN, *C. andrusi* G. POST, *C. floribunda* WORONOW, *C. cucullata* subsp. *floribunda* (WORONOW) SUNDERMANN, *Limodorum turkestanicum Litwinow*.

Description Rhizomatous, often producing several stems, each (10-) 15-70cm tall, robust, grooved towards tip; leaves 2-4, short, elliptical to oval-lanceolate, 2.5-5cm x 1-2.5cm, keeled, pointed, rather leathery, (near) clasping and held erect; bracts similar to leaves, decreasing in size up stem but upper bracts still longer than ovary; inflorescence rather dense to lax, elongated, occupying more than half of stem; flowers (2-) 10-40 (-50), half-opening, near horizontal, often distributed in 3-4 ranks; buds greenish-yellow to creamy-white, on opening flowers intense pink; sepals lanceolate, 20-25 (-30)mm x 5-8 (-10)mm, acuminate, keeled, leathery, with papillae on outer surfaces, lateral sepals spreading; petals oval to broadly lanceolate, 16-18mm x 6-11mm, connivent with upper sepal; lip 14-18mm long; hypochile pink, concave, with 2 erect, triangular-rounded lateral lobes surrounding column; epichile whitish, 8-10mm x 6-10mm, heart-shaped, near obtuse, margins reflexed, with 6-7 creamy to brownish-yellow longitudinal ridges; spur conical, curving slightly forward, 3-4mm long; column tipped crimson; ovary near sessile, twisted at base.

Flowering Season (III-) IV-VI; slightly earlier than *C. epipactoides*.

Habitat Mid-shade to shade on dry to moist, usually alkaline substrates. Bare ground in open broadleaved forests and pinewoods, sometimes scrub and woodland edges, up to 2000m asl.

Distribution The Near East. Southern and eastern Anatolia, from Antalya to Turkish and Iraqi Kurdistan, as well as the eastern Black Sea coastlands (Çorum, Rize), south to Lebanon and east to Iran. Rather local but can be quite abundant where found.

Countries An Ls.

Photos An, Antalya, 13.V.1990. P. DELFORGE.

45

Cephalanthera cucullata
BOISSIER & HELDREICH ex REICHENBACH fil.

Etymology *cucullata*: shaped like a hood (the leaves and bracts). **Type** Cr, Lassithi (1853). **Synonym** *Epipactis cucullata* (BOISSIER & HELDREICH ex REICHENBACH fil.) WETTSTEIN.

Description Height (10-) 15-30cm; stem flexuous, hairless, rather robust, grooved towards tip, lowest leaf almost at soil level; leaves 2-4, near clasping, short, 2.5-6cm long, oblong-lanceolate, hooded, pointed, erect, dark glaucous-green; bracts similar to leaves, lower bracts exceeding flowers, upper bracts longer than ovary, inflorescence near lax, 4-15cm long; flowers (4-) 7-24 (-30), half-opening, white, creamy-white or pinkish; sepals oblong-lanceolate, pointed, 14-20mm x 4-7mm; petals shorter and blunter, oval-oblong; lip 11-13mm long; hypochile concave, lateral lobes rounded, surrounding column; epichile heart-shaped, near pointed, concave, with 4-7 yellow to ochre longitudinal ridges; spur 1-2mm long, conical, obtuse; ovary hairless.

Flowering Season V-VI; sporadic.

Habitat Mid-shade on dry to moist, alkaline substrates. Mixed forests with oak (*Quercus calliprinos*), cypress (*Cupressus horizontalis*) and maple (*Acer creticum*), 700-1500m asl.

Distribution Endemic to Crete, where known from a few stations at Mont Ida (Iraklio), the gorges of Samaria (Chania) and in the eastern mountains (Lassithi). Very rare and local, and restricted to a rare and fragile habitat.

Countries Cr.

Photos Cr, Lassithi (loc. typ.), 26.V.1999. C.A.J. KREUTZ.

Hybrids in the genus *Cephalanthera*

The 3 possible hybrids between *C. rubra*, *C. damasonium* and *C. longifolia* have been described, as well as *C. damasonium* × *C. kotschyana*, *C. longifolia* × *C. epipactoides* and *C. longifolia* × *C. cucullata*; all seem to be extremely rare. *C. epipactoides* and *C. kurdica* can produce hybrids in their contact zone. All these intermediates are particularly difficult to distinguish from their parents, and it should not be forgotten that these may show anomalous coloration. As for the only 2 intergeneric hybrids to be described – *C. damasonium* with, respectively, *Epipactis helleborine* (× *Cephalopactis hybrida* (HOLUBY EX SOÓ) DOM.) and *E. atrorubens* (× *Cephalopactis speciosa* (WETTSTEIN ASCHERSON & GRÄBNER) – they are dubious.

Epipactis
ZINN 1757 (nom. cons.)

Etymology A name given by Theophrastus, around 50 BC, probably to a hellebore. **Characteristics** Rhizomatous geophyte; bracts leaf-like; petals and sepals similar; lip jointed; hypochile concave, without a spur; epichile fixed or mobile, ± heart-shaped; anther suspended; clinandrium often present; 2 smooth pollinia; ovary not twisted, stalked; 2n=16, 18, 32, 36, 38, 40, 52, 60.

Discussion An essentially Eurasian genus (1 endemic American species, *E. gigantea* DOUGLAS EX HOOKER, and 1 African species, *E. africana* RENDLE). Monophyletic. In this guide there are 59 species divided into 8 groups; most are found in the temperate and submeridional zones, often associated with relict deciduous forests, in Europe, principally beechwoods. During the last glaciation these species had their distributions restricted to the south, to the Iberian, Italian and Balkan peninsulas as well as the Caucasus. With the amelioration of the climate that began *c.* 10,000 BC beechwoods moved slowly north and west, reaching Scandinavia only *c.* AD 500 This recent arrival in mid Europe may perhaps explain why *Epipactis* seems to be in the process of an evolutionary radiation and that the taxonomic treatment of the genus is tentative. Difficulties arise from the marked plasticity of *Epipactis* species, which have a different appearance depending on their habitat, this morphological variability is probably amplified by the high incidence of self-pollination and aneuploidy (the source, notably, of degenerate variants). The attention given to relict European old-growth forests in recent years has led to the description, in addition to those species of broad distribution that are ± well defined and have been recognised for many years, of numerous new taxa with restricted ranges. These new taxa are sometimes represented by a small number of populations or indeed just one, comprising a few scattered plants.

The genus is divided into two monophyletic sister sections, distinguished by the shape of the lip. 1. Section *Arthrochilium* Irmisch, in which the hypochile has lateral lobes (rather than being cup-shaped) and the epichile is mobile. In this guide it comprises the *Epipactis palustris* group, with 2 species confined to damp habitats. 2. Section *Euepipactis* Irmisch, with a cup-shaped hypochile, lacking lateral lobes, and the epichile firmly fixed to the hypochile. It is derived from the previous section and comprises 7 groups, although these are not consistently defined by molecular and genetic analyses. The *E. phyllanthes* group, which may be monophyletic and the most derived, is made up of 6 species that have a (near) hairless stem and a greenish-yellow

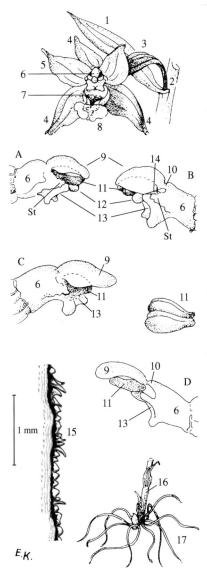

Figure 5: **A**. *Epipactis helleborine*. **B**. *E. palustris*. **C**. *E. muelleri*. **D**. *E. leptochila*. **1**. Bract. **2**. Pedicel. **3**. Ovary. **4**. Sepal. **5**. Petal. **6**. Column. **7**. Hypochile. **8**. Epichile. **9**. Anther. **10**. Anther stalk. St. Staminode. **11**. Pollinia. **12**. Viscidium. **13**. Stigmatic surface. **14**. Clinandrium. **15**. Denticulation along margin of leaf (*E. phyllanthes*). **16**. Collar. **17**. Underground parts.

47

Epipactis meridionalis Hypochromatic. **Photo:** It, Reggio di Calabria, 19.VII.1989. P. DELFORGE.

A male of the social wasp *Paravespula vulgaris* (L.), alighting on the epichile of *Epipactis purpurata* and sinking its head into the hypochile to lap up nectar. The two pollinia that it was already carrying at the base of its forehead when it arrived come into contact with the stigmatic surface; simultaneously, the top of the wasp's head knocks the tip of the column, rupturing a membrane protecting a sticky substance which, released, glues 2 new pollinia above the eyes, between the insect's antennae. Continuing its visits, this wasp pollinated in a few minutes 23 flowers on 6 different *E. purpurata* and carried up to 8 pollinia.

Photo: Ga, Ardennes, 21.VII.1990. P. DELFORGE.

base to the pedicel. Together with the *E. leptochila* group (16 species with a ± pubescent stem and a pedicel base lacking violet tones), the *E. purpurata* group (7 species with small leaves, ± hairy stems, the plants only slightly purplish or becoming greenish on flowering) and the *E. helleborine* group (11 species with ± hairy to villous stems, median leaves longer than their internode and the base of the pedicel pigmented violet), it forms a monophyletic cluster, sister to the *E. atrorubens* group (7 species with a strongly hairy stem, pedicel and ovary, the pedicel pigmented violet, as well as a very ornate epichile, characters that are very probably primitive). These ensembles are probably connected by 2 groups, the *E. tremolsii* group (5 species appearing intermediate between *E. atrorubens* s.l. and *E. helleborine* s.l.) and the *E. albensis* group (5 species appearing intermediate between *E. leptochila* s.l. and *E. phyllanthes* s.l.).

Hypochromy in genus *Epipactis*

Some *Epipactis* species are normally devoid of anthocyanin pigments and have only green or white flowers. Other species are dramatically varied in flower coloration; *E. helleborine* plants with purplish-red flowers may be found next to plants with green flowers; more often yet, *E. palustris* may have, at the same site, plants with reddish-brown sepals and others with white and yellow flowers. In the species that are usually reddish or purplish, such as *E. atrorubens*, hypochromy is exceptional or rare and may complicate identification. Very rarely, plants of *E. purpurata* and *E. helleborine* lack chlorophyll, an anomaly probably caused by a particularly virulent fungal partner; these plants are entirely purplish-pink (if anthocyanins are produced) or pure white (thus albinos in the strict sense) (see p. 24).

Pollination of *Epipactis*

The genus has numerous species that are regularly self-pollinating (sometimes even cleistogamous) or becoming rapidly self-pollinating due to withering of the viscidium and associated break-up of pollinia onto the stigma. The species that are regularly insect-pollinated attract their pollinators with nectar. Their visitors are usually diverse and numerous but only few of them pollinate the flowers, either because they do not reach the viscidium when entering the hypochile due to their small size, or because, like Lepidoptera or bumblebees, their long proboscis allows them to reach the nectar without touching the column with their head.

Depending on the region and habitat, the pollinators of an *Epipactis* may vary dramatically. The presence of beehives next to a site may, for example, mean that honey bees are the sole pollinators at that site. Nevertheless, the pollinators are generally social wasps (Hymenoptera, Vespidae) and, to a lesser extent, bumblebees *Bombus*. Visits from social wasps increase at the end of the summer, when their populations are at their maximum and before the dispersal of fertile females ('queens'). The flowers are mostly visited by males or old workers that have no larva to feed anymore or have become unable to hunt other insects to feed the larva and are thus making do with sweet substances. Some authors think that the nectar of *E. helleborine* and its allies may be toxic or may ferment due to the action of yeasts; drunken wasps would then be unable to remove the pollinia from their heads or leave the colony of helleborines. Becoming addicted, they would increase their visits to the flowers and therefore increase the rate of successful pollinations.

Early-flowering plants of *Epipactis atrorubens* seem to be pollinated by various *Bombus* species, which visit the orchids when their usual feeding plants produce less nectar. *Epipactis palustris*, very different in both floral morphology and ecology, also attracts social wasps, but these only pollinate an average of 10% of flowers. Its other true pollinators are very diverse, depending on the location of the population, climatic conditions and season. All of them are relatively light due to the mobile epichile, which bends under excessive weight, thereby deflecting the insect's head from the column. Pollen-gathering flies, like syrphids, may effect the majority of pollinations in mid-summer. Beetles, including click beetles and soldier beetles, are also frequently seen carrying the pollinia of *E. palustris*.

Hybrids in the genus *Epipactis*

Two intergeneric hybrids, both recorded extremely rarely and doubtfully, have been described with *Cephalanthera* (× *Cephalopactis* ASCHERSON & GRÄBNER) (see p. 46). Because of the dramatic variability of *Epipactis* species, interspecific hybrids are often difficult to detect with certainty, apart from the extremely rare *E. palustris* × *E. atrorubens* which involves 2 morphologically very distinct species.

Key to the genus *Epipactis*

1   hypochile with 2 lateral lobes, epichile flexible (section *Arthrochilium*)
.... *E. palustris* group (p. 50)

1*   hypochile cup-shaped, without lateral lobes; epichile fixed (section *Euepipactis*) 2

2   stem, ovary and pedicel strongly villous; epichile with prominent, very wrinkled bosses .... *E. atrorubens* group (p. 52)

2*   plants lacking these characters 3

3   base of pedicel washed purple 4

3*   base of pedicel greenish-yellow or bronze ....
....6

4   leaves ± erect, grouped together at base of stem, at least at the onset of flowering; inflorescence elongated .... *E. tremolsii* group (p. 59)

4*   leaves spreading, distributed over more than half the length of the stem 5

5   median leaves small, shorter than their internode; plants lightly coloured or ± purplish-grey then turning green ....
.... *E. purpurata* group (p. 79)

5*   median leaves longer than their internode; plants and flowers usually highly coloured ...
.... *E. helleborine* group (p. 65)

6   upper stem with fine greyish hairs ± obscuring the colour of the stem 7

6*   upper stem hairless to very slightly puberulous ..... *E. phyllanthes* group (p. 102)

7   base of pedicel greenish-yellow ....
.... *E. leptochila* group (p. 81)

7*   base of pedicel bronze ....
.... *E. albensis* group (p. 97)

Epipactis atrorubens subvar. *barbosii* × *E. bugacensis* (= *E.* × *robatschii* A. GÉVAUDAN & P. DELFORGE). **Photo:** Hu, Bács-Kiskun, 18.VI.2004. P. DELFORGE.

49

The *Epipactis palustris* group

Characteristics Stem, pedicel and ovary villous; hypochile concave (not cup-shaped), with 2 lateral lobes; epichile with a mobile joint; ovary spindle-shaped; pedicel elongated. A Eurasian group, monophyletic, with 2 species in this guide.

Epipactis veratrifolia
BOISSIER & HOHENACKER

Etymology *-folia*: [with] leaves; *-veratri*: like *Helleborus*. **Type** Ro, mont Elbrouz (1853). **Synonyms** *E. somaliensis* ROLFE, *E. consimilis* HOOKER fil., *E. abyssinica* PAX.

Description Rhizomatous, producing groups of villous aerial stems 20-120 (-150)cm tall; 3-10 cauline leaves, sheathing, lanceolate, pointed, stiff, keeled, erect to spreading, 8-25cm x 1.2-5cm, largest around centre of stem, upper leaves bract-like; lower bract far longer than flower; inflorescence lax, up to 60cm tall; flowers cross-pollinated, 4-40, large, pendant to horizontal, near bell-shaped; sepals and petals greenish to crimson-brown and villous on outer surface, green, ± broadly bordered purplish-brown on inner face, keeled, near spreading, lanceolate, 9-21mm x 4-10mm, lateral sepals asymmetric; hypochile 7-12mm long, whitish to greenish outside, reddish inside, concave, wedge-shaped (when spread), with 2 narrow lobes at base, floor dark red, granular, nectariferous; epichile flexible, 9-11mm long, narrowly triangular, concave, yellowish to reddish in centre, with 2 pale (sometimes white), erect, triangular lateral lobes at base, central lobe elongated to a pointed white tip; column and ovary as *E. palustris* but anther greenish. **Variation** Very distinct, but varied in flower size and the timing of flowering; there are populations with small flowers (sepals 9-12mm long) and large flowers (sepals 15-21mm long) and 2 waves of flowering; a long, early period (XII-III Sn; I-V Cy) and a shorter later period (IV-VI North Ij; VI-VII Cy); the taxonomic value of these differences is not known.

Flowering Season (XII-) I-VIII. **Habitat** Wet sites in full sun on very calcareous substrates. Seepages and springs on rocky cliffs, marshy depressions in the mountains, 200-2500m asl.

Distribution Afro-Asian, very fragmented. Himalayas west to Anatolia (west to Anamur) and Sinai; a few isolated stations in Somalia. Very local but abundant where found.

Countries An Cy Ij Ls Sn. **Photos A, C** Cy, Limassol, 31.III.1989; **B** An, Artvin, 21.V.1990. P. DELFORGE.

Epipactis palustris
(L.) CRANTZ

Etymology palustris: of marshes. **Type*** Be, Brabant (1753).

Description Rhizome long, horizontal, stoloniferous, producing one to several aerial stems, 15-60 (-90)cm tall, hairless at base, villous and often washed purple at tip; 4-8 cauline leaves, sheathing, narrowly lanceolate, keeled, erect-spreading, margins undulate, 7-18cm x 1.5-4cm, upper leaves bract-like; lower bract equal in length to the flower; inflorescence lax, 6-20cm tall; flowers cross-pollinated, (4-) 7-20, rather large, pendant to horizontal; sepals 8-13.5mm x 3.5-5.5mm long, lanceolate, villous and ashy-green to crimson-brown on outer surfaces, yellowish-green to purple inside, lateral sepals spreading, keeled, asymmetric, upper sepal near equal, near erect; petals 8-12.5mm x 3.5-5mm long, hairless, white washed pale purple, connivent then spreading, sometimes tinted greenish on outer surface; lip 9.5-13mm long; hypochile near cup-shaped, 5.5-7.5mm long, white veined purple, triangular (when spread), with 2 erect ear-shaped lateral lobes, sometimes undulate or connivent, and with weakly nectariferous, raised yellow ridges at base; epichile flexible, 7-8.5mm long, heart-shaped (when spread), concave, white, margins scalloped, undulate-crisped, base narrow, formed by an unguis bordered by 2 orange-yellow ridges; column yellowish-green, narrow at base; anther yellowish; viscidium and clinandrium well developed; stigma near oval; pollinia coherent; spindle-shaped ovary and elongated pedicel pubescent, glaucous-green washed violet; 2n=40, 44, 46, 48. **Variation** A very distinct species; forms ± lacking purple pigments are frequent.

Flowering Season VI-VIII. **Habitat** Damp to wet sites in full sun, mostly on alkaline substrates. Seepages, springs, damp grassland, dune slacks, rich fens, up to 2100m asl.

Distribution Europe and Asia in the submeridional and temperate zones; occurs east to Siberia and south to western Iran. Rather widespread and often found in dense colonies; rare in the boreal and meridional zones (Scandinavia, southern Italy, Balkans, northern Anatolia).

Countries Al An Au Be Br Bu Co Cz Da Fe Ga Ge Gr Hb He Ho Hs Hu It Ju Lu Lx No Pb Po Rm Ro Su Tu. **Photos** Br, Anglesey, 12.VII.1994. P. DELFORGE.

Key to the *Epipactis palustris* group

1   lower bract much longer than flower ....*E. veratrifolia*

1*   lower bract as long as flower ..... *E. palustris*

The *Epipactis atrorubens* group

Characteristics Stem, pedicel and ovary very villous, washed reddish or violet; margins of leaves regularly toothed, serrations very small, barely visible; hypochile cup-shaped, without lateral lobes; epichile rigidly attached to hypochile, with 2 prominent, very wrinkled bosses at base; margins of epichile scalloped.

Epipactis microphylla
(EHRHARDT) SWARTZ

Etymology *micro-*: [with] small; *-phylla*: leaves. **Type** Ge, Brunswick-Lüneburg (1789). **Synonym** *E. helleborine* subsp. *microphylla* (EHRHARDT) RIVAS GODAY & BORGA.

Description Rhizome short, producing a single aerial stem (occasionally 2), 15-55cm tall, glaucous-green and densely hairy almost to base (hairs soft, grey, stellate); 3-9 (-12) short cauline leaves, near sheathing, greyish-green, near keeled, erect to spreading, well-spaced, 2.5-5cm x 0.5-2.5cm, shorter than their respective internode (rarely longer), oval-lanceolate, upper leaves bract-like; bracts narrow, lower bract equalling the flower, upper bracts shorter; inflorescence lax, near one-sided, 4-22cm tall; flowers 4-30, small, facultatively self-pollinating, held dropping to nearly horizontal, bell-shaped, greenish-white washed violet, vanilla-scented; sepals and petals keeled, near spreading, oval-pointed, 5-8mm x 2-5mm, pubescent on outer surface; hypochile cup-shaped, nectariferous, interior shiny dark green, sometimes washed violet, outer surface whitish to greenish; epichile heart-shaped, whitish-green to green, sometimes washed pink, 2.5-4mm x 2.5-4mm, near spreading, margins wavy-scalloped, 2 strongly wrinkled bosses at base, extended into a longitudinal central strip; column short, whitish; anther greenish-yellow; viscidium well developed in the bud but rapidly withering after anthesis; clinandrium developed; pollinia yellow, at first cohesive but then disintegrating and may fall onto the stigma after anthesis; ovary pear-shaped, short, rather thick, pedicel relatively short, green washed violet, very hairy; 2n=32, 40. **Variation** Slight. Distinguished by its small leaves.

Flowering Season V-VIII. **Habitat** Predominantly shady sites, on deep, moist, principally calcareous substrates. Dense deciduous forests, rarely pine forests, scrub, woodland edges, up to 1700m asl. **Distribution** Euro-Caucasian. The temperate and submeridional zones, from Belgium to the Caspian Sea. Local and often rare. **Countries** Ae Al An Au Be Bl Bu Co Cr Cy Cz Ga Ge Gr Hs Hu It Ju Lx Po Rm Ro Sa Si. **Photos** It, Rieti, 13.VII.1989. P. DELFORGE.

Epipactis atrorubens
(HOFFMANN ex BERNHARDI) BESSER

Etymology *atrorubens*: dark red. **Type** Ge (1804). **Synonyms** *E. rubiginosa* (CRANTZ) W.D.J. KOCH, *E. atropurpurea* auct. non Rafinesque, *E. atrorubens* subsp., var. vel f. *borbasii* SoÓ, *E. atrorubens* subsp. *triploidea* J. GELDBRECHT & HAMEL, *E. atrorubens* var. *triploidea* (J. GELDBRECHT & HAMEL) KREUTZ.

Description Rhizome short, bearing 1 (-3) aerial stems, greyish-green to purplish, (10-) 20-80 (-100)cm tall, very villous towards tip; 5-11 cauline leaves, sheathing, often in two opposite rows, green, sometimes washed violet below, keeled, erect-spreading, margins finely toothed, lowest leaf short, oval, higher leaves oval-lanceolate, 4-12cm x 1-5cm, longer than their internode, upper 1-5 leaves bract-like; large gap between uppermost leaf and base of inflorescence; lower bract longer than flowers; inflorescence near lax, near one-sided, (5-) 10-25 (-35)cm long; flowers (7-) 12-50 (-70), medium-sized, cross-pollinated, vanilla-scented, pendant to near horizontal, bell-shaped, dark violet-purple often washed green or brown; sepals and petals keeled, near spreading, outer surfaces pubescent, oval-pointed, 5-10mm x 2.5-4.5mm; hypochile cup-shaped, nectariferous, 4-6mm long, brownish-purple with a shiny interior; epichile heart-shaped, 2.5-4mm x 4-5mm, spreading, margins scalloped, tip often turned down, base with 2 prominent wrinkled bosses that sometimes merge; column short; anthers bright yellow; viscidium and clinandrium present; stigma near quadrangular; pollinia yellow; pear-shaped ovary and elongated pedicel dark crimson-green, very villous; 2n=38, 40, 60. **Variation** Distinctive, but varied in stature and occasionally in coloration, the flowers sometimes ± lacking purple pigments (= *E. atrorubens* var. *pallens* Beckhaus). 'borbasii': Often sturdy, with short, small leaves (shorter than their internode); a taxon linked to the nominate form by numerous intermediates. **Countries** Hu. *'triploidea'* a triploid, rather late-flowering form. **Countries** Ge.

Flowering Season VI-VII. **Habitat** Full sun to partial shade on calcareous, dry to moist, often sandy, skeletal substrates. Scree, short grassland, dunes, open woodland, up to 2400m asl. **Distribution** The boreal, temperate and submeridional zones from Europe to Siberia. Relatively widespread and often abundant, although rare in the Mediterranean zone and Caucasus; reports from Portugal probably refer to *E. lusitanica*. **Countries** Ae Al Au Be Br Bu Cz Da Fe Ga Ge Gr Hb He Ho Hs Hu It Ju Lx No Pb Po Rm Ro Su. **Photos** It, L'Aquila, 10.VII.1989; Be, Luxembourg, 11.VII.1991. P. DELFORGE.

Epipactis cardina
BENITO AYUSO & HERMOSILLA

Etymology *cardina*: dark purple. **Type** Hs, Teruel (1998).

Description Often appears as clusters of 2-8 stems, 25-55 (-75)cm tall, flexuous, entirely violet, very hairy; leaves 5-8, large, ± in two opposite rows, spreading to arched, dark green, lanceolate, far exceeding their internode, the largest up to 10cm x 5cm, margins wavy with regular, minute and hard-to-see serrations; inflorescence relatively short, near one-sided; flowers 15-35, rather large, cross-pollinated; sepals 9-10mm x 4.5-5mm, green, washed violet; petals 8-9mm x 3.9-4.3mm, more purplish than sepals; lip shorter than sepals; interior of hypochile shiny carmine, exterior greenish; epichile 3.8-4.2mm x 3.6-4mm, heart-shaped, violet, tip reflexed, base redder, with 2 ± wrinkled bosses; anthers pale greenish-white; viscidium well developed in fresh flowers; pollinia cohesive; ovary near spherical, ± hairy, dark green with brownish sides; pedicel 4-5mm long, purplish or crimson, hairy.

Flowering Season VII-VIII. **Habitat** Mid-shade on basic substrates. Open pine forests and their edges, scrub, 1400-1800m asl. **Distribution** Known from the central massifs of the Iberian mountains, notably in the provinces of Alicante, Teruel and Cuenca. Very local but sometimes abundant where found. **Countries** Hs. **Photos** Hs, Teruel, 20.VII.2001. P. DELFORGE.

Epipactis kleinii
M.B. Crespo, M.R. Lowe & Piera

Etymology Named after E. Klein, a modern Austrian orchidologist. **Type** Hs, Albacete (1971). **Synonyms** *E. atrorubens* subsp. *parviflora* A. NIESCHALK & C. NIESCHALK, *E. parviflora* (A. NIESCHALK & C. NIESCHALK) E. KLEIN nom. illeg.

Description As *E. atrorubens* but more spindly, height 15-40 (-50)cm; leaves relatively more elongated, greyish-green, often washed violet, sometimes strongly so, median leaves 3-7cm x 1-3.5cm, longer than their internode; inflorescence 8-25cm long; flowers 10-40, very small, cross-pollinated, less scented than *atrorubens* but brighter; sepals and petals 4-6mm x 2-3mm, exterior greenish, interior yellowish-green, often washed pale violet; lip 4-5.5mm long; interior of hypochile shiny brown, exterior whitish to greenish; epichile 2-2.8mm long, heart-shaped, greenish-white to pinkish, broadly washed darker crimson-pink in centre, margins less scalloped than *atrorubens*, the 2 basal bosses much smaller and less wrinkled; anther greenish-yellow; ovary near spherical, pedicel long, both greyish-green washed violet with greyish hairs. **Variation** Distinguished from *E. microphylla* by having the lower leaves longer than their respective internode and by the size and coloration of the flowers.

Flowering Season V-VII. **Habitat** Mostly mid-shade on dry to moist, alkaline, skeletal substrates. Pine and oak forests and their margins, 700-500m asl.

Distribution Endemic to the mountains of central and eastern Spain (Pyrenean foothills, Sierra Alcaraz and Segura foothills, Serranía de Cuenca...), with some populations reaching France (Pyrenées-Orientales). Very rare and local. **Countries** Ga Hs. **Photos** Hs, Burgos, 17.VI.1994; Albacete (loc. typ.), 18.VI.1989. P. DELFORGE.

Key to the *Epipactis atrorubens* group

1   largest leaf shorter than its respective internode .... *E. microphylla*

1*   median leaves longer than their respective internodes 2

2   leaves ± spirally arranged, violet on both sides .... *E. subclausa*

2*   leaves ± in two opposite rows, green or washed violet, but only rarely on both sides . 3

3   sepals 4-6mm long, greenish on outer surface .... *E. kleinii*

3*   sepals 5-11mm long, greenish-white, yellowish, purple or brownish on outer surface... 4

(continued overleaf)

Epipactis subclausa
Robatsch

Etymology *subclausa*: [with flowers] almost closed. **Type** Gr, Mount Olympus (1988). **Synonyms** *E. atrorubens* subsp. *subclausa* (ROBATSCH) KREUTZ, *E. atrorubens* auct., *E. thessala* B. BAUMANN & H. BAUMANN.

Description As *E. atrorubens* but general coloration more violet; stem 15-50cm tall, purple or purplish-green, all except base very densely hairy, hairs long and greyish; 7-11 cauline leaves, spirally arranged, green, strongly washed violet on both sides, median leaves (3-) 4-7cm x 1.3-2.6cm, longer than their respective internode; inflorescence near one-sided, 5-15cm tall; flowers 10-30, cross-pollinated, ± fully opening, rapidly withering; sepals and petals 5-8mm x 2.5-5mm, outer surfaces pubescent, brownish-green washed violet, inner faces hairless, greenish washed violet or reddish; interior of hypochile shiny, green washed violet, exterior of cup whitish to greenish; epichile heart-shaped, 2-3mm x 3.5-5mm, greenish-white, extensively washed purplish-pink in centre, margins less scalloped than *atrorubens*, basal bosses smaller and less wrinkled; anther greenish-yellow; ovary and pedicel purplish-green with long, dense greyish hairs. **Variation** Differentiated from *E. kleinii* (of which it may seem to be an eastern vicariant) notably by its overall more violet coloration, larger flowers and broader base to the epichile.

Flowering Season VII-VIII; late and fleeting. **Habitat** Mid-shade to shade on moist, calcareous, dolomitic, often rocky substrates. Pine and deciduous forests and their edges, 700-1700m asl.

Distribution Endemic to the mountains of north-western Greece. Very rare and local. **Countries** Gr. **Photos** Gr, Imathia, 24.VII.2003; Pieria, 26.VII.2003. P. DELFORGE.

Key to the *Epipactis atrorubens* group *(continued)*

4   median leaves flat, broad (length/width < 2), flowers generally yellowish .. *E. spiridonovii*

4*   leaves channelled, narrower (length/width > 2), flowers generally purple, whitish-green, purplish-green or pinkish-green 5

5   interior of flower dark purple; anther bright yellow .... *E. atrorubens*

5*   flower of another colour 6

6   petals pink to crimson; epichile crimson
.... *E. cardina*

6*   petals whitish to pale pink, epichile whitish ..
.... *E. condensata*

Epipactis spiridonovii

J. DEVILLERS-TERSCHUREN & P. DEVILLERS

Etymology Named after G. Spiridonov, modern Bulgarian naturalist. **Type** Bu, massif of Pirin (1995). **Synonym** *E. atrorubens* subsp. *spiridonovii* (J. Devillers-Terschuren & P. Devillers) Kreutz.

Description Rather spindly, 20-50cm tall; leaves 5-7, relatively large for this group, flat, held horizontally, ± in two opposite rows, green, lacking violet tones, broadly oval to rounded, median leaves 3-7.5cm x 1.9-5.1cm, far longer and broader than their respective internode; inflorescence 5-20cm long; flowers 6-17, small, facultatively self-pollinated; sepals and petals 5.5-7.5mm x 2.5-3.5mm, outer face yellowish-green to olive-green, inner surface whitish-green, often washed pink; lip 5-6mm long; interior of hypochile brown, shiny, exterior whitish to greenish; epichile heart-shaped with a reflexed tip, yellowish, 2 very wrinkled bosses at base, yellowish or sometimes pinkish; anther pale greenish-yellow; viscidium well developed in fresh flowers; pollinia frequently crumbling; ovary near spherical, hairy, green with mauve ridges or entirely mauve; pedicel washed reddish, prominently hairy.

Variation Differentiated from *E. microphylla* by its leaves, which are far longer than their respective internode, and from *E. subclausa* particularly by the lack of any violet tones in the leaves.

Flowering Season VII-VIII. **Habitat** Shady sites on calcareous substrates. Climax pine forests with *Pinus heldreichii* and mixed pine forests, 1400-1800m asl.

Distribution Apparently endemic to the Pirin and Vihrenfrom massifs of Bulgaria, but should be looked for in the neighbouring mountains of Greece and Macedonia (Ju). Very local and rare. **Countries** Bu.

Photos Bu, Pirin, (loc. typ.), 3.VIII.1994. J. DEVILLERS-TERSCHUREN.

Discussion of the *Epipactis atrorubens* group

A Eurasian group, monophyletic, with 7 species in this guide, of which *E. atrorubens*, with its vast distribution, seems to be the central species. *E. microphylla* is closely related; it probably differentiated early on, probably by ecological isolation. *E. subclausa* and *E. kleinii* appear to be geographical vicariants that replace *E. atrorubens*, the first in the southern Balkans, the latter in Spain. *E. spiridonovii* seems restricted to a very specific and limited climatic zone; similarly *E. condensata*, which may be an ancestral species close to the common ancestor of both the *atrorubens* and *tremolsii* groups.

Epipactis condensata
BOISSIER ex D.P. YOUNG

Etymology *condensata*: condensed. **Type** An, Izmir (1970). **Synonym** *E. helleborine* subsp. *condensata* (BOISSIER EX D.P. YOUNG) SUNDERMANN.

Description Rhizomatous, often producing clusters of sturdy aerial stems, 20-75cm tall, pale green, hairless at base, very hairy and sometimes washed brownish-purple towards tip; 4-10 cauline leaves, greyish-green to yellowish-green, sometimes washed violet on upper side, relatively small, median leaves (oval-)lanceolate, 3.5-6 (-9.5)cm x 2-3.5 (-4.5)cm, spirally arranged, erect, keeled, sometimes arched, relatively stiff, with slightly wavy margins, upper leaves bract-like; bracts longer than flowers; inflorescence dense, ± elongated, open; flowers large, cross-pollinated, held horizontally or pendant; sepals whitish-green to pinkish, keeled, oval-lanceolate, 9-11mm x 5-7mm; petals hairless, near equal, whitish towards the centre, sometimes washed with pinkish and yellowish towards the tip; hypochile cup-shaped, open widely at its junction with the epichile, *c.* 5-6mm x 5-6mm, nectariferous, exterior greenish, sometimes bordered purple, interior shiny dark greenish-brown; epichile *c.* 5mm x 6mm, heart-shaped, whitish, near spreading, margins scalloped, sometimes reflexed, the tip turned down and back, two poorly developed, relatively wrinkled bosses at rear, pinkish to purple, divided by a longitudinal groove that is more intensely purple; clinandrium developed; viscidium functional but then withering; pollinia cohesive but then powdering, probably causing self-pollination at end of flowering period; ovary spindle-shaped, villous, green, sometimes washed violet; pedicel elongated, hairy, lightly washed violet at base.

Flowering Season Mid VI-VIII; 2-3 weeks before *E. helleborine* but at the same time as *E. microphylla* (often syntopic in Anatolia).

Habitat Full sun to mid-shade on dry to moist, alkaline substrates, often on skeletal soils. Open woodland and its edges, 600-2000m asl.

Distribution Primarily Anatolia. Described from a few scattered sites in Anatolia, Cyprus and Lebanon, as well as the Caucasus (Azerbaijan, Georgia); also maybe in Samos (Ae). Very rare and local.

Countries ?Ae An Cy Ls Ro.

Photos Cy, Troodos, 26.VI.2002. P. DELFORGE.

Notes Probably polytypic, even within the restricted definition used here, but at least part of the range of variation, as illustrated here, belongs with the *E. atrorubens* group.

The *Epipactis tremolsii* group

Characteristics Stem strongly villous, hairs obscuring ground colour, with 300-400 coloured elements per mm^2; persistent, bunched and tangled, some hairs may be over 1mm long. Leaves often short and broad, grouped together at base of stem to form a cone; serrations on leaf margins fine and rather regular; inflorescence elongated, occupying more than half length of stem; coloration and ornamentation of flowers often similar to *E. atrorubens*; ovary and pedicel villous, the latter more or less strongly coloured purple at base.

Epipactis turcica
KREUTZ

Etymology *turcica*: Turkish. **Type** An, Ankara (1997). **Synonym** *E. tremolsii* subsp. *turcica* (Kreutz) Kreutz.

Description Rather spindly, 25-60cm tall; stem rather thick, flexuous, pale green, washed red at base and rather densely hairy towards tip; leaves pale to dark green, ± spirally arranged, clustered at base of stem and then distributed along its lower half, margins ± wavy, an average of 7 cauline leaves, longer then their respective internode, largest leaf up to 10cm x 3.5cm, lower leaves broadly oval-lanceolate, median leaves narrower, upper leaves bract-like; lower bract up to 4.5cm long; inflorescence near one-sided, elongated, near lax; up to 40 medium-sized flowers, cross-pollinated, often half-opening, pendant; sepals variably dark olive-green, sometimes edged purple on outer surfaces, olive-green to purple on inner face, 6.5-10mm x 3.5-7mm; petals near equal, pinker or more crimson than sepals; hypochile nectariferous, interior blackish-brown and shiny, exterior olive-green, whitish or purple; epichile broadly heart-shaped, whitish or yellowish-green to olive-green or purple, tip turned downwards, 2 well developed, greenish-olive to brownish-purple, wrinkled bosses at base; anther yellow; viscidium functional; ovary very narrowly pear-shaped, hairy, light to dark green; pedicel hairy, washed violet at base.

Flowering Season Mid V-mid VII. **Habitat** Full sun to mid-shade on dry, basic substrates. Short grassland, scrub, pine forests, open oak woodland and hazel plantations, 300-1500m asl. **Distribution** Poorly known due to confusion with, for example, *E. condensata*; currently recorded from *c.* 50 stations in Anatolia. Records from Azerbaidjan (Ro), Lesbos and Samos (Ae) need further confirmation. Very local and scattered. **Countries** ?Ae An ?Ro. **Photos** An, Ankara (holotyp.), 20.VI.1996; Denizli 4.VII.1996. C.A.J. KREUTZ

Epipactis lusitanica
D. TYTECA

Etymology *lusitanica* from Portugal. **Type** Lu, Algarve (1988). **Synonyms** *E. tremolsii* subsp. lusitanica (D. TYTECA) M.R. LOWE & M.B. CRESPO, *E. tremolsii* subsp. *lusitanica* (D. TYTECA) KREUTZ isonym., *E. duriensis* BERNARDOS et al., *E. tremolsii* subsp. *duriensis* (BERNARDOS et al.) Kreutz, *E. lusitanica* var. *duriensis* (BERNARDOS et al.) P. DELFORGE.

Description As *E. tremolsii* but produces 1 (-2) aerial stems, 20-40 (-50)cm tall; 4-9 cauline leaves, green, sometimes clustered at base of stem (to form a cone), often alternate, erect to spreading, relatively stiff with wavy margins, oval-rounded, median leaves 3-6.5cm x 2-4cm, upper leaves bract-like; lower bracts barely longer than flowers; inflorescence lax, 6-17cm long; flowers (7-) 15-25, medium-sized, pale, held near horizontally, near bell-shaped; sepals and petals near spreading, oval-pointed, 7-10mm x 3.5-6.5mm, outer surfaces yellowish or olive-green or purplish-brown and slightly villous, inner surfaces hairless, greenish-white, often washed purple; lip 6-9mm long; interior of hypochile olive-green to shiny brown, exterior pinkish; epichile pale pinkish to greenish, rarely purplish, broadly heart-shaped, 3.3-4.6mm x 4.3-5.7mm, spreading, with blunt tip and 2 relatively unmarked bosses at base; ovary olive-green to purplish-brown with abundant short grey hairs; pedicel elongated. **Variation** Varied in habit and coloration, from near *E. kleinii* to *E. tremolsii*; may sometimes appear as an ecotype of *E. tremolsii* occurring on acidic soils. 'duriensis' is an intermediate form, with leaves as *E. tremoslsii*, flowers as *E. lusitanica* and very dull, often green, pedicels; it is known from 2 small populations from the upper Douro (Trás-os-Montes, Lu).

Flowering Season IV-V. **Habitat** Mid-shade to shade on moist, acidic substrates. Forests of pine and Cork Oak, chestnut groves, eucalyptus woods and scrub, 150-700m asl. **Distribution** Southern Portugal (Alentejo, Algarve) and south-west Andalucia (Hs, Huelva). Rare and local. **Countries** Hs Lu. **Photos** Lu, Algarve, 6.IV.1990. P. DELFORGE.

Epipactis tremolsii
C. PAU

Etymology Named after F. Tremols y Borrell, Catalan botanist (1831-1900). **Type** Hs, Barcelona (1914). **Synonyms** *E. helleborine* subsp. *tremolsii* (C. PAU) E. KLEIN, *E. atropurpurea* var. *tremolsii* (C. PAU) SCHLECHTER.

Description Rhizomatous, producing 1 (sometimes more) sturdy aerial stems, often isolated; stems thick, (30-) 40-65cm tall, green, washed violet at base and with red, at least at the tip, densely to sparsely hairy, hairs short; 6-11 cauline leaves, olive-green, sometimes washed with red, initially clustered at base and then often spaced along stem up to inflorescence, near spirally arranged, erect, oval-rounded to lanceolate or orbicular with wavy margins, median leaves 5-10cm x 4-8cm; lower bract far exceeding flowers; inflorescence dense, occupying up to *c.* 3/4 of the stem's length; 20-60 large flowers, cross-pollinated, reddish-green, analogous to those of *E. helleborine*; sepals and petals spreading, lanceolate, concave, keeled, 8-12.5mm x 4.5-6.5mm; hypochile nectariferous, outer surface greenish, interior shiny blackish-brown, often whitish washed pink around edges; epichile broadly heart-shaped, 3-5mm x 4-5.5mm, spreading, tip bent down and back, yellowish-green washed pink, ± strongly red or crimson in centre, with 2 well-marked wrinkled bosses at base; viscidium and clinandrium developed; ovary pear-shaped, yellowish-green, villous; pedicel rather elongated, slightly to strongly purplish at base; 2n=16, 20, 24, 30, 32, 36, 38, 40, 60.

Flowering Season IV-VI; 3-6 weeks earlier than *E. helleborine*. **Habitat** Full sun to mid-shade on dry to moist, calcareous substrates. Short grassland, garrigue, clearings, scrub and pine and oak forests, up to 1600m asl. **Distribution** Western Mediterranean. North to Drôme (Ga) and south to the Maghreb. Rather local and often rare. **Countries** Ag Ga Hs Lu Ma Sa. **Photos** Hs, Tarragona, 8.VI.1989; Cuenca, 8.VI.1988. P. DELFORGE.

Discussion of the *Epipactis tremolsii* group

This group may be monophyletic, and has 5 species (*E. turcica, E. lusitanica, E. tremolsii, E. latina, E. neerlandica*) adapted to xeric habitats. They may have differentiated after the fragmentation of the range of a common ancestor that was adapted to this kind of environment and close to the root of the *E. atrorubens* and *E. helleborine* groups. It is also plausible, however, that they each originated in separate speciation events from populations of a *E. proto-helleborine*, adapting to extreme habitats, some of these being influenced by *E. atrorubens*.

Epipactis latina
(W. ROSSI & E. KLEIN) B. BAUMANN & H. BAUMANN

Etymology *latina*: from Latium. **Type** It, Rieti (1987). **Synonyms** *E. helleborine* subsp. *latina* W. ROSSI & E. KLEIN, *E. tremolsii* subsp. *latina* (W. ROSSI & E. KLEIN) S. HERTEL & A. RIECHELMANN.

Description Rhizomatous, bearing (1-) 2-6 aerial stems, often grouped, 35-100cm tall, sturdy, relatively thick, pale green, sometimes lightly washed red, densely to sparsely hairy (except at base), hairs short; 5-9 cauline leaves, green, initially clustered and forming a cone at base of stem, ± in two opposite rows, erect to spreading, oval-rounded to lanceolate, margins ± wavy, median leaves 5-9cm x 4-7cm, upper leaves bract-like; a prominent gap between uppermost leaf and base of inflorescence; bracts relatively short and narrow; inflorescence dense to near lax; 15-50 large flowers, cross-pollinated, near bell-shaped, analogous to those of *E. helleborine*; sepals lanceolate, keeled, yellowish-green, exterior surfaces near hairless, 8-12mm long; petals hairless, near equal, greenish-white washed with pink or purple; hypochile cup-shaped, nectariferous, interior glossy brown, exterior greenish to pinkish; epichile broadly heart-shaped, tip turned down and back, whitish, washed violet, red or sometimes ochre in centre, with 2 poorly-marked bosses at base, often separated by a darker longitudinal groove; viscidium and clinandrium developed; ovary pear-shaped, green, often rather dark, villous; pedicel elongated, purple at base.

Flowering Season V-VII (-VIII); 3-5 weeks earlier than *E. helleborine*. **Habitat** Full sun to mid-shade on calcareous substrates, sometimes rocky but above all dry. Scree, banks, short grassland, mountain pastures, the edge of beechwoods and open oak forests, 500-1700m asl. **Distribution** Centre of Italian peninsula and Calabre; similar plants have been reported in Croatia and Slovenia (Ju). Local and relatively rare. **Countries** It Ju. **Photos** It, L'Aquila, 10.VII.1989. P. DELFORGE.

Epipactis neerlandica
(VERMEULEN) J. DEVILLERS-TERSCHUREN & P. DEVILLERS

Etymology *neerlandica* from Holland. **Type** Ho, Noord-Holland (1949). **Synonyms** *E. helleborine* var. *neerlandica* VERMEULEN, *E. helleborine* subsp. *neerlandica* (VERMEULEN) BUTTLER.

Description Stems sturdy, arising singly (rarely several together), 10-50cm tall, thick, green (often pale), hairy, densely so towards tip (hairs short); 5-8 cauline leaves, dark green to yellowish-green, clustered at base of stem, held ± in two opposite rows, erect, sheathing, slightly leathery, oval-rounded to near orbicular, shortly pointed with ± wavy margins, median leaves 4-8cm x 3-6cm, upper leaves lanceolate, bract-like, 2-5cm x 0.75-1.5cm; bracts relatively short; inflorescence dense to near lax, short to elongated; 10-40 large flowers, cross-pollinated, near bell-shaped, only slightly opening, analogous to those of *E. helleborine*; sepals dark green, outer surface slightly pubescent, inner face greenish, sometimes washed with pink, 7-11mm x 4-7.5mm; petals greenish-white to pale purplish-pink; hypochile nectariferous, interior glossy brown, exterior pinkish; epichile heart-shaped, greenish-white, ± washed with pink or green in centre, with 2 poorly developed and sparsely wrinkled bosses at base, separated by a darker longitudinal groove; viscidium and clinandrium ± developed; ovary pear-shaped, green, often pale, densely hairy (hairs short); pedicel relatively short, villous, usually purplish at base.

Variation Distinguished from *E. helleborine* by its overall shape and its ecology; plants growing in open woodland are more slender, with more spreading leaves. This taxon is well adapted to hot, dry summers; '*renzii*' see next page.

Flowering Season VIII-IX; late.

Habitat Full sun to mid-shade on dry to moist, calcareous sands. Dunes, mostly in willow scrub (*Salix repens* subsp. *argentea*); more rarely in pine plantations and open woodland on dunes, up to 40m asl.

Distribution Known from a few areas on the Atlantic littoral from Manche (Normandy, Ga) to northern Holland, Jutland (Da) and Pomerania (Ge), as well as Wales (Br). Extremely rare and local.

Countries Be Br Da Ga Ge Ho.

Photos Ho, Noord-Holland (loc. typ.), 19.VIII.1989. P. DELFORGE.

63

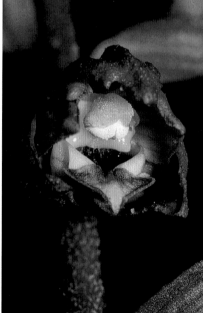

Epipactis neerlandica
(VERMEULEN) J. DEVILLERS-TERSCHUREN & P. DEVILLERS
var. *renzii*
(ROBATSCH) CLAESSENS, KLEYNEN & WIELINGA

Etymology Named after J. Renz, Swiss orchidologist (1907-1999). **Type** Da, Jutland (1988). **Synonyms** *E. renzii* ROBATSCH, *E. helleborine* subsp. *renzii* (ROBATSCH) LØJTNANT.

Description As *E. neerlandica* but usually with one-sided inflorescence; self-pollinating flowers, which average redder and do not open as widely, sometimes remaining closed; column similar to that of *E. pontica*; anther whitish, with the top overhanging the stigma; clinandrium much-reduced and not holding the pollinia; viscidium reduced or lacking, rapidly withering and non-functional; stigmatic surface erect towards the anther, with a depression at its centre; pollinia yellow, compact to powdering, tips making contact with stigma.

Flowering Season VII-VIII. **Habitat** As *E. neerlandica*. **Distribution** Known only from the dunes of northern Jutland. Extremely rare and local. **Countries** Da. **Photos** Da, Jutland. 5.VIII.1995. H. PRESSER.

Notes The Danish 'Sahara' is known for its aridity. The frequent strong winds severely limit insect flight and thus the availably of pollinators, proffering an advantage to plants in which mutations of the column allow self-pollination. This is especially so when a reduction in the clinandrium is associated with the straightening of the anther towards the stigmatic surface and the disappearance of the viscidium. Similar modifications to the column have also arisen sporadically in other places away from Danish Jutland, so that the ± completely self-pollinating populations from Denmark are here treated at the rank of variety.

Key to the *Epipactis tremolsii* group

1   plant late flowering (VIII-IX), growing below 100m asl .... *E. neerlandica*
1*   plant earlier flowering [IV-VII (-VIII)], growing above 100m asl 2

2   stem dark green, tinged purple towards tip ..3
2*   stem pale green, rarely washed red towards tip 4

3   plant robust, largest leaf 4-8cm long .... *E. tremolsii*
3*   plant spindly, largest leaf 2-4cm long .... *E. lusitanica*

4   leaves ± in two opposite rows; flowers large; sepals 8-12mm long .... *E. latina*
4*   leaves ± spirally arranged; flowers medium-sized; sepals 6.5-10mm long .... *E. turcica*

The *Epipactis helleborine* group

Characteristics Upper stem villous; hairs obscuring ground colour of stem rather well, with 200-365 elements (papillae, denticles and hairs) per mm^2, grey or sometimes purplish, persistent, grouped and tangled, with hairs up to 1mm long or even longer; leaves with short and relatively regular serrations along edges; at least median leaves longer than their respective internode; inflorescence occupying less than half stem's length; epichile less well-marked than *E. atrorubens* and often without clearly scalloped edges; ovary sparsely hairy; pedicel villous, mostly clearly purple at base.

Key to the *Epipactis helleborine* group

1	efficient viscidium and cohesive pollinia present for at least 2-3 days after flower opens 2	
1*	viscidium absent, evanescent or inefficient (because the pollinia are not cohesive after flower opens) 7	
2	median leaves shorter than, or equal to, their respective internode .... *E. helleborine* var. *orbicularis*	
2*	leaves longer than their internode 3	
3	largest leaves (3-) 4-10cm wide 4	
3*	largest leaves less than 3 (-3.5)cm wide 5	
4	leaves with very undulate margins .... *E. densifolia*	
4*	leaves with margins not undulate .... *E. helleborine*	
5	bosses at base of epichile brightly coloured .. .. *E. meridionalis*	
5*	bosses not very colourful 6	
6	leaves leathery and erect .... *E. heraclea*	
6*	leaves soft and spreading .... *E. voethii*	
7	late flowering (VIII-IX), well after *E. helleborine* .... *E. nordeniorum*	
7*	early flowering (V-VII (-VIII)), before *E. helleborine* 8	
8	median leaves far longer than their respective internode 9	
8*	leaves shorter than, or equal to, their internode .... *E. rhodanensis*	
9	growing below 300m asl 10	
9*	growing above 500m asl 11	
10	flowers small, sepals 6-8.5mm long x 2.5-4mm wide .... *E. dunensis*	
10*	flowers medium-sized, sepals 8-11mm long x 5-6mm wide .... *E. helleborine* var. *youngiana*	
11	flowers small, sepals 6-8mm long 12	
11*	flowers large, sepals 9-13mm long................ .... *E. molochina*	
12	plant small, 17-32cm tall .... *E. pontica*	
12*	plant 30-90cm tall .... *E. schubertiorum*	

Discussion of the *Epipactis helleborine* group

Found in Europe and Asia, this group is probably monophyletic, with 11 species in this guide, of which *E. helleborine*, with its vast range, seems to be the central figure. The other members of the group are probably all independently derived from *E. helleborine* through temporal, ecological or geographical isolation and are often confined to ancient relict forests (flood-plain forests and their substitutes: *E. rhodanensis*, *E. nordeniorum*; Calabrian pine forests: *E. schubertiorum*; Italo-Sicilian acidophilous deciduous forests: *E. meridionalis*; mid-European acidophilous oak-hornbeam woods: *E. voethii*; sub Mediterranean basiphilous fir plantations with *Abies cephalonica*: *E. heraclea*; sub Mediterranean and central Iberian calcareous pinewoods: *E. molochina*).

The other species in this cluster probably evolved through the development of regular self-pollination (*E. pontica*) and the ability to colonise extreme habitats (*E. dunensis*). *E. pontica* is a polytypic taxon that is probably heterogeneous, but it is unfortunately poorly-documented and its demarcation and affinities remain hard to pin down.

Epipactis helleborine
(L.) CRANTZ

Etymology *helleborine*: Helleborus, an ancient name for *Veratrum album* and *Epipactis*. **Type*** Ge, Baden-Württemberg (1753). **Synonyms** *Serapias helleborine* L. var. *latifolia* L., *Helleborine latifolia* (L.) MOENCH, *Epipactis latifolia* (L.) ALLIONI, *E. leutei* ROBATSCH, *E. helleborine* var. vel subsp. *minor* ENGEL.

Description Rhizomatous, producing 1-6 aerial stems, isolated or grouped, flexuous, often robust, (20-) 35-90 (-130)cm tall, hairless at base, where whitish ± washed violet, densely hairy towards the tip, where green, sometimes crimson; 4-9 (-15) cauline leaves, longer than their respective internode, spirally arranged, spreading horizontally, soft, near orbicular to lanceolate; median leaves 7-17cm x 3-10cm, green (darker

than stem), margins straight, finely toothed (see figure), upper 1-5 leaves lanceolate, uppermost bract-like, sometimes pendant; lower bract 2-3x longer than flower; inflorescence lax to dense, near one-sided, elongated, (10-) 20-40cm tall, comprising 1/4-1/3 (-1/2) of stem's length with up to 100 flowers; flowers cross-pollinated, opening, pendant to near horizontal, greenish, ± strongly washed brownish-pink or violet; sepals oval-lanceolate, 7-15mm x 4-9mm, exterior pubescent; petals near equal, more richly coloured than sepals; hypochile nectariferous, exterior greenish-white, interior shiny blackish-brown to olive-green; epichile 3-5mm x 4-6.5mm, heart-shaped, greenish-white to deep purplish, tip turned down, 2 ± prominent bosses at base, ± wrinkled and separated by a longitudinal groove that is often dark; anther broad, yellowish; clinandrium well developed; viscidium functional; pollinia cohesive; ovary pear-shaped, dark green, hairy; pedicel quite short, tinted violet at base; 2n=18, 20, 32, 38-40.

Variation Due to it tolerance of a wide range of ecological conditions this species is very varied in size and habit, and is distinguished by the shape and disposition of the leaves and the structure of the flowers. '*leutei*' has few leaves, pendant flowers and bracts and a reddish stem base, it is only known from a single population (Au, southern Carinthie, the Karawanken massif, Kleinobir forest). '*Minor*' is small, it grows in small calcareous zones within acidic regions [NE France, forest of Rambouillet (Yvelines)…]. Both of these taxa fall within the range of variation of *E. helleborine*.

Flowering Season (V-) VI-VIII (-IX).

Habitat Mid-shade to shade on moist, deep substrates. Mostly edges and clearings in open or dense woodland, up to 2000m asl. This species is rather indifferent as to habitat and behaves as a pioneer; it may appear spontaneously in town parks and gardens.

Distribution Eurasia, north to Scandinavia and east to central Siberia and the Himalayas. Introduced to the northeastern USA 150 years ago and rapidly spreading. Records from southern areas (Ag An Ma Hs Lu) often refer to related taxa; those from Crete need to be confirmed. Widespread and sometimes abundant. **Countries** Ae Al An Au Be Bl Br Bu Co ?Cr Cz Da Fe Ga Ge Gr Hb He Ho Hs Hu Ij It Ju Lx No Pb Po Rm Ro Sa Si Su Tu.

Photos It, L'Aquila, 10.VII.1989; Be, Brabant, 21.VII.1996. P. DELFORGE.

Epipactis helleborine (L.) CRANTZ
var. *orbicularis* (K. RICHTER) VERMEULEN

Etymology *orbicularis*: [with] orbicular [leaves].
Type Au, Basse-Autriche (1887). **Synonyms**
E. orbicularis K. RICHTER, *E. helleborine* (L.) CRANTZ
subsp. *orbicularis* (K. RICHTER) E. KLEIN, *E. latifolia*
(L.) ALLIONI var. *orbicularis* K. RICHTER vel (K. RICHTER)
E.G. CAMUS, BERGON & A. CAMUS, *E. latifolia* (L.) ALLIONI
?var. *subrotundifolia* f. *parvifolia* ZAPALOWICZ,
E. distans auct. non ARVET-TOUVET.

Description Differs from *E. helleborine* in its
small rounded leaves, often far shorter than their
respective internode, and more elongated
inflorescence, as well as in its flowering period,
1-2 weeks earlier than the nominative variety
when growing in sunny sites (which is often the
case). The flowers are similar to those of
E. helleborine, cross-pollinated, generally richly
coloured at the start of the flowering period; the
epichile has distinct wrinkled bosses and more
often than not is colourful at the base.

Distribution Appears sporadically throughout
the range of *E. helleborine*, usually with plants
that have normal leaves, but sometimes in their
absence in very sunny situations or if the autumn
preceding the growing season was marked by a
severe drought affecting all the plants in a
population. Plants identifiable as var. *orbicularis*
may also flower in dense, moist, shady forests
and var. *orbicularis* is therefore not strictly
heliophilous or xerophilous.

Notes The majority of references to *E. distans*
from the Austrian Tyrol (Au), Switzerland, the
Dolomites (It), Dutch Limburg (Ho), northern
France and the Pyrenean region (Ga), Bavaria,
Brandenburg and Baltic islands (Ge, Po), as well
as the Czech Republic and Slovakia (Cz), Poland
and Sweden, sometimes from sea level, and from
very diverse habitats, concern plants that flower
hardly any earlier than *E. helleborine* and more
often have well-coloured flowers. These should,
most probably, be referred to *E. helleborine* var.
orbicularis or sometimes to other taxa which may
be un-named. Records of *E. distans* from the
Iberian peninsula refer to *E. molochina* and
atypical forms of *E. tremolsii*, those from
Sardinia also concern *E. tremolsii*; records of
E. helleborine var. *orbicularis* or *E. distans* from
the Balkans (Ju, Gr) and Anatolia usually refer to
other taxa (notably *E. greuteri*, *E. halacsyi*,
E. olympica, *E. condensata*, *E. bithynica*,
E. turcica), but it should nevertheless be noted
there are small populations attributable to
E. helleborine var. *orbicularis* in mainland
Greece, notably Pindhos.

Photos Au, Tirol, 25.VII.1998. P. DELFORGE.

67

Epipactis helleborine (L.) CRANTZ var. *youngiana* (A.J. RICHARDS & A.F. PORTER) KREUTZ

Etymology Named after D.P. Young, English botanist (1917-1972). **Type** Br, Northumberland (1982). **Basionym** *E. youngiana* A.J. RICHARDS & A.F. PORTER

Description Overall greenish-yellow; the rhizome produces 1-2 (-5) relatively robust stems, flexuous, 30-60cm tall and, for the *E. helleborine* group, rather weakly hairy; leaves 4-7, ± in two opposite rows, ± broadly lanceolate, spreading-erect, slightly keeled, sometimes grouped at base of stem, median leaves 5-8 (-12)cm x 1-5 (-6)cm, far longer than their respective internode, margins weakly undulate with fine, irregular serrations; lower bract elongated, up to 6.5 (-8.8)cm long; inflorescence often dense, (near) unilateral; flowers 10-40, quite large, usually self-pollinated, opening slightly; sepals 8-11mm x 5-6mm, greenish, sometimes fringed pale pinkish; petals near equal, greenish washed pink, sometimes rather strongly pink; hypochile cup-shaped, weakly nectariferous, greenish spotted with purple; epichile 3-4mm x 3.5-5mm, lightly coloured, whitish, pink or greenish, tip spreading to turned down, 2 poorly-marked greenish to purplish bosses at base, slightly wrinkled and separated by a ± coloured furrow; clinandrium poorly developed; viscidium rudimentary, very elongated, apparently not functional except perhaps when flower first opens and then rapidly withering; pollinia powdery, disintegrating onto the stigma; stigma straightened-up towards anther; ovary near hairless; pedicel rather elongated, lightly tinted violet at base; 2n= probably 32.

Flowering Season VII-VIII, slightly earlier than *E. helleborine.*

Habitat Full sun to mid-shade on moist, sandy or clayey substrates, often polluted with heavy metals, up to 300m asl.

Distribution Known from 3 mine sites in Northumberland; may also be present in dunes in Wales. Very rare and local in its stations; probably threatened.

Countries Br. **Photos** Br, Northumberland (loc. typ.), 6.VIII.1996. P. DELFORGE.

Discussion Genetic analysis has led to the conclusion that *E. youngiana* is probably not a hybrid (at least not *E. helleborine* × *E. phyllanthes*) as had been supposed; it is probably often cross-pollinated and is genetically very similar to *E. helleborine*, from which it is not completely isolated; it comprises a species in the process of formation. Populations of *E. 'youngiana'* reported from Glasgow (Scotland, Br) are probably unstable hybrid swarms between *E. helleborine* and *E. leptochila*.

Epipactis dunensis
(T. Stephenson & T.A. Stephenson) Godfery

Etymology *dunensis*: of dunes. **Type** Br, Lancashire (1918). **Synonyms** *E. leptochila* subsp. *dunensis* T. & T.A. Stephenson, *E. helleborine* subsp. *dunensis* (T. & T.A. Stephenson) Soó, *Helleborine viridiflora* (Rchb.) sensu Wheldon & Travis.

Description Stems 1 (-2), isolated, relatively spindly, 20-40 (-50)cm tall, whitish-green, densely hairy towards tip (hairs grey); 3-8 cauline leaves, oval-lanceolate, much longer than their internode, greenish-yellow, erect, channelled, with the margins slightly undulate and with fine regular serrations 0.03-0.06mm high; lower bract rather short; inflorescence lax; 4-25 small, yellowish-green bell-shaped flowers that are self-pollinating, only partially open, held horizontally and then pendant; sepals oval-acuminate, yellowish-green, keeled, 6-8.5mm x 2.5-4.5mm; petals near equal, paler, sometimes pinkish; hypochile not very nectariferous, whitish outside, shiny brown inside; epichile pinkish-white, 2.5-3.5mm x 3-4.5mm, heart-shaped, the tip often turned down, 2 small bosses at base, pinkish to greenish, separated by a groove; anther greenish-yellow; clinandrium ± developed, sometimes almost absent; viscidium rudimentary, evanescent; pollinia crumbly; ovary pear-shaped, glabrescent, 8-9.5mm long; pedicel short, washed violet at base. **Variation** Plants from pine plantations are sturdier, more brightly coloured and have more flowers. A taxon, as yet unnamed, with only a few riverside micro-populations in the South Tyne valley (Northumberland, Br), may represent a var. of *E. dunensis*; it is generally pale green, has more elongated leaves and lacks violet at base of pedicel.

Flowering Season VI-VII, earlier than *E. helleborine*. **Habitat** Full sun to mid-shade on moist, alkaline substrates. Coastal dune slacks amongst willow scrub (*Salix repens*), more rarely in pine plantations, up to 100m asl. **Distribution** Endemic to the north coast of England (Lancashire, Cumbria) and Wales. Very rare and local. **Countries** Br. **Photos** Br, Anglesey, 7.VII.1993. P. Delforge.

Epipactis molochina
P. DELFORGE

Etymology *molochina*: pale purple. **Type** Hs, Teruel (2004). **Synonyms** *E. helleborine* subsp. *molochina* (P. DELFORGE) KREUTZ, *E. distans* auct. Hispan. non ARVET-TOUVET.

Description Rhizomatous, producing 1-5 (-21) stems lined-up in a row or grouped, rather thick and 15-65 (-75)cm tall; upper stem densely hairy, well-concealing ground colour, with *c.* 290-365 grey to purplish hairs per mm²; (2-) 3-11 cauline leaves, yellowish-green to green, often washed violet, at least at base, rather leathery, margins undulate, edges serrated as *E. helleborine* but often purplish; largest leaf 5-9.5cm x 2.5-4.8cm, median leaves usually far longer than their respective internode, lanceolate, near erect, arched; upper 1- 3 (-5) leaves narrow and bract-like; inflorescence dense, elongated, near one-sided; up to 75 medium-sized to rather large flowers, opening, cross-pollinated but then rapidly self-pollinating, colourful, near horizontal; sepals keeled, whitish-green to purplish-green or purple, veined purple on outside, paler inside, 9-13mm x 4.5-9mm, petals near equal, relatively broad, 7-9mm x 5-6mm, pale to rather intense purple; hypochile nectariferous, pinkish to pale greenish-purple outside, dark and shiny inside; junction of hypochile and epichile narrow; epichile 3.5-4.7mm x 2.5-4,1mm, whitish to pinkish, base with 2 ± well developed and ± wrinkled bosses, pinkish to purple washed green, sometimes dark, often with a central ridge that is slightly more colourful, the combination heart-shaped; anther stalked, withering quite rapidly, clinandrium well developed; viscidium present but quickly rendered ineffective by rather rapid disintegration of pollinia onto upper margin of stigma; ovary thick, hairy, with prominent ribs, often purplish; pedicel elongated, often entirely purplish.

Flowering Season LateVI-VII. **Habitat** Mid-shade on dry, calcareous substrates. Montane pinewoods and their edges, 600-1700m asl. **Distribution** Endemic to the central massif of Spain. **Countries** Hs. **Photos** Hs, Teruel, 6, 9 & 11.VII.2004. P. DELFORGE.

Epipactis rhodanensis
A. GÉVAUDAN & ROBATSCH

Etymology *rhodanensis*: from the [river] Rhône
Type Ga, Rhône (1994). **Synonyms**
E. bugacensis ROBATSCH subsp. *rhodanensis* (A.
GÉVAUDAN & ROBATSCH) WUCHERPFENNIG, *E. hispanica*
BENITO AYUSO & HERMOSILLA var. *hispanica*.

Description Rhizomatous, producing 1 (-4) rather
spindly stems, 20-50 (-70)cm tall, green, rather
densely hairy towards tip (280-360 rather long
hyaline elements per mm², hairs <0.8mm
long); 4-6 (-7) cauline leaves, ± in two
opposite rows, small (often shorter than
their respective internode, largest 6cm x
3.5cm), oval-lanceolate, near erect, green
(often washed yellowish), margins undulate
with rather irregular serrations (formed by
hyaline teeth that are blunt and broader than
long) see left; lower bracts longer than
flowers, lowest up to 3cm long;
inflorescence (near) lax, near one-sided,
with up to 50 (-70) small flowers; flowers
well-open, self-pollinating, near horizontal
to pendant; sepals green outside, lighter
inside, oval-lanceolate, 7-8mm x 4mm;
petals hairless, near equal, slightly paler;
hypochile nectariferous, greenish-white to

0,2 mm

green washed pinkish outside, shiny green
washed brown (± deeply) inside); epichile 3.5mm
x 4mm, broadly heart-shaped, whitish (sometimes
washed purple or green in centre), spreading,
margins only slightly scalloped, 2 small bosses at
base, only slightly wrinkled and not highly
coloured, separated by a crimson groove;
clinandrium very deep; viscidium developed but
inefficient; pollinia crumbly, disintegrating onto
upper stigma; ovary spindle-shaped, elongated,
green, densely hairy; pedicel elongated, usually
clearly washed violet-purple. **Variation**
Identification sometimes complicated by presence
of syntopic individuals or populations of
E. fageticola and *E. campeadorii*, which are
distinguished principally by their very pale
flowers, lacking violet tint to pedicel.

Flowering Season VI-VII, earlier than
E. helleborine. **Habitat** Mid-shade on basic to
neutral substrates, often sandy alluvia. Disturbed
river banks liable to flooding (poplar plantations
with *Populus nigra*, alder or ash woods), sometimes pine plantations, 100-1600m asl.

Distribution Spain: upper Ebro basin, and, in the
south, from Valladolid to Teruel; France: Rhône
basin, north to Doubs, west to Allier and Puy-de-
Dôme, south to Alpes-Maritimes, Vaucluse and
Pyrénées Orientales; in the east: Switzerland,
Bavaria and neighbouring regions of Austria.

Countries Au Ga Ge He Hs. **Photos** Ga, Rhône,
14.VII. 1997. P. DELFORGE.

Epipactis meridionalis
H. BAUMANN & R. LORENZ

Etymology *meridionalis*: southern. **Type** It, Reggio de Calabre (1988).

Description Rhizomatous, bearing 1 (-2) isolated stems, spindly, flexuous, 15-40cm tall, washed violet and hairless at base, green washed violet and densely hairy at tip; 4-8 cauline leaves, rather short, often in two opposite rows (the 3-5 median leaves spreading), green sometimes washed violet, oval-lanceolate, 4-6cm x 1.4-2.7cm, upper 1-2 leaves bract-like; bracts small, up to 1.6cm long; inflorescence lax, often near one-sided, up to 12cm tall; 5-17 medium-sized flowers, opening, cross-pollinated, near horizontal, near bell-shaped; sepals green washed violet-purple outside, green inside, oval-lanceolate, 8-10mm x 4.5-6mm; petals hairless, near equal, greenish-white to pale violet; lip 9-10mm long; hypochile cup-shaped, nectariferous, greenish-white outside, shiny green to dark brown inside, 3.5-5mm x 3.5-5mm; epichile 3-4mm x 5-6mm, heart-shaped, greenish-white, spreading, margins ± scalloped, tip turned down and back, 2 bosses at base, slightly wrinkled, strongly crimson, sometimes green (see p. 48); anther whitish to yellowish; clinandrium well developed; viscidium efficient; ovary spindle-shaped, rather thin, dark green, densely hairy; pedicel elongated, hairy, purplish.

Variation Distinct from *E. helleborine* in its more spindly general appearance and shorter leaves, and from *E. schubertiorum* especially in its much shorter leaves.

Flowering Season VII-VIII; relatively late.

Habitat Mid-shade to shade on deep, moist, acidic substrates. Old-growth beechwoods, mixed oak woodland, sometimes chestnut woods, 500-1600m asl.

Distribution Southern Italy, from Latium and Mount Gargano (Foggia) to Sicily. Very rare and local. **Countries** It Si. **Photos** It, Reggio di Calabria (loc. typ.), 19.VII.1989. P. DELFORGE.

Epipactis schubertiorum
BARTOLO, PULVIRENTI & ROBATSCH

Etymology Named after the Schubert family, modern Austrian naturalists. **Type** It, Calabre, Cosenza (1997). **Synonym** *E. helleborine* subsp. *schubertiorum* (BARTOLO, PULVIRENTI & ROBATSCH) KREUTZ.

Description Rhizomatous, bearing 1-10 spindly, flexuous stems, 30-100cm tall, green, near hairless and washed red at base, densely hairy at tip; 6-10 cauline leaves, spirally arranged, lowest leaf placed quite high on stem, the median 4-5 (-6) leaves soft, spreading-arched, green, oval-lanceolate to narrowly lanceolate, 3-12cm x 2-4cm, upper 1 (-2) leaves bract-like, *c.* 9cm x 1.5cm; bracts small, lowest up to 3cm long; inflorescence lax, near one-sided; 10-40 small flowers, opening, facultatively self-pollinating, (near) horizontal; sepals whitish-green on both sides, sometimes finely edged pale purple, oval-lanceolate, *c.* 7mm x 3-4mm; petals hairless, near equal, green washed pink outside, greenish-white inside, ± washed lilac in centre with margins pale violet to entirely pale purple; hypochile cup-shaped, nectariferous, greenish-white to green washed pinkish outside, shiny dark brownish-green inside; epichile *c.* 4mm x 4mm, broadly heart-shaped, whitish, spreading, margins clearly undulate-scalloped, tip turned down, 2 small bosses at base, slightly wrinkled, slightly coloured, separated by a narrow groove; anther yellowish; clinandrium well developed; viscidium functional and efficient for first 2-3 days after flower opens; pollinia cohesive and then powdery, pollen grains overflowing the clinandrium and reaching the upper stigma; ovary spindle-shaped, relatively elongated, green, densely hairy; pedicel elongated, hairy, washed violet-purple at base.

Flowering Season Mid VII-mid VIII; relatively late.

Habitat Shady sites on deep, moist, acidic to neutral substrates. Old-growth coniferous forests above 900m asl.

Distribution Known only from Calabria (Serra San Bruno). Extremely local but abundant where it occurs.

Countries It.

Photos Si, Cosenza, 4.VII.1990. E. GÜGEL; 18.VII.1989. P. DELFORGE.

Epipactis voethii
ROBATSCH

Etymology Named after W. Vöth, modern Austrian orchidologist. **Type** Au, Basse-Autriche (1993). **Synonyms** *E. moravica* P. BATOUSEK, *E. nordeniorum* subsp. *moravica* (P. BATOUSEK) KREUTZ.

Description Rhizomatous, bearing 1 (-2) spindly, near flexuous stems, 15-45cm tall, green, near hairless and washed red at base, densely hairy at tip (hairs grey); (5-) 6-8 cauline leaves, ± spirally arranged, edged with fine, hyaline, rather irregular serrations formed by narrow teeth, maximum 0.2mm high (see left); median (3-) 4-5 leaves longer than their respective internode, soft, spreading-arched, green, narrowly lanceolate, 6-10cm x 1-2.5cm, upper leaf bract-like, *c.* 5cm x 0.5cm; bracts small, lowest up to 3cm long; inflorescence lax, near one-sided; up to 30 relatively small flowers, opening, majority cross-pollinated, (near) horizontal to pendant; sepals green outside, lighter inside, oval-lanceolate, 9-10mm x 4-5mm; petals

0,2 mm

hairless, near equal, green outside, greenish-white or sometimes crimson inside; hypochile cup-shaped, rather wide-mouthed, nectariferous, greenish-white to green washed pinkish outside, olive-green to shiny dark chestnut-brown inside; epichile 4mm x 4mm, broadly heart-shaped, whitish sometimes washed with purple, spreading, margins slightly crenate, tip strongly turned down, 2 small bosses at base, slightly wrinkled, lightly washed olive-green or purple, separated by a slight groove; anther yellowish; clinandrium rather poorly developed; viscidium functional and relatively efficient; pollinia powdery, sometimes leading to self-pollination, ovary spindle-shaped, elongated, green, sparsely hairy; pedicel elongated, *c.* 5mm long, hairy, ± clearly washed violet-purple.
Variation Identification sometimes complicated by intermediates between this species and *E. helleborine.*

Flowering Season VII, slightly earlier than *E. helleborine.*

Habitat Mid-shade to shade on deep, moist, acidic to neutral substrates. Oak-hornbeam woods, mixed conifer plantations and their edges, up to 400m asl.

Distribution Eastern Austria (Lower-Austria, Burgenland) and neighbouring regions.

Countries Au Cz Hu.

Photos Au, Burgenland, 20.VII.1998. P. DELFORGE; 25.VII.2004. S. HERTEL.

Epipactis nordeniorum
ROBATSCH

Etymology Named after Norden, contemporary Austrian botanist who discovered the species. **Type** Au, Styrie (1991).

Description Usually small; stem isolated, flexuous, robust, 4-15 (-38)cm tall, near hairless and washed red at base, green and densely hairy at tip; 1-3 (-4) cauline leaves, + in two opposite rows, dark green to yellowish-green, strongly veined, spreading-arched, soft, orbicular to oval, 3-5.5cm x 3-4cm, margins undulate, uppermost 1-2 leaves bract-like; bracts relatively short, the lowest 1-2cm long; inflorescence few-flowered, relatively lax, near one-sided; 3-8 (-30) small flowers, half-opening, self-pollinating, horizontal to pendant, quickly withering; sepals 5-8mm x 3-4mm, greenish outside, paler green inside; petals near equal, washed pink; hypochile green to whitish outside, nectariferous, shiny, pinkish-brown to reddish inside; epichile whitish to pinkish, 3-4mm x 3-4mm, heart-shaped, junction with the hypochile very narrow, margins slightly scalloped, tip spreading and then turned down, heart-shaped boss at base, poorly marked, lightly wrinkled, often washed pale violet; anther yellow, broad, obtuse; clinandrium short but deep; viscidium present but evanescent and inefficient; pollinia powdery, overflowing the clinandrium and breaking up onto stigma; ovary pale yellowish-green, puberulous to near hairless; pedicel washed violet at base.

Flowering Season Late VII-IX, late and fleeting. **Habitat** Shady sites on deep, moist to damp substrates. Damp, old-growth, oak-alder riverine woodland, mixed oak-hornbeam woods, up to 400m asl.

Distribution Eastern Austria and neighbouring regions. Extremely rare and local; threatened by the ongoing exploitation of most of its habitats.

Countries Au Cz Hu. **Photos A&B** Au, Niederösterreich, 24.VII.1999. C.A.J. KREUTZ; C Steiermark, 9.VIII.1995. A. GÉVAUDAN.

Epipactis pontica
TAUBENHEIM

Etymology *pontica*: of the Black sea. **Type** An, Bolu (1975). **Synonym** *E. helleborine* subsp. *pontica* (TAUBENHEIM) SUNDERMANN.

Description 1 (-2) isolated stems, spindly, 15-32cm tall, green, with rather long, dense hairs; 3-7 cauline leaves, dark green, ± spirally arranged, spreading-erect, 4.5-8.5cm x 1-2.5cm; lower bracts 1.2-4cm long, projecting beyond flower; inflorescence short, lax, often near one-sided, 3-7cm tall; 7-14 small flowers, self-pollinating, sometimes cleistogamous, yellowish-green, half-opening, bell-shaped, pendant to sometimes near horizontal; sepals 6.5-8mm long; petals hyaline; hypochile greenish-white outside, shiny green to olive-green inside; epichile whitish, green in centre, 2.3-3mm x 3-4.2mm, heart-shaped, margins undulating, tip spreading and then turned down and back, 2 very attenuated pale green bosses at base, junction with hypochile narrow; anther whitish, large, near stalked, projecting above viscidium; clinandrium much reduced to near absent; viscidium inefficient, evanescent; pollinia crumbly then powdery, breaking up onto stigma; pedicel short, tinted violet at base; 2n=40.

Flowering Season VI-VIII. **Habitat** Shady sites on deep, moist, slightly acidic to neutral substrates. Damp, old-growth deciduous forests, in Anatolia mostly found in damp beech-woods with rhododendrons, 500-1500m asl. **Distribution** Poorly known. Sometimes considered to be endemic to the Pontic Mountains (northern An), but also reported west to Austria and Slovenia. Extremely rare and local. **Countries** An Au Bu Hu Ju Rm. **Photos A&B** An, Zonguldak, 8.VIII.1996. C.A.J. KREUTZ; **C** Au, Burgenland, 20.VII.1998. P. DELFORGE.

Epipactis heraclea
P. DELFORGE & KREUTZ

Etymology Named after Heracles, son of Zeus.
Type Gr, Phthiotida (2003). **Synonym** *E.
tremolsii* subsp. *heraclea* (P. DELFORGE & KREUTZ)
KREUTZ.

Description Rhizomatous, producing up to 21
robust stems, (20-) 30-45 (-50)cm tall, whitish-
green; upper stem hairy (210-250 grey, hyaline
elements per mm^2); 4-7 cauline leaves, dark green
to yellowish-green, growing on average along
more than two-thirds of stem's length, almost in
two opposite rows, erect, arching, rather leathery,
median leaves lanceolate, longer than their
respective internode, 3.2-7.1cm x 1.4-4cm,
margins slightly undulate, with fine, rather regular
serrations, upper 1-2 leaves bract-like; bracts
often only just longer than flowers; inflorescence
near lax, near one-sided, 8-19cm tall, usually (1/2)
1/3-1/4 of stem length; (10-) 12-30 (-50) medium-
sized flowers, cross-pollinated, opening, near
horizontal; sepals green to whitish-green, keeled,
9-10mm x 4-5mm; petals near equal, pink or
crimson; hypochile cup-shaped, margins narrowed
at the junction with epichile; epichile larger than
hypochile, 5-6.5mm x 5mm, heart-shaped-
acuminate, pale pinkish, tip spreading then turned
down, 2 bosses at base, well developed, only
slightly wrinkled, ± strongly washed pinkish,
purple or brown, separated by a longitudinal
groove; anther yellow, slightly stalked;
clinandrium well developed; viscidium functional,
efficient; pollinia cohesive; ovary rather narrowly
pear-shaped, slightly hairy, green, far shorter than
floral bud; pedicel short, hairy, ± strongly washed
purplish at base.

Flowering Season Mid VII-mid VIII. **Habitat**
Full sun on dry to damp, calcareous substrates.
Rocky places, banks, woodland edges, up to
1800m asl. **Distribution** Abundant on Mount Eta
(Iti), probably also on mountains in mainland
Greece. Local and rather rare. **Countries** Gr.
Photos Gr, Phthiotida. 21.VII.2003.
P. DELFORGE.

Epipactis densifolia
W. Hahn, J. Passin & R. Wegener

Etymology *densifolia*: densely-leaved. **Type** An, Konya (2003). **Synonym** *E. tremolsii* subsp. *densifolia* (W. Hahn et al.) Kreutz.

Description Stems 1-5, robust, 30-90cm tall, green, washed purple at tip; upper stem villous; 6-16 dark green to yellowish-green cauline leaves, spreading, lower rounded, median leaves broadly lanceolate, far longer than their internode, 6-10.2cm x 4-7.2cm, margins very undulate; inflorescence dense, near one-sided, 10-30cm tall, comprising 1/3-1/4 of stem; 25-65 large flowers, well-coloured, cross-pollinated, opening, near horizontal; sepals whitish-green to lilac, keeled, 12mm x 7mm; petals near equal, oval-acuminate, pink or crimson; hypochile cup-shaped, nectariferous, dark brown inside, margins rather constricted at junction with epichile; epichile broadly heart-shaped, 6mm x 7.5mm, reddish-purple to dark magenta, tip turned down, 2 well developed wrinkled bosses at base; anther yellow, broad; clinandrium well developed; viscidium functional and efficient; pollinia cohesive; ovary purplish-green, hairy; pedicel hairy, purplish-green at base.

Flowering Season Mid VI-VII. **Habitat** Full sun to mid-shade on dry, calcareous substrates. Banks, the edges of open oak- and pinewoods, 1300-1600m asl. **Distribution** Known from south-central Anatolia, in Konya and Karaman provinces; perhaps also further west, to Samos (Ae). Local and quite rare. **Countries** ?Ae An. **Photos A** An, Konya. 18.VI.2002. J. Passin; **B&C** 14 & 16.VII.2004. W. Hahn.

The *Epipactis purpurata* group

Characteristics Closely related to *E. helleborine*, but coloration pale purplish, then turning green or even pale green, sometimes saprophytic (or mycoheterotrophic); leaves small, median leaves often shorter than their respective internode, with fine regular serrations on edges; inflorescence elongated; epichile with bosses not as well-marked as *E. helleborine* s.l. **Discussion** This group is probably monophyletic, with 7 species in this guide, all but one limited to the deep shade of beechwoods; *E. purpurata* is the only species in the group to have an extensive distribution, mainly northern, all the other species seem to be isolated.

Epipactis rechingeri
Renz

Etymology Named after K.H. Rechinger, Austrian botanist (1906-1998). **Type** Iran, Sang-Deh (1973).

Description Stems 1 (-3), elongated, 20-70cm tall, purplish-green, rather shortly-hairy at tip; few cauline leaves, spreading along stem, dark green, washed violet at least on lower side, near rounded to oval-oblong, acuminate, far shorter than their respective internode, 3-5 (-6)cm x 2-3cm, upper 1-2 leaves bract-like; lower bract elongated, up to 5cm long; inflorescence near dense, up to 35cm tall; flowers rather large, well-open, cross-pollinated, near horizontal to pendant; sepals hairless, oval-lanceolate, 11-14mm x 5-7mm; petals near equal, 10-12mm x 5-7mm; hypochile greenish-white outside, shiny dark green to olive-green inside, 5-6mm; junction of hypochile and epichile rather broad; epichile pinkish-green, broadly triangular, 4-5mm x 5-6mm, tip turned down and back, 2 attenuated bosses at base, pale green washed pink to deep purplish-pink; column short; anther whitish; clinandrium well developed; viscidium efficient; pollinia cohesive; pedicel 5mm long, tinted violet at base; ovary near hairless.

Flowering Season Mid VIII-IX. **Habitat** Shady sites on deep, moist, calcareous and schistose substrates. Damp oak- and beechwoods, 1400-2200m asl. **Distribution** Thought to be endemic to the mountains of northern Iran. Very rare and local. **Countries** Iran ?Ro (see below). **Photos** Iran, Mt. Elbrouz, 12 & 22.VIII.1972. J. Renz. **Notes** This species probably falls outside the region covered in this guide. It has recently been reported from Georgia (Ro) but probably in error, the records in all likelihood referring to *E. condensata*.

Epipactis bithynica
ROBATSCH

Etymology *bithynica*: from Bithynia, an ancient country in northwestern Asia Minor (An). **Type** An, Bursa (1991). **Synonym** *E. helleborine* subsp. *bithynica* (ROBATSCH) KREUTZ.

Description Rhizomatous, frequently bearing clumps of 4-40 thick, robust stems, 40-85cm tall, whitish-green, densely hairy towards tip (hairs grey); 5-9 cauline leaves, yellowish-green, often washed with violet or reddish, erect and then spreading, sometimes arched, quite straight, median leaves lanceolate, 4-8cm x 3-4cm, upper leaves bract-like; bracts clearly longer than flowers, lowest up to 6cm long; inflorescence compact to dense, 20-35cm tall; flowers large, cross-pollinated, well-open, horizontal; sepals green, ± intensely so, washed and edged with purple outside, 11mm x 5mm; petals hairless, near equal, broadly lanceolate-acuminate, pinker or more crimson than sepals; hypochile cup-shaped, aperture rather closed, nectariferous, shiny dark brown inside, walls narrowed at junction with epichile; epichile 5mm x 5mm, heart-shaped, whitish, greenish-yellow or pinkish, tip spreading and then turned down, 2 poorly developed bosses at base, not very wrinkled but ± strongly washed pinkish, greenish or brownish, separated by a longitudinal groove; anther whitish-yellow to greenish; clinandrium well developed; viscidium functional and efficient; pollinia cohesive; ovary rather narrowly pear-shaped, villous, green, sometimes washed violet; pedicel hairy, ± strongly washed purple.

Flowering Season VII-mid VIII. **Habitat** Mid-shade to shade on moist to damp, acidic to neutral substrates. Dense pine forests, beechwoods and mixed forest with deep humus and, rarely, their edges, 1300-1800m asl. **Distribution** Poorly known due to confusion with closely related taxa. Apparently endemic to Anatolia, where reported from Mount Olympus of Mysia (loc. typ., Bursa = Ulu Dag) and a few sites in the Pontic chain and the centre of southern Anatolia. Very local but sometimes quite abundant in its stations. **Countries** An. **Photos A&C** An, Bursa (loc. typ.), 3.VII.1994. C.A.J. KREUTZ; **B** 15.VII.1990. K. ROBATSCH.

Key to *Epipactis purpurata* group

1   viscidium efficient 2
1*   viscidium lacking or vanishing when flower opens .... *O. pseudopurpurata*

2   flowering early (VI-VII), often found in exposed sunny sites, not very brightly coloured, leaves erect, slightly leathery .... *E. distans*
2*   flowering later (mid VII-IX), in shady sites, washed violet, leaves not leathery 3

80

(continued next page)

Epipactis halacsyi
ROBATSCH

Etymology Named after E. von Halácsy, Austrian botanist (1842-1913). **Type** Gr, Messénie (1990). **Synonyms** *E. graeca* HALÁCSY nom. nud., *E. purpurata* auct. non J.E. SMITH.

Description Rhizomatous, bearing (1-) 3-10 stems, 20-35 (-40)cm tall, spindly, flexuous, washed red and near hairless at base, green tinted violet and densely hairy at tip; hairs on upper stem short, 0.1-0.4mm long, and greyish, well-concealing colour of stem; 4-7 cauline leaves, in two opposite rows, edges rather irregularly serrated, lower 1-2 leaves short, rounded and acuminate, median 3-4 leaves spreading, green ± washed violet, elliptic, 2.5-4cm x 0.5-2cm, shorter or slightly longer than their respective internode; lower bracts only just longer than flowers; (15-) 25-35 cross-pollinated flowers; sepals green, washed purple inside, lanceolate, 9-10mm x 5-6mm; petals hairless, near equal, red; hypochile broadly open, pale reddish-green outside, dark olive-brown inside; epichile strongly turned down and back, *c.* 4mm x 5.5mm, heart-shaped, reddish, 2 smooth, poorly developed bosses at base; anther broad; viscidium rapidly becoming inefficient; ovary sparsely hairy; pedicel elongated, purplish at base.

Flowering Season VII, fleeting. **Habitat** Shady sites on moist, alkaline substrates. Old-growth deciduous, fir and pine forests, 900-1500m asl. **Distribution** The Taygete massif (Peloponnese). Extremely local and very rare. **Countries** Gr. **Photos** Gr, Messinia (loc. typ.), 20.VII.2003. P. DELFORGE.

Key to *Epipactis purpurata* group

(continued)

3   plant robust, frequently more than 50cm tall 4

3*   plant spindly, rarely to 40cm tall 6

4   leaves very small, largest leaves 3-5 (-6)cm x 2-3cm .... *E. rechingeri*

4*   largest leaves longer and/or broader 5

5   largest leaves narrower, 2.7-5x as long as broad .... *E. purpurata*

5*   largest leaves broader, 1.3-2.2x as long as broad .... *E. bithynica*

6   flowering mid VII-end VII, sepals coloured inside .... *E. halacsyi*

6*   flowering VIII-IX, sepals whitish inside .... *E. pollinensis*

Epipactis purpurata
J.E. SMITH (nom. cons. prop.)

Etymology *purpurata*: crimson. **Type*** Ge, Harz massif (1814). **Synonyms** *E. viridiflora* HOFFMANN ex KROCKER, *E. violacea* (DURAND-DUQUENEY) BOREAU, *E. helleborine* subsp. *varians* (CRANTZ) SOÓ, *E. sessilifolia* PETERMANN.

Description Rhizomatous, frequently producing clusters of (1-) 5-30 (-38) thick, stiff stems, 20-70 (-120)cm tall, greenish-grey washed violet, hairless and shiny at base and with short, dense hairs at tip; 4-13 cauline leaves, quite small, spirally arranged, spreading, stiff, near keeled, hardly longer than their respective internode, (oval-)lanceolate, 5-10cm x 1-3cm, greyish-green washed violet, margins slightly undulate, upper 2-3 leaves narrow and bract-like; bracts all longer than flowers; inflorescence dense, elongated, 10-50cm tall; (6-) 20-50 (-100) large flowers, cross-pollinated, opening widely, slightly scented, pendant to near horizontal; sepals purplish and hairy on outer surface, green to whitish, ± washed with violet, keeled, oval-lanceolate, 8-13mm x 4-6mm; petals near equal, often hyaline; hypochile cup-shaped, nectariferous, greenish-white outside, shiny bright purplish-brown inside; epichile 3.5-5mm x 4.5-6mm, heart-shaped, whitish to pale lilac, margins undulate-contorted, tip turned down and under, 2 well-marked bosses at base, wrinkled, ± purplish, separated by a longitudinal groove; anther whitish to yellowish; clinandrium well developed; viscidium efficient; ovary spindle-shaped, glabrescent, dark green, sometimes washed violet; pedicel rather short, 2-5mm long, pubescent, tinted violet at its base; 2n=40. **Variation** Distinct in its general aspect and overall coloration. After an area of forest has been felled, plants may appear a few times in the resultant exposed, sunny sites; they are greener and rarely appear as clusters of stems. Extremely rarely plants are saprophytic and completely lack chlorophyll; such plants are entirely pink or ± pale violet.

Flowering Season Late: mid VII-IX. **Habitat** Shady sites on deep, heavy, moist, acidic to neutral substrates, often clayey. Mostly the shadier and barest parts of beech and hornbeam woods, sometimes in conifer forests, up to 1500m asl.

Distribution The temperate zone of mid-Europe; fragmented. Southern England (Br) and Lithuania (Pb) to Romania and Moldavia (Ro); may reach the meridional zone in old-growth montane beechwoods as far as the Apennines (It). Local but often rather abundant. **Countries** Au Be Br ?Bu Cz Da Ga Ge He Hu It Ju Lx Pb Po Rm Ro. **Photos A&B** Ga, Ardennes, 1.VIII.1982; **C** 21.VII.1990. P. DELFORGE.

Epipactis pollinensis
B. BAUMANN & H. BAUMANN

Etymology *pollinensis*: from Mount Pollino (Calabre/Basilicate, It). **Type** It, Mount Pollino (2000). **Synonym** *E. viridiflora* var. *pollinensis* (B. BAUMANN & H. BAUMANN) KREUTZ.

Description As *E. purpurata* but smaller in all parts, the rhizome producing one to a few stems 17-33cm tall, reddish-brown, near hairless at base, washed violet and with dense grey hairs at tip; 2-8 cauline leaves, ± alternate, longer than their respective internode, keeled, arching, dark green, washed with purplish-red, especially on lower side, lanceolate, 2.5-5cm x 0.5-2.1cm, upper leaf often the largest, *c.* 3.8-6.3cm long; bracts dark green, rather small, lowest bract longer than flower, central bracts 16-24mm long; inflorescence near lax to lax, 4-14cm tall, near one-sided; 6-33 small flowers, well-open, cross-pollinated, (near) horizontal to pendant; sepals pale olive-green, washed violet outside, a little whiter inside, oval-lanceolate, 8.5-11mm x 3.5-5mm; petals hairless, near equal, a little paler and more whitish than sepals; hypochile cup-shaped, nectariferous, greenish-white outside, shiny pale brownish inside, 4.5-5.5mm x 4.5-5.5mm, more widely open at junction with epichile than in *E. purpurata*; epichile 2.5-3.5mm x 3.8-5mm, broadly heart-shaped, whitish to cream, spreading, margins not markedly scalloped, the tip strongly turned down, 2 small bosses at base, hardly scarred or wrinkled, washed pale purplish, separated by a slight groove; anther yellow; clinandrium well developed; viscidium functional and efficient; pollinia cohesive; ovary spindle-shaped, 10-12mm long, reddish-brown, near hairless; pedicel elongated, 3.5-4mm long, sparsely hairy, purplish-brown at base.

Flowering Season Late: VIII-IX, after *E. helleborine* and *E. gracilis* have flowered in the same sites. **Habitat** Shady sites on moist, deep alkaline to neutral substrates. Old-growth montane beechwoods at *c.* 1500m asl.

Distribution Described and known with certainty only from Mount Pollino (Calabre/Basilicate, It). The rare populations of *E. purpurata* reported from centre of the Italian peninsula (Apennines, Abruzzi) do not seem to belong to *E. pollinensis*. **Countries** It. **Photos** It, Monte Pollino, 2 & 3.VIII.1988. J. DEVILLERS-TERSCHUREN.

Discussion The presence on Mount Pollino of plants with dimensions intermediate between *E. pollinensis* and *E. purpurata* lead some specialists to consider the taxon of short plants from Mount Pollino to be more likely a variety or simple form of *E. purpurata*.

Epipactis pseudopurpurata
MERED'A.

Etymology *pseudo-*: false + purpurata i.e. false-*[E.] purpurata*. **Type** Cz, *Slovaquie, Carpates*, Trencin Teplice (1996). **Synonym** *E. viridiflora* subsp. *pseudopurpurata* (MERED'A.) KREUTZ.

Description Rhizomatous, usually bearing 1 (-2) spindly stems, (10-) 15-30 (-41)cm tall, dark greenish-grey, near hairless and washed violet at base, densely hairy at tip (hairs grey); 1-3 cauline leaves, slightly longer than their respective internode, keeled, arching, margins often undulate on outer half of leaf, dark greyish-green, washed purplish on underside, oval to narrowly lanceolate and pointed, largest leaf (2.5-) 3.5-6 (-7.2)cm x (0.7-) 1-2 (-2.8)cm; bracts dark greyish-green, lowest (1.5-) 2-4 (-6.2)cm x 0.3-1 (-1.8)cm; inflorescence lax, few-flowered, near one-sided; (1-) 3-12 (-20) rather small flowers, well-open and almost exclusively self-pollinating to closed and cleistogamous, horizontal to pendant; sepals pale to dark greyish-green, sometimes yellow-ochre, ± washed violet, lighter inside, lanceolate, keeled, 8.5-11.5mm x 3-5mm; petals hairless, near equal, 8-9.5mm x 3.5-5mm, paler than sepals, whitish, greenish in centre, yellowish at tip, washed purplish-pink; hypochile cup-shaped, not very deep, nectariferous, whitish outside, yellow to pale green ± washed with pale violet inside; epichile 3-4mm long, 4-5.5mm broad, broadly heart-shaped, whitish, spreading and then tip turned down, margins not crenate, tip yellowish, 2 small bosses at base, hardly scarred or wrinkled, washed pale purple, separated by a slight groove; anther pale yellow, reduced, short-stalked; clinandrium well developed; viscidium usually lacking or evanescent and inefficient; pollinia rapidly crumbling; ovary spindle-shaped, sparsely hairy, maximum 11mm long, pale green at tip, greyish-purple green at base; pedicel short, hairy, purplish. 2n=40.

Flowering Season End VII-VIII.

Habitat Shady sites on moist, acidic to neutral substrates. Beech, hornbeam or oak forests in mountain valleys, 370-850m asl.

Distribution Known from ± 20 stations in the Strázovski mountains (Cz, Slovakia, south-western Carpathians) and the Bakony massif (Hu, transdanubian Hungary, southwestern Carpathians).

Countries Cz Hu.

Photos Hu, Bakony, 7.VIII.1991. J. DEVILLERS-TERSCHUREN; CZ, Trencin Teplice (loc. typ.), 1.VIII.2003. H. PRESSER.

Epipactis distans
C. ARVET-TOUVET

Etymology *distans*: differing [from others], or with distant [leaves]. **Type*** Ga, Drôme (1872). **Synonym** *E. helleborine* (L.) CRANTZ subsp. *distans* (C. ARVET-TOUVET) ENGEL & QUENTIN.

Description General coloration pale green, with a rhizome bearing up to 20 grouped stems, 15-60 (-85)cm tall, thick, pale green, hairy at tip, but hairs only slightly concealing colour of stem (200-270 grey elements per mm²); 3-6 (-8) cauline leaves, often shorter than their respective internode, matt pale green, ± alternate, slightly leathery, median leaves lanceolate, upper leaf narrow, (near) erect, slightly arched and bent into a gutter-shape, the larger 4.8-6.6cm x 2.5-3.6cm, margins undulate, serrations on edges as *E. helleborine*; inflorescence relatively dense, elongated, near one-sided; 15-40 (-70) flowers, rather well-open, cross-pollinated and then facultatively self-pollinating, lightly coloured, near horizontal to pendant; sepals keeled, whitish-green to yellowish-green, paler inside, 9-14mm x 4.5-8mm, petals near equal, keeled, relatively broad, 7-10.5mm x 5-6.6mm, whitish to greenish-white, sometimes slightly washed pink; hypochile cup-shaped, nectariferous, whitish to greenish-white outside, shiny dark greenish-brown inside; epichile 4-4.5mm x 3.8-4.6mm, whitish, 2 bosses at base (poorly developed and only slightly wrinkled), white or slightly washed greenish, brownish or pinkish, with a slightly more colourful central ridge; viscidium effective for a long time; clinandrium very deep and broad; pollinia cohesive and then powdery, able to break up onto the upper margin of stigma; ovary thick, hairy, with well-marked ribs; pedicel dark green, ± clearly purplish at base.

Flowering Season VI-VII, 2-4 weeks before *E. helleborine*. **Habitat** Full sun to shade on calcareous substrates, often on marly soils, sometimes dry in summer, but frequently flushed. Principally xeric pinewoods in intra-alpine valleys, 800-2200m asl. **Distribution** Probably only the western Alps; known from Haute-Savoie and Isère to Alpes-de-Haute-Provence (Ga), as well as in the Italian mountains bordering the Briançon area; widespread in this region and sometimes abundant; also reported from a few stations in the Massif Central (Ga) where it is far rarer and more local (for other reports, see especially *E. molochina* p. 70 and *E. helleborine* var. *orbicularis*, Note, p. 67). **Countries** ?Au ?Co Ga ?Ge It. **Photos** Ga, Hautes-Alpes, 19.VII. 1992; Drôme 18.VI.1998. P. DELFORGE.

Note One station holding atypical *E. distans* has been reported at low altitude, on acidic sands, in the Vaucluse.

The *Epipactis leptochila* group

Characteristics Upper stem pubescent, hairs ± concealing ground colour of stem and imparting a silvery appearance; pubescence comprising either 250-360 hyaline elements (papillae, teeth and hairs) per mm^2, each less than 0.5mm long, persistent, grouped and tangled, or 50-100 elements per mm^2, each up to 1mm long, grouped or isolated; leaves edged either with short and regular serrations or with irregular hyaline strips; pedicel green to yellowish-green, without purple at base.

Discussion of the *Epipactis leptochila* group

Probably monophyletic, this group from temperate Eurasia is represented by 16 species in this guide. Usually self-pollinating, they are often dependent upon stable climax habitats, usually beechwoods. The group can be divided into 3 distinct lineages that differ in the structure of the column and epichile, characters nevertheless sometimes inconsistent within the group. The first subgroup contains *E. provincialis*, *E. maestrazgona*, *E. leptochila* and its varieties and probably also *E. tallosii* and *E. danubialis*; these species are characterised by a pointed epichile, with 2 longitudinal bosses at the base and a well-developed clinandrium, a viscidium is sometimes present. The placement of *E. guegelii* with this group needs confirmation. The second subgroup contains *E. nauosaensis*, *E. olympica*, *E. degenii*, *E. greuteri* and perhaps *E. komoricensis*, *E. aspromontana* and *E. campeadorii*, species that have an epichile that is sometimes coloured and often ornamented with basal bosses that are well developed, as well as having the clinandrium reduced so that the pollinia (which are not very cohesive) jut out from it and pollen grains can fall on the stigmatic surface, which is near vertical, ± perpendicular to the axis of the column. The third subgroup, the most westerly and probably the most derived, is formed by *E. muelleri* and its sister species *E. placentina*, along with *E. sancta*; this group is characterised by a relatively smooth epichile and an extreme reduction of the clinandrium, leading to an orientation of the stigmatic surface towards the anther, the pollinia falling directly on this (Fig. 5c p. 47). The majority of the species in the group perhaps originate from the fragmentation of the range of a common ancestor, of eastern origin, speciation facilitated by the development of routine self-pollination. Radiations from refugia in sub-Mediterranean beechwoods, where the ancestral taxa may have survived the last glaciation, are plausible. A few species in this group, with very restricted distributions, still occur in such regions (Aspromonte, Calabria, It: *E. aspromontana*; Mount Olympus, Gr: *E. degenii* and *E. olympica*; Pindhos, Gr: *E. nauosaensis*).

86

Epipactis guegelii
ROBATSCH

Etymology Named after E. Gügel, modern German orchidologist. **Type** Ro, Danubian delta (1997).

Description Stems single, 30-45cm tall; (4-) 5-9 lanceolate leaves, spreading-arched, glaucous-green, median leaves 5-8.5cm x 1.8-3.5cm, longer than their respective internode, margins undulate; inflorescence rather dense; 10-20 small, cross-pollinated flowers; sepals 7.5-8mm x 4-4.5mm, green to greenish; petals near equal, pinkish; hypochile nectariferous, shiny greenish-brown inside, greenish outside; junction of hypochile and epichile broad; epichile broadly heart-shaped, 3.5mm x 4.5mm, whitish to pinkish, margins undulate, tip reflexed, 2 bosses at base, slightly wrinkled, slightly more colourful; viscidium highly developed and efficient; clinandrium broad; pollinia cohesive.

Flowering Season VII. **Habitat** Mid-shade to shade on damp to wet substrates. Mixed alluvial forests of oak, ash, willow and poplar, prone to flooding, *c.* 5m asl. **Distribution** Danube delta. Probably very local and extremely rare. **Countries** Rm. **Photo** Holotype (cult.). K. ROBATSCH

Epipactis campeadorii
P. DELFORGE

Etymology Named after R. Díaz de Vivar, known as El Cid Campeador (1043-1099). **Type** Hs, Burgos (1995). **Synonyms** *E. hispanica* BENITO AYUSO & HERMOSILLA var. *viridis* BENITO AYUSO & HERMOSILLA.

Description Rhizomatous, bearing 1 or a few stems, clustered, very robust, 25-61 (-75)cm tall, yellowish-green, densely pubescent at tip (formed by (100-) 250-360 hyaline elements per mm², not more than 0.5mm long); 4-8 (-10) cauline leaves, yellowish-green to green, erect, (near) sheathing, rather leathery, margins undulate, with fine regular serrations, median leaves lanceolate, far longer than their respective internode, 5-8.5 (-11)cm x 2-4cm, upper leaf bract-like; bracts erect, longer than flower, lowest bract up to 5cm long; inflorescence elongated, dense; up to 45 relatively small flowers, self-pollinating, yellowish-green, half-opening, near horizontal; sepals (6-) 7-8 (-9)mm long, yellowish-green on both sides; petals near equal, yellowish-green, sometimes whitish or slightly pinkish inside; hypochile only slightly nectariferous, greenish-white outside, yellowish-green or pinkish inside; junction of hypochile and epichile rather narrow and not very depressed; epichile white, greenish at tip or sometimes pinkish at base and in central groove, 3-4mm x 3-4mm, heart-shaped, tip slightly turned down and back, 2 distinct, sharply-defined bosses at base, only slightly wrinkled; anther shortly stalk; clinandrium well developed, almost flat; viscidium present but inefficient; pollinia cohesive in the bud and then crumbling, disintegrating onto stigma; pedicel elongated, ± 5mm long, yellowish-green at base. *'viridis'* is a heterogeneous taxon gathering together forms with leaves that are slightly larger, greener and more spreading, a normal tendency in *E. campeadorii* growing in shadier sites, as well as, probably, plants introgressed with *E. helleborine* s.l. and hybrid *E. campeadorii* × *E. helleborine* s.l., characterised by flowers that are a little more colourful and pedicels that are washed pale purple.

Flowering Season Late VI-late VII, relatively early. **Habitat** Full sun to mid-shade on dry to moist, calcareous substrates, often sandy. Predominantly riverine woodland, waterside poplar plantations and their edges, sometimes xeric, 400-800m asl.

Distribution Centred on the upper Ebro basin (northern Iberian peninsula); extends south to the central Iberian mountains (Iberian system, Teruel province). **Countries** Hs. **Photos** Hs, Burgos, 17.VII.2001; (loc. typ.), 26.VI.1992. P. DELFORGE.

0,2 mm

87

Epipactis maestrazgona
P. Delforge & A. Gévaudan

Etymology *Maestrazgona*: Maestrazgo, land of the maestres (masters). **Type** Hs, Teruel (2004). **Synonyms** *E. leptochila* subsp. *maestrazgona* (P. DELFORGE & A. GÉVAUDAN) KREUTZ, *E. provincialis* auct. Hispan. non AUBENAS & ROBATSCH.

Description Overall coloration decidedly green; rhizomatous, bearing (1-) 3-8 stems, clustered, thick, 25-50cm tall; upper stem with hairs almost concealing ground colour (250-325 hyaline purplish elements per mm^2); 4-9 cauline leaves, uniformly green, rather leathery, longer than their respective internode, median leaves lanceolate, near erect to spreading, biggest 4-8cm x 1.5-3.4cm, upper 1-5 leaves narrow and bract-like, margins undulate, with regular, often purplish, serrations; upper internode large; lower bract large, leaf-like, 4.5-6.9mm long; inflorescence at first dense and then quite lax, elongated, near one-sided; up to 45 medium-sized flowers, half-opening, self-pollinating, near horizontal; sepals keeled, green, 10.5-12mm long; petals near equal, rather lanceolate; lip appearing as long as lateral sepals; hypochile cup-shaped, with narrowed edges, often undulate-contorted, nectariferous, blackish and shiny inside; junction of hypochile and epichile rather broad but clearly distinct; epichile heart-shaped, longer than broad, 5-6.3mm x 4.3-5mm, green, washed pinkish in the centre, 2 well developed bosses at base, slightly wrinkled, pinkish or frequently bright amethyst, sometimes joined by a less brightly coloured central ridge, the whole structure then heart-shaped; anther sessile; stigma quadrangular, staminodes well developed, their tip reaching the clinandrium; viscidium poorly developed, very quickly becoming inefficient; pollinia not very cohesive and then crumbling, disintegrating onto the upper edge of the stigma; ovary hairy, dark green; pedicel rather elongated, 3-5mm long, entirely dark green.

Flowering Season Late, mid VII-VIII. **Habitat** Mid-shade to shade on dry, calcareous substrates. Cool montane pine forests and their edges at 1400-1700m asl. **Distribution** Endemic to the southern Iberian mountains (Iberian system). **Countries** Hs.**Photos** Hs, Teruel (loc. typ.), 19.VII.2001. P. DELFORGE.

Epipactis provincialis
AUBENAS & ROBATSCH

Etymology *provincialis*: from Provence. **Type** Ga, Drôme (1996).

Description Overall yellowish-green, with a rhizome bearing 1 (-3) thick stems, 17-40 (-50)cm tall, yellowish-green, base hairless, slightly purplish, tip pubescent (60-100 elements, sometimes up to 1mm long, per mm^2); 4-8 (-10) cauline leaves, yellowish-green, sometimes in two opposite rows, erect, arching, channelled, margins undulate, with fine, rather irregular serrations (see figure), median leaves oval-lanceolate, 3.5-5cm x 2-4cm; lowest bract up to 4.5cm long, sullied yellow at base (Photo C); inflorescence near lax, near one-sided to spirally arranged, occupying up to half the stem's length; (7-) 10-23 (-30) quite small flowers, self-pollinated to cleistogamous, yellowish-green, half-opening, near horizontal to pendant; sepals oval-lanceolate, keeled, 10-11mm x 6-7mm; petals shorter, oval-acuminate, whitish-green inside; lip clearly shorter than lateral sepals; hypochile cup-shaped, wide-

0,2 mm

mouthed, nectariferous, green, sometimes slightly crimson outside, pink to reddish-brown, wrinkled and shiny inside; junction of hypochile and epichile very broad, epichile greenish to pinkish-white, washed with magenta at base, triangular-acuminate, 4.5-6mm x 4.5-6mm, spreading, concave, margins reflexed, tip only rarely bent down and back, 2 marked rounded bosses at base, whitish to magenta, delineating a deep central groove (sometimes very narrow); anther large, yellowish, withering very quickly; clinandrium well developed, broad, not very deep; viscidium reduced, inefficient even in the bud; pollinia granular and crumbling, jutting out from clinandrium and disintegrating onto stigma (sometimes even in the bud); pedicel yellowish-green. **Variation** Plants growing in shady sites have leaves that are greener and not as leathery.

Flowering Season Late V-mid VI, early for this genus.

Habitat Full sun to mid-shade on dry, calcareous substrates. Thermophilous woodland of Downy Oak and associated (sub-) Mediterranean xeric garrigue, 200-500m asl.

Distribution Endemic to northern and central Provence, France; known from the departments of Ardèche, Drôme, Var and Vaucluse. Very local and rather rare in its stations.

Countries Ga.

Photos Ga, Drôme, 8.VI.1997, 13.VI.1998. P. DELFORGE.

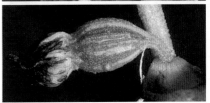

Epipactis leptochila
(GODFERY) GODFERY

Etymology *lepto*- thin; *-cheilos* lips (i.e. epichile). **Type** Br, Surrey (1919). **Synonyms** *E. viridiflava* U. LÖW, *E. helleborine* subsp. *leptochila* (GODFERY) SOÓ, *E. leptochila* var. *altensteinia* H. KÜMPEL, *E. cleistogama* C. THOMAS.

Description Overall pale green, with a rhizome bearing 1 (-5) stem, rather thick, flexuous, sometimes sterile, 20-80cm tall, yellowish-green, pubescent at tip; 3-6 (-10) cauline leaves, yellowish-green, spreading, curved downwards, margins undulate, with either fine, rather regular serrations similar to *E. helleborine*, or irregular hyaline projections (see right); median leaves oval to lanceolate, 5-11cm x 2.5-5cm, upper 2-3 leaves narrowly lanceolate, 8-10cm long; lowest bracts resembling upper leaf, very long, often pendant, up to 8cm long; inflorescence ± lax, near one-sided, 7-30cm tall; 8-35 rather large flowers, more often than not self-pollinating, ± opening or remaining closed, slightly bell-shaped, near horizontal to pendant, whitish-green to yellowish, sometimes washed purple; sepals lanceolate, acuminate, keeled, near hairless, 10-15mm long; petals near equal, 8-11mm long, not as keeled and often more pink; hypochile cup-shaped, nectariferous, greenish-pink outside, reddish-brown and shiny inside; epichile whitish to greenish, 4-7 (-9)mm x 3-5mm, narrowly heart-shaped, ± acuminate, with 2 small rounded bosses at base, sometimes pink, and, in centre, a larger and often more colourful boss, the combination forming a heart-shaped, steep-sided swelling, an extension of the inner walls of the hypochile; column variously shaped; anther narrow, stalked; clinandrium ± developed; viscidium present in the bud, poorly developed, withering rapidly and quickly ineffective; pollinia friable then crumbling, disintegrating onto stigma; pedicel 3-5mm long, greenish-yellow at base. Var. *leptochila* has junction of hypochile and epichile rather broad; epichile spreading, directed obliquely forward, with reflexed margins. *'altensteinia'* is an unstable morph, ± cleistogamous; perianth segments sometimes remaining fused at the tip; hypochile olive-green; epichile green, lacking bosses.

0,2 mm

Flowering Season (VI-) VII-VIII, 1-3 weeks earlier than *E. helleborine*. **Habitat** Shady sites on heavy, moist, calcareous substrates. Mostly on bare soils in young beechwoods up to 1500m asl. **Distribution** Temperate Europe, from southern England and Denmark to the former Yugoslavia and Pyrenees. Extremely local and often rare in Continental Europe, more frequent in Britain. **Countries** Au Be Br Cz Da Ga Ge He Hu It Ju Lx. **Photos** Ga, Ardennes, 21.VII.1990. P. DELFORGE.

Epipactis leptochila (GODFERY) GODFERY var. neglecta (H. KÜMPEL) A. GÉVAUDAN

Etymology *neglecta*: neglected, forgotten. **Type** Ge, Thuringe (1982). **Synonyms** *E. leptochila* var. *praematura* KRÖSCHE nom. inval., *E. leptochila* subsp. *neglecta* H. KÜMPEL, *E. neglecta* (H. KÜMPEL) H. KÜMPEL.

Description As *E. leptochila* but with leaves darker green; flowers often a little more colourful and more open; hypochile averages not so deep; junction of hypochile and epichile narrow, upper margins of hypochile's walls almost touching each other there; tip of epichile frequently twisted down asymmetrically to one side. Plants resembling var. *neglecta* ± closely, but with pedicels extensively washed purple, are most probably the hybrid *E. helleborine* × *E. leptochila*, which is apparently not rare.

Flowering Season VI-VII, 1-2 weeks earlier than *E. leptochila*. **Habitat** More tolerant than *E. leptochila*; mid-shade to shade, beechwoods, thermophilous Oak-Hornbeam woods and other mesophilous deciduous forests, on dry to moist, calcareous substrates, up to 1500m asl.

Distribution Almost throughout the range of var. *leptochila*, often with intermediates. **Photo A** Ga, Isère, 9.VII.1997. P. DELFORGE.

Epipactis leptochila (GODFERY) GODFERY var. peitzii (H. NEUMANN & WUCHERPFENNIG) P. DELFORGE

Etymology Named after E. Peitz, German botanist (1913-1984). **Type** Ge, Taunus mountains (1997). **Synonyms** *E. peitzii* H. NEUMANN & WUCHERPFENNIG, *E. muelleri* var. *peitzii* (H. NEUMANN & WUCHERPFENNIG) P. DELFORGE, *E. leptochila* subsp. *peitzii* (H. NEUMANN & WUCHERPFENNIG) KREUTZ.

Description As *E. leptochila* but with stems isolated, robust, 15-35cm tall; cauline leaves darker green, erect, median 2-4 leaves lanceolate, acuminate, 4-7cm x 2-4cm; inflorescence near lax, 4-10cm tall; 6-20 near horizontal flowers, more widely open; junction of hypochile and epichile very narrow; column of the *E. muelleri*-type (Fig. 5c p. 47): anther overhanging stigma; clinandrium absent or nearly so; viscidium absent or rudimentary; stigma perpendicular to the axis of column; pollinia erect, their bases touching the stigma.

Flowering Season Late VII-mid VIII. **Habitat** Shady sites on moist, neutral substrates. Old-growth beechwoods 200-300m asl. **Distribution** Known only from 2 very small populations in the Taunus mountains. Extremely rare and local; threatened by forestry works. **Countries** Ge. **Photo B** Ge, Taunus (loc. typ.), 2.VIII.1997. C.A.J. KREUTZ.

Epipactis leptochila (Godfery) Godfery
var. *dinarica* (S. Hertel & Riechelmann) P. Delforge

Etymology *dinarica*: from the Dinaric Alps. **Type** Ju, Istria, Croatia (2003). **Basionym** *E. leptochila* subsp. *dinarica* S. Hertel & Riechelmann.

Description As *E. leptochila* but leaves a little longer and near erect, largest 4.7-9.4cm x 2.2-4.7cm; flowers often less open, less pendant; hypochile with splayed edges, often greenish-olive rather than reddish-brown inside; epichile more broadly heart-shaped, 4.5-5.7mm x 3.1-4.2mm; viscidium present after flower has opened.

Flowering Season VII, slightly earlier than *E. leptochila*. **Habitat** More tolerant than *E. leptochila*; from mid-shade to shade on dry to moist, calcareous substrates. Thermophilous Oak-Hornbeam woods, 600-1000m asl. **Distribution** Apparently endemic to the U´cka massif in northern Istria (Croatia). **Countries** Ju. **Photo A** Ju, Istria (loc. typ.), 6.VII.2002. S. Hertel.

Epipactis leptochila (Godfery) Godfery
var. *futakii* (Mered'a. & Potucek) P. Delforge

Etymology Named after J. Futák, Slovakian botanist (1914-1980). **Type** Cz, Slovakia, Strázovské vrchy (1998). **Synonyms** *E. futakii* Mered'a fil. & Potucek, *E. leptochila* subsp. *futakii* (Mered'a fil. & Potucek) Kreutz.

Description As *E. leptochila* but regularly cleistogamous, forming groups of, at most, 2-3 stems, 15-35 (-60)cm tall; 2-10 (-33) flowers; sepals 9-12 (-13.5)mm x 3.5-6mm, frequently washed violet at base on outer side; petals more acuminate; junction of hypochile and epichile narrower; epichile much smaller, 3.5-5.5mm x 3-43mm, greenish, whitish only at base; anther sessile; viscidium present but inefficient.

Flowering Season Mid VII-end VII. **Habitat** Shady sites on moist, acidic to neutral substrates. Beechwoods, oak-hornbeam woods, 300-600m asl. **Distribution** Known only from small populations in the Carpathians and neighbouring massifs in Slovakia. Extremely rare and local. **Countries** Cz. **Photos B** Cz, Slovakia, Partizúnske, 16.VII.2004. S. Hertel; **C** (below), **D** (opposite): Trenciaske Teplice, 17.VII.1999. E. Gügel.

Epipactis komoricensis
MERED'A.

Etymology *komoricensis*: from Komoric, part of the Strázovské massif, a south-western outlier of the Carpathians. **Type** Cz, Slovakia, Strázovské vrchy (1996). **Synonym** *E. leptochila* subsp. *komoricensis* (MERED'A fil.) KREUTZ.

Description As *E. leptochila* but with 1(-4) robust stem, (16-) 20-50 (80)cm tall; cauline leaves weakly erect, not as dark, the (2-) 3-6 (-8) median leaves narrowly lanceolate, 4-9.5cm x 1-3.5cm; bracts rather short; 3-38 pendant flowers, half-opening, self-pollinating, often cleistogamous; sepals 9-12.5mm long; petals near equal, edged pale violet; junction of hypochile and epichile not so narrow; epichile triangular to heart-shaped, 3.5-4.3mm x 3-4.3mm, tip often turned down, sometimes with an asymmetric lateral twist, 2 small bosses at base, often crimson; column of *E. muelleri*-type.

1 mm   d'après MERED'A

Flowering Season mid VII-mid VIII. **Habitat** Mid-shade to shade on moist, calcareous substrates. Old-growth beechwoods, 300-800m asl. **Distribution** The southwestern Carpathians and neighbouring massifs. Very rare and local. **Countries** Cz Hu. **Photos** Cz, Strázovské vrchy (loc. typ.), 11.VII.2000. C.A.J. KREUTZ.

E. leptochila var. *futakii*

Epipactis tallosii

A. MOLNÁR & ROBATSCH

Etymology Named after P. Tallós, Hungarian botanist. **Type** Hu, Nyirad (1997).

Description Rhizomatous, bearing 1 (-2) thick stem, (14-) 18-35 (-42)cm tall, yellowish-green, pubescent at tip; 3-5 (-8) cauline leaves, yellowish-green, spreading, erect, slightly channelled, with undulate margins; median leaves rather small, rounded to lanceolate, 2-5cm x 1-2.5cm, uppermost leaf narrowly lanceolate, bract-like; lower bracts shorter or equal to flowers; inflorescence ± lax, near one-sided, 7-30cm tall; up to 50 rather small flowers, self-pollinating, opening, near horizontal to pendant; sepals pale green, 9-10mm long; petals near equal, white to pinkish inside; hypochile nectariferous, greenish-pink outside, green or reddish brown and shiny inside; junction of hypochile and epichile rather narrow; epichile whitish to pinkish, 4.5mm x 4mm, triangular-acuminate, spreading-arched, margins reflexed, 3 small, rounded swellings at base, forming a heart-shaped, strongly grooved boss, an extension of hypochile walls; anther broad; clinandrium well developed; viscidium present in the bud, developed but inefficient; pollinia friable and then crumbling, already disintegrating onto stigma in the bud; pedicel 2.5-5mm long, base greenish-yellow.

Flowering Season VII-VIII. **Habitat** Shady sites on moist, acidic substrates. Oak woodland with *Quercus cerris* and *Q. robur*, *c.* 100m asl. **Distribution** Poorly known, but apparently endemic to the Danube valley and the interfluve between the Danube and Tisza. Very rare and local. **Countries** Hu. **Photos** Hu, Nyirad (loc. typ.), 9.VII.2000. C.A.J. KREUTZ; Tiszadersz, 30.VII.2004. S. HERTEL.

Epipactis aspromontana
BARTOLO, PULVIRENTI & ROBATSCH

Etymology *aspromontana*: from Aspromonte, a Calabrian granite massif (It). **Type** It, Reggio de Calabre (1996). **Synonym** *E. leptochila* subsp. *aspromontana* (BARTOLO, PULVIRENTI & ROBATSCH) KREUTZ.

Description As *E. greuteri* but rhizomatous, more frequently producing groups of robust stems, 30-60cm tall; 4-10 cauline leaves, median leaves lanceolate, 3.5-6cm x 1.5cm-3cm, upper 1-3 leaves bract-like; bracts pendant, lowest up to 5cm long; inflorescence elongated, dense, up to 30cm tall; 10-30 (-45) medium-sized flowers, cross-pollinated, but then self-pollinating at end of flowering period, coloration as *E. greuteri* or a little more purplish and more open; sepals 10-11mm long; petals near equal, pinkish-white; epichile *c*. 5mm x 5mm, triangular, margins undulate and reflexed; anther shortly stalked; clinandrium well developed; viscidium efficient; stigma orientated downwards; pollinia cohesive for a long time but then crumbling; pedicel not as long, 4-5mm.

Flowering Season Mid VII-mid VIII. **Habitat** Mid-shade to shade on deep, moist, siliceous substrates. The fringes of acidophilous montane beechwoods, 1100-1500m asl.

Distribution Apparently endemic to the Aspromonte massif in Calabria. Extremely rare and local.

Countries It.

Photos It, Reggio di Calabria (loc. typ.). 19.VII.1989. P. DELFORGE.

Note On Photo C (below), the raised anther reveals the pollinia in the clinandrium.

Epipactis nauosaensis
ROBATSCH

Etymology *nauosaensis*: rom. Naoussa [sic], a small town in Macedonia (Gr, Veroia). **Type** Gr, Veroia (1989). **Synonym** *E. leptochila* subsp. *nauosaensis* (ROBATSCH) KREUTZ.

Description Rhizomatous, often carrying grouped stems, thin, ± flexuous, 20-50cm tall, green, hairy (dense at tip, the short whitish elements may almost conceal colour of stem); 5-7 cauline leaves, green, rather yellowish, ± spirally arranged, spreading, margins almost lacking serrations, 1 (-2) lower leaf short, orbicular, 3-4 median leaves lanceolate, 7-9cm x 1.8-3.5cm, uppermost leaf narrowly lanceolate, 7-8.5cm long; lower bracts broad, 4-6cm long, upper bracts even longer than the flowers; inflorescence rather dense; 10-30 (-40) self-pollinating flowers, opening, bell-shaped, pendant; sepals oval-acuminate, green washed yellowish-pink inside, 8-9mm x 4-5mm; petals near equal, pinker; hypochile nectariferous, pinkish outside, pinkish-brown and shiny inside; epichile pinkish-white, narrow at junction with hypochile, 4-6mm x 3-5mm, heart-shaped, tip turned down and back, 2 purplish bosses at base, separated by a longitudinal groove that is sometimes washed green; anther yellow, acuminate, projecting beyond the rostellum; clinandrium poorly developed; rostellum elongated; viscidium very inefficient, sometimes lacking; stigmatic surface near vertical; pollinia friable and then crumbling, breaking up onto stigma; pedicel elongated, 4-5mm long, curved, with a pale yellowish base.

Flowering Season VII-VIII. **Habitat** Shady sites on deep, moist to damp, alkaline substrates. Bare depressions in montane beechwoods, up to 1800m asl. **Distribution** Bulgaria, extending southwest to Mount Vermion (Gr, Veroia and Imathia). Extremely rare and local. **Countries** Bu Gr. **Photos** Gr, Veroia (loc. typ.), 23.VII.2003. P. DELFORGE. **Notes** Often forms hybrid swarms with *E. helleborine*; these intermediates are recognisable because the base of the pedicel is washed purple and the viscidium remains functional for several days (to be confirmed!).

Epipactis greuteri
H. Baumann & Künkele

Etymology Named after W. Greuter, contemporary Swiss botanist. **Type** Gr, Trikala (1981). **Synonyms** *E. flaminia* P.R. SAVELLI & ALESSANDRINI, *E. greuteri* subsp. *flaminia* (P.R. SAVELLI & ALESSANDRINI) H. BAUMANN *et al.*, *E. greuteri* var. *flaminia* (P.R. SAVELLI & ALESSANDRINI) KREUTZ.

Description Rhizomatous, bearing 1 or a few stems, clustered, robust, 20-60 (-76)cm tall, dark green, sometimes washed violet, with a dense, hyaline pubescence; 4-8 cauline leaves, dark green, ± spirally arranged, spreading-erect, narrow, arching, edges regularly serrated, lower 1-3 leaves short and rounded, median leaves lanceolate, 5-8cm x 2-3cm, upper 1-2 leaves bract-like; bracts pendant, the lower bract up to 4.5cm long; inflorescence elongated, up to 18cm tall, occupying up to half the stem; 5-25 medium-sized flowers, self-pollinating, green to olive-green, ± opening, bell-shaped, pendant; sepals oval-acuminate, keeled, pale green, 9-12mm x 4-5mm; petals near equal, pinkish; lip 7-9mm long; hypochile nectariferous, greenish-white outside, yellowish-green to reddish-brown and shiny inside; junction of hypochile and epichile rather broad and depressed; epichile white, greenish or pinkish, 3-4mm x 4-5mm, heart-shaped, margins undulate, tip slightly turned down and backwards, base with 2 attenuated bosses; anther sessile, projecting beyond rostellum; clinandrium poorly developed or almost absent; viscidium inefficient, often absent; stigma orientated downwards (if clinandrium is sufficiently developed) or towards the anther (when clinandrium is near absent); structure then analogous to that of *E. muelleri*); pollinia friable and then crumbling, disintegrating onto the stigma; ovary pear-shaped, narrow, glabrescent, yellowish-green; pedicel very elongated, 5-10mm long, green at base, washed yellowish. The morph *'flaminia'* from Italy has a column lacking a clinandrium; it lies within the range of variation of *E. greuteri*.

Flowering Season Late VI-VIII (-early IX), just after *E. helleborine*. **Habitat** Shady sites on deep, moist calcareous substrates. Beechwoods, mixed woodland with beech and coniferous forests, up to 1500m asl. **Distribution** Disjunct. Thessalia (Gr, Pindhos and Olympus mountains) and the eastern Alps, from northern Italy to Croatia (Ju) and south to Émilie-Romagne. Very rare and local. **Countries** Au Cz Ge Gr It Ju. **Photos** Gr, Trikala, 24.VII.2003. P. DELFORGE.

97

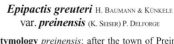

Epipactis greuteri H. Baumann & Künkele
var. ***preinensis*** (K. Seiser) P. Delforge

Etymology *preinensis*: after the town of Prein a. d. Rax. **Type** Au, Lower Austria (2001). **Basionym** *E. greuteri* subsp. *preinensis* K. Seiser.

Description As *E. greuteri* but varied, sometimes more colourful, recalling a hybrid swarm with a taxon from the *E. helleborine* complex of species; leaves a little longer, 6-7cm x 2cm, longer than their respective internode; flowers more open, less pendant; viscidium always lacking; pedicel shorter, 3-6mm long, sometimes lightly washed violet at base; ovary longer.

Flowering Season VIII. **Habitat** Shady sites on moist to dry, calcareous substrates. Mixed oak woodland, 800-900m asl. **Distribution** Apparently endemic to the Rax massif (Au). **Countries** Au. **Photos** Au, Niederösterreich (loc. typ.), 15.VII.2002. S. Hertel; 30.VII.2003. E. Gügel.

Epipactis danubialis
Robatsch & Rydlo

Etymology *danubialis*: from the River Danube. **Type** Rm, Danube delta (1989). **Synonym** *E. atrorubens* subsp. *danubialis* (Robatsch & Rydlo) Ciocărlan & R. Rös.

Description As *E. leptochila* but 1 stem, 15-40cm tall, reddish at base; 3 (-4) cauline leaves, spreading, oval, 2.2-4cm x 1-2cm, upper 1-2 leaves bract-like; the lowest bract up to 3cm long; inflorescence 3.5-15cm tall; 5-40 self-pollinating flowers, half-opening or closed; sepals 9-10mm x 4-6mm; petals near equal, yellowish; hypochile green outside, brownish inside; epichile *c.* 4mm x 3.5mm, triangular, margins undulate, tip yellowish; anther broad, obtuse; clinandrium well developed; viscidium viscous in the bud, evanescent, inefficient.

Flowering Season VI (-VII). **Habitat** Moderately shady sites on damp to wet substrates. Clearings in oak and ash woods, in depressions liable to flooding, *c.* 5m asl. **Distribution** Danube delta. Very local and very rare. **Countries** Rm.

Drawing: Rm, delta of the Danube (holotype), 20.VI.1988. E. Klopfenstein.

98

Epipactis olympica
ROBATSCH

Etymology *olympica*: from Mount Olympus.
Type Gr, Thessalia, Mount Olympus (1990).

Description As *E. greuteri* but 1 (-2) isolated stem, 35-55cm tall, pubescent at tip; 6-10 cauline leaves, green, spreading, oval-lanceolate, 4-6.5cm x 1-4cm, the upper 3-4 leaves narrowly lanceolate, up to 6cm long; lowest bract up to 4cm long, longer than the flower; 30-45 flowers, opening, mainly self-pollinating, near horizontal to pendant, withering rapidly; sepals greenish, 9-10mm x 3.5-5mm; petals near equal, greenish-pink inside; hypochile green outside, brownish-pink inside; epichile *c.* 5mm x 4mm, triangular, broad at its junction with the hypochile, with 2 small basal bosses prolonged by a central lamella; anther narrow; clinandrium poorly developed; rostellum long, narrow, dry at its tip; viscidium becoming rapidly non-functional; stigmatic surface angled slightly up towards anther; pedicel elongated, longer than ovary, base green.

Flowering Season Late VI-VII. **Habitat** Shady sites on deep, moist substrates. Old-growth montane forest, 1100-1200m asl. **Distribution** Apparently endemic to Mount Olympus. Extremely local and extremely rare. **Countries** Gr. **Photos** Gr, Mount Olympus (loc. typ.), 15.VII.1998. A. GÉVAUDAN.

Key to the *Epipactis leptochila* group

1   early flowering (late V-mid VI); bracts yellow at base .... *E. provincialis*
1*   later flowering; bracts lacking yellow at base 2

2   viscidium efficient; pollinia cohesive; flowers always cross-pollinated .. *E. guegelii*
2* viscidium absent or inefficient; pollinia crumbling; flowers self-pollinated 3

3   growing on coastal dunes .... *E. sancta*

3* growing in other habitats 4

4   junction of hypochile and epichile broad, clinandrium lacking; base of pollinia resting directly on the upright stigmatic surface 5
4* flowers lacking these characters 6

5   flowers intensely tinted magenta .... *E. placentina*
5* flowers pale, epichile whitish to pale pinkish .... *E. muelleri*

(continued on next page)

Epipactis degenii
SZENTPÉTERI & MÓNUS

Etymology Named after Á. Dégen, Hungarian naturalist (1866-1934). **Type** Gr, Thessalia, Mount Olympus (1999). **Synonym** *E. halacsyi* subsp. *degenii* (SZENTPÉTERI & MÓNUS) KREUTZ.

Description Thickset, with a rhizome bearing 1-3 (-12) stems, 8-25 (-50)cm tall, pubescent at tip; 3-8 cauline leaves, green, leathery, clasping to sheathing, oval-lanceolate, upper leaf bract-like, 2-6cm x 0.5-2.6cm; lower bract up to 5.4cm long, longer than the flower; inflorescence dense; 7-30 flowers, opening, principally cross-pollinated, near horizontal; sepals greenish, sometimes edged purple, 8-11.5mm x 4-6mm; petals near equal, whitish, veined and edged with pink on the outside, often pinker inside; hypochile nectariferous, greenish outside, brownish to reddish inside; epichile darker pink than petals, 3.5-4.5mm x 4.5-6mm, heart-shaped, rather narrow at junction with hypochile, with 2 small basal bosses prolonged by a central lamella; anther narrow; clinandrium well developed; viscidium present and functional; stigmatic surface slightly erect; pollinia cohesive then crumbling; pedicel rather long, 4-5mm, with a green base.

Flowering Season Late VII-mid VIII.

Habitat Full sun to shade on moist, calcareous substrates. Pine forests with *Pinus nigra* and their margins 1500-2200m asl.

Distribution Apparently endemic to the southern slopes of Mount Olympus. Extremely local and extremely rare. Threatened by grazing.

Countries Gr. **Photos** Gr, Mount Olympus (loc. typ.), 31.VII.1997. L.J. SZENTPÉTERI.

Key to the *Epipactis leptochila* group

(continued from previous page)

6   pedicel long, 5-10mm long 7
6*   pedicel shorter 9

7   flowers very pendant, half-opening, usually lacking pink tones .... *E. greuteri*
7*   flowers otherwise 8

8   junction of hypochile and epichile broad .... *E. olympica*
8*   junction of hypochile and epichile narrow .... *E. nauosaensis*

9   stocky, 8-25cm tall, growing over 1500m asl .... *E. degenii*
9*   plant lacking these characters 10

(continued next page)

Epipactis placentina
BONGIORNI & GRÜNANGER

Etymology *placentina*: from Plaisance, a town in Lombardy (It). **Type** It, Plaisance (1993). **Synonym** *E. muelleri* subsp. *cerritae* GRASSO.

Description As *E.muelleri* but stems solitary, 16-40 (-50)cm tall; 3-5 (-8) cauline leaves, near alternate, spreading-near arching to flat, edged with fine irregular serrations; inflorescence rather lax; 8-32 flowers, pink to magenta; sepals 7-10mm long, pink to green, the edges in that case crimson; petals pink to magenta on both sides; hypochile nectariferous, ± intensely pink outside, reddish inside; epichile pink to dark magenta, base with 2 bosses, attenuated to distinct and wrinkled.

Flowering Season Late VI-early VIII.

Habitat Mid-shade to shade on deep, moist, slightly acidic to neutral substrates. The edges of mixed forests, beech, ash and pine plantations, 600-1400m asl.

Distribution Highly fragmented. Centred on northern Italy, with a few stations in Isère (Ga), on the slopes of Etna and Mount Faito (Si), Dalmatia (Croatia Ju) and in Slovakia (Cz). Very rare and local.

Countries Cz Ga He It Ju Si. **Photos** Ga, Isère, 9.VII.1997. P. DELFORGE.

Key to the *Epipactis leptochila* group

(continued from previous page)

10   flowers small; sepals 6-8 (-9)mm long .... *E. campeadorii*
10* flowers larger, with longer sepals 11

11   early flowering (VI) .... *E. danubialis*
11* late flowering (VII-IX) 12

12   overall coloration markedly green, upper stem densely hairy, with purplish reflections; junction of hypochile and epichile broad .... *E. maestrazgona*
12* plant lacking these characters 13

13   epichile longer than broad .... *E. leptochila*
13* epichile as long as broad 14

14   leaves short and broad (length/breadth=2) .15
14* leaves elongated (length/breadth=3) ....*E. komoricensis*

15   growing below 300m asl .... *E. tallosii*
15* growing over 1000m asl .... *E. aspromontana*

Epipactis muelleri
GODFERY

Etymology Named after F. Müller, German botanist (1829-1883). **Type** Ga, Alpes-Maritimes (1918). **Synonyms** *E. viridiflora* RCHB. sensu MÜLLER, *E. helleborine* subsp. *muelleri* (GODFERY) O. BOLÓS, MASALLES & VIGO, *Parapactis epipactoides* ZIMMERMANN.

Description Rhizomatous, bearing 1-2 rather spindly stems (rarely a few clustered stems), 20-65 (-90)cm tall, yellowish-green, base hairless, purplish, tip greyish, pubescent; 5-10 cauline leaves, green to yellowish green, sometimes in two opposite rows, spreading-erect, arching, channelled, margins undulate, median leaves oval-lanceolate, acuminate, (4-) 5-10 (-12)cm x 2-4cm, upper 1-3 leaves bract-like; the lowest bract up to 4.5cm long; inflorescence dense to near lax, 5-20 (-28)cm tall; 10-40 rather large flowers, self-pollinating, yellowish-green to whitish-green, half-opening, bell-shaped, near horizontal to pendant; sepals oval-lanceolate, near obtuse, yellowish-green, keeled, 7-12mm x 3.5-5mm; petals near equal, oval-acuminate, whitish-green, hyaline, sometimes tinted pink inside; hypochile cup-shaped, nectariferous, white or greenish-pink outside, brown (± dark) and shiny inside; junction of hypochile and epichile broad; epichile whitish, 4-5mm x 2.5-4mm, heart-shaped, obtuse, spreading, tip forward-pointing to turned down and backwards, 2 very attenuated bosses at base, pinkish, sometimes reduced to a longitudinal groove; anther stalked, yellowish, overhanging the stigma (Fig. 5c p. 47); clinandrium (near) absent; viscidium absent or rudimentary, present only within the bud; stigma perpendicular to the axis of column; pollinia erect, their bases touching the stigma; ovary pear-shaped, near hairless, green; pedicel yellowish -green, not very pubescent; 2n=38, 40.

Flowering Season Mid VI-early VIII, 2-4 weeks before *E. helleborine*. **Habitat** Mainly full sun to mid-shade on dry to moist, alkaline substrates. Thermophilous short grassland and moorland, woodland edges, scrub, open woodland, up to 1300m asl.

Distribution Mid-Europe, from the Ardennes (Be Ga) to Slovakia, and from the Pyrenees to Istria (Ju) and the centre of the Italian peninsula (for Holy Island, England, see next page). Local and often rare. **Countries** Au Be Cz Ga Ge He Ho Hs Hu It Ju Lx. **Photos** Be, Luxembourg, 11.VII.1990; It, Rieti, 13.VII.1989. P. DELFORGE.

Variation Plants growing in shady sites or at high altitudes have smaller flowers, darker leaves and a general appearance similar to *Epipactis persica*. Intermediates with *E. helleborine* are sometimes reported.

Epipactis sancta
(P. DELFORGE) P. DELFORGE

Etymology *sancta*: holy (in reference to Holy Island). **Type** Br, Cheviotland, Holy Island (2000). **Synonyms** *E. peitzii* var. *sancta* P. DELFORGE, *E. leptochila* subsp. *sancta* (P. DELFORGE) KREUTZ, *E. dunensis* auct. non (T. STEPHENSON & T.A. STEPHENSON) GODFERY, *E. leptochila* var. vel subsp. *dunensis* auct. Britain. p.p., "Lindisfarne" *Epipactis* auct. Britain.

Description Differs from *E. muelleri* in its more spindly habit (stem 15-40cm tall), greenish-yellow overall coloration, channelled leaves that are more distinctly in two opposite rows, more leathery and smaller (the largest leaf 6cm x 3cm), inflorescence almost spirally arranged, smaller flowers (sepals 8mm long), very narrow junction of hypochile and epichile, smaller hypochile, 3.5mm broad, often washed with green inside, longer epichile, 3mm x 3mm, longer rostellum, pollinia already crumbling in the bud, and ecology. 2n=32.

Flowering Season VII. **Habitat** Full sun, on shell-sand among bushes of Creeping Willow *Salix repens* at sea level. **Distribution** Dunes on Holy Island. Very local and quite rare. **Countries** Br. **Photos** Br, Holy Island (loc. typ.), 12.VII.1994. P. DELFORGE.

Discussion From recent molecular analysis, this species does not appear to be closely related to *E.muelleri*, *E. leptochila* or *E. dunensis*.

103

The *Epipactis albensis* group

Characteristics Upper stem pubescent, with 60-100 hyaline elements (papillae, teeth and hairs) per mm², almost concealing the colour of the stem; leaves rather long, often narrowly lanceolate, edged with irregular serrations formed by hyaline teeth or lamina 0.1-0.3mm long; pedicel hairless, bronze-green to yellowish-green, mostly without purple at base.

Epipactis albensis
NOVÁKOVÁ & RYDLO

Etymology *albensis*: from the Elbe. **Type** Cz, central Bohemia (1978).

Description Rhizomatous, bearing 1-2 (-5) thin, spindly stems, 8-30 (-47)cm tall, base hairless, yellowish-green, tip dark green, pubescent; 3-5 cauline leaves, rather pale green, sometimes in two opposite rows, gently spreading, curved, edges slightly undulating, median leaves lanceolate, acuminate, 2-6.3cm x 1.4-3.6cm, longer than their respective internode, upper leaf bract-like; the lowest bract ± 4cm long, longer than the flower; inflorescence lax, sometimes near one-sided, up to 16cm tall; (2-) 3-12 (-25) self-pollinating flowers, yellowish-green, ± opening to closed, bell-shaped, horizontal to pendant; sepals oval-lanceolate, near obtuse, keeled, near hairless outside, whitish-green inside, 6-9.5mm x 2.5-5mm; petals near equal, whitish-green, sometimes pinkish; hypochile cup-shaped, nectariferous, whitish outside, shiny ochre to crimson or brownish, often rather pale inside; epichile short, whitish, 2.7-4mm x 2.8-4.5mm, heart-shaped, spreading, tip forward-pointing to turned down and backwards, 2 very attenuated bosses at base, pinkish, separated by a greenish longitudinal groove; anther yellowish, overhanging the stigma; clinandrium well developed; viscidium usually absent, sometimes present in the bud but quickly drying; pollinia friable; ovary narrowly spindle-shaped, shorter than the bud, glabrescent, darker green than sepals; pedicel glabrescent, washed greenish-yellow at base.

Flowering Season Late: (VII-) VIII-X (-XI). **Habitat** Mid-shade to shade on deep, moist to damp, acidic substrates. Slopes and small valleys, principally in old-growth alluvial forests, up to 500m asl. **Distribution** Continental mid-Europe, principally the basins of the Elbe (Bohemia, Saxony), upper Vistula (Poland), Morava and Oder (Moravia), Vah and Hron (Moravia and Slovakia), March and upper Danube (Lower-Austria, Hungary). **Countries** Au Cz Ge Hu Po.

Photos: Cz, Böhmen, 1.VIII.1991. J. DEVILLERS-TERSCHUREN.

E. mecsekensis

A. MOLNÁR & ROBATSCH.

Etymology *mecseksensis*: from the Mecsek massif (Hu). **Type** Hu, Mecsek massif (1996). **Synonym** *E. nordeniorum* subsp. *mecseksensis* (A. MOLNÁR & ROBATSCH) KREUTZ.

Description As *E. albensis* but 1 (-3) stems 20-40cm tall, base hairless, yellowish-green, tip pubescent; 3-5 (-7) cauline leaves, green, in two opposite rows or spirally arranged, median leaves lanceolate, rather short, acuminate, 3-5.5cm x 1-2.3cm; lower bract *c*. 2.5cm long, only slightly longer than flower; inflorescence lax, one-sided; 6-20 flowers, opening, self-pollinating, yellowish-green to pinkish, near horizontal to pendant; sepals oval-lanceolate, whitish-green on both sides, 8mm x 4mm; petals near equal, pinkish outside, pink inside; hypochile cup-shaped, nectariferous, greenish outside, dark brownish and shiny inside; junction of hypochile and epichile rather narrow; epichile rather broad, pink, 4mm x 3mm, heart-shaped, spreading, tip turned down, 2 well-developed bosses at base, pinkish to reddish, divided by a brownish longitudinal groove; anther rather broad; viscidium present but inefficient; clinandrium well developed, flat; pollinia rather friable; ovary glabrescent, narrowly spindle-shaped, longer than the bud, green, concolourous with the sepals; pedicel long, glabrescent, washed with greenish-yellow or slightly brownish at base.

Flowering Season Late VII-VIII.

Habitat Mid-shade to shade on deep, moist to damp, basic to neutral substrates. Forested ravines, often near water, up to 500m asl.

Distribution Apparently endemic to the Mecsek massif (Hu).

Countries Hu.

Photos Hu, Mecsek massif, 2.VIII.2004. S. HERTEL.

Epipactis fibri
SCAPPATICCI & ROBATSCH

Etymology *fibri*: beaver [a reference to l'île du Castor (Rhône, Ga)]. **Type** Ga, Rhône (1995).
Synonym *E. albensis* var. *fibri* (SCAPPATICCI & ROBATSCH) P. DELFORGE.

Description Differs in morphology only slightly from *E. albensis*; *E. fibri* apparently has, on average, a yellow pedicel that is more often bronzy-green at base, leaves fringed with more irregular serrations (see right), an anther with a more pointed tip and a slightly longer rostellum, but it always lacks a viscidium. The ecology of the two taxa is similar as they are both late flowering and both are limited to deep shade in acidophilous flood-plane forests at low altitudes. Molecular analysis, however, clearly separates them.

Flowering Season Late: end VII-IX (-X).

Habitat Shady sites on deep, moist to damp, acidic substrates. Poplar woods (natural or plantations), prone to flooding, wet ash-elm woodland; 90-160m asl.

Distribution The Rhône valley downstream of Lyon. Very rare and local.

0,2 mm

Countries Ga.

Photos Ga, Rhône (loc. typ.), 29.VII.1999; 31.VII.1997. P. DELFORGE.

Discussion of the *Epipactis albensis* group

A group of 5 species that has diagnostic characters intermediate between those of the *E. leptochila* group and the *E. phyllanthes* group, and until very recently included in the latter. Recent morphological, biogeographical and molecular studies show that *E. albensis* and *E. fibri* are well-differentiated species that are neither directly related to each other nor to *E. phyllanthes*; the demarcation and affinities of *E. confusa* remain less clear; *E.mecsekensis* and *E. bugacensis* have not yet been investigated genetically and are provisionally placed here. The 5 species of the group demand high humidity and are associated with flood-plain forests and their substitutes. They perhaps constitute a monophyletic group of 'alluvial' *Epipactis* that may have been able to survive in Europe not far from the ice-sheets during the last glaciation. Nevertheless, more recent hybrid origins, between species of the *E. helleborine* and *E. leptochila* groups on the one hand and *E. phyllanthes* s.l. on the other, are also plausible.

Epipactis confusa

D.P. YOUNG

Etymology *confusa:* source of confusion. **Type** Da, Teglværkskoven (1953). **Synonyms** *E. helleborine* subsp. *confusa* (D.P. YOUNG) SUNDER-MANN, *E. phyllanthes* subsp. *confusa* (D.P. YOUNG) LØJTNANT, *E. persica* (SOÓ) NANNFELDT p.p.

Description As *E. albensis* but more robust, up to 70cm tall; largest leaf up to 8cm long; leaves edged with blunt serrations that are shorter and more regular; the lowest bract up to 5.5cm long; up to 30 flowers, opening more widely; lip more colourful; epichile *c.* 4mm x 3.5mm, the tip strongly turned down, 2 larger bosses, rather wrinkled, often crimson; anther stalkless; pollinia crumbling, breaking up onto the stigma during anthesis; ovary obovoid, 11-14mm long; 2n=40.

Flowering Season VI-VIII (-IX). **Habitat** The margins of beechwoods and acidoclinous pinewoods, up to 200m asl.

Distribution Southern Sweden, Denmark and the German Baltic islands; records from the north of continental Germany probably refer to *E. albensis*. Very local and very rare. **Countries** Da Ge Su. **Photos** Da, Sjælland, 20.VII.1999. A. GÉVAUDAN.

0,2 mm

Key to the *Epipactis albensis* group

1 early flowering (late V-VI) .... *E. bugacensis*
1* flowering later 2

2 ovary shorter than the bud; sepals whitish-green 3
2* ovary longer than the bud; sepals tinted pink 4

3 tip of anther pointed; rostellum long, viscidium always absent .... *E. fibri*
3* tip of anther rounded; rostellum short, viscidium sometimes present but always inefficient and withering rapidly . *E. albensis*

4 often robust (up to 70cm tall); lowest bract up to 5cm long, rather longer than the flower .... *E. confusa*
4* less robust (up to 40cm tall); lowest bract *c.* 2.5cm long, rather short, only slightly longer than the flower .... *E. mecsekensis*

Epipactis bugacensis
ROBATSCH

Etymology *bugacensis*: from Bugaʹc, a locality in the Hungarian plains. **Type** Hu, Bács-Kiskun (1990).

Description Stems 1 (-6), (15-) 20-60cm tall, green, hairy towards tip (hairs hyaline, rather dense and long:100-160 elements per mm², > 0.8mm long); (2-) 3-5 well developed cauline leaves, ± in two opposite rows, elliptical to lanceolate, often mucronate, 3.5-6.5cm x 1.8-3.6cm, ± equal their internode, near spreading to near erect, green, often tinged yellowish, margins undulate, edged with hyaline, rather irregular serrations; upper (1-) 3-9 leaves bract-like; bracts short; inflorescence lax, near one-sided; up to 30 small flowers, half-opening, not very colourful, near horizontal to pendant; sepals green outside, yellowish-green inside, oval-lanceolate, acuminate, 9-12mm x 3.5-6mm; petals near equal, yellowish-green, sometimes with a pale pink border; hypochile nectariferous, greenish-white outside, shiny brown, ± strongly washed greenish inside; junction of hypochile and epichile very narrow; epichile 3.5-5mm x 3.5-5mm, triangular to heart-shaped, greenish-white, washed pink in centre, spreading, tip turned down, borders scalloped, 2 bosses at base, slightly wrinkled, nor very colourful, separated by a pinkish central groove; anther long-stalked, very narrow, not covering the pollinia, the sides rapidly withering; clinandrium well developed, rather flat, enclosed at the sides by the staminodes; viscidium ± developed, often inefficient, even in the bud, due to a frequent lack of cohesiveness in the pollinia; stigma quadrangular, with a well-developed basal callus and emarginate at its centre; pedicel elongated, up to 10mm long, hairy, pale green, ± washed with bronze at base.

Flowering Season Early: end V-VI. **Habitat** Shady sites on deep, moist to damp substrates. Old-growth poplar and oak woodland on alluvium at up to 300m asl. **Distribution** Known from ± ten stations in the Pannonian plain, between the Danube and the Theiss. **Countries** Hu. **Photos** Hu, Bács-Kiskun, 17.VI.2004. P. DELFORGE.

The *Epipactis phyllanthes* group

Characteristics Upper stem weakly pubescent, glabrescent or hairless; the hairs not concealing the colour of stem, with (0-) 10-100 (-110) hyaline elements (papillae, teeth and hairs) per mm², not persistent, isolated, rarely clustered, usually less than 0.3mm long; leaves fringed with (very) irregular serrations, sometimes formed by untidy tufts of hyaline teeth or lamina 0.1-0.3mm long; pedicel hairless, green to yellowish-green, lacking purple at base.

Epipactis persica
(Soó) NANNFELDT

Etymology *persica*: from Persia. **Type** Iran, Tehran (1927). **Synonyms** *Helleborine persica* Soó, *Epipactis helleborine* subsp. *persica* (Soó) SUNDERMANN.

Description Rhizomatous, bearing 1 (-5) spindly stem, 10-60cm tall, green, hairless and sometimes purplish at base, hairless to slightly puberulous at tip; 2-5 cauline leaves, often dark green, spreading, curved, edged very irregularly with small hyaline teeth, median 1-4 leaves oval to lanceolate, 3-8mm x 1.5-4.5cm, placed rather high on stem; bracts leaf-like, lowest bract as upper leaf, 3.5-6cm long; inflorescence lax; 5-30 flowers, opening, bell-shaped, facultatively cross-pollinated; sepals oval-lanceolate, 9-10mm x 4-5mm, pale green; petals near equal, more whitish; lip 8-10mm long; hypochile cup-shaped, nectariferous, whitish-green to olive-green, sometimes purplish outside, dark brown and shiny inside; epichile heart-shaped, greenish-white, sometimes washed crimson-pink, 3-4mm x 3-4mm, spreading, tip turned down, 2 ± pronounced, ± rough bosses at base, separated by a longitudinal groove; clinandrium poorly developed; viscidium persisting for rather a long time in the open flower; pollinia cohesive then crumbling, breaking up onto the stigma; ovary spindle-shaped, elongated, near hairless; pedicel pale green. **Variation** Probably a heterogeneous taxon, about which various authors may hold very different opinions.

Flowering Season VI-VIII. **Habitat** Shady sites on deep, moist, alkaline substrates. Scrub, bare ground in beech and conifer woods, sometimes also in hazel or poplar plantations, 200-2700m asl. **Distribution** Huge but fragmented, from Anatolia to the Himalayas; similar plants have been reported from old-growth European beechwoods (Ae Gr It Ju Tu); their status is not always clear. Records from Denmark refer to *E. confusa*. Very rare and local. **Countries** ?Ae An ?Gr ?It ?Ju ?Tu. **Photos** An, Zonguldag, 8.VIII.1996. C.A.J. KREUTZ.

0,2 mm

Epipactis troodi
H. Lindberg fil.

Etymology *troodi*: from Mount Troodos. **Type** Cy, Mount Troodos (1942). **Synonym** *E. helleborine* subsp. *troodi* (H. Lindberg fil.) Sundermann.

Description Rhizomatous, bearing 1(-4) thick stem, 20-45cm tall, green washed violet, central third of stem papillose, tip pubescent with very short elements that do not conceal the ground colour; 1-4 leaves, oval-lanceolate, 3-7cm x 1-3.3cm, spreading-erect, spirally arranged, keeled, rather leathery, sometimes washed violet on one (or both) sides, edged with irregular, hyaline, purplish serrations; lowest bract leaf-like, up to 5cm long; inflorescence dense to lax, near one-sided; up to 30 medium-sized flowers, yellowish-green, facultatively cross-pollinated, opening, (near)horizontal; sepals 10-12mm long, greenish-yellow to olive-green; petals near equal, paler green, often washed violet; hypochile nectariferous, whitish-green washed violet outside, greenish-red to bronze and glossy inside; epichile heart-shaped, 3-5mm x 3-5mm, purplish, 2 bosses at base, wrinkled, separated by a distinct longitudinal groove; anther stalkless, rather narrow; clinandrium ± developed; viscidium present in the newly opened flower; pollinia cohesive and then crumbling; pedicel short, greenish, ovary papillose.

Flowering Season VI-VII. **Habitat** Full sun to shade on dry to moist, acidic substrates. Mostly pine woodland, sometimes deciduous woods, 800-2100m asl. **Distribution** Endemic to Cyprus. Rare and local. **Countries** Cy. **Photos** Cy, Troodos, 21 & 22.VI.2002. P. Delforge.

Discussion of the *Epipactis phyllanthes* group

A monophyletic group, the most derived, comprising 6 species, usually self-pollinating, often confined to stable environments, principally forests that may have been glacial refuges. One subgroup contains *E. persica*, *E. troodi*, *E. cretica* and *E. exilis*, species associated with temperate forest from the Mediterraneo-hyrcano-pontic zone, i.e. either with a very broad distribution (continued on next page)

Epipactis cretica
KALOPISSIS & ROBATSCH

Etymology *cretica*: from Crete. **Type** Cr, mounts Ida and Dikti (1980).

Description As *E. troodi* but stem flexuous, 10-40 (-50)cm tall; 2-5 leaves, near erect, leathery, the edges near hairless, dark glaucous-green, tinted violet on lower surfaces, (1-) 2-4 median leaves sheathing, 2-5cm x 1-3.5cm, ± equal to their internode; lowest bract leaf-like, up to 4.5cm long; up to 20 small flowers, bronze-green, a little waxen, frequently self-pollinating, hardly opening, horizontal to pendant, near bell-shaped, slightly scented; sepals up to 9mm x 5mm; petals reddish-green inside; hypochile greenish outside, dark green or brown and shiny inside, the edges sometimes tinted purple; epichile 4-5mm x 4-5mm, greenish, sometimes pink in centre, the sides ± reflexed, often whitish to crimson-pink; anther narrow; viscidium present for 3-4 days in the newly opened flower.

Flowering Season Late V-VI; fleeting. **Habitat** Moderately shady sites on dry to moist, alkaline substrates. Mostly mixed forests of oak (*Quercus calliprinos*), cypress (*Cupressus horizontalis*) and Cretan Maple (*Acer creticum*), 700-1500m asl. **Distribution** Endemic to the Ida and Dikti massifs. Very local and extremely rare, confined to a rare and fragile habitat. **Countries** Cr. **Photos** Cr. Lassithi, 2.VI.1999. C.A.J. KREUTZ.

Discussion of the *Epipactis phyllanthes* group
(continued from previous page)

(from the Himalayas to the Alps: *E. persica*, probably a heterogeneous taxon; from northern Greece to Sardinia *E. exilis*), or with a very limited island distribution (Cyprus *E. troodi*; Crete *E. cretica*). *E. phyllanthes*, very polymorphic, is a hyper-Atlantic species, probably the most derived in the genus.

Key to the *Epipactis phyllanthes* group

1	outer face of sepals paler than ovary in freshly opened flowers	2
1*	ovary and sepals concolourous	*E. phyllanthes*
2	leaves near erect, leathery, keeled	3
2*	leaves ± spreading, soft	4
3	sepals 10-12mm long	*E. troodi*
3*	sepals up to 9mm long	*E. cretica*
4	lowest bract 3.5-6cm long	*E. persica*
4*	lowest bract 2-3.5cm long	5
5	pedicel very short	*E. exilis*
5*	pedicel 3-4mm long	*E. fageticola*

Epipactis exilis
P. DELFORGE

Etymology *exilis*: spindly. **Type** Gr, Imathia (1988). **Synonyms** *E. gracilis* B. BAUMANN & H. BAUMANN nom. illeg., *E. persica* subsp. *gracilis* W. ROSSI, *E. persica* subsp. *exilis* (P. DELFORGE) KREUTZ, *E. baumanniorum* STRÖLHE.

Description Rhizomatous, bearing 1 or a few thin stems, 11-35 (-49)cm tall, green, ± dark, hairless and purplish at base, slightly puberulous at tip; 4-6 cauline leaves, dark green, sheathing, spreading, curved, spirally arranged, edged with irregular serrations, the 2-4 leaves oval-acuminate, 2.5-6.5cm x 0.8-3.3cm, placed high on stem; bracts often all longer than flowers, lowest bract 2.8-3.5cm long; inflorescence lax, near one-sided; 3-9 (-15) pale green flowers, self-pollinating, ± opening, bell-shaped, pendant to near horizontal; sepals near keeled, oval-lanceolate, 7.5-10mm x 3.5-4.5mm, glabrescent on outside, whitish-green inside; petals near equal, whiter; lip 7-8.5mm long, greenish-white; hypochile cup-shaped, only slightly nectariferous, brown to dark green, shiny inside; epichile heart-shaped, 3.5-4.5mm x 3.9-5mm, spreading, tip greenish, pointed, ± turned down and backwards, 2 well-marked bosses at base, slightly wrinkled, whitish to pinkish, separated by a narrow longitudinal groove; anther pale yellow, narrow; clinandrium ± well developed, stigma slightly raised towards anther; rostellum long, not sticky, viscidium inefficient, evanescent; pollinia crumbling, breaking up onto stigma; ovary spindle-shaped, very elongated, up to 15mm long, glabrescent; pedicel short, yellowish-green.

Flowering Season VI-VIII. **Habitat** Shady sites on moist, calcareous to slightly acidic substrates. Bare ground in forests of beech and Holm Oak, 700-1700m asl. **Distribution** Highly disjunct. In the east: northern Greece, south to Pindhos and neighbouring regions; in the west Mount Günser (Au/Hu), Croatia and Italy, Sardinia. Very local and very rare. **Countries** Au Bu ?Co Gr Hu It Ju Sa. **Photos A&C** It, Potenza, 16.VII.1989; **B** Gr, Kalambaka, 24.VII.2003. P. DELFORGE

Epipactis fageticola
(HERMOSILLA) J. DEVILLERS-TERSCHUREN & P. DEVILLERS

Etymology *fageticola*: inhabiting beechwoods.
Type Hs, La Rioja (1998). **Synonyms**
E. phyllanthes var. *fageticola* HERMOSILLA,
E. phyllanthes subsp. *fageticola* (HERMOSILLA)
KREUTZ, *E. phyllanthes* auct. non G.E. SMITH, *E. stellifera* M. DI ANTONIO & VEYA.

Description Spindly to quite sturdy; stems 1 (-4),
whitish-green, (15-) 30-50 (-65)cm tall, tip
sparsely hairy, with (40-) 60-110 (-130) elements
per mm²; (2-) 3-7 shiny green leaves, darker than
stem, ± in two opposite rows, rather soft,
channelled to almost flat, spreading to near erect,
± arching downwards, oboval-acuminate to
lanceolate, often slightly longer than their
respective internode, second from bottom 3.5-7cm
x 1.2-4cm; the first leaf is placed relatively high
on the stem (up to 25cm), the following leaves are
regularly distributed; borders gently undulate,
often with translucent green serrations, sometimes
mica-tinted, irregular but without tufts of small
teeth; lower bract rather broad; inflorescence near
one-sided, occupying (1/3-)1/4 -1/5 (-1/6) of stem
length; 5-30 pendant flowers, closed or well-
opened; perianth segments appearing narrow,
elongated, acuminate; sepals lanceolate, keeled,
9mm x 3mm, whitish-green outside, a little paler
than the ovary; petals near equal; lip averages
8mm long, appearing rather small; hypochile cup-
shaped, green inside, nectariferous; junction
between epichile and hypochile broad; epichile
elongated, whitish to white edged with green, tip
spreading, always turned down by end of
flowering, 2 distinct bosses at base, slightly
wrinkled to smooth, white to slightly washed
pink, separated by a rather broad groove; anther
narrower than stigma; clinandrium rather deep, ±
developed; rostellum short; viscidium present,
often evanescent, inefficient; pollinia quite
cohesive but then rapidly becoming very friable;
pedicel long, yellowish-green. 2n=36, 40.

Flowering Season mid VI-VII (early IX);
sporadic. **Habitat** Mid-shade on deep,
moist to wet, slightly acidic to calcareous
substrates. Deep humus bordering streams and
watercourses, and seepages on associated slopes,
alluvial forests, old-growth poplar and willow
forests, moist mixed and deciduous forests, up to
1600m asl. **Distribution** In the east: the Rhône
basin, from the canton of Vaud (He) to Crau
(Bouches-du-Rhône, Ga) and in the eastern
Pyrenees; in the west: Spain, mainly in the upper
basin of the Ebro, and a few isolated stations
(Galicia, Salamanca, Saragossa, Teruel) south to
Andalusia (Granada, Almeria); two stations in
Portugal. Very local and often rare. **Countries** Ga
He Hs Lu. **Photos A&C** Hs, Logroño (loc. typ.),
17.VII.2001; **B** Ga, Pyrénées-Orientales,
16.VII.2001. P. DELFORGE

Epipactis phyllanthes
G.E. Smith

Etymology *-anthes*: [with] flowers; *phyll-*: [with] leaves [shape] (a reference to the petaloid lip of the nominative var.). **Type** Br, Sussex (1852). **Synonyms** *E. helleborine* subsp. *phyllanthes* (G.E. Smith) Sundermann, *E. cambrensis* C. Thomas.

Description General coloration yellowish-green; 1-2 (-5) sturdy stems, (8-) 20-45 (-65)cm tall, hairless to sometimes slightly puberulous at tip; 3-7 cauline leaves, spreading-erect, irregularly edged with disorderly tufts of hyaline serrations (see right), median leaves near quadrangular-oval, mucronate, 3.5-7.5cm x 1.5-3.5cm, placed high on stem, margins undulate, upper leaf bract-like; lowest bract leaf-like, longer than the flower; inflorescence dense to lax, near one-sided, up to 15cm tall; 5-35 self-pollinating flowers, often cleistogamous, closed or ± opening and bell-shaped, pendant; sepals and petals equal, 5-11mm long, waxen, green, sometimes with weak purplish reflections; lip 6-9mm long, green to white, of various forms, petal-like (= '*phyllanthes*'), poorly differentiated or divided in hypochile and epichile; hypochile ± cup-shaped, slightly nectariferous, green inside; epichile

0,2 mm

heart-shaped, white, spreading, tip pointed, 2 small, attenuated bosses at base, sometimes washed pinkish; structure of column varied, rapidly withering; anther stalked or stalkless; clinandrium poorly developed; viscidium absent or very quickly non-functional and evanescent; pollinia crumbling, the pollen germinating rapidly, often in the bud, forming pollen tubes on upper part of stigma; ovary green, very elongated, up to 17mm long, (near) hairless, swelling rapidly; pedicel short, yellowish-green; 2n=36. **Variation** A polytypic species (see next page).

Flowering Season VI-IX. **Habitat** Full sun (rarely) to shade on dry to moist, alkaline substrates, often calcareous sands. Dunes, scrub, bare ground in beech, oak and conifer forests, up to 200m asl.

Distribution Atlantic, highly fragmented. In the south, Galicia and Cantabria (Hs), then Landes (Ga) and to northern England, Ireland and Denmark. Very local and often rare. For records away from the Atlantic zone, see especially *E. fageticola*, and in Scandinavia *E. confusa*. **Countries** Be Br Da Ga Ge Hb Hs. **Photos** Br, Northumberland, 23.VII.1994 (*vectensis*); Ga, Landes, 18.VI.1997 (*pendula*). P. Delforge

Epipactis phyllanthes G.E. Smith
var. *olarionensis* P. Delforge

Etymology *olarionensis*: from l'île d'Oléron.
Type Ga, Charente-Maritime, île d'Oléron (1997).

Description Flowers often opening, often near horizontal; lip well differentiated; pollinia ± cohesive; viscidium often present, sometimes efficient; cross-pollination possible in newly opened flowers. **Distribution** Charente-Maritime, Vendée (Ga). **Photo A** Charente-Maritime (loc. typ.), 10.VI.1995. P. Delforge.

Epipactis phyllanthes G.E. Smith
var. *pendula* (C. Thomas) D.P. Young

Etymology *pendula*: pendulous. **Type** Br, Lancashire (1942). **Basionym** *E. pendula* C. Thomas.

Description Flowers pendant, ± opening, rarely cleistogamous; lip well differentiated; no viscidium. **Photo B** Ga, Landes, 18.VI.1997. P. Delforge.

Epipactis phyllanthes G.E. Smith
var. *vectensis* (T. & T.A. Stephenson) D.P. Young

Etymology *vectensis*: from [the Isle of] Wight. **Type** Br, Isle of Wight (1952). **Synonyms** *E. leptochila* var. *vectensis* T. & T.A. Stephenson, *E. vectensis* (T. & T.A. Stephenson) Broocke & F. Rose.

Description Lip differentiated, divided into a small cup-shaped hypochile, 2.5-3.5mm long, surrounding the column, and a triangular, elongate epichile; flowers quite often cleistogamous.

Epipactis phyllanthes G.E. Smith
var. *degenera* D.P. Young

Etymology *degenera*: degenerate. **Type** Br, Wiltshire (1952).

Description Lip weakly differentiated, with a rudimentary hypochile; flowers cleistogamous, only slightly opening. **Photo C** Be, Brabant, 13.VIII.1989. P. Delforge.

Limodorum
BOEHMER in C.G. LUDWIG 1760

Etymology *Liemodôron*: a name used by Theophrastus, probably for broomrapes (Orobanche). **Characteristics** Entirely violet, lacking green leaves, with a short rhizome and thick roots; sepals and petals free; column elongated; 2 undivided pollinia, held by a single viscidium; 2n=56, 58, 60, 64. A monospecific genus.

Limodorum abortivum
(L.) SWARTZ

Etymology *abortivum*: aborted (a reference to leaves that are aborted, i.e. reduced to small sheaths). **Type*** Ga, Seine-et-Marne, Fontainebleau (1753). **Basionym** *Orchis abortiva* L.

Description Sturdy, 20-80cm tall; stem violet or brownish, surrounded by bract-like leaves for its entire length; bracts similar to the leaves, sheathing, slightly longer than ovary; inflorescence lax, 10-33cm tall; 4-25 flowers, erect, often closed; sepals oval-lanceolate, 16-25mm x 5-11mm; lateral sepals spreading, upper sepal curved over column; petals linear, slightly shorter than sepals; lip jointed, 14-22mm long; hypochile slightly concave, 4-7mm x 4-7mm, yellowish striped with violet inside; epichile oval or heart-shaped, 10-15mm x 7-12mm, channelled, sides rolled-up and scalloped; spur slender, nectariferous, ± as long as ovary, straight or slightly curved, pointing downwards; ovary erect, stalked, 14-25mm long.

Flowering Season IV-VII; very sporadic. **Habitat** Mostly mid-shade on cool, calcareous substrates (rarely siliceous). Thermophilous woodland fringes, scrub, sometimes short grassland, banks, up to 2300m asl.

Distribution Mediterranean-Atlantic, east to Iran and the Caucasus and reaching the Belgian frontier in the north. Local but sometimes rather abundant in the south, very local and very rare in the north. **Countries** Ae Ag Al An Au Be Bl Bu Co Cr Cy Cz Ga Ge Gr He Hs Hu Ij It Ju Ls Lu Lx Ma Rm Ro Sa Si Tn Tu. **Photos** Hs, Burgos, 11.VI.1993; Gr, Kiklades, Naxos, 21.IV.1995. P. DELFORGE.

L. abortivum f. *gracile* (B. WILLING & E. WILLING) P. DELFORGE [*L. abortivum* subsp. *gracile* B. WILLING & E. WILLING, *L. abortivum* var. *gracile* (B. WILLING & E. WILLING) KREUTZ]: Spindly, 10-30cm tall, paler and smaller in all parts; flowering a little earlier (V). Known from a few stations around Megalopolis (Gr, Arcadia).

L. abortivum f. *rubrum* RÜCKBRODT [*L. abortivum* var. *rubrum* SUNDERMANN ex KREUTZ, *L. rubriflorum* BARTOLO & PULVIRENTI]: Flowers redder; a variant lacking evolutionary significance. **Countries** An Cy.

Limodorum abortivum (L.) SWARTZ
var. *trabutianum* (BATTANDIER) SCHLECHTER

Etymology Named after the French botanist L. Trabut (1853-1929). **Type*** Ag, Mount Zaccar (1886). **Synonyms** *L. trabutianum* BATTANDIER, *L. lusitanicum* GUIMARÃES, *L. abortivum* subsp. *occidentale* ROUY, *L. abortivum* subsp. *thracum* H. PRESSER, *L. brulloi* BARTOLO & PULVIRENTI, *L. trabutianum* var. *brulloi* (BARTOLO & PULVIRENTI) P. DELFORGE.

Description As *L. abortivum* but more spindly, 20-55cm tall; stem rather pale purplish-green with numerous dark violet streaks; inflorescence 10-20cm tall; up to 20 flowers, half-opening, regularly self-pollinating, vertically upright; sepals and petals directed forward; lip sepaloid, not jointed, entire, spatulate, 13-18mm x 3-5mm, flat or very slightly convex, pointing upwards, sometimes pendant; spur rudimentary, often imperceptible, 0.5-4mm long; 1 petaloid staminode in front of stigma. **Distribution** Appears rarely and sporadically in the western half of the range of *L. abortivum*. **Photos** (var. *trabutianum*): Lu, Estrémadura, 3.IV.1990. P. DELFORGE.

Variation *'thracum'*: Lip very narrow; spur 1mm long, 2 petaloid staminodes; flowers later than *L. abortivum*. **Distribution** Thrace (Gr). *'brulloi'*: Lip weakly divided in hypochile and epichile; spur 4-6mm long; 5 petaloid staminodes. **Distribution** Calabre (It).

Discussion These 3 taxa constitute degenerate and teratological variations of *L. abortivum*, due to the frequent self-pollination in this species (a situation comparable to the variation in *Epipactis phyllanthes* or *Ophrys apifera*).

Biology of *Limodorum*

The biology of *Limodorum* is not well known; reputed to be saprophytic (or mycoheterotrophic), its roots have been found connected to the roots of trees or *Cistus*, leading some authors to think it is a parasite. Be that as it may, the plant is dependent throughout its life on mycorrhizal fungi, and it also contains chlorophyll: the stem is green in section and apochromatic plants are a greenish-yellow colour. The flowers are sometimes pollinated by Hymenoptera of the genera *Bombus* and *Anthidium*, nevertheless cleistogamy is significant in *Limodorum*. Frequently, a ± large proportion of the spike does not open; flowering and fruiting entirely underground has been recorded. This species is known for its prolonged absences and can disappear for several years, particularly during drought or when the vegetation becomes too dense.

Epipogium

J.G. GMELIN ex BORKHAUSEN 1792

Etymology *epi-*: above; *-pôgôn*: lip (a reference to the position of the lip). **Characteristics** Terrestrial, saprophytic plants, with a coral-like rhizome, stoloniferous, lacking roots; stem surrounded by scales, lacking green leaves; lip 3-lobed, pointing upwards; spur ascending; column short. The genus comprises 2 species: *E. pinkum* (D. Don) Lindley, from tropical Asia, Africa and Oceania, and *E. aphyllum* from Eurasia.

Epipogium aphyllum

SWARTZ

Etymology *a-*: without; *-phyllon*: leaf. **Type*** Ro, Siberia (1753). **Basionym** *Satyrium epipogium* L.

Description Saprophytic, 5-20 (-30)cm tall; stem thickened at base, thick but fragile, whitish, yellowish or purplish, sometimes streaked red, with a few clasping scales; bracts membranous, thin, sheathing, longer than ovary; inflorescence lax; (1-) 2-8 (-10) flowers, pendant, not resupinate; sepals and petals almost identical, facing downwards, yellowish to pinkish, erect, elongated, lanceolate, channelled, 8-15mm long; lip whitish, globular, 6-9mm long, jointed; hypochile formed by 2 very short lateral lobes bordering a broad nectariferous cup, which is prolonged into a large, curved, upward-pointing spur, white washed violet; epichile heart-shaped, concave, borders scalloped, translucent-white, with 2-3 reddish or crimson papillose ridges; column 4-7mm long, yellow, thickened at tip; ovary stalked, not bent; 2n=68.

Flowering Season VI-VIII (-IX); very sporadic.

Habitat Shady sites on cool, deep substrates, alkaline to slightly acidic substrates: dense beech and conifer forests up to 1800m asl.

Distribution Temperate Eurasia east to Japan. Widespread but rare.

Countries Al An Au Br Bu Co Cz Da Fe Ga Ge Gr He Hu It Ju Lu Lx No Pb Po Rm Ro Su.

Photos Gr, Kalambaka, 24.VII.2003; Ge, Baden-Württemberg, 7.VIII.1982. P. DELFORGE.

Notes The flowers are pollinated by bees, attracted by the nectar, which has the scent of fermented banana. This species is hard to see and very irregular at its sites; it may not flower for several years or flower underground. Axillary bulbils on the underground stolons lead to the formation of large clusters of spikes and to the apparent movement of plants between appearances.

Neottia

GUETTARD 1750

Etymology *neottia*: bird's nest. **Characteristics** Terrestrial plant, sometimes saprophytic, with many non-tuberised roots or with a short rhizome; sepals and petals alike, connivent into a hood; lip elongate, 2-lobed, without a spur, often with a central nectariferous groove; column short, stigma moves forwards as soon as pollinia removed; viscidium producing a viscous drop at the slightest touch and sticking the 2 pollinia onto the head of a visiting insect. Molecular analyses have recently shown that *Listera* and *Neottia* form a single genus of *c.* 50 species spread over the cool temperate regions of both the eastern and western hemispheres; 3 species of *Neottia* in this guide.

Neottia nidus-avis

(L.) L.C.M. RICHARD

Etymology *nidus-avis*: bird's nest (after the shape of the rhizome). **Type*** Br, ?southern England (1753). **Basionym** *Ophrys nidus-avis* L.

Description Resembles a broomrape (*Orobanche*); sturdy, entirely brownish-yellow, rarely whitish, (10-) 15-35 (-50)cm tall; stem thick, emerging laterally from the rootstock, surrounded by 4-6 sheaths 2-6cm long, the upper sheaths longer and more bulging; bracts linear; inflorescence 5-20 (-30)cm tall, cylindrical, elongated, denser towards the tip, the lower flowers frequently well-spaced; sepals and petals oval-elliptic, forming a loose hood 4-6mm long; lip pendant, often pointing forward, 9-12mm long, hollowed at base into an elongated, nectariferous cup without a spur, centre with bulbous sides, tip divided into 2 broad, divergent lobes; ovary elongated, near cylindrical, 8-10mm long; pedicel twisted; 2n=36.

Flowering Season V-VII; relatively sporadic. **Habitat** Shady sites on deep, moist, alkaline to neutral substrates: dense beechwoods and conifer forests up to 2000m asl. **Distribution** Eurasia, in temperate to southern zones east to Japan. Widespread but rather rare. **Countries** Ag Al An Au Be Bl Br Bu Co Cz Da Fe Ga Ge Gr Hb He Ho Hs Hu It Ju ?Lu Lx No Pb Po Rm Ro Sa Si Su Tu. **Photos** Be, Hainaut, 6.VI.1983. J. DEVILLERS-TERSCHUREN; Ga, Aisne, 9.VI.1991. P. DELFORGE.

Notes Mostly self-pollinating, sometimes pollinated by flies, but frequently forming groups by vegetative multiplication starting from the rhizome. May flower and fruit underground. Old, dry spikes and capsules, very leathery, often persist for several years.

Neottia ovata
(L.) Bluff & Fingerhuth

Etymology *ovata*: oval (a reference to the shape of the leaves). **Type*** Ge, Baden-Württemberg (1753). **Synonyms** *Ophrys ovata* L., *Epipactis ovata* (L.) Crantz, *Listera ovata* (L.) R. Brown, *Neottia latifolia* (L.) L.C.M. Richard.

Description Sturdy, entirely green, 20-60cm tall; stem thick, with whitish hairs at the tip; leaves 2 (-3), opposite, clearly veined, slightly erect, near sheathing, inserted into lower third of stem, oval, mucronate, 4-13cm x 3-8cm; bracts 3-5mm long; inflorescence lax, 7-25cm tall; 20-80 yellowish-green flowers; sepals and petals oval, forming a loose hood 4-5mm long; sepals sometimes crimson, 2mm wide; petals 1mm wide; lip pendant, elongated, 7-15mm long, abruptly kinked, with a nectariferous cup at base (spur absent), longitudinally grooved, and divided at tip into 2 elongated lobes; ovary globular, strongly ribbed, 4-6mm long; pedicel twisted, *c.* 3mm long; 2n=32, 34, 38, 42.

Flowering Season V-VII. **Habitat** Found in a wide range of habitats up to 2400m asl. **Distribution** Eurasia; also reported from Ontario (Canada). Very widespread and common in the temperate zone, rare in Mediterranean Europe. **Countries** Ae Al An Au Be Br Bu Co Cr Cz Da Fe Ga Ge Gr Hb He Ho Hs Hu Is It Ju Lx No Pb Po Rm Ro Sa Si Su. **Photos** Be, Luxembourg, 25.V.1991; Namur, 2.VI.1991. P. Delforge.

Notes A robust species, it can live without mycorrhiza and flower for over 20 years; pollinated by the numerous insects attracted to the abundant nectar: Coleoptera, Diptera, Hymenoptera (mostly wasps and ichneumons).

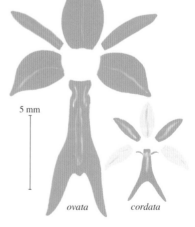

5 mm

ovata   cordata

Neottia cordata
(L.) L.C.M. RICHARD

Etymology *cordata*: heart-shaped (a reference to the shape of the leaves). **Type*** Su, Småland (1753). **Synonyms** *Ophrys cordata* L., *Epipactis cordata* (L.) ALLIONI, *Listera cordata* (L.) R. BROWN, *L. nephrophylla* LYDBERG.

Description Spindly, very small, 5-20 (-25)cm tall; stem fine, whitish and hairless below the leaves, coppery and slightly pubescent towards tip; 2 leaves, opposite, inserted in centre of stem, finely veined, horizontal, heart-shaped, dark green and shiny on the upper side, margins undulate, 1-2.5cm long; bracts 1mm long; inflorescence rather lax; 6-15 (-25) minuscule flowers, pale green to dark brownish red; sepals and petals spreading, oval to elliptic; sepals 2-3mm x 1mm; petals near equal; lip elongate, 3-4.5mm long, with a longitudinal groove, there is no spur, but the base, nectariferous, often bears 2 erect, horn-like projections, tip divided into 2 linear lobes, sometimes separated by a small appendage; ovary globular, not curved, with prominent ribs, 2-4mm long; pedicel small, twisted; 2n=36, 38, 40, 42.

Flowering Season (V-) VI-VII (-VIII). **Habitat** Full sun to shade on acidic, damp to wet substrates: cool conifer forests, amongst the mosses of boreal *Sphagnum* bogs, often in association with Bilberry (*Vaccinium myrtillus*), up to 2300m asl (above 1000m in the south of the range). **Distribution** Circumpolar (Eurasia, North America). Widespread and common in the boreal zone, less frequent in the subarctic zone, and rare and local in southern Europe, where only found in the mountains. **Countries** An Au Br Bu Cz Da Fa Fe Ga Ge Gr Hb He Ho Hs Hu It Ju No Pb Po Rm Ro Su. **Photos** Ga, Isère, 12.VI.1997. P. DELFORGE.

Notes Very difficult to spot, but often forming large populations over small areas. The flowers, facultatively self-pollinating, are pollinated by tiny Diptera and Hymenoptera. The withered flower lasts a long time on the ripe capsule.

Key to the genus *Neottia*

1   plant lacking chlorophyll, with leaves reduced to sheaths .... *N. nidus-avis*

1*   plant green, with 2 opposite leaves 2

2   sturdy, more than 20cm tall, leaves oval, more than 4cm long, stem thick, with whitish hairs .... *L. ovata*

2*   spindly, less than 20cm tall, leaves heart-shaped, less than 2.5cm long, stem slender, apparently hairless .... *L. cordata*

Spiranthes

L.C.M. Richard 1817 (nom. cons.)

Etymology *spir-*: spirally arranged; *-anthes*: flowers (inflorescence spirally arranged). **Characteristics** 2-6 spindle-shaped root-tubers, inflorescence spirally arranged; divisions of perianth near equal, usually forming a tube; lip oblong, entire, nectariferous, broadening at the tip, spur absent; rostellum split into 2 parts. Primarily an American and Asian genus, with 30 to 300 species, depending on the classification adopted; 4 species in this guide.

Spiranthes spiralis

(L.) Chevallier

Etymology *spiralis*: spirally arranged. **Type*** Ga, near Strasbourg (1753). **Synonyms** *Ophrys spiralis* L., *Neottia spiralis* (L.) Willldenow, *Spiranthes autumnalis* L.C.M. Richard.

Description Spindly, 6-30 (-40)cm tall; stem greyish-green, pubescent, surrounded by 3-7 sheaths; leaves from the current season withered by flowering, 3-7 leaves for the next season present in a rosette just next to the inflorescence, hairless, dull blue-green, oval to elliptical, acuminate, 2-3.5cm long; bracts 6-7mm long, longer than ovary, pubescent outside; inflorescence lax, helical, 3-15cm tall; 6-30 small flowers, near horizontal, greenish-white; sepals and petals near equal, oblong, 4-7mm long; dorsal sepal, petals and lip forming a narrow, bell-shaped tube; lateral spreading sepals; lip oblong, channelled, 6-7mm long, greenish-yellow edged with white, 2 visible nectaries at base, tip broader, strongly scalloped; ovary erect, sessile, puberulous; 2n=30.

Flowering Season VIII-X; sporadic.

Habitat Full sun on slightly acidic to alkaline substrates, dry (but damp in winter) to damp. Short, close-cropped vegetation on grassland, abandoned cultivation and dunes, more rarely marshes, garrigue and open pinewoods, up to 1400m asl.

Distribution Mediterranean-Atlantic, north to southern Sweden, east to Iran, and south to North Africa; absent from the boreal zone. Widespread but rare throughout the range.

Countries Ae Ag Al An Au Be Bl Br Bu Co Cr Cy Cz Da Ga Ge Gr Hb He Ho Hs Hu Ij It Ju Ls Lu Me Pb Po Rm Ro Sa Si Su Tn Tu. **Photos** Ho, Zuid-Holland, 7.IX.1980; Be, Liège, 15. VIII.1998. P. Delforge.

Notes Decreasing dramatically in many areas following the abandonment of extensive grazing and eutrophication via nitrogen fall-out.

Spiranthes sinensis
(PERSOON) AMES

Etymology *sinensis*: from China. **Type** China, nearby Canton (1807). **Synonyms** *Neottia sinensis* PERSOON, *N. amoena* M.-BIEB., *Spiranthes amoena* (M.-BIEB.) SPRENGEL, *S. sinensis* var. *amoena* (M.-BIEB.) H. HARA, *S. australis* LINDLEY.

Description Spindly, 10-40 (-50)cm tall; 3-6 (-7) basal leaves, clasping, linear-lanceolate, green, erect, (3-) 7-20cm x 0.4-2cm; 1-3 cauline leaves, bract-like, clasping; bracts narrowly oval-acuminate, 5-8mm long; inflorescence rather dense, helical, glandular-tomentose, 4-15cm tall; 6-50 flowers, small, scented, horizontal, usually pink, rarely white; perianth 5-8mm long, bell-shaped, glandular outside, closely encompassing the column; sepals and petals elongate, near equal; lip oblong, concave, with 2 small bosses at base, papillose in centre, tip projecting from the tube, crimson-pink, borders scalloped; ovary erect, sessile, puberulous.

Flowering Season (IV-) VII-VIII (-IX) (in temperate Asia).

Habitat Full sun on acidic to alkaline substrates, damp, submerged in winter. Flushed slopes, damp grassland, fens, river banks, around waterfalls; up to 2500m asl.

Distribution Principally the Urals east to Japan and Korea, as well as the Himalayas and Malaysia south to New Guinea, Australia and New Zealand. Local but often abundant in its stations.

Countries Ro.

Photos Malaysia, Tana Rata, 16.X.1999. J.-M. HERVOUET.

Notes A species with a huge distribution, very probably polytypic. Reaches Europe in the Volga-Kama region (Urals) and in the Ukrainian Carpathians (3 stations). Recently a substantial population has been reported in Georgia (Ro) under the name of *S. amoena*, an epithet considered by most authors to be a synonym of *S. sinensis*. The site, a vast acidic peat bog to which the orchids, like *Calluna vulgaris*, seem to have been introduced, lies 1,800km from the known range of *Spiranthes sinensis - amoena*. These 'Georgian' *Spiranthes* probably originate from seed of Asian plants dispersing from the nearby Batumi Botanic Gardens.

123

Spiranthes aestivalis
(POIRET) L.C.M. RICHARD

Etymology *aestivalis*: summer. **Type*** Ga, nearby Paris (1798). **Basionym** *Ophrys aestivalis* Poiret.

Description Spindly, 12-30 (-40)cm tall; stem yellowish-green, puberulous at tip; 4-6 basal leaves, clasping, linear-lanceolate, bright green, erect, 5-12cm x 0.4-1cm; 1-3 cauline leaves, bract-like; bracts acuminate, puberulous at base on outside, 6-9mm long, longer than ovary; inflorescence lax, helical, 3-10cm tall; 6-24 flowers, small, horizontal, white; perianth 5-7mm long, forming a bell-shaped tube, puberulous outside, closely encompassing the column; sepals and petals elongated, near equal; lip oblong, concave, bordered by 2 small ridges at base, tip projecting from the tube, broader, with scalloped borders; ovary erect, sessile, puberulous; 2n=30.

Flowering Season V-VIII (-IX); sporadic.
Habitat Full sun on damp, slightly acidic to neutral substrates, oligotrophic or mesotrophic. Damp dune slacks, areas with Cross-leaved Heath (*Erica tetralix*), peat bogs, damp grassland with Purple Moor-grass (*Molinia caerulea*), up to 1400m asl.

Distribution Mediterranean-Atlantic, north to Pas-de-Calais (Ga). Widespread but rare, and very rare in the north of the range. **Countries** Ag Au †Be Br Co Cz Ga Ge He †Ho Hs Hu It Ju Lu †Lx Ma Sa. **Photos** Ga, Hérault, 18.VI.1988. P. DELFORGE.

Notes Has decreased dramatically due to drainage, eutrophication or habitat destruction; apparently extinct in most of temperate ('median') Europe.

Pollination of *Spiranthes*

The flowers are pollinated by insects, usually bees, in a highly evolved mechanism that favours efficient out-crossing. On opening the flowers have the perianth so tight around the column that an insect cannot reach the nectar at the base of the lip; in trying to do so it touches the viscidium and carries off the pollinia. Once the pollinia have been removed from the flower, the rostellum slowly rises away from the lip, allowing access to the stigma. The insect, now carrying the pollinia, visits another inflorescence, always starting with the older, lower flowers. If a flower has already been visited and its pollinia removed, the insect can reach the nectar and its pollinia will touch the flower's stigma. The insect visits the flowers from the bottom of the spike upwards until it reaches a newly-opened flower where it cannot reach the nectar and leaves with a new pollinia, going on to the older flowers of another plant.

Spiranthes romanzoffiana
CHAMISSO

Etymology Named after N. Romanzoff, Russian minister (1754-1826) (Alaska belonged to Russia at this time). **Type** USA, Alaska, Aleutian islands (1828). **Synonyms** *Neottia gemmipara* SMITH, *Gyrostachys stricta* RYDBERG.

Description 15-25 (-30)cm tall; stem puberulous at tip; 3-6 basal leaves, linear-lanceolate, pointed, erect, 7-12 (-22)cm x 0.5-1.3cm, often reaching base of inflorescence; 1-3 cauline leaves, clasping, bract-like; bracts puberulous on outer side, 10-17mm long, oval, acuminate, sheathing, longer than ovary; inflorescence dense, 3-8cm tall, in a tight spiral bearing flowers in 3-4 vertical ranks; 12-35 small horizontal flowers, white or yellowish, scented; perianth 8-12mm long, tubular for half its length, tip bell-shaped; sepals and petals elongate; lip oblong, concave, channelled, pinched at the centre, streaked greenish, broadening and turned down and back at tip, edges scalloped, 2 visible nectaries at base, in the form of white bosses; ovary erect, sessile, 8mm long; 2n=30, 60.

Flowering Season VII-VIII; sporadic. **Habitat** Full sun on damp to wet, acidic substrates. In Europe, peat bogs and coastal marshes. **Distribution** USA, in the boreal and temperate zones, west to the Aleutian islands and east to the British Isles. Very local and extremely rare in Europe, where only known from a few stations in Ireland, western Scotland and England. **Countries** Br Hb. **Photos** Hb, Galway, 27.VII.1996. P. DELFORGE. **Notes** Sometimes considered a pre-glaciation relict, but seeds of *S. romanzoffiana* may have been brought to Europe by migratory birds as most of its stations in the British Isles seem to be stopovers for birds coming from the west, for example, Greenland White-fronted Goose (*Anser albifrons flavirostris*).

Key to the genus *Spiranthes*

1   flowers pink .... *S. sinensis*
1* flowers whitish to yellowish 2

2   leaves oval-elliptic, spreading, in rosette adjacent to flowering stem .... *S. spiralis*
2* leaves narrower, erect at base of flowering stem 3

3   inflorescence a lax spiral .... *S. aestivalis*
3* inflorescence a tight spiral, the flowers arranged into 3-4 vertical ranks
    .... *S. romanzoffiana*

Goodyera
R. Brown 1813

Etymology Named after J. Goodyer, English botanist (1592-1664). **Characteristics** Closely related to *Spiranthes*, with a similar pollination mechanism, but lacking root-tubers and having instead a rhizome and stolons that produce leafy shoots; leaves with reticulate veins; inflorescence less helical, sometimes one-sided or cylindrical; lip smaller than sepals, with a nectariferous hypochile that is hollowed into a cup-shape and a triangular epichile. Cosmopolitan genus, with *c.* 40 species; 2 species in this guide.

Goodyera macrophylla
Lowe

Etymology *macro-*: with large; *-phylla*: leaves. **Type** Mi (1851). **Synonym** *Epipactis macrophylla* (Lowe) A.A. Eaton.

Description Rhizome thick, producing numerous large roots; stem erect, sturdy, 20-60 (-70)cm tall, shiny green, hairless; 6-9 basal leaves, spreading-erect, elliptic-oblong, acuminate, 12-20cm x 3-7cm, dark green, shiny, ± marked with white reticulate veins; numerous small cauline leaves, bract-like, 1-2.5cm long; bracts longer than ovary; inflorescence dense to near lax, near cylindrical, up to 20cm long; up to 60 small whitish flowers, *c.*13mm long, similar to those of *G. repens*; lateral sepals spreading, 8-9mm long; dorsal sepal and petals forming a hood; sepals and ovary with a whitish pubescence on outside.

Flowering Season (VIII-) IX-XI; very sporadic. Flowering in this species is extremely rare and apparently may not take place for up to *c.* 20 years. Flowers start to open from the base of the inflorescence, in successive series lasting ± 3 weeks, flowers at the tip of the spike open 2 months after those at base. By the end of flowering the leaves have withered.

Habitat Mostly mid-shade on acidic, damp to wet substrates. Cliffs and ravines in evergreen forest in the trade-wind cloudforest zone, 1000-1400m asl.

Distribution Endemic to Madeira. Very local and extremely rare, known from a few inaccessible stations in the north of the island. A relict Macaronesian species close to extinction; a few plants are preserved in Ribeiro Frio Botanic Gardens.

Countries Mi. **Photos** Mi, Ribeiro Frio Botanic Gardens, 19.IX.1991. D. Rückbrodt.

Goodyera repens

(L.) R. Brown

Etymology *repens*: creeping (a reference to the stolons). **Type*** Ge, Bavaria, Nürnberg (1753). **Synonyms** *Satyrium repens* L., *Epipactis repens* (L.) CRANTZ, *Neottia repens* (L.) SWARTZ, *Goodyera repens* var. *ophioides* FERNALD.

Description Spindly, 6-25 (-30)cm tall; stem pale green, pubescent at tip; 3-7 basal leaves, spreading in a rosette, oval-oblong, acuminate, 1-4 cm x 0.5-2cm, blue-green or yellowish, stalked, ± marked with white reticulate veins (Photo C); a few small, bract-like cauline leaves; bracts pale green, lanceolate, longer than ovary; spike rather dense, one-sided or slightly helical, 3-7cm tall; 5-30 small white flowers, horizontal, scented, pubescent outside, 3-5mm long; sepals concave, lanceolate, lateral sepals spreading; petals oblong, near spatulate; dorsal sepal and petals forming a hood; lip jointed, pointing downwards; hypochile globular, nectariferous, sometimes slightly pinkish, epichile 2mm long, triangular, channelled, directed forwards; column short; pollinia yellow; ovary erect, sessile, pubescent; 2n=28, 30, 32, 40.

Flowering Season VI-IX. **Habitat** Mid-shade to shade on dry to damp, acidic to slightly alkaline substrates. Conifer forests, more rarely broad-leaved woodland, up to 2000m asl.

Distribution Circumpolar in the temperate and boreal zones. Widespread but rather rare; spreading in temperate Europe following the coniferisation of forests.

Countries An Au Be Br Bu Cz Da Fe Ga Ge Gr He Ho Hs Hu It Ju Lx No Pb Po Rm Ro Su.

Photos Be, Luxembourg, **A&C** 11.VII.1992; **B** 12.VII.1981. P. DELFORGE.

Key to the genus *Goodyera*

1   leaves 12-20cm long .... *G. macrophylla*
1*   leaves 1-4cm long .... *G. repens*

Corallorhiza

GAGNEBIN 1755 (nom. & orth. cons.)

Etymology *korallion*-: coral; -*rhiza*: roots (in reference to the shape of the rhizome). **Characteristics** Saprophytic, with a branched, angular rhizome that resembles a piece of coral and produces one or several spindly stems that lack leaves and are surrounded by sheaths; anther terminal, 4 yellow pollinia, waxy, attached to the viscidium by a thin elastic caudicle. A poorly known genus with 10 species, exclusively American with the exception of *C. trifida*.

Corallorhiza trifida

CHÂTELAIN

Etymology *trifida*: with 3 points (shape of lip). **Type*** Su, Norrbotten (1760). **Synonyms** *C. intacta* CHAMISSO, *C. innata* R. BROWN.

Description 7-30cm tall; stem hairless, yellowish, surrounded by 2-4 sheaths; bracts scale-like; inflorescence lax; 2-10 (-12) small flowers, slightly pendant, perianth greenish-yellow; sepals and petals oblong, 4-6mm x 1-2mm; lateral sepals near spreading; dorsal sepal and petals forming a loose hood; petals sometimes lightly spotted brownish-red inside; lip 3-lobed, white, spotted brownish-red at base, shorter than sepals, 4-5.5mm x 2.5-3mm, with 2 slight ridges and a central groove (probably nectariferous); lateral lobes small, pointed; centre lobe broadly oval; spur rudimentary; column curved, 4mm long; ovary not twisted, greenish, with a twisted pedicel; 2n=38, 40, 42.

Flowering Season V-VII (-VIII); sporadic.

Habitat Very diverse, on damp, acidic, neutral or basic substrates. Montane woodland and marshes, tundra, wet dune slacks, often in small groups in the leaf-litter of beechwoods or conifer forests, up to 2300m asl.

Distribution Circumpolar (Eurasia, North America). Widespread in boreal Europe, more local in the temperate and sub-Mediterranean zones.

Countries Al An Au Be Br Bu Cz Da Fe Ga Ge Gr He †Ho Hs Hu Is It Ju No Pb Po Rm Ro Su.

Photos Ga, Alpes-de-Haute-Provence, 5.VI.1980; Isère, 11.VI.1997. P. DELFORGE.

Notes Difficult to find, with a largely subterranean life cycle. Self-pollinating, but sometimes pollinated by Hymenoptera and small flies of the genus *Scatiphaga*. The brownish capsules, surmounted by the dried-out divisions of the perianth, may remain hanging on the stem for a long time.

Calypso
SALISBURY 1807 (nom. cons.)

Etymology *Kalypso*: the queenly nymph in Homer's *Odyssey*. **Characteristics** Rhizome coral-shaped, poorly developed; 1 ovoid pseudobulb, originating from a swelling of the stem; a single leaf, stalked, growing from the pseudobulb; one stem with a solitary flower; sepals and petals similar; lip clog-like; column thickened, petaloid; viscidium functional, bursicle absent. Monospecific genus (various American taxa seem to be merely varieties), without close relatives. The clog-like lip recalls *Cypripedium*, but the single stamen and 2 pairs of pollinia point to a separate evolution to that of the Cypripedioidae.

Calypso bulbosa
(L.) OAKES

Etymology *bulbosa*: bulbous. **Type*** Su, Lapland; Ro, Siberia (1753). **Synonyms** *Cypripedium bulbosum* L, *Calypso borealis* (SWARTZ) SALISBURY, *C. americana* R. BROWN.

Description 8-20cm tall; stem hairless, surrounded by 2-3 sheaths; 1 long-stalked leaf, glaucous-green, pleated, oval, near pointed at tip, 3-6cm x 2-5cm; bract pink, 10-12mm x 2-3mm, as long as pedicel; 1 (-2) flowers, vanilla-scented; sepals and petals crimson-pink, lanceolate, pointed, 12-22mm x 2.5-4mm, spreading or erect; lip white or pink, 15-23mm long, clog-shaped, tip spreading, base hollowed into a cup, with long yellow hairs at throat and strongly streaked with purple inside (more lightly marked on exterior), this extending forward as a 2-lobed yellow spur that lies below tip of lip; column very thickened, pink, petaloid; ovary elongate, not twisted.

Flowering Season V-VI; early, as soon as the snow melts.

Habitat Shady sites on acidic, damp to wet substrates. *Sphagnum* bogs in boreal conifer forests.

Distribution Circumpolar (Eurasia, North America); not growing south of 57° N in Europe. Local but sometimes abundant in Scandinavia, more widespread in Asia and North America.

Countries Fe Ro Su.

Photos Su, Västerbotten, 22.V.1994. D. TYTECA.

Note The flower has no nectar and attracts its pollinators – female bumblebees of the genus *Bombus* – by deception; it resembles a nutritive flower in its scent and the shape of the lip, and the cluster of yellow hairs mimics pollen (see p. 14, visual lures).

Liparis
L.C.M. RICHARD 1817 (nom. cons.)

Etymology *liparos*: shiny (a reference to the leaves). **Characteristics** Leaves shiny green; petals often filiform; lip curved; column more elongated than in Malaxis, tip winged; 4 waxy pollinia; rostellum much reduced. A cosmopolitan genus, with *c*. 300 species, 1 species in Europe.

Liparis loeselii
(L.) L.C.M. RICHARD

Etymology Named after J. Loesel, German professor of medicine (1607-1657). **Type*** Su, Uppland (1753). **Synonyms** *Ophrys loeselii* L., *Malaxis loeselii* (L.) SWARTZ, *Liparis loeselii* subsp. *ovata* RIDDELSDELL, *L. loeselii* var. *ovata* (RIDDELSDELL) Q.O.N. KAY & R.F. JOHN.

Description Spindly, entirely green, 6-25cm tall, with a horizontal rhizome bearing 2 adjacent pseudobulbs, the older topped for a long time by the dead inflorescence and dried capsules; stem hairless, 3-5 angled at base, near winged at tip; 2 (-3) basal leaves, 2.5-11cm x 1-2.5cm, oval-lanceolate, erect, surrounding younger pseudobulb and base of stem; bracts scale-like; inflorescence lax, 2-10cm tall; 2-15 (-18) greenish-yellow flowers, facing upwards, probably self-pollinating; sepals and petals in a horizontal plane, 4-6mm long, margins very recurved, forming very fine tubes 0.5-1mm in diameter; lip without a spur, 5mm long, oblong, concave, entire, curved, erect, far broader than sepals, margins scalloped; column elongated, 3mm long; ovary vertical, 6mm long, with a short pedicel; 2n=26, 32. *'ovata'* leaves broad and oval; a variant without evolutionary significance, known from Wales (Br) and Finistère (Ga).

Flowering Season (V-) VI-VII (-VIII); sporadic. **Habitat** Full sun to shade on wet, alkaline to neutral substrates. Amongst mosses in fens, the margins of damp dune slacks, up to 900m asl. **Distribution** Circumboreal (Eurasia, North America). Widespread but very rare in temperate and sub-Mediterranean Europe. **Countries** Au Be Br †Bu Cz Da Fa Fe Ga Ge He Ho Hs Hu It ?Ju No Pb Po Rm Ro Su. **Photos** Ga, Isère, 12.VI.1997. P. DELFORGE. **Notes** A pioneer species associated with the initial stages in the development of alkaline or basiclinous bogs, often growing on moss surrounding tussocks of Black Bog-rush (*Schoenus nigricans*), but disappearing as soon as the vegetation increases in height or when the substrate dries out. On the road to extinction following drainage of its habitats and urbanisation of coastal areas.

Malaxis
SWARTZ 1788

Etymology *malaxos*: soft (a reference to the leaves). **Characteristics** Soft green leaves; inflorescence with numerous very small flowers; perianth recurved backwards, freeing up access to the stigma; petals often filiform; lip nectariferous; column very short, with 4 waxy pollinia. Essentially a pan-tropical genus with more than 200 species; 2 species in Europe.

Malaxis monophyllos
(L.) SWARTZ

Etymology *mono-*: single; *-phyllos*: leaf. **Type** Su, Medelpad (1753). **Synonyms** *Ophrys monophyllos* L., *Microstylis monophyllos* (L.) LINDLEY.

Description Spindly, entirely greenish-yellow, 10-30 (-50)cm tall; stem hairless, grooved at tip, growing from a vertical rhizome that has a single subterranean pseudobulb, 8-10mm diameter, enveloped by sheaths of dead leaves; 1 (-2) basal leaf, oval-elliptic, 3-10cm x 1.5-5cm, spreading, curved; bracts tiny; inflorescence rather lax, 3-15 (-25)cm tall; up to 35 very small green flowers; sepals 2-3mm long, oval-lanceolate, margins recurved, lateral sepals vertically erect; petals filiform, 1.7-2.4mm long, spreading, ± curved backward; lip 1.3-2.5mm long, broadly triangular, acuminate, concave, cone-shaped, entire or with small pointed lateral lobes, most often pointing upwards with base of ovary and pedicel twisted through 360°; spur absent; ovary short, 5mm long, stalked; 2n=28, 30.

Variation The flowers more remote from the stem give the spike a laxer appearance than that of *M. paludosa*.

Flowering Season VI-VII (-VIII).

Habitat Mid-shade on damp to wet, neutral or slightly alkaline substrates. Flushed slopes, bogs in coniferous and deciduous forests, peat bogs, fens, up to 1900m asl.

Distribution Circumpolar (Eurasia, North America); temperate and boreal Europe, but absent from the western Alps. Relatively widespread and rather rare.

Countries Au Cz Fe Ge He It Ju No Pb Po Rm Ro Su.

Photos Au, Steiermark, 19.VII.1998: Ge, Garmisch-Partenkirchen, 2.VII.1989. P. DELFORGE.

Malaxis paludosa
(L.) SWARTZ

Etymology *paludosa*: of boggy ground. **Type** Su, Uppsalaland (1753). **Synonyms** *Ophrys paludosa* L., *Hammarbya paludosa* (L.) O. KUNTZE.

Description Small, entirely greenish-yellow, 5-20 (-25)cm tall, often forming groups; stem hairless, 3-5-angled, growing from a vertical rhizome that has 2-3 pseudobulbs 4-8mm diameter, separated by 1-2cm, the upper visible; usually 2 (-3) clasping leaves at base of stem, surrounding upper pseudobulb, largest 0.8-3cm x 0.5-1.3cm, sometimes with a row of bulbils at tip; bracts tiny; inflorescence 2-15cm tall; up to 35 tiny green flowers; sepals oval, 2-3mm long, lateral sepals vertically erect; petals 1.4-2mm long, oval, strongly reflexed and bent backwards; lip 1.5-2mm long, concave, entire, cone-shaped, spur absent; lip orientated upwards due to 360° twist in pedicel and ovary; ovary very short, 3mm long; 2n=28.

Flowering Season VII-VIII (-IX); rather sporadic.

Habitat Confined to areas saturated with water, amongst *Sphagnum*, in acidic, oligotrophic mires, up to 1100m asl.

Distribution Circumpolar (Eurasia, North America); temperate and boreal Europe. Widespread and rare; very rare in submeridional Europe. Threatened due to eutrophication and destruction of its habitats. **Countries** Au Be Br Cz Da Fa Fe Ga Ge Hb Ho It Ju No Pb Po Rm Ro Su.

Photos Su, Medelpad, 6.VII.1988. P. DELFORGE.

Note Flowers pollinated by tiny flies. The intermittent presence of bulbils on the margins of the leaves and the vertical arrangement of the pseudobulbs do not justify the creation of a monospecific genus (*Hammarbya*) for this species if one considers the range of variation in vegetative parts in the entire genus *Malaxis*.

Key to the genus *Malaxis*

1   a single leaf 3-10cm long .... *M. monophyllos*
1*   2-3 leaves 0.8-3cm long .... *M. paludosa*

Note on the subtribe Liparinae

Liparis loeselii, *Malaxis monophyllos* and *M. paludosa*, growing on mosses and *Sphagnum*, with pseudobulbs adapted to the annual growth of their support, may be considered to be the only 3 epiphytic orchids in Europe.

Gennaria
PARLATORE 1860

Etymology Named after P. Gennari, Sardinian botanist (1820-1897). **Characteristics** Underground parts made up of 1 atrophied rhizome and 2 successive ovoid-oblong root-tubers, solitary at flowering time; root-tubers for the following year appear after anthesis, at the extremities of long runners; stem with 2 alternate leaves; inflorescence rather dense with small flowers; perianth segments free; column very short; rostellum triangular; retinacles without bursicles; 2n=34, 40. A monospecific genus.

Gennaria diphylla
(LINK) PARLATORE

Etymology *di-*: 2; *-phylla*: leaves. **Type** Lu, Setubal (1800). **Synonyms** *Satyrium diphyllum* LINK, *Orchis diphylla* (LINK) SAMPAIO, *Coeloglossum diphyllum* (LINK) FIORI & PAOLETTI.

Description Entirely greenish-yellow, 10-50cm tall; 2 unspotted leaves, alternate, clasping, inserted rather high on stem, broadly heart-shaped, acuminate, lower leaf 3-12.5cm x 2.2-8cm, upper leaf far smaller, green, glossy on underside, with marked longitudinal and fine intermediate veins that form an obvious web on dried leaves; bracts shorter than flowers; inflorescence elongated, rather dense, usually one-sided; 10-45 small flowers; perianth segments connivent, bell-shaped, 3-4mm long; sepals oblong, obtuse, slightly concave; petals rhomboidal, obtuse, a little longer and paler than sepals; lip oblong, 3-lobed, shorter than, to as long as, petals; lateral lobes linear-lanceolate, divergent; median lobe broader and longer than laterals, pendant; spur 1-2mm long, short, obtuse, flattened, tip bilobed; ovary spindle-shaped, twisted, stalked; 2n=34.

Flowering Season I-IV (-V).

Habitat Usually mid-shade, on acidic to slightly alkaline substrates. Rock fissures, garrigue, maquis, pinewoods, laurel forests, up to 1000m asl.

Distribution Mediterranean-Atlantic zone. Recorded from Madeira and Porto Santo (Mi), the Canaries, although absent from Lanzarote and Fuerteventura, and Minorca in the Balearics. Very local and rather rare in the centre and west of its range, extremely rare in Sardinia, Corsica and Tunisia.

Countries Ag Bl Ca Co Hs Lu Ma Mi Sa Tn.
Photos Co, Corse-du-Sud, 5.IV.1996. P. DELFORGE.

Habenaria
WILLDENOW 1805

Etymology *habena*: strip (a reference to the linear lobes of the lip). **Characteristics** 1-2 entire root-tubers, ovoid to spindle-shaped; flowers often greenish; lateral sepals spreading; dorsal sepal concave; petals often lobed; lip usually 3-lobed, spurred; stigma with 3 distinct lobes; 2 granular pollinia; 2 caudicles and 2 distinct retinacles, without bursicles. A pantropical genus with *c.* 600 species; 1 species in the guide.

Habenaria tridactylites
LINDLEY

Etymology *tri-*: 3; *-dactylos*: finger (a reference to the 3-lobed lip). **Type** Ca (1835).

Description 10-30 (-60)cm tall; stem erect, leafless; 2 (-3) basal leaves, near erect to spreading, oblong-lanceolate, acuminate, (1.5-) 5-18cm x (1-) 1.5-7cm; bracts equal to ± 1/2 length of ovary; inflorescence lax, cylindrical; 2-12 (-24) greenish-yellow flowers, scented; lateral sepals 5-7mm x 1-2.5mm, bent backwards, linear to narrowly falcate, tips reflexed; dorsal sepal broadly oval, concave, 4-6mm long, forming a hood with petals; petals oval-elongate, asymmetrical, with a tooth at base; lip 7-9mm long, strongly 3-lobed; lobes near equal, lateral lobes linear, spreading, divergent, median lobe slightly broader, pendant; spur elongate-club-shaped, pendant, curving forward, 9-14.5 (-20)mm long, as long as, to slightly longer than, ovary.

Flowering Season XI-II.

Habitat Full sun to mid-shade on moist to damp, slightly acidic substrates. Fissures in shaded cliffs, mossy, rocky slopes in open woodland, old terraces, up to 1400m asl.

Distribution Endemic to the Canary Islands. Widespread and sometimes quite common in the western side of the archipelago, far rarer on Lanzarote, doubtfully recorded from Fuerteventura.

Countries Ca.

Photos Ca, Tenerife, 16.I.1999. P. DELFORGE.

Note A relict of an ancient Atlantic flora, *H. tridactylites* was probably restricted to laurel forests, only fragments of which survive today. Its closest relative, *H. aitchinsonii*, is found in Nepal.

Herminium
L. 1758

Etymology *hermis, inos*: foot of the bed (a reference to the shape of the root-tuber). **Characteristics** 2 basal leaves; perianth segments erect, connivent, bell-shaped; lip 3-lobed; median lobe elongated; retinacle distinct; bursicle rudimentary. Eurasian genus, with *c.* 20 species, but only 1 in Europe.

Herminium monorchis
(L.) R. Brown

Etymology *mon-*: single; *-orchis*: tuber. **Type*** Su, Scanie (1753). **Synonyms** *Ophrys monorchis* L, *Herminium clandestinum* Grenier.

Description Entirely greenish, with an atrophied rhizome and 1 root-tuber: apparently solitary at flowering time (there are, in fact, 2-5 secondary root-tubers at the end of long rhizomes); stem 7-25 (-30)cm tall; 2 opposite basal leaves, oval to linear-lanceolate, 2-10 (-12)cm long; 1-2 (-3) bract-like cauline leaves; bracts 2-4mm long; inflorescence spindly, cylindrical, rather elongated, 1.5-10cm tall; up to 100 tiny flowers, yellowish-green, bell-shaped; sepals oval-oblong, 2-3mm x 1-2mm, slightly greener than petals; petals linear, 3-4.2mm long, obtuse, longer and yellower than sepals, frequently 3-lobed, median lobe tapering, tooth-shaped; lip 3-4.5mm long, distinctly 3-lobed, the same colour as the petals, with a small, nectariferous cup and a rudimentary spur at the base; lateral lobes linear, divergent; median lobe elongate; column short; ovary stalkless; 2n=40, 42.

Flowering Season V-VII (-VIII); sporadic. **Habitat** Full sun on dry to damp, calcareous to neutral substrates. Dune slacks, fens in the plains, short grassland and marshes in hills and mountains, up to 2400m asl.

Distribution Eurasia, east to Japan. Locally abundant in temperate Europe, local in the boreal zone, found in mountains in the submeridional zone.

Countries Au Be Br Bu Cz Da Fe Ga Ge He Ho Hu It Ju No Pb Po Rm Ro Su.

Photos Ga, Savoie, 9.VII.1997. P. Delforge.

Notes The flowers are honey-scented and pollinated by diverse small insects, but produce little seed. Propagation is apparently principally vegetative, and this species can form populations of several thousand plants. There are large fluctuations in the number of flowering plants from one year to the next.

135

Neottianthe
SCHLECHTER 1919

Etymology *Neottia*: a genus of orchids; *-anthos*: flower (a reference to a resemblance to the flowers of certain Asian *Neottia*). **Characteristics** 2 ovoid to ellipsoidal root-tubers, sometimes slightly cut; 2 basal leaves; sepals and petals forming a hood; lip 3-lobed, spurred; retinacles parallel, close, without bursicles; caudicles very short. A monospecific genus.

Neottianthe cucullata
(L.) SCHLECHTER

Etymology *cucullata*: hooded (a reference to the hood formed by the sepals). **Type*** Ro, Siberia, Lake Baikal (1753). **Synonyms** *Orchis cucullata* L., *Gymnadenia cucullata* (L.) L.C.M. RICHARD.

Description Spindly, 10-30 (-40)cm tall; 2 (-3) near opposite basal leaves, oblong to rounded, 1.5-7 (-9)cm x 1-5cm; 1-2 (-4) bract-like clasping leaves; bracts pointed, equal to, or longer than, ovary; inflorescence lax, often near one-sided, 3-8cm tall; 3-20 (-30) narrow flowers, pink to reddish, sometimes crimson; sepals lanceolate, pointed, together with the linear petals forming an acuminate hood, 6-8mm long, ± bell-shaped at tip; lip deeply 3-lobed, directed forwards, 7-9mm long, margins pink, centre white, with 2-8 dark spots; lateral lobes linear; median lobe tongue-shaped, broader and longer than laterals; spur narrow, near cylindrical, pendant, curved forwards, 5-6.5mm long; ovary stalkless.

Flowering Season (VI-) VII-VIII (-IX).

Habitat Mid-shade to shade on deep, damp, acidic substrates. Primary forests of conifers, more rarely mixed or oak woodland, up to 500m asl. May grow up to 2000m in alkaline marshes in Japan.

Distribution Temperate Eurasia from the Baltic to Japan. Rare and local.

Countries Pb Po Ro. **Photos** Po, Augustow, 8.VIII.1985. C.A.J. KREUTZ.

Notes Morphologically very stable throughout the range, has the habit of a *Gymnadenia* with large pink flowers and often grows together with *Goodyera repens*. Pollinators poorly known, but most probably bees.

Traunsteinera
REICHENBACH 1841

Etymology Named after J. Traunsteiner, Austrian pharmacist (1798-1850). **Characteristics** 2 entire, ovoid root-tubers; leaves glaucous-green, not forming a basal rosette; inflorescence globular; sepals and petals spatulate at tip, connivent in a hood; spur short; column short, obtuse; rostellum 3-lobed, median lobe erect, linear, hooded; retinacles enclosed in a rudimentary bursicle that does not completely envelop them; 2n=42. **Discussion** An apparently isolated genus, difficult to place in a phylogeny. Recent molecular analyses tend to place it close to the genus *Chamorchis*, whose morphology is nevertheless very divergent; these 2 genera then form a clade, close to the *Plantanthera-Gymnadenia-Dactylorhiza* group.

Traunsteinera sphaerica
(M.-BIEB.) SCHLECHTER

Etymology *sphaerica*: spherical (shape of inflorescence). **Type** Ro, Iberia (1808). **Synonyms** *Orchis sphaerica* M.-BIEB., *Traunsteinera globosa* subsp. *sphaerica* (M.-BIEB.) SOÓ.

Description Habit (leaves, as well as shape of inflorescence, sepals and petals), similar to *T. globosa*, differing mainly in flower colour and dimensions and shape of lip. Flowers cream or pale yellow (sometimes a little greenish), without spots; lateral sepals 8-12.5mm long; petals 4.5-7.5mm long; lip 5-9mm long; lateral lobes rhomboidal, sometimes slightly falcate; median lobe 2-4mm long, tongue-shaped, sometimes with a mucro at tip; spur spindly, conical, 3-5mm long.

Flowering Season VI-VII. **Habitat** Probably as *T. globosa*, in full sun on slightly acidic to alkaline, dry to damp substrates. Poor grassland, mountain pastures, montane marshes, the fringes and more open areas in conifer forests, 1600-2700m asl. **Distribution** The montane and subalpine zones of the Caucasus and mountains bordering the eastern Black Sea; in eastern Anatolia as far as Giresun; reports from further west in Anatolia, notably from mountains around Bursa, may refer to *T. globosa*. Very rare and local in Anatolia. **Countries** An Ro. **Photos** An, Giresun, 27.VI.1994. C.A.J. KREUTZ.

Key to the genus *Traunsteinera*

1   flowers pink to deep lilac; lip spotted with purple .... *T. globosa*

1*   flowers pale yellow or cream; lip unspotted .... *T. sphaerica*

Traunsteinera globosa
(L.) REICHENBACH

Etymology *globosa*: spherical (shape of mature inflorescence). **Type** He (1759). **Synonyms** *Orchis globosa* L., *Nigritella globosa* (L.) REICHENBACH.

Description Spindly and slender, 20-60 (-70)cm tall; stem flexuous, yellowish-green; 4-6 leaves, erect, sheathing, arranged all along stem, dark glaucous-green on both sides, unspotted, narrowly lanceolate, slightly hooded, diminishing in size, lowest leaf 5.5-13cm x 1-3cm, intermediate leaves more pointed, uppermost bract-like; bracts membranous, green, edged violet; inflorescence very dense, initially shortly conical then longer and globular, 1.5-6cm x 1.5-3cm; numerous small flowers, pink to deep lilac, very rarely white; sepals (4.5-8 (-9)mm long) and petals (3.5-6 (-7)mm long) oval-lanceolate, terminating in a long-spatulate point, forming a hood, tight at base, bell-shaped at tip, sometimes spotted purple; lip spreading, wedge-shaped, 3-lobed, 3.5-6 (-8)mm long, pink or lilac, whitish or yellowish at base, spotted purple over entire surface, rarely unspotted in centre; lateral lobes small, triangular to rhomboidal, obtuse or scalloped; median lobe longer, truncated, often with elongated mucro at tip; spur spindly, slightly curved, 2.5-3mm long; ovary near linear, stalkless, hardly twisted.

Variation Very distinctive, showing very little variation.

Flowering Season (V-) VI-VIII.

Habitat Full sun on dry to damp, slightly acidic to alkaline substrates. Poor short grassland, mountain pastures, montane marshes, (500-) 1000-2700m asl.

Distribution European, montane and subalpine: the Pyrenees, Massif Central, Vosges, Alps and Carpathians, north to southern Poland, south to the Apennines, perhaps to Abruzzi (It); eastern limits poorly known in the Balkans and in Anatolia, where reports from west of Giresun and in the mountains around Bursa most probably refer to *T. sphaerica*. Not very widespread and rather rare.

Countries ?Al Au Bu Cz Ga Ge He Hs Hu It Ju Rm Ro.

Photos It, Trento, 12.VII.1987; Ga, Isère, 11.VI.1983. P. DELFORGE.

Note The 2 species in this genus apparently never produce hybrids, neither interspecific nor intergeneric.

Chamorchis

L.C.M. RICHARD 1817

Etymology *kamai*: on the ground; *-orchis*: [the genus] *Orchis* (a reference to the height of the plant). **Characteristics** 2-3 entire, ellipsoid root-tubers; numerous grass-like basal leaves; lip lacking a spur; 2 pollinia; retinacles contiguous; 2n=?42. A monospecific genus that may be closely related to *Traunsteinera* (see Discussion p. 137).

Chamorchis alpina

(L.) L.C.M. RICHARD

Etymology *alpina*: alpine. **Type*** Su, Luleå Alps (1753). **Synonyms** *Ophrys alpina* L., *Herminium alpinum* (L.) LINDLEY, *Orchis alpinum* (L.) SCHRANK.

Description Very small, entirely greenish, often forming 2 young root-tubers; stem pale green, (3-) 5-12 (-15)cm tall, slightly angular at tip; 4-10 leaves, all basal, narrowly linear, channelled, reaching tip of inflorescence or longer; bracts green, linear, acuminate, longer than their flowers; inflorescence dense, oval, 1-4cm tall; 2-12 (-15) very small flowers, green washed with brown; sepals alike, yellowish, brownish or greenish, oval, 3-4.2mm long, forming a tight hood; petals linear, 2-3mm long, concealed in hood; lip without a spur, yellowish, brownish, greenish or bright green, oval, 3-4mm long, obscurely 3-lobed, rarely entire, 2 bosses at base forming a small nectariferous cup that is prolonged into a groove on median lobe; column short; ovary stalkless, twisted.

Flowering Season VII-VIII. **Habitat** Full sun, mainly on dry, calcareous substrates. Short, exposed alpine grassland above the tree line, at (1500-) 2000-2700m in the Alps, sometimes at sea level in Scandinavia; often associated with Mountain Avens (*Dryas octipetala*).

Distribution The European boreal-alpine zone in the Alps, Carpathians and Scandinavian Alps, north almost to the Kola Peninsula (Ro). Very local but often abundant in its stations. **Countries** Au Cz Fe Ga Ge He It Ju No Po Rm Ro Su. **Photos** He, Uri, 25.VII.1989. P. DELFORGE.

Notes The flowers lack a perceptible scent and are pollinated by various small insects, often minuscule flies. This, the smallest European orchid, is very difficult to see, even though it may form colonies of many hundreds, thanks to significant vegetative propagation via the root-tubers. Sometimes in the company of Edelweiss (*Leontipodium alpinum*) in the Alps.

Platanthera

L.C.M. RICHARD 1817

Etymology *plat-*: thickened; *-anthera*: anther (a reference to the separation of the base of the housings of the pollinia). **Characteristics** 2 entire root-tubers, ovoid to spindle-shaped; lateral sepals spreading; dorsal sepal and petals connivent in a hood; spur nectariferous; stigma single, flat; 2 distinct retinacles, lacking bursicles. This genus is probably paraphyletic, close to *Gymnadenia*, with *c.* 80 species; 8 species in the guide.

Platanthera bifolia

(L.) L.C.M. RICHARD

Etymology *bifolia*: with 2 leaves. **Type*** He, Zürich (1753). **Synonyms** *Orchis bifolia* L., *P. solsticialis* BÖNNINGHAUSEN, *Platanthera solsticialis* var. *latiflora* DREJER, *P. bifolia* subsp. *latiflora* (DREJER) LØJTNANT.

Description As *P. chlorantha* but often smaller and more spindly, (8-) 15-50 (-90)cm tall; 12-25 (-45) white flowers; tip of lip greenish-yellow; spur arched, neither flattened nor broadening at tip; housings of pollinia (theca) parallel and close to each other; 2n=42.

Flowering Season V-VIII.

Habitat Not specialised. Short grassland, moorland, open woodland, sometimes marshes, up to 2500m asl.

Distribution Temperate Eurasia, north to Lapland and east to central Siberia. Widespread and sometimes quite common, except in southern regions.

Countries Ag Al An Au Be Bl Br Bu ?Co Cz Da Fa Fe Ga Ge Gr Hb He Ho Hs Hu It Ju Lu Lx No Pb Po Rm Ro Sa Si Su Tn Tu.

Photos Hs, Tarragona, 10.VI.1989; Ga, Bouches-du-Rhône, 10.V.2001. P. DELFORGE.

Variation Rather varied. In mid-Europe, 2 ecotypes can be distinguished. The most frequent (photos) is limited to short grassland and open woodland on dry to moist, neutral and basic soils; it is relatively distinct due to its early flowering season, sturdiness and larger flowers (lip 10-16mm long, spur 20-41mm long). The second ecotype, associated with acidic habitats, flowers *c.* 3 weeks later and has smaller flowers (see var. *robusta*, next page); it is quite frequent at low altitudes from Belgium to Scandinavia, growing in grassland, open forest and acidic peat bogs. The distinction between these 2 ecotypes has rarely been made and their relative distribution is poorly known. Moreover, the distinction runs into a nomenclatural imbroglio.

Platanthera bifolia (L.) L.C.M. Richard
var. *robusta* Seemen

Etymology *robusta*: robust; **Type** Ge, Borkum island (1894). **Synonym** *P. bifolia* subsp. *graciliflora* Bisse.

Description Spindly to robust, 8-30cm tall; inflorescence often dense; small yellowish flowers; tips of sepals rounded; lip 6-10 (-12)mm long, spur 13-23mm long.

Flowering Season 2-3 weeks after *P. bifolia*. **Habitat** Full sun to shade on moist to wet, acidic substrates. Dune slacks, short grassland, open woodland, peat bogs, up to 600m asl. **Distribution** The Atlantic zone, from Belgium and the British Isles to northern Scandinavia. Very rare and local. **Countries** Be Br Ge Da Hb Su No. **Photo A** Be, Luxembourg, 25.VI.1994. P. Delforge.

Platanthera bifolia (L.) L.C.M. Richard
var. *kuenkelei* (H. Baumann) P. Delforge

Etymology Named after S. Künkele, German orchidologist (1931-2004). **Type** Ag, Azazga (1981). **Synonyms** *P. kuenkelei* H. Baumann, *P. bifolia* subsp. *kuenkelei* (H. Baumann) Kreutz.

Description 45-90cm tall; basal leaves up to 30cm long; inflorescence lax and elongated; 15-80 spindly flowers; lip 11-13mm long.

Flowering Season IV-VII. **Habitat** Shady sites on acidic substrates. Oak woodland with *Quercus suber*, up to 1300m asl. **Distribution** Known from a few stations in eastern Algeria and extreme northwest Tunisia. Very rare and local. **Countries** Ag Tn.

Platanthera bifolia (L.) L.C.M. Richard
var. *atropatenica* (B. Baumann et al.) P. Delforge

Etymology *atropatenica*: from Atropatene, a region of Media. **Type** Ro, Azerbaijan, Talysch massif (2003). **Basionym** *P. bifolia* subsp. *atropatenica* [*"atropatanica"*] B. Baumann *et al.*

Description As var. *bifolia* but more slender, averages taller, with broader leaves and a more elongated inflorescence, petals smaller (6-6.7mm x 1.9-2.5mm vs 7-8.4mm x 2.5-3.6mm for var. *bifolia*) and spur shorter (18-25mm vs 26-32mm, according to the description of var. *atropatenica*).

Flowering Season V-VI. **Habitat** As var. *bifolia* but mid-shade to shade. Mostly forest and forest edge. **Distribution** Caucasus. Rare and local. **Countries** Ro. **Photo B** Ro, Azerbaïdjan, Mt. Talysch. 23.V.1996. H.-W. Zaiss.

Platanthera chlorantha
(CUSTER) REICHENBACH

Etymology *-antha*: [with] flowers, *chlor-*: green; **Type** He (1827). **Synonyms** *Orchis montana* auct., *Platanthera montana* auct., *P. bifolia* subsp. *chlorantha* (CUSTER) ROUY, *P. chlorantha* var. *gselliana* H. BAUMANN et al.

Description Sturdy, (20-) 40-80cm tall; 2 (-3) large basal leaves, near erect to spreading, broadly elliptic to oval, 5.5-20cm x 1.75-8cm, shiny, green (sometimes bluish); bracts broad, leaf-like, the lower a little shorter than flowers; inflorescence near lax, cylindrical, up to 27cm tall, appearing broad; 8-27 rather large flowers, whitish with yellowish-green extremities, rarely entirely white or pale greenish-yellow, scented, especially at night; lateral sepals spreading, narrowly oval to slightly falcate, 9-12mm x 5-6mm; dorsal sepal broadly heart-shaped, 6.5-10mm x 6.5-10mm, forming a hood with petals, which are narrowly falcate, 6.5-10mm x 2-3mm; lip narrowly tongue-shaped, usually pendant, 9-18mm x 2.3-4.2mm, the tip brightly tinted yellowish, greenish-yellow or pale green; spur club-shaped, tip obtuse, 18-41mm long, far longer than ovary, slightly curved into an S-shape, upper half broader, compressed and greener; housings of pollinia divergent, well separated at their base; 2n=42.

Flowering Season V-VIII, 2-3 weeks before *P. bifolia*. **Habitat** Shade to full sun on alkaline, often calcareous, dry or damp substrates. Short grassland, damp meadows, fens, open woodland (more rarely dense), with moist soils, up to 2300m asl.

Distribution Mediterranean-Atlantic; north to the coast of central Norway, south to Sicily. South-eastern and south-western limits poorly known as a result of confusion with neighbouring taxa. Widespread but uncommon. **Countries** Ae Al An Au Be Br Bu ?Co ?Cy Cz Da Fe Ga Ge Gr Hb He Ho Hs Hu ?Ij It Ju ?Ls Lx ?Ma No Pb Po Rm Ro ?Sa Si Su Tu. **Photos** Be, Hainaut, 25.V.1991; Luxembourg, 2.VI.1991. P. DELFORGE.

Pollination of *P. bifolia* and *P. chlorantha*

These 2 species are broadly sympatric, completely interfertile, and their flowering seasons overlap. They are only isolated by pre-zygotic barriers due to subtle mechanisms that illustrate a highly specialised adaptation to their pollinators, crepuscular and nocturnal moths of the families Sphingidae, Noctuidae and Geometridae. Despite having different scents, the 2 species attract similar pollinators, although in unequal frequencies.

(continued on next page)

Platanthera algeriensis
BATTANDIER & TRABUT

Etymology *algeriensis*: from Algeria. **Type** Ag, the Algiers region (1892). **Synonyms** *P. chlorantha* subsp. *algeriensis* (BATTANDIER & TRABUT) EMBERGER.

Description Robust, (25-) 40-80cm tall; 2 (-3) large basal leaves, near erect to spreading, oblong-lanceolate, channelled, 9-30cm x 2-5cm; 4-6 small, bract-like cauline leaves; bracts broad, leaf-like, the lowest at least longer than the flowers; inflorescence rather dense, cylindrical, 6-25cm tall, appearing narrow, with flowers close to stem; 8-30 rather small flowers, entirely green or greenish-yellow; lateral sepals spreading, oval-obtuse, 8-11mm x 4-6mm; dorsal sepal broadly heart-shaped, petals ovoid, together forming a hood 5.5-8mm long; lip narrowly tongue-shaped, pendant or curved backward, 8-14mm x 1.7-3.9mm; spur club-shaped, attenuated at the base, 15-24mm long, the upper half compressed and flattened, tip obtuse; anther with housings of pollinia divergent, well separated at their base.

Flowering Season V-VII. **Habitat** Full sun on damp or wet, acidic substrates. Boggy depressions in the mountains at 700-2000m asl.

Distribution Western sub-Mediterranean. The Moroccan and Saharan Atlas, east to the vicinity of Algiers (Ag). Reported in Europe from Corsica, Sardinia and Abruzzi (It), as well as from Spain, as far as southern Aragon (Teruel province). Very rare and local. **Countries** Ag Co Hs It Ma Sa. **Photos** Hs, Teruel, 11.VII.2004. P. DELFORGE.

Pollination of *P. bifolia* and *P. chlorantha*
(continued from previous page)

Nevertheless, due to its shorter spur and closely-placed retinacles, the pollinia of *P. bifolia* are fixed to the proboscis of a visiting moth, while those of *P. chlorantha* are attached to the eyes, so that the transfer of pollen between the two is greatly reduced and only takes place from short-spurred flowers to those with long spurs. Hybrids are disadvantaged in that their scent is less attractive to pollinators and the intermediate location of their retinacles results in their pollinia being fixed to the base of a moth's proboscis, where the palps prevent a firm attachment: either they are not carried away or they rapidly fall off. Hybrids, poorly-pollinated, function only as female receptacles and are rapidly absorbed into the parent species. Nevertheless, in regions where *P. bifolia* and *P. chlorantha* have spurs with similar lengths, the isolation mechanism is less effective, giving rise to hybrid populations with flowers close to those of *P. bifolia*, but with the housings of the pollina clearly divergent.

Platanthera holmboei
H. LINDBERG fil

Etymology Named after J. Holmboe, Norwegian botanist (1880-1943). **Type** Cy (1942). **Synonym** *P. chlorantha* subsp. *holmboei* (H. LINDBERG fil.) J.J. WOOD, *P. montana* subsp. *holmboei* (H. LINDBERG fil.) STRÖHLE.

Description As *P. algeriensis* but smaller and less robust, 15-40cm tall, and with fewer flowers; (1-) 2-3 (-4) basal leaves, 6-18cm x 2-5cm; inflorescence lax; up to 25 entirely green flowers; lateral sepals 7-10mm x 3-4mm; hood 5-7mm long; lip pendant, sometimes slightly curved backwards at the tip, 7-10mm x 1.5-3mm; spur 15-30mm long, cylindrical, little or not at all flattened at tip.

Flowering Season IV-VI.

Habitat Mid-shade to shade on dry to moist substrates. Pinewoods, scrub, up to 2000m asl.

Distribution Eastern Mediterranean: reported from the coastal mountains from southern Anatolia south to Israel; may reach the Greek islands in the eastern Aegean. Rare and local.

Countries ?Ae An Cy Ij Ls.

Photos A&B Cy, Limassol. 21.VI.2003; **C** 9.IV.1989. P. DELFORGE.

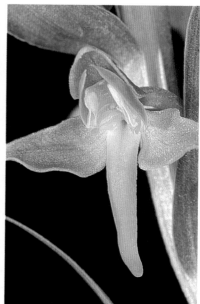

Platanthera hyperborea
(L.) LINDLEY

Etymology *hyperborea*: northern (a reference to its range). **Type** Is, Oxeraa (1767). **Synonym** *P. convallenifolia* (FISCHER) LINDLEY, *P. koenigii* LINDLEY, *Orchis hyperborea* L., *Habenaria hyperborea* (L.) R. BROWN, *Limnorchis hyperborea* (L.) RYDBERG, *Gymnadenia hyperborea* (L.) LINK.

Description On Iceland, compact, (6-) 10-30 (-45)cm tall; 4-8 cauline leaves, near erect, the lower leaf short, hooded, 2-3 median leaves lanceolate, 5-15cm x 1-3cm, upper 1-5 leaves small, bract-like; inflorescence rather dense, 2-9cm tall; numerous small, sweetly-scented flowers, facultatively self-pollinating or cleistogamous, greenish-yellow to green; lateral sepals spreading or deflexed, lanceolate, asymmetric, 4-6mm long; dorsal sepal rhomboidal, with a broad, truncate base, concave, obtuse, 3-5mm long, forming a hood with the petals; petals lanceolate to falcate; lip tongue-shaped, obtuse, usually pendant, 4-7mm x 1.5-3mm; spur 3-6mm long, slightly shorter than the lip, curved downward.

Variation Highly polymorphic, poorly-delimited, may reach a height of 100cm in North America. Numerous variants have been described at various taxonomic ranks. In Iceland, only the nominative var. can be found: small, compact and few-flowered.

Flowering Season (VI-) VII-VIII (-IX).

Habitat Full sun on damp to wet, acidic substrates. Fens in the taiga and tundra, rarely poor, dry, short grassland, up to 3000m asl in North America.

Distribution North America in the subarctic to cold temperate zones, east to Greenland and Iceland, west to Japan and Kamchatka. In Iceland rather widespread and abundant in its stations.

Countries Is.

Photos Is, Bingrellir, 10.VII.1995. D. RÜCKBRODT.

Notes Although the spur is slightly nectariferous and the column morphologically similar to that of *Platanthera chlorantha*, *P. hyperborea* is regularly self-pollinating in the more northerly parts of its range, where moths of the family Noctuidae are absent. With the least vibration the pollinia come out of their housings and fall onto the stigma. The predominance of autogamy may explain the intense radiation that characterises the various populations of *P. hyperborea*, perplexing botanists and resulting in the various taxonomic treatments that have been applied to this taxon.

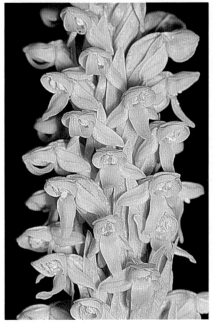

145

Platanthera micrantha
(HOCHSTETTER ex SEUBERT) SCHLECHTER

Etymology *micro-*: small; *-anthos*: flower. **Type** Az (1844). **Basionym** *Habenaria micrantha* HOCHSTETTER ex SEUBERT.

Description 12-35cm tall; 2 basal leaves, erect to spreading, oblong-lanceolate to elliptic, 6-17cm x 2-6.5cm; 2-6 smaller cauline leaves, decreasing in size, the uppermost bract-like; bracts often shorter than ovary; inflorescence rather dense, narrowly cylindrical, 8-13cm tall, *c.* 1cm broad; numerous small yellowish-green flowers; lateral sepals spreading, elliptical, asymmetrical, 2.5-4mm long; petals triangular-rounded, slightly fleshy, connivent with dorsal sepal in a hood 2.5-4mm long; lip oblong, rounded at tip, horizontal, curved downward, 2-4mm long; spur obtuse, 2-3.5mm long, curved downward, 1/4-1/3x length of ovary; housings of pollinia parallel.

Flowering Season V-VI. **Habitat** Full sun to mid-shade on damp, acidic substrates. Amongst *Sphagnum* in herbaceous maquis with the heather *Erica azorica*, 200-1400m asl. **Distribution** Endemic to the Azores, although absent from Gracioso. Local and rather rare. **Countries** Az. **Photos** Az, São Miguel, 14.VI.2003; Pico, 12.VI.2003. P. DELFORGE. **Discussion** The specific status of *P. azorica* is sometimes disputed; some authors consider it to be a variety of, or synonym for, *P. micrantha*. Nevertheless, although *P. micrantha* and *P. azorica* are often syntopic and their flowering times overlap, they produce very few hybrids, indicating that they are separated by efficient isolating mechanisms, including, perhaps, a rather frequent tendency towards self-pollination due to the disintegration of the pollinia.

Problems of the *P. chlorantha* group

Although they are better differentiated than the different variants of *P. bifolia*, the status of the 3 taxa in this group is not well established. They do not, apparently, come into contact but the limits of their distributions are not known with certainty. Variation, cytology, pollinators, and the chemistry of the nectar have only been well studied in *P. chlorantha*, so that a phylogenetic reconstruction of this group would be premature. The remaining morphological differences do not appear to be decisive: the spur length may be correlated with the flower size or be a function of selective pressures exerted by the available pollinators; Greek populations of *P. chlorantha* often show, with their smaller and greener flowers, a similarity with *P. holmboei*; finally, although well-separated geographically and ecologically, *P. algeriensis* and *P. holmboei* are rather similar.

146

Platanthera azorica
SCHLECHTER

Etymology *azorica*: from the Azores. **Type** Az (1920). **Synonym** *Habenaria longibracteata* HOCHSTETTER ex SEUBERT.

Description As *Platanthera micrantha* but more robust, 25-40 (-60)cm tall, overall coloration more whitish; leaves larger, up to 23cm long; bracts often longer than ovary; inflorescence laxer, up to 2cm in diameter; flowers a more whitish green, larger, although sepals and petals smaller; lateral sepals more elongated, directed downwards; lip narrowly tongue-shaped, 2-4mm long, horizontal, curved upwards, often hiding the entrance of the spur and the pollinia; spur slender, 7-9mm long, ± equal to ovary.

Flowering Season VI-VII.

Habitat As *P. micrantha*, 500-1000m asl.

Distribution Endemic to the Azores; reported from Santa Maria, São Miguel, São Jorge, Pico and Flores. Rarer than *P. micrantha*.

Countries Az.

Photos Az, Pico, 12.VI.2003. P. DELFORGE.

Key to the genus *Platanthera*

1	basal and cauline leaves present	 2
1*	only basal leaves present	 4
2	lowest leaf short, much smaller than the next leaf	*P. hyperborea*
2*	2 lowest leaves large	 3
3	spur 7-9mm long	*P. azorica*
3*	spur 2-3mm long	*P. micrantha*
4	a single basal leaf	*P. oligantha*
4*	2 (-3) basal leaves	 5
5	housings of pollinia parallel	*P. bifolia*
5*	housings of pollinia divergent at base	 6
6	lip usually white, at least at the base	*P. chlorantha*
6*	flowers entirely green	 7
7	full sun, in wet sites (marshes, seepages, margins of streams)	*P. algeriensis*
7*	mid-shade to shade, in pinewoods, garrigue	*P. holmboei*

Platanthera oligantha
TURCZANINOW

Etymology *olig-*: few; *-antha*: flowers. **Type** Ro, Siberia (1854). **Synonyms** *Platanthera parvula* SCHLECHTER, *P. obtusata* (BANKS ex PURSH) LINDLEY subsp. *oligantha* (TURCZANINOW) HULTÉN, *Lysiella oligantha* (TURCZANINOW) NEVSKI.

Description 6-20cm tall; 1 basal leaf, erect, oval-lanceolate, 4-7.5cm x 1.2-2.1cm; 1 (-2) small, bract-like cauline leaf; bracts ± equal to ovary; inflorescence rather dense; 2-9 small greenish-white flowers; lateral sepals deflexed, oval, asymmetric, 2.2mm-2.8mm long; dorsal sepal broadly heart-shaped, concave, obtuse, 2-2.3mm long, connivent in a hood with the petals, which are oblong, asymmetric, 2.5-3mm long; lip tongue-shaped, near pointed, slightly down-curved, 3-3.5mm x 1mm, with 2 small bosses at base; spur linear, curved downwards, 2.5-3mm long.

Flowering Season VI-VII. **Habitat** Full sun to mid-shade on damp, alkaline or decalcified substrates. Arctic and subarctic tundras, mountains, 500-1200m asl. **Distribution** Eurosiberia in the boreal and arctic zones, extending to the temperate zone in Asia. In Europe, only present in Lapland, where very local and extremely rare. **Countries** Fe No Ro Su. **Photos** Su, Abisko, 4.VII.1991. C.A.J. KREUTZ. **Note** The flowers are pollinated by mosquitoes.

Discussion Sometimes considered as a var. or subsp. of *P. obtusata*, an American species that is more robust, up to 35cm tall, with larger and more numerous flowers, longer lateral sepals, 3.5-4.5mm long, a linear-lanceolate lip, 4-10mm long, and a conical spur 5-10mm long. Depending on the author, either a: forms intermediate between *P. obtusata* and *P. oligantha* are only found in Alaska, which is thus the contact zone between the 2 species, which are not present in Greenland or Iceland, or b: numerous plants similar to *P. oligantha* grow here and there, with intermediates, in many American populations of *P. obtusata* and therefore *P. oligantha* is a variety of *P. obtusata*.

Hybrids in the genus *Platanthera*

With the exception of the interspecific hybrid *P. bifolia* × *P. chlorantha* (*P.* × *hybrida* Brügger), which is perhaps quite frequent, some intergeneric hybrids have been described: with *Dactylorhiza* (×*Rhizanthera*), *Gymnadenia* (×*Gymnaplatanthera*), *Orchis* (×*Orchiplat-anthera*), *Anacamptis* (×*Anacamptiplatanthera*) and *Coeloglossum* (×*Coeloplatanthera*). They are all extremely rare and very unconvincing.

Gymnadenia

R. BROWN 1813

Etymology *gymn-*: naked; *-adên*: gland (a reference to the absence of a bursicle). **Characteristics** Root-tubers flattened, digitate for at least half their length; numerous small flowers; dorsal sepal and petals forming a hood; lip obscurely to clearly 3-lobed; spur nectariferous; column short; retinacles without bursicles. Eurasian and North Atlantic genus, close to *Platanthera* and *Dactylorhiza*, with *c.* 30 species; 19 species in this guide.

The *Gymnadenia albida* group

Characteristics Lip turned downwards; lateral sepals not spreading; root-tubers deeply divided; 2n=40, 42; 2 species in this guide. **Discussion** This group is probably paraphyletic. Often considered to form a distinct genus (= *Leucorchis*, = *Pseudorchis*), apparently primitive, similar to the common ancestor of the genera *Platanthera* and *Gymnadenia*.

Gymnadenia straminea

(FERNALD) P. DELFORGE

Etymology *straminea*: straw yellow. **Type*** Canada, Newfoundland (1926). **Synonyms** *Habenaria straminea* FERNALD, *Pseudorchis albida* subsp. *straminea* (FERNALD) A. LÖVE & D. LÖVE, *P. straminea* (FERNALD) SOÓ, *Leucorchis straminea* (FERNALD) A. LÖVE, *Leucorchis albida* subsp. *straminea* (FERNALD) A. LÖVE, *Platanthera albida* var. *straminea* (FERNALD) LUER, *Gymnadenia albida* subsp. *straminea* (FERNALD) LØJTNANT.

Description As *G. albida* but more thickset, 15-31cm tall; 2-5 leaves, the largest 2-7cm x 1-4cm; inflorescence often short; up to 50 pale yellow flowers, much larger; bracts 10-15mm long, clearly longer than the flower; sepals and petals 2.7-4mm x 1.5mm; lip 3-5mm long, 3-lobed, the 3 lobes near equal in length; spur 2.5-3.1mm long (see figure, next page).

Flowering Season VII-VIII. **Habitat** In Europe full sun, on very alkaline, dry to damp substrates. Meso-hygrophilic grassland, up to 1000m asl.

Distribution Boreal-subarctic amphi-Atlantic, from Canada and Greenland to northern Scandinavia, south to the Faeroe Islands. Rare and local. **Countries** Fa Fe Is No Ro Su. **Photos** Is, Austur Skaftafell, 7.VII.2000. J. DEVILLERS-TERSCHUREN; Su, Abisko, 5.VII.1991. C.A.J. KREUTZ.

Gymnadenia albida
(L.) L.C.M. RICHARD

Etymology *albida*: whitish. **Type*** It, Pistoia (1753). **Synonyms** *Leucorchis albida* (L.) E. MEYER, *L. albida* var. *subalpina* (NEUMAN) HYLANDER nom. nud., *Pseudorchis albida* (L.) A. LÖVE & D. LÖVE, *P. albida* subsp. *tricuspis* (BECK) E. KLEIN, *Gymnadenia albida* f. *subalpina* NEUMAN, *G. albida* var. *tricuspis* BECK, *G. aschersonii* BRÜGGER & KILLIAS.

Description (6-) 10-40cm tall; 3-7 oblong-elliptic to lanceolate leaves, near erect, 2.5-8cm x 1-2.5cm, positioned all along stem, the 2-3 uppermost bract-like; bracts equal to, or longer than, ovary, 5-8mm long, shorter than flower; inflorescence dense, cylindrical, elongated, 2-8 (-10)cm tall; up to 60 small pendant flowers, half-opening, greenish-yellow to whitish, facultatively self-pollinating or cleistogamous; divisions of perianth loosely connivent; sepals and petals near equal, oval, 2-3mm long; lip 2.4-4mm x 2-3mm, base concave, 3-lobed, cut to centre; lateral lobes linear or tooth-shaped; median lobe frequently longer and broader than lateral lobes; spur yellowish, descendent, curved, 1.5-2.3mm long; ovary stalkless, erect, 2n=40, 42. **Variation** 2 ecotypes can be distinguished, with similarly-sized flowers: *'albida'*, an acidophilous taxon, has lateral lobes of the lip clearly shorter than median lobe; *'tricuspis'* (= subalpina, = aschersonii), a taxon of calcareous habitats, has lateral lobes of the lip almost as long as median lobe (Photos A & B).

Flowering Season V-VIII. **Habitat** Full sun on acidic to alkaline, dry to damp substrates. Poor or eutrophic short grassland, montane fens, sometimes open woodland, up to 2700m asl. **Distribution** Eurasia in the boreo-alpine and temperate zones, east to Kamchatka, south to the Pyrenees and Apennines. Rather widespread and sometimes abundant in the mountains, rarer elsewhere. **Countries** Al Au Be Br Bu Co Cz ?Fa Fe Ga Ge Gr Hb He †Ho Hs ?Is It Ju No Pb Po Ro Su. **Photos** He, Graubünden, 6.VII.1987; Ga, Isère, 18.VII.1976. P. DELFORGE.

albida

tricuspis

straminea

2 mm

d'après KLEIN, modifié

150

The *Gymnadenia conopsea* group

Characteristics Lip turned downwards; lateral sepals spreading; root-tubers flattened, digitate for half their length; 2n=40, 80, 100, 120; 3 species in this guide (*G. alpina* (RCHB. f.) CZEREPANOV, *G. conopsea* subsp. *serotina* (SCHÖNHEIT) DWORSCHAK, *G. graminea* DWORSCHAK, *G. splendida* DWORSCHAK, *G. splendida* subsp. *odorata* DWORSCHAK, *G. vernalis* DWORSCHAK are considered synonyms of *G. conopsea*.

Gymnadenia frivaldii
HAMPE ex GRIESEBACH

Etymology Named after Frivaldszky de Frivald, Hungarian botanist (1799-1870). **Type** Roumelia (1844). **Synonyms** *Pseudorchis frivaldii* (HAMPE ex GRIESEBACH) P.F. HUNT, *Leucorchis frivaldii* (HAMPE ex GRIESEBACH) SCHLECHTER.

Description 10-30cm tall; 3-5 erect leaves, the 2-3 lower leaves close together, oblong-lanceolate, near obtuse, 4-9cm x 0.8-1.5cm, upper leaves cauline, bract-like; bracts lanceolate, pointed, washed pink, longer than ovary; inflorescence dense, short, initially conical then ovoid, 1.5-4cm tall; 15-40 (-50) small flowers, slightly inclined, pinkish-white, pink or cream; dorsal sepal oval, 3-3.5mm long, forming a hood together with petals; lateral sepals spreading horizontally, 3.5-4.5mm long, margins strongly rolled; petals oblong, obtuse, shorter than sepals; lip entire to obscurely 3-lobed, 3.5-4mm x 3.5-4mm, lateral lobes rounded, central lobe wedge-shaped, recurved; spur filiform, 1.5-3mm long, slightly curved, no more than 1/2 length of ovary.

Flowering Season VI-VII (-VIII).

Habitat Full sun on damp, siliceous substrates. The drawdown zone of montane fens, 1000-2300m asl.

Distribution The Balkans. Montenegro to northern Greece and Bulgaria; also the southern Carpathians. Very local but often abundant.

Countries Al Bu Gr Ju Rm.

Photos Gr, Kastoria, 16.VI.1987; 17.VI.1990. P. DELFORGE.

Discussion Often considered close to *G. albida* and, since 1920, placed with it in the genus *Leucorchis* (or *Pseudorchis*) because the structure of the column recalls *Gymnadenia albida*. Nevertheless, the shape of the root-tubers, flower colour, spreading lateral sepals, and the shape of the lip and spur suggest a closer relationship with *G. conopsea*, a conclusion confirmed by molecular analysis.

Gymnadenia conopsea
(L.) R. BROWN

Etymology *konos*: fly; *-opsis*: [with the] appearance of. **Type*** Ge, Baden-Württemberg (1753). **Synonyms** (see p. 151) *Orchis conopsea* L., *Gymnadenia conopsea* var. *insulicola* HESLOP-HARRISON.

Description Slender, 20-60cm tall; 5-12 leaves, erect, green (sometimes bluish), linear-lanceolate, channelled, the 2-5 lower leaves close together and clasping, 6-25cm x 0.5-4cm; upper leaves cauline, bract-like; bracts linear, sometimes washed violet, equal to ovary; inflorescence dense, cylindrical, 5-25cm tall; 20-80 flowers, intense purplish-pink, lilac, more rarely pale pink or white, giving off, mostly towards dusk, a generally pleasant scent; sepals oval, obtuse, 4-7mm long, margins rolled up; petals shorter, asymmetric, forming hood with dorsal sepal; lip deeply 3-lobed, appearing broader than long, 3.5-6mm long, centre often white; lateral lobes ± equal to triangular median lobe; spur filiform, curving downwards, 10-20mm long, 1.5-2x ovary; 2n=40. **Variation** *'insulicola'*, with reddish flowers and an unpleasant scent has been described from the Hebrides (Br).

Flowering Season V-VIII. **Habitat** Full sun on dry to wet, mostly calcareous, substrates. Short grassland, meadows, fens, flushed slopes, scrub, up to 2800m asl. **Distribution** Boreal and temperate Eurasia, east to China; montane in the southern parts of the range. Widespread and sometimes abundant. **Countries** Ae Al An Au Be Bl Br Bu Co Cz Da Fe Ga Ge Gr Hb He Ho Hs Hu It Ju Lu Lx No Pb Po Rm Ro Si Su. **Photos** Ho, Zuid-Limbourg, 15.VI.1991; Be, Luxembourg, 11.VII.1990. P. DELFORGE.

Discussion Polytypic. Numerous taxa have been described, differentiated on the basis of general aspect, height, the dimensions of the leaves or inflorescence and the diameter, colour or scent of the flowers; their status is controversial. Three ecotypes can be distinguished. 1. var. *conopsea*, a calcicole from dry, mesophilic grassland and scrub; 2. var. *densiflora*, a calcicole from base-rich fens, mostly montane; 3. var. *borealis*, an acidophile from damp meadows and acidic to neutral peat bogs. These 3 taxa are often difficult to distinguish in the field due to the existence of numerous intermediates with var. *conopsea*; var. *borealis*, moreover, is an integral part of the normal range of morphological variation of var. *conopsea*. Nevertheless, molecular studies, although still incomplete, reveal considerable differences between the 3 taxa, which may thus be sufficiently distinct to be considered distinct species; this point of view requires further confirmation.

Gymnadenia conopsea (L.) R. BROWN
var. *densiflora* (WAHLENBERG) LINDLEY

Etymology *densiflora*: with a dense inflorescence. **Type** Su, Scanie (1806). **Synonyms** *Orchis densiflora* WAHLENBERG, *Gymnadenia conopsea* subsp. *densiflora* (WAHLENBERG) E.G. CAMUS.

Description Robust, flowering late (VII-VIII); up to 100cm tall; up to 150 flowers, lip with undulate-crisped margins; polyploid (2n=80, 100, 120). **Distribution** Throughout the range of *G. conopsea*, mostly in montane alkaline marshes, but also at low altitude and sometimes in dune slacks in the Atlantic zone; at times in pure populations, more often together with var. *conopsea* and intermediates linked to the ecotones. **Photos A&B** Ga, Drôme, 18.VI.1998. P. DELFORGE.

Gymnadenia conopsea (L.) R. BROWN
var. *borealis* (DRUCE) SOÓ

Etymology *borealis*: boreal. **Type** Br, Cumberland (1918). **Synonyms** *Habenaria gymnadenia* var. *borealis* DRUCE, *Gymnadenia conopsea* subsp. *borealis* (DRUCE) F. PINK, *G. borealis* (DRUCE) R.M. BATEMAN, PRIDGEON & M.W. CHASE, ?*G. conopsea* subsp. *montana* BISSE.

Description Not distinguishable from a small, spindly *G. conopsea*, barely later-flowering; 2n=40. **Habitat** Damp meadows and acidic to neutral fens. **Photo C** Br, Scotland, 16.VI.1995. C.A.J. KREUTZ.

153

Gymnadenia odoratissima
(L.) L.C.M. Richard

Etymology *odoratissima*: highly-scented. **Type*** Ga, Haut-Rhin (1759).

Description As *G. conopsea* but more spindly, smaller in all parts, 12-30 (-50)cm tall; leaves narrow, glaucous-green, erect, linear, 4-8 (-10)mm wide; inflorescence near cylindrical, dense at tip, laxer at base; numerous small flowers, slightly inclined, paler, from bright pink to pale pink, sometimes white, with a strong vanilla scent; lateral sepals 3-4mm long; lip 3-lobed, longer than broad; lateral lobes rounded; median lobe broader, obtuse, clearly longer than lateral ones; spur filiform, slightly curved, 3-6mm long, ± equal to ovary; 2n=40. **Variation** Less varied than *G. conopsea*; nevertheless see following page.

Flowering Season V-VIII. **Habitat** Mostly full sun, on moist to damp, calcareous substrates. Grassy places: meadows, flushed slopes, hillsides, marshes, mountain pastures, rarely xerophitic short grassland, up to 2700m asl. **Distribution** Europe in the submeridional and temperate zones, from southern Sweden to northern Spain and east to the Carpathians. Rather local but sometimes abundant in its stations. **Countries** Au Be Cz Ga Ge Gr Hb He Hs Hu It Ju Lx Pb Po Rm Ro Su. **Photos** Ga, Drôme, 9.VI.1997; It, Bolzano, 18.VII.1987. P. Delforge.

Discussion of the genus *Gymnadenia*

In the sense used in this guide, the genus *Gymnadenia*, which is probably monophyletic, is a sister section to a clade formed by the genera *Platanthera* and *Galearis*. Within the genus, *Gymnadenia* is divided into the *G. nigra* and *G. conopsea* groups. *G. nigra* is monophyletic and the most derived, comprising 13 very closely-related species with non-resupinate flowers, restricted to boreo-alpine European grassland. The *G. conopsea* group is also monophyletic, with 3 species that have a broader ecological tolerance and wider distribution. These 2 groups are connected by a species of hybrid origin, *G. runei*. This cluster constitutes a monophyletic section whose sister section is the *G. albida* group, formed by 2 closely-related species, near to both the common ancestor of the *Gymnadenia* group and to the *Galearis-Platanthera* clade. The position of the *G. albida* group is confirmed by morphological, cladistic and molecular analyses, and is reflected in the diverse taxonomic treatments of *G. albida*, often considered as a *Platanthera* sp. by American botanists, or as a representative of a distinct genus (*Leucorchis* or *Pseudorchis*), intermediate between *Platanthera* and *Gymnadenia*, by European authors.

Gymnadenia odoratissima (L.) L.C.M. Richard var. *pyrenaica* (K. Richter) P. Delforge

Etymology *pyrenaica*: from the Pyrenees. **Type** Ga, Hautes-Pyrénées (1890). **Synonyms** *Orchis pyrenaica* Philippe nom. illeg., *Gymnadenia pyrenaica* Giraudias, *G. conopsea* subsp. *pyrenaica* (Philippe) E.G. Camus & A. Camus comb. illeg., *G. conopsea* var. *pyrenaica* Gautier, ?*G. comigera* Rchb. pat., *G. odoratissima* subsp. *longicalcarata* Hermosilla & Sabando.

Description Habit of a robust *G. odoratissima*; spur up to 10 (-12)mm long, up to 1/3 longer than ovary. **Distribution** The Pyrenees (Ga Hs), often with *G. conopsea* and its hybrids. Some ± pure populations have also been reported in southern France. **Photo A** Hs, Burgos, 5.VI.1994. P. Delforge.

Hybrids in the genus *Gymnadenia*

The inclusion in *Gymnadenia* of the 'vanilla orchids' (formerly *Nigritella*) and the *G. albida* group has considerably increased the number of interspecific hybrids as it leads to the disappearance of the intergeneric hybrids ×*Gymnigritella*, ×*Leucadenia* (= ×*Pseudadenia*) and ×*Leucotella* (= ×*Pseuditella*). Hybrids between *Gymnadenia conopsea* and *G. odoratissima* (= *G.* ×*intermedia* Petermann) are neither rare nor difficult to determine. Hybrids involving *G. albida* or *G. straminea* are far less frequent. Hybrids between the vanilla orchids seem to be rather frequent but are very difficult to detect. The more spectacular hybrids, which may be relatively frequent in some parts of the Alps, notably the Dolomites (It), are those between vanilla orchids and *G. conopsea* or *G. odoratissima*. They can often be distinguished by their intense colours, and their inclined flowers, the lip pointing obliquely upwards, forming an angle of 45-90° with the vertical axis, a position intermediate between that of the vanilla orchids (whose flowers are non-resupinate) and the remaining *Gymnadenia* (whose lip points downwards, often inclined). *G. conopsea* × *G. rhellicani* (= *G.* ×*suavolens* (Villars) Wettstein) is the most frequent combination; it is easily detected from a distance by its very saturated purplish tints; *G. odoratissima* × *G. rhellicani* (= *G.* ×*heufleri* (A. Kerner) Wettstein) has brighter flowers (Photo B) that are a little more inclined and have a shorter spur, characteristics that also distinguish *G. odoratissima* from *G. conopsea*. The combinations *G. odoratissima* × *G. rubra* (= *G.* × *abelii* Hayek nom. inval.) and *G. conopsea* × *G. corneliana* (= *G.* × *truongae* (Démares) W. Foelsche) are far rarer.

Photo B *G. odoratissima* × *G. rhellicani* (*G.* × *heufleri* (A. Kerner) Wettstein). It, Trento, 11.VII.1987. P. Delforge.

The *Gymnadenia runei* group

Characteristics Ovary stalkless, not twisted; lip pointing upwards; lateral sepals spreading; root-tubers flattened and digitate for half their length; 2n=80, allopolyploid: 60 chromosomes from *Gymnadenia nigra* and 20 from *G. conopsea* s.l., probably from var. *borealis*.

Gymnadenia runei
(TEPPNER & E. KLEIN) ERICSSON

Etymology Named after O. Rune, the contemporary Swedish botanist that discovered the plant. **Type** Su, Västerbotten (1989). **Synonyms** *Gymnigritella runei* TEPPNER & E. KLEIN, *Nigritella runei* (TEPPNER & E. KLEIN) KREUTZ.

Description Appearance as vanilla orchids (see following group), 10-16cm tall; 3-8 erect leaves, lower leaves narrowly lanceolate, cauline leaves bract-like, narrowly triangular; lower bract with near hairless margins; inflorescence ovoid to hemispherical; flowers small, not very numerous, apomictic, claret with a blue sheen, buds darker than opened flowers, which fade further; weakly-scented (recalling *G. conopsea*); perianth segments paler at the base than at the tip; lateral sepals widely spreading-arched, 6-8.5mm x 1.7-2.8mm; petals near equal; lip of basal flowers 6.5-8.5mm x 3.5-5.7mm, wide-open, tip pointed, margins slightly undulate; spur bag-like, 1.9-2.3mm long.

Flowering Season VII. **Habitat** Full sun on alkaline substrates. Short grassland with Mat-grass *Nardus stricta* and Mountain Avens *Dryas octipetala*, *c.* 800m asl.

Distribution Known from a few stations in southern Lapland (Su). Extremely local and rare. **Countries** Su. **Photos** Su, Västerbotten, 20.VII.2000. E. KONGSHAUG; Jämtland, 19.VII. 1995. D. RÜCKBRODT.

Discussion A taxon of hybrid origin, between *G. conopsea* s.l. and *G. nigra*, that acquired an independent identity due to apomixis. Its existence demonstrates that it is possible for apomictic species to be pollinated by insects searching for nectar and carrying pollinia or pollen grains from closely related, sexually reproducing species.

Pollination in the *G. conopsea* group

Dark forms of *G. conopsea* are apparently pollinated by a variety of day-flying butterflies or moths, while those with whitish flowers and *G. odoratissima* attract instead night-flying moths; the pollinia are attached by their retinacles to its proboscis as an insect drinks the abundant nectar from the tip of the spur.

The *Gymnadenia nigra* group

Characteristics Root-tubers deeply digitate; leaves linear; inflorescence short and compact; flowers small, often pleasantly scented; lip pointing upwards; spur, short, nectariferous; ovary stalkless, not twisted. Monophyletic group, with 13 very closely-related species, confined to the boreal-alpine zones and sometimes grouped into the genus or subgenus *Nigritella* (vanilla orchids).

Gymnadenia rhellicani
(TEPPNER & E. KLEIN) TEPPNER & E. KLEIN

Etymology Named after J. Müller, known as Rhellicanus, Swiss naturalist († 1542). **Type** Au, Gurktaler Alps (1990). **Synonyms** *Nigritella rhellicani* TEPPNER & E. KLEIN, *N. nigra* subsp. *rhellicani* (TEPPNER & E. KLEIN) H. BAUMANN et al., *N. nigra* auct. non (L.) RCHB. fil.

Description 5-30cm tall; 7-11 leaves in a basal rosette, thick, linear, pointed, channelled, dark green on upper side, pale green below, margins finely serrated; 2-3 upper leaves cauline, bract-like, sometimes edged red; bracts green washed purple, the lower bracts, ± equalling their flowers, have teeth 0.05-0.1mm long on their margins; inflorescence dense, short, initially conical and then (hemi-)ovoid, becoming near cylindrical by end of flowering; flowers numerous, small, cross-pollinated, blackish-purple, very rarely red, pink, yellowish, orange or white, with a strong vanilla or spicy scent; perianth segments pointed, spreading star-like; sepals lanceolate, 4.5-7.5mm x 1.1-2.5mm; petals near equal; lip entire or very slightly 3-lobed, oval-acuminate to near rhomboidal, 4.5-7mm x 3-5mm, saddle-shaped on lower quarter, margins scalloped, sometimes revolute; spur short, 1-1.6mm long, bulbous, purplish-pink to whitish; 2n=40.

Flowering Season Late VI-mid VIII.

Habitat Full sun, mostly on dry to moist, calcareous substrates. Short grassland and alpine meadows, 1000-2800m asl.

Distribution Mid-European alpine zone, from the Alps to the Carpathians. Rather local and often abundant in its stations.

Countries Al Au Bu Cz Ga Ge Gr He Hu It Ju ?Ro Rm.

Photos It, Trento, 22.VII.1998; Ga, Savoie, 9.VII.1997. P. DELFORGE.

Note Nectariferous, attracting numerous different insects, including 53 species of pollinator (48 of them Lepidoptera).

Key to the genus *Gymnadenia*

1   lip pointing downwards 2
1* lip pointing upwards (flowers non-resupinate) 6

2   flowers yellow to yellowish; lateral sepals connivent with petals and dorsal sepal in a loose hood 3
2* flowers purple, lilac, pink or white; lateral sepals spreading 4

3   lower bracts 10-15mm long; spur 2.5-4.1mm long .... *G. straminea*
3* lower bracts 5-8mm long; spur 1.5-2.3mm long .... *G. albida*

4   inflorescence short, up to 2x taller than broad .... *G. frivaldii*
4* inflorescence elongated, at least 2.5x taller than broad 5

5   spur more than 12mm long, 1.5-2x as long as ovary .... *G. conopsea*
5* spur less than 10 (-12)mm long, 0.6-1.3x as long as ovary .... *G. odoratissima*

6   stem very sturdy, compressible, angular, with a diameter that may reach 10mm below the inflorescence 7
6* stem thin, not or not very compressible, not or not very angular at tip 8

7   flowers dark brownish-red
    .... *G. rhellicani* var. *robusta*
7* flowers reddish then pale bluish-pink
    .... *G. buschmanniae*

8   flowers dark purplish-red 9
8* flowers dark brownish-red to blackish, or ruby-red, bluish-pink, pink or whitish (exceptionally orange or yellow) 10

9   growing below 1000m asl; lower bracts with near hairless margins .... *G. runei*
9* growing above 2000m asl; bracts with clearly serrated margins .... *G. dolomitensis*

10 flowers dark brownish-purple to blackish-red (exceptionally orange or yellow) 11

10* flowers luminous ruby-red, pink or whitish
    14

11 lower bracts with hairless margins; lip open
    12

11* lower bracts edged with distinct serrations, tight or lax; lip strongly in-rolled, the base forming a tube 13

(continued on p. 162)

Gymnadenia rhellicani
(TEPPNER & E. KLEIN) TEPPNER & E. KLEIN
var. *robusta* P. DELFORGE

Etymology *robusta*: robust. **Type** Ga, Savoie (2003). **Synonyms** *Nigritella cenisia* G. FOELSCHE et al., *N. rhellicani* var. *robusta* (P. DELFORGE) KREUTZ, *Gymnadenia cenisia* (G. FOELSCHE et al.) G. FOELSCHE et al., *G.* ×*robatschiana* O. GERBAUD & W. FOELSCHE.

Description As *G. rhellicani* but more robust and more floriferous; stem up to 10mm in diameter below the inflorescence; up to 25 leaves; 50-125 flowers, often redder; buds blackish.

Flowering Season Due to the greater number of flowers, flowering is more prolonged than in *G. rhellicani*, (end VI-) VII-VIII.

Habitat With *G. rhellicani* and numerous intermediates, 1800-2600m asl. **Distribution** Western Alps, centred on Mount Cenis. Local and sometimes abundant in its stations.

Countries Ga It. **Photo** Ga, Savoie (loc. typ.) 25.VII.1999. P. DELFORGE.

Gymnadenia gabasiana
(TEPPNER & E. KLEIN) TEPPNER & E. KLEIN

Etymology *gabasiana*: [from the Centre of Alpine Ecology] of Gabas. **Type** Hs, Huesca (1993). **Basionym** *Nigritella gabasiana* TEPPNER & E. KLEIN.

Description As *G. rhellicani* but (6-) 10-23cm tall; up to 15 leaves; lower bracts with lax, near pointed teeth; inflorescence initially conical then ovoid to near cylindrical; flowers rather small, cross-pollinated, dark red, not or hardly scented; lip 6.5-9.1mm x 3.5-5mm, basal third strongly contracted, margins almost touching, distal part flared and then spreading; spur relatively spindly, 0.8-1.4mm long; 2n=40.

Flowering Season Mid VI-VIII. **Habitat** As *G. austriaca* var. *gallica* and sometimes found with it, 1500-2100m asl. **Distribution** Cantabrian Pyrenees. Local and sometimes abundant in its stations. **Countries** Ga Hs. **Photos** Hs, León (Picos de Europa), 15.VI.1992. P. DELFORGE.

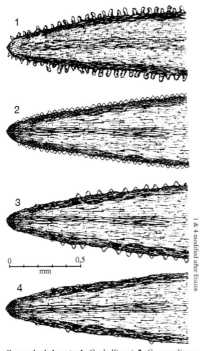

1 & 4 modified after EGGER

Gymnadenia **bracts**: 1. *G. rhellicani*; 2. *G. corneliana*; 3. *G. gabasiana*; 4. *G. austriaca*.

159

Gymnadenia corneliana
(BEAUVERD) TEPPNER & E. KLEIN

Etymology Named after Cornelia Rudio. **Type** Ga, Alpes du Lautaret (1925). **Synonyms** *Nigritella nigra* subsp. *corneliana* BEAUVERD, *N. corneliana* (BEAUVERD) GÖLZ & H.R. REINHARD, *N. lithopolitanica* subsp. *corneliana* (BEAUVERD) TEPPNER & E. KLEIN, *N. corneliana* subsp. *bourneriasii* E. BREINER & R. BREINER, *N. corneliana* var. *bourneriasii* (E. BREINER & R. BREINER) E. KLEIN.

Description As *G. rhellicani* but with 8-18 basal leaves; lower bracts edged with less pointed teeth; inflorescence initially conical then globular-elongate; bud cinnabar-red, darker than flowers, which fade markedly; perianth segments two-toned, base pale (pure white, pinkish or yellowish), tip flesh-pink, warm-toned, rather dark; lip 6-10mm x 3-5mm, often obscurely 3-lobed, margins slightly turned up, forming a tube at very base, rarely spreading and lacking rolled-up margins at base. *'bourneriasii'* is a slightly sturdier variety; inflorescence uniformly red, flowers not fading after anthesis.

Flowering Season Late VI-mid VIII. **Habitat** Short, calcareous alpine grassland, 1500-2500m asl. **Distribution** Southwest Alps, from Chartreuse (Isère) and Savoie to the Mediterranean, on both sides of the Franco-Italian frontier. Rare and local. **Countries** Ga It. **Photos A&B** Ga, Savoie (loc. typ.), 21.VII.1992; **C** (*bourneriasii*): Hautes-Alpes, 19.VI.1998. P. DELFORGE.

Gymnadenia lithopolitanica
(V. RAVNIK) TEPPNER & E. KLEIN

Etymology *lithopolitanica*: from Kamnik (= Stein), a Slovenian town (Ju). **Type** Ju, Slovenia (1978). **Synonyms** *Nigritella lithopolitanica* V. RAVNIK, *N. nigra* var. *rosea* GOIRAN.

Description As *G. rhellicani* but 8-20cm tall; 6-13 cauline leaves; inflorescence hemispherical; flowers cross-pollinated, whitish to pale, slightly bluish, pink, buds darker – pink, intensely washed bluish with a rather cold tone; lateral sepals 5-8mm x 2mm; petals 1-1.5mm wide; lip 6.5-8.5mm x 3.5-4.5mm, margins slightly turned upwards, forming a tube close to the base; spur 0.9-1.2mm long; 2n=40.

Flowering Season Mid VI-mid VII; earlier than *N. rhellicani*.

Habitat Short, calcareous alpine grassland, 1500-2000m asl.

Distribution The Alps from Kamnik-Savinja in northern Slovenia to Koralpe and Karawanken in Austria. Very rare and local.

Countries Au Ju.

Photos A&B Au, Klagenfurt, 25.VI.2001. P. DELFORGE; **C** Karawanken, 2.VII.1992. C.A.J. KREUTZ.

Gymnadenia carpatica
(Zapalowicz) Teppner & E. Klein

Etymology *carpatica*: from the Carpathians.
Type Rm, Stanalui Verticu - Trojaga (1906).
Synonyms *Nigritella angustifolia* Rich. var.
carpatica Zapalowicz, *N. nigra* var. *carpatica*
(Zapalowicz) Pawlowski, *N. carpatica* (Zapalowicz)
Teppner, E. Klein & Zagulskij.

Description As *G. corneliana* but 7.5-18cm tall;
lower bracts with hairless margins; inflorescence
dense, hemi-ovoid then ovoid; flowers small, not
very open, with a strong scent of chocolate; buds
bluish-red, darker than flowers, which fade
markedly, becoming pale pink to whitish;
perianth segments 2-toned, slightly paler at base
than at tip; lip 4.5-5.9mm x 2-2.5mm, saddle-
shaped, forming a bulging tube at base,
tip spreading, margins rolled-up; spur 1-1.1
(-1.5)mm long; 2n=40 (-60).

Flowering Season VI-VIII. **Habitat** Short,
moist, alkaline to decalcified alpine
grassland, 1000-1800m asl. **Distribution** Eastern
Carpathians, on both sides of the Romania-
Ukraine frontier. Very local and very rare.

Countries Rm Ro. **Photos** Ro, the Ukraine,
Dzogul-Pass, 14 & 15.VI.1993. E. Klein.

Key to the genus *Gymnadenia*

(continued from p.158)

12 growing over (1100-) 1400m asl; lip up to
10mm long .... *G. austriaca*
12* growing below 1300m asl; lip up to 12mm
long .... *G. nigra*

13 lower bracts fringed with closely-spaced
teeth; lip 4.5-7mm long .... *G. rhellicani*
13* lower bracts fringed with laxer serrations; lip
(6.5-) 7-9.1mm long .... *G. gabasiana*

14 flowers well-open; sepals and petals
spreading 15
14* flowers half-opening, sepals, petals and lip
rolled up, forming tubes
.... *G. archiducis-joannis*

15 flowers luminous ruby-red, fading a little
after anthesis 16
15* flowers pink 17

16 spur 0.9-1.2mm long
.... *G. corneliana* var. *bourneriasii*
16* spur 1.3-1.7mm long .... *G. rubra*

(continued on next page)

Gymnadenia nigra
(L.) Reichenbach fil.

Etymology *nigra*: black. **Type*** Su, Jämtland (1753). **Synonyms** *Satyrium nigrum* L., *Nigritella nigra* (L.) Reichenbach fil., *N. nigra* f. *apomicta* Gustafsson, *N. angustifolia* Rich. nom. illeg.

Description As *G. rhellicani* but 9-22cm tall; bracts hairless or, more rarely, 1-3 lower bracts slightly papillose; inflorescence more hemispherical; flowers apomictic, larger, dark red-brown to brownish-purple; sepals 6.9-10.5mm x 1.4-2.2mm; lip spreading, (6.8-) 7-12mm x 2.7-4.9mm; spur relatively shorter and more bulbous, 0.8-1.1mm long; 2n=60.

Flowering Season VI-VII (-VIII).

Habitat As *G. rhellicani* but only up to 1300m asl.

Distribution Endemic to Scandinavia. Range disjunct: northern Norway (Tromsø), central Sweden (Jämtland) and neighbouring regions of Norway. Local and rather rare.

Countries No Su.

Photos No, Sør-Trøndelag, 17 & 15.VII.2000. E. Kongshaug.

Key to the genus *Gymnadenia*

(continued from previous page)

Gymnadenia austriaca
(Teppner & E. Klein) P. Delforge

Etymology *austriaca*: from Austria. **Type** Au, Styrie (1990). **Synonyms** *Nigritella nigra* subsp. *austriaca* Teppner & E. Klein, *N. austriaca* (Teppner & E. Klein) P. Delforge, *Gymnadenia nigra* subsp. *austriaca* (Teppner & E. Klein) Teppner & E. Klein.

Description As *G. rhellicani* but bracts hairless or, more rarely, 1-5 lower bracts slightly papillose (10% of plants); inflorescence initially hemispherical and then near ovoid; flowers rather large, apomictic, more open, dark red-brown to brownish-purple; lip 6.8-10mm long, open; spur relatively shorter and more bulbous, 1-1.3mm long; 2n=80.

Flowering Season Relatively early, mid VI-VIII.

Habitat As *G. rhellicani*, 1500-2400m.

Distribution The centre and east of the eastern Alps, west from the Dolomites (It). Local and sometimes abundant in its stations.

Countries Au Ge He It.

Photo A It, Bolzano, 7.VII.1989. P. Delforge.

Gymnadenia austriaca
(Teppner & E. Klein) P. Delforge
var. *gallica*
(E. Breiner & R. Breiner) P. Delforge

Etymology *gallica*: from France. **Type** Ga, Savoie (1993). **Synonyms** *N. nigra* subsp. *gallica* E. Breiner & R. Breiner, *N. rhellicani* subsp. *gallica* (E. Breiner & R. Breiner) Kerguélen, *?N. nigra* var. *pyrenaica* Schlechter, *N. nigra* subsp. *iberica* Teppner & E. Klein, *N. rhellicani* subsp. *iberica* (Teppner & E. Klein) Kerguélen, *Gymnadenia nigra* subsp. *iberica* (Teppner & E. Klein) Teppner & E. Klein.

Description As *G. austriaca* var. *austriaca* but spike carrying a few more flowers; spur averages 0.1mm longer; molecular analysis also reveals a few differences.

Flowering Season Early VI-mid VII, slightly earlier than *G. austriaca* var. *austriaca*.

Habitat As *G. austriaca* var. *austriaca*, (1100-)1400-2100m asl.

Distribution The periphery of the western Alps (north to the Jura), Massif Central and Pyrenees. Local and sometimes abundant in its stations.

Countries Ga He Hs ?It.

Photo B Ga, Isère, 13.VI.1997; **C** (p. 165) 10.VI.1997. P. Delforge.

Gymnadenia widderi
(Teppner & E. Klein) Teppner & E. Klein

Etymology Named after F.J. Widder (1892-1974), Austrian botanist, who was the first to draw attention to this species. **Type** Au, Styrie (1985). **Basionym** *Nigritella widderi* Teppner & E. Klein.

Description As *G. rhellicani* but 6-17cm tall; 7-10 cauline leaves; inflorescence short, semi-globular to ovoid; flowers apomictic, whitish to pale pink, slightly paler than buds, which are a more intense pink, with a rather cold, slightly bluish, tone; lateral sepals (4.5-) 6-9mm x 1.3-2.5mm; petals 4.5-8mm x 1.2-1.7mm; lip (4.7-) 6-9mm x 2.5-5mm, margins turned up, forming a narrow tube in centre of lip, base rather 'pot-bellied', 2.6-3.2mm wide, as broad or a little broader than distal half (slightly narrower in Italian populations); 2n=80.

Flowering Season VI-VIII; slightly earlier than *G. rhellicani*.

Habitat Short, calcareous alpine grassland, 1500-2200m asl; rarely with *G. rhellicani*.

Distribution Currently known from a few stations in Styrie (Au), Bavaria (Ge) and Abruzzi (It); should be looked for elsewhere. Very local and extremely rare.

Countries Au Ge It.

Photos It, Rieti, 12.VII.1989. P. Delforge.

Below: *Gymnadenia austriaca* var. *gallica*

(*see page 164*)

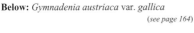

Gymnadenia archiducis-joannis
(Teppner & E. Klein) Teppner & E. Klein

Etymology Named after Archduke Jean of Austria. **Type** Au, Styrie (1985). **Basionym** *Nigritella archiducis-joannis* Teppner & E. Klein.

Description As *G. widderi* but inflorescence semi-globular to globular; flowers apomictic, with a slight vanilla scent, always not widely open, crimson-pink, slightly lighter than buds; lateral sepals only slightly spreading, *c.* 8mm long, slightly broader than petals; dorsal sepal and petals forming a hood that projects horizontally forwards, forming, with the lip, a narrow tube; lip *c.* 8mm x 2-4mm, the margins undulate and turned upwards, forming a tube throughout almost its entire length; 2n=80.

Flowering Season VII-VIII.

Habitat Short, calcareous alpine grassland, 1800-2000m asl.

Distribution The eastern Alps; currently known from a few stations in the Dachstein, Salzkammergut, Totes Gebirge and Eisener massifs. Extremely local and rare.

Countries Au. **Photos** Au, Steiermark (loc. typ.), 18.VII.1998. P. Delforge.

Gymnadenia stiriaca
(K. RECHINGER) TEPPNER & E. KLEIN

Etymology *stiriaca*: from Styrie (Au). **Type** Au, Styrie (1906). **Synonyms** *Gymnadenia rubra* WETTSTEIN var. *stiriaca* K. RECHINGER, *Nigritella stiriaca* (K. RECHINGER) TEPPNER & E. KLEIN.

Description As *G. rubra* but leaves rather broad; lower bracts edged with irregular serrations; inflorescence elongated, near cylindrical and then becoming cylindrical; flowers apomictic, crimson-pink or purplish, with a slight vanilla scent; tip of perianth segments paler than base, only tip whitish before anthesis, entire distal half tip whitish after anthesis; lateral sepals slightly broader than dorsal sepal, far broader than petals; lip 5.5-6.5mm x 3-4mm, margins turned upwards, forming a tube for the basal quarter; spur 1-1.3mm long; 2n=80.

Flowering Season Mid VI-mid VII, brief. **Habitat** Short, calcareous alpine grassland, 1800-2000m asl. **Distribution** Eastern Alps; currently known from a few stations in the Dachstein, Salzkammergut and Grazer Bergland massifs. Extremely local and very rare. **Countries** Au. **Photos A&B** Au, Steiermark (loc. typ.), 26.VI.2001. P. DELFORGE; **C** 1.VII.1992. C.A.J. KREUTZ.

167

Gymnadenia rubra
WETTSTEIN

Etymology *rubra*: red. **Type** Au (1889).
Synonyms *Gymnadenia nigra* subsp. *rubra*
(WETTSTEIN) SUNDERMANN, *Nigritella nigra* subsp.
rubra (WETTSTEIN) BEAUVERD, *N. rubra* (WETTSTEIN)
K. RICHTER, *Orchis miniata* CRANTZ (nom. confusum)
p.p., *Nigritella miniata* (CRANTZ) JANCHEN,
Gymnadenia miniata (CRANTZ) HAYEK.

Description As *G. rhellicani* but with 7-12 basal
leaves; 2-8 bract-like cauline leaves;
inflorescence initially conical, then hemi-ovoid,
more elongated than in *G. rhellicani*; flowers
probably rather often apomictic, intense,
luminous ruby-red colour, rarely pink; lateral
sepals 4-7mm long; lip 5.5-8mm x 3.5-4.5mm,
concave, usually with the margins turned
upwards to form a narrow tube in the lower
quarter, but sometimes merely spreading. As
G. rhellicani; spur 1.3-1.7mm long, with a
narrower throat; 2n=80.

Flowering Season Mid VI-early VIII; 2 weeks
before *G. rhellicani*. **Habitat** Only on alkaline
substrates (limestone and calcareous schists).
Short alpine grassland, (1200-) 1600-2600m asl.
Distribution Dolomites (It), central and eastern
Alps, east of the Rhin valley, Carpathians. Less
frequent than *G. rhellicani*. **Countries** Au Ge He
It Rm. **Photos** It, Belluno, 7.VII.1989.
P. DELFORGE.

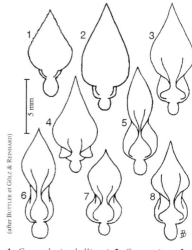

(after BUTTLER et GÖLZ & REINHARD)

1. *Gymnadenia rhellicani*. **2**. *G. austriaca*. **3**. *G.
corneliana*. **4**. *G. lithopolitanica*. **5**. *G. widderi*.
6. *G. archiducis-joannis*. **7**. *G. stiriaca*. **8**. *G. rubra*.

Gymnadenia dolomitensis
TEPPNER & E. KLEIN

Etymology *dolomitensis*: from the Dolomites. **Type** It, Bolzano (1998). **Synonyms** *Nigritella dolomitensis* (TEPPNER & E. KLEIN) HÉDREN, E. KLEIN & TEPPNER, *N. rubra* var. *dolomitensis* (TEPPNER & E. KLEIN) R. LORENZ & PERAZZA.

Description As *G. rubra*, but 5-12cm tall; bracts edged with pointed serrations, formed by regular hyaline papillae; inflorescence initially conical, then cylindrical, elongating strongly towards end of flowering, hemispherical when few-flowered; flowers apomictic, well opened, dark purplish-pink, fading after anthesis, sometimes slightly chocolate scented; lateral sepals elongated, curved, 5.9-7.5mm long, far longer and broader than petals; lip 6.8-8mm x 3-4mm, forming a bulbous tube in the basal quarter, tip spreading; spur globular, 1.2-1.3mm long; 2n=80.

Flowering Season VII. **Habitat** Short, calcareous alpine grassland, from 2150m to more than 2500m asl. **Distribution** Dolomites and neighbouring areas. Rather local and rare. **Countries** ?Au ?Ge It. **Photos** It, Trento, 24.VII.1998; Bolzano (loc. typ.) 24.VII.1999. P. DELFORGE.

The problem of the *Gymnadenia nigra* group

The *G. nigra* group (vanilla orchids) contains 13 very closely related species. It is very near to the *G. conopsea* group, from which it is distinguished by the density of the inflorescence and the position of the lip. Two species with a very broad distribution, *G. rhellicani* and *G. rubra*, form 2 distinct poles between which all the other taxa are arranged, sometimes represented by only a few tens of plants. *G. stiriaca* and *G. dolomitensis* seem to be very close to *G. rubra*. *G. gabasiana*, *G. carpatica*, *G. corneliana*, *G. nigra* and *G. austriaca* seem close to *G. rhellicani*. The chemistry of pigments, whose results are not confirmed by molecular analysis, reinforces this classification. Cytological analysis demonstrates the existence of a group of 5 diploid species (2n=40), reproducing sexually (*G. rhellicani*, *G. gabasiana*, *G. corneliana*, *G. lithopolitanica*, *G. carpatica*) and another group of 8 polyploid species, probably independently derived from species in the diploid group by aneuploidy or autopolyploidy combined with the acquisition of apomixy – a completely effective isolating mechanism. Independent of pollinators, these species can colonise extreme habitats that are not favourable to insects. This polyploid group contains *G. nigra* (triploid, 2n=60), *G. austriaca*, *G. rubra*, *G. dolomitensis*, *G. widderi*, *G. archiducis-joannis*, *G. stiriaca* (tetraploid, 2n=80) and *G. buschmanniae* (pentaploid, 2n=100). Of this group, only *G. austriaca* and *G. rubra* (sometimes cross-pollinated) have an extensive distribution.

Gymnadenia buschmanniae
(Teppner & Ster) Teppner & E. Klein

Etymology Named after Mme A. Buschmann, Austrian botanist (1908-1989). **Type** It, Trento (1998). **Basionym** *Nigritella buschmanniae* Teppner & Ster.

Description Sturdy; 5-14cm tall; stem angular, very thick even below the inflorescence; basal leaves 1.5-4.5mm broad; cauline leaves and lower bracts edged with a marked hyaline serration, highly visible, up to 0.1mm long; inflorescence very dense, initially hemispherical and then hemi-ovoid; flowers apomictic, not very open, intense bluish-pink, fading after anthesis, with a slight cinnamon scent; buds dark purplish-red; lateral sepals 4.8-8mm long; lip 5.9-7.7mm x 2.5-3.8mm, bulbous at base, saddle-shaped, margins coming close together in central part, tip spreading, pointed, with undulate margins; spur globular, 1-1.5mm x 1-1.5mm; 2n=100.

Flowering Season Mid VII-early VIII. **Habitat** Short, calcareous alpine grassland, 2300-2400m asl. **Distribution** Only known from the Brenta range (Dolomites). Extremely local and abundant in its few stations. **Countries** It. **Photos** It, Trento (loc. typ.), 22.VII.1998. P. Delforge.

Coeloglossum

HARTMAN 1820

Etymology *koilo-*: hollow; *-glôssa*: tongue (a reference to the depression at the base of the lip). **Characteristics** Root-tubers palmate; column short; pollinia divergent; bursicle rudimentary; 2n=40. A monospecific genus. Recent molecular analyses give contradictory results: either the maintenance of the genus or its subsumption within *Dactylorhiza*.

Coeloglossum viride

(L.) HARTMAN

Etymology *viride*: green. **Type*** Pb, Kœnigsberg (1753). **Synonyms** *Satyrium viride* L., *Coeloglossum alpinum* SCHUR, *C. viride* var. *islandicum* (LINDLEY) SCHULZE, *C. viride* var. *bracteatum* (WILLDENOW) K. RICHTER, *C. viride* var. *longibracteatum* (DE BRÉBISSON) ASCHERSON & GRÄBNER, *Dactylorhiza viridis* (L.) R.M. BATEMAN, PRIDGEON & M.W. CHASE nom. illeg.

Description 5-40cm tall; 3-5 (-7) leaves, unspotted, clasping, near erect, 2-10cm x 1-5cm, lower leaves oval-elliptic, upper leaves more lanceolate, the uppermost bract-like; bracts equal to or longer than flowers; inflorescence near lax, cylindrical; 5-25 (-30) flowers; sepals 3.5-6.5mm x 2-3mm, oval-triangular (lateral sepals asymmetrical), green, sometimes edged purple, forming an obtuse hood; petals linear, 3-6.5mm long, concealed within the hood; lip flat, pendant or reflexed backwards, 5-10mm x 2-3mm, with a central longitudinal groove, green, sometimes edged with purple and, chiefly at higher altitudes, tinted brown or purple throughout, with a basal depression with 2 nectariferous pits, tip 3-lobed, lateral lobes parallel, median lobe tooth-shaped; spur globular, nectariferous, with a narrow entrance, 2-3mm long; ovary stalkless. **Variation** With the exception of the last, which is lacking in Europe, these variants are of little significance: *'islandicum'*, *'alpinum'*, small, few-flowered; *'longibracteatum'* with long bracts; *'bracteatum'*, robust, up to 80cm tall, leaves up to 18cm long; shady places of dense forests in eastern Asia and America.

Flowering Season V-VIII. **Habitat** Full sun to mid-shade on acidic or alkaline, dry to damp substrates. Short, poor grassland, fens, mountain pastures, woodland fringes, open woodland, rarely forests, up to 2900m asl. **Distribution** Circumboreal. Not widespread and rather rare, montane in the south. **Countries** Al An Au Be Br Bu Cz Da Fa Fe Ga Ge Gr Hb He Ho Hs Hu Is It Ju Lx No Pb Po Rm Ro Su. **Photos** He, Uri, 25.VII.1989; It, Trento, 11.VII.1986. P. DELFORGE. **Note** Flowers very nectariferous, pollinated by a large number of insects: wasps, bees, ants, beetles and small nocturnal moths.

171

Dactylorhiza

NECKER ex NEVSKI 1937

Etymology *dactylo-*: finger; *-rhiza*: root (a reference to the digitate root-tubers). **Characteristics** 2 (-3) root-tubers, clustered or ± deeply digitate, often flattened, rarely entire (*D. iberica*), then spindle-shaped; emerging inflorescence without clasping leaf; leaves usually arranged along length of stem, upper 1-4 leaves often bract-like; bracts leaf-like, often green, lowest always longer than ovary; flower structure very similar to that of *Orchis* (see p. 278); lateral sepals usually spreading to erect; dorsal sepal connivent in a hood with the petals; lip orientated downwards, entire or 3-lobed; spur present, lacking nectar; column short; 2n= 40, 60, 80, 100, 120 (-122).

Discussion Eurasian genus, monophyletic, comprising 7 groups and 60 species in the guide. Distributed principally in the boreal and temperate zones, from northern Scandinavia south to North Africa and the Himalayas, west to Iceland and Madeira and east to Siberia; reaches the far west of Alaska via the Aleutian Islands; the single station of the genus in the New World (*D. maculata* s.l., Ontario, Canada) is probably not native.

Long considered members of the genus *Orchis*, they were separated by Klinge in 1937 and by Vermeulen in 1947 (sub nom. *Dactylorchis*), and the *Dactylorhiza* now comprise a distinct genus, almost universally recognised today, which occupies a position intermediate between Gymnadeniinae and Serapiadinae. Intergeneric hybrids are rare, and mostly formed with species that have digitate root-tubers: *Coeloglossum* (=× *Dactyloglossum*), *Gymnadenia* (see × *Dactylodenia*, p. 26), and much more rarely with *Orchis* (see × *Orchidactylorhiza*, p. 26).

The *Dactylorhiza* are arranged into a group of diploid species (2n=40) and autotetraploid species (2n=80) with a thin, solid stem (the *D. maculata* group, 15 species) and a group of diploid species that have a very hollow, thick stem (the *D. incarnata* group, 10 species; *D. aristata* from the Aleutian islands may also belong here). These 2 groups are linked by a suite of allopolyploid species, all originating from recurrent hybridisation events involving the same diploid ancestors, *D. fuchsii* s.l. on the one hand, and *D. incarnata* s.l. or *D. euxina* s.l on the other. These hybridogenous taxa are sometimes considered to form a single biological mega-species, but this treatment is not acceptable under the evolutionary species concept. They are therefore here placed in 3 convenient groups: the *D. majalis* group (7 early-flowering allotetraploid species); the *D. praetermissa* group (14, often robust, late-flowering allotetraploid species); and the *D. traunsteineri* group (8 rather spindly

species, sometimes hexaploid, with characters clearly intermediate between the 2 previous groups). These 3 groups form in turn a monophyletic section whose sister section is the *D. sambucina* group (5 diploid species, morphology and ecology rather similar to the *Orchis mascula* group). This clade, in turn, is sister to the isolated ancestral species, *Dactylorhiza iberica*.

The presence of numerous hybridogenous species in this genus, originating, at various times and places, from the same 2 parents, and the frequent interbreeding of these taxa, both between themselves and with their parental species, prevents the clear demarcation of most of them. There are, consequently, major problems in field identification.

Despite centuries of observations, and whatever methods of analysis are used today – statistical, genetic, molecular – it is very difficult to isolate variants that are stabilised and characteristic of a

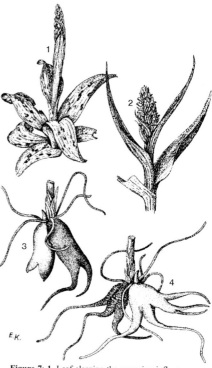

Figure 7: **1**. Leaf clasping the emerging inflorescence in the genus *Orchis* (*O. militaris*). **2**. Emerging inflorescence without leaves in the genus *Dactylorhiza* (*D. coccinea*). **3**. Root-tubers slightly digitate (*D. sambucina*). **4**. Root-tubers flattened and deeply digitate (*D. maculata*).

species, from those produced by unstable hybrid swarms or those due to environmental differences, to which *Dactylorhiza* species are very sensitive.

In addition, the dramatic reduction in wetlands due to human land management has resulted in the increased scarcity or even extinction of the most hygrophilous species and the reduction and isolation of marsh orchid populations. Many type localities have been destroyed and this, together with the sometimes vague type descriptions, makes it difficult to determine whether newly-discovered 'critical' populations can be matched with old existing names.

All these reasons explain why there is no consensus on the systematics of *Dactylorhiza*, neither the number of taxa in the genus (which, moreover, can be increased on a whim), nor, accordingly, on nomenclature. Studies of the genus in the field, therefore, rely on the observation of a large set of characteristics from a significant sample of plants, where hybrids will be frequently very difficult to detect. Even then, one should be aware that there will always be plants, or even whole populations, that will resist any attempt at accurate identification.

Hypochromy in the genus *Dactylorhiza*

With the probable exception of the *Dactylorhiza sambucina* group, every species in this genus may throw up, with various frequencies, hypochromic plants. These have pure white, unmarked flowers and unspotted leaves. These occasional variations should not be confused with species that normally have white flowers, such as *D. okellyi*.

Pollination of *Dactylorhiza*

Dactylorhiza are generally held to be cross-pollinated, although exceptional cases of self-pollination have been reported, and in certain taxa apomixis is sometimes suspected. Like most *Orchis* spp., they lack nectar and seem to attract their pollinators by giving the appearance of a nectariferous flower (see Pollination in *Orchis*, p. 279).

Photo A: Hypochromatic *Dactylorhiza elata*. Hs, Albacete, 18.VI.1989. P. DELFORGE.

Photo B: A long-horned beetle, *Strangalia maculata* Poda, on *Dactylorhiza saccifera* – it visited 3 flowers as it climbed the inflorescence. Two green pollinia are glued to the labrum, below the head; arriving at the top of the plant, the beetle descends, head-down. When it begins to eat the column of the first open flower that it finds, the pollinia come into contact with the stigma. In this case, it is geitonogamy, because it is pollen from the same plant that fertilises the flower. Experiments in cultivation have shown that the pollen of *Dactylorhiza* obtained in this manner are as fertile as others. Gr, Florina, 13.VII.1985. P. DELFORGE.

Some species, like *Dactylorhiza sambucina*, are only visited by bumblebee queens (*Bombus* spp.) that have recently emerged from pupation and are therefore inexperienced; they rapidly forsake orchids for truly nutritive species. Most other *Dactylorhiza* are, however, more frequently visited as they attract recently emerged young worker bees, far more numerous than queens. Outcrossing is favoured by this method of attraction; insects that do not find food often visit just one flower per spike. The great variability in the shape, colour and markings of the lip is without doubt an advantage; uniform flowers would probably be quickly abandoned. The flowers are, however, not the only attraction offered by *Dactylorhiza*; some visitors are able to lick or eat a viscous substance from the stigmatic surface. This exudation, which contains sugars and amino acids, functions in all the Orchidaceae to retain the dry pollen at the moment of pollination. The study of pollinators in *D. fuchsii* shows that this is visited by a large number and variety of insects that assiduously forage for these nutritive substances, which may even sometimes make them drunk. Among the visitors, some are too small or do not possess the correct morphology to carry off the pollinia (e.g. butterflies). Most are, however, efficient pollinators, among which *c*. 60% are beetles, 30% flies and 5% bees and wasps; almost 90% of the beetles are long-horned beetles (Cerambycidae). This method of attracting pollinators seems efficient, as up to 50% of ovaries can mature in *D. fuchsii*. It is likely that not only do most *Dactylorhiza* species have the same pollination mechanism, but also that it is shared by other genera, notably *Orchis* and *Ophrys*, although probably less frequently.

This diversity of pollinators, which visit, apparently indiscriminately, the majority of species, coupled with the low efficiency of postzygotic isolation mechanisms, probably explains the dramatic number of hybrids produced by *Dactylorhiza*.

Hybrids in the genus *Dactylorhiza*

Most *Dactylorhiza* hybridise easily, and more than a hundred natural interspecific hybrids have already been described or reported. As they are often interfertile with their parent species, amongst which there is usually a wide range of variation, and hybridogenous species are not infrequent in the genus, hybrids are difficult to report with certainty and can only be legitimately identified in the field, amongst living plants. Identification as a hybrid is then aided by a large number of intermediate characteristics. Frequent polyploidy in *Dactylorhiza* hybrids often produces plants that are far more robust than the parents, and this may be the first character to attract attention.

D. sambucina × *D. romana* = *D.* × *fasciculata* (Tineo pro sp.) H. Baumann & Künkele. **Photo** Si, Catania, 19.IV.1989. P. Delforge.

Key to the genus *Dactylorhiza*

1   Sepals connivent with petals to form a loose hood; lip 6-9mm broad .... *D. iberica*
1*   lacking these 2 characteristics 2

2   flowers yellow 3
2*   flowers of another colour 4

3   plants growing on dry soils: meadows, open woodland .... *D. sambucina* group (p. 176)
3*   plants growing in marshes
      .... *D. incarnata* group (p. 181)

4   stem solid, thin; leaves often spotted on upper side .... *D. maculata* group (p. 227)
4*   stem hollow, ± compressible below inflorescence 5

5   flowers red or magenta, with a bright red or yellow centre, unspotted or finely spotted red
      .... *D. sambucina* group (p. 176)
5*   flowers otherwise 6

6   clearly hygrophilous plants; stem hollow, very compressible (diameter of central hollow > 1/2 total stem diameter); flowers small to medium-sized; lip as long as, or longer than, broad, (near) rhomboidal
      .... *D. incarnata* group (p. 181)
6*   plants otherwise 7

7   stem rather thin, not very compressible; leaves few, narrow; flowers rather large
      .... *D. traunsteineri* group (p. 201)
7*   stem rather thick, very compressible; leaves often numerous and broad 8

8   flowering early, before other marsh orchids in the same sites .... *D. majalis* group (p. 194)
8*   flowering late, after the majority of the species in other groups
      .... *D. praetermissa* group (p. 210)

The *Dactylorhiza iberica* group

Characteristics Root-tubers spindle-shaped; stem stoloniferous; sepals and petals connivent to form a ± loose hood; 2n=40. Monospecific.

Dactylorhiza iberica
(M.-Bieb. ex Willdenow) Soó

Etymology *iberica*: from Iberia (eastern Georgia). **Type** Ro, Georgia (1806). **Synonyms** *Orchis iberica* M.-Bieb. ex Willdenow, *O. angustifolia* M.-Bieb., *O. leptophylla* K. Koch, *O. natolica* Fischer & Meyer.

Description 2 narrow, ribbon-like root-tubers, elongated, slightly digitate; stolons rhizomatous; stem 20-60cm tall; 3-7 cauline leaves, well-spaced, obliquely erect to spreading, unspotted, linear-lanceolate, slightly keeled, narrowly sheathing, 10-25cm x 1-2 (-3)cm, upper leaves smaller; bracts green, ± equal to ovary; inflorescence initially ovoid, then cylindrical, dense to lax; flowers pale to deep lilac; sepals and petals forming a tight hood, rarely lax; sepals oval-pointed, 5-9mm x 2-4mm; petals near equal; lip spreading, rounded, near entire or 3-lobed, 7.5-11mm x 6-9mm, base wedge-shaped, narrow, centre pale, with varied markings, margins darker, sometimes scalloped, curved forwards; median lobe tooth-shaped; spur spindly, cylindrical, descendent, arched downwards, 5-7mm x *c.* 1mm; 2n=40.

Variation Varies in the colour of the flowers as well as the shape and markings of the lip.

Flowering Season V-VIII; late.

Habitat Full sun to mid-shade on calcareous, very damp to wet substrates. Marshy meadows, flushed slopes, stream banks, 600-2600m asl.

Distribution Mediterranean-pontic; from the northern Peloponnese and Greek Macedonia to the Caucasus and Iran, and north to the Crimea; absent from the Aegean zone with the exception of the island of Euboea (Gr). Local and often occurring in small populations in its stations.

Countries An Cy Gr Ls Ro.

Photos Cy, Troodos, 23.VI.2002. P. Delforge.

Note Considered by most authors to be very isolated and ancestral, due to its distinctive morphology and the presence of non-digitate root-tubers and stolons. Molecular analyses initially placed *D. iberica* in the *D. maculata* group, a result now considered erroneous. *D. iberica* thus returns to the basal place in the phylogeny of the genus that it occupied in the first edition.

The *Dactylorhiza sambucina* group

Characteristics Root-tubers flattened, near entirely to shortly palmate; stem hollow; leaves unspotted; 2n=40, 42, 60. A monophyletic group of 5 species which, in their ecology and the shape of the root-tubers and flowers, seems rather close to the *Orchis pallens* subgroup.

Dactylorhiza sambucina
(L.) Soó

Etymology *sambucina*: [with a scent of] elder. **Type** Su, Stockholm (1755). **Synonyms** *Orchis latifolia* L. p.p., *O. sambucina* L., *O. lutea* DULAC nom. illeg., *O. sambucina* var. *zimmermanii* A. CAMUS, *Dactylorhiza latifolia* (L.) Soó vel H. BAUMANN & KÜNKELE nom. illeg..

Description Robust and squat, 10-30 (-45)cm tall; stem thick, hollow; 4-7 leaves, unspotted, pale green, well-spaced along stem, lower leaves lanceolate, 5-12cm x 1-3cm, uppermost 1-2 leaves smaller, linear-lanceolate, bract-like; bracts, green, equal or longer than the flowers; inflorescence dense, initially ovoid then near cylindrical; flowers yellow or purple, with a slight scent of elder; lateral sepals spreading to vertically erect, tips recurved, oval, 8-13mm x 4-5.5mm, dorsal sepal near equal, forming a hood with the petals; lip elliptical, near entire or obscurely to clearly 3-lobed, slightly convex, 7.5-11mm x 11-17mm, centre yellow spotted red, margins often scalloped; spur robust, near cylindrical to conical, 10-15mm x 3mm, descendent, curving downwards parallel to ovary. 2n=40, 60.

Variation Slight. Plants with red flowers are often rarer and slightly earlier-flowering than yellow ones; the 2 forms often grow together. *'zimmermanii'*: An intermediate form with salmon-pink flowers, is rare.

Flowering Season (III-) IV-VII; quite early.

Habitat Mostly full sun, on calcareous to slightly acidic, dry to damp substrates. Short, poor grassland, meadows, mountain pastures, open woodland, mostly montane, up to 2600m asl.

Distribution European. Central Spain to the Crimea, south to Sicily and north to central Scandinavia. Distribution fragmented, absent from mid-and Atlantic Europe. Quite local and often abundant in its stations.

Countries Al Au Bu Co Cz Da Fe Ga Ge Gr He Hs Hu It Ju No Rm Ro Si Su. **Photos** Ga, Isère, 10.VII.1997; Aveyron, 10.V.1988. P. DELFORGE.

Dactylorhiza insularis
(Sommier) Landwehr

Etymology *insularis*: island. **Type** Sa, Giglio (1895). **Synonyms** *Orchis insularis* SOMMIER, *Dactylorhiza sambucina* subsp. *insularis* (SOMMIER) SOÓ, *D. romana* subsp. *bartonii* HUXLEY & P.F. HUNT, *D. insularis* f. *bartonii* (HUXLEY & P.F. HUNT) GATHOYE & D. TYTECA.

Description As *D. sambucina* but slender, 20-50cm tall; 5-9 near erect leaves, linear-lanceolate, up to 15cm x 2cm; inflorescence laxer, near cylindrical; flowers yellow; sepals 7-10mm long; lip 5-9mm x 5.5-11mm, the same shade as the sepals; spur cylindrical, 7.5-11mm long, horizontal, straight to slightly downcurved; 2n=60. 60+1B. **Variation** Lacks a red form; lip unspotted or adorned with 4 red dots at base, more rarely with 2 broad red spots (= **photo C** '*bartonii*').

Flowering Season IV-VI. **Habitat** Full sun to mid-shade on dry to moist, often acidic, substrates. Short, poor grassland, meadows, open woodland, up to 2000m asl. **Distribution** Western Mediterranean, east to Grosseto (It), north to Corbières (Ga). Local and sometimes abundant. **Countries** Co Ga Hs It Lu Sa. **Photos A&B** Sa, Sassari, 3.V.1996; **C** Hs, Cuenca, 11.V.1988. P. DELFORGE.

177

Dactylorhiza markusii
(TINEO) H. BAUMANN & KÜNKELE

Etymology Named after Dr Markus, doctor to the Russian empress. **Type** Si, Palerme (1846). **Synonyms** *D. romana* subsp. *markusii* (TINEO) J. HOLUB, *D. sambucina* subsp. *siciliensis* (KLINGE) SUNDERMANN, *D. romana* subsp. *siciliensis* (KLINGE) SOÓ, *D. sulphurea* subsp. *siciliensis* (KLINGE) FRANCO nom. inval., *D. sicula* (TINEO) AVERYANOV.

Description 15-40cm tall; 4-7 leaves, unspotted, pale green, attenuated at base, arched, spreading in a basal rosette, linear-lanceolate, 10-18cm x 1-1.6cm; 2-5 smaller, well-spaced cauline leaves, the upper bract-like; bracts green, the lower rather longer than the flowers; inflorescence rather dense, initially ovoid then cylindrical; 10-40 flowers, usually whitish-yellow; lateral sepals oval, asymmetrical, vertically erect and often touching back-to-back, 5.5-10mm x 2.5-4mm; dorsal sepal near equal; petals narrower; dorsal sepal and petal forming a hood; lip yellow, brighter than sepals, 3-lobed, slightly convex, 7-10mm x (8-) 10-14mm, base obcordiforme, centre unspotted; lateral lobes rounded, margins often scalloped; median lobe emarginate, narrower and longer than lateral lobes; spur robust but rather thin, cylindrical, as long as, or shorter than, ovary, 9-13mm (-15) x 1.2-2mm, ascendant, tip rounded, upcurved. 2n=40. 40+1B.

Variation Red form extremely rare, reported from Sicily: lip unspotted magenta with a bright red centre (photo C).

Flowering Season III-VI; early. **Habitat** Full sun to mid-shade on dry to moist acidic substrates. Short, poor grassland, open montane woodland, 700-2000m asl.

Distribution Western Mediterranean, east to Calabria; more southerly than *D. insularis*. Local and often rather rare. **Countries** Ag Bl Hs It Lu Ma Sa Si.

Photos A&B Hs, Jaén, 12.IV.1990; **C** (below) Si, Messina, 18.IV.1987. P. DELFORGE.

Dactylorhiza flavescens
(K. KOCH) J. HOLUB

Etymology *flavescens*: turning yellow. **Type** Ro, Caucasus (1849). **Synonyms** *Orchis flavescens* K. KOCH, *Orchis mediterranea* subsp. *georgica* KLINGE, *Dactylorhiza ruprechtii* AVERYANOV, *D. sambucina* subsp. *georgica* (KLINGE) SUNDER- MANN, *D. romana* subsp. *georgica* (KLINGE) RENZ & TAUBENHEIM.

Description As *D. markusii* but 10-40cm tall; leaves slightly narrower; bracts slightly shorter; flowers pale whitish-yellow or purple, the 2 forms often growing together; lip narrower, shape more varied, entire or ± clearly 3-lobed, 5-10mm x 5-10 (-13)mm, margins pale yellow, centre brighter yellow, unspotted, or margins magenta, centre red, base and central groove yellow (as often in *D. romana*); spur 7-11 (-14)mm long, not as upcurved.

Flowering Season (III-) IV-VI; quite early.

Habitat Full sun to mid-shade on dry to moist, alkaline to acidic substrates. Short, poor grassland, scrub, open montane woodland, 900-2200m asl.

Distribution Caucasian; from northeast Anatolia to Turkmenistan. Local and sometimes in scattered populations.

Countries An Ro.

Photos An, Bitlis, 19.V.1990. P. DELFORGE.

Key to the *Dactylorhiza sambucina* group

1 spur descendant, downcurved parallel to ovary .... *D. sambucina*
1* spur horizontal or ascendant 2

2 spur (13-) 17-25mm long, longer than ovary .... *D. romana*
2* spur 7-15mm long 3

3 spur horizontal, straight or slightly down- curved .... *D. insularis*
3* spur ascendant, ± upcurved 4

4 lip (spreading), usually broader than long, 10-14mm wide .... *D. markusii*
4* lip usually as broad as long, 5-10mm wide .... *D. flavescens*

Dactylorhiza romana
(Sebastiani) Soó

Etymology *romana*: Roman. **Type** It, Latina (1813). **Synonyms** *Orchis romana* Sebastiani, *O. mediterranea* Klinge, *O. pseudosambucina* Tenore, *O. romana* subsp. *libanotica* Mouterde, *Dactylorhiza libanotica* (Mouterde) Averyanov, *D. sulphurea* Franco, *D. sulphurea* subsp. *pseudosambucina* (Tenore) Franco, *D. sambucina* subsp. *pseudosambucina* (Tenore) Sundermann.

Description 15-35 (-50)cm high; 3-9 leaves, unspotted, pale green, slightly arched, spreading in a basal rosette, linear-lanceolate, 9-20cm x 1-3.5cm; 1-4 cauline leaves, well-spaced, smaller, the uppermost bract-like; bracts green, slightly longer than flowers; inflorescence initially ovoid-elongate then near cylindrical, dense then lax; flowers rather pale whitish-yellow or light to dark magenta, the 2 forms often growing together; lateral sepals broadly oval, asymmetrical, vertically erect and often touching back-to-back, 6-10 (-13)mm x 3.5-7 (-9)mm; dorsal sepal near equal, petals rather broad; dorsal sepal and petals forming a hood; lip yellow (brighter than sepals) or magenta (as sepals), 3-lobed, slightly convex, 7.5-12mm x (8-) 10-18mm, base near quadrangular, centre unspotted, usually yellow, rarely red in the magenta form; lateral lobes broadly falcate; median lobe emarginate, as wide as lateral lobes but much longer; spur robust, cylindrical, longer than ovary, (13-) 17-25mm x 1.5-3mm, ascendant to vertical, slightly up-curved. 2n=40. 40+1B.

Variation Intermediates between red and yellow forms are rather frequent; the red form is absent from Cyprus.

Flowering Season III-VI; quite early.

Habitat Full sun to shade on dry to moist, alkaline to acidic substrates. Garrigue, scrub, open woodland, up to 2000m asl.

Distribution Central and eastern Mediterranean, north to Grosseto Province (It), Hvar Island (Ju) and the Crimea, east to Syria, south to Crete; limits in the Pontic zone not well known (see Notes). Rather local, sites usually holding a few plants, sometimes larger populations.

Countries Ae Al An Bu Cr Cy Gr It Ju Ls Ro Si Tu.

Photos It, Brindisi, 30.III.1991; Si, Enna, 18.IV.1987. P. Delforge.

Notes The contact zones with *D. markusii* (Sicily, Calabria) and *D. flavescens* (northeastern Anatolia, Caucasus) are poorly known; intermediate populations are sometimes reported in these regions.

The *Dactylorhiza incarnata* group

Characteristics Clearly hygrophilous; root-tubers flattened, long-digitate; stem hollow, central cavity with a diameter over half total stem diameter; lip (near-) entire, longer than, or as long as, broad, often rhomboidal and rather small; 2n=40 (-80). A Euro-Siberian group, probably monophyletic, containing at least 15 species, essentially Asian; 10 species in this guide.

Dactylorhiza ochroleuca
(WÜSTNEI ex BOLL) J. HOLUB

Etymology *ochroleuca*: yellowish-white. **Type** Ge, Mecklembourg (1860). **Synonyms** *D. incarnata* subsp. *ochroleuca* (WÜSTNEI ex BOLL) P.F. HUNT & SUMMERHAYES.

Description As *D. incarnata* but taller and more robust, (30-) 50-90cm tall; 4-6 leaves, unspotted, very erect, placed against the stem, relatively short, not or only just reaching base of inflorescence; inflorescence more cylindrical; flowers whitish-yellow; lip slightly more elongate, more clearly 3-lobed, median lobe very well-defined and longer, base and centre bright yellow, lateral lobes strongly reflexed backwards. 2n=40.

Variation Not very varied. Well defined and clearly separated from the yellow form of *D. incarnata* (see '*ochrantha*') which is smaller, with longer leaves, more divergent at base, a more ovoid inflorescence, flowers that are more whitish and more translucent, with a less colourful lip, sometimes faintly spotted in centre, less clearly 3-lobed, central lobe less well developed, lateral lobes shorter and more spreading, with the sides reflexed.

Flowering Season (V-) VI-VII; slightly after *D. incarnata*.

Habitat Full sun on wet, alkaline substrates. The intermediate zones of rich fens, above all stands of sedges and reeds colonising calcareous peat, up to 900m asl.

Distribution The centre of Europe and Scandinavia. Limits poorly known; in the east perhaps extends to the Crimea; the numerous reports from England probably refer to yellow forms of *D. incarnata* and *D. pulchella*. Very rare and local, and in decline following the disappearance of its habitats.

Countries Au Br Da Ga Ge He Hs Hu No Po Pb Rm ?Ro Su.

Photos Su, Mjølby, 4.VII.1988; Ge, Garmisch-Partenkirchen, 2.VII.1989. P. DELFORGE.

Dactylorhiza incarnata
(L.) Soó

Etymology *incarnata*: flesh-coloured. **Type*** Su, Uppsala (1755). **Synonyms** *Orchis latifolia* L. sensu Pugsley, *O. strictifolia* Opiz, *O. impudica* Crantz, *O. haematodes* Rchb. nom. illeg., *Dactylorhiza gemmana* (Pugsley) Averyanov, *D. incarnata* var. *drudei* (Schulze) Soó, *D. incarnata* var. *latissima* (Zapal.) Hylander, *D. incarnata* var. *brevibracteata* Landwehr, *D. incarnata* subsp. *lobelii* (Vermeulen) H.Æ. Pedersen, *D. incarnata* var. *lobelii* (Vermeulen) Soó, *D. incarnata* var. *hyphaematodes* (Neumann) Landwehr, *D. incarnata* var. *reichenbachii* Gathoye & D. Tyteca, *D. incarnata* subsp. *baumgartneriana* B. Baumann et. al., *D. incarnata* var. *baumgartneriana* (B. Baumann et. al.) P. Delforge, *D. incarnata* f. *ochrantha* Landwehr.

Description 15-80cm tall; stem hollow; 4-8 leaves, yellowish-green, usually unspotted, sheathing, erect, keeled, tip hooded, narrowly lanceolate, broadest at base, 8-20cm x 1.5-4cm, longest leaves exceeding base or even tip of inflorescence, uppermost 1-2 bract-like; bracts clearly longer than flowers; inflorescence dense, initially ovoid then near cylindrical, 4-15cm tall; up to 70 (-220) small flowers, pale to dark flesh-pink, sometimes lilac, very rarely yellowish or white; sepals lanceolate, 7-9mm x 2.5-4mm, marked with dots and thin loops, the laterals spreading to erect, tip recurved; petals oval, narrow, forming a hood with the dorsal sepal; lip near rhomboidal, entire or obscurely 3-lobed, 4.5-8 (-9)mm x 4.5-8 (-9)mm, the base pale yellowish, the centre pink, convex, finely marked with well-defined dots, loops and streaks, margins spreading, recurved, median lobe poorly developed; spur robust, conical, pinkish-white, descendent, slightly curved, 5-9mm long, 2-3.5mm thick, shorter than ovary. 2n=40.

Variation Very varied, and numerous infraspecific taxa have been described (see following pages).

Flowering Season V-VII (-VIII); after *D. majalis*. **Habitat** Full sun on alkaline to neutral, damp to wet substrates. Coastal marshes, oligotrophic fens and damp meadows, stream banks, up to 2400m asl.

Distribution Euro-Siberian. West to central Spain and northern Scandinavia; south to northern Italy, northern Greece and northwest Anatolia; east to the Caucasus and to Lake Baikal and China. Widespread but becoming rare due to the disappearance of its habitats; often absorbed by *D. majalis* s.l. when the substrate dries out.

Countries Al An Au Be Br Bu Cz Da Fe Ga Ge Gr Hb He Ho Hs Hu It Ju †Lu Lx No Pb Po Rm Ro Su. **Photos** Ga, North, 16.VI.2002; Su, Öland, 3.VII.1988. P. Delforge.

182

Variation *'gemmana', 'latissima'*: Robust, up to 100cm tall; here and there through the range; probably ecotypes.

'lobelii': Very short but sturdy, up to 20cm tall; stem very short and thick; inflorescence usually elongate, its base almost at ground level; leaves slightly broader than those of var. *incarnata*. **Habitat** Damp shell sands that are flooded over the winter. Dune slacks, coastal marshes; probably an ecotype. **Countries** Br Ho. **Photo A** Ho, Zuid-Holland, 9.VI.2001. P. DELFORGE.

'brevibracteata': Plants with more purplish flowers and shorter leaves, described from central Spain, may approximate to *D. pulchella*. Populations of *D. incarnata* from the southwest Massif Central (Ga) are often more purple. **Photo B** Hs, Cuenca, 13.VI.1988. P. DELFORGE.

'ochrantha': Flowers pale yellow. Occurs here and there with the normal pink-flowered form but very rare; often mistakenly identified as *D. ochroleuca* (see p. 181). **Photo C** Ga, Somme, 16.VI.1985. J. DEVILLERS-TERSCHUREN.

'reichenbachii' (= *haematodes*): Leaves blotched purple on upper side; a variant that sometimes results from the introgression of *D. incarnata* by *D. majalis* s.l.

183

'*hyphaematodes*': Leaves spotted purple on both sides; found here and there throughout the range, sometimes in pure populations, rare. **Photo A** Su, Ostersund, 9.VII.1988. P. DELFORGE. **Discussion** Described from Sweden, where *D. incarnata* and *D. cruenta* are clearly distinct, this variety does not seem to originate as a hybrid between these species, nor to be influenced by *D. majalis*. The situation is often more complex in the Alps where, next to plants with spotted leaves that are not hybrids, there are hybrid swarms that are tricky to identify.

'*drudei*': Spindly, 10-20cm tall; 3-5 short, narrow leaves, 4-6cm x 0.4-1cm; flowers as var. *incarnata*, but less numerous. **Habitat** Acidic marshes, damp heathland. **Countries** Br Fe No Su. **Photo B** Su, Rotvik, 7.VII.1988. P. DELFORGE.

'*baumgartneriana*': As var. *incarnata*, but spindly, 12-35cm tall; leaves on average more numerous, 5-9, relatively short, rather broad, 6-18cm x 1.2-4.3cm; 14-65 smaller flowers; lateral sepals shorter, spreading, not erect; petals (5.7-7.6mm x 2.2-2.8mm), spur (61-7.2mm x 1.7-2.5mm) and ovary all shorter. **Habitat** Damp meadows in the course of drainage, which threatens the survival of this recently described taxon (2003). **Countries** Ro, Azerbaijan. **Watercolour** Ro, Azerbaijan, 25.IV.2000. M. WALRAVENS.

Dactylorhiza pulchella
(DRUCE) AVERYANOV

Etymology *pulchella*: beautiful. **Type** Ge, Thuringe (1884). **Synonyms** *O. incarnata* var. *pulchella* DRUCE, *?O. latifolia* var. *serotina* HAUSSKNECHT, *?O. serotinus* (HAUSSKNECHT) SCHWARZ, *?O. angustifolia* var. *haussnechtii* KLINGE, *?Orchis incarnata* var. *borealis* NEUMANN, *Dactylorhiza incarnata* var. *borealis* (NEUMANN) HYLANDER.

Description As *D. incarnata* but more spindly, 15-40cm tall; 3-4 leaves, unspotted, less numerous, slightly shorter, 0.7-2cm wide, but the same habit as those of *D. incarnata*; bracts washed violet; inflorescence 4-7cm tall; 10-40 flowers, strongly fuchsia-pink to violet; lip with pronounced thick dark violet dots, loops and streaks. 2n=40. **Variation** A form with yellow flowers probably exists, but without doubt hardly different from *D. incarnata* f. *ochrantha*.

Flowering Season VI-VIII; 2 weeks after *D. incarnata*. **Habitat** Full sun on acidic to alkaline, very damp to wet substrates. Various oligotrophic mires, at least up to 1500m asl. **Distribution** Probably endemic to British Isles. **Countries** ?Au ?Be Br ?Cz ?Da ?Ga ?Ge Hb ?He ?Hs No ?Pb ?Po ?Ro ?Su. **Photos** Br, Wales, Anglesey, 6 & 7.VII. 1993. P. DELFORGE.

Discussion In some regions of the British Isles *D. pulchella* is commoner than *D. incarnata*; intermediate forms or hybrid swarms with *D. purpurella* (Br, Hb) and *D. incarnata* seem to be quite frequent. Some late-flowering, dark forms of *D. incarnata* may be reported as *D. pulchella*, for example, *D. incarnata* var. *brevibracteata* in central Spain. There are certainly hybrid swarms between *D. incarnata* and *D. majalis* that have been mistakenly identified as *D. pulchella*. The identity of British populations ('*pulchella*') and Continental ('*serotina*') has sometimes been advocated but not formally established; if this happens, the name *serotina* will take priority.

Key to the *Dactylorhiza incarnata* group

1   flower yellow 2
1*   flowers of another colour 3

2   centre of lip bright yellow ..... *D. ochroleuca*
2*   lip pale .... *D. incarnata* f. *ochrantha*

3   flowers scarlet-red .... *D. coccinea*
3*   flowers of another colour 4

(continued on next page)

Dactylorhiza bohemica
BUSINSKY

Etymology *bohemica*: from Bohemia. **Type** Cz, Ceska Lípa (1989).

Description Spindly, 20-50cm tall; stem thin, hollow; 3-4 cauline leaves, lightly spotted to unspotted on basal half, narrowly lanceolate, ± channelled and hooded, obliquely erect, sometimes reaching base of inflorescence, 7-21cm x 0.9-2cm, distal half broadest, tip of largest leaf obtuse-rounded; inflorescence lax to near dense, shortly cylindrical, 3.5-8cm tall; 7-15 (-20) medium-sized flowers, amethyst to dark purple; lateral sepals 7.9-9.7mm x 2.9-3.4mm; lip broadly oboval, weakly 3-lobed, strongly folded longitudinally, very convex, (5.8-) 6.7-8.7mm x 9.4-12.4mm, base and centre whitish, marked with thick dark patterns, forming streaks and loops; lateral lobes rounded; median lobe small; spur elongated, conical, near horizontal to directed obliquely downwards, 7.3-9.2mm long, 1.5-2.4mm thick; 2n=40.

Flowering Season Late VI-VII. **Habitat** Full sun on damp to wet, basic substrates. Fens on the plains, 200-300m asl.

Distribution Northern Bohemia (Czech).

Countries Cz. **Photos** Cz, Cseska Lipa, 11.VII.1999. C.A.J. KREUTZ.

Key to the *Dactylorhiza incarnata* group

(*continued from previous page*)

4   lip 5-8 (-9)mm long 5

4*   lip (6-) 8-16mm long 8

5   flowers mauve, lip marked with thick, dark violet patterns 6

5*   flowers pink to lilac, lip marked with ± fine patterns 7

6   leaves slightly spotted, at least on distal half; cauline leaves broadest in distal half .... *D. bohemica*

6*   leaves unspotted; cauline leaves broadest in basal half .... *D. pulchella*

7   lip markings blood-red; leaves short .... *D. cruenta*

7*   lip markings purplish-pink; leaves elongated .... *D. incarnata*

(*continued on next page*)

Dactylorhiza coccinea
PUGSLEY) AVERYANOV

Etymology *coccinea*: scarlet-red. **Type** Br, Anglesey (1884). **Synonyms** *Orchis latifolia* var. *coccinea* PUGSLEY, *Dactylorhiza incarnata* subsp. *coccinea* (PUGSLEY) SOÓ, *Orchis incarnata* var. *atrirubra* GODFERY, *Dactylorhiza incarnata* f. *dunensis* (DRUCE) SOÓ.

Description As *D. incarnata* but squat, 5-15 (-25)cm tall; stem washed with purple at tip; 5-10 leaves, unspotted, dark green, more strongly curved outwards, erect to spreading on the ground, broader, up to 21cm x 4.5cm, uppermost 1-3 leaves bract-like, sometimes edged purple; inflorescence dense, with 20-40 (-100) small brick-red to scarlet flowers; sepals and petals slightly larger; lip a little more spreading; 2n=40.

Variation Very distinct, linked to *D. pulchella* by intermediate populations in acidic fens in Ireland; dwarf plants growing mostly in dune slacks (*'dunensis'*); populations of dwarf plants with pink flowers and pale yellowish-green leaves are probably best placed with a variety of *D. incarnata* (?*'lobelii'*).

Flowering Season VI-VII; 2 weeks after *D. incarnata*.

Habitat Full sun on slightly acidic to alkaline, damp to wet substrates. Marshy dune slacks, more rarely damp meadows and fens further away from the coast, up to 200m asl.

Distribution Principally around the coasts of the Irish Sea and Scotland. Very rare and local.

Countries Br Hb. **Photos** Br, Wales, Anglesey, 6.VII.1993; Outer Hebrides, 17.VII.1994. P. DELFORGE.

Key to the *Dactylorhiza incarnata* group

(*continued from previous page*)

8	lip streaked reddish to edges 9
8*	lip marked in centre only, with violet loops and streaks 10
9	leaves marked with violet streaks on both sides .... *D. euxina*
9*	leaves unspotted .... *D. armeniaca*
10	short spur, 1/2x or 2/3x length of ovary .... *D. osmanica*
10*	spur elongated, ± equal to ovary .... *D. umbrosa*

Dactylorhiza cruenta
(O.F. Müller) Soó

Etymology *cruenta*: bloody. **Type** Da, Röraas (1782). **Synonyms** *Orchis cruenta* O.F. Müller, *Dactylorhiza incarnata* subsp. *cruenta* (O.F. Müller) P.D. Sell.

Description Robust and thickset, 15-35 (-50)cm tall; stem often washed purple at tip; 3-5 leaves, spotted ± intensely brownish-purple on both sides, rarely unspotted, spreading to near erect, often curved downwards, not or slightly keeled, tip not hooded, oval-lanceolate, broadest on basal half, 4-10 (-15)cm x 1-2.5 (3.5)cm, not reaching base of inflorescence, uppermost 1-2 leaves bract-like; bracts often spotted with purple; inflorescence frequently few-flowered, ovoid, short, then near cylindrical, 3-8cm tall; 8-30 (-35) flowers similar to those of *D. incarnata* but often darker pink, sometimes lilac or red, sepals and lip marked with thick bright red dots, loops and streaks; 2n=40. **Variation** Shape and colour of flowers constant; nevertheless, an exceptional morph with unmarked yellow flowers has been reported. Shape and colour of leaves more varied, from rather narrow to broad, entirely brownish-purple to slightly spotted with purple on both sides, rarely unspotted; the different forms are often found together.

Flowering Season VI-VII (-VIII).

Habitat Full sun on very calcareous, very wet substrates. In Scandinavia found in coastal marshes, fens with *Sphagnum* and boggy coniferous forests, up to 1000m asl. In the Alps damp meadows, marshy depressions, stream banks and flushes, 1100-2500m asl.

Distribution Probably Euro-Siberian; slightly more northerly and less widespread than *D. incarnata*.

Countries ?Br †Da Fe Ga Ge ?Hb He No ?Pb ?Po Ro Su. **Photos** Ga, Hautes-Alpes, 19.VI.1998; It, Belluno, 6.VII.1989.

Discussion Sometimes difficult to distinguish from *D. incarnata* on the basis of leaf characters, particularly from vars. *hyphaematodes* and *drudei*. When growing in sympatry, a rather frequent occurrence in the Alps, the 2 species preserve their identity well, although intermediate forms are found. The distribution of *D. cruenta* is rather poorly understood away from the Alps and Scandinavia; its presence as far east as Siberia has not been established; reports from the British Isles probably refer to *D. purpurella* and *D. incarnata* var. *hyphaematodes*.

Dactylorhiza osmanica
(KLINGE) SOÓ

Etymology *osmanica*: from the Ottomans. **Type*** An, Pont (1898). **Synonyms** *Orchis orientalis* subsp. *cilicica* KLINGE p.p., *O. cataonica* H. FLEISCHMANN, *Dactylorhiza elata* subsp. *anatolica* E. NELSON, *D. olocheilos* (BOISSIER) AVERYANOV.

Description Robust, 20-90 (-120)cm tall; stem hollow, thick; 4-10 leaves, unspotted, sheathing, spreading to near erect, keeled, often hooded at tip, shape very varied, broadly to rather narrowly lanceolate, largest leaf broadest around the lower third, 9-22cm x 2-5cm, upper 1-3 leaves smaller; lower bracts longer than flowers; inflorescence dense, initially long-ovoid then near cylindrical, up to 20cm tall; numerous medium-sized flowers, usually rather deep mauve or magenta; lateral sepals spreading to vertically erect, sometimes spotted, oval-lanceolate, 8-16mm x 3-5.5mm; dorsal sepal and petals near equal, 6-12mm long, forming a hood; lip entire to obscurely 3-lobed, near rhomboidal to elliptic, (7-) 9-16mm x (7-) 9-16mm, tip sometimes tooth-shaped, margins ± spreading, centre convex, whitish to pink, marked with thick dark violet patterns, formed by dots and streaks surrounded by loops, often unbroken; spur short and broad, 5-11mm x 3-4.5mm, cylindrical to conical, slightly descendent, 1/3-1/2x length of ovary; 2n=40.

Variation Rather distinct from *D. umbrosa* and *D. euxina* in its sturdiness, flower colour and relatively short spur, but very varied in the shape of the leaves and flowers; forms intermediate with *D. umbrosa*, very polymorphic itself, have been reported. *'anatolica'*: Very robust, up to 120cm tall, found throughout the range; a taxon that recalls *D. elata*, but a member of the diploid group.

Flowering Season V-VII.

Habitat Full sun on very damp to wet, mostly alkaline to slightly acidic substrates. Meadows and open marshy woodland, stream banks, flushed slopes, 500-2400m asl.

Distribution Anatolia. Mostly in the quadrilateral formed by Erzurum, Samsun, Antalya and Iskenderun; may reach Syria. Local, but some sites hold very large populations.

Countries An ?Ls.

Photos An, Sivas, 28.V.1990; Erzincan, 25.V.1990. P. DELFORGE.

Dactylorhiza umbrosa
(Karelin & Kirilow) Nevsky

Etymology *umbrosa*: dark **Type** Ro, Songorie (central Asia) (1842). **Synonyms** *Orchis turcestanica* (Klinge) Klinge, *Dactylorhiza sanasunitensis* (H. Fleischmann) Averyanov, *D. vanensis* E. Nelson, *D. persica* (Schlechter) Soó, *D. chuhensis* Renz & Taubenheim, *D. umbrosa* var. *chuhensis* (Renz & Taubenheim) Kreutz, *D. merovensis* (Grosheim) Averyanov.

Description Slender, 10-60 (-80)cm tall; stem hollow, thick; 4-9 leaves, unspotted, or spotted with purple on both sides (*'chuhuensis'*, photo **B**), sheathing, spreading to near erect, keeled, sometimes hooded at tip, shape varied, very broadly to very narrowly lanceolate, 6-30cm x 2-6cm, largest leaf often broadest towards centre, 1-3 upper leaves smaller, frequently extending beyond base of inflorescence; bracts often shorter than flowers; inflorescence dense to near lax, initially conical then long-ovoid or near cylindrical, 5-25cm tall; flowers numerous, pale purplish-pink to rather dark magenta; lateral sepals spreading forward to erect, oval-lanceolate, 6.5-13mm x 2.5-5mm; dorsal sepal near equal, petals narrow, 5-10mm long, dorsal sepal and petals forming a hood; lip usually entire, rhomboidal, 6-13mm x 4-12mm, tip long tooth-shaped, sides ± spreading or reflexed, centre convex or flat, pale, marked with rather thick, very varied, dark violet patterns formed by dots and streaks surrounded by irregular loops; spur near cylindrical, downcurved, descendent, rather thin, 7-15 (-18)mm x 1.5-3.5 (-5)mm, ± equal to ovary; 2n=40.

Flowering Season V-VII; rather early. **Habitat** As *D. osmanica*, 1000-3800m asl. **Distribution** Central Asia: west to Erzincan (An) and perhaps to Maras (An); south to Iraqi Kurdistan; east to Afghanistan and Kazakhstan. Widespread, often in large populations. **Countries** An Ro. **Photos A&C** An, Van, 20.V.1990; Bitlis, 19.V.1990. P. Delforge; **B** (*'chuhuensis'*): Van, 23.V.2004. C.A.J. Kreutz.

Dactylorhiza euxina
(NEVSKI) CZEREPANOV

Etymology *euxina*: from Pontus Euxinus (ancient name given to the Black Sea). **Type** Ro, Caucasus (1898). **Synonyms** *Orchis monticola* subsp. *caucasica* (LIPSKY) KLINGE, *Dactylorhiza majalis* subsp. *caucasica* (LIPSKY) SUNDERMANN, *D. euxina* (NEVSKI) H. BAUMANN & KÜNKELE isonym.

Description (5-) 10-35cm tall; stem green, often marked all over with violet streaks; 3-6 cauline leaves, near erect, unspotted (= var. *markowitschii*, see next page) or much more often, marked with violet streaks on both sides, 3-9cm x 1-5cm, lanceolate to elliptic-oblong; lower bracts longer than flowers; inflorescence short, dense, ovoid, 2.5-5cm tall; flowers dark, reddish-purple or purplish; lateral sepals oval-lanceolate, 8-14mm long, spreading; lip 7-13mm x 8-15mm, entire or obscurely 3-lobed, near rhomboidal to near heart-shaped, margins scalloped, often undulate-crisped, densely marked from the convex centre to the edge with abundant thick red streaks, rarely with complete loops; spur 6-9mm x 3-4mm, conical, descendent, forming an acute angle with the lip; 2n=40.

Flowering Season V-VIII.

Habitat Full sun to mid-shade on alkaline to slightly acidic, moist to wet substrates. Short grassland, damp meadows and fens, 850-2900m asl.

Distribution Mostly the Caucasus; in Anatolia found in the northeast, west to Giresun and south to Erzurum and Agri. Rare and local.

Countries An. **Photos** An, Rize, 22.V.1990; 4.VI.1990. P. DELFORGE.

Notes The identity of this taxon is not always clear. On the one hand it was considered to be associated with marshes over 1700m asl, where it flowers with *D. umbrosa*, and on the other, as an 'eastern *D. cruenta*', colonising more diverse habitats, at least in Anatolia. Although showing constant floral characters, *D. euxina* may be heterogeneous, which may explain the disparity in the reported chromosome number. Recent molecular studies show, nevertheless, that this taxon is diploid and constitutes an ancestral eastern species with a wide distribution, close to *D. incarnata*, at the root of the emergence of the allopolyploid hybridogenous species through repeated crosses with diploid species of the *D. maculata* group, notably *D. saccifera*. This is the case of *D. urvilleana*, an allotetraploid species, whose genome is half made up of chromosomes from *D. saccifera,* the other half from *D. euxina*.

191

Dactylorhiza euxina
(NEVSKI) CZEREPANOV
var. *markowitschii*
(SOÓ) RENZ & TAUBENHEIM

Etymology Named after Vasil Vasilevitch Marcowitch [sic], Russian botanist (1865-1942).**Type** Ro, Caucasus (1926). **Synonyms** *Orchis caucasica* var. *markowitschii* SOÓ, *O. caucasica* var. *alpina* SCHLECHTER, *D. marko-witschii* (SOÓ) AVERYANOV.

Note This taxon was considered by its describers, Soó (var. *markowitschii*) and Schlechter (var. *alpina*), as growing at high altitudes, with a very thickset habit, rarely reaching 7-10cm high, with, in consequence, the leaves grouped at the base of the stem and a very dense, few-flowered spike. Other morphological differences with *D. euxina*: leaves elliptic-lanceolate, broader; flowers smaller, with the lip, obscurely 3-lobed, more often with a tooth-shaped central lobe. Nowadays, *D. euxina* var. *markowitschii* is interpreted as a robust variant of *D. euxina*, with the leaves and stem unspotted. In this interpretation, as used here, this taxon seems very close in its morphology to the recently described *D. armeniaca*, from which it is only distinguished by chromosome number and molecular analysis (see next page).

Description As *D. euxina* but often squat and sturdy, (10-) 20-40cm tall; stem usually without markings but washed violet at tip; leaves on average broader, 3-8cm x 2.5-5.5cm; lip usually slightly broader and more often obscurely 3-lobed.

Flowering Season V-mid VII.

Habitat As *D. euxina* var. *euxina*.

Distribution As *D. euxina* var. *euxina*, but very rare; very rarely in pure populations.

Countries An, Ro.

Photos Ro, Azerbaijan, Kuba-Amsar, 5.VI.2000. C.A.J. KREUTZ.

Dactylorhiza armeniaca
HEDRÉN

Etymology *armeniaca*: from Armenia. **Type** An, Ardahan (2001). **Synonym** *D. euxina* subsp. *armeniaca* (HEDRÉN) KREUTZ.

Description Robust, 25-70cm tall; stem thick, compressible; (4-) 5-7 cauline leaves, unspotted, lanceolate-pointed, obliquely erect, straight or slightly arched outwards, keeled and then spreading, up to 14cm x 3cm, largest leaf broadest at base, uppermost 1-2 leaves bract-like; bracts dark green, sometimes washed purple, elongate, 30-52mm x 6-10mm, lower bracts longer than the flowers; inflorescence rather dense; up to 30 flowers, intense purple; lateral sepals spreading, marked with blotches or, more rarely, with rings, oval-lanceolate, asymmetrical, 11-12mm x 5mm; petals *c.* 10mm x 3.5mm; lip rather clearly 3-lobed, very convex transversely, 8-12mm x 8-15mm, base whitish to entrance of spur, marked with red to dark purple loops and streaks in centre, streaks on margins; spur rather robust, near cylindrical, straight to slightly descendent, horizontal or pointing downwards, 8.5-11.5mm x 2.5-3.5mm, *c.* 2/3x length of ovary; 2n=80.

Flowering Season V-VI.

Habitat Full sun to mid-shade on moist to wet alkaline substrates. Short grassland, damp meadows and fens, stream banks. Montane, but altitudinal range not yet defined.

Distribution Extreme northeast Anatolia, in Artvin, Ardahan and Kars province. Very local and very rare.

Countries An.

Photos An, Ardahan, 24.VI.1996. C.A.J. KREUTZ.

Discussion Recently described on the basis of caryological and molecular studies that demonstrated it was a hybridogenous species originating from crosses between *D. euxina* and *D. incarnata* and, although it is tetraploid, this is sufficient to place it in the group of *D. incarnata*. The range of *D. armeniaca* is very poorly known; it could also be present in the eastern Caucasus and could already have been described from this area. Its demarcation vis-à-vis *D. euxina* var. *markowitschii* should be clarified.

193

The *Dactylorhiza majalis* group

Characteristics Rather hygrophilous; stem hollow, diameter of central cavity less than half total stem diameter; leaves often broad, rather large, spotted; flowering early, before *D. incarnata*; 2n=80. Essentially a European group, with 7 species that replace each other geographically, all originating from hybridisation between *D. incarnata* and *D. maculata* s.l., but resulting from distinct speciation events.

Dactylorhiza alpestris
(PUGSLEY) AVERYANOV

Etymology *alpestris*: from Alps. **Type** Au, Vorarlberg (1935). **Synonyms** *Orchis alpestris* PUGSLEY, *Dactylorhiza majalis* subsp. *alpestris* (PUGSLEY) SENGHAS, *D. fistulosa* subsp. *alpestris* (PUGSLEY) H. BAUMANN & KÜNKELE nom. illeg.

Description As *D. majalis* but often stocky, 10-25 (-35)cm tall; 3-5 leaves, the lower leaves shorter and broader, oval to elliptical, sometimes near orbicular, 6-10cm x 2.5-5cm, clearly spotted, uppermost 1-2 leaves bract-like; inflorescence shorter and more few-flowered, often not so dense; lip less deeply 3-lobed, often near entire, on average slightly bigger, up to 15mm broad, strongly marked with purple to violet loops, lines and streaks, blurred, often muddled; lateral lobes entire.

Variation More constant than *D. majalis*.

Discussion A controversial taxon, frequent and often flowering in pure populations, but intergrading widely with *D. majalis*, of which it may sometimes appear to be a mere variety or altitudinal ecotype. It seems nevertheless to have fixed, clear-cut characteristics. It is sometimes considered to have a hybrid origin, resulting from the complete absorption of *D. cordigera* by *D. majalis* in alpine zones when sympatry was re-established after the last glaciation.

Flowering Season VI-VIII.

Habitat Full sun on damp to wet, slightly alkaline to slightly acidic substrates. Springs, seepages and marshy hollows in the mountains, 1500-2600m asl.

Distribution The Alps and probably the Pyrenees; eastern limits of range poorly known due to confusion with *D. cordigera*. Rather local but sometimes rather abundant.

Countries Au Ga Ge He Hs It Ju No. **Photos** It, Belluno, 8.VII.1989; Ga, Savoie, 1.VII.1984. P. DELFORGE.

194

Dactylorhiza majalis
(REICHENBACH) P.F. HUNT & SUMMERHAYES

Etymology *majalis*: from the month of May.
Type Ge, Dresden (1828). **Synonyms** *Orchis majalis* REICHENBACH, *O. latifolia* L. p.p., *Dactylorhiza latifolia* (L.) Soó nom. conf., *Orchis fistulosa* MOENCH nom. illeg., *Dactylorhiza fistulosa* (MOENCH) H. BAUMANN & KÜNKELE nom. illeg., *?Orchis comosa* SCOPOLI, *Dactylorhiza comosa* (SCOPOLI) P.D. SELL.

Description Robust, 20-40 (-70)cm tall; stem hollow, thick, tip angular and violet purple; 4-10 leaves, dark green, spotted brownish-purple to blackish on upper side, rarely unspotted, slightly keeled and then flat, obliquely erect to spreading, oblong-lanceolate, 8-16cm x 1.5-3.5cm, broadest towards middle, upper 1-3 leaves bract-like; bracts often longer than flowers; inflorescence dense, ovoid, conical or cylindrical, (2-) 5-10 (-16)cm tall; up to 50 flowers, deep violet-purple, rarely pale lilac; lateral sepals spreading to erect, tip often reflexed, oval-lanceolate, 7-12.5mm x 2.5-5mm; dorsal sepal near equal, petals 5-9mm long, dorsal sepal and petals forming a hood; lip (5-) 8-12mm x (7-) 10-14mm, 3-lobed, rarely near entire, lip index >1.25 (see p. 229), base convex, wedge-shaped, almost white, marked, from entrance of spur to median lobe, with dark violet patterns, often muddled, formed by dots and pale loops; lateral lobes near rhomboidal to rounded, margins ± scalloped, curved forwards or flat; median lobe tooth-like, convex, obtuse; spur conical to near cylindrical, slightly descendent, 8-14mm long, parallel to, and slightly shorter than, ovary.

Variation Large variations in vegetative characters but floral characters rather constant.

Flowering Season V-VII; early.

Habitat Full sun on damp to wet, slightly alkaline to slightly acidic substrates. Mostly moist, marshy unimproved meadows up to 1800m asl.

Distribution Atlantic Europe. Northern Spain and the Dolomites (It) to the far south of Scandinavia; southeastern limits of range poorly known due to confusion with closely related taxa. Rather widespread and sometimes abundant.

Countries Au Be Cz Da Ga Ge He Ho Hs Hu It Ju No Po ?Rm ?Ro Su.

Photos Be, Namur, 2.VI.1991. P. DELFORGE.

Dactylorhiza cordigera
(Fries) Soó

Etymology *cordi-:* heart, *-gera:* bearing. **Type** Rm, Banat (1842). **Synonyms** *Orchis cordigera* Fries, *Dactylorhiza majalis* subsp. *cordigera* (Fries) Sundermann, *D. cordigera* var. *vermionica* B. Willing & E. Willing, *D. lagotis* (Rchb. fil.) H. Baumann, *D. cordigera* subsp. *bosniaca* (G. Beck) Soó, *D. bosniaca* (G. Beck) Averyanov, *D. cordigera* subsp. *siculorum* (Soó) Soó.

Description 15-40cm tall; stem hollow; 3-7 cauline leaves, spotted blackish-violet on upper side, sometimes densely so, erect to spreading, often arched downwards, broadly oval to lanceolate, 4-15cm x 1.5-5.5cm, largest leaf frequently broadest in the upper third, uppermost 1-2 leaves bract-like; bracts sometimes far longer than lower flowers; inflorescence dense, short, ovoid to cylindrical, 3-12cm tall; 5-40 flowers, dark purplish, rarely lilac; sepals lateral spreading to erect, tip often reflexed, oval-lanceolate, 10-16mm x 3.5-6mm; dorsal sepal near equal, petals broadly oval, 8-12.5mm long, dorsal sepal and sepal forming a hood; lip varied, oval, rhomboidal or broadly heart-shaped, entire or 3-lobed (median lobe then broadly tooth-like), 8-16mm x (8-) 10-20mm, spreading or, more often, abruptly contracted and convex in centre, margins flattened or concave, undulate, broadly washed deep purple, base white with a pattern of thick deep purple streaks and irregular loops, rarely extending to centre of lip; spur robust, conical, descendent, 5-12mm x 2-5mm, 0.5x-1x as long as lip.

Variation Significant variations in vegetative characters but floral characters rather constant. *'cordigera'*: Spindly and squat, small in all parts; high altitudes throughout the range. *'bosniaca'*: Small, with big flowers and short spur; mostly northern half of range. *'lagotis'*: Robust; mostly southern part of range. *'siculorum'*: Tall, flowers with long spur, rather similar to those of *D. majalis*. *'vermionica'*: Spindly, perhaps influenced by *D. saccifera*; here and there in Macedonia (Gr).

Flowering Season V-VIII. **Habitat** Full sun on damp to wet, acidic to alkaline substrates. Marshy mountain meadows, seepages, stream banks, 900-2400m asl.

Distribution Balkans. From the Carpathians to northern Greece and from Bosnia (Ju) to Bulgaria. Rather widespread and sometimes abundant in its stations.

Countries Al Bu Gr Ju Rm Ro. **Photos** Gr, Ioannina, 14.VI.1990; Kastoria, 16.VI.1987. P. Delforge.

Dactylorhiza occidentalis
(PUGSLEY) P. DELFORGE

Etymology *occidentalis*: western. **Type** Hb, Clare (1935). **Synonyms** *Orchis majalis* var. *occidentalis* PUGSLEY, *O. occidentalis* (PUGSLEY) WILMOTT, *Dactylorhiza majalis* subsp. *occidentalis* (PUGSLEY) P.D. SELL, *D. comosa* subsp. *occidentalis* (PUGSLEY) P.D. SELL.

Description Thickset, 10-25 (-40)cm tall; 6-8 cauline leaves, often grouped at base of stem, often spotted in various ways on upper side, near erect, curving downwards, lanceolate, keeled, 5-11cm x 1.5-3cm, uppermost 1-3 leaves bract-like; inflorescence dense, ovoid to near cylindrical, 3-10cm tall; flowers numerous, crimson-violet; lip 6-9mm x 8-12mm, near entire to clearly 3-lobed, obcordate, marked with patterns that are similar to those of *D. majalis*, but more distinct; median lobe reduced, sometimes protuberant; spur near cylindrical, straight, near horizontal, 7-10mm x 2-4mm. **Variation** Distinguished from *D. purpurella* by paler flowers and a larger lip.

Flowering Season (IV-) V-VI (-VII); early. **Habitat** Full sun on damp to wet, alkaline to acidic substrates. Marshy dune slacks, coastal meadows, up to 200m asl.

Distribution Western Ireland. Many records from Scotland probably refer to *D. purpurella*. Local and sometimes abundant.

Countries Br Hb. **Photos** Hb, Galway, 10.VII.1993. P. DELFORGE.

Key to *Dactylorhiza majalis* group

1   very short, 6-10 (-18)cm tall .... *D. ebudensis*
1*   (10-) 15-70cm tall 2

2   flowers large; lip (8-) 9-16mm long 3
2*   flowers small; lip 4.5-9mm long 5

3   markings confined to base of lip
     .... *D. cordigera*
3*   markings more extensive 4

4   leaves oblong; lip deeply 3-lobed; lateral lobes scalloped on margins .... *D. majalis*
4*   leaves oval to near orbicular; lip near entire or slightly 3-lobed; lateral lobes entire
     .... *D. alpestris*

(*continued on p. 198*)

Dactylorhiza ebudensis
(WIEFELSPÜTZ ex R.M. BATEMAN & DENHOLM) P. DELFORGE

Etymology *ebudensis*: from Hebrides. **Type** Br, Hebridean (1995). **Synonyms** *Dactylorhiza majalis* subsp. *occidentalis* var. *ebudensis* WIEFELSPÜTZ nom. inval., *D. majalis* subsp. *occidentalis* var. *ebudensis* WIEFELSPÜTZ ex R.M. BATEMAN & DENHOLM, *D. majalis* subsp. *ebudensis* (WIEFELSPÜTZ ex R.M. BATEMAN & DENHOLM) M.R. LOWE, *D. majalis* subsp. *scotica* E. NELSON nom. inval., *D. comosa* subsp. *scotica* (E. NELSON) P.D. SELL nom. inval., *D. majalis* subsp. *occidentalis* var. *scotica* (E. NELSON) R.M. BATEMAN & DENHOLM nom. inval.

Description Very squat, 6-10 (-18)cm tall; stem slightly hollow, washed red; 2-3 (-5) oblong-lanceolate leaves, pointed, gathered at base of stem, spreading to near erect, slightly channelled and curved, usually marked with large purplish-brown blotches on upper side, largest leaf extending past base of inflorescence, uppermost bract-like; bracts sometimes spotted, slightly longer than flowers; inflorescence dense, up to 6cm x 3cm; 5-20 flowers, similar to those of *D. occidentalis*, intense purple; lip obscurely 3-lobed, 6-8.5mm x 8-11.5mm; median lobe poorly developed; spur longer than ovary.

Flowering Season V-VI; early.

Habitat Full sun on moist to wet shell-sand overlying peat. Low growing vegetation in dune depressions (machair), up to 100m asl.

Distribution Known only from North Uist (Hebrides, Scotland); may be present in northern Scotland. Very local and not very abundant.

Countries Br. **Photos** Br, North Uist (loc. typ.), A&C 7.VI.1988. D.M.T. ETTLINGER; **B** 13.VI. 1995. C.A.J. KREUTZ.

Discussion A remarkable taxon. Peripheral, isolated in time and space; a species resulting from an old hybridisation between *D. coccinea* and *D. hebridensis*.

Key to *Dactylorhiza majalis* group

(continued from previous page)

5 robust and slender, 25-70cm tall; median leaves elongated, at least 6x longer than broad .... *D. longifolia*
5* thickset or spindly, 10-30 (-40)cm tall; median leaves shorter, less than 5x longer than broad 6

6 spindly; 2-5 leaves .... *D. lapponica*
6* rather robust, thickset; 6-8 leaves .... *D. occidentalis*

Dactylorhiza baltica
(KLINGE) ORLOVA EX AVERYANOV

Etymology *baltica:* Baltic. **Type** Pb, probably Estonia (1898). **Synonyms** *Orchis latifolia* subsp. *baltica* KLINGE, *Dactylorhiza latifolia* subsp. *baltica* (KLINGE) SOO, *D. majalis* subsp. *baltica* (KLINGE) SENGHAS, *D. majalis* subsp. *baltica* (KLINGE) SUNDERMANN ISONYM., *D. longifolia* AUCT. NON (NEUMANN) AVERYANOV.

Description Robust, 25-70cm tall; stem hollow, relatively slender, a maximum of 1cm thick at base; 6-9 cauline leaves, marked on upper side with numerous small light to dark brown blotches, rarely unspotted, obliquely erect, arching outwards, oblong-lanceolate, 9-25cm x 1.5-4cm, largest leaf broadest towards centre, uppermost 1-2 leaves bract-like; bracts slightly longer than flowers; inflorescence dense, ovoid to cylindrical, (2-) 3-10cm tall; flowers numerous, lilac to crimson-red, rather pale; lateral sepals oval, asymmetrical, spreading to erect, tip often reflexed, 8-10mm x 3-4.5mm, often spotted; dorsal sepal 6.5-8mm long, forming a hood together with petals; lip 6-9mm x (7-) 8-13mm, 3-lobed, oboval to obcordate, base and centre pale, convex, marked with distinct deep purple patterns formed by numerous streaks surrounded with 1-2 almost complete loops; lateral lobes broadly rounded, spreading to abruptly turned down and then reflexed, dark, covered, almost to the edges, with rather thick streaks and/or rings; median lobe reduced, tooth-like, ± as long as laterals; spur near cylindrical, straight, near horizontal, 6-9mm x 2-3mm.

Flowering Season VI-VII; rather early.

Habitat Full sun on damp to wet, slightly alkaline to slightly acidic substrates. Fens and marshy meadows, mostly coastal, up to 400m asl (in Europe).

Distribution Probably boreal and temperate Eurasia. Extends west to the Baltic (Su: Gotland; Fe: Åland Island); eastwards, may reach central Mongolia and Siberia, but more probably only western Russia. Rather local and rather rare.

Countries Fe Pb Po Ro Su.

Photos Pb, Estonia, 1.VII.1978. E. VIMBA; 25.VI.1994. D. RÜCKBRODT.

Discussion A species resulting from an old hybridisation between *D. incarnata* and *D. fuchsii.*

Dactylorhiza lapponica
(LAESTADIUS ex REICHENBACH fil.) SOÓ

Etymology *lapponica*: from Lapland. **Type*** Su, Lapland (1850). **Synonyms** *Dactylorhiza traunsteineri* subsp. *lapponica* (HARTMAN) SOÓ, *D. cruenta* subsp. *lapponica* (HARTMAN) E. NELSON, *D. majalis* subsp. *lapponica* (HARTMAN) SUNDERMANN, *D. lapponica* subsp. *parvimajalis* (D. TYTECA & GATHOYE) KREUTZ, *D. pseudocordigera* (NEUMAN) SOÓ, *D. pycnantha* (NEUMAN) AVERYANOV.

Description Rather spindly, 10-30 (-40)cm tall; stem rather robust, hollow, washed reddish-violet at tip; 2-5 leaves, densely to slightly spotted purple on upper side, erect, well-spread along stem, shape very varied, narrowly to broadly lanceolate, 3-12cm x 0.6-2.5cm, largest leaf broadest at centre or in lower half, uppermost 1-2 leaves bract-like; bracts at least equal to flowers; inflorescence rather lax and few-flowered, cylindrical; 5-20 flowers, dark, reddish-magenta to purplish; lateral sepals spreading to vertically erect, oval-lanceolate, 6-10mm x 2-4mm, often spotted purple; dorsal sepal near equal, petals 5-8mm long, dorsal petal and sepals forming a loose hood; lip varied, near rhomboidal to obcordate, 4.5-9mm x 6-11mm, often longer than broad, spreading to abrupt longitudinal fold, frequently slightly kinked at base, near entire to 3-lobed, lateral lobes rounded, shorter than the median lobe which is broadly tooth-like, often pale in the centre, marked with thick red to dark purple patterns, formed by dots and streaks surrounded by often-complete loops; spur conical, horizontal to descendent, rather thin, 6.5-11mm x 2-3mm, ± equal to ovary. **Variation** Very diverse. Scandinavian populations, probably influenced by *D. curvifolia*, have a range of variation sometimes shifted slightly towards *D. traunsteineri* s.l. Alpine populations are more influenced by *D. majalis* or *D. alpestris*; some intermediates have been described as species (for example, *D. parvimajalis* D. Tyteca & Gathoye).

Flowering Season (V-) VI-VII. **Habitat** Chiefly full sun, on slightly acidic (Scandinavia) to clearly calcareous (Alps) substrates; damp (rarely dry in the Alps). Meadows and boggy woods, stream banks, up to 1000m asl (500-2400m in Alps). **Distribution** Boreal-alpine. From Gotland (Su) north to Tromsø (No). In the Alps chiefly the peripheral calcareous massifs in France, the Dolomites (It) and Switzerland; also reported from Bavaria, the Salzburg region (Au) and Scotland (Br). Local and often rare. **Countries** Au Br Cz Fe Ga Ge He It No Su. **Photos** It, Bolzano, 15.VII.1987; No, Saltdal, 17.VII.1988. P. DELFORGE.

The *Dactylorhiza traunsteineri* group

Characteristics Rather hygrophilous; stem slender, not very compressible; leaves few, narrow; flowers not numerous, often rather large; lip longitudinally folded; spur large; Flowering season intermediate between the *D. incarnata* and *D. praetermissa* groups; 2n=80, 120 (122). Essentially European, polyphyletic, with 8 species and an indeterminate number of taxa, all of a complex hybrid origin, but all arising from distinct speciation events.

Dactylorhiza traunsteineri
(SAUTER ex REICHENBACH) SOÓ

Etymology Named after J. Traunsteiner, Austrian pharmacist (1798-1850). **Type** Au, North Tyrol (1830). **Synonyms** *Dactylorhiza majalis* subsp. *traunsteineri* (SAUTER ex RCHB.) SUNDERMANN, *Orchis angustifolia* RCHB. pat.

Description Spindly, (10-) 20-40cm tall; stem slender, very slightly compressible, washed violet at tip; 3-5 cauline leaves, bluish-green, obliquely erect, often slightly arched outwards, unspotted or spotted on upper side, linear-lanceolate, pointed, keeled, 5-16cm x 0.5-1.5cm, the largest leaf usually broadest close to the base, uppermost 1-2 leaves bract-like; bracts coloured, often shorter than flowers; inflorescence lax, few-flowered, ovoid to near cylindrical, 3-10cm tall; (3-) 8-12 (-20) rather large flowers, purple to magenta, dark; lateral sepals lanceolate, 8-11mm x 2.5-4mm, often spotted, spreading to erect, tip ± reflexed; dorsal sepal turned down and, together with the rather large petals, forming a ± tight hood; lip 6-10mm x 7-13mm, oboval to obcordate, 3-lobed, folded longitudinally, base and centre pale, marked with rather distinct dark reddish-purple or purplish patterns, formed by streaks and dots surrounded by an almost complete loop; lateral lobes rounded, turned down and then slightly reflexed, sometimes spotted with diffuse dots; median lobe tooth-like, protuberant, near pointed; spur robust, conical, elongate, 7-12mm x 2-3.5mm, (near) horizontal, straight or slightly descendent.

Flowering Season V-VII (-VIII). **Habitat** Full sun to mid-shade on wet, alkaline substrates. Most probably narrowly specialised in alpine alkaline peat bogs, up to 2100m asl. **Distribution** Probably the central Alps (see Notes, next page). Very rare and local following the disappearance of its habitat. **Countries** Au Ga Ge He It. **Photos** Ge, Garmisch-Partenkirschen, 2.VII.1989. P. DELFORGE.

Notes Of the genus, *D. traunsteineri* poses one of the thorniest problems, probably insoluble. Apart from British (see *D. traunsteinerioides*), northern (see *D. curvifolia*) and alpine taxa (see *D. traunsteineri*), there is (was) a large number of ± similar populations in Western Europe that have been the subject of abundant literature and several tens of descriptions.

The majority of these taxa are on the verge of extinction or have already disappeared due to the dramatic reduction in wetlands and to introgression with closely related species that are more resistant to drainage of the habitat. *D. traunsteineri* s.l. therefore encompasses a mosaic of micropopulations, now very isolated and ± hybridised, for which it is often now impossible to reconstruct their morphological characters, their probable hybrid origin or their affinities with the better-circumscribed western groups. In this regard, the 'parents' cited in the literature represent almost all the western taxa in the genus, and also *D. sambucina*.

Nevertheless, in this mosaic, sometimes named *'D. pseudotraunsteineri'* [*Orchis pseudo-traunsteineri* Fuchs], 3 groups can be distinguished.

1. Populations from alkaline rich fens at low altitudes, mostly extinct, often with a shift in the range of variation towards *Dactylorhiza majalis*, *D. incarnata* or *D. maculata* s.l. and therefore frequently described as hybrids; for example, *D. deweveri* (Vermeulen) Landwehr, sometimes identified as *D. sphagnicola* [*D. sphagnicola* subsp. *deweveri* (Vermeulen) D. *Wenker*] (**Countries** †Ho) or even *Orchis rhenana* Höppner, *O. rigida* Höppner, *O. pseudo-traunsteineri* subsp. *konigveeniana* Fuchs (see also *Dactylorhiza wirtgenii*, next page).

2. Populations from acidic fens all around the Alps, probably ecotypes of *D. traunsteineri*, notably in Baden-Württemberg (Ge), Jura and Vosges (Ga) as well as in Bohemia (Cz) [= *D. majalis* subsp. *turfosa* Procházka, *D. traunsteineri* subsp. *turfosa* (Procházka) Kreutz].

3. Hybrid swarms, ± stabilised, between *D. incarnata*, *D. majalis* and *D. maculata* s.l. or intermediate populations from alkaline to neutral fens, often intermediate between *D. majalis* s.l. and *D. traunsteineri*, reported from the Alps as well as from more distant massifs (Pyrenees, Carpathians). **Photo A** Ga, Hautes-Alpes, 20.VII. 1992. P. DELFORGE.

To the latter group, to which many names have been applied but which, if it has to be named, may perhaps be called *D. angustata* (Arvet-Touvet) D. Tyteca & Gathoye [**Synonyms** *D. dufftiana* (Schulze) Soó, *D. delphinensis* D. Tyteca & Gathoye] probably also belongs *D. majalis* subsp. *brevifolia* Bisse. **Photo B** Ge, Garmisch-Partenkirchen, 3.VII.1989. P. Delforge.

Dactylorhiza wirtgenii
(HÖPPNER) SOÓ

Etymology Named after F. Wirtgen, German botanist (1848-1924). **Type** Ge, Rhenanie (1916). **Synonyms** *Orchis wirtgenii* HÖPPNER (pro hybr.), *D. traunsteineri* subsp. *wirtgenii* (HÖPPNER) KREUTZ, *Dactylorhiza traunsteineri* auct.

Description As *D. traunsteineri* but slightly more robust, 20-45cm tall; stem compressible; 4-7 cauline leaves, 1.3-4cm wide, averaging slightly longer and broader, slightly to clearly spotted, lower bracts longer than the flowers; inflorescence denser, ovoid to near cylindrical, more floriferous; up to 28 flowers, slightly larger and darker; lip not so folded longitudinally, (8-) 9-12mm long, sides of lateral lobes often recurved, base and centre rarely whitish, marked with thicker patterns; spur conical, sometimes curved, near horizontal or frequently pointing obliquely downwards, 6-9mm long, less often crossing the ovary.

Flowering Season Late V-VI. **Habitat** Full sun to mid-shade on damp to wet, slightly to very alkaline substrates. Peat bogs and fens on the plains, 200-600 (-900?)m asl.

Distribution Very poorly known due to confusion with var. and spindly plants of *D. praetermissa* and *D. elata*, with *D. traunsteinerioides*, as well as with unstable hybrid swarms between *D. incarnata*, *D. majalis* and *D. maculata* s.l. (see previous page). Probably eastern France and the mid-Rhine valley. Very rare and local, and threatened by habitat destruction and absorption by closely related taxa, in particular *D. incarnata*. **Countries** Ga Ge. **Photos** Ga, Haute-Marne, 7.VI.1997. P. DELFORGE.

Key to the *Dactylorhiza traunsteineri* group

| 1 | growing above 1000m asl .... 2 |
| 1* | growing below 600m asl .... 5 |

| 2 | leaves spotted .... *D. baumanniana* |
| 2* | leaves unspotted or only slightly spotted .... 3 |

| 3 | 3-5 leaves, 0.5-1.5cm wide .. *D. traunsteineri* |
| 3* | 4-7 leaves 1.5-3.2cm wide .... 4 |

| 4 | 2nd leaf 14-20cm long, 8-25 flowers, spur spindly .... *D. graeca* |
| 4* | 2nd leaf 8-13cm long, 17-31 flowers, spur robust .... *D. smolikana* |

(continued on p. 204)

Dactylorhiza carpatica
(P. BATOUSEK & KREUTZ) P. DELFORGE

Etymology *carpatica*: from the Carpathians.
Type Cz, White Carpathians (1999). **Synonyms**
D. traunsteineri subsp. *carpatica* P. BATOUSEK &
KREUTZ, *D. fuchsii* subsp. *carpatica* (P. BATOUSEK &
KREUTZ) KREUTZ.

Description Spindly, 30-55cm tall; stem hollow,
thick; 3-5 cauline leaves, strongly spotted, linear-
lanceolate, pointed, ± channelled and hooded,
obliquely erect, 8.5-16.5cm x 1-1.9cm, largest
leaf broadest in the basal half; inflorescence
dense, near ovoid, 6-10cm tall; 7-26 (-32)
flowers, rather small, lilac to reddish-pink; lateral
sepals often spotted, 6.6-8.7mm x 2.2-3.1mm; lip
broadly wedge-shaped at the base, spreading to
slightly convex, 3-lobed, 5.8-7.5mm x 6.3-
10.6mm, base and centre whitish, marked with
thick dark purple to red patterns formed by dots,
streaks and concentric loops; lateral lobes broadly
rounded; median lobe not very large; spur
elongated, near cylindrical, directed obliquely
downwards, 5.6-8.1mm x 1.6-2.1mm.

Flowering Season Late V-VI.

Habitat Full sun on damp to wet, alkaline
substrates. Fens and flushed slopes, *c.* 500m asl.

Distribution Currently known from a few
stations in the White Carpathians.

Countries Cz.

Photos Cz, Bílé Karpaty (loc. typ.), 29.V.1994.
C.A.J. KREUTZ.

Key to the *Dactylorhiza traunsteineri* group

(*continued from previous page*)

5   stem hollow, clearly compressible 6
5*   stem not or not very compressible
     .... *D. traunsteinerioides*

6   lip 5.8-9mm long 7
6*   lip (8-) 9-12mm long .... *D. wirtgenii*

7   leaves strongly spotted, obliquely erect,
     broadest in the basal half .... *D. carpatica*
7*   leaves not or not very spotted, often arched
     downwards, broadest towards the middle
     .... *D. curvifolia*

Dactylorhiza traunsteinerioides
(PUGSLEY) LANDWEHR

Etymology *-eidês*: similar to [*D.*] *traunsteineri*.
Type Hb, Wicklow (1936). **Synonyms** *Orchis majalis* subsp. *traunsteinerioides* PUGSLEY, *O. latifolia* var. *eborensis* GODFERY, *Dactylorhiza traunsteineri* subsp. *traunsteinerioides* (PUGSLEY) Soó, *D. francis-drucei* (WILMOTT) AVERYANOV, *D. traunsteinerioides* subsp. *hibernica* LANDWEHR.

Description Spindly, 10-40cm tall; stem not very compressible, slender; 3-5 cauline leaves, unspotted or lightly spotted close to tip, linear-lanceolate, keeled, almost vertically erect to obliquely erect, often arched outwards, 6-12cm x 0.5-1.5 (-2)cm, broadest in the lower half, often close to the base; upper leaf rarely bract-like; bracts washed purple, lowest longer than the flowers; inflorescence short, dense, conical to cylindrical, 3-6cm tall; (5-) 10-25 (-30) flowers, medium-sized, lilac to pale purple; lateral sepals often spotted, spreading to erect; lip near rhomboidal to obcordate, spreading or folded longitudinally, near entire or 3-lobed, 7-9mm x 9-11mm, base and centre pale, broadly marked with distinct dark purple patterns formed by dots and streaks surrounded by often-fragmented loops; median lobe obtuse, broad, protuberant; spur spindly, near cylindrical, descendent, 7-11mm x 2-3.5mm.

Variation Very diverse, often very introgressed with *D. praetermissa* in south of range. Distinguished from *D. traunsteineri* by a denser inflorescence, the leaves broader at the base, the flowers on average more numerous, with a paler lip and markings that are more contrasting and more extensive. **'francis-drucei':** Spindly, 5-15cm tall; leaves very small, unspotted; inflorescence lax, with 5-8 flowers; lip 7mm x 6mm, whitish with dark purplish patterns. Extremely rare in Scotland. **'eborensis':** Stocky, 7-15cm tall; leaves sometimes ring-spotted; inflorescence with 3-8 pale flowers, spur long, up to 8.5mm. Very rare in Yorkshire. These 2 variants are probably ecotypes; in cultivation *'eborensis'* is no longer distinguishable from *'traunsteinerioides'*.

Flowering Season V-VI. **Habitat** Full sun on damp to wet, neutral to alkaline substrates. The flooded parts of rich fens, up to 200m asl (in Europe). **Distribution** British Isles, Picardy, perhaps the Parisian tertiary basin. Rather widespread, in decline due to habitat destruction and its frequent absorption by closely related taxa. **Countries** Br Ga Hb. **Photos** Br, Anglesey, 22.VI.1985. P. DEVILLERS; 20.VI.1983. D.M.T. ETTLINGER.

205

Dactylorhiza curvifolia
(F. NYLANDER) CZEREPANOV

Etymology *curvifolia*: with curved leaves. **Type** Fe, Olonetz (1844). **Synonyms** *Orchis curvifolia* RCHB. fil., *O. angustifolia* var. *russowi* KLINGE, *Dactylorhiza traunsteineri* subsp. *curvifolia* (F. NYLANDER) SOÓ, *D. russowi* (KLINGE) J. HOLUB.

Description Spindly, 15-45cm tall; stem hollow, relatively thick, washed reddish-brown at tip; 3-4 cauline leaves, glaucous-green, spotted or not, narrowly lanceolate, near obtuse to pointed, channelled then spreading, obliquely erect, straight to strongly arched downwards, 6-15cm x 0.5-1.5cm, broadest towards middle, the uppermost bract-like; bracts ± equal to flowers; inflorescence dense, sometimes lax, ovoid to cylindrical, 3-7cm tall; 6-22 flowers, rather small, lilac to reddish-pink, pale to dark; lateral sepals often spotted, broadly lanceolate, spreading to vertically erect and sometimes touching back-to-back, 6-9mm x 3-4.5mm; dorsal sepal near equal, together with petals forming a hood, sometimes spotted outside; lip varied, wedge-shaped, or obcordate to rhomboidal, spreading to slightly convex and longitudinally folded, near entire or 3-lobed, 7-9mm x 9-12mm, base and centre rather pale, marked with thick purple to dark red patterns, sometimes bright, formed by dots and streaks surrounded by a marked loop; lateral lobes rounded, flat or slightly turned down and backwards, margins often reflexed; median lobe not large; spur elongated, near cylindrical, straight or descendent, horizontal or pointing slightly downwards, 7-10mm x 2-3mm; 2n=80, 120 (122).

Variation A very varied taxon, rarely flowering in pure populations. Distinguished from *D. traunsteineri* by a more hollow stem, more frequently spotted leaves, an inflorescence that is denser on average, flowers that are on average smaller, more numerous and redder. Strongly arched leaves, which should be a characteristic of '*curvifolia*', apparently constitute an extreme variation without evolutionary significance.

Flowering Season VI-VII. **Habitat** Full sun on damp to wet, alkaline substrates. Chiefly coastal fens, up to 200m asl (in Europe). **Distribution** The southern half of the Baltic and perhaps formerly Bohemia (Cz); also reported from continental Russia and east to central Siberia. Rather local and not very abundant in its stations. Probably in decline due to habitat destruction and its frequent absorption by closely related taxa. **Countries** ?†Cz Fe Pb Po Ro Su. **Photos** Pb, Eesti (loc. typ. for *Orchis angustifolia* var. *russowi*), 27.VI.1994. D. Rückbrodt; Su, Uppland, 5.VII.1988. P. DELFORGE.

Dactylorhiza baumanniana
HÖLZINGER & KÜNKELE

Etymology Named after H. Baumann, contemporary German orchidologist. **Type** Gr, Grevena (1981).

Description Robust, 15-40cm tall; stem not very compressible, washed purple at tip; 3-5 (-6) cauline leaves, often densely spotted, mostly the upper half, very rarely unspotted, lanceolate, obliquely erect, keeled and then spreading, 6-15cm x 0.8-3 (-4.2)cm, broadest towards middle, uppermost 1-2 leaves bract-like; bracts washed purple, ± equal to flowers; inflorescence dense to near lax, near cylindrical, 3-9 (-12)cm tall; 6-25 flowers, dark magenta, rarely pale lilac; lateral sepals obliquely erect to vertical, sometimes touching back-to-back, narrowly oval, 8.5-12.5mm x 3-4.8mm; dorsal sepal near equal, petals broadly oval, asymmetrical, 6-10mm long; dorsal sepal and petals forming a hood; lip obcordate to oboval, spreading to slightly convex, near entire or obscurely 3-lobed, 7.5-12mm x 7.5-15mm, base white, centre often dark, densely spotted with diffuse, thick, dark, purple to violet lines and dots, rarely with distinct loops and streaks; lateral lobes rounded, turned slightly down and backwards, margins sometimes scalloped and flat; median lobe slightly protuberant; spur robust, near cylindrical, straight to slightly descendent, horizontal or pointing downwards, 6.5-10 (-12)mm x 2-3mm.

Variation Very diverse but nevertheless rather well characterised by its size and habit, spotted leaves and dark flowers, slightly convex lip, with thick, diffuse, often rather red markings. Forms hybrid swarms with closely related species.

Flowering Season V-VI.

Habitat Full sun to mid-shade on neutral to acidic, moist to damp substrates. Marshy hollows, stream banks, seepages, 1000-1800m asl.

Distribution The Balkans. Reported from the entire Pindhos massif and a station in the Peloponnese (Gr), as well as southern Bulgaria; probably also found in other massifs in Macedonia. Rather local and not very abundant in its stations.

Countries Bu Gr.

Photos Gr, Grevena (loc. typ.), 11.VI.1990; 11.VI.1987. P. DELFORGE.

Dactylorhiza smolikana
B. WILLING & E. WILLING

Etymology *smolikana*: from Mount Smolikas (Pindhos mountains, Gr). **Type** Gr, Ioannina (1989).

Description Robust, 30-61cm tall; stem robust but slender, rather compressible; (4-) 5-7 cauline leaves, unspotted, lanceolate, obliquely erect, straight or slightly arched outwards, keeled then spreading, (6-) 8-13 (-19.5)cm x (1.2-) 2-3.2cm, broadest toward the middle, uppermost 1-2 leaves bract-like; bracts green or washed purple, lower bracts longer than flowers; inflorescence rather dense, elongate, cylindrical, 7-16cm tall; (15-) 17-31 (-42) flowers, lilac to purple; lateral sepals often spotted, spreading to erect, rarely touching back-to-back, oval-lanceolate, asymmetrical, 10-15mm x 3-5.2mm; dorsal sepal near equal, petals 7-12mm long, together forming a hood; lip orbicular to broadly oboval, slightly folded longitudinally, 3-lobed, 9-15mm x 10-18.5mm, base and centre pale, marked with rather fine, distinct, dark purple patterns, formed by dots and streaks surrounded by a full loop, often complete, extending as far as base of median lobe; lateral lobes rounded, dark, often unspotted, slightly turned down, edges flat or reflexed; median lobe tooth-like, not very prominent but clearly incised, rounded to pointed, spreading or pointing forwards; spur robust, near cylindrical, straight to slightly descendent, horizontal or pointing downwards, 6-12mm x 2.5-5mm, *c.* 3/4x ovary.

Variation Morphologically rather stable. Morphs with spotted leaves may exist. Distinguished from *D. baumanniana* by its flowers which are, on average, paler, with lip markings that are narrower, more distinct and better circumscribed. *D. pindica* has, on average, 2 more leaves, much larger and often more strongly spotted, as well as a denser inflorescence with 2-4 times more flowers that have broader lips.

Flowering Season V-VI.

Habitat Full sun on damp, alkaline to neutral substrates. The drawndown zones of marshy depressions, 1200-1500m asl.

Distribution Endemic to the centre of the Pindhos massif. Very local and sometimes found in small populations.

Countries Gr.

Photos Gr, Ioannina (loc. typ.), 15.VI.1990. P. DELFORGE.

Dactylorhiza graeca
H. BAUMANN

Etymology *graeca*: Greek. **Type** Gr, Serres (1983). **Synonyms** *D. cordigera* var. *graeca* (H. BAUMANN) H. PRESSER, *D. cordigera* subsp. *graeca* (H. BAUMANN) KREUTZ, *D. cordigera* var. *rhodopeia* H. PRESSER.

Description Spindly, 20-45cm tall; stem rather compressible; 4-6 cauline leaves, unspotted or slightly spotted, narrowly lanceolate, erect to spreading, arching outwards, keeled, 13-20cm x 1.5-2.5cm, broadest in centre of upper third, uppermost 1-2 leaves bract-like; inflorescence lax, elongated, cylindrical, 5-10.5cm tall; 8-25 flowers, pink to magenta; lateral sepals erect, upper half reflexed, oval-lanceolate, 10-12mm x 3-4mm; lip rhomboidal, near entire or obscurely 3-lobed, 9-11mm x 10-12mm, weakly convex to flat, margins flat or slightly reflexed, base and centre pale, marked with varied purple patterns, ± extensive, formed by streaks and distinct dots surrounded by 1 (-2) loop (often entire); spur spindly, near cylindrical, slightly descendent, 8-10mm long.

Flowering Season VI-VII.

Habitat Mostly full sun, on damp to wet, alkaline to neutral substrates. Marshy depressions, 1400-1600m asl.

Distribution Endemic to Mount Vrondou. Very rare and local.

Countries Gr.

Photos Gr, Serres (loc. typ.), 8.VI.1990. P. DELFORGE.

Discussion A controversial taxon, sometimes considered a hybridogenous swarm between *D. cordigera* (sympatric) and *D. kalopissii* or *D. baumanniana*, itself very polymorphic, or even *D. incarnata*.

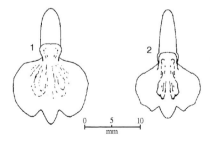

1. *Dactylorhiza smolikana*; 2. *D. baumanniana*.
(modified after GÖLZ & REINHARD)

The *Dactylorhiza praetermissa* group

Characteristics Rather hygrophilous, often robust; stem thick, hollow, the central cavity with a diameter less than half that of the stem; leaves often large, unspotted or spotted on upper side; flowers numerous; late flowering, after the 3 previous groups; 2n=80. A group of convenience, essentially from the Euro-mediterranean and Pontic zones, containing 14 species of recent hybrid origin (*D. incarnata* s.l. × *D. maculata* s.l. for the western taxa), but resulting from distinct speciation events.

Dactylorhiza kerryensis
(WILMOTT) P.F. HUNT & SUMMERHAYES

Etymology *kerryensis*: from Kerry. **Type** Hb, Kerry (1936). **Synonyms** *Orchis kerryensis* WILMOTT, *O. occidentalis* subsp. *kerryensis* (WILMOTT) CLAPHAM, *Dactylorhiza majalis* subsp. *kerryensis* (WILMOTT) SENGHAS.

Description Rather robust, (8-) 10-20 (-30)cm tall; stem compressible; 5-10 cauline leaves, often grouped at base of stem, glaucous-green, unspotted, lanceolate, keeled, strongly arched downwards, 6-10cm x 1-2cm, uppermost 1-2 leaves bract-like; bracts unspotted; inflorescence rather dense, ovoid to (near)cylindrical, 5-10cm tall; flowers magenta to crimson-pink, pale to, less often, dark; lateral sepals oval, asymmetrical, spreading horizontally, sometimes spotted, 6.5-9mm x 2-4mm; dorsal sepal near equal, forming a hood with petals; lip 6-10mm x 8-13mm, 3-lobed, clearly incised, broadly elliptic to obcordate, slightly folded longitudinally, centre whitish, marked with varied, rather distinct, dark violet-purple patterns, formed by dots, streaks and sometimes ± entire loops; lateral lobes often almost flat, sometimes turned slightly down and backwards, margins undulate, sometimes scalloped; median lobe tooth-like, not very large to clearly protuberant; spur often robust, near cylindrical, 5-10mm x 2-3.5mm.

Flowering Season (V-) VI-VII. **Habitat** Full sun on damp to wet substrates. Damp meadows and coastal fens, up to 200m asl. **Distribution** South-west and western Ireland; reports from Scotland and the Hebrides (Br) probably refer to closely related taxa. Widespread and sometimes abundant. **Countries** ?Br Hb. **Photos** Hb, Galway, 10.VII.1993. P. DELFORGE.

Discussion Controversial, often either ignored or considered to be a variant of *D. occidentalis*; appears, however, well-separated by floral characters and its rather later flowering season.

Dactylorhiza purpurella
(T. STEPHENSON & T.A. STEPHENSON) SOÓ

Etymology *purpurella*: purplish. **Type** Br, Wales (1920). **Synonyms** *Orchis purpurella* T. STEPHENSON & T.A. STEPHENSON, *O. purpurella* var. *pulchella* (PUGSLEY) T. STEPHENSON, *Dactylorhiza majalis* subsp. *purpurella* (T. STEPHENSON & T.A. STEPHENSON) MORESBY MOORE & SOÓ, *D. occidentalis* subsp. *maculosa* (T. STEPHENSON & T.A. STEPHENSON) R.M. BATEMAN & DENHOLM.

Description Robust, often thickset, 10-30 (-40)cm tall; stem not very compressible; 4-8 cauline leaves, often grouped at base of stem, unspotted or finely spotted on upper half, oblong-lanceolate, slightly keeled, sometimes hooded, often spreading, 5-10 (-16)cm x 1.5-3.5cm, broadest in centre, uppermost 1-2 leaves sometimes bract-like; bracts shorter than, to as long as, flowers; inflorescence dense, ovoid to near cylindrical, 3-7 (-10)cm tall; 10-30 (-80) flowers, bright pale purple to deep blackish-purple; lateral sepals oval, rarely spotted, 6-8.5mm x 2.5-3.5mm, spreading to vertically erect, tip reflexed; dorsal sepal near equal, petals 5-6mm long; dorsal sepal and petals forming a hood; lip 5-9mm x 6-12mm, entire, broadly rhomboidal to orbicular, flat, base and centre (sometimes slightly convex) marked very broadly with diffuse purple to deep carmine streaks and broken lines that form irregular and incomplete loops, sometimes extending to sides; lateral lobes almost flat, margins reflexed forwards; median lobe poorly developed, sometimes protuberant; spur rather robust, 6-10mm x 2-3.5mm, conical to near cylindrical.

Variation Very varied in stature, shape and leaf-spotting, but clearly distinguished by its floral characters. *'pulchella'* (NB not *D. pulchella* p. 185): Dwarf, few-flowered.

Flowering Season VI-VII (-VIII); after *D. occidentalis* at the same sites.

Habitat Full sun on neutral to slightly acidic, moist to wet substrates. Dune slacks, damp coastal meadows, sometimes drier dune slopes, up to 500m asl.

Distribution Atlantic. Northern and western British Isles, southern Scandinavia, north to Sør Trøndelag (No), east to Jutland (Da). Widespread (Br Hb) to local and sometimes abundant.

Countries Br Da Fa Hb No Su.

Photos Br, Wales, Anglesey, 7.VII.1993. P. DELFORGE.

211

Dactylorhiza cambrensis
(R.H. Roberts) Averyanov

Etymology *cambrensis*: Welsh. **Type** Br, Wales (1961). **Synonyms** *Dactylorhiza majalis* subsp. *cambrensis* (R.H. Roberts) R.H. Roberts, *D. majalis* var. *cambrensis* (R.H. Roberts) R.M. Bateman & Denholm, *D. purpurella* subsp. *majaliformis* E. Nelson ex Løjtnant.

Description Robust, often thickset, 15-35cm tall; stem not very compressible, yellowish-green, washed red at tip; 4-7 cauline leaves, dark green, sometimes clustered at base of stem, spotted, sometimes strongly so, often with ring-shaped markings, rarely unspotted, oblong-lanceolate, channelled, slightly hooded, erect, arched, 1-2.5cm broad, up to 7x longer than broad, often extending past base of inflorescence, uppermost 1-3 leaves bract-like; bracts often spotted; inflorescence dense, up to 20% of stem length; flowers numerous, often rather dark, boldly-coloured, magenta to lilac, analogous to those of *D. purpurella*, but paler; lip near entire or obscurely 3-lobed, near rhomboidal, marked, often with heavy loops, dispersed or concentrated at centre, more contrasting than in *D. purpurella*; lateral lobes ± flat or reflexed; spur over 3.5mm thick.

Flowering Season VI-VII. **Habitat** Full sun on damp to wet neutral substrates. Marshy dune slacks, damp areas near rivers, up to 100m asl. **Distribution** Great Britain. Essentially the Welsh coast and perhaps also Yorkshire and northwest Scotland. Very local and rather rare. **Countries** Br. **Photos** Br, Wales, Anglesey, 6.VII.1993; P. Delforge. **Discussion** A controversial taxon, considered sometimes to be an assemblage of hybrid swarms or a variant of *D. purpurella* that is strongly introgressed with *D. maculata* s.l.

Key to the *Dactylorhiza praetermissa* group

1   lip large, (8-) 14-24mm wide 2
1*   lip small, 6-14 (-17)mm wide 5

2   leaves clearly spotted, rather broad (length/breadth =3-6) 3
2*   leaves narrower (length/breadth = 4-12), without spots or only slightly spotted 4

3   spur descendent, 8-11mm long .... *D. pindica*
3*   spur horizontal, 11-17mm long
      .... *D. urvilleana*

(*continued on next page*)

Dactylorhiza ruthei
(M. SCHULZE ex RUTHE) SOÓ

Etymology Named after R. Ruthe, German entomologist (1823-1905). **Type** Ge, Pomerania (1897). **Basionym** *Orchis ruthei* M. SCHULZE ex RUTHE.

Description As *D. sphagnicola* but 25-50cm tall; stem hollow, compressible; 4-6 (-7) cauline leaves, yellowish-green, unspotted, linear-lanceolate, tiered (all internodes near equal), almost vertically erect, often reaching base of inflorescence, 13-23cm x 2-3.3cm, broadest in basal half, uppermost 1-3 leaves bract-like; bracts longer than flowers, often crimson; inflorescence dense, short, near ovoid to cylindrical, 4-7 (-8)cm tall; up to 40 flowers. rather small, crimson to lilac, pale; lateral sepals oblong, often spotted, 9-10mm long; lip 8-10.5mm long, near entire to clearly 3-lobed, rhomboidal to subcordate, clearly longitudinally folded, margins recurved, marked from centre to tip of median lobe with purplish streaks that form neither lines nor loops; median lobe not very large, often protuberant; spur rather robust, 10-12mm long, near conical, descendent, parallel to ovary.

Flowering Season VI. **Habitat** Full sun to mid-shade on damp to wet, basiclinous substrates. Fens and marshy meadows, mostly coastal, up to 200m asl. **Distribution** Southern Baltic. Known from 3 stations on the island of Usedom (Ge/Po), and 1 site in coastal Estonia; perhaps also Slovakia. Extremely local and rare. Declining due to habitat destruction and absorption by *D. incarnata*, *D. fuchsii* and *D. baltica*. **Countries** ?Cz Ge Pb ?†Po. **Photos** Pb, Eesti, 16.VI.1994. D. RÜCKBRODT.

Key to the *Dactylorhiza praetermissa* group

(continued from previous page)

4   lip clearly 3-lobed, flat or very slightly convex .... *D. nieschalkiorum*
4* lip 3-lobed to near entire, ± strongly folded longitudinally .... *D. elata*

5   thickset, 10-30 (-40)cm tall 6
5* elongate, (15-) 25-90cm tall 8

6   lip clearly 3-lobed 7
6* lip rhomboidal, lip (near) entire 8

7   leaves erect, placed all along stem
    .... *D. pontica*
7* leaves arching downwards, clustered at base of stem .... *D. kerryensis*

(continued on p. 217)

213

Dactylorhiza sphagnicola
(Höppner) Soó

Etymology *sphagnicola*: growing among *Sphagnum* **Type** Ge, Cologne (1926). **Synonyms** *Orchis sphagnicola* Höppner (pro hybr.), *Dactylorhiza incarnata* subsp. *sphagnicola* (Höppner) Soó, *D. majalis* subsp. *sphagnicola* (Höppner) H.Æ. Pedersen & Hedrén, *D. majalis* subsp. *calcifugiens* H.Æ. Pedersen, *D. sphagnicola* subsp. *hoeppneri* (A. Fuchs) Dalkowski et al. comb. inval.

Description 20-60cm tall; stem rather compressible; 4-8 cauline leaves, unspotted, linear-lanceolate, channelled, hooded, almost vertically erect, 10-25cm x 1-3 (-3.5)cm, broadest towards the middle, uppermost 1-3 leaves bract-like; bracts longer than flowers, hooded, incurved within inflorescence; inflorescence dense, rather short, ovoid to near cylindrical, 5-10cm tall; 20-50 (-60) flowers, pink to lilac, pale to rather dark; lateral sepals oblong, often spotted, 9-12.5mm x 3-5mm, spreading horizontally to vertically erect and touching back-to-back, tip slightly reflexed; lip 7-11.5mm x 8.5-14mm, near entire or 3-lobed, mostly rhomboidal, sometimes orbicular to obcordate, slightly folded longitudinally to flat, marked over entire surface with fine purplish dots, sometimes forming diffuse streaks, rarely with lines or rudimentary loops; sides recurved, sometimes scalloped, with a narrow coloured margin; median lobe not very large, often pointed and protuberant; spur rather spindly, 8-14mm x 2-3.5mm, near cylindrical, descendent, often parallel to ovary.

Variation Varied, often introgressed with *D. maculata*. Clearly distinct from *D. praetermissa* in its ecological requirement and thus sometimes considered as an ecotype; *D. praetermissa* is nevertheless distinguished on average by being more robust, with slightly more numerous, longer leaves, and a shorter spur. Populations in the north of the range appear to be influenced by *D. curvifolia*. *'calcifugiens'*: Described from Denmark, as *D. sphagnicola* but leaves not so erect, flowers whiter and lip smaller.

Flowering Season VI-VII. **Habitat** Full sun to mid-shade on damp to wet, acidic substrates. Raised bogs, swampy deciduous and coniferous woodland, up to 600m asl.

Distribution Atlantic. From the French Ardennes and Belgium Lorraine north to southern Scandinavia; in Sweden, north to at least Dalsland. Local and rather rare; in widespread decline due to habitat destruction and absorption by closely related taxa. **Countries** Be Da Ga Ge ?†Ho No Su. **Photos** Be, Luxembourg, 21.VI.1981; 23.VI. 1990. P. Delforge.

Dactylorhiza sennia
VOLLMAR

Etymology *sennia*: from Senne (Westphalia, Ge).
Type Ge, Ostwestfalen (2002). **Synonyms**
Dactylorhiza maculata subsp. *sennia* (VOLLMAR)
KREUTZ, *Orchis sphagnicola* auct., *Dactylorhiza
sphagnicola* auct..

Description As *D. sphagnicola* but 19-42.5cm
tall; 4-7 cauline leaves, unspotted, averaging
slightly broader, narrowly lanceolate, erect then
curving outwards, 7-19cm x 0.6-2.7cm; bracts
slightly shorter, the lower 10-18mm x 1.4-
3.8mm; inflorescence dense, rather short, conical
to ovoid; 12-44 flowers, smaller, pink to lilac,
pale, upper bracts pink; petals 4.5-6.5mm x 1.7-
3.2mm; lip 4.7-8 x 6.3-10mm, obscurely 3-lobed,
more lightly spotted with fine purplish dots,
sometimes forming diffuse streaks; median lobe a
little more distinct and more prominent; spur
more spindly, 8-13mm x 1.3-2.6mm.

Flowering Season VI.

Habitat Full sun on damp to wet, acidic to
almost neutral substrates. Damp heathland with
Cross-leaved Heath *Erica tetralix* bordering
raised bogs, *c.* 300m asl.

Distribution Known from an isolated group of
bogs in the Senne region. Very local but rather
abundant in its stations.

Countries Ge.

Photos Ge, Ostwestfalen (loc. typ.), 20.VI.2000.
J. VOLLMAR.

Discussion Distinguished from *D. sphagnicola*
by its broader leaves, growing further out from
the stem, few-flowered inflorescence and smaller,
differently coloured flowers. According to its
describer, this species may have originated from
a separate speciation event from that of *D.
sphagnicola*. The arguments advanced to
distinguish *D. sennia* from *D. sphagnicola* rely
essentially on morphometrics and the statistical
analysis of these. It is certainly very difficult to
give precise characters or gaps in measurements
that allowing easy demarcation of *D. sennia* from
D. sphagnicola, itself highly polymorphic. For
example, the position of the leaves, well-spaced
along the stem, and the smaller flowers, are also
shown by *D. majalis* subsp. *calcifugiens*, a
Danish taxon that probably falls within the range
of variation of *D. sphagnicola*. *D. sennia* is
therefore here given specific status but with
reservations; it may only be one of the very
numerous forms of *D. sphagnicola*.

Dactylorhiza praetermissa
(Druce) Soó

Etymology *praetermissa*: neglected. **Type*** Br, South of England (1914). **Synonyms** *Orchis praetermissa* Druce, *Dactylorhiza praetermissa* subsp. *integrata* (E.G. Camus ex Fourcy) Soó, *D. integrata* (E.G. Camus ex Fourcy) Averyanov, *D. praetermissa* var. *junialis* (Vermeulen) Senghas.

Description Robust, (20-) 30-70 (-90)cm tall; stem hollow; 5-9 cauline leaves, unspotted (spotted in var. *junialis*), oblong-lanceolate, keeled and then flat, almost vertically to obliquely erect, straight or arched outwards, 8-25cm x 1.5-4.5cm, broadest towards middle, uppermost 1-3 leaves bract-like; bracts equal to or longer than the flowers; inflorescence dense, rather short, conical to cylindrical, 5-15cm tall; 20-60 (-80) flowers, lilac to crimson-pink; lateral sepals oval-elongate, sometimes spotted, 8-11mm x 3-4.5mm, spreading horizontally to vertically erect, tip reflexed; petals 6-8mm x 2.5-4mm, connivent with dorsal sepal; lip 7-10mm x 8-14mm, entire or 3-lobed, mostly near rhomboidal to obcordate, flat to longitudinally folded, base and centre pale, marked, sometimes broadly, with fine, purplish dots, often arranged into a fan-like pattern, margins more richly coloured, unspotted, clearly reflexed forwards; median lobe not very prominent, tooth-like, rounded; spur (5-) 7.5-11 (-12.5)mm x 2-3.5mm, conical, slightly descendent, pointing downwards.

Flowering Season VI-VII (-VIII).

Habitat Full sun on damp to dry, alkaline to neutral substrates. Marshy dune slacks, fens and damp oligotrophic meadows, sometimes short calcareous grassland, up to 600m asl.

Distribution Atlantic, mostly around the North Sea coasts. Principally southern England and northwest France (up to Lorraine). Local but sometimes abundant.

Countries Be Br Da Ga Ge Ho.

Photos Be, Hainaut, 29.VI.1991; Ga, Aisne, 18.VI.1980. P. Delforge.

Variation Very varied, polymorphic. Its range of morphological variation overlaps with those of *D. elata*, *D. sphagnicola* and *D. baltica* amongst others, and it is often introgressed with *D. maculata* s.l., which may explain the uncertainty about the limits of its range (notably in central France, regions around the Alps, Rhine basin and Scandinavia).

'*Integrata*' a variant with the lip entire, near rhomboidal (lip index > 1.25, see p. 229), darkly coloured, and sometimes with slightly bolder markings; here and there throughout the range. **Photo A** Ho, Zuid-Holland, 15.VI.1991. P. DELFORGE.

Dactylorhiza praetermissa (DRUCE) SOÓ
var. *junialis* (VERMEULEN) SENGHAS

Etymology *junialis*: of the month of June. **Type** Ho (1930). **Synonyms** *D. praetermissa* subsp. *junialis* (VERMEULEN) SOÓ, *D. majalis* subsp. *parda-lina* (PUGSLEY) E. NELSON comb. inval., *D. pardalina* (PUGSLEY) AVERYANOV.

Description Averages slightly spindlier, leaves marked with violet rings, rarely small solid blotches; flowers darker; lip often slightly more clearly 3-lobed, with dark violet patterns, sometimes broad, clearly formed by complete loops surrounding a few streaks and ring-spots.

Distribution Throughout the range, but rarer than the nominative var.; often with the latter and numerous intermediates. **Photo B** Ho, Zuid-Holland, 9.VI.2001. P. DELFORGE. **Discussion** A dark variant, evidence of a hybrid origin for *D. praetermissa*, in which *D. maculata* s.l. played a role.

Key to the *Dactylorhiza praetermissa* group

(continued from p. 213)

8 flowers very dark; leaves unspotted or finely spotted .... *D. purpurella*

8* flowers paler; leaves spotted . *D. cambrensis*

9 growing above 600m asl 10

9* growing below 600m asl 11

10 bracts shorter than flowers; spur 4-10 (-11.5)mm long .... *D. kalopissii*

10* bracts longer than flowers; spur 9-14.5mm long .... *D. pythagorae*

11 leaves elongated [length/breadth = (6-) 7-10] 12

11* leaves shorter [length/breadth = 4-6 (-7)] .... *D. praetermissa*

12* growing in damp, alkaline to neutral habitats .... *D. ruthei*

12 growing on acidic moorland and peat bogs 13

13 leaves almost vertically erect, spur 2.3-5mm thick .... *D. sphagnicola*

13* leaves less erect, spaced along the stem; spur 1.3-2.6mm thick .... *D. sennia*

Dactylorhiza elata
(POIRET) SOÓ

Etymology *elata:* high. **Type** Ag, Mazoula (1786). **Synonyms** *D sesquipedalis* (WILLDENOW) VERMEULEN, *D. munbyana* (BOISSIER & REUTER) AVERYANOV, *D. durandii* (BOISSIER & REUTER) M. LAINZ, *D. elata* var. *corsica* (REVERCHON) SOÓ.

Description Robust, (25-) 40-100 (-125)cm tall; stem hollow; 5-10 cauline leaves, unspotted or, more rarely, lightly spotted, narrowly to broadly oval-lanceolate, (near)erect, 15-25 (-45)cm x 1.5-4.5 (-6)cm, 4-6x as long as broad, broadest in the lower half; uppermost 1-4 leaves bract-like; bracts longer than flowers; inflorescence elongated, dense to near lax, (5-) 16-32 (-50)cm tall; (10-) 30-120 (-150) flowers, pink to lilac, sometimes purple, often dark; lateral sepals oval-lanceolate, sometimes spotted, 9-18mm x 3-6mm, vertically erect, often touching back-to-back; petals 7-14mm long, forming a hood with dorsal sepal; lip 9-15mm x (8-) 10-22mm, near entire or 3-lobed, near rhomboidal to obcordate, longitudinally folded, base and centre rather pale, marked with a ± distinct, crimson pattern of streaks, lines, rings and 1-3 concentric loops (often entire); lateral lobes dark, sometimes marked with streaks and rings; median lobe not very large, rarely protuberant; spur robust, 9-19mm x 2-4mm, conical to near cylindrical, descendent, parallel to the ovary.**Variation** Floral characters rather constant but vegetative characters highly polymorphic. A large number of variants have been described, at various taxonomic levels, but these cannot be adequately defined as their 'diagnostic' characters can appear irregularly in (micro)populations throughout the range:
1. Very robust: leaves large – *'munbyana'*; lax inflorescence – *'durandii'*; dense inflorescence – *'sesquipedalis'*;
2. Small, sometimes spindly, probably intermediate with *D. praetermissa*; see following pages.

Flowering Season IV-VII.

Habitat Mostly full sun, on moist to wet, alkaline substrates. Fens, damp meadows, seepages, sometimes banks, up to 2500m asl.

Distribution Near) western Mediterranean. North to at least Indre (Ga); 2 isolated localities reported from Zeeland (Ho) are the result of an introduction by an enthusiast amateur and have disappeared. Rather widespread and often abundant in its stations.

Countries Ag Co Ga Hs Lu Ma Sa Tn.

Photos Hs, Cuenca, 16.VI.1988; Ga. Aveyron, 9.VI.1982. P. DELFORGE (see also p. 173).

Dactylorhiza elata (POIRET) SOÓ
var. *brennensis* (E. NELSON) P. DELFORGE

Etymology *brennensis*: from Brenne. **Type** Ga, Indre (1976). **Synonyms** *D. elata* subsp. *brennensis* E. NELSON, *D. brennensis* (E. NELSON) D. TYTECA & GATHOYE.

Description As *D. elata*, but spindlier, 20-45 (-60)cm tall, with narrow leaves and flowers a little smaller. **Distribution** Brenne (Indre, Ga), often with var. *elata*. **Photos A&B** Ga, Indre, 27.V.1999. P. DELFORGE.

Dactylorhiza elata (POIRET) SOÓ
var. *iberica* (T. Stephenson) SOÓ

Etymology *iberica*: [from the] Iberian [peninsula]. **Type** Hs, Asturia (1928). **Basionym** *Orchis sesquipedalis* WILLDENOW var. *iberica* T. STEPHENSON.

Description As *D. elata*, but spindlier, 20-35cm tall; cauline leaves linear to narrowly lanceolate, 7-12x as long as broad; bracts shorter; sinuses in lip deeper. **Distribution** Rarely found in pure population; Iberian Peninsula (Hs, ?Lu, here and there), central (Massif Central) and northwest French range (Sarthe, Maine-et-Loire), where incorrectly identified as *D. traunsteineri*. **Photo C** Hs, Cantabria, Santander, 8.VI.1992. P. DELFORGE.

Dactylorhiza elata (Poiret) Soó
var. ambigua (Martrin-Donos) Soó

Etymology *ambigua*: dubious. **Type** Ga, Tarn (1864). **Synonyms** *Orchis ambigua* Martrin-Donos, *O. sesquipedalis* var. *ambigua* (Martrin-Donos) Rouy, *O. elata* subsp. *ambigua* (Martrin-Donos) Soó, *Dactylorhiza elata* subsp. *ambigua* (Martrin-Donos) Kreutz, *D. occitanica* Geniez et al.

Description As *D. elata*, but stockier, 20-50 (-70)cm tall; bracts shorter; inflorescence averages denser and flowers darker; lip 8-11mm x 11-14mm. **Distribution** Lower Rhône valley and neighbouring massifs, from Tarn and Hérault in the west to the Alpes-Maritimes in the east, often with robust plants, indistinguishable from var. *elata*. **Photos A&B** Ga, Ardèche (**B** loc. typ. for *D. occitanica*), 15.V.1999. P. Delforge.

Dactylorhiza isculana
K. Seiser

Etymology *isculana*: from Bad Ischl (Au). **Type** Au, Salzkammergut (2002).

Description Spindly, 16-27cm tall; flowers small, lip narrow, pinkish, marked with 2 longitudinal purple lines. A 'monstrous' or hybridogenous taxon, known from a single small population, now virtually extinct. An example of the many hybrid swarms in *Dactylorhiza* that are occasionally ± aberrant and sometimes formally named. **Photo C** Au, holotype, 6.VI.1992. K. Seiser.

Dactylorhiza kalopissii
E. NELSON

Etymology Named after Y. Kalopissis, contemporary Greek botanist. **Type** Gr, Ioannina (1976). **Synonyms** *D. macedonica* HÖLZINGER & KÜNKELE, *Dactylorhiza kalopisii* subsp. *macedonica* (HÖLZINGER & KÜNKELE) KREUTZ.

Description Slender, (14-) 18-56 (-74)cm tall; stem rather compressible; 5-9 erect cauline leaves, erect, unspotted or finely spotted on the upper half, lanceolate, slightly keeled and then flat, arching outwards, 8-19cm x (1.4) 2-4.5 (-6.4)cm, broadest towards middle, uppermost 1-3 leaves bract-like; bracts shorter than flowers; inflorescence rather dense, elongate, long-ovoid to cylindrical, (3.5-) 5-12 (-19.5)cm tall; (10-) 15-50 (-70) rather pale flowers, pink to lilac; lateral sepals sometimes narrowly-oval, unspotted or finely spotted, 8-13 (-16)mm x 3-6mm, spreading to erect, tip slightly reflexed; dorsal sepal near equal, forming a hood with petals; lip 6-12 (-15)mm x (4.5-) 6-14 (-17)mm, varied, entire or obscurely 3-lobed, narrowly obcordate, rarely orbicular, longitudinally folded, base and centre whitish, unspotted or spotted with thin violet-purple dots, rarely streaks, clearly defined adjacent to base and then diffuse, arranged into a fan-shape, sometimes surrounded with a diffuse, incomplete loop, margins more colourful, turned down to spread, rarely reflexed, sometimes finely dotted; median lobe often elongated and protuberant; spur robust, 4-10 (-11.5)mm long, conical to near cylindrical, straight to descendent, near horizontal. **Variation** Rather diverse. Robust plants with spotted leaves, broad, clearly 3-lobed lips, marked with distinct streaks surrounded by ± complete loops, are very probably hybrids with *D. saccifera*. *'macedonica'* is slightly earlier flowering; flowers pale, pink to lilac; lip rather small, 6-8mm x 8-10mm, unspotted or faintly dotted; median lobe large. This taxon, sometimes considered a separate species, is most probably merely a variant of *D. kalopissii*. It is rather rare, occurring here and there throughout the range, rarely in a pure population, often with *D. kalopissii* and numerous intermediates.

Flowering Season (V-) VI-VII. **Habitat** Full sun on damp to wet, neutral to slightly acidic substrates. Marshy depressions, seepages, stream banks, 600-1700m asl.

Distribution Greek and ex-Yugoslavian Macedonia (Fyrom), south to Metsovo (Ioannina). Local but sometimes abundant in its stations. **Countries** Gr Ju. **Photos** Gr, Ioannina, (loc. typ.) 13.VI.1990; 19.VI.1987 P. DELFORGE.

Dactylorhiza pindica
B. WILLING & E. WILLING

Etymology *pindica*: from Pindhos, Greek mountain range. **Type** Gr, Kastoria (1986).

Description Robust, (25-) 35-77 (-90)cm tall; stem hollow, green, often washed purple at tip; (3-) 4-6 (-7) cauline leaves, strongly spotted, very rarely unspotted, broadly oval-lanceolate, keeled and then flat, (near)erect, lower 1-2 leaves sometimes spreading, 8-16cm x 3-6cm, broadest towards middle, uppermost 1-2 bract-like; bracts washed purple, prominent, up to 36mm long, but hidden within spike; inflorescence cylindrical, dense, 8-21cm tall; (20-) 25-60 (-130) flowers, relatively large, magenta to crimson-pink, often rather dark; lateral sepals oval-lanceolate, sometimes spotted, 12-14mm x 4-5.5mm, vertically erect, touching back-to-back at base, tip reflexed, sometimes horizontally; petals 8-11mm x 3.5-4.5mm, forming a hood with dorsal sepal; lip 10-13 (-15)mm x (15-) 16-20 (-24)mm, 3-lobed, broadly oboval, longitudinally folded, base and centre pale, marked with ± distinct, rather fine, purple dots and lines surrounded by 1-3 ± entire concentric loops, sometimes extending to the median lobe, very rarely unmarked; lateral lobes ± strongly turned down, flat, margins rarely reflexed, dark, sometimes with a few dots and streaks; median lobe rather prominent, tooth-like, often protuberant, 1-3.5mm long; spur robust, 8-11mm x 3-4.5mm, near cylindrical, descendent, parallel to ovary.

Variation Rather distinctive due to its robust habit, broad spotted leaves and large flowers with a robust spur and more extensive markings than *D. cordigera*. Sometimes forms hybrid swarms with *D. saccifera* and *D. baumanniana*.

Flowering Season V-VII.

Habitat Full sun on damp to wet, alkaline to slightly acidic substrates. Marshy depressions and meadows, seepages, stream banks, 1200-1800m asl.

Distribution Balkans. The Pindhos mountains (Gr) and central Bulgaria; probably more widespread. Local and sometimes rather abundant.

Countries Bu Gr. **Photos** Gr, Kastoria, (loc. typ.) 14.VI.1987; Ioannina, 15.VI.1990. P. DELFORGE.

Dactylorhiza nieschalkiorum
H. BAUMANN & KÜNKELE

Etymology Named after A. and C. Nieschalk, German orchidologists (1904-1985; 1913-). **Type** An, Bolu (1981). **Synonyms** *D. osmanica* auct. non SOÓ, *D. maculata* subsp. *osmanica* (KLINGE) SUNDERMANN.

Description Robust, (20-) 40-70cm tall; stem thick, hollow; 4-9 cauline leaves, unspotted or sometimes very finely and lightly spotted, oval-lanceolate, keeled and then flat, erect, often almost vertically, lower 1-2 leaves sometimes spreading, 8-20 x 2-6.5cm, broadest towards middle; uppermost 1-2 leaves bract-like; bracts green, longer than flowers; inflorescence long-ovoid to near cylindrical, dense, 8-20cm tall; 20-90 large flowers, purple purplish-violet, dark, rarely pale; lateral sepals oval-lanceolate, 11-17mm x 4-6mm, spreading to vertically erect, tip reflexed; petals 8.5-13mm long, forming a hood with dorsal sepal; lip 10-20mm x 14-23mm, 3-lobed, oboval to obcordate or orbicular, usually spreading, base and centre slightly convex, pale, with a distinct pattern of purple dots and streaks surrounded by 1-3 ± entire, well-marked concentric loops; lateral lobes broadly rounded to near rhomboidal, margins sometimes undulate-scalloped, often marked with streaks and dots; median lobe prominent, broadly tooth-like, protuberant but much smaller than lateral lobes; spur robust, (8-) 10-15mm x 3-6mm, conical to near cylindrical, straight to descendent, horizontal to clearly pointing downwards.

Variation Rather varied. Distinctive in its robust habit and large flowers.

Flowering Season VI-VII.

Habitat Full sun to mid-shade on damp to wet, alkaline to neutral substrates. Marshy depressions, flushes in open woodland, 1000-1800m asl.

Distribution Endemic to the coastal mountains on northwest Anatolia, centred on the *vilayet* (provinces) of Bolu and Kastamonu. Local but sometimes rather abundant.

Countries An.

Photos An, Bolu (loc. typ.), 6.VI.1990. P. DELFORGE.

223

Dactylorhiza pythagorae
GÖLZ & H.R. REINHARD

Etymology Named after Pythagoras, Greek philosopher and mathematician (580-497 A.C.). **Type** Ae, Samos (1992). **Synonym** *D. kalopisii* subsp. *pythagorae* (GÖLZ & H.R. REINHARD) KREUTZ.

Description Slender; stem thick, 20-50cm tall; 4-7 cauline leaves, unspotted, obliquely erect, narrowly lanceolate, 3-20cm x 1.4-5cm, uppermost 1-2 leaves bract-like; bracts green, elongated, up to 40mm long, longer than flowers; inflorescence ± dense and many-flowered; 6-65 flowers, rather large, pale pink, more rarely dark pink or violet; lateral sepals 11-15.5mm x 3.2-5mm; lip 8.8-15mm x 10-14.5mm, obscurely 3-lobed, elliptic to near rhomboidal, base whitish, slightly folded longitudinally and convex in centre and then spreading-recurved, unspotted or with lightly-marked, fine, reddish dots and longitudinal streaks; median lobe small; spur robust, 9-14.5mm x 3.8-5mm, conical, straight, (near) horizontal.

Flowering Season VI. **Habitat** Full sun to mid-shade on moist to damp, alkaline substrates. Damp meadows and the banks of perennial streams in oak woodland, 800-900m asl. **Distribution** Known only from Samos. Local but sometimes abundant. **Countries** Ae. **Photos** Ae, Samos, 15.VI.1991. P. GÖLZ.

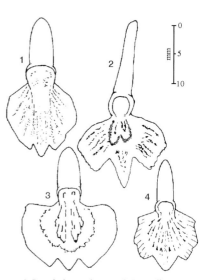

1. *Dactylorhiza pythagorae*; 2. *D. urvilleana*;
3. *D. pindica*; 4. *D. kalopissii*.

(1, 3, 4 modified after GÖLZ & REINHARD)

Dactylorhiza urvilleana
(STEUDEL) H. BAUMANN & KÜNKELE

Etymology Named after Jules Dumont d'Urville, French sailor (1790-1841). **Type** Ro, Colchide (1841). **Synonyms** *Orchis urvilleana* STEUDEL, *O. lancibracteata* K. KOCH, *O. cartaliniae* KLINGE, *O. amblyoloba* NEVSKI.

Description Slender, (15-) 25-70 (-90)cm tall; stem solid to slightly hollow, grooved at tip; 4-8 cauline leaves, marked on upperside, often with ring marks, (near) erect, oval-lanceolate, 8-25cm x 1.5-6.5cm, broadest in upper third, uppermost 1-2 leaves bract-like; bracts often spotted, longer than flowers; inflorescence dense, (near) cylindrical, 5-25cm tall; (10-) 20-90 flowers, lilac to crimson, pale to rather dark; lateral sepals oval-lanceolate, 10-17mm x 4-6mm, often spotted, spreading to vertically erect; dorsal sepal forming hood with petals; lip 10-16mm x 14-23mm, clearly 3-lobed or rarely near entire, elliptic to obcordate, base whitish, longitudinally folded and convex in centre and then spreading, sometimes flat, marked over the whole surface with bold patterns, formed by thick purple to deep magenta dots, streaks, rings and 1-3 ± distinct incomplete central loops; median lobe rather prominent, triangular, smaller than lateral lobes; spur robust, 11-17mm x 2.5-5mm, near cylindrical, straight, (near) horizontal, sometimes slightly upcurved at tip.

Flowering Season V-VIII.

Habitat Full sun to shade on damp to wet, alkaline substrates. Damp meadows and undergrowth, marshy depressions, flushed slopes, up to 2700m asl.

Distribution Northern Anatolia and the Caucasus, west to Kastamonu and south to Erzincan and Erzurum. Local and sometimes abundant.

Countries An Ro.

Photos An, Rize, 4.VI.1990. P. DELFORGE.

Note Sometimes considered as diploid (2n=40) and assigned to the *D. fuchsii* subgroup, which comprises the diploid species in the *D. maculata* group. Molecular analysis has shown that *D. urvilleana* is in fact an allotetraploid (2n=80), whose genome is made up of n chromosomes from *D. maculata* s.l. (probably *D. saccifera*) and n chromosomes from *D. euxina*. It should therefore be placed in the *D. praetermissa* group, here polyphyletic, comprising recent hybridogenous species between *D. maculata* s.l. and *D. incarnata* s.l., all late flowering.

Dactylorhiza pontica
(H. FLEISCHMANN & HANDEL-MAZZETTI) P. DELFORGE

Etymology *pontica*: Pontic. **Type** An, Trabzon and Giresun (1909). **Synonyms** *Orchis pontica* H. FLEISCHMANN & HANDEL-MAZZETTI, *O. maculata* subsp. *lancibracteata* var. *pontica* (H. FLEISCHMANN & HANDEL-MAZZETTI) SOÓ, *Dactylorhiza saccifera* subsp. *lancibracteata* var. *pontica* (H. FLEISCHMANN & HANDEL-MAZZETTI) SOÓ, *D. ilgazica* KREUTZ, *D. urvilleana* subsp. *ilgazica* (KREUTZ) KREUTZ.

Description Relatively small; stem rather robust, hollow, 20-40cm tall; 4-7 cauline leaves, slightly and irregularly spotted, channelled, obliquely erect, ± narrowly lanceolate, broadest in basal half or towards middle, 5-11cm x 1.2-2.5cm, uppermost 1-3 leaves bract-like; bracts only slightly longer than flowers or equal to them; inflorescence rather dense, relatively short and few-flowered, ovoid to near cylindrical; 10-30 flowers, rather small, ± dark pink to lilac; lip 7-10mm x 9-12.5mm, clearly 3-lobed, folded longitudinally with the sides turned down or, more often, flat or concave with the margins recurved; base pale, centre or entirety of lip marked with numerous thick, reddish to dark purple dots and streaks that sometimes form 1-3 concentric loops; lateral lobes rounded, often scalloped; median lobe prominent, obtusely-triangular; spur robust, equal to ovary, 9-12mm long, near conical, straight, pointing downwards.

Flowering Season End V-mid VIII.

Habitat Full sun to mid-shade on damp to wet, alkaline substrates. Damp meadows, flushed slopes and road margins, up to 1800m asl.

Distribution Poorly known due to confusion with closely related taxa. Pontic Anatolia, west to the Ilgaz massif (Kastamonu) and east to the Trabzon region; a station reported from central Anatolia (Malatya province), requires confirmation. Local and sometimes abundant.

Countries An.

Photos An, Kastamonu, 29.VI.1996. C.A.J. KREUTZ.

Note Apparently close to *D. urvilleana* and probably also of a recent hybridogenous origin, with *D. euxina* and *D. saccifera* as parents.

The *Dactylorhiza maculata* group

Characteristics Stem slender, rarely slightly hollow; leaves usually spotted on upper side; leaves normally developed, often clustered in the lower third of stem. A Euro-Siberian group, with 2 subgroups: the *D. fuchsii* subgroup, paraphyletic, with 6 diploid species (2n=40), mainly associated with alkaline substrates, and the *D. maculata* subgroup, derived from the first, with 10 (auto)tetraploid species (2n=80) mostly acidophilous.

Dactylorhiza saccifera
(BRONGNIART) SOÓ

Etymology *-fera*: bearing; *sacci-*: bags; (a reference to the shape of spur). **Type** Gr, Messenie (1832). **Synonyms** *Orchis macrostachys* TINEO, *Dactylorhiza gervasiana* (TODARO) H. BAUMANN & KÜNKELE, *D. saccifera* subsp. *gervasiana* (TODARO) KREUTZ, *D. bithynica* H. BAUMANN, *D. saccifera* subsp. *bithynica* (H. BAUMANN) KREUTZ.

Description Robust and slender, 25-90cm tall; stem solid, grooved at tip; 4-12 cauline leaves, erect to spreading and arched downwards, spotted on upper side, median leaves lanceolate, ± obtuse, 10-20cm x 2-6cm, broadest towards middle, uppermost 1-4 leaves bract-like; bracts far longer than flowers; inflorescence dense to near lax, conical and then (near) cylindrical, 6-22cm tall; 15-80 flowers, whitish or crimson-pink to purplish, very pale to dark; lateral sepals 7-14mm long, sometimes spotted; lip 7-11mm x 8.5-16mm, deeply 3-lobed, kidney-shaped to wedge-shaped at base, flat to slightly convex, marked with rather thick, bold, purple to dark magenta dots, streaks and 1-3 ± entire central loops; lateral lobes near rhomboidal to broadly falcate; median lobe prominent, triangular to rhomboidal, 0.5-1x breadth of lateral lobes; lip index 1.30-1.63 (see p. 229); spur robust, 9-15mm x 2-4.5mm, near cylindrical to conical, straight, sometimes slightly curved upwards at tip, horizontal to pointing downwards; 2n=40.

Flowering Season V-VII. **Habitat** Full sun to shade on moist to wet, mostly alkaline substrates. Damp woods, flushed slopes, marshy depressions in the mountains, up to 2000m asl.

Distribution Central and eastern Mediterranean and the Pontic region. From Corsica and Tuscany (It) in the west, probably to Kurdistan in the east. Rather widespread but often rare in its stations. **Countries** Al An Bu Co Gr It Ju Ls Rm Sa Si Tu.

Photos Gr, Florina, 14.VII.1985; It, Rieti, 15.VII.1989. P. DELFORGE (see also p. 230).

Dactylorhiza fuchsii
(DRUCE) Soó nom. cons. prop

Etymology Named after L. Fuchs, German professor (1501-1566). **Type** Br, Kent (1914). **Synonyms** *Orchis longibracteata* F.W.SCHMIDT, *O. fuchsii* DRUCE, *Dactylorhiza maculata* subsp. *fuchsii* (DRUCE) HYLANDER, *O. maculata* var. *trilobata* DE BRÉBISSON, *Dactylorhiza maculata* auct. non L., *D. maculata* subsp. *meyeri* (RCHB. fil.) TOURNAY, *D. meyeri* (RCHB. fil.) AVERYANOV.

Description Slender, (15-) 30-50 (-70)cm tall; solid stem, slender, sometimes slightly hollow, grooved; 5-11 (-15) cauline leaves, erect, arching outwards, keeled and then flat, densely spotted on upper side, rarely unspotted, lower side shiny greyish-green, lowermost leaf short, oval, spreading, median leaves lanceolate, ± obtuse, 8-21cm x 2-5cm, broadest in the upper half, uppermost 2-4 (-8) leaves bract-like; bracts rather short; inflorescence dense to lax, initially conical then near cylindrical, 4-10cm tall; (15-) 20-50 flowers, medium-sized, whitish to deep lilac, sometimes crimson; lateral sepals 6.5-10mm long; lip 6-10mm x 8-16mm, deeply 3-lobed, wedge-shaped to obcordate at base, flat to convex, marked, mostly around the median axis, with rather thick, often dark, purplish dots, streaks, rings and 1-3 central loops, ± regular; lateral lobes widely spread, rounded, obliquely truncated or falcate, margins sometimes scalloped; median lobe prominent, triangular to near rhomboidal, almost as broad as, and longer than, lateral lobes; lip index 1.32-1.52 (see p. 229); pale spur, 6-10mm x 1.2-2.5mm, narrowly near cylindrical, ± straight, horizontal to pointing downwards; 2n=40.

Variation Very varied. Distinguished from *D. maculata* mainly by the obtuse tip of the lowest leaf, the leaves being broadest in their upper half, and the shape of the lip with the markings more central. *'meyeri'*: Rather spindly with few leaves and a lax, few-flowered inflorescence.

Flowering Season VI-VII (-VIII).

Habitat Full sun to shade on dry to wet, alkaline substrates. Short grassland, marshes, woodland edges, secondary woodland, forests, up to 2300m asl.

Distribution Poorly known due to confusion with *D. maculata* s.l. Probably Euro-Siberian, in the boreal to temperate zones. Widespread and often abundant in its stations. **Countries** Au Be Br Cz Da Fe Ga Ge Hb He Ho Hs ?Hu It Ju No Pb Po ?Rm Ro Su.

Photos Be, Luxembourg, 4.VII.1985; Ho, Zuid-Limburg, 15.VI.1991. P. DELFORGE.

Dactylorhiza psychrophila
(SCHLECHTER) AVERYANOV

Etymology *-phila*: loving; *psychro-*: cold(ness). **Type*** Fe, Lapland, Muonia (1927). **Synonyms** *Orchis maculata* var. *psychrophila* SCHLECHTER, *Dactylorhiza fuchsii* subsp. *psychrophila* (SCHLECHTER) J. HOLUB.

Description Dwarf, 5-17 (-25)cm tall; stem slender; 2-4 cauline leaves, sometimes basal, 2-5cm x 0.3-1 (-1.5)cm, lanceolate, the tip obtuse-rounded, broadest in distal half, often heavily marked with elongated spots; 1-2 leaves bract-like, very small; inflorescence dense and few-flowered; flowers small, pale, lip deeply 3-lobed, slightly convex, marked with a few thick, reddish to dark purple, curved streaks; median lobe generally large and protuberant; 2n=40.

Flowering Season VI-VII (-VIII). **Habitat** Full sun to mid-shade on damp to wet, neutral to acidic substrates. Tundra, peat bogs, seepages in montane meadows, up to 1000m asl. **Distribution** Poorly known due to confusion with closely related taxa. Probably boreal Europe. Northern Scandinavia (Lapland), the Urals and northwest Siberia. Rare and local in its stations. **Countries** Fe No Ro Su. **Photo** No, Trøms, 21.VII.1988. P. DELFORGE.

Discussion When it was described as *Orchis maculata* var. *psychrophila*, the high altitude zones of the Alps were included in its range, but reports of *D. psychrophyla* from the Alps and other massifs in mid-Europe (e.g. Massif Central, Ga) are dubious. Besides, they often refer to more slender plants, whose leaves and flowers differ in length and structure from those in Lapland; reports from central Europe often refer to *D. sudetica* (and not *D. savogiensis*) or related taxa.

Problems in the *D. maculata* group

A particularly difficult group, the object of very diverse systematic treatments in which even the division into 2 groups, the first diploid and calcicolous, the other tetraploid and acidophilous, is controversial. Even if, in many areas (British Isles, Scandinavia, France...), the distinction between *D. fuchsii* and *D. maculata* is rather easy, in the centre of Europe there is a morphological convergence between the 2 species that often leads Continental botanists to refuse to separate them.

Nevertheless, an ecological separation apparently exists throughout their common range; moreover, within the 2 subgroups, the species appear to be both geographically and morphologically distinct. The situation is complicated by the presence of intermediate forms, associated with ecotones, more rarely by hybrid swarms, as well as the very great variability of vegetative and floral characters

influenced by the plant's age and by ecological and climatic factors. Within the same species, populations from woodland and from open ground such as dry grassland or peat bogs may, at similar altitudes, vary greatly in sturdiness, habit, number of leaves or flower colour. Uncertainties in the determination of some plants has led to different chromosome numbers being attributed to some species.

This diversity, often increased by introgression with species from other groups, has led to the description of numerous taxa whose validity, demarcation and range are all the more difficult to establish because of the disappearance of many wetlands, the source of several type specimens. If the diploid species appear less varied and better delineated than the tetraploid species, there remain, nevertheless, populations that are difficult to identify.

lip index:

$$\frac{2a}{b+c}$$

229

Dactylorhiza hebridensis
(WILMOTT) AVERYANOV

Etymology *hebridensis*: from the Hebrides. **Type** Br, Hebrides (1939). **Synonyms** *Orchis hebridensis* WILMOTT, *O. fuchsii* var. *hebridensis* H.-HARRISON fil., *Dactylorhiza fuchsii* subsp. *hebridensis* (WILMOTT) SOÓ, *D. maculata* subsp. *hebridensis* (WILMOTT) H. BAUMANN & KÜNKELE, *D. fuchsii* var. *cornubiensis* (PUGSLEY) AVERYANOV.

Description As *D. fuchsii* but thickset, robust, 10-35cm tall; 6-10 cauline leaves, near erect, arching outwards, ± clearly spotted or unspotted, uppermost 3-5 leaves bract-like; lower bracts longer than flowers; inflorescence short and dense, conical to ovoid, 5-7cm tall; flowers rather large, dark, pink or bright crimson-red; lateral sepals oval to lanceolate, spotted within, spreading, pointing forwards; lip 5-10mm x 10-15mm, spreading, sides reflexed forwards, orbicular, entire or ± clearly 3-lobed, the whole surface densely marked with dark purple streaks and lines, forming 1-4 concentric loops in the centre; lateral lobes broadly rounded, sometimes scalloped; median lobe ± prominent, protuberant; spur spindly, 4-10mm long, 1-2mm thick; 2n=40.

Flowering Season (VI-) VII.

Habitat Full sun on dry to wet, calcareous substrates. Stabilised grassy dunes, damp coastal meadows (machair), up to 100m asl.

Distribution Northwest Ireland and Scotland, Hebrides, Cornwall. Local and rather rare in its stations. **Countries** Br Hb.

Photos Br, Outer Hebrides, 16.VII.1994. P. DELFORGE.

Key to the *Dactylorhiza maculata* group

1 lateral sepals forming loose hood with dorsal sepal and petals .... *D. foliosa*
1* lateral sepals spreading or erect 2

2 lip with prominent median lobe, longer than lateral lobes (lip index > 1.3)
.... (*D. fuchsii* subgroup) 3
2* median lobe not prominent, not as long as lateral lobes (lip index < 1.3)
.... *D. maculata* subgroup (key p. 236)
3 spur very robust, 9-17mm long, 2-5mm thick
.... *D. saccifera*
3* spur finer, 6-10mm long, 1.5-2.5mm thick
.... 4

(continued on next page)

Dactylorhiza okellyi
(DRUCE) AVERYANOV

Etymology Named after P. O'Kelly, Irish botanist (1852-1937). **Type** Hb, Clare (1909). **Synonyms** *Orchis maculata* var. *okellyi* DRUCE, *O. okellyi* (DRUCE) DRUCE, *O. maculata* subsp. *okellyi* (DRUCE) DRUCE, *Dactylorhiza fuchsii* subsp. *okellyi* (DRUCE) SOÓ, *D. maculata* subsp. *okellyi* (DRUCE) H. BAUMANN & KÜNKELE.

Description As *D. fuchsii* but often spindly, (15-) 20-40cm tall; 5-8 cauline leaves, rather narrow, erect to spreading and arching downwards, often keeled, unspotted, up to 8cm x 2cm, uppermost 2-4 leaves bract-like; bracts shorter than flowers; inflorescence short and dense, near cylindrical to near ovoid, 3-5cm tall; flowers small, scented, usually pure white, unspotted; lip averages 5.5mm x 8mm, spreading, clearly 3-lobed; 2n=40.

Variation A unique taxon, showing very little variation. Nevertheless, there are plants transitional towards *D. fuchsii* and these are sometimes considered to belong with *okellyi*. In this broader conception, *D. okellyi* may then include plants with lightly spotted leaves (usually close to the tip), and with flowers lightly washed pink and very faintly spotted.

Flowering Season V-VII.

Habitat Full sun on moist, calcareous substrates. Mostly in the grykes of limestone pavements away from the coast (the Burren), up to 500m asl.

Distribution Western Ireland, Scotland, ?Isle of Man (Br). Other reports in the British Isles probably refer to occasional hypochromatic forms of *D. fuchsii*. Very local and rather rare in its stations.

Countries Br Hb.

Photos Hb, Clare (loc. typ.), 13.VII.1993. P. DELFORGE.

Key to the *Dactylorhiza maculata* group

(continued from previous page)

4   flowers white, unspotted (in populations!) .... *D. okellyi*

4*   flowers coloured and spotted 5

5   (15-) 30-70cm tall .... *D. fuchsii*

5*   5-30 (-35)cm tall 6

6   robust, 6-10 leaves .... *D. hebridensis*

6*   spindly, 2-4 leaves .... *D. psychrophila*

Dactylorhiza foliosa
(Solander ex Lowe) Soó

Etymology *foliosa*: leaf-like. **Type** Mi (1831).
Synonyms *Orchis foliosa* Solander ex Lowe,
O. maderensis Summerhayes.

Description 30-70cm tall; stem solid, sometimes
thick, grooved at tip; 7-16 leaves, sheathing,
cauline, decreasing in sizes, bright green,
unspotted to rarely very faintly spotted,
lanceolate, up to 20cm x 7cm, upper 3-5 leaves
small, bract-like; bracts often shorter than flowers;
inflorescence short, conical, 5-13cm tall; flowers
rather large, pale to dark crimson-pink; lateral
sepals 8-11mm x 2.5-4mm, lanceolate, pointing
obliquely forwards, keeled, asymmetrical, tip
sometimes slightly reflexed; petals and dorsal
sepal near erect, forming with lateral sepals an
open hood; lip broadly elliptic, 8-17mm x 9.5-
20mm, near entire to 3-lobed, spreading,
sometimes with a convex longitudinal fold,
unspotted or unobtrusively marked with a fan of
purple or deep purplish-violet dots or streaks,
margins scalloped, reflexed; median lobe reduced,
much smaller than lateral lobes; stigmatic cavity
edged with purple; spur spindly, cylindrical, 5-
11mm x *c.* 1mm, straight to slightly descendent,
inclined downwards, *c.* 1/2x ovary; 2n=40.

Flowering Season V-VII. **Habitat** Mid-shade to
shade on moist to rather dry, acidic substrates
(very rarely damp). Cliff fissures and open
woodland in the trade-wind cloudforest zone,
400-1150m asl. **Distribution** Endemic to the
northern part of Madeira. Very rare and local;
sometimes cultivated in gardens. **Countries** Mi.
Photos A&B Mi, San Vicente. 27.V.2003.
P. Delforge; **C** Portela, 30.V.1993. D. Tyteca.

Dactylorhiza sudetica
(PÖCH ex REICHENBACH fil.) AVERYANOV

Etymology *sudetica*: from the Sudety [mountains]. **Type** ?Cz, ?Po (1851). **Synonyms** *Orchis maculata* var. *sudetica* PÖCH ex REICHENBACH fil., *Dactylorhiza fuchsii* subsp. *sudetica* (PÖCH ex REICHENBACH fil.) VERMEULEN, *D. fuchsii* var. *sudetica* (PÖCH ex REICHENBACH fil.) H. BAUMANN, KÜNKELE & LORENZ, *D. psych(r)ophila* auct. non (SCHLECHTER) AVERYANOV.

Description Spindly, 15-25 (-30)cm tall; stem solid, washed violet at tip; 3-5 leaves, ovoid-oblong, spatulate, weakly keeled and then flat, uppermost 1-2 leaves bract-like; lower bracts equal to flowers; inflorescence very short, few-flowered, near lax, conical to ovoid; up to 20 small flowers; lip varied, ± clearly 3-lobed to near rhomboidal, averages 6.6mm x 8.7mm, flat or slightly convex in the centre, pale pink, marked, often over the entire surface, with large purple spots and streaks, sometimes forming 1-2 ± distinct central loops; lateral lobes rounded and spreading, margins sometimes recurved; median lobe prominent, narrower than lateral lobes, ± clearly projecting; lip index 1.10-1.50 (see p. 229); spur shorter than ovary, near cylindrical, downcurved; 2n=80.

Flowering Season VII-VIII.

Habitat Full sun on damp to wet, acidic substrates. Peat bogs and damp arctic-alpine grassland *c.* 1200-500m asl.

Distribution Poorly known due to confusion with closely related taxa. May be endemic to the Sudety mountains, a very isolated range with a distinctive climate; may also be present in Thüringen (Ge) and in Austria. Extremely local and extremely rare; threatened by eutrophication of its habitat due to nutrient fall-out.

Countries ?Au Cz ?Ge Po.

Photos Cz, Karkonosze, 27 & 28.VII.1999. J. DEVILLERS-TERSCHUREN.

Note A novel species, apparently far closer to southern Scandinavian taxa that have sinuses and lip markings intermediate between those of *D. fuchsii* and *D. maculata* (e.g. *D. kolaensis*), than to Alpine taxa, such as *D. savogiensis*, with which it is often confused.

233

Dactylorhiza kolaensis
(Montell) Averyanov

Etymology *kolaensis*: from the Kola [peninsula]. **Type** Ro, Kola peninsula (1947). **Synonyms** *Orchis spotstus* var. *kolaensis* Montell, *Dactylorhiza maculata* subsp. *elodes* var. *kolaensis* (Montell) Soó, *D. maculata* subsp. *kolaensis* (Montell) Kreutz comb. illeg., *Dactylorchis maculata* subsp. *montellii* Vermeulen, *D. maculata* subsp. *montellii* (Vermeulen) Landwehr, *D. montellii* (Vermeulen) P. Delforge, *D. maculata* subsp. *deflexa* Landwehr.

Description Spindly, 5-22 (-30)cm tall; stem slender, solid, often flexuose and washed violet at tip, sometimes spotted violet to the base; 3-4 leaves, oblong-lanceolate, tip ± obtuse, spreading to arching downwards, sometimes bent and in-rolled, short, up to 8cm x 1.5cm, broadest in the upper half, heavily spotted on upper side, uppermost bract-like; bracts often spotted, lower bracts shorter than flowers; inflorescence short, dense, ovoid; 5-15 flowers, relatively large, pale to rather dark pink; lateral sepals lanceolate, spreading forwards, tip reflexed upwards, spotted within; petals and dorsal sepal forming a ± loose hood; lip near entire or 3-lobed, shape and markings intermediate between those of *D. fuchsii* and *D. maculata*, 8.5-12mm x 7-10.5mm, flat to slightly convex, margins reflexed, orbicular, broadly elliptic, sometimes near rhomboidal or obcordate at base, centre thick pink to dark magenta dots and streaks, sometimes forming 1-2 central loops (rarely entire); lateral lobes rounded; median lobe often poorly marked (i.e. lip ± rhomboidal), prominent, longer than laterals; spur spindly, purplish, straight to slightly descendent, 0.5x-0.7x ovary; 2n=80.

Flowering Season VII-VIII.

Habitat Full sun to mid-shade on wet, acidic substrates. Sheltered, flushed areas in depressions and peat bogs in the subarctic tundras, up to 200m asl.

Distribution Scandinavian and Russian Lapland, eastwards perhaps to Siberia. Rare and local.

Countries Fe No Ro Su.

Photos No, Finnmark, 28 & 29.VII.1988. P. Delforge.

234

Dactylorhiza ericetorum
(E.F. Linton) Averyanov

Etymology *ericetorum*: with heather. **Type** Br, Bornemouth (1900). **Synonyms** *Orchis maculata* subsp. *ericetorum* Linton, *Dactylorhiza maculata* subsp. *ericetorum* (Linton) P.F. Hunt & Summerhayes, ?*D. maculata* var. *praecox* (Webster) Soó, *D. maculata* var. *schurii* (Klinge) Soó, *D. maculata* subsp. *schurii* (Klinge) Soó.

Description Rather spindly, 10-35 (-50)cm tall; stem slender, solid; 3-5 leaves, shape and habit varied, narrowly lanceolate to linear, keeled, sometimes hooded, 6-15cm x 0.8-2cm, erect to spreading and arching downwards, spotted on upper side, the longer leaves little more than *c.* 1/2 the height of the plant; uppermost 1-2 (-5) leaves bract-like; bracts short; inflorescence (2-) 3-6 (-9)cm tall, dense, conical to ovoid; 15-35 flowers, relatively large, often pale, whitish to lilac; lateral sepals lanceolate, 7-11mm x 2.5-4mm, near erect to spreading horizontally, tip reflexed, often strongly spotted inside; petals and dorsal sepal forming a ± loose hood; lip rather broadly orbicular, 3-lobed but only slightly incised, 7-10mm x 8-12 (-14)mm, flat to slightly convex, with fine, unobtrusive pink to lilac markings, sometimes reduced to sparse fine dots, more often formed by streaks and lines that form 1-2 central, ± entire, loops; lateral lobes rounded, margins often undulate-scalloped; median lobe much reduced, usually shorter than laterals; lip index 1.05-1.25 (-1.3) (see p. 229); spur spindly, 6-13mm x 1.3-2mm, sometimes equal to ovary, whitish, straight or slightly descendent, pointing downwards; 2n=80.

Variation Very varied. Distinguished from *D. maculata* by its ecological requirements, but often linked to it by intermediate forms associated with ecotones. Identified mostly by its narrower and less numerous leaves and by its large, subtly-marked lips. Distinguished from *D. maculata* var. *elodes* mostly by the habit and length of the leaves. *'schurii'* is a variant from the Carpathians.

Flowering Season (V-) VI-VII. **Habitat** Full sun to mid-shade on very acidic, damp to wet substrates. Peaty heathland, marshes with *Sphagnum*, seepages, often growing with Cross-leaved Heath (*Erica tetralix*).

Distribution More western than *D. maculata*. The Atlantic zone of Europe, from northern Portugal to northern Scandinavia. Rather local and often rare.

Countries Be Br Da Fa Fe Ga Ge Hb Ho Hs Lu ?Lx No Ro Su. **Photos** Br, Wales, 6.VII.1993; Scotland, Highland, 14.VII.1994. P. Delforge.

235

Dactylorhiza islandica
(A. Löve & D. Löve) Averyanov

Etymology *islandica*: from Iceland. **Type** Is, Kaldalon (1948). **Synonyms** *Dactylorchis maculata* (L.) Vermeulen subsp. *islandica* A. Löve & D. Löve, *Dactylorhiza maculata* subsp. *islandica* (A. Löve & D. Löve) Soó, *D. maculata* var. *islandica* (A. Löve & D. Löve) Hylander.

Description As *D. maculata* but stocky, 5-20cm tall; stem thick, solid; 3-5 leaves, clearly spotted, at least in distal half, 1-2 basal leaves relatively large, lanceolate, tip ± obtuse, 5-10mm x 2-3.5cm, obliquely erect to spreading and near arched, 1 sheathing cauline leaf, erect, narrowly lanceolate, uppermost leaf (12) bract-like; bracts short; inflorescence short, dense, few-flowered, ovoid to near cylindrical; flowers pale, pinkish to lilac; lateral sepals often slightly spreading; lip as *D. ericetorum*, flat, margins recurved, marked in the centre, from base to tip, with fine dots and scattered streaks, purple to deep violet, highly contrasting, rarely forming a single, ± entire central loop; spur spindly, down-curved, pointing downwards; 2n=80.

Flowering Season Late VI-VII. **Habitat** Full sun to mid-shade on damp, acidic substrates. Peaty heathland, often growing with Crowberry (*Empetrum nigrum*). **Distribution** Endemic to Iceland; recent reports from Norway probably refer to other taxa from the group or hybrids. Local and sometimes abundant in its stations. **Countries** Is. **Photos** Is, Arnes, 5.VII.2000. J. Devillers-Terschuren; Snæfellsnes, 14.VII. 1995. D. Rückbrodt.

Key to the *Dactylorhiza maculata* subgroup

1   spur spindly, less than 2mm thick at entrance 2

1* spur more robust, more than (1.7-) 2mm thick at entrance 9

2   plant slender, often robust, (20-) 25-60cm tall 3

2* plant small, thickset or spindly, 5-20 (-30)cm tall 4

3   4-10 leaves, 1.5-3cm wide; lip clearly spotted .... *D. maculata*

3* 3-5 leaves, narrow, 0.8-1.5cm wide; lip subtly spotted .... *D. ericetorum*

4   largest leaf as long as the stem or almost so 5

4* largest leaf reaching *c.* 1/2 way up stem 7

(continued on p. 242)

Dactylorhiza savogiensis
D. TYTECA & GATHOYE

Etymology *savogiensis*: from Savoy. **Type** Ga, Haute-Savoie (1990). **Synonyms** *Dactylorhiza maculata* subsp. *savogiensis* (D. TYTECA & GATHOYE) KREUTZ, *Orchis maculata* var. *brachystachys* A. CAMUS, *Dactylorhiza sudetica* auct. non (PÖCH EX REICHENBACH fil.) AVERYANOV.

Description (20-) 23-46 (-52)cm tall; stem solid, grooved and often washed violet at tip; 3-5 (-6) leaves, linear-lanceolate, weakly keeled and then flat, lowest leaf broader than the following leaf, largest leaf 7-16cm x 1-2.5cm, broadest towards the middle, marked with blackish-violet blotches of various sizes, uppermost 2-4 leaves bract-like; lower bracts shorter than flowers; inflorescence dense to near lax, initially conical then near cylindrical or ovoid, 3.5-11cm tall; 12-35 flowers, large, purplish-red, often rather dark; lateral sepals lanceolate, erect to spreading horizontally, often spotted inside, 8-13.5mm x 2.8-4.2mm; petals 6-10mm long, forming a loose hood with the dorsal sepal; lip orbicular, clearly 3-lobed, 8-11.5mm x 10-15.2mm, flat or slightly convex in the centre, pale at base, with thick, dark violet-purple streaks, large dots, rings and 1-2 ± entire central loops spread over the whole surface; lateral lobes rounded, often dark, turned down and back or spreading, margins then sometimes reflexed; median lobe broad, projecting ± clearly beyond lateral lobes; lip index 1.13-1.37 (see p. 229); spur 7.5-13mm x 1.7-2.9mm, near cylindrical, slightly down-curved; 2n=80.

Flowering Season VI-VII (-VIII).

Habitat Full sun on damp to wet, acidic substrates. Peat bogs and damp alpine meadows, 1200-2000m asl.

Distribution Poorly known due to confusion with closely related taxa; probably the western Alps, Massif Central (Ga) and Pyrenees (Ga/Hs). Rather local and often rare.

Countries Ga Ge He Hs It.

Photos Ga, Haute-Savoie, 22.VII.1992; Savoie, 10.VII.1984. P. DELFORGE.

Discussion Distinguished by its few leaves, dark flowers and the sinuses in the lip, intermediate between those of *D. fuchsii* and *D. maculata*; may replace the latter at altitude in the western Alps. Its distinction from hybrid swarms of *D. maculata* or *D. fuchsii* × *D. majalis* is not always easy.

Dactylorhiza maculata
(L.) Soó

Etymology *maculata*: spotted. **Type*** ?Su, Uppsala (1753). **Synonyms** *Orchis maculata* L., *Dactylorhiza maculata* subsp. *arduennensis* (ZADOKS) TOURNAY.

Description Slender, often robust, 20-60cm tall; stem slender, solid or slightly hollow, grooved and ± washed violet at tip; 4-10 leaves, oblong-lanceolate, 10-15mm x 1.5-3cm, broadest in the basal half, near erect to spreading and slightly arching outwards, ± densely spotted on upper side, rarely unspotted, underside often matt grey-green, lowest leaf ± pointed at tip, uppermost 1-5 leaves bract-like; bracts rather short; inflorescence 5-10cm tall, dense, conical and then (near) cylindrical; 15-50 flowers, often pale, whitish to pinkish, sometimes dark lilac; lateral sepals narrowly lanceolate, 7-10mm x 2-3mm, near erect to spreading, tip reflexed or turned down, often spotted inside; lip (near) orbicular to obcordate, sometimes near rhomboidal, 3-lobed or near entire, 7-11mm x 9-13.5mm, flat to slightly convex, with purple to purplish-violet dots, streaks and lines, ± uniformly spread, often forming loops in the centre; lateral lobes rounded; median lobe very narrow; lip index 1.07-1.27 (see p. 229); spur spindly, (4-) 6-10.5mm x 1-1.8mm, whitish, descendent parallel to ovary; 2n=80.

Flowering Season VI-VII (-VIII).

Habitat Full sun to shade on moist to wet, acidic substrates. Unimproved enriched meadows, woodland edges, clearings, drawdown zones in peat bogs, mostly in associations with Purple Moor-grass (*Molinia caeruleae*) and Marsh Marigold (*Caltha palustris*), up to 2300m asl.

Distribution Poorly known due to confusion within the group. Temperate to boreal Euro-Siberia. Widespread and sometimes abundant.

Countries Au Be Bu Co Cz Da ?Fa Fe Ga Ge He Ho Hs Hu It Ju Lx No Pb Po Rm Ro Su.

Photos Be, Luxembourg, 11.VII.1990; Su, Kalmarland, 4.VII.1988. P. DELFORGE.

Variation Very varied, distinguished from *D. fuchsii* by its ecology, lip-sinuses and markings and more pointed leaves. Numerous variants have been described; *'arduennensis'*: Slender and robust, with numerous leaves and flowers (Photo A). **Countries** Be (Ardenne) ?Ga Lx.

Dactylorhiza maculata (L.) Soó
var. *transsilvanica* (SCHUR) P. DELFORGE

Etymology *transsilvanica*: from Transylvania.
Type Ro, Transylvania (1886). **Synonyms**
Orchis transsilvanica SCHUR, *Dactylorhiza*
maculata subsp. *transsilvanica* (SCHUR) Soó,
D. fuchsii subsp. *transsilvanica* (SCHUR) FRÖHNER,
D. transsilvanica (SCHUR) AVERYANOV.

Description Slender, robust; flowers large, often
but not exclusively white or greenish-yellow,
unspotted; lip up to 16mm wide; spur up to
12mm long. An eastern variant, linked to var.
maculata by numerous intermediates. **Countries**
Ju Rm Ro. **Photo A** Ju, Slovenia, 13.VII.1999.
C.A.J. KREUTZ.

Dactylorhiza maculata (L.) Soó
var. *elodes* (GRISEBACH) AVERYANOV

Etymology *elodes*: marshy. **Type*** Ho, Bour-
tanger Moor (1845). **Synonyms** *Orchis elodes*
GREYEBACH, *Orchis maculata* var. *elodes*
(GREYEBACH) RCHB. fil., *Dactylorhiza maculata*
subsp. *elodes* (GREYEBACH) Soó, *D. elodes*
(GREYEBACH) AVERYANOV, *D. maculata* var. vel subsp.
averyanovii JAGIELLO.

Description Very spindly, 10-35cm tall; stem
slender, solid; 3-4 leaves, frequently unspotted,
narrowly lanceolate to linear, 9-16cm x 0.8-
1.5cm, erect, ± touching the stem, the largest
almost reaching base of inflorescence;
inflorescence short, 2-6cm tall; 15-35 flowers,
whitish to lilac; lateral sepals near erect; lip
weakly cut, with distinct dark markings forming
1-2 ± entire central loops; median lobe reduced;
lip index 1-1.15 (see p. 229); spur very spindly, 6-
9mm x 0.9-1.4mm, shorter than ovary.

Flowering Season V-VI (-VII). **Habitat** Full sun
to mid-shade on very acidic, damp to wet
substrates. Without doubt, predominantly
Sphagnum bogs and damp depressions on acidic
heathland.

Distribution Impossible to delineate. Plausibly
recorded from the bogs of the Benelux and
Ardennes (Ga), but also reported from the British
Isles and Russia. Probably local and rare.

Photo B Ho, Limburg, 9.VI.1991. C.A.J. KREUTZ
(see also p. 241).

Discussion A very controversial taxon, rather
varied, isolated from *D. maculata* by its relatively
early flowering and ecological requirements,
which place it closer to *D. ericetorum*.
Distinguished from the latter by its more spindly
habit, less numerous leaves, which are more erect
and relatively longer, by the markings on the lip,
which are on average more pronounced, and by
its very spindly spur.

(continued on p. 240)

239

(*continued from p. 239*)

Described from a bog that is now almost destroyed, this variety is reported ± sporadically from the more acidic parts of the damp areas, where the few remaining plants often appear to be introgressed with *D. maculata* s.l.; it may therefore be on the edge of extinction. It is variously considered to be an ecotype of *D. maculata*, an extreme form of *D. ericetorum*, or as a distinct species with a vast European range.

Dactylorhiza maculata (L.) Soó
var. *rhoumensis*
(HESLOP-HARRISON) D.M.T. ETTLINGER ?comb. inval.

Etymology *rhoumensis*: from Rhum (Hebrides, Br). **Type** Br, Rhum (1948). **Synonyms** *Orchis fuchsii* subsp. *rhoumensis* HESLOP-HARRISON, *Dactylorhiza maculata* subsp. *rhoumensis* (HESLOP-HARRISON) SOÓ.

Description Very thickset, 5-12 (-20)cm tall; stem thick, solid; 3-4 leaves, often heavily spotted, rather long for such a low growing plant, broadest in the distal half; lower bracts slightly longer than flowers; inflorescence near ovoid, short, very dense and many-flowered; flowers often larger than those of var. *maculata*, whitish to lilac or dark purple; lip weakly cut, marked, often over the whole surface with numerous dark purple dots and streaks, forming 1-2 ± entire central loops.

Flowering Season VII-VIII, relatively late.

Habitat Full sun on moist to damp, acidic substrates. Acidic moorland with heather.

Distribution Poorly known. Western Scotland. Probably local but sometimes abundant in its stations.

Countries Br. **Photos** Br, Scotland, Skye, 15.VII.1994. P. DELFORGE.

Note A morphologically similar taxon, but early-flowering, has been described from Terschelling Island (Ho) (= *D. maculata* var. *podesta* LANDWEHR, *D. maculata* subsp. *podesta* (LANDWEHR) KREUTZ); it is considered an ecotype of *D. maculata*. However, in cultivation plants from Terschelling became more slender but retained their leaf and floral characters, contradicting the hypothesis of an ecotype. Similarly, *D. maculata* var. *rhoumensis*, which appears to be rather frequent on the western side of Scotland, is held to be merely a dwarf form of *D. ericetorum* or *D. maculata*, but this is probably not a completely adequate treatment.

Dactylorhiza caramulensis
(VERMEULEN) D. TYTECA

Etymology *caramulensis*: from [Serra de] Caramulo. **Type** Lu, Beira Alta (1970). **Basionym** *D. maculata* subsp. *caramulensis* VERMEULEN.

Description As *D. maculata* but a little more slender and more robust, 30-65cm tall; stem thicker, diameter 2.6-7.5mm below the inflorescence; 5-9 leaves, 7-20cm x 1.5-3cm, near erect to spreading, lower leaves placed rather low on stem, uppermost 2-4 leaves bract-like; bracts large, up to 35mm long, longer than lower flowers; inflorescence 5-15cm tall, dense, conical then near cylindrical; (20-) 30-70 flowers, large and rather pale, white to lilac or sometimes crimson; lateral sepals 8.5-13mm long, erect to spreading, margins often rolled up; petals 6.5-10mm long; lip orbicular to obcordate, ± clearly 3-lobed, 8.5-16mm x 11.5-17mm, flat to slightly convex, with numerous distinct, dark, purple or purplish-violet dots, streaks and lines over the whole surface, forming 1-2 ± entire loops in the centre; lateral lobes rounded, margins scalloped, sometimes reflexed; median lobe rather small, rarely protuberant; lip index 1.10-1.32 (see p. 229); spur prominent, relatively robust, 8-15mm x 1-3mm, descendent parallel to ovary and often equal to it in length. **Variation** Rather distinct, notably in its robustness and the length of the bracts and spur; varies in the sinuses of the lip. Sometimes recalls *D. elata* in its habit; it is perhaps only a robust variant of *D. maculata*.

Flowering Season V-VII. **Habitat** Full sun to mid-shade on moist to wet, acidic substrates. Damp meadows, moist woods, flushed slopes, 600-1400m asl.

Distribution The northern half of Portugal, Galicia and León (Hs) and the western Spanish Pyrenees. Local but sometimes rather abundant. **Countries** ?Ga Hs Lu.

Photos Hs, León, 10.VI.1992. P. DELFORGE.

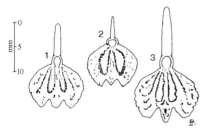

1. *D. maculata* (Be). 2. *D. maculata* var. *elodes* (Be).
3. *D. caramulensis* (Lu). (3 modified after TYTECA)

241

E.K.

Dactylorhiza battandieri
RAYNAUD

Etymology Named after J.A. Battandier, French botanist (1848-1922). **Type** Ag, Petite Kabylie (1985). **Synonyms** *Orchis maculata* subsp. *baborica* MAIRE, *Dactylorhiza maculata* subsp. *battandieri* (RAYNAUD) H. BAUMANN & KÜNKELE.

Description Spindly, 20-55cm tall; stem solid or slightly hollow; 5-9 leaves, oval-oblong, keeled, bright green, ± spotted purple, lowest leaf shorter and broader than second lowest, uppermost 2-4 leaves bract-like; bracts shorter than flowers; inflorescence dense to near lax, conical and then cylindrical; flowers large, crimson-pink to purplish, pale to rather dark; lateral sepals narrowly lanceolate, 9-11mm x 2-3mm, near erect, tip reflexed; petals 7-8mm long, forming a loose hood with dorsal sepal; lip orbicular to obcordate, ± clearly 3-lobed, 9-10mm x 10-15mm, flat to slightly convex, slightly folded longitudinally, base pale, sides reflexed, with diffuse dots and streaks forming a vague, ± entire loop in centre; lateral lobes rounded; median lobe reduced; spur descendent, near cylindrical, 8-10mm x 2-3mm, pointing downwards, ± equal to ovary.

Flowering Season VI-VII. **Habitat** Full sun to mid-shade on damp to wet, acidic substrates. Marshy depressions, from 1300m to over 1600m asl. **Distribution** Endemic to Djebel Babor (Petite Kabylie). Very rare and local. **Countries** Ag. **Watercolour** Ag, Petite Kabylie, 25.V.1971. E. KLOPFENSTEIN.

Key to the *Dactylorhiza maculata* subgroup

(continued from p. 236)

5   very thickset 6

5*   slender and very spindly
     .... *D. maculata* var. *elodes*

6   lower bracts equal to, or slightly longer than, flowers .... *D. maculata* var. *rhoumensis*

6*   lower bracts shorter than flowers
     .... *D. islandica*

7   lip finely and subtly spotted; median lobe very small, shorter than lateral lobes
     .... *D. ericetorum*

7*   lip clearly spotted; median lobe often large and protuberant 8

8   lip 8.5-12mm long .... *D. kolaensis*

8*   smaller lip, averaging 6.6mm long
     ....*D. sudetica*

(continued on next page)

Dactylorhiza maurusia
(EMBERGER & MAIRE) J. HOLUB

Etymology *maurusia*: from Mauritania. **Type** Ma, Djebel Tidighin (1930). **Synonyms** *Orchis maurusia* EMBERGER & MAIRE, *Dactylorhiza maculata* subsp. *maurusia* (EMBERGER & MAIRE) SOÓ.

Description Rather spindly, 25-50cm tall; stem solid or slightly hollow, finely grooved at tip; 5-7 leaves, oblong-lanceolate, channelled then flat, green, unspotted, obliquely erect, slightly arched, 6-18cm x 1.5-2.5cm; lower bracts equal to flowers; inflorescence near lax, conical then near cylindrical; 10-25 flowers, medium-sized, pale lilac, sometimes whitish; lateral sepals oval-lanceolate, 9-10mm x 3-4mm, spreading to erect; petals 7-9mm long, forming a loose hood with dorsal sepal; lip orbicular to oboval, 3-lobed, 8-10mm x 10-12mm, folded longitudinally, margins turned downwards then recurved, marked with purple blotches and lines that form 2-3 ± entire concentric loops in the centre; median lobe triangular, reduced, only slightly longer than laterals; spur spindly, slightly descendent to strongly arched, pointing downwards, near cylindrical, 10-12mm x 2-3mm, ± equal to ovary.

Flowering Season IV-VII. **Habitat** Full sun to mid-shade on damp to wet, siliceous or calcareous substrates. The edges of streams, marshy depressions from 700m to more than 1900m asl.

Distribution Endemic to the Rif. Very rare and local. **Countries** Ma. **Watercolour** Ma, Tazekka, 12.VI.1972. E. KLOPFENSTEIN.

Key to the *Dactylorhiza maculata* subgroup

(continued from previous page)

9 flowers often unspotted, greenish-yellow or white .... *D. maculata* var. *transsilvanica*
9* flowers not as above 10

10 leaves unspotted .... *D. maurusia*
10* leaves spotted 11

11 Lowest leaf not as broad as 2nd; bracts longer than flowers .... *D. caramulensis*
11* Lowest leaf broader than 2nd; bracts not longer than flowers 12

12 5-9 leaves; flowers rather pale, median lobe of lip reduced .... *D. battandieri*
12* 4-6 leaves; flowers dark, median lobe of lip prominent .... *D. savogiensis*

E.K.

Serapias L. 1753

Etymology *Serapis*: Egyptian god, master of fertility, to whom an orgiastic cult was devoted. By analogy, Dioscorides named an orchid Serapias; this was probably a species of *Orchis*, reputedly an aphrodisiac.

Characteristics 2-5 ovoid root-tubers, the 1-3 younger tubers long-stalked; leaves narrow, channelled, sheathing, upper leaves cauline, often bract-like; bracts coloured as sepals and similarly marked with dark veins; sepals elongated, lanceolate, lateral sepals slightly asymmetrical, margins coalescent (but not joined) often almost to the tip, connivent to form an acuminate hood; petals hairless, entirely concealed in hood, very different to sepals, often purple at base, broad, orbicular, long-tapering towards the tip; lip without a spur, 3-lobed, ± strongly hairy in the centre with, at the base, a narrow unguis surmounted by 2 lamellae or 1 (-2) rounded, blackish boss; basal part (hypochile) concave, often entirely hidden within the hood; median lobe (epichile) pendant to turned down and backwards, rarely projecting forwards; column very elongated, inclined forwards, terminating in a long-tapering connective; 2 pollinia with distinct caudicles; 1 retinacle; 1 bursicle; ovary sessile, not twisted, erect; 2n=36 (72).

Discussion Essentially Mediterranean, ranging west to the Azores and Canaries, east to the Caucasus and north to Brittany (Ga). The genus *Serapias* is monophyletic, isolated, well-characterised and made up of very similar species; as a result, the number recognised varies greatly between authors. Problems arise from the difficulty in defining the various taxa when their ranges of variation overlap ± broadly, the apparent abundance of intermediate forms and the very different appearence presented by populations from one year to the next and even between times within the same flowering season.

The genus is divided into 2 sister sections. One contains the *Serapias lingua* group, a monophyletic assemblage of 6 species that have 1 (-2) rounded blackish boss, ± deeply grooved, at the base of the lip. The other section is a monophyletic assemblage of species which have 2 lamellae at the base of the lip and either 1: an orbicular base to the petals (the *S. vomeracea* group, 18 species), or 2: more-or-less acuminate drop-shaped petals (the *S. parviflora* group, 3 species). Only *S. lingua* seems to be clearly isolated from other members of the genus; the 5 other species in its group appear to be intermediate to various degrees between *S. lingua* and the 'bi-lamellar' taxa without it being possible to say whether they have a hybridogenous origin or represent species with primitive characters, close to the common ancestor of the 2 sections.

Figure 8: **1**. Bract. **2**. Hood. **3**. Lateral lobe of hypochile. **4**. Epichile. **5**. Ovary. **6**. Lateral sepal. **7**. Petal. **8**. Dorsal sepal. **9**. Unguis. **10**. Basal lamellae. **11**. Basal boss (*Serapias lingua*). **12**. Loculus or theca enclosing a pollinium. **13**. Tip of column. **14**. Bursicle. **15**. Viscidium. **16**. Caudicle. **17**. Pollinium. **18**. Stigmatic surface. **19**. Underground portion of *Serapias lingua*. **20**. Neck. **21**. Root-tuber. **22**. Rhizome.

244

The closest relatives of the genus *Serapias* are the genera *Anacamptis* and *Orchis*. *Serapias* is linked to *Anacamptis* by its chromosome number, 3-lobed lip with 2 lamellae at the base and a single retinacle enclosed within a bursicle. A hybrid with *S. lingua* has been reported (× *Serapicamptis forbesii* GODFERY), but only very rarely. With the genus *Orchis*, on the other hand, although still very rare, hybrids are more numerous and more frequent (see × *Orchiserapias*, p. 27). Moreover the morphological similarities with *Orchis papilionacea* (sepals veined with purple and petals connivent in a hood, lip with a central hairy area, and contracted at the base into a narrow unguis with 2 crests) as well as with *O. coriophora* (sepals coalescent, connivent in a hood, lip 3-lobed in the centre, contracted at the base, grooved, often hairy) are remarkable. The relationship with the genus *Ophrys* is probably more distant than with *Orchis*; similarities are limited to an identical chromosome number and lack of a spur. The structure of the lip (a central hairy area and 2 basal crests divided by a groove) is only evoked by section *Pseudophrys*; moreover there are no hybrids between the 2 genera.

Hypochromy in the genus *Serapias*

Certain species may normally be very pale (*S. neglecta*, *S. parviflora*, *S. lingua*, *S. perez-chiscanoi*, *S. stenopetala*). Examples with yellowish or greenish lips and lightly-coloured bracts and hood are rather frequent in *S. bergonii* and *S. orientalis*. Plants totally devoid of anthocyanins are very rare.

Pollination of *Serapias*

Serapias lack nectar, so what mechanisms do they use to attract their pollinators? In the narrow tube formed by the hypochile concave and the hood the temperature is 1-3°C higher than outside. A large number of hymenopterans (solitary bees and wasps) have been observed, sluggish, in the flowers of *Serapias*, where they remain for a while during rain, on cold days or overnight. When the outside temperature rises sufficiently they leave the shelter of the flower, carrying off the pollinia whenever the size of their head allows them to insert it between the basal lamella and the column and touch the retinacle. Small pollen beetles (Coleoptera, Scarabaeidae),

Serapias vomeracea hypochromatic. **Photo A**: Ga, Var, 13.V.1988. P. DELFORGE.

A solitary bee (*Osmia versicolor*) carrying the pollinia of a flower of *Serapias ionica* in which it sheltered from the rain. **Photo B**: Gr, Kefallinia, 4.IV.1991. P. DELFORGE.

feeding on pollen, have also been observed leaving the flowers of *S. cordigera* and *S. olbia* with pollinia glued to their heads. Some spiders also live in *Serapias* flowers, but they do not seem to facilitate cross-pollination. Two of the more specialised species, *S. parviflora* and *S. lingua*, are equally original in their pollination mechanism. *S. parviflora* is regularly cleistogamous, while *S. lingua* is not used as shelter, rather it seems to exert a sexual attraction on its pollinators analogous to that of the genus *Ophrys*. Males of the small bee *Ceratina cucurbitina* emerge from their pupae before the females and start looking for a partner. They are attracted by the shiny boss at the base of the lip of *Serapias lingua*, probably also by scents emitted by the flower that mimic female pheromones. Through the heat of the day they frantically visit the flowers and attempt pseudocopulation with the basal boss, touching the retinacle with their head and carrying off the pollinia.

Hybrids in the genus *Serapias*

The majority of *Serapias* species appear to hybridise frequently whenever they are syntopic, and the number of hybrid plants may greatly exceed that of the parent species. This interfertility, the morphological proximity of *Serapias*, the range of their variation and their hybridogenous origin often make the location and identification of hybrids very uncertain. The characters that allow any progress towards a diagnosis are few: the habit of the plant or shape of the leaves are not often of much use; the colour and size of the flowers, shape of the petals, hypochile and epichile, as well as the degree of hairiness and details of the basal boss of the lip are characters that are only truly useful when the parent species differ significantly in one or more of these. It is therefore best to identify hybrid plants *in situ*, comparing as many living plants as possible; useful characters are usually hidden within the hood, and photographs are not much help in determining plants *a posteriori*. Frequently, plants cannot be precisely determined, especially when several species of *Serapias* are syntopic; it is sometimes good to monitor hybrid swarms over several years in order to understand their composition.

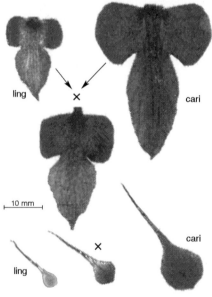

S. carica × *S. lingua* = *S.* × *walravensiana* P. Delforge. Hybrids involving *S. lingua* can often be recognised by their intense coloration and entire but strongly hollowed basal boss. **Photo**: Gr, Kiklades, Amorgos, 15.IV.1997. P. DELFORGE. **Below**: Lip and petals of *S.* x *walravensiana* between those of its parents. (herbar. P. Delforge).

The *Serapias parviflora* group

Characteristics Base of lip with 2 lamellae; petals acuminate-drop-shaped. A monophyletic group with 2 species and 1 hybridogenous species, *S. politisii*.

Serapias nurrica
CORRIAS

Etymology *nurrica*: from Nurra, a region in northwest Sardinia. **Type** Sa, Sassari (1982).

Description Often slender, (15-) 20-35 (-42)cm tall; base of stem and leaves streaked red; 5-8 leaves, erect, linear-lanceolate, 10-18cm x 0.8-1.6cm, channelled-keeled, pointed, uppermost 1-2 leaves bract-like, near clasping; bracts 32-36mm long, colour as hood but shorter; inflorescence short and dense; 4-8 flowers, medium-sized; hood matt lilac-grey outside, red with brown veins inside, usually obliquely erect; sepals lanceolate, 20-26mm x 5-7mm; petals slightly shorter, drop-shaped, very acuminate, 4.5-6.5mm wide, blackish-purple at base; lip (18-) 23-30mm long, 2 glossy, purple, divergent lamellae at base; hypochile concave, rectangular-rounded to near kidney-shaped, (8-) 11-13mm x (13-) 15-18mm, red and densely hairy in centre; lateral lobes lilac-grey on outside, concealed within hood; epichile oval-lanceolate, pointed, much narrower than hypochile, (10-) 14-18mm x (5-) 7-10mm, pendant to slightly recurved, bicoloured, pale reddish to dark brownish-red, bordered by a narrow paler lilac-grey strip; weakly convex to flat in centre, margins curved forwards, slightly scalloped; pollinia greenish-yellow.

Flowering Season IV-V (-VI); rather late.
Habitat Full sun to mid-shade on dry, acidic substrates. Coastal garrigue, up to 200m asl.

Distribution Central-west Mediterranean. Known from Sardinia, southern Corsica, north-west Minorca (Bl) and a few stations in Sicily and Calabria (It). Very rare and local. **Countries** Bl Co It Sa Si. **Photos** Sa, Sassari, 25.IV.1996. P. DELFORGE.

Note Close to *S. parviflora* in its drop-shaped petals and narrow hypochile, remarkable because its epichile always has a pale margin. A few reports from Portugal and the single record from France (*S. nurrica* 'subsp. *argensi*') concern occasional plants of other species that show a pale margin (Lu *S. ?cordigera*; Ga *S. gregaria*).

Serapias parviflora
PARLATORE

Etymology *parviflora*: with small flowers. **Type** Si, Palermo (1837). **Synonyms** *S. occultata* GAY ex CAVALIER, *S. elongata* TODARO, *S. mascaensis* H. KRETZSCHMAR, G. KRETZSCHMAR & KREUTZ, *S. parviflora* subsp. *mascaensis* (H. KRETZSCHMAR, G. KRETZSCHMAR & KREUTZ) KREUTZ.

Description Slender; stems usually arising singly, (10-) 15-30 (-40)cm tall; base of stem and leaves; 4-7 leaves, sheathing, (near) erect, linear-lanceolate, channelled-keeled, pointed, 6-15cm long, upper 1-3 leaves much smaller, near clasping; bracts relatively large, 25-40mm long, often longer than hood and similarly coloured; inflorescence narrow, dense to near lax, rather pale; 3-8 (-12) small flowers, usually cleistogamous; hood greenish-grey to pale lilac grey, veined red outside, red-brown inside, horizontal to near erect; sepals lanceolate, (10-) 13-16 (-18)mm x 3-4mm, briefly coalescent; petals slightly shorter, drop-shaped, elongated (see p. 273), 3-4mm wide, purple-brown to purplish at the base; lip only just as long as the hood, (13-) 14-19 (-22)mm long, with 2 shiny greenish-purple to purplish, slightly divergent lamellae at the base; hypochile concave, obcordate, (6-) 8-10mm x (7-) 9-12mm, centre pale with rather sparse, short hairs, rarely almost hairless; lateral lobes darker, almost entirely concealed within hood; epichile lanceolate, pointed, short, much narrower than hypochile, (5-) 6-10 (-13)mm x 3-5mm, pale, brownish-pink to greenish-yellow, usually slightly convex at centre, turned down and curved backwards below hypochile; pollinia yellow, powdery, generally breaking up onto the stigmatic surface in the bud; ovaries large, erect, greenish-yellow, swollen. **Variation** Not very varied, distinguished by its small pale flowers and yellow pollinia, usually breaking up in the bud. *'mascaensis'* has cohesive pollinia, even after the flower has opened. **Countries** Tenerife (Ca).

Flowering Season (III-) IV-V (-VI); rather late. **Habitat** Full sun to mid-shade on dry to damp, alkaline to slightly acidic substrates. Damp coastal meadows, garrigue, scrub, olive groves, open woodland, up to 1200m asl. **Distribution** Mediterranean-Atlantic. East to the Aegean Islands and Cyprus, west to the Canaries and north to Brittany (Côtes-du-Nord, Ga). Rather widespread but rather rare. **Countries** Ae Ag Al Bl Ca Co Cr Cy Ga Gr Hs It Ju Lu Ma Me Sa Si Tn. **Photos** Hs, Malaga, 10.IV.1990; Gr, Messinia, 20.IV.1991. P. DELFORGE.

Serapias politisii
RENZ (pro hybr.)

Etymology Named after V. Politis, Athens professor. **Type** Gr, Corfu (1928).

Description Slender and spindly; stems arising singly, 13-35 (-40)cm tall; base of stem and leaves; 4-8 leaves, sheathing, erect, linear-lanceolate, rather short, not reaching base of inflorescence, 7-15cm x 0.7-1.2cm, channelled-keeled, pointed, uppermost 2-3 leaves bract-like; bracts ± as long as hood and similarly coloured; inflorescence near lax to lax, dark red; 2-7 small flowers; hood pale grey to reddish, veined red outside, dark red inside, obliquely erect to almost vertical; sepals 13-18mm x 3-4.5mm; petals 2-3.8mm wide, violet-purple at base; lip 17-23mm long, 2 parallel shiny reddish lamellae at the base; hypochile concave, kidney-shaped to obcordate, 6-11mm x 7-12mm, centre pale pinkish with rather sparse whitish hairs; lateral lobes dark brownish-purple, almost entirely concealed within hood; epichile lanceolate, pointed, far narrower than hypochile, 8-13mm x 3-5mm, reddish-brown, rather pale to dark, pendant or folded below the hypochile; pollinia green.

Variation Clearly intermediate between *S. bergonii* (general habit, coloration) and *S. parviflora* (small flowers, shape of petals, ?ability to self-pollinate).

Flowering Season IV-V; rather late. **Habitat** Full sun to mid-shade on dry to moist substrates. Garrigue, scrub, olive groves, up to more than 400m asl. **Distribution** Corfu, Epirus coasts, central Aegean, reported further east, to the Mediterranean region of western Anatolia, as well as from Italy (Puglia). Very rare and local. **Countries** Ae An Gr It. **Photos** Gr, Thesprotia, 7.V.1990. P. DELFORGE.

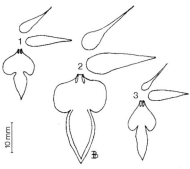

1. *S. parviflora* (Gr). 2. *S.nurrica* (Sa).
3. *S. politisii* (Gr).

249

The *Serapias vomeracea* group

Characteristics Base of lip with 2 distinct lamellae; base of petals orbicular. Monophyletic group with 18 species.

Serapias aphroditae
P. DELFORGE

Etymology Named after the goddess Aphrodite, said to have been born on Cyprus. **Type** Cy, Akamas Peninsula (1990).

Description As *S. bergonii* but small; stem arising singly, (5-) 11-24 (-30)cm tall; 4-8 leaves, unspotted at base, rather short, 5-9cm long, rarely reaching base of inflorescence; bracts ± equal in size to hood of lower flowers; inflorescence lax, dark; (1-) 3-6 (-10) small, cross-pollinated flowers; hood purplish-grey veined purple, reddish at the base outside, dark reddish inside, obliquely erect; sepals 10-15mm x 3-4mm; petals slightly shorter, orbicular and crimson at base, subulate and paler towards tip, 3-4.2mm wide; dorsal sepal and petals coalescent; lip 16-21mm long, 2 shiny, dark purple, near-parallel lamellae at the base; hypochile semi-orbicular to wedge-shaped, 8-12mm x 9-13mm, centre pale purple, with rather sparse, short, whitish hairs; lateral lobes dark brownish-purple, almost entirely concealed inside hood; epichile lanceolate, pointed, much narrower and sometimes shorter than hypochile, (6-) 8-11mm x 4-6mm, red to deep purple, projecting forward, pendant or turned down under the hypochile; pollinia purple.

Variation Rather constant. Close to *S. bergonii*, but distinguished by its smaller overall size and small epichile. Distinguished from *S. parviflora* by the shape of the petals, dark coloration and routine cross-pollination.

Flowering Season III-IV; rather early.

Habitat Full sun on dry to moist, alkaline substrates. Coastal garrigue, field margins, olive groves, up to 500m asl.

Distribution Apparently endemic to western Cyprus (Akamas and Akrotiri Peninsulas). Very rare and local.

Countries Cy.

Photos Cy, Polis (loc. typ.), 5.IV.1989. P. DELFORGE.

Serapias bergonii
E.G. Camus (pro hybr.)

Etymology Named after P. Bergon, French botanist (1863-1912). **Type** Gr, Corfu (1908). **Synonyms** *S. laxiflora* Chaubard nom. illeg., *S. cordigera* subsp. *laxiflora* (Soó) Sundermann, *S. vomeracea* subsp. *laxiflora* (Soó) Gölz & Reinhard, *S. columnae* auct. non Rchb. fil., *S. hellenica* Renz.

Description As *S. vomeracea* but slender, 15-42 (-50)cm tall; base of stem and leaves often streaked red; 6-9 leaves, lanceolate, 6-14cm long, uppermost 1-2 bract-like; bracts 18-55mm long, washed purple, longer than hood; inflorescence lax, elongate, up to 20cm tall, rather dark; 3-12 (-18) flowers, medium to small, cross-pollinated; hood lilac-grey, obliquely erect; sepals 15-21 (-24)mm x 4-5.5mm; petals subulate, 19-27.5mm x 2-4.5mm, base orbicular, crimson; lip 18-29 (-35)mm long, rather pale red to deep violet-purple, 2 small, parallel, whitish to dark purple ridges at base; hypochile 10-13mm x 11-15mm, kidney-shaped to obcordate, rarely wedge-shaped, centre greenish-yellow to pale pinkish, sometimes ochre, with short hairs; lateral lobes blackish-purple, concealed within hood; epichile lanceolate, (10-) 12-18 (-20)mm x 4-7.5mm, near hairless, pendant to turned down and back; pollinia greenish. **Variation** Varied. May grow either as isolated stems or in groups. The range of variation partly overlaps that of *S. vomeracea*, with which intermediates exist. Isolated and polymorphic populations, apparently in part attributable to *S. bergonii* and reported from central Italy (Parma, Siena), may be *S. vomeracea*.

Flowering Season III-V; rather early. **Habitat** As *S. vomeracea* but up to 1500m asl.

Distribution Eastern Mediterranean. East to Antioch (Hakkari, An), west to Calabria (It) and Sicily. Rather widespread and often abundant. **Countries** Ae Al An Cr Cy Gr It Ju Si Tu. **Photos** Gr, Lakonia, 18.IV.1991; Ae, Lesvos, 11.IV.1991. P. Delforge.

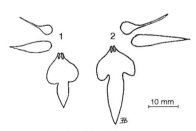

1. *S. aphroditae* (Cy). 2. *S. bergonii* (Gr).

10 mm

251

Serapias vomeracea
(N.L. BURMAN) BRIQUET

Etymology *vomeracea*: shaped as a ploughshare.
Type* It, Verona (1770). **Synonyms** *S. lancifera*
ST. AMAND, *S. pseudocordigera* (SEBASTIANI) MORIC.,
S. longipetala (TENORE) POLLINI, *S. cordigera* subsp.
vomeracea (N.L. BURMAN) SUNDERMANN, *S. vomeracea*
subsp. *longipetala* (TENORE) H. BAUMANN & KÜNKELE.

Description Robust, (17-) 25-60cm tall; base of
stem and leaves rarely spotted; 4-7 leaves, erect,
sometimes curved, linear-lanceolate, channelled-
keeled, 6-19cm long; 1-2 bract-like cauline
leaves; bracts very large (see p. 253), acuminate,
up to 70mm x 20mm, longer than the hood and
similarly coloured; inflorescence near lax,
elongate; 3-12 large cross-pollinated flowers;
hood lilac-grey, veined deep purple outside, dark
red inside, very acuminate, obliquely erect; sepals
20-31mm x 5-8.5mm, long-coalescent, slightly
keeled; petals subulate, 19-27.5mm x 4-8.5mm,
base orbicular, crimson; lip 28-44mm long, rather
pale red to dark violet-purple, rarely ochre,
densely hairy to centre of epichile, 2 parallel
whitish to dark purple lamellae at base; hypochile
concave, 12-17mm x 17-25mm, broadly kidney-
shaped to obcordate, centre paler, sometimes
greenish-yellow, lateral lobes blackish-purple,
concealed within hood; epichile lanceolate, 18-
30mm x 8-13mm, often turned down and back,
sometimes pendant or pointing obliquely
forwards, straight, convex at centre, margins
reflexed; pollinia violet washed with green.

Variation Varied. Usually distinguished by its
habit and the shape and length of the bracts, hood
and epichile. Nevertheless, the range of variation
partly overlaps that of *S. bergonii*, of *S. orientalis*
and of its allies, so that the limits of this species
are not always clear. The variations in *S.
vomeracea* do not appear sufficiently consistent
to distinguish infraspecific taxa within it.

Flowering Season (III-) IV-VI; rather late.
Habitat Full sun to mid-shade on moist to damp,
alkaline to slightly acidic substrates. Short, poor
grassland, damp meadows, garrigue, olive groves,
open woodland, up to 1200m asl. **Distribution**
Mediterranean-Atlantic. North to Charente-
Maritime (Ga) and the foothills of the Alps (He)
and east to Cyprus. Rather widespread and
sometimes abundant in its stations. **Countries** Ae
Ag Al Bl Co Cy Ga Gr He Hs It Ju Li Ma Me Si.
Photos Gr, Messinia, 21.IV.1991; Ga, Var,
13.V.1988. P. DELFORGE.

Serapias perez-chiscanoi
C. ACEDO

Etymology Named after J.L. Pérez Chiscano, contemporary Spanish botanist. **Type** Hs, Badajoz (1990). **Synonym** *S. viridis* PÉREZ CHISCANO nom. illeg.

Description As *S. vomeracea* but 20-40cm tall; stem pale green; leaves 11-14cm x 0.8-2cm; bracts pale green, veined and sometimes finely spotted purple; inflorescence short and dense; 3-13 rather large self-pollinating flowers, very often cleistogamous; sepals pale green, sometimes washed pink, veined dark green or purple, 21-25mm x 5-7mm; petals subulate, pale green, base orbicular, sometimes dark or pinkish; lip with 2 slightly divergent lamellae at the base, green to sometimes pinkish; hypochile 7-10mm x 12-19mm, pale green, lateral lobes sometimes crimson-pink, concealed inside hood; epichile lanceolate, 17-22mm x 9-14mm, folded down and backwards, pale green, veined green or purple, centre with whitish or pinkish hairs; pollinia whitish, rapidly disintegrating onto stigma. **Variation** Isolated by self-pollination. Distinguished from *S. vomeracea*, from which it probably derives, by its hypochromy, shorter inflorescence and smaller flowers.

Flowering Season (III-) IV-V. **Habitat** Full sun to mid-shade on moist to damp, acidic substrates, often siliceous. Damp, unimproved meadows, degraded garrigue, up to 400m asl. **Distribution** Apparently endemic to Extremadura (Hs) and neighbouring regions of Portugal. Very rare and local. **Countries** Hs Lu. **Photos** Hs, Badajoz (loc. typ.), 22.IV.1994. C.A.J. KREUTZ.

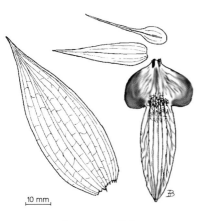

S. vomeracea (Ga).

10 mm

253

Serapias levantina
H. Baumann & Künkele

Etymology *levantina*: from the Levant, from the Near East. **Type** Ij, Palestine (1989). **Synonym** *S. orientalis* subsp. *levantina* (H. Baumann & Künkele) Kreutz.

Description As *S. vomeracea* but 16-30cm tall; stem often washed red; 4-8 leaves, lanceolate, near pointed, 3-15cm long, uppermost 1-2 leaves much smaller, clasping; bracts 25-42mm x 11-17mm, ± equal to hood and similarly coloured; inflorescence lax; 3-6 (-10) flowers; hood lilac-grey, veined violet outside, dark red inside; sepals 18-25mm x 5-6mm; petals slightly shorter, 4.5-6.2mm wide; lip 23-32mm long, rather dark brick-red, 2 divergent violet lamellae at base, centre with long, dense, purplish hairs; hypochile near kidney-shaped to obcordate, 8.5-12mm x 14-20mm; epichile oval-lanceolate, 14-25mm x 8-12mm, pendant to bent down and backwards, flat or with margins reflexed.

Variation Rather critical, this taxon appears to be polymorphic and intermediate between *S. orientalis* and *S. vomeracea*; often appears hardly different from *S. vomeracea* in Cyprus. The range of variation, distribution and status of this taxon require confirmation.

Flowering Season (II-) III-IV; early. **Habitat** As *S. vomeracea* but up to 600m asl.

Distribution Eastern Mediterranean. From Cyprus and Hatay (An) to Jerusalem (Ij); in the east perhaps to Diyarbakir (An) and as far as Kurdistan. Local but sometimes abundant. **Countries** An Cy Ij Ls.

Photos Ij, Tel-Aviv, 25.III.1992. C.A.J. Kreutz.

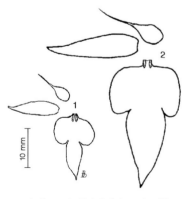

1. *S. patmia* (Ae). 2. *S. levantina* (Ij).

Serapias feldwegiana
H. BAUMANN & KÜNKELE

Etymology Named after O. Feldweg, German orchidologist (1917-1996). **Type** An, Ordu (1989). **Synonym** *S. orientalis* subsp. *feldwegiana* (H. BAUMANN & KÜNKELE) KREUTZ.

Description Slender, 15-45cm tall; 5-9 leaves, unspotted, lanceolate, long-acuminate, 5.5-16cm long, lower 2-4 leaves arched, erect to spreading, median 1-2 leaves erect, clasping, reaching base of inflorescence; uppermost 1-2 leaves bract-like; bracts 30-49mm long, equal to, or slightly longer than, hood and more crimson; inflorescence near lax; 3-8 (-10) large flowers; hood horizontal, grey veined with violet-purple outside, deep purple inside; sepals 20-30mm x 5-8mm; petals slightly shorter, subulate, base orbicular, 5.5-9mm wide; lip 25-36mm long, bright ochre-red to deep brick-red, 2 divergent violet lamellae at base, centre with long, dense, whitish hairs; hypochile near kidney shaped to obcordate, 10-14mm x 15-22mm, lateral lobes blackish-purple, concealed inside hood or projecting slightly from it; epichile lanceolate, 14-25mm x 8-12mm, flat or with margins recurved, pendant to slightly turned down and backwards. **Variation** Little variation. Distinguished by its habit, large flowers with large bracts and very broad petals.

Flowering Season V-VI; late. **Habitat** Full sun to mid-shade on moist to wet, alkaline to acidic substrates, up to 1000m asl.

Distribution Eastern Pontics. The Black Sea coastlands, from Bolu (An) in the west to Abkhasis (Ro) in the east. The only representative of the genus in this area; sympatric only with *S. bergonii* at the western extremity of its range. Local but sometimes abundant in its stations. **Countries** An Ro. **Photos** An, Trabzon, 4.VI.1990. P. DELFORGE.

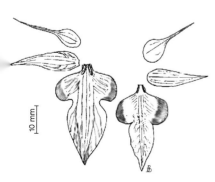

1. *S. orientalis* (Cr). 2. *S. feldwegiana* (An).

Serapias patmia
HIRTH & SPAETH

Etymology *patmia*: from [the island of] Patmos.
Type Ae, Patmos Island (1994). **Synonym**
S. cordigera subsp. *patmia* (HIRTH & SPAETH) KREUTZ.

Description Thickset, 3-15.5cm tall; stem
sometimes washed red, no red streaks at base; 4-6
basal leaves, narrowly lanceolate, 2-8cm x 0.5-
1.3cm, channelled-keeled, arched, uppermost 1-2
leaves bract-like, clasping, tinted red; bracts oval,
purple, 18-28mm x 8-15mm, equal to or slightly
longer than hood; inflorescence, short, dark and
dense, 2.5-6cm tall; 2-7 medium-sized flowers,
cross-pollinated; hood shiny deep red, veined
purple outside, dark blackish-red inside; sepals
14-17mm x 3-5mm, slightly keeled; petals
subulate, base orbicular, deep violet-purple, 3-
6mm wide; lip 15-22mm long, dark reddish-
brown to blackish-purple, 2 shiny, near parallel
blackish-purple lamellae at the base; hypochile
projecting slightly from hood, 7-10.5mm x 10-
16mm, base kidney-shaped, centre slightly paler,
with dense, crimson hairs; lateral lobes rounded,
projecting slightly from hood; epichile reddish-
brown, sometimes orange, oval-lanceolate, 9-
14mm x 4.5-7.5mm, pendant, pointing forwards,
rarely slightly turned down and back, flat, margins
curved forwards.

Flowering Season Late III-mid IV. **Habitat** Full
sun to mid-shade on dry, volcanic, alkaline to
slightly acidic substrates. Garrigue and scrub, up
to 200m asl. **Distribution** Endemic to an
archipelago of small islands south of Samos:
Patmos, Lipsi and Agathonisi. Rare and local.
Countries Ae. **Photos** Ae, Patmos, 14.IV.1992;
Agathonisi, 1.IV.1994. H. SPAETH.

Key to the *genus Serapias*

1   2 lamellae at base of lip, parallel or divergent
.... 2

1* single boss at base of lip, entire or ± deeply
grooved, channelled, sometimes divided into
2 contiguous bosses (*S. lingua* group, p. 270)
.... 23

2   petals orbicular at the base (*S. vomeracea*
group) 5

2* petals shaped like an elongated drop at the
base (*S. parviflora* group) 3

3   epichile bicoloured .... *S. nurrica*

3* epichile monochrome 4

4   flowers pale, pollinia yellow, generally
disintegrating onto the stigma .. *S. parviflora*

4* flower dark, pollinia green .... *S. politisii*

(continued on p. 258)

Serapias orientalis
(GREUTER) H. BAUMANN & KÜNKELE

Etymology *orientalis*: eastern. **Type** Cr, Lassithi (1972). **Synonyms** *S. orientalis* E. NELSON nom. illeg., *S. vomeracea* near sp. *orientalis* GREUTER, *S. orientalis* var. *cordigeroides* E. NELSON.

Description Robust, 10-30cm tall, isolated; base of stem and leaves sometimes marked with purple streaks; 4-8 (-10) leaves, lanceolate, 5-14cm x 1.2-2cm, channelled-keeled, arched, spreading to erect, upper 1-3 leaves smaller, near clasping, washed purple, upper leaf bract-like; bracts large, up to 52mm x 25mm, ± equal to hood and the same colour; inflorescence often pale, ovoid, dense, short; 3-8 (-10) flowers, rather large; hood horizontal to slightly erect, pale greenish-grey to, more rarely, lilac, veined dark crimson-green outside, sometimes washed red inside; sepals 20-32mm x 6-9mm, slightly keeled, long-coalescent; petals slightly shorter, subulate, base orbicular, violet-purple, 5-9mm wide; lip 28-40 (-48)mm long, often ochre and pale, brownish-yellow, salmon-pink, sometimes dark brick-red, with a prominent patch of dense, long, whitish hairs near tip of epichile and 2 parallel orange lamellae at the base; hypochile varied, (near) kidney-shaped to (ob) cordate, 12-19mm x 18-26 (-31)mm; lateral lobes crimson, often projecting slightly from hood; epichile arched and turned down and back, near heart-shaped to lanceolate, much narrower than hypochile, 14-26 (-33)mm x 9-14 (-20)mm, centre flat to convex, edges slightly undulate, reflexed; pollinia greenish. **Variation** Varied, rather distinctive in its thickset habit, often pale flowers and markedly hairy lip. In the north of the Peloponnese (Gr), forms transitional towards *S. vomeracea* are frequent. '*cordigeroides*': Lip dark violet-purple; here and there throughout the range (Photo A).

Flowering Season III-IV (-V); rather early.
Habitat Full sun to mid-shade on dry to damp, mostly alkaline substrates. Short, poor grassland, damp meadows, garrigue, terraces, olive groves, up to 1000m asl.

Distribution Eastern Mediterranean, centred on Crete and southern Greece; limits of range poorly-known due to confusion with closely related taxa. Rather widespread and sometimes abundant.

Countries Ae An Cr Cy Gr ?Ij ?Ls Tu.

Photos Gr, Messinia, 21.IV.1991; Cr, Lassithi, 7.IV.1982. P. DELFORGE.

257

Serapias orientalis

(GREUTER) H. BAUMANN & KÜNKELE

var. *siciliensis* (BARTOLO & PULVIRENTI) P. DELFORGE

Etymology *siciliensis*: from Sicily. **Type** Si, Caltanissetta (1972). **Basionym** *S. orientalis* subsp. *siciliensis* BARTOLO & PULVIRENTI.

Description As *S. orientalis*, but slightly more robust; leaves 10-16cm x 0.7-2cm; inflorescence dense, with 3-8 large flowers; lip 32-45mm long; hypochile with very pale centre and dark purple margins; epichile 20-31mm x 11-17mm.

Flowering Season III-IV. **Habitat** Full sun to mid-shade on dry to moist, alkaline to neutral substrates. Garrigue, terraces, olive groves, the margins of Cork Oak woodland, up to 1100m asl. **Distribution** Described as endemic to southern Sicily. Local and sometimes abundant. **Countries** ?It Si. **Photo A** Si, Catania, 22.IV.2000. P. DELFORGE. **Discussion** A critical taxon, which most often appears to fall within the normal range of variation of *S. orientalis* var. *orientalis*. Populations from Palermo appear to approach *S. neglecta*. There are, on the other hand, populations (sometimes large) in the south of peninsular Italy, notably Basilicata, that flower late, are more slender, and have slightly smaller flowers, which may be an isolated taxon close to *S. orientalis* var. *siciliensis*. **Photo B** It, Potenza, 24.V.2000. P. DELFORGE.

Key to the genus *Serapias*

(continued from p. 256)

5   epichile 4-7.5mm wide 6
5*   epichile 8-26mm wide 8

6   thickset, 3-15.5cm tall; inflorescence dense and short .... *S. patmia*
6*   slender, (5-) 11-50cm tall; inflorescence lax, elongated 7

7   epichile 6-11mm long .... *S. aphroditae*
7*   epichile 12-20mm long .... *S. bergonii*

8   epichile   entirely   pale   green .... *S. perez-chiscanoi*
8*   epichile pink, ochre or red, ± dark 9

9   flower solitary 10
9*   at least 2 flowers 11

10   bracts small, *c.* 25mm long, late flowering (V) .... *S. cycladum*
10* bracts large, up to 50mm long, flowering earlier (III-IV) .... *S. carica* var. *monantha*

(continued on next page)

Serapias carica
(H. BAUMANN & KÜNKELE) P. DELFORGE

Etymology *carica*: from Caria, a region in
ancient Anatolia. **Type** An, Mugla, Bodrum
(1989). **Basionym** *S. orientalis* subsp. *carica* H.
BAUMANN & KÜNKELE.

Description As *S. orientalis* but 9-35cm tall; base
of stem and leaves unmarked; 5-11 leaves,
lanceolate, 5-16cm long, often passing base of
inflorescence, upper 1-2 leaves smaller, bract-like;
bracts up to 50mm x 20mm, shorter than hood,
similarly coloured or often more crimson;
inflorescence, dark, ovoid, dense, often elongated;
(2-) 3-10 large flowers; hood horizontal, lilac-
grey, veined dark purple outside, purple inside;
sepals 21-34mm x 6-9mm, keeled, long-
coalescent; petals slightly shorter, base orbicular,
5.5-9.5mm wide; lip (see p. 246) 20-42 (-50)mm
long, dark violet-purple, with a prominent, dense
patch of long pale hairs extending almost to tip of
epichile, and 2 orange to blackish-purple
divergent lamellae at base; hypochile 10-18mm x
18-24 (-34)mm, lateral lobes blackish-purple,
often projecting slightly from hood; epichile
curved, turned down and back, lanceolate, 16-30
(-35)mm x 10-17 (-23)mm, centre flat to convex,
edges slightly undulate, reflexed. **Variation** Very
close to *S. apulica* and *S. orientalis*; distinct from
S. orientalis in its relatively early flowering, more
elongated inflorescence, and much darker and
slightly larger bracts and flowers.

Flowering Season III-IV; before *S. orientalis*.
Habitat As *S. orientalis*, up to 400m asl.
Distribution Central Aegean. Mediterranean coast
of Anatolia between Bodrum and Fethiye, the
eastern Aegean islands (Lesbos, Samos and
Rhodes) (Ae) and the Cyclades (Gr). Local but
sometimes rather abundant. **Countries** Ae An Gr.
Photos Gr, Kiklades, Amorgos, 16.IV.1997; Ae,
Lesvos, 14.IV.1991. P. DELFORGE.

Key to the genus *Serapias*

(continued from previous page)

11 base of lip with 2 parallel or almost parallel
    lamellae 12
11* base of lip with 2 clearly divergent lamellae
    17

12 bracts longer than hood 13
12* bracts ± equal to, or shorter than, hood 15

13 slender, (17-) 25-60cm tall ...... *S. vomeracea*
13* thickset, 12-28 (-34)cm tall 14

(continued on p. 261)

Serapias carica

(H. Baumann & Künkele) P. Delforge

var. *monantha* P. Delforge

Etymology *mon-:* single; *antha*: flower. **Type** Gr, Cyclades, Kimolos island (1999).

Description As *S. carica* but shorter, bearing a single flower.

Flowering Season, Habitat As *S. carica.*

Distribution Known from a few islands in the Cyclades (Andros, Tinos, the Milos group, Paros-Antiparos, Amorgos, Astypalea). Local and rare, often growing with var. *carica*, sometimes as isolated individuals, rarely in pure populations.

Countries Gr.

Photo A Gr, Kiklades, Kimolos (loc. typ.), 21.IV.1998. P. Delforge.

Serapias cycladum

H. Baumann & Künkele

Etymology *cycladum*: from the Cyclades. **Type** Gr, Andros island (1989). **Synonym** *S. orientalis* subsp. *cycladum* (H. Baumann & Künkele) Kreutz.

Description As *S. orientalis* but short, less than 20cm tall, with a single flower; bract ± 25mm long, shorter than hood; hood horizontal, grey outside; sepals ± 21mm long; petals slightly shorter, subulate, base orbicular, ± 9mm wide; lip ± 30mm long, pale and very hairy in centre; hypochile ± 22.5mm wide, lateral lobes of hypochile blackish-purple, projecting from hood; epichile lanceolate, ± 17mm x ± 10mm, pendant.

Flowering Season ?(IV-) V; rather late.

Habitat Full sun to mid-shade on dry, alkaline to acidic substrates, up to 560m asl.

Distribution Known from a few sites in the south of Andros island. Extremely rare and local. **Countries** Gr.

Photo B Gr, Kiklades, Andros, 10.IV.1994. P. Delforge.

Discussion A controversial taxon, whose only known measurements are from the type. For reasons unknown, *Serapias* with a single flower are frequent in the Cyclades, but mostly flower in April; those with pale flowers vary greatly in the size of the flowers, recalling hybrid swarms, and this does not match the description of *S. cycladum*. Those with dark flowers are better-defined and more frequent; they constitute a variety of *S. carica* (see above).

Serapias istriaca
M.L. Perko

Etymology *istriaca*: from Istria. **Type** Ju, Croatian, Istrian (1998). **Synonym** *S. vomeracea* subsp. *istriaca* (M.L. Perko) Kreutz.

Description Robust, (14-) 20-28 (-34)cm tall; base of stem and leaves unmarked; 4-7 leaves, lanceolate, 4-13cm x 0.6-1.8cm, channelled, often arched, upper 1-2 leaves bract-like, clasping; bracts up to 50mm x 22mm, colour as hood but longer; inflorescence ovoid, dense and then near lax; (1-) 3-6 (-7) large flowers; hood veined dark purple, crimson-lilac-grey outside, dark red inside; sepals 20-25mm long; petals slightly shorter, subulate, base orbicular, dark violet-purple, 5-8mm wide; lip rather elongated, 33-47mm long, dark red to dark violet-purple, with a dense patch of long, whitish to crimson hairs extending to centre of epichile and 2 near-parallel blackish-purple lamellae at base; hypochile rounded-rectangular to kidney-shaped, 11-14mm x 19-21mm, pale in centre; lateral lobes dark blackish-purple, projecting slightly from hood; epichile dark, pendant, shape varied, narrower than hypochile, lanceolate, 22-35mm x 10-14mm, flat to convex in centre; pollinia dark olive-green.

Flowering Season Mid V-mid VI; rather late.
Habitat Full sun on dry, calcareous substrates. Short grassland, abandoned cultivation and coastal garrigue, up to 100m asl.

Distribution Endemic to southern Istria and Losinj island (Croatia). Local and sometimes abundant. **Countries** Ju. **Photos** Ju, Hrvatska, Istria (loc. typ.), 28.V.2002. P. Delforge.

Key to the genus *Serapias* (continued from p. 259)

14   sepals 20-25mm long .... *S. istriaca*
14* sepals 26-34mm long .... *S. apulica*

15   bract much shorter than hood 16
15* bract ± equal to hood................. *S. orientalis*

16   lip pale .... *S. neglecta*
16* lip dark .... *S. ionica*

17   lateral lobes of hypochile (flattened) slightly covering base of epichile 18
17* lip otherwise 20

18   lip 21-30mm long .... *S. azorica*
18* lip 30-48mm long 19

(continued on p. 263)

Serapias apulica
(H. BAUMANN & KÜNKELE) P. DELFORGE

Etymology *apulica*: from Puglia. **Type** It, Foggia (1989). **Synonym** *S. orientalis* subsp. *apulica* E. NELSON nom. illeg., *S. orientalis* subsp. *apulica* H. BAUMANN & KÜNKELE.

Description Thickset and robust, 12-25 (-32)cm tall; base of stem and leaves unmarked; 5-7 leaves, lanceolate, 4-12cm x 0.7-2cm, channelled, lower leaves arched, upper 1-2 leaves bract-like, clasping; bracts up to 55mm x 24mm, colour as hood but longer; inflorescence dark, ovoid, dense then near lax; 2-6 (-7) large flowers; hood veined dark purple, crimson-lilac-grey outside, dark red inside, often horizontal; sepals 26-34mm x 5.5-8.5mm, long-coalescent; petals slightly shorter, subulate, base orbicular, dark violet-purple, 6-9.5mm wide; lip rather elongated, 30-45 (-52)mm long, orange-red, sometimes ochre, to dark violet-purple, with a dense patch of long, whitish to crimson hairs extending to centre of epichile and 2 near-parallel blackish-purple lamellae at base; hypochile rounded-rectangular to kidney-shaped, 12-16mm x 17-25mm; lateral lobes entirely concealed within hood; epichile pendant, shape varied, narrower than hypochile, near heart-shaped to lanceolate, 18-28 (-33)mm x 10-18 (-23)mm, flat to convex in centre, margins sometimes reflexed; pollinia olive-green.

Variation Varied. Range of variation in flower dimensions overlaps slightly with those of *S. orientalis*, *S. neglecta*, *S. vomeracea* and *S. cordigera*; populations intermediate with the last two species have been reported at the edge of the range.

Flowering Season III-IV (-V); rather early.

Habitat Full sun on dry to moist, often alkaline substrates. Short, poor grassland, coastal garrigue, terraces, olive groves, up to 300m asl.

Distribution Endemic to the coast of Puglia, from Mont Gargano to Tricase (Lecce). Local but abundant. **Countries** It.

Photos It, Brindisi, 30.III.1986. P. DELFORGE.

262

Serapias ionica
E. NELSON ex H. BAUMANN & KÜNKELE

Etymology *ionica*: from Ionia. **Type** Gr, Cephalonia island (1988). **Synonym** *S. neglecta* subsp. *ionica* E. NELSON.

Description As *S. neglecta* but 5-15 (-20)cm tall; 3-7 leaves, linear-lanceolate, strongly arched to spiral, spreading, 4-9cm long, upper 1-2 leaves bract-like; inflorescence dense, short, ovoid and then lax; 2-8 (-13) large flowers; hood pale lilac-grey, veined violet outside, dark red inside, often horizontal; sepals 19-28mm x 5-7mm, long-coalescent; petals slightly shorter, 4.5-6.5mm wide; lip 29-38mm long, rather dark brick-red, sometimes ochre, with long, dense, whitish hairs; hypochile 11.5-16mm x 17-21mm; lateral lobes projecting less from hood; epichile more narrowly heart-shaped, 16-27mm x 10-16mm, slightly covering the hypochile (flattened), margins strongly reflexed, tip turned down and back.

Flowering Season III-IV; early.

Habitat Full sun to mid-shade on moist to damp, alkaline substrates. Grassy places in garrigue and maquis, olive groves, open woodland of cypress and pine, up to 400m asl.

Distribution Range disjunct. The Ionian Islands (Gr: Corfu, Cephalonia, Zante) and islands of the Dalmatian Archipelago (Ju, Croatia: Korçula, Hvar, Brac). Very rare and local; threatened by agriculture and urbanisation of the coast.

Countries Gr Ju.

Photos Gr, Kefallinia, 4.IV.1991. P. DELFORGE.

Key to the genus *Serapias*

(continued from p. 261)

19	early flowering (III-IV) .... *S. cossyrensis*
19*	later flowering (IV-VI) .... *S. cordigera*

20	late flowering (V-VI) .... *S. feldwegiana*
20*	earlier flowering (III-IV) 21

21	base of stem and leaves heavily streaked reddish .... *S. lorenziana*
21*	base of stem and leaves without red streaks 22

22	inflorescence lax, with 3-6 (-10) flowers, epichile 8-12mm wide .... *S. levantina*
22*	inflorescence dense, with (3-) 5-10 flowers, epichile 10-17 (-23)mm broad .... *S. carica*

(continued on p. 267)

263

Serapias neglecta
DE NOTARIS

Etymology neglecta: neglected. **Type** It, Genoa region (1848). **Synonym** *S. cordigera* subsp. *neglecta* (DE NOTARIS) K. RICHTER.

Description Thickset, 10-30 (-35)cm tall; base of stem and leaves unmarked; 4-8 (near) erect leaves, arched, lanceolate, channelled, 5.5-11cm long; bracts 27-42mm long, colour as hood but shorter; inflorescence short and dense; 3-8 (-18) large, pale, scented flowers; hood greenish-grey to pale lilac-grey outside, obliquely erect; sepals 20-28mm x 6-7.5mm, free; petals subulate, 18-24mm x 6-8mm, base orbicular, purplish; lip 33-45 (-52)mm long, ochre, pink (often salmon-pink), brownish-red, usually pale, veined red, 2 parallel, rather well spaced, pale to dark lamellae at base, centre with a dense covering of long whitish hairs; hypochile 14-18.5mm x 22-26mm, lateral lobes often truncated, lightly coloured, projecting broadly from hood; epichile oval to heart-shaped, 20-28 (-33)mm x 15-21 (-24)mm, pendant to directed obliquely forwards, edges slightly undulate, reflexed.

Flowering Season III-V; rather early, before *S. cordigera.*

Habitat Full sun to mid-shade on moist to damp, alkaline to slightly acidic substrates. Damp meadows, garrigue, olive groves, open woodland, up to 600m asl.

Distribution Tyrrhenian. Coastal zones of the Var (Ga) to Elba (It), Corsica, Sardinia and perhaps the Palermo region (Si). Rather local and rather rare.

Countries Co Ga It Sa ?Si.

Photos Ga, Var, 19.IV.1973; It, Genova, 13.V.1988. P. DELFORGE.

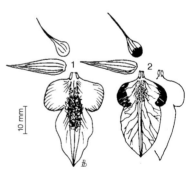

1. *S. neglecta* (Ga). 2. *S. ionica* (Gr).

Serapias atlantica

D. RÜCKBRODT & U. RÜCKBRODT

Etymology *atlantica*: of the Atlantic. **Type** Az, Pico (1994). **Synonyms** ? *S. azorica* SCHLECHTER, ?*S. cordigera* subsp. *azorica* (SCHLECHTER) SOÓ.

Description As *S. cordigera* but small, thickset, 8-25cm tall; inflorescence compact, with 3-12 flowers, smaller and often (± 30% of individuals) paler, pink, greenish-pink or yellowish-white; sepals 17.5-23.5mm x 5-7.5mm; lip 21-30mm long; petals with a more slender base, hypochile 8-13mm x (13-) 16-22mm, usually completely hidden within hood; epichile more transverse, 15-23.5mm x (10-) 12-18.5mm, not usually covering the hypochile when spread out.

Flowering Season Late V-VI.

Habitat Full sun on dry to moist, acidic, volcanic substrates. Rocky slopes, path-sides, meadows, in the trade-wind cloud zone, 400-1000m asl.

Distribution Endemic to the Azores; absent from Corvo, Flores and Santa Maria, extinct on Terceira and Faial. Extremely rare and local, threatened by the expansion of grazing; endangered on São Miguel. **Countries** Az.

Photos Az, Pico, 10 & 11.VI.2003. P. DELFORGE.

265

Serapias cordigera L.

Etymology *-gera*: bearing; *cordi-*: heart (shape of epichile). **Type*** Hs, Cadiz region (1763). **Synonym** *S. ovalis* L.C.M. RICHARD nom. illeg.

Description (9-) 15-40 (-55)cm tall; base of stem and leaves streaked red; 4-9 leaves, linear to lanceolate, 4-16cm long, channelled-keeled, upper 1-2 leaves bract-like, clasping; bracts broad, washed purple, slightly shorter than hood; inflorescence dark, ovoid, dense and short; 3-10 (-20) large flowers; hood veined purple, light grey outside, very dark red inside, often horizontal, tip slightly upturned; sepals 20-28 (-35)mm x 5-9mm, slightly keeled, long-coalescent; petals slightly shorter, subulate, base orbicular, dark violet-purple, 6-9mm wide; lip rather elongated, 30-42 (-48)mm long, reddish-brown to blackish-purple, with a dense area of long purplish hairs extending to at least centre of epichile and 2 divergent, shiny, blackish-purple lamellae at base; hypochile, 12-18mm x 18-26mm, base heart-shaped; lateral lobes rounded, projecting slightly from hood; epichile broadly heart-shaped to orbicular or lanceolate, usually covering a little of the hypochile (flattened) and almost as broad as it, (14-) 19-29 (-34)mm x (8-) 16-23 (-26)mm, pendant, flat to convex in centre, outer half often slightly turned down and back; pollinia dark green washed violet.

Variation Distinctive in its habit and the width of the epichile, but with a certain range of variation throughout the vast distribution, and there are sometimes intermediates with neighbouring species.

Flowering Season (III-) IV-VI.

Habitat Full sun to mid-shade on moist to damp substrates, mostly acidic, siliceous or schistose. Damp meadows, garrigue, scrub, terraces, open woodland, up to 1000m asl.

Distribution Mediterranean-Atlantic. East to Crete and Anatolia, west to Portugal and north to Finistère (Ga). Rather local but sometimes abundant in its stations.

Countries Ae Ag Al An Bl Co Cr Ga Gr Hs It Ju ?Li Lu Ma Me Sa Si Tn Tu.

Photos It, Potenza, 26.V.2000; Lecce, 26.IV.1991. P. DELFORGE.

Serapias cordigera L.

var. cretica (B. Baumann & H. Baumann) P. Delforge

Etymology *cretica*: from Crete. **Type** Cr, Panormos (1999). **Basionym** *S. cordigera* subsp. *cretica* B. Baumann & H. Baumann.

Description As *S. cordigera* but 14-22cm tall; 5-8 leaves, linear-lanceolate, 6.5-11.5cm x 0.6-1cm long; inflorescence dense, short; (1-) 2-7 medium-sized flowers; sepals 19-27mm x 5.8-7.2mm; base of petals orbicular, 6-7.7mm wide; lip 24-34mm long, red-brown to blackish-purple, dense patch of long, whitish hairs in centre; hypochile 9-13.5mm x 17-23mm, base kidney-shaped; lateral lobes rounded, projecting slightly from hood; epichile heart-shaped to lanceolate, narrower than, and rarely slightly covering, the hypochile (flattened), 17-24mm x 10-14mm, often undulate, pendant to turned down and back.

Flowering Season Late IV-V, rather late.

Habitat Full sun to mid-shade on dry to damp, acidic, siliceous or schistose substrates. Garrigue, scrub, terraces, damp meadows, up to 700m asl.

Distribution Thought to be endemic to Crete, but populations of similar plants have been reported from the central Aegean basin. Rare and local.

Countries Cr ?Gr.

Photos Cr, Rethimnon, 20.V.2004. A. Gévaudan

Key to the genus *Serapias*

(continued from p. 263)

23 basal boss blackish 24

23 basal boss lemon-yellow .... *S. stenopetala*

24 basal boss entire or lightly grooved and emarginate .... *S. lingua*

24* basal boss strongly grooved or channelled 25

25 epichile over 6mm wide 26

25* epichile 2.5-6mm wide 27

26 flowers dark .... *S. olbia*

26* flowers pale .... *S. elsae*

27 petals acuminate, with an oval base 2-4mm wide .... *S. strictiflora*

27* petals shaped like an elongated drop, 3.5-5.3mm wide at base .... *S. gregaria*

Serapias lorenziana
H. Baumann & Künkele

Etymology Named after R. Lorenz, contemporary German orchidologist. **Type** Ma, Mohammedia (1989). **Synonyms** *S. pseudocordigera* var. *mauritanica* E.G. Camus, Bergon & A. Camus, *S. cordigera* var. *mauritanica* (E.G. Camus, Bergon & A. Camus) E. Nelson, *S. cordigera* subsp. *lorenziana* (H. Baumann & Künkele) Kreutz.

Description As *S. cordigera* but thickset, averages 14cm tall; base of stem and leaves strongly marked with purple streaks; inflorescence few-flowered and compact and with 2-4 (-5) flowers, slightly smaller, paler brownish-red; bracts long-acuminate, much shorter than hood; hood (near) horizontal; sepals average 23.2mm long; lip averages 29mm long; hypochile averages 18.8mm wide, projecting slightly from hood; epichile much narrower, averaging 9.9mm x 16.8mm, not covering margins of hypochile (flattened).

Flowering Season Mid III-mid IV, early, ± 4 weeks before *S. cordigera*. **Habitat** Full sun on dry to moist, alkaline substrates. Garrigue and abandoned cultivation, up to 700m asl. **Distribution** Endemic to western Morocco. The Casablanca region to Oulmès and east to foothills of the Middle Atlas. Very rare and local. **Countries** Ma.

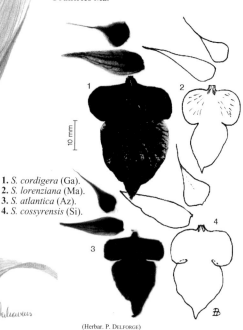

1. *S. cordigera* (Ga).
2. *S. lorenziana* (Ma).
3. *S. atlantica* (Az).
4. *S. cossyrensis* (Si).

10 mm

Watercolour M. Walravens.

(Herbar. P. Delforge)

268

Serapias cossyrensis
B. BAUMANN & H. BAUMANN

Etymology *cossyrensis*: from Cossyra (ancient name for the island of Pantelleria). **Type** Si, Pantelleria (1999). **Synonym** *S. cordigera* subsp. *cossyrensis* (B. BAUMANN & H. BAUMANN) KREUTZ.

Description As *S. cordigera* but leaves slightly broader and inflorescence shorter; lower bracts 25-36mm x 10-17mm, slightly longer than hood; 3-11 large flowers; hood pale purplish-grey outside; sepals 22-29mm long; base of petals 7-10mm wide; lip 30-35mm long, wine-red to pale reddish-brown, with a dense patch of long whitish hairs, extending to at least centre of epichile; hypochile 10-15mm x 20-25mm, entirely concealed by, or projecting slightly from, hood; epichile broadly heart-shaped, 18-25mm x 18-26mm, pendant, flat to convex.

Flowering Season
Late III-IV. **Habitat**
Full sun to mid-
shade on dry,
acidic, volcanic
substrates.
Garrigue, scrub,
open woodland,
120-820m asl.
Distribution
Endemic to the
island of
Pantelleria. Very
rare and local.
Countries Si.
Photos Si, Pantelleria,
23.IV.2004. C.A.J.
KREUTZ.

Watercolour M. WALRAVENS.

269

The *Serapias lingua* group

Characteristics More than 2 root-tubers, the younger stalked; base of lip with a shiny blackish-purple boss, entire or ± deeply grooved or channelled. A group of 6 species, several probably of hybrid origin.

Serapias lingua L.

Etymology *lingua*: tongue. **Type*** It, Naples (1753). **Synonyms** *S. laxiflora* var. *columnae* RCHB. fil., *S. parviflora* var. *columnae* (RCHB. fil.) ASCHERSON & GRÄBNER, *S. columnae* (RCHB. fil.) LOJACONO, *S. excavata* SCHLECHTER.

Description 10-30 (-50)cm tall, with (2-) 3-5 root-tubers, the younger ones long-stalked, often forming large groups; base of stem and leaves sometimes streaked red; 4-8 leaves, linear-lanceolate, erect, arched, channelled-keeled, 5-13cm long, upper 1-3 leaves bract-like; bracts shorter than hood, base green washed red, veined violet-purple; inflorescence elongated, lax; 2-6 (-8) medium-sized flowers, rather pale; hood horizontal, pale lilac-grey, veined violet-purple; sepals 13-25mm x 3-6mm, keeled, long-coalescent; petals slightly shorter, subulate, base orbicular, 1.5-4.5mm wide; lip 15-29mm long, colour varied, yellowish, fleshy- or salmon-pink, reddish, slightly hairy, with a shiny blackish-purple boss at base, entire, sometimes emarginate, often extended back into 2 fine ridges (see p. 244); hypochile kidney-shaped to obcordate, 8-15mm x 13-18mm, concave, centre pale; lateral lobes darker, crimson, often entirely concealed inside hood; epichile narrower than hypochile, lanceolate, 8-18mm x 4-12mm, projecting forwards, pendant or more rarely turned down and back; pollinia greenish-yellow; 2n=72.

Variation Characterised by the 'coffee bean like' boss at the base of the lip.

Flowering Season III-VI. **Habitat** Full sun to mid-shade on moist to wet, alkaline to acidic substrates. Short, poor grasslands, damp and marshy meadows, garrigue, scrub, open woodland, up to 1200m asl.

Distribution Mediterranean-Atlantic. East to Rhodes (Ae) and north to Morbihan (Ga). Rather widespread and often abundant.

Countries Ae Ag Al Bl Co Cr Ga Gr Hs It Ju Lu Ma Me Sa Si Tn. **Photos** Gr, Lakonia, 18.IV.1991. P. DELFORGE.

Note For details of pollination see p. 245.

Serapias stenopetala
MAIRE & STEPHENSON

Etymology *-petala*: with petals; *steno-*: narrow.
Type Ag, Bône (Annaba, wilaya El Tarf) (1930).
Synonym *S. lingua* subsp. *stenopetala* (MAIRE & STEPHENSON) MAIRE.

Description Slender, 25-30cm tall, with (2-) 3 root-tubers, the younger long-stalked; base of stem and leaves sometimes streaked red; bracts erect, shorter or equal to hood and similarly coloured, lemon-yellow to greenish-yellow; inflorescence very short, dense; 2-3 (-5) medium-sized flowers, usually entirely lemon-yellow; hood horizontal to near erect, lemon-yellow; sepals 20-21mm x 4-5mm, keeled, coalescent to tip; petals slightly shorter, base oval, 1-3mm wide, lemon-yellow; lip 25-30mm long, basal boss always shiny lemon-yellow, entire, emarginate, ± deeply channelled; hypochile kidney-shaped, 7-11mm x 15-20mm, concave, centre yellowish, sometimes pubescent; lateral lobes concolourous or rarely washed pale purple, entirely hidden inside hood; epichile much narrower than hypochile, lanceolate, 12-22mm x 4-9mm, forward-projecting, lemon-yellow, rarely ± strongly washed pale purple and then salmon pink.

Flowering Season IV-VI, late.

Habitat Full sun on wet, acidic substrates. Peaty places in woodland with Cork Oak (*Quercus suber*), their edges and degraded areas, wadi banks, ditches.

Distribution The east coast of Algeria. Very rare and local, seriously threatened by grazing and the cultivation of its habitats.

Countries Ag.

Photos Ag, wilaya El Tarf, El Frin. 3.V.2003, 7.V.2004, 11.VI.2003. G. DE BÉLAIR.

271

Serapias olbia
VERGUIN

Etymology *Olbia*: ancient Greek colony, now Hyères (Var). **Type** Ga, Var (1907).

Description 10-30cm tall, with 3-4 root-tubers, the younger stalked; base of stem and leaves often streaked purple; 5-7 leaves, lanceolate, erect, arched, 4-10cm long, upper 1-3 leaves bract-like; bracts much shorter than hood or sometimes equal to it, concolourous or more purple; inflorescence short, near lax to lax; 2-4 (-5) medium-sized flowers; hood horizontal, pale lilac-grey, veined violet outside, blackish-purple inside; sepals 19-25mm x 5.5-7.5mm, long-coalescent; petals slightly shorter, subulate, base orbicular, 5.5-7mm wide; lip 20-31mm long, deep brick-red to blackish-purple, dense purplish hairs extending almost to tip of epichile and a shiny blackish-purple boss at base, deeply grooved, sometimes divided into 2 contiguous bosses; hypochile kidney-shaped to obcordate, 11.5-15mm x 13-21mm, lateral lobes sometimes truncated, projecting slightly from hood; epichile oval to lanceolate, 12-20mm x 6-9.5mm, convex, often turned down and back against hypochile, rarely pendant; pollinia yellow to dark green.

Variation Rather distinct in the habit, length and colour of the flowers, but varied and sometimes difficult to separate from neighbouring taxa and occasional hybrids.

Flowering Season IV-V.

Habitat Full sun on dry to damp, acidic substrates, often siliceous or sandy. Damp dune slacks, meadows and coastal garrigue, up to 200m asl.

Distribution The coast of Var and Alpes-Maritimes (Ga); reports from Corsica and Asturias (Hs) probably refer respectively to occasional hybrids or to hybrid swarms. Very rare and local.

Countries Ga.

Photos Ga, Var, 22.V.1982; 16.IV.1999. P. DELFORGE.

Discussion Probably of hybrid origin (*S. lingua* × *S. cordigera*), but may, like *S. strictiflora*, show primitive characteristics that are close to the common ancestor of the 2 principal radiations, the *S. lingua* group on the one hand and the bi-lamellate *Serapias* on the other.

Serapias gregaria
GODFERY

Etymology *gregaria*: gregarious (an allusion to the groups of plants formed by this species). **Type** Ga, Var (1921). **Synonyms** *S. strictiflora* subsp. *gregaria* (GODFERY) KREUTZ, *S. strictiflora* auct. non WELWITSCH ex VEIGA, *S. nurrica* subsp. *argensii* M. GERBAUD & O. GERBAUD.

Description As *S. olbia* but 15-30cm tall; 5-9 leaves; bracts large, up to 57mm long, clearly longer than hood; inflorescence dense to near lax; 2-5 (-6) flowers; hood near horizontal to obliquely erect; sepals 20-26mm x 3.4-5.5mm; petals drop-shaped but less attenuated, similar to those of *S. parviflora*, base rounded, 3.5-5.3mm wide; lip 18-27mm long; hypochile kidney-shaped to obcordate, 9-13.5mm x 12-17.5mm, lateral lobes entirely concealed inside hood; epichile narrowly but clearly lanceolate, 11-18mm x 3.4-5.5mm, flat to convex, pendant to turned down and back against the hypochile. *'argensii'*: a dozen plants in a population of *S. gregaria* that had bleached margins to the epichile; this clone has probably disappeared.

Flowering Season Late IV-V. **Habitat** Full sun on dry to moist, alkaline to neutral substrates. Grasslands and garrigue, up to 200m asl.

Distribution Var and probably Alpes-Maritimes, but less coastal than *S. olbia* (Ga). Very rare and local. **Countries** Ga. **Photos** Ga, Var, 19.IV.1999. P. DELFORGE.

Discussion A controversial taxon, often ignored or thought either to comprise unstable hybrid swarms or to fall within the range of variation of *S. olbia*. It is, however, distinct from *S. olbia* in a number of morphological characteristics (notably the size of the bracts and the shape of the lip and petals), showing an approach to *S. parviflora*. For the same reasons, this taxon cannot be assimilated into *S. strictiflora*, a species that has a far narrower and less lanceolate epichile and narrower and more subulate petals, and whose range, at the closest, lies in the extreme south of the Iberian Peninsula, in the Mediterranean-Atlantic zone 1,200km from the sites in Var.

Petals of *S. parviflora* (Lu), *S. gregaria* (Ga), *S. strictiflora* (Lu) and *S. olbia* (Ga). The attenuated, drop-shaped petal of *S. gregaria* approaches *S. parviflora*, unlike *S. strictiflora* and *S. olbida*.

(Herbar. P. DELFORGE)

273

Serapias strictiflora
WELWITSCH ex VEIGA

Etymology *strictiflora*: with narrow flowers.
Type Lu, Extremadura (1886). **Synonyms** *S. stricta* WELWITSCH ex WOODS, *S. lingua* var. *durieui* RCHB. fil., *S. mauretanica* SCHLECHTER, *S. gracilis* KREUTZ, *S. strictiflora* var. *distenta* H. PRESSER.

Description Spindly, 10-35 (-45)cm tall, with 2-3 long-stalked root-tubers, often forming groups; 5-7 leaves, linear-lanceolate, erect, 4-14cm long, lower leaves arched, erect, sometimes reaching base of inflorescence, upper 1-2 leaves bract-like; bracts 17-35mm x 4-11mm, a little more purple than hood and no longer; inflorescence elongated, lax; 1-4 (-5) small flowers; hood ± horizontal, acuminate, pale lilac-grey washed purple, veined deep violet-purple outside, blackish-purple inside; sepals 16-25mm x 2.5-5mm, keeled, long-coalescent; petals subulate, base oval, 2-4mm wide; lip 16-30mm long, dark red to dark blackish-purple, with a dense patch of long, pale hairs extending to centre of epichile and a shiny blackish-purple boss at base, emarginate, deeply channelled, the margins surmounted by 2 ridges; hypochile rectangular-near rounded to near kidney-shaped, 7-13mm x 7.5-14mm; lateral lobes almost entirely concealed inside hood; epichile much narrower than hypochile, very narrowly lanceolate to, more often, very narrowly triangular, 9-16 (-19)mm x 2.5-4.5 (-6)mm, straight or curved backwards, pendant or, more rarely, bent under the hypochile.

Variation Distinct in its habit and in its very narrow epichile, very often with straight margins.

Flowering Season (III-) IV-V; rather early.

Habitat Full sun to mid-shade on dry to damp, calcareous or acidic substrates. Short, poor grassland, damp meadows, garrigue, maquis, open woodland, up to 900m asl.

Distribution Mediterranean-Atlantic. Eastern Algeria to Morocco, southern Portugal and Andalucia (Cadiz). Local but often abundant. Reports from France refer to *S. gregaria*.

Countries Ag Hs Lu Ma.

Photos Lu, Algarve, 6.IV.1990. P. DELFORGE.

Discussion Considered to be of hybrid origin, involving *S. lingua*, to which it is close, and *S. parviflora*, but it could also be a species showing primitive characters, like *S. olbia* (see Discussion, p. 272).

Serapias elsae
P. Delforge

Etymology Named after Elsa Delforge, daughter of the author. **Type** Lu, Extremadura (2004). **Synonyms** *S. lingua* subsp. *elsae* (P. Delforge) Kreutz, *S. stenopetala* auct. non Maire & Stephenson.

Description Slender, 20-40cm tall; base of stem and leaves sometimes streaked red; 4-6 leaves, linear-lanceolate, erect, arched, channelled-keeled, 5-11cm long, upper 1-2 leaves bract-like; bracts up to 50mm long, longer than hood but similarly coloured; inflorescence elongated, lax; 3-8 (-13) medium-sized flowers, rather pale; hood obliquely erect, pale grey washed green, veined purple outside, red inside; sepals 14-21mm x 3-6mm, keeled, long-coalescent; petals slightly shorter, subulate, base oval, 2.5-5mm wide, ochre to dark red; lip 20-30mm long, with a patch of dense whitish hairs extending almost to centre of epichile and a shiny blackish-purple boss at base, entire, emarginate, ± deeply channelled; hypochile kidney-shaped, 7-14mm x 12-32mm, concave, centre yellowish to pinkish; lateral lobes slightly darker, entirely concealed inside hood; epichile narrower than hypochile, lanceolate, 14-21mm x 6-12mm, pendant, yellowish to pale ochre-red.

Flowering Season III-V. **Habitat** As *S. strictiflora.*

Distribution Central Portugal, southern Spain. Very local but sometimes abundant in its stations.

Countries Hs Lu.

Photos Lu, Extremadura (loc. typ.), 4.IV.1990; Hs, Badajoz, 1.IV.1990. P. Delforge.

Discussion Not a variant of *S. lingua*. Although it is intermediate between *S. lingua* and *S. strictiflora*, it has autonomy, stability, and its own peculiar characters that suggest that it is not an occasional hybrid between these 2 species.

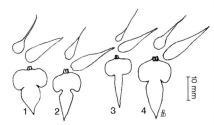

1. *S. olbia* (Ga). 2. *S. gregaria* (Ga).
3. *S. strictiflora* (Lu). 4. *S. elsae* (Lu).

275

Anacamptis
L.C.M.Richard 1818

Etymology *anacamptos*: bent back (an allusion to the position of the pollinia). **Characteristics** Monospecific genus, close to *Orchis* (see Discussion of that genus, p. 278); but distinguished by the 2 ridges at the base of the lip and the single retinacle bearing both pollinia.

Anacamptis pyramidalis
(L.) L.C.M. Richard

Etymology pyramidalis: pyramidal (inflorescence) **Type*** Br, Oxford (1753). **Synonyms** *A. pyramidalis* var. *brachystachys* (D'Urville) Boissier, *A. brachystachys* Nyman, *A. pyramidalis* var. *tanayensis* Chenevard, *A. pyramidalis* var. *sanguinea* (Druce) Kreutz, *A. tanayensis* (Chenevard) Soó, *A. urvilleana* Sommier & Gatto.

Description Slender, 20-60 (-80)cm tall; 4-10 leaves, lower erect, linear-lanceolate, pointed, 8-25cm x 0.7-2cm, upper leaves almost bract-like; bracts often purplish, longer than ovary; inflorescence dense, initially conical then oblong, 3-12cm tall; flowers rather small, pink to pale or dark lilac, rarely white or red; sepals and petals oval-lanceolate, pointed, slightly keeled; lateral sepals spreading, 4-8mm long, dorsal sepal near erect, connivent with petals in a loose hood, 3.5-6mm long; lip wedge-shaped, 3-lobed, 6-9mm long, with 2 prominent, near parallel ridges at base; lobes near equal, oblong to ovoid, median lobe slightly longer and often narrower than laterals; spur filiform, spindly, curved downwards, 10-16mm long; 2n=36, 54, 72.

Flowering Season (III-) IV-VII. **Habitat** Full sun on calcareous substrates, usually dry. Short grassland, garrigue, up to 2000m asl. **Distribution** Mediterranean-Atlantic. Morocco to the Caspian Sea and the Baltic islands. Widespread and sometimes abundant. **Countries** Ae Ag Al An Au Be Bl Br Bu Co Cr Cy Cz Da Ga Ge Gr Hb He Ho Hu Hs Ij It Ju Ls Lu Lx Ma Me Pb Po Rm Ro Sa Si Tn Tu. **Photos** Lu, Extremadura, 30.III.1990; Be, Hainaut, 29.VI.1991. P. Delforge.

Notes The flowers are pollinated by a variety of butterflies and moths in a very precise mechanism. The proboscis is directed towards the entrance of the spur by the basal ridges and the pollinia are attached to the proboscis by the single retinacle while the insect is drinking nectar. Hybridises very rarely with a few species of *Orchis* (× *Anacamptorchis*), extremely rarely with *Serapias* and *Gymnadenia*, and doubtfully with *Dactylorhiza* and *Platanthera*.

Variation Distinctive. Varies in size, shape of inflorescence and degree of indentation and colour of lip. Several variants have been named which, on

account of numerous intergrades, probably have little evolutionary significance.

'urvilleana': Rather early, with small pale flowers; 2n=36 (Me Cr); probably inseparable from the following.

'brachystachys': Inflorescence near globular, rather lax, flowers pale; scattered in Mediterranean region, mostly in the east, but also Portugal; 2n= ?54. **Photo A** Gr, Kiklades, Amorgos, 27.IV.1997. P. DELFORGE.

'tanayensis': Inflorescence dense; flowers bright red; median lobe of lip prominent, broad and protuberant; spur rather short; frequent above 1300m in the Alps; also reported from the Carpathians (also *'sanguinea'* a red-flowered morph from Ireland). **Photo B** Ga, Haute-Savoie, 23.VII.1992. P. DELFORGE.

Anacamptis pyramidalis (L.) L.C.M. RICHARD
var. *nivea* P. DELFORGE

Etymology *nivea*: snow-white. **Type** Gr, Etolia and Acarnania (2000).

Description Flowers pure white; basal ridges reduced, formed by 2 sinuous lamellae; spur very short and fine, 5-10mm long. Forms stable, homogenous populations in Etolia and Acarnania (Gr), where it seems to be completely isolated from var. *pyramidalis* (which is, nevertheless, syntopic), and in southern peninsular Italy and Dalmatia (Ju), where intermediates are more frequent. **Photo C** (below): Gr, Etolia-Akarnania, 23.IV.1991. P. DELFORGE.

277

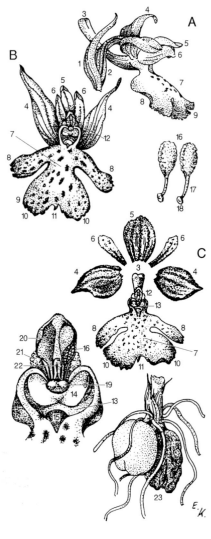

Orchis L. 1753

Etymology *orchis*: testicle (an allusion to the shape of the root-tubers). **Characteristics** 2 (-3) root-tubers, entire, ovoid to ellipsoid; a single leaf sheathing the emerging inflorescence (see Fig. 7, p. 172); bracts usually membranous and coloured; lateral sepals spreading, erect, or connivent with dorsal sepal and petals to form a hood; lip orientated downwards, entire or lobed, usually with a spur; column short; 2 retinacles enclosed within a 2-lobed bursicle; ovary sessile, twisted; 2n= 32, 36, 38, 40. 42, 80, 84.

Discussion A Euro-Mediterranean genus, containing 7 groups and 60 species in this guide. Present from Madeira and the Canaries in the west to the Caucasus and Iran in the east, and to northern Scandinavia, the genus *Orchis* occupies a central position within the subtribe Serapiadinae and has been the subject of various taxonomic treatments. Notably, until recently the genera *Coeloglossum*, *Dactylorhiza* and *Himantoglossum* were not treated as distinct from it and conversely component parts are still periodically removed from *Orchis* and treated as distinct genera.

Unfortunately, recent investigative techniques have yielded contradictory results that still do not permit the demarcation of confirmed monophyletic groups. For example, chemical analysis of floral pigments suggests that the *Orchis coriophora* group forms a distinct genus, with primitive characters in this respect (= *Anteriorchis* E. Klein & D. Strack), but this is contradicted by caryological and molecular analyses. Depending on the techniques used and the statistical treatment of the results, molecular and genetic analyses place *Anacamptis pyramidalis* either in the *Orchis morio* group (whose members can therefore be considered as members of the genus *Anacamptis*), or within the genus *Serapias*. These contradictory results are even sometimes obtained using the same DNA sequences and the same procedures.

These uncertainties encourage, provisionally, the conservation of *Anacamptis* as a mono-specific genus and the retention in *Orchis* of the 4 lineages formed by the groups *O. palustris-morio-coriophora-papilionacea* (2n=36, 38, 42), as well as the monophyletic groups *O. mascula*, *O. militaris* (with *Aceras*) and *O. tridentata* (with *Neotinea*), which have the chromosome number 2n=40, 42, 80, 84.

In this presentation, a contribution to a stable nomenclature, the genus *Orchis* is paraphyletic. It is very likely that at least the genus *Serapias* and probably also *Ophrys* would have to be returned to *Orchis* for it to be monophyletic.

The *Orchis palustris* group, with leaf characteristics and an ecology similar to those of *Dactylorhiza* constitutes, with the *Orchis morio*

Figure 9. A. *Orchis mascula*. B. *Orchis tridentata*. C. *Orchis purpurea*. **1**. Bract. **2**. Ovary. **3**. Spur. **4**. Lateral sepal. **5**. Dorsal sepal. **6**. Petal. **7**. Lip. **8**. Lateral lobe of lip. **9**. Median lobe of lip. **10**. Secondary lobes of median lobe of lip. **11**. Appendage. **12**. Column. **13**. Stigmatic cavity. **14**. Stigma. **15**. Entrance to spur. **16**. Pollinium. **17**. Caudicle. **18**. Viscidium. **19**. Bursicle. **20**. Loculus or theca enclosing a pollinium. **21**. Auricle. **22**. Median lobe of rostellum. **23**. Underground parts.

and *O. papilionacea* groups, a primary clade from which may derive, via aneuploidy, the *O. coriophora* group (2n=38); species from this assemblage hybridise rather frequently with each other and with the genera *Serapias*, *Anacamptis*, and, exceptionally, with species from the *Dactylorhiza sambucina* group.

A second clade, formed by the *Orchis mascula-O. spitzelii* group, perhaps mono-phyletic, contains species with 2n=(40) 42 (80) chromosomes, spreading lateral sepals and a 3-lobed lip with a reduced median lobe. These species, which do not seem to hybridise with other *Orchis* species, appear to be close to *Himantoglossum*, but without the support of intergeneric hybrids or molecular analyses, the proximity suggested by their morphology cannot be confirmed. The remaining 2 clades, the monophyletic *O. militaris* and *Orchis tridentata* groups (the latter the most derived), are very isolated; their members have the sepals and petals connivent in a hood and a lip in which the median lobe is deeply cut to form a quasi-anthropomorphic figure.

Hypochromy in the genus *Orchis*

Hypochromatic individuals are known for all species of *Orchis*. Pure white flowers are regular in large populations of *O. quadripunctata*, *O. morio* or *O. fragrans* (the hood is still veined with green in the latter 2 species). The phenomenon is rarer in the *O. mascula* and *O. papilionacea* groups. In the *O. palustris* group, hypochromy produces individuals with pink flowers, rarely white. In the *O. militaris* group, hypochromatic individuals are rather rare. They have a white lip with greenish-yellow markings, similarly the hood, and are very spectacular in *O. purpurea*.

Pollination in *Orchis*

There are apparently no self-pollinating species in this genus. The methods by which insects are attracted are diverse and often still poorly known. Only the mechanism in the *O. coriophora* group is obvious as the flowers are strongly scented and abundantly nectariferous; many species of insect visit assiduously to feed and 90% of ovaries are fertilised. By contrast, the remaining *Orchis* lack nectar and have nothing to offer insects. How, then, are they attracted? It seems that there are two different types of mechanism: predominantly visual, sometimes replaced by tactile stimulants, and predominantly olfactory.

Orchis pinetorum hypochromatic. **Photo A**: An, Eskisehir, 30.V.1990. P. DELFORGE.
In *Orchis militaris*, the tufts of dark hairs on the lip stimulate the underside of the abdomen of various bees and bumblebees, and they position themselves on the lip with their heads directed towards the entrance of the spur.
Photo B: Ho, Zuid-Limburg, 15.VI.1991. P. DELFORGE.

Some *Orchis*, for example, *O. mascula* and *O. morio*, mimic nectariferous flowers (spur, landing platform, markings), on the whole recalling the flowers of Lamiaceae or Fabaceae. Inexperienced bees, just recently emerged from the pupa, visit the orchid but rapidly lose interest in favour of truly nectariferous species. The imitation may be associated with a particular 'model', as has been described for *Orchis pallens* (see p. 327) and *O. israelitica* (see p. 294); the orchid 'mimic' is visited far more often in the presence of the 'model' than when it is absent. The combination of colours in the flower is, in certain cases, perhaps the principal factor triggering a visit. *O. ustulata*, for example, is assiduously visited by *Echinomyia magnicornis* Zett., a rather large fly (Tachinidae) that seems to be attracted by the colour of the hood. It settles, head downwards, on the buds at the tip of the spike. Its legs have long sensory hairs for detecting sweet liquids and these touch the tufts of papillae on the lip of recently open flowers. This leads to the following reaction: the insect pushes aside the hood of the flower and plunges its proboscis towards the mouth of the spur, whose structure is finely adapted to its mouthparts. Although there is no nectar to stimulate it, the fly continues its quest, visiting other flowers and carrying off pollinia. The adaptation of *Orchis ustulata* to its pollinator is so finely tuned that it does not attract any other insect, which may explain its isolation within the genus.

Orchis papilionacea (see p. 296) seems to benefit from an olfactory lure in addition to its floral mimicry, as males of a solitary bee mark the lip with pheromones to indicate a swarming site. Other lures, predominantly olfactory and originating with the plant, are utilised by *O. galilaea*, whose musky scent attracts only males of the social bee *Halictus marginatus*, even in the presence of females. Settled on the lip, the male adopts a precopulatory position and plunges its head into the entrance of the spur. The scent of the flower, which probably mimics the female's pheromones, is so strongly attractive to the male that visual stimuli are incidental: *Orchis galilaea* shows great variation in its coloration. This kind of lure, also utilised by *O. punctulata*, seems to herald further evolution which has led to the development of pseudocopulation in the genus *Ophrys*.

Hybrids in the genus *Orchis*

There are relatively few hybrids between *Orchis*. They are usually not difficult to determine. Their intermediate coloration is usually the first criterion in their detection. The identification should, of course, be corroborated by the presence of other morphologically intermediate characteristics.

Orchis pallens × *O. spitzelii* = *O.* × *klopfensteiniae* P. DELFORGE. **Photo** Ga, Isère, 18.VI.1984. P. DELFORGE.

Key to subgroups within the genus *Orchis*

1 leaves inserted along the length of the stem .... *O. palustris* group (p. 281)
1* leaves in a basal rosette, upper leaves long-clasping 2

2 sepals and petals forming a hood, ± compact 3
2* later sepals near spreading to vertically erect .... *Orchis mascula* group (p. 306)

3 lip entire, orbicular, fan-shaped .... *O. papilionacea* group (p. 296)
3* lip 3-lobed 4

4 median lobe of lip entire, longer than lateral lobes .... *O. coriophora* group (p. 302)
4* median lobe emarginate or 2-lobed 5

5 median lobe emarginate or weakly 2-lobed, not prominent, ± as long as lateral lobes .. *O. morio* group (p. 287)
5* median lobe clearly 2-lobed, prominent, much longer than lateral lobes 6

6 flowers usually large; median lobe of lip divided into 2 secondary lobes, rather similar to lateral lobes and separated by a prominent tooth, lip 'anthropomorphic', resembling a puppet.................. *O. militaris* group (p. 330)
6* flowers usually small; median lobe divided into 2 secondary lobes, but these rarely separated by a small tooth .... *O. tridentata* group (p. 341)

The *Orchis palustris* group

Characteristics Moisture-loving plants; leaves narrow, unmarked, arranged along the length of the stem rather than in a basal rosette; bracts leaf-like.

Discussion A group composed of taxa whose status is controversial. It is less and less considered to comprise 1-2 polytypic species, rather several species whose contact zones contain large intermediate populations. A Eurasian group, monophyletic, with 5 species, close to the common ancestor of *Orchis-Dactylorhiza* and probably separated from other *Orchis* when colonising very moist habitats. Arranged into 2 subgroups of which the most derived is characterised by the reduction of the median lobe of the lip (*O. laxiflora*). Following on from the frequency of hybrids, its closest relationships are with the *O. morio* and *O. coriophora* groups and, less clearly, the *O. papilionacea* group as well as the genus *Serapias* (see × *Orchiserapias*, p. 27). Hybrids with other *Orchis* species or with *Anacamptis* are extremely rare; those with *Dactylorhiza* are mostly dubious.

Orchis robusta
(STEPHENSON) GÖLZ & H.R. REINHARD

Etymology *robusta*: robust, solid. **Type** Ag, the Algiers region (1931). **Synonyms** *O. palustris* var. *robusta* STEPHENSON, *O. laxiflora* subsp. *robusta* (STEPHENSON) SUNDERMANN, *O. palustris* subsp. *robusta* (STEPHENSON) KREUTZ, *Anacamptis palustris* subsp. *robusta* (STEPHENSON) R.M. BATEMAN, PRIDGEON & M.W. CHASE, *A. robusta* (STEPHENSON) R.M. BATEMAN.

Description As *O. palustris* but more robust, up to 90cm tall; leaves larger, up to 30cm x 4.5cm; bracts longer than ovary; flowers large, very pale pink to strongly magenta; lip 13-20mm x 16-23mm, spreading to slightly convex, densely streaked and dotted lilac or pale purple, centre pale, sometimes yellowish, margins undulate; median lobe emarginate, slightly longer than lateral lobes; spur 9-14mm long, conical, rather spindly, horizontal, straight to slightly curved downwards.

Flowering Season III-IV (-V). **Habitat** As *O. palustris*, but only in the plains.

Distribution Reported from Majorca, the Algiers region and a site in Morocco (Chaonia marshes), and also Crete. Very rare and local, greatly threatened by habitat destruction. **Countries** Ag Bl Cr Ma. **Photos** Bl, Mallorca, 9.IV.1985. P. DELFORGE (see also p. 286). **Note** This taxon probably groups together a heterogeneous assemblage of robust, large-flowered individuals.

Orchis palustris
JACQUIN

Etymology *palustris*: from marshes. **Type** Ge, Himberg (1786). **Synonyms** *O. laxiflora* subsp. *palustris* (JACQUIN) BONNIER & LAYENS, *Anacamptis palustris* (JACQUIN) R.M. BATEMAN, PRIDGEON & M.W. CHASE, *Orchis michaelis* SENNEN, *O. mediterranea* GUSSONE.

Description Slender, 20-60cm tall; 3-5 leaves arranged along the stem, sheathing, near erect to erect, linear-lanceolate, keeled, 7-15cm x 1-2.5cm, unmarked, upper leaf bract-like; bracts leaf-like, washed red, ± equal to ovary; inflorescence elongated, dense to near lax, near ovoid, becoming near cylindrical; flowers rather large, pink or pale purple to dark magenta; lateral sepals oval, elongated, 7-12mm x 3-5.5mm, spreading horizontally to near erect and directed forwards; petals near equal, forming a hood with dorsal sepal; lip 3-lobed, broadly oboval to obcordate, 9-15mm x 9-18mm, spreading, base whitish, contracted into 2 attenuated ridges, separated by a broad groove, centre convex, pale, densely marked with purplish streaks and dots; lateral lobes rounded, sometimes crenate, recurved forwards; median lobe slightly longer than lateral lobes, spatulate, emarginate; spur 10-18mm long, rather thick, cylindrical, tip rounded, near horizontal to very slightly ascendant, straight to slightly curved; 2n=36, 42.

Variation Rather diverse. *'mediterranea'*: More robust, larger in all parts, up to 100cm tall, with pale flowers; probably lacking evolutionary significance, described from Calabria (It) but also reported from Sicily, Lesbos (Ae) and Catalonia (Ga, Hs = *O. michaelis*); records from northern Greece probably refer to populations intermediate between *O. palustris* and *O. elegans*. For reports from Crete, see *O. robusta*.

Flowering Season IV-VII.

Habitat Full sun on damp to wet, basic, sometimes saline substrates. Calcareous dune slacks, marshy meadows, fens, up to 1800m asl.

Distribution Euro-Mediterranean. Range poorly known due to confusion with closely related taxa. North to Gotland (Su), south to Andalusia (Hs) and northern Tunisia and east to at least central Anatolia. Local but often abundant in its stations; declining dramatically due to habitat destruction. **Countries** Ae Al An Au †Be Bu Co Cr Cz Ga Ge Gr He Hs Hu It Ju No ?Ro Si Su Tn.

Photos An, Malatya, 28.V.1990; Ga, Hérault, 7.VI.1986. P. DELFORGE (see also p. 286).

Orchis elegans

HEUFFEL

Etymology *elegans*: delicate, refined. **Type** Ju, Zaidóvár (1835). **Synonyms** *O. laxiflora* var. *elegans* (HEUFFEL) ASCHERSON & GRÄBNER, *O. laxiflora* subsp. *elegans* (HEUFFEL) SOÓ, *O. palustris* subsp. *elegans* (HEUFFEL) NYÁRADY, *Anacamptis palustris* subsp. *elegans* (HEUFFEL) R.M. BATEMAN, PRIDGEON & M.W. CHASE.

Description As *O. palustris* but 50-80cm tall; leaves larger, 10-25cm x 1.5-3cm; bracts longer than ovary; flowers average darker; sepals slightly shorter and more pointed; lip near entire or obscurely 3-lobed, spreading, almost flat, 9-13mm x 8-15mm, centre less spotted; lateral lobes narrower; median lobe as long as, or slightly longer than, lateral lobes; spur near cylindrical, ascendant, 12-18mm long.

Flowering Season IV-VI. **Habitat** As *O. palustris*, but substrates may be acidic.

Distribution Poorly known, probably centred on the northern Balkans. Local but sometimes abundant in its stations. **Countries** ?An Bu ?Gr Hu Ju Rm Ro ?Tu.

Photos Ju, Slovenia, 28.V.1988. C.A.J. KREUTZ (see also p. 286).

Key to the *Orchis palustris* group

1   median lobe of lip longer than lateral lobes or lip near entire 2

1*   median lobe of lip much shorter than lateral lobes or absent (*O. laxiflora* subgroup) 5

2   lip near entire or with median lobe hardly distinct .... *O. elegans*

2*   lip 3-lobed 3

3   spur conical, shorter than lip ....*O. robusta*

3*   spur (near) cylindrical, as long as, or longer than, lip 4

4   inflorescence dense to near lax, spur rather thick, ± horizontal .... *O. palustris*

4*   inflorescence near lax to lax, spur spindly, ascendant .... *O. pseudolaxiflora*

5   lip 6-8mm long, base of lip pale, spotted .... *O. dinsmorei*

5*   lip 8-12mm long, base and centre of lip pale, usually unmarked .... *O. laxiflora*

283

Orchis pseudolaxiflora
CZERNIAKOVSKA

Etymology *pseudo-*: false; *-laxiflora*: [*Orchis*] *laxiflora* **Type** Ro, Ouzbekistan (1941). **Synonym** *O. laxiflora* subsp. *dielsiana* Soó.

Description As *O. palustris* but robust, 30-105cm tall; 3-7 leaves, 10-22cm x 1.2-2.5cm, keeled, pointed, unmarked, erect; bracts leaf-like, margins washed violet, ± equal to ovary; inflorescence elongated, near cylindrical, near lax then becoming lax, 7-50cm tall; (13-) 20-60 medium-sized flowers, violet-purple to deep violet; sepals oval, 7-12mm x 3.5-5mm, lateral sepals spreading and directed forwards; dorsal sepal near erect, petals near equal, dorsal sepal and petals forming a hood; lip rather varied, obscurely to clearly 3-lobed, 8-18mm x 10-19mm, base whitish, slightly contracted into 2 lamellae separated by a groove, centre convex, pale, marked with rather pale streaks; lateral lobes broadly rounded, recurved forwards; median lobe obscurely bilobed, undulate; spur fine, cylindrical, straight to slightly curved upwards, ascendant, 7-19mm long. **Variation** Distinct from *O. palustris* in its laxer inflorescence, darker and less well spotted flowers and shorter lip in comparison to the hood and spur.

Flowering Season III-VII.

Habitat Full sun on damp to wet, alkaline to slightly acidic substrates. Damp to marshy meadows, fens, streamsides, damp mountain hollows, 700-2300m asl.

Distribution Eastern sub-Mediterranean and Asia. Central Anatolia east to Afghanistan and south to Yemen. Local but often abundant in its stations.

Countries An Ro.

Photos An, Tunceli, 26.V.1990; An, Andyaman, 16.V.1990. P. DELFORGE.

Hybrids within the *Orchis palustris* group

Due to the variability of some taxa and the existence of intermediate populations few authors attempt to describe the occasional hybrids within this group. *O. laxiflora* and *O. palustris*, separated by different ecological requirements (tolerance of acidity, of salinity, staggered flowering seasons) are rarely sympatric and form relatively few hybrids. Within the *O. palustris* subgroup, intermediates are rather frequently encountered but little-studied. The occasional hybrids are often spectacular due to their robustness, height and very numerous flowers.

Orchis laxiflora
LAMARCK

Etymology *laxiflora*: with a lax inflorescence. **Type*** Ga, near Paris (1778). **Synonyms** *O. palustris* var. *laxiflora* FRIEDRICHSTHAL, *Anacamptis laxiflora* (LAMARCK) R.M. BATEMAN, PRIDGEON & M.W. CHASE, *O. ensifolia* VILLARS, *O. laxiflora* subsp. *ensifolia* (VILLARS) ASCHERSON & GRÄBNER.

Description Slender, (20-) 30-60cm tall; stem washed violet at tip; 3-8 leaves, arranged along the stem, sheathing, near erect to erect, linear-lanceolate, 7-15cm x 1-2.5cm, keeled, folded into a gutter, pointed, unmarked, upper leaves bract-like, near clasping; bracts leaf-like, washed violet-purple at tip, ± equal to ovary; inflorescence elongated, lax, near cylindrical, up to 25cm tall; flowers numerous, dark violet-purple, rarely pink; sepals oval, 7-14mm x 3-6mm, lateral sepals vertically erect, backs touching; dorsal sepal near erect or forming a hood with the more elongated petals, 6-9mm x 3-5mm; lip 3-lobed, wedge-shaped, much broader than long, 8-12mm x 12-18mm, centre pale, unmarked or very rarely lightly marked with very pale blotches, sharply folded longitudinally; lateral lobes broadly rounded, slightly crenate, tips touching below the lip; median lobe far shorter than lateral lobes, truncated, scalloped, sometimes almost absent, lip thus obcordate; spur straight to very slightly curved upwards, ascendant, 10-19mm long, tip thick, often bilobed; 2n=36, 42.

Variation Little variation. Distinct from *O. palustris* particularly in its flower colour and strongly convex lip, with the median lobe short or absent.

Flowering Season (III-) IV-VII; usually after *O. palustris.*

Habitat Full sun on damp to wet, alkaline to slightly acidic substrates. Damp to marshy meadows, fens, streamsides, seepages, up to 1600m asl.

Distribution Mediterranean-Atlantic, northwest to the Channel Islands, east to Anatolia (to at least Kastamonu). Local but often abundant in its stations; decreasing due to habitat destruction.

Countries Ae Al An †Be Bl Co Cr Cy Ga Gr He ?†Ho Hs It Ju Lu Sa Si Tu.

Photos Ga, Ardèche, 15.V.1999; Gr, Ioannina, 15.VI.1990. P. DELFORGE (see next page).

Orchis dinsmorei
(SCHLECHTER) H. BAUMANN & DAFNI

Etymology Named after J.E. Dinsmore, English botanist (1862-1951). **Type** Ij, Palestine (1941). **Basionym** *O. laxiflora* var. *dinsmorei* SCHLECHTER.

Description As *O. laxiflora* but earlier flowering, more slender, more spindly, 45-70cm tall; 5-8 leaves, 10-27cm x 1.5-3cm; inflorescence lax, 10-28cm tall; 15-60 small flowers, dark violet-purple; sepals oval, 9-11mm x 4-5mm, lateral sepals vertically erect; lip 3-lobed, convex, 6-8mm x 9-13mm, base whitish or very pale, marked with a few violet dots or streaks, contracted into 2 attenuated lamellae separated by a groove, centre and margins dark, colourful; lateral lobes triangular-rounded to broadly falcate, ± strongly turned down under lip; median lobe far shorter than lateral lobes, emarginate, sometimes near absent; spur straight or slightly curved upwards, thick, conical, ascendant, 9-13mm long.

Flowering Season (II-) III-IV (-V), early. **Habitat** As *O. laxiflora* but up to 1000m asl **Distribution** Eastern Mediterranean. From Israel north to Cilicia (An). Very local but sometimes abundant. **Countries** An Ij Ls. **Photos** Ij, Galilee, 2 & 28. IV.1992. C.A.J. KREUTZ.

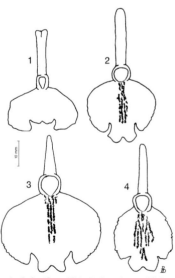

1. *O. laxiflora* (Ga). **2**. *O. palustris* (Ga).
3. *O. robusta* (Bl). **4**. *O. elegans* (Ju).

(3 and 4 after GÖLZ & REINHARD)

286

The *Orchis morio* group

Characteristics Sepals oval, veined green; sepals and petals forming a hood; lip broad, weakly 3-lobed; lateral lobes rounded. 8 species in the group. **Discussion** A monophyletic group, clearly composed of 2 subgroups. The first subgroup comprises 6 taxa very close to *O. morio*, the second comprises *O. boryi* and *O. israelitica*, notably distinct in that flowering starts from the tip of the spike.

Orchis champagneuxii
BARNÉOUD

Etymology Named after A.B. Champagneux, French botanist (1774-1845). **Type** Ga, Var (1843). **Synonyms** *O. morio* subsp. *champagneuxii* (BARNÉOUD) E.G. CAMUS, *O. morio* var. *champagneuxii* (BARNÉOUD) GUIMARÃES, Anacamptis *champagneuxii* (BARNÉOUD) R.M. BATEMAN, PRIDGEON & M.W. CHASE, *O. champagneuxii* var. *mesomelana* (RCHB. fil.) D. TYTECA.

Description Spindly, 10-25 (-40)cm tall, with 3 root-tubers, of which 1-2 are located at the end of long subterranean rhizomes, thus forming groups; 5-9 basal leaves, near erect, unmarked, narrowly lanceolate, 3-8cm x 0.7-1.5cm; 2-3 smaller cauline leaves, sheathing; bracts membranous, purplish, slightly shorter than ovary; inflorescence lax, few-flowered; hood ovoid, closed, violet to purple, rarely pink, veined purplish-green; sepals broadly oval, 6.5-10mm x 3-5mm; petals 4.5-6.5mm long; lip 3-lobed, broader than long (when flattened), 6-8.5mm x 11-14mm, folded longitudinally, centre white, sometimes washed lilac, unmarked or with very pale, almost imperceptible spots; lateral lobes concolourous with hood, rounded, sometimes toothed, folded down and touching each other below the lip; median lobe ± as long as lateral lobes, tip indented; spur thick, 10-15mm long, 1.5-2x as long as lip, ascendant, near vertical, cylindrical, straight to slightly curved, tip thickened, truncated, often bilobed; 2n=72. **Variation** Not very varied; *'mesomelana'* has centre of lip clearly spotted lilac, sometimes broadly so; occurs with nominative variety.

Flowering Season (III-) IV-VI. **Habitat** Full sun to mid-shade on alkaline to acidic, dry to moist substrates. Garrigue, scrub, open woodland, up to 1500m asl.

Distribution Western Mediterranean, centred on the Iberian peninsula; in France as far as Alpes-Maritimes. Local but often abundant. **Countries** Bl Ga Hs Lu Ma. **Photos** Hs, Jaén, 12.IV.1990; Cuenca, 12.VI.1988. P. DELFORGE.

Orchis longicornu
POIRET

Etymology *longi-*: long; *-cornu*: horn [shape] (an allusion to the length of the spur). **Type** Ag (1789). **Synonym** *Anacamptis longicornu* (POIRET) R.M. BATEMAN, PRIDGEON & M.W. CHASE.

Description As *O. champagneuxii* but probably only 2 root-tubers; slightly more robust, 10-35cm tall; basal leaves 3-12cm long; inflorescence more elongated, with 5-15 flowers; hood usually pink or violet, far paler than the blackish-violet lateral lobes; lip (when flattened) fuller, 6-8mm x 12-18mm, centre whitish, marked with 2 rows of 3-6 dark purple spots; spur larger, up to 17mm long, very thickened at tip, straight to slightly curved, often vertical.

Flowering Season (I-) II-V. **Habitat** Full sun on acidic to calcareous, dry or moist substrates. Garrigue, maquis, short montane grassland, up to 2000m asl.

Distribution Western Mediterranean. Majorca (Bl) and southern Corsica to Calabria (It), Cape Bon (Tn) and Algerian Tell. Very local and often rare. **Countries** Ag Bl Co It Me Sa Si Tn. **Photos** Sa, Nuoro, 13.IV.1996; Si, Palermo, 16.IV.2000. P. DELFORGE.

Key to the *Orchis morio* group

1   flowers opening from bottom to top of spike
.... 2
1*   flowers opening from top to bottom of spike
.... *O. boryi* subgroup (p. 278)

2   centre of lip pale, unmarked 3
2*   centre of lip spotted 4

3   lip with dark lateral lobes and pale centre
.... *O. champagneuxii*
3*   lip with lateral lobes as pale as the centre
.... *O. syriaca*

4   lateral lobes of lip far darker than hood and coloured differently .... *O. longicornu*
4*   lateral lobes of lip and hood concolourous
.... 5

5   lip (when flattened) narrow, 1.2-1.4x as broad as long, 6-9mm wide .... *O. albanica*
5*   lip full, 1.5-2x as broad as long, 9-16mm wide 6

6   plant robust, spur thick .... *O. morio*
6*   plant spindly, spur fine .... *O. picta*

Orchis morio L.

Etymology *morio*: jester (name given to the species in the Renaissance). **Type*** Ge, Baden-Württemberg (1753). **Synonym** *Anacamptis morio* (L.) R.M. BATEMAN, PRIDGEON & M.W. CHASE.

Description Usually robust, 10-50cm tall; stem thick, washed violet at tip; 5-10 basal leaves, narrowly to broadly lanceolate, pointed to obtuse, spreading to near erect, 2.5-11cm x 0.5-2cm; 2-4 smaller cauline leaves, long-clasping; bracts membranous, purplish, slightly longer than ovary; inflorescence short, rather dense, near cylindrical; 15-20 (-25) medium-sized flowers, colour varied, often violet, purple or lilac, more rarely pink, sometimes white; hood near globular, obtuse, tight to loose, clearly veined green, washed green at base; lateral sepals oval-oblong, asymmetrical, 7.5-11mm x 3.5-6mm; dorsal sepal and petals near equal, 6-8.5mm long; lip much broader than long (when spread), 6.5-10mm x 12-18mm, often kidney-shaped, almost flat to convex and sharply folded, centre pale, densely marked with violet-purple to pink blotches, often broad; lateral lobes broadly rounded, margins scalloped or slightly undulate-crisped; median lobe longer than lateral lobes, broad, emarginate; spur robust, club-shaped, slightly shorter than lip, 9-14mm long, straight to ascendant, horizontal to vertical, dilated, flattened, tip truncated and bilobed; 2n=36.

Variation Very varied in size and habit, the variation often appears to be linked to ecological conditions: more robust plants growing on damp or wet substrates, spindlier plants growing in shady sites. Coloration varies even within the same population. The hood and lip are sometimes discoloured, the lip rarely unmarked. Hypochromatic plants, with a white lip and green hood, are rather frequent.

Flowering Season III-VI. **Habitat** Shows a broad ecological tolerance, but mostly in full sun. Short, poor grassland, unimproved meadows, alpine pastures, forest fringes, open woodland in the south, up to 2000m asl.

Distribution Euro-Mediterranean. Extends north to southern Norway and east to Iran. Southern limits of range poorly known due to confusion with *O. picta*; perhaps absent from southern zones where *O. picta* may replace it. Widespread and sometimes very abundant (up to several thousand plants). In general decline, however, following the improvement of meadows.

Countries Ae Al An Au Be Bl Br Bu Co Cz Da Ga Ge Gr Hb He Ho Hs Hu It Ju Lu Lx Ma ?†Me No Pb Po Rm Ro Si Su Tu. **Photos** Be, Luxembourg, 13.V.1994; 29.IV.1990. P. DELFORGE.

Orchis picta
LOISELEUR

Etymology *picta*: ornate. **Type** Ga, Var (1827).
Synonyms *O. morio* var. *picta* (LOISELEUR)
REICHENBACH fil., *O. morio* subsp. *picta* (LOISELEUR)
K. RICHTER, *Anacamptis morio* subsp. *picta*
(LOISELEUR) P. JACQUET & SCAPPATICCI, *A. picta*
(LOISELEUR) R.M. BATEMAN, ?*Orchis skorpilii*
VELENOVSKI.

Description As *O. morio* but more spindly, 12-
30cm tall, sometimes with 3 root-tubers; leaves
smaller, 2.5-8cm x 0.5-1.3cm; inflorescence more
pyramidal, often not so dense; 5-15 medium-
sized to small flowers, more colourful, often dark
violet, coloration less varied than *O. morio*;
lateral sepals 6-8.5mm x 4.5-6mm; petals 4.5-
6.5mm long; lip 4-6mm x 8-12mm, centre pale,
densely spotted deep violet-purple; median
lobe often shorter than lateral lobes; spur
8-11mm long, robust, ± curved upwards, tip
slightly dilated.

Flowering Season III-V (-VI).

Habitat As *O. morio* but on drier, more often
alkaline, substrates.

Distribution Mediterranean. Range poorly
known due to confusion with *O. morio*, which it
may replace in some areas; reported throughout
the southern part of the range of *O. morio*, north
to the southern Alps. Widespread and
sometimes abundant.

Countries Ae ?Ag Al An Bl Co Ga Gr ?He Hs It
Ju Lu Ma Me ?Rm ?Ro Si Tu.

Photos Ga, Var, 15.IV.1999; Ju, Macedonia
(FYROM), Nis, 5.V.1990. P. DELFORGE.

Discussion Polytypic and probably
heterogeneous, *O. picta* groups together an
assemblage of Mediterranean populations that are
as different from each other as they are from *O.
morio*. The type of *O. picta* is few-flowered and
richly coloured, with a broad, spreading, kidney-
shaped lip and a fine spur that is strongly curved
upwards. Iberian and French populations often
show transitions towards *O. morio*, to the point
that *O. picta* may sometimes appear in these
regions to be merely part of a clinal variation.
Italian and eastern populations are sometimes
better demarcated but often show denser
inflorescences, sharply folded lips and straighter
spurs. Balkan populations sometimes have an
attenuated base to the lip (?*'skorpilii'*),
intermediate between that of *O. picta* and
O. albanica.

Orchis albanica
GÖLZ & H.R. REINHARD

Etymology *albanica*: from Albania. **Type** Al, Lushnjë (1984). **Synonym** *O. morio* subsp. *albanica* (GÖLZ & H.R. REINHARD) BUTTLER.

Description As *O. morio* and *O. picta* but much more spindly, 15-30cm tall; stem pale green; 4-8 basal leaves, 4-8cm x 0.5-1.5cm; 2-3 cauline leaves, smaller, clasping; bracts pale, slightly shorter than ovary; inflorescence laxer; 5-15 pale flowers, whitish, pinkish or lilac, rarely deep violet; sepals 5.5-8mm x 2.5-3.5mm; petals 4-5.5mm long; lip 4.5-7mm x 6-9mm, slightly convex, centre white, with 2-3 rows of fine purple dots, more rarely large spots; lateral lobes shorter than median lobe, margins sometimes slightly reflexed; spur 7-10mm long, spindly, ± curved, cylindrical, tip usually not dilated, merely obtuse.

Flowering Season IV-VI.

Habitat Full sun to mid-shade on diverse substrates. Grassy places, often open pinewoods, up to 1500m asl.

Distribution Central Albania. Hybridogenous or intermediate populations occur elsewhere in Albania and probably north to central Yugoslavia, in northern Greece and on Corfu. Very rare and local.

Countries Al ?Gr ?Ju.

Photos Al, Vlorë, 15.IV.1982; 19.V.1980. H.R. REINHARD.

Hybrids in the *Orchis morio* group

No hybrid between *O. boryi* or *O. israelitica* and the other members of the group has ever been reported. The frequent presence of populations intermediate between the 6 taxa in the *O. morio* subgroup make it risky to identify hybrids within this subgroup. With the exception of *O. albanica* and *O. syriaca*, all members of the *O. morio* group have a hybrid with *O. papilionacea* described; these hybrids are frequent and illustrate the genetic proximity of these 2 groups. Hybrids of *O. morio* with members of the *O. palustris* group are rarer, those with *O. collina*, *O. mascula*, *O. coriophora* and *O. fragrans* are extremely rare. Finally, *O. morio* and its allies also hybridise with the genus *Anacamptis* (× *Anacamptorchis*) and above all with the genus *Serapias*, with which they produce the majority of × *Orchiserapias* (see p. 27).

Orchis syriaca
BOISSIER ex H. BAUMANN & KÜNKELE

Etymology *syriaca*: from Syria. **Type** Ls, Syria (1862). **Synonyms** *O. morio* subsp. *syriaca* E.G. CAMUS, *O. morio* subsp. *libani* RENZ, *Anacamptis syriaca* (BOISSIER ex H. BAUMANN & KÜNKELE) R.M. BATEMAN, PRIDGEON & M.W. CHASE.

Description As *O. morio* but more spindly, 10-30cm tall; bracts violet, 3/4x ovary; inflorescence lax to dense, with 5-30 flowers; hood lax, violet, lilac or rather bright purple; sepals 5-7mm long, lateral sepals sometimes near erect; lip convex, 3-lobed, unmarked, pale, usually whitish, base grooved, margins sometimes washed violet or pink; lateral lobes rounded, turned down and back; median lobe protuberant, often crisped at base; spur concolourous with hood, slender, slightly curved upwards.

Flowering Season II-IV (-V).

Habitat Full sun to mid-shade on dry to moist, often calcareous substrates. Short grassland, garrigue, olive groves, open woodland, up to 1300m asl.

Distribution Eastern Mediterranean. Southern Turkey, Cyprus, Syria, perhaps also Lebanon and Israel. Local and often rare.

Countries An Cy ?Ij Ls. **Photos** Cy, Larnaca, 28.III.1989. P. DELFORGE.

Problems in the *Orchis morio* group

With the exception, perhaps, of *O. syriaca* and *O. champagneuxii*, all taxa in the subgroup show a wide range of variation (habit, size, coloration) which ± overlap. For example, it is common, in some seasons, to find plants displaying the characters of *O. picta* or *O. champagneuxii* in southern populations of *O. morio*, or plants with the coloration of *O. syriaca* in western populations. It is evident that, as usual, the characteristics of the whole population should be used for identification and in the use of the keys. On the other hand, with the apparent exception of *O. syriaca*, all members of the subgroup have numerous contact zones or intermediate populations that vary in size from year to year. It is difficult to know whether these are composed of hybrids or represent stages along a cline. They pose major identification problems, make the determination of the occasional hybrid very tricky, and are the origin of numerous erroneous reports – for example, *O. longicornu* in the Iberian peninsula and continental France, *O. champagneuxii* in Corsica and Italy.

Orchis boryi
REICHENBACH fil.

Etymology Named after J.-B. Bory de Saint-Vincent, French general and botanist (1778-1840). **Type** Gr, Messinia (1851). **Synonyms** *O. morio* subsp. *boryi* (RCHB. fil.) SOÓ, *Anacamptis boryi* (RCHB. fil.) R.M. BATEMAN, PRIDGEON & M.W. CHASE.

Description 10-35 (-45)cm tall; 4-9 leaves in a basal rosette, 5-11cm x 1-3.5cm; 2-3 cauline leaves, smaller, clasping; bracts membranous, clasping, lower bract as long as ovary; inflorescence rather short and lax, flowers at tip opening first; 5-20 flowers, growing away from stem; sepals and petals dark, reddish-lilac to violet, rarely pink, veined green inside, dark purplish-green outside, forming a loose hood; lateral sepals sometimes near erect, oval, asymmetrical, near pointed, 6-10mm x 3-6mm; dorsal sepal and petals near equal, 4-7.5mm long; lip wedge-shaped, 3-lobed to near entire, 7-10mm x 9-12mm (when spread), base grooved, centre flat, whitish to pinkish, marked with 2 rows of 2-4 violet dots, rarely unmarked, margins coloured as hood, often slightly scalloped and undulate-crisped; lobes poorly defined, near equal; median lobe broad, slightly longer than lateral lobes, slightly emarginate; spur fine, elongated, cylindrical, horizontal to slightly descendent, 12-18mm long, ± as long as ovary.

Flowering Season IV-V. **Habitat** Full sun to mid-shade on moist to damp, calcareous or schistose substrates. Short grassland, garrigue, maquis, open woodland, up to 1300m asl.

Distribution Endemic to southern Greece. Range disjunct: Phocide, Peloponnese, Skiathos (Sporades), Eubee, Cyclades, and Crete in the south. Local and rather rare. **Countries** Cr Gr.

Photos Cr, Iraklion, 12.IV.1982; Gr, Lakonia, 18.IV.1991. P. DELFORGE.

Discussion A unique taxon, close to *O. morio* s.l. but with an obscure origin. Sometimes considered to be hybridogenous, with *O. picta* and *O. quadripunctata* as parents, but this seems unlikely; very close to *O. israelitica*, a sister-species with which it shares, importantly, an inverse (top to bottom) flowering sequence.

Key to the *Orchis boryi* subgroup

1   hood dark, spur 12-18mm long .... *O. boryi*
1*   hood pale, spur 11-13mm long
    .... *O. israelitica*

293

Orchis israelitica
H. BAUMANN & DAFNI

Etymology *israelitica*: from Israel. **Type** Ij, Galilee (1979). **Synonym** *Anacamptis israelitica* (H. BAUMANN & DAFNI) R.M. BATEMAN, PRIDGEON & M.W. CHASE.

Description As *O. boryi* but 10-25 (-30)cm tall; 3-6 basal leaves, 5-12cm x 1.5-3cm; 1-2 cauline leaves, smaller, long-clasping; bracts pinkish to greenish, *c*. 2/3x ovary; inflorescence (near) lax, flowers at tip opening first; 5-15 (-20) small flowers; sepals and petals pale, whitish to pinkish or lilac, centre pale green; lateral sepals oval-obtuse, 6-8mm x 3-4.5mm; lip more clearly 3-lobed and more convex, 5-8mm x 7-10mm (when spread), centre whitish, marked with 2 rows of 1-3 large dark purple spots, margins scalloped (less undulate-crisped); lateral lobes smaller, obliquely truncated, sometimes falcate; median lobe obscurely bilobed, clearly longer than lateral lobes; spur 11-13mm long.

Variation Coloration rather varied, the range of colour variation can overlap slightly with that of *O. boryi*, which is, without doubt, a geographical vicariant.

Flowering Season I-III (-IV).

Habitat Full sun to mid-shade on dry, calcareous substrates. Open garrigue, open mixed woodland with *Quercus calliprinos*, 400-800m asl.

Distribution Endemic to northern Israel. Known from a few stations from Upper and Lower Galilee. Very local and very rare.

Countries Ij. **Photos** Ij, Low Galilee, 23.III.1992. C.A.J. KREUTZ.

Note Exclusively cross-pollinated, by bees of the genera *Bombus*, *Eucera* and *Anthophora*, attracted by the similar appearance of *Orchis israelitica*, which lacks nectar, to the lily *Bellevalia flexuosa* Boissier, which is nectariferous and therefore offers nourishment. In the presence of *B. flexuosa*, 25-50% of *Orchis israelitica* flowers are pollinated; in its absence, only 5%. *O. israelitica* attracts all the pollinators of *Bellevalia flexuosa*. It exhibits facultative floral mimicry, because the mimic, which has nothing to offer to pollinators, is still visited even when its model is absent.

The *Orchis papilionacea* group

Characteristics lip entire, fan-shaped to near rhomboidal; 2n=32, 36.

Orchis cyrenaica
E.A. DURAND & BARATTE

Etymology *cyrenaica*: from Cyrenaica (Li) **Type** Li, Koubba (1910). **Synonyms** *O. papilionacea* var. *cyrenaica* (E.A. DURAND & BARATTE) P. DELFORGE, *Dactylorhiza cyrenaica* (E.A. DURAND & BARATTE) HAUTZINGER, ?*Orchis melchifafii* HAUTZINGER.

Description Robust, 20-35cm tall; 4-6 basal leaves in a rosette, near erect, broadly lanceolate, shortly pointed, shiny, unmarked, up to 10cm x 2.5cm, broader than those of *O. papilionacea*; 1-2 cauline leaves, clasping, often reaching base of inflorescence; bracts lanceolate, purplish, lower bracts up to 30mm long; inflorescence dense, ovoid to near cylindrical; 5-21 flowers; sepals and petals forming a very loose hood, clearly veined, near obtuse, crimson-red or purple; lateral sepals oval-obtuse, asymmetrical, *c*. 10mm x 5mm, directed forwards; dorsal sepal near erect; petals near equal, narrower; lip 8-12mm x 6.5-11mm, pendent, convex, near entire, rhomboidal to oboval-wedge-shaped, sometimes with a small, subtle central lobe, margins entire, broadly deep purple, without lines or veins, turned down or slightly recurved, the base contracted, grooved, white, with 2 dark purple spots around the spur entrance, centre white, with 1-4 streaks, sometimes 3 longitudinal rows of spots; spur pale purple, conical, spindly, descendent, 15-28mm long, often longer than the ovary; stigmatic surface narrow.

Flowering Season Late II-III (-mid IV). **Habitat** Usually full sun, on dry, calcareous substrates. Short, poor grassland, open garrigue, edges and clearings in thermophilous woods, up to 1000m asl.

Distribution Endemic to Cyrenaica. Very local but sometimes in large populations. **Countries** Li. **Photos** Li, Benghazi, 14.III.2003. C.A.J. KREUTZ.

Key to the *Orchis papilionacea* group

1	spur large, sack-like	*O. collina*
1*	spur fine, elongated	2

2   margins of lip unstreaked, not scalloped; spur 15-28mm long .... *O. cyrenaica*

2* margins of lip scalloped and/or marked fan-like with streaks; spur 8-14mm long ....*O. papilionacea*

Orchis papilionacea L.

Etymology *papilionacea*: in the shape of a butterfly. **Type*** It (1759). **Synonyms** *Anacamptis papilionacea* (L.) R.M. Bateman, Pridgeon & M.W. Chase, *Orchis rubra* Jacquin in Murray, *O. decipiens* Todaro, *O. papilionacea* var. *vexillifera* Terraciano.

Description 15-40 (-55)cm tall; 3-9 basal leaves, spreading to near erect, linear-lanceolate, pointed, unmarked, 3-18cm x 0.5-2cm; 2-5 cauline leaves, smaller, clasping, upper 1-2 leaves bract-like, sometimes washed red; bracts membranous, washed red, almost equalling ovary or longer than it; inflorescence initially dense then lax, ovoid to (near-) cylindrical; 4-15 (-22) flowers; sepals and petals forming a loose hood, clearly veined, near obtuse, pink, crimson-red or purple; lateral sepals linear-lanceolate, asymmetrical, 8-22mm x 4-7.5mm, directed forwards to spreading; dorsal sepal near erect; petals narrower; lip pendent, entire, orbicular, 9-26mm x 7-27mm, concave to flat, concolourous with hood but brighter and shinier, unmarked or veined with lines, streaks and dark dots, base pale, contracted into 2 ridges separated by a groove, then abruptly widening to a wedge- or heart-shape, margins scalloped, sometimes undulate; spur 8-14mm long, conical, appearing spindly, initially horizontal then curved or bent downwards; 2n=32.

Flowering Season (I-) II-V.

Habitat Full sun to mid-shade on dry to moist substrates, above all alkaline, often calcareous. Short, poor grassland, garrigue, maquis, open woodland, up to 1800m asl.

Distribution Mediterranean and eastern. North to the foothills of the Alps and east to the Caspian Sea. Rather widespread and often abundant.

Countries Ae Ag Al An Bl Bu Co Cr Cy Ga Gr ?†He Hs Ij It Ju ?Li Ls Lu Ma Rm Ro Sa Si Tn Tu.

Photos It, Brindisi, 30.III.1986; Foggia, 31.III.19991. P. Delforge.

Orchis papilionacea L. var. *papilionacea*

Description Flowers medium-sized; lateral sepals 14-19mm long, lip (9-) 12-17 (-20)mm long.

Photos It, Brindisi, 30.III.1986; Foggia, 31.III.1991. P. Delforge.

This variety has 2 variants:

1. 'rubra' Type Around Rome. **Description** Hood deep crimson-red; lip unmarked, shiny, paler than hood, sometimes almost white, more

often lilac, base wedge-shaped, often whitish.
Distribution Rather frequent in centre of range.
Countries It Ju, but also Ag in the south, An in the east (photos previous page).

2. As *'rubra'* but hood often with a pale background and dark veins; lip pale, veined fanwise with rather thick lines and streaks, often concolourous with veins on hood, margins sometimes purple.

Variation Range of variation from *'bruhnsiana'* to *'grandiflora'* and to *'rubra'*; often mixed in the field with the latter 2, apparently sometimes with intermediates, especially in island populations (Co, Cr, Sa, Si).

Distribution Probably throughout the range but more frequent in the centre; France, mostly east of the Rhône.

Photo A Ga, Alpes-Maritimes, 14.V.1988. P. DELFORGE.

'vexillifera': rather large, described from Sardinia but present in Italy, mostly in the north, but also in the south and on Corsica; in Sicily =?*'decipiens'* **Photo B** Sa, Nuoro, 10.IV.1996. P. DELFORGE.

This last variant is also rather frequent in Yugoslavia; it is the principal variant in continental Greece. **Photo C** (below) Gr, Imathia, 9.V.1990. P. DELFORGE.

Orchis papilionacea L.
var. *grandiflora* Boissier

Etymology *grandiflora*: with large flowers. **Type** Hs, Seville (1842). **Synonyms** *O. papilionacea* subsp. *grandiflora* (Boissier) E. Nelson vel Malagarriga vel H. Baumann, *O. expansa* Tenore, *O. rubra* var. *expansa* (Tenore) Lindley, *O. papilionacea* subsp. *expansa* (Tenore) Raynaud.

Description Flowers large; hood dark to pale; lateral sepals 16-23mm long; lip 15-26mm x 16-29 (-32)mm, pure white to pink or rather dark lilac, obscurely or, more often, clearly spotted fan-wise, flat to concave, margins sometimes undulate, base heart-shaped, narrow but widening abruptly. **Variation** Range of variation from *'vexillifera'* to *'heroica'*.

Distribution Mostly the west of the range. North Africa, Iberian peninsula, ?France, also reported, although less frequently, from Corsica, the Italian peninsula and islands (Sa Si), where it appears mostly as the variant *'expansa'*, as well as Greece, Crete and Anatolia, most probably due to confusion with var. *heroica*. **Photos** Lu, Extremadura, 5.IV.1990; Hs, Malaga, 10.IV. 1990. P. Delforge.

Discussion of *Orchis papilionacea*

This species is made up of a mosaic of morphs that vary principally in the size of the floral parts, colour of the hood, and markings on the lip, but without clear-cut boundaries emerging. Furthermore, it should be noted that throughout the centre of the range there are groups with a dark hood and unmarked lip (*papilionacea 'rubra'*), in the east of the range groups of small plants with the lip marked fan-wise (*bruhnsiana*), in the centre of the range groups of medium-sized plants (*papilionacea 'vexillifera'*) and in the west of the range groups of large plants (var. *grandiflora*). These trends have, however, numerous exceptions, as the ranges of variation overlap and intermediate populations are frequent, so that the species currently seems polymorphic, no one form (variant) or variety can be given a specific or subspecies rank.

Pollination of *Orchis papilionacea*

In southern Greece, pollination is effected by solitary bees (*Eucera bidentata*, *Nomada imperialis*) in a mechanism of facultative floral mimicry, analogous to that of *Orchis pallens* or *O. israelitica*. In Italy (observations from Elba), however, it seems that males of another solitary bee, *Eucera tuberculata*, deposit their pheromones on the lip of *Orchis papilionacea*, thus establishing swarming routes that attract females; their repeated patrols and the occasional visits of females ensure pollination.

Orchis papilionacea L.
var. *heroica* (E.D. CLARKE) P. DELFORGE

Etymology *heroica*: heroic (an allusion to ancient heroes of the Trojan War). **Type** An, Çanakkale, archaeological site of Troy (1812). **Synonyms** *O. heroica* E.D. CLARKE, *O. papilionacea* subsp. *heroica* (E.D. CLARKE) H. BAUMANN.

Description Close to *'grandiflora'* but often more thickset; inflorescence short and dense; 2-10 flowers, large relative to length of stem; hood often dark red, sometimes slightly purplish; lateral sepals 13-20mm long; lip 12-21mm x 12-21mm, often concave, finely marked fan-wise with pink, crimson-red or purple streaks and dots, rarely unbroken lines, margins sometimes undulate, base constricted broadly wedge-shaped to abruptly heart-shaped, usually pale, often pure white.

Variation Range of variation from *'papilionacea'* to *'grandiflora'*. An early variant (late I-early IV), with slightly larger flowers, and a late variant (mid IV-V, *'alibertis'*, below) with smaller flowers, have been reported; they are linked by numerous intermediates which make their demarcation risky.

Distribution Mostly the Ionian Islands and Aegean basin. **Countries** Ae An Cr Gr. **Photo A** Cr, Lassithi, 26.II.1990. P. DELFORGE.

Orchis papilionacea L.
var. *alibertis*
(G. KRETZSCHMAR & H. KRETZSCHMAR) P. DELFORGE

Etymology Named after A. Alibertis, contemporary Cretan botanist. **Type** Cr, Agios Ioannis (2000). **Basionym** *O. papilionacea* subsp. *alibertis* G. KRETZSCHMAR & H. KRETZSCHMAR.

Description As var. *heroica* but later flowering, much more spindly, few-flowered; inflorescence denser, flowers grouped at tip of stem, smaller, coloration as var. *heroica*; lip less than 15mm x 10mm, pink, spotted fan-wise; spur *c.* 1/2 length of ovary.

Distribution Reported from 9 stations in Crete but probably occurs elsewhere in the range of var. *heroica*. Very rare and local. **Photo B** Cr, Lassithi, 18.IV.2000. H. KRETZSCHMAR.

Hybrids in the *Orchis papilionacea* group

Orchis papilionacea often hybridises with members of the *O. morio* group; the hybrids are easy to detect due to their coloration and their intermediate spurs. Hybrids with *O. laxiflora* are far less frequent, those with *O. collina* very rare; finally, hybrids with the genera *Serapias* and *Anacamptis* are extremely rare.

Orchis papilionacea L. var. *messenica* RENZ

Etymology *messenica*: from Messinia. **Type** Gr, Messinia (1928).

Description As var. *heroica* but inflorescence dense; hood and lip white veined with violet.

Distribution Southern Peloponnese. **Countries** Gr.

Photo A Gr, Lakonia, 18.IV.1991. P. DELFORGE.

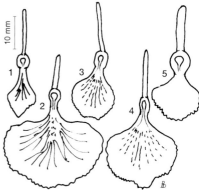

Orchis papilionacea: **1**. ?'*bruhnsiana*' (northern Gr). **2**. '*grandiflora*' (Hs). **3**. '*papilionacea*' (western Gr). **4**. '*heroica*' (Cr). **5**. '*papilionacea*' (It).

Orchis papilionacea L. var. *bruhnsiana* GRUNER

Etymology *bruhnsiana*: named after Bruhns, who collected the plant. **Type** Ro, Azerbaijan, Baku (1867). **Synonyms** *O. bruhnsiana* (GRUNER) MAJOROV in GROSSHEIM, *O. papilionacea* subsp. *bruhnsiana* (GRUNER) SOÓ, *O. caspia* TRAUTVETTER, *O. schirwanica* WORONOW, *O. papilionacea* subsp. *schirwanica* (WORONOW) SOÓ.

Description Inflorescence dense and sometimes elongated; up to 22 small flowers; lateral sepals 8-13mm long; lip often concave, 9-12mm x 9-12mm, base wedge-shaped, whitish to pinkish or decidedly purple, margins sometimes undulate, darker, crimson-pink to purple, spotted fan-wise with thick, dark streaks and dots, rarely unbroken lines.

Variation Probably the best-defined variety, sometimes considered a distinct species.

Distribution Range disjunct. Caucasus and Transcaucasus, Near East.

Pays: An Cy Ij Ls.

Photo B Ij, Galilee, 23.III.1992. C.A.J. KREUTZ.

Orchis collina
BANKS & SOLANDER ex RUSSEL

Etymology *collina*: hilly **Type** Ls, near Alep (1798). **Synonyms** *Anacamptis collina* (BANKS & SOLANDER ex RUSSEL) R.M. BATEMAN, PRIDGEON & M.W. CHASE, *Orchis saccata* TENORE, *O. fedtschenkoi* CZERNIAKOWSKA, *O. saccata* subsp. *fedtschenkoi* (CZERNIAKOWSKA) SOÓ, *O. chlorotica* WORONOW, *O. leucoglossa* O. SCHWARZ.

Description Robust, 10-40cm tall; upper half of stem purplish-brown; 2-6 basal leaves in a rather spreading rosette, broadly lanceolate, shortly pointed, shiny, unmarked, 3-12cm x 1-3.5cm; 1-4 cauline leaves, smaller, clasping; bracts lanceolate, purplish-brown, hooded, lower bracts longer than flowers; inflorescence broad, near cylindrical, rather dense; 3-20 flowers; sepals and petals purplish-brown, sometimes olive-green; sepals oval-oblong, 9-12mm x 3-4mm, lateral sepals erect, slightly reflexed; petals slightly falcate, obtuse, 7-10mm long, forming a hood with the dorsal sepal; lip entire, near orbicular, emarginate at tip, red, pink, white or dingy green, sometimes veined fan-wise, throat of spur pale, centre slightly convex, margins reflexed, undulate, weakly scalloped, base slightly kinked, contracted into 2 rounded ridges, angular when viewed in profile; spur whitish to pale pink, 5-7 (-10)mm long, large, sack-like, descendent, slightly curved, shorter than ovary; 2n=36.

Variation Not very varied. Plants from the second wave of flowering are often more robust and have more flowers (Photo A). **'leucoglossa'**: A rather rare hypochromatic form, lip white bordered with green.

Flowering Season (XII-) I-IV; in two successive waves.

Habitat Mainly full sun, on dry, alkaline, often calcareous substrates. Short, poor grassland, open garrigue, edges and clearings in thermophilous woods, often near the coast, up to 1300m asl.

Distribution Mediterranean. From Portugal to the Caucasus and Iran. Rather widespread but often rare, except in Crete and Malta where it can be rather abundant. In France only in Var, but perhaps extinct.

Countries Ae Ag ?Al An Bl Cr Cy ?†Ga Gr Hs Ij It Li Ls Ma Me Sa Si Tn Tu.

Photos Gr, Kiklades, Milos, 18.IV.1998; Me, Malta, 22.II.1993. P. DELFORGE.

The *Orchis coriophora* group

Characteristics Sepals long-coalescent; sepals and petals forming a tight hood; lip 3-lobed; median lobe entire, longer than lateral lobes; spur thick, nectariferous; 2n= (36), 38. A monophyletic group with 3 species.

Orchis coriophora L.

Etymology -*phora*: bearing; corio-: bugs (an allusion to the unpleasant scent of the flowers). **Type*** Be, Brabant, Louvain (1753). **Synonyms** *Anteriorchis coriophora* (L.) E. KLEIN & STRACK, *Anacamptis coriophora* (L.) R.M. BATEMAN, PRIDGEON & M.W. CHASE.

Description 15-40 (-60)cm tall; stem robust, pale green, often with leaves up to the tip; 4-10 basal leaves, (near -)erect, unmarked, linear-lanceolate, slightly keeled, 5-15cm x 1-4cm; 2-6 cauline leaves, smaller, clasping, upper leaves bract-like; bracts membranous, green washed red, longer than ovary; inflorescence dense, ovoid to cylindrical, up to 8cm tall; flowers numerous, deep dark red to olive-green, often wine-purple, rarely pink washed green, with a bug-like scent; hood ovoid-pointed, 6.5-10mm long; sepals oval-pointed; petals linear-lanceolate, 4-6mm long; lip fleshy, thick, 3-lobed, 5-8 (-10)mm long, base pale, often grooved and hairy, centre convex, abruptly kinked, with red to brownish papillose spots; lateral lobes near rhomboidal, obliquely pointed, irregularly scalloped; median lobe oblong to lanceolate, entire, slightly longer than lateral lobes, turned down and back; spur conical, 4-8mm long, descendent, slightly curved, usually shorter than lip; 2n=36, 38. **Variation** Less varied than *Orchis fragrans*.

Flowering Season IV-VII.

Habitat Mostly full sun, on damp, slightly acidic to slightly alkaline, clayey-calcareous substrates. Grassy places derived from 'molinaies': boggy meadows and moorland, flushed slopes, woodland edges prone to flooding, up to 2500m asl.

Distribution Central and southern Europe. Confined to the mountains in the Mediterranean region; eastwards perhaps as far as the Caucasus; southern limits of range poorly known due to confusion with *O. fragrans*. Very local and often rare, in general decline.

Countries Al An Au †Be Bu Cz Ga Ge Gr He †Ho Hs Hu It Ju Lu †Lx Pb Po Rm Ro.

Photos Ga, Ardèche, 15.V.1999. P. DELFORGE.

Orchis coriophora L.
var. *carpetana* WILLKOMM

Etymology *carpetana*: from Carpetani, ancient peoples of central Iberia. **Type** Hs, Madrid (1870). **Synonyms** *O. coriophora* subsp. *carpetana* (WILLKOMM) K. RICHTER, *Anacamptis coriophora* subsp. *carpetana* (WILLKOMM) BERNARDOS, *Orchis martrinii* auct. non TIMBAL-LAGRAVE.

Description As *O. coriophora* var. *coriophora* but slenderer, 30-50cm tall; inflorescence elongated, dense and many-flowered; flowers large with little or no scent, wine-red; spur paler, appearing very thick in profile, often longer than lip (see Discussion below); 2n=36.

Flowering Season VI-VII, rather late. **Habitat** Short grassland and damp, acidic to neutral areas, sometimes open oak woodland, often at altitude. Local but abundant, sometimes in pure populations. **Distribution** Central and southern Iberia. **Countries** Hs Lu ?Ma. **Photo A** Hs, Madrid, 14.VI.1994. P. DELFORGE.

Orchis coriophora L.
var. *martrinii* (TIMBAL-LAGRAVE) GAUTIER

Etymology Dedicated to V. de Martrin-Donos (1802-1870). **Type** Hs, Gérone (1856). **Synonyms** *O. martrinii* TIMBAL-LAGRAVE, *O. coriophora* subsp. *martrinii* (TIMBAL-LAGRAVE) NYMAN, *Anteriorchis coriophora* subsp. *martrinii* (TIMBAL-LAGRAVE) P. JACQUET, *Orchis fragrans* var. *apricorum* DUFFORT, *O. coriophora* subsp. *martrinii* var. *apricorum* (DUFFORT) A. CAMUS, *O. coriophora* subsp. *apricorum* (DUFFORT) MALAGARRIGA.

Description As *O. coriophora* var. *carpetana* but small, 14-22cm tall; inflorescence elliptic, short and few-flowered; flowers without any scent; centre of lip white, finely spotted purple, margins strongly purple; spur bulbous, pinkish to whitish; '*apricorum*', variant with a vanilla scent (of *O. fragrans* ?).

Flowering Season IV-VI. **Habitat** Acidic to neutral short grassland. Local and not very abundant, rarely in pure populations. **Distribution** Central and southern Iberia, Pyrenees. **Countries** Ga Hs ?Lu. **Photo B** Hs, Burgos, 11.VI.1993. P. DELFORGE.

Discussion The validity of these two varieties is not confirmed. They are often mixed with *O. coriophora* and in size they appear to lie within its range of variation. The most spectacular feature of these taxa is the large size of the spur, particularly broad in profile in var. *martrinii*. The circumference of the entrance to the spur is equal to that of var. *coriophora*, but is ± circular in var. *coriophora* and narrowly oval in *martrinii-carpetana*, and it is this which gives the appearance of great thickness to the spur when viewed in profile.

Orchis fragrans
POLLINI

Etymology *fragrans*: perfumed. **Type** It, Verona (1811). **Synonyms** *O. coriophora* subsp. *fragrans* (POLLINI) SOUTHRE, *Anteriorchis coriophora* subsp. *fragrans* (POLLINI) P. JACQUET, *Anacamptis coriophora* subsp. *fragrans* (POLLINI) R.M. BATEMAN, PRIDGEON & M.W. CHASE, *A. fragrans* (POLLINI) R.M. BATEMAN, *Orchis cassidea* M.-BIEB.

Description As *O. coriophora* but more spindly; stem finer, often with fewer leaves; up to 100 flowers, coloration less vinous, less dirty but more varied, often pale, sometimes with a white lip and green hood; pleasantly vanilla-scented; hood slightly more acuminate; lip and hood may be coloured differently; median lobe often clearly longer than lateral lobes and less curved backwards; spur usually as long as lip. **Variation** Polymorphic. More diverse than *O. coriophora*, notably in its size, coloration and the shape of the lip and spur; 2n=38.

Flowering Season III-VI. **Habitat** Mostly full sun, often on dry, calcareous substrates, sometimes saline. Short, poor grassland, garrigue, scrub, open woodland, up to 1100m asl. **Distribution** Mediterranean, east to Iran. Range more southerly than *O. coriophora*, but poorly known due to confusion with that species. Rather widespread and often abundant. **Countries** Ae Ag Al An ?Au Bl Bu Co Cr Cy Ga ?Ge Gr ?He Hs Ij It Ju Li Ls Lu Ma Me ?Rm Ro Sa Si Tn Tu. **Photos** Gr, Kiklades, Kimolos, 26.IV. 1998; Nissia Ioniou, Zakynthos, 17.VI.1993. P. DELFORGE.

Problems in the *Orchis coriophora* group

This group has characteristics that are sometimes interpreted as primitive (flower structure, presence of nectar, limited range of colorants), but its chromosome count seems to be more recent than that of the preceding groups, and this is partly confirmed by molecular analysis. Its closest relatives are the *O. palustris* and *O. papilionacea* groups, and hybrids are sometimes reported with species from these groups; hybrids with members of the *O. morio* group, *Anacamptis* and *Serapias* are rare to extremely rare.

The distinction between *O. coriophora* and *O. fragrans* is clear in many areas. In the mountains of the southern Mediterranean basin and in Anatolia, however, populations can contain a mosaic of forms and an interpenetration of characters which may demonstrate that there is a vast contact zone and consequent hybridisation. This situation has resulted in the frequent refusal of botanists to separate them as 2 species and they are consequently poorly studied.

Orchis sancta L.

Etymology *sancta*: holy (a reference to the holy places of Palestine, the Type locality). **Type*** Ij, Haifa (1759). **Synonyms** *O. coriophora* var. *sancta* (L.) REICHENBACH fil., *O. coriophora* subsp. *sancta* (L.) HAYEK, *Anteriorchis sancta* (L.) E. KLEIN & STRACK, *Anacamptis sancta* (L.) R.M. BATEMAN, PRIDGEON & M.W. CHASE.

Description The habit of *O. coriophora*; 15-45cm tall; 5-15 basal leaves, spreading to erect, unmarked, linear-lanceolate, slightly keeled, 4-12cm x 0.8-1.5cm, often withered by anthesis; 3-6 cauline leaves, smaller, clasping, upper leaves bract-like; bracts membranous, pale, longer than ovary; inflorescence near lax, cylindrical, 6-11cm tall; flowers rather large, pink, purple or pale carmine, slightly scented; hood elongated, very acuminate, sometimes washed green, 9-15mm long; sepals narrowly oval-pointed, asymmetrical; petals linear-lanceolate, 8-13mm long; lip unmarked, 3-lobed, 8-15mm x 3.5-6mm, base grooved, contracted into 2 ridges framing entrance to spur; lateral lobes rhomboidal, broad, clearly toothed; median lobe oblong-lanceolate, entire, curved forward to pendent; spur conical, rather slender, 6-10mm long, descendent, curved forwards. **Variation** A constant species, very isolated, that only hybridises with *O. fragrans* (*O. × callithea* E. Klein), but this may result in large hybrid swarms.

Flowering Season IV-VI (-VII); late. **Habitat** Full sun to mid-shade on dry, calcareous substrates. Short, poor grassland, garrigue, scrub, open woodland, up to 900m asl.

Distribution Eastern Mediterranean. Very rare and local. **Countries** Ae An Cr Cy Gr Ij Ls. **Photos** Gr, Kiklades, Naxos, 24.IV.1995; Milos, 10.IV.1998. P. DELFORGE.

Key to the *Orchis coriophora* group

1   lip unmarked .... *O. sancta*
1*   lip with centre spotted 2

2   stem robust, with leaves along its entire length; flowers dark, dirty, brownish-red to olive-green; scent fetid; on moist substrates.
.... *O. coriophora*
2*   stem more spindly, with fewer leaves; flowers of various colours, often pale, rarely dirty, purple to whitish-green; vanilla-scented; usually on dry substrates.
.... *O. fragrans*

The *Orchis mascula* group

Characteristics Lateral sepals near spreading to erect; petals folded over column; lip with a spur, 3-lobed; lateral lobes broad; median lobe longer than lateral lobes, divided into 2 secondary lobes; 2n=40, 42, 80. A monophyletic group with 23 species in the guide.

Orchis brancifortii
BIVONA-BERNARDI

Etymology Named after Prince Brancifortis, protector of Bivona-Bernardi. **Type** Si, Palermo (1813). **Synonyms** *O. quadripunctata* subsp. *brancifortii* (BIVONA-BERNARDI) E.G. CAMUS, *O. quadripunctata* var. *brancifortii* (BIVONA-BERNARDI) BOISSIER, *Anacamptis brancifortii* (BIVONA-BERNARDI) LINDLEY.

Description As *O. quadripunctata* but more spindly, 10-25cm tall; basal leaves unmarked, 4-10cm x 1-1.5cm; bracts *c.* 2/3x ovary; inflorescence lax, ovoid to near cylindrical; 3-24 flowers, very small, pink, lilac or crimson; lateral sepals 3-5mm long; lip flat, strongly 3-lobed, 3-5mm long, with (1-) 2 blackish-red dots at the base and (1-) 2 other dots hidden in the spur entrance, sometimes forming a streak, centre pale, sometimes washed dark red; lateral lobes linear-obtuse, near horizontal, divergent; median lobe broader, obtuse; spur horizontal, slightly sinuous, ± equal to ovary; 2n=42. **Variation** Not very varied.

Flowering Season IV-VI.

Habitat Full sun to mid-shade on dry, stony, mostly calcareous substrates. Open garrigue, scrub, open woodland, up to 1300m asl.

Distribution Endemic to the eastern half of Sardinia and northern Sicily; also known from one site in Calabria. Very rare and local.

Countries It Sa Si. **Photos** Si, Trapani, 16.IV.1987; Catania, 28.IV.2000. P. DELFORGE.

Key to the *Orchis mascula* group

1 spur large, short, broadly open
.... *O. spitzelii* subgroup (p. 308)
1* spur elongated 3

2 spur very elongated, conical, broad at base, fine at tip ..... *O. anatolica* subgroup (p. 308)
2* spur elongated, cylindrical, thickened at tip
.... *O. mascula* subgroup (p. 322)

Orchis quadripunctata
CYRILLO ex TENORE

Etymology *quadripunctata*: with 4 dots (an allusion to the spotted base of the lip). **Type** It, Naples (1811). **Synonyms** *Anacamptis quadripunctata* LINDLEY, *O. hostii* TRATTINNICK.

Description 10-30 (-40)cm tall; stem often purplish-red at tip; 2-6 basal leaves, spotted or unspotted, oblong to narrowly lanceolate, 4-12cm x 1-2.5cm; 1-3 cauline leaves, smaller, clasping; bracts membranous, reddish, almost as long as ovary; inflorescence lax to dense, cylindrical; 8-35 flowers, small, pink, lilac, purple or sometimes white; sepals oval-obtuse, spreading, slightly curved backwards, lateral sepals 4-7mm x 1.5-4mm, dorsal sepal near equal, vertically erect; petals 2-5mm long, folded down into a tight hood over the column; lip broadly wedge-shaped, ± deeply 3-lobed, 4-7.5mm x 6-11mm, centre flat, white, with 4 (-8) blackish-purple papillose dots, of which 2 (-6) are visible at the base and 2 are hidden in the spur entrance; lateral lobes broad, quadrangular to rhomboidal, rounded; median lobe near quadrangular, rounded, slightly convex, sometimes obscurely bilobed, shorter than, to as long as, lateral lobes and ± as broad; spur 8-14mm long, filiform, hardly broader at base, descendent, slightly curved, sometimes sinuous, ± equal to ovary.

Flowering Season III-VI. **Habitat** Full sun to mid-shade on dry, stony, mostly calcareous substrates. Short grassland, garrigue, open woodland, up to 1600m asl. **Distribution** Central and eastern Mediterranean. Range disjunct, from Mount Gargano (It) and Campania (It) in the west to Cyprus in the east, and from Dalmatia in the north to Crete in the south; probably absent Sicily and Sardinia where replaced by *O. brancifortii*. Local but often occurs in groups. **Countries** Ae Al An Cr Cy Gr It Ju. **Photos** Ju, Hrvatska, Hvar, 12.IV.2004; Cy, Larnaca, 29.III.1989; Gr, Kefallinia, 5.IV.1991. P. DELFORGE.

Orchis (×) sezikiana
B. BAUMANN & H. BAUMANN (pro hybr.)

Etymology Dedicated to E. Sezik, contemporary Turkish botanist. **Type** An, Lydia, Çesme (1991). **Synonym** *O. anatolica* subsp. *sezikiana* (B. BAUMANN & H. BAUMANN) KREUTZ.

Description Habit, leaves and flowers intermediate between *O. anatolica* s.l. and *O. quadripunctata*. Stem 7-21cm tall; 4-7 leaves, spotted or not; sepals 5.5-8.2mm long, dorsal sepal sometimes near erect; lip 5.8-10mm long, with at least 8 dark purple spots or thick streaks from throat of spur to centre of median lobe; spur near horizontal, ± sinuous, 7-16mm x 0.9-1.5mm. Flowering season and habitat as parent species.

Distribution Reported here and there in the Aegean basin (Ae Cr), from Anatolia (An) and Cyprus (Cy). **Photo** An, Çesme, 2.IV.1996. C.A.J. KREUTZ.

Discussion A heterogeneous taxon that has not stabilised, made up of hybrid swarms involving *O. quadripunctata* on one hand and *O. anatolica, O. sitiaca* or *O. troodi* on the other, and ambiguously described as an occasional hybrid that may also be considered as a fully-fledged species. The independence of *O. × sezikiana* from its parent species is not effective. All reported populations are in narrow contact with their parents, making their delimitation very difficult and their status as isolated species of little relevance. Moreover, as constituted, *O. × sezikiana* is a heterogeneous taxon because it groups hybrids of different origins, springing from crosses between *O. quadripunctata* and 3 different species. Within the genus *Orchis*, and particularly the *O. mascula* group, there are other examples of non-stabilised hybrid populations that are not isolated and sometimes wrongly considered fully-fledged species; this is the case, notably, in *O. × colemanii* (= *O. mascula* × *O. pauciflora*) from peninsular Italy.

Key to the *O. anatolica* and *O. spitzelii* subgroups

1   spur very elongated, fine at tip 2
1*   spur large, short, broadly open 6

2   sepals oval, lateral sepals spreading horizontally, dorsal sepal vertically erect ... 3
2*   sepals otherwise 4

3   lip 4-7.5mm long; lateral lobes quadrangular .... *O. quadripunctata*
3*   lip 3-5mm long; lateral lobes linear .... *O. brancifortii*

4   flowers often dark, lateral sepals without central green markings .... *O. anatolica*
4*   flowers often pale, lateral sepals with central green blotches 5

5   lip broader than long, median lobe unspotted .... *O. troodi*
5*   lip longer than broad, median lobe spotted to the tip .... *O. sitiaca*

6   sepals olive-green to reddish-brown outside 7
6*   sepals pink to crimson-lilac outside 8

7   lip very convex, folded; spur almost as long as lip .... *O. spitzelii*
7*   lip not very convex, rather spreading; spur *c.* 1/2x length of lip .... *O. cazorlensis*

8   sepals pale, with a central green mark inside, not prominent, without purple dots .... *O. canariensis*
8*   sepals dark, with a central green mark inside, dotted purple 9

9   spur purple, horizontal or ascendant .... *O. ligustica*
9*   spur pale pink, descendent 10

10   spur rather elongated, often pointed, 2-3.5mm thick at base .... *O. prisca*
10* rather short spur, obtuse, 4-4.5mm thick at base .... *O. patens*

Orchis anatolica
BOISSIER

Etymology *anatolica*: from Anatolia. **Type** An, Carie (1844). **Synonyms** *O. anatolica* var. *taurica* REICHENBACH fil., *O. anatolica* var. *kochii* BOISSIER, *O. rariflora* K. KOCH.

Description 10-40cm tall; stem rather dark reddish-brown; 2-6 basal leaves, spreading in a rosette, green dark, rather matt, spotted violet, rarely pale green and unmarked, oblong to lanceolate, near obtuse, (3-) 6-12cm x 0.8-2.3cm; 1-2 cauline leaves, smaller, clasping; bracts membranous, reddish, almost as long as ovary; inflorescence lax, up to 12cm tall; 2-15 flowers, pale pink to violet or rich purple, rarely white; sepals narrowly oval to lanceolate, slightly concave, lateral sepals spreading to near erect, (2-) 3 veined, 6-9mm x 3-4.5mm, dorsal sepal near equal, near erect or forming a hood with petals; petals 2- (3-) veined, 4-8mm x 2-3mm; lip wedge-shaped, ± deeply 3-lobed, 8-12mm x 8-13mm, centre convex, grooved, whitish, with 2 rows of papillose purple spots; lateral lobes broad, near quadrangular, rounded, often curved forward; median lobe near rhomboidal, sometimes obscurely bilobed, slightly longer than lateral lobes; spur 15-23mm long, conical, horizontal to near vertical, straight to slightly curved, concolourous with hood, base thick, tip long-attenuated.

Variation *'taurica'*, *'kochii'*, variants with (near) entire lips.

Flowering Season (II-) III-V.

Habitat Mid-shade on stony, dry to moist, calcareous to neutral substrates. Garrigue, pinewoods and open woodland, up to 2000m asl.

Distribution Eastern Mediterranean. From the Cyclades and Crete in the west to Iran in the east (reports from Tunisia refer to *O. olbiensis*). Local and rather rare.

Countries Ae An Cr Cy Gr Ij Ls

Photos Gr, Kiklades, Tinos, 6.IV.1994; Paros, 8.IV.1995. P. DELFORGE.

Discussion Morphologically close to heavily spotted eastern populations of *O. quadripunctata* and sometimes considered to be a subspecies of the latter. *O. anatolica* is, however, clearly distinct in its elongated, veined sepals, larger size, the spotting and indentation of the lip, and the shape and position of the spur. Its status is confirmed by molecular analysis.

Orchis troodi
(Renz) P. Delforge

Etymology *troodi*: from the Troodos mountains, Cyprus. **Type** Cy, Troodos mountains (1929). **Synonyms** *O. anatolica* subsp. *troodi* Renz, *O. anatolica* var. *troodi* (Renz) Soó.

Description As *O. anatolica* but often with a more robust habit, larger in all parts; 15-50cm tall; stem sometimes with reduced red wash; leaves more broadly oval, lighter green, less spotted, up to 20cm x 3.5cm, basal leaves sometimes near erect; lower bracts ± equal to ovary; inflorescence near lax to dense, up to 20cm tall; 3-18 flowers, larger, paler, pink to purplish, turning dark carmine on withering; lateral sepals broadly oval, inside washed or blotched green in the centre, 7-11mm x 3.5-5mm; dorsal sepal often near erect; lip wedge-shaped, proportionally larger, spreading to convex, deeply 3-lobed, up to 17mm x 22mm, centre whitish to yellowish, spotted on the lower two-thirds; lateral lobes near quadrangular, rounded, broad; median lobe bilobed to scalloped, unmarked; spur 20-25mm long, horizontal to near vertical, often ascendant.

Flowering Season III-IV.

Habitat Mostly mid-shade, on dry to moist, acidic to neutral substrates, usually lava rubble. Principally open pinewoods and mixed oak woodland with *Quercus alnifolia*, in association with *Dactylorhiza romana*, more rarely garrigue. Usually occurs 700-1000m, but up to 1700m asl.

Distribution Endemic to the mountains of Cyprus. Local but sometimes abundant in its stations.

Countries Cy.

Photos Cy, Troodos mountains, 03.IV.1989. P. Delforge.

Discussion *O. troodi* and *O. anatolica* are rarely distinguished and the presence of *O. anatolica* on Cyprus is sometimes questioned. The 2 species are certainly present on Cyprus, with *O. troodi* confined to the higher, more acidic habitats.

Orchis sitiaca
RENZ) P. DELFORGE

Etymology *sitiaca*: from (the region of) Sitia (Cr). **Type** Cr, Lassithi (1932). **Basionym** *O. anatolica* subsp. *sitiaca* RENZ.

Description As *O. anatolica* but with a more robust habit, 8-35cm tall; leaves greyish-green, shiny, slightly marked to unmarked, up to 14cm long, basal leaves sometimes near erect; bracts greener, lower longer than ovary, upper bracts shorter, 1/2 length of ovary; inflorescence near lax, up to 15cm tall; 3-16 flowers, slightly larger, usually pale, whitish to purplish, washed green; sepals more elongated, lateral sepals blotched green in the centre, 7-11mm x 3-4mm; petals more acuminate, 6-9mm x 2.5-4mm; lip wedge-shaped, narrower and proportionally smaller, very convex to abruptly folded, deeply 3-lobed, 8-14mm x 7-12mm, centre more extensively paler, often yellowish; lateral lobes near rhomboidal to triangular, narrow, not strongly coloured, turned down under the lip; median lobe much longer than lateral lobes, quadrangular, truncated, sometimes obscurely bilobed, usually whitish and spotted to the tip; spur 15-22mm long, horizontal, often spindly, tip ascendant.

Flowering Season (III-) IV-V, 2-3 weeks after *O. anatolica.*

Habitat Full sun to mid-shade on slightly acidic to alkaline, dry to moist substrates. Grassy areas in garrigue, scrub, more rarely pinewoods, up to 1400m asl.

Distribution Endemic to the mountains of eastern and central Crete. Local and rather rare.

Countries Cr.

Photos Cr, Rethimnon, 11.IV.1982. P. DELFORGE.

Notes Hybrid swarms with *O. anatolica* have been reported (see p. 308). Molecular analysis suggests that *O. anatolica* and *O. quadripunctata* are a clade that may derive from *O. sitiaca*, a species which appears to be an archetype.

Orchis spitzelii
SAUTER ex W.D.J. KOCH

Etymology Named after A. von Spitzel, Bavarian botanist (1807-1853). **Type*** Au, Salzburg (1837). **Synonyms** *O. viridifusca* ALBOFF, *O. patens* subsp. *orientalis* (RCHB. fil.) K. RICHTER, *O. patens* subsp. *spitzelii* (SAUTER ex W.D.J. KOCH) LÖVE & KJELLQVIST, *O. patens* var. *asiatica* RENZ, *O. spitzelii* var. *sendtneri* RCHB. fil., *O. spitzelii* var. *gotlandica* PETTERSSON.

Description Slender, 20-40 (-60)cm tall; upper half of stem tinted brownish-red; 2-7 basal leaves, oval-lanceolate, spreading to near erect, unmarked, 6-12cm x 1.6-3.3cm; 1-3 cauline leaves, smaller, clasping; inflorescence near cylindrical, rather dense; (6-) 12-25 (-35) flowers; sepals and petals olive-green, washed purplish-brown outside, rather pale green, spotted purple, inside, forming a rather loose hood; sepals oval, 7-11mm x 3-5mm, lateral sepals sometimes slightly spreading; petals near equal, 5.5-8mm long; lip deeply 3-lobed, pink to carmine-lilac, often densely spotted lilac (sometimes crimson), 9-14mm x 11-18mm (when spread), convex to strongly folded; lateral lobes spatulate, usually turned down, rarely reflexed; median lobe broadly spatulate, incised at tip, sometimes slightly scalloped; spur entrance framed by 2 protuberant lamellae which form a pointed projection when viewed in profile; spur often pale, conical, obtuse, straight to slightly curved, descendent, 6-11mm x 3-4mm (at entrance), ± equal to lip and forming an acute angle with it; 2n=40.

Variation Polymorphic but not polytypic, distinctive notably in the shape and position of the spur. The described varieties have, without doubt, little evolutionary value. *'gotlandica'*: Spindly plants from Gotland (Su) (whether the Swedish populations are native is sometimes questioned); *'asiatica'* from Lebanon; *'sendtneri'*: Spindly plants from Bosnia (Ju).

Flowering Season IV-VII. **Habitat** Mostly mid-shade on dry to moist, alkaline, often calcareous, substrates, well covered by snow in winter. Open woodland, short mountain grasslands, often growing with Bearberry (*Arctostaphylos uva-ursi*), 1000-2100m asl, rarely at lower altitudes, but at sea level on Gotland (Su).

Distribution Sub-Mediterranean montane. Range very disjunct. Gotland (Su) in the north, the Pyrenees, Alps, Balkans, Anatolia and Lebanon in the east, Algeria in the south; reports from Morocco and Majorca (Bl) may refer to *O. cazorlensis*. Very rare and local.

Countries Ag Al An Au ?Bl Co Ga †Ge Gr He It Ju Ls ?Ma Su. **Photos** Ga, Hautes-Alpes, 12.VI. 1982; Isère, 10.VI.1997. P. DELFORGE.

Orchis cazorlensis
LACAITA

Etymology *cazorlensis*: from [Sierra de] Cazorla (Hs, Jaén). **Type** Hs, Jaén (1930). **Synonyms** *O. spitzelii* subsp. *cazorlensis* (LACAITA) RIVERA NUÑEZ & LÓPEZ VÉLEZ, *O. laxiflora* subsp. *cazorlensis* (LACAITA) O. DE BOLOS & VIGO.

Description As *O. spitzelii* but more slender; 2-6 basal leaves, rarely near erect, proportionally shorter, 4-11cm x 1.5-3.5cm; inflorescence laxer; 8-25 (-32) flowers, paler, not so purplish; hood greener, unspotted or lightly spotted inside; sepals more lanceolate, 7-10mm long, lateral sepals sometimes spreading horizontally; lip longer and broader by an average of 3mm, paler, pink to white, densely spotted rather pale lilac-pink, only slightly folded, convex to spreading, margins strongly scalloped, often reflexed; lateral lobes rounded to triangular-obtuse; median lobe broadly spatulate, very scalloped, sometimes toothed; lamellae framing entrance to spur often more attenuated and more rounded when viewed in profile; spur shorter, 5-9mm x 3-4mm (at entrance), *c.* 1/2x lip; 2n=42.

Flowering Season (IV-) V-VI. **Habitat** Principally mid-shade, on dry to moist, slightly acidic to neutral substrates, snow-covered in winter. Open woodland, mostly of conifers, in short, sometimes dense, vegetation, often with lavanders (*Lavandula* spp.) and Bracken (*Pteridium aquilinum*), more rarely Bearberry (*Arctostaphylos uva-ursi*), 900-1900m asl. **Distribution** Western sub-Mediterranean. Apparently endemic to the mountains of central and southern Spain; perhaps also Majorca and Morocco. Very local but sometimes abundant. **Countries** ?Bl Hs ?Ma. **Photos** Jaén, 15.VI.1989 (loc. typ.); Hs, Cuenca, 15.VI. 1988. P. DELFORGE.

Discussion of the *Orchis mascula* group

Probably monophyletic, with 29 species, this group has not yet been extensively examined using isozyme, molecular or genetic analyses. It appears very isolated from other *Orchis*, with which known hybrids seem to be exceptional.

The *Orchis mascula* group is probably the sister group of the *O. militaris* group, in which the majority of species also have a chromosome number of 2n=42. It can be divided into 3, probably monophyletic, lineages, the oldest of which, according to molecular, biogeographical and cladistic analyses, seems to be the *O. anatolica - O. quadripunctata* clade (and its sister species *O. brancifortii*), probably sister of the *O. troodi - O. sitiaca* clade, and this monophyletic assemblage in its turn is probably a sister section to *Orchis spitzelii* and its allies, a monophyletic cluster of 6 species (with perhaps a seventh in Iran (*O. bungii Hautzinger*), made up of species with various chromosome numbers,

(continued on next page)

Orchis canariensis
LINDLEY

Etymology *canariensis*: from the Canaries. **Type** Ca, Tenerife (1835). **Synonym** *O. patens* subsp. *canariensis* (LINDLEY) ASCHERSON & GRÄBNER.

Description 15-40 (-60)cm tall; 3-5 basal leaves in a rosette, sometimes spreading, usually near erect, lanceolate, acuminate, shiny, unmarked, 5.5-18cm x 2-4cm; 1 (-2) cauline leaf, smaller, clasping; bracts lanceolate, purplish, longer than ovary; inflorescence appears short and dense, slightly conical; 5-20 flowers, whitish to reddish-pink; sepals oval, margins more colourful, with a small green central patch inside and often also outside, rarely spotted green or pink, lateral sepals slightly concave, 8-13mm x 4-6mm, near erect, slightly reflexed, directed obliquely forwards; dorsal sepal forming a loose hood with petals, which are narrowly oval, 7-10mm long; lip 3-lobed, hardly convex, spreading, near horizontal to pendent, pinkish-white to pale lilac-pink, with reddish-pink lines, streaks or spots, 12-17mm long, almost as broad, base not kinked, with 2 attenuated ridges framing entrance to spur; lateral lobes near rhomboidal, spreading to slightly turned down and back; median lobe longer, rounded, weakly emarginate; spur 5-7mm long, thick, obtuse, sack-like, slightly ascendant, shorter than ovary; 2n=80.

Flowering Season I-IV (-V). **Habitat** Full sun to mid-shade on moist, slightly acidic substrates, usually lava rubble. Open pinewoods, the fringes of maquis with Tree Heath (*Erica arborea*), bushy ravines, shady rock faces, in areas exposed to the trade winds, 800-1400m asl.

Distribution Endemic to the Canaries; absent Lanzarote and Fuerteventura. Very local but sometimes rather abundant.

Countries Ca. **Photos** Ca, Tenerife, 20.I.1989. D. TYTECA.

Discussion of the *Orchis mascula* group (*continued*)

diploids 2n=40 (*O. prisca, O. spitzelii*), 2n=42 (*O. cazorlensis, O. ligustica*) and tetraploids 2n=80 (*O. patens, O. canariensis*). With its very fragmented distribution, the *O. anatolica* sub-group appears to be an assemblage of preglacial relicts originating from the fragmentation of one or several ancient species that had a vast distribution in the Mediterranean-Atlantic region and were endowed with a purplish lip and sepals that were tinted or spotted with green.

(*continued on next page*)

Orchis prisca
HAUTZINGER

Etymology *prisca*: ancient, forgotten. **Type** Cr, Iraklion (1976). **Synonyms** *O. patens* subsp. *nitidifolia* TESCHNER, *O. spitzelii* subsp. *nitidifolia* (TESCHNER) SOÓ, *O. patens* subsp. *falcicalcarata* WILDHABER.

Description 15-40cm tall; upper half of stem purplish-brown; 3-7 basal leaves, oval-lanceolate, channelled, unmarked, 6-17mm x 1.6-3cm; 1-3 cauline leaves, clasping; lower bracts ± equal to ovary; inflorescence near lax to lax; 5-25 flowers, appearing large, pink to lilac, rather reddish and often dark; margins of sepals and petals more intensely coloured, centre rather dark green, spotted purple inside; sepals oval-lanceolate, 8-13mm x 4-5.5mm, lateral sepals spreading to erect; dorsal sepal forming a loose hood with petals, which are near equal; lip deeply 3-lobed, slightly to very convex, pink to reddish-lilac, usually dark, centre pale, spotted with crimson-lilac, (8-) 10-16mm long and wide; lateral lobes falcate, ± turned down and backwards; median lobe longer, broadly spatulate, emarginate; entrance of spur bordered by 2 ridges that join at base of lip and clearly protruding when viewed in profile; spur varied, 7-11mm x 2-3.4mm (at entrance), conical, descendent, sometimes falcate and pointed when viewed in profile; 2n=40.

Flowering Season Late IV-V (-VI). **Habitat** Full sun to mid-shade on dry, decalcified substrates. Open woodland with pines and Cretan Maple (*Acer creticum*), bushy phrygana, 600-1700m asl. **Distribution** Endemic to Crete. Known from calcareous areas in the mountains in the west (Lefka Ori), centre (Ida) and east (Thripti). Very local and very rare. **Countries** Cr. **Photos** Cr, Lassithi, 17.IV.1989. C.A.J. KREUTZ.

Discussion of the *Orchis mascula* group (*continued*)

Defined in this way, the *Orchis anatolica* sub-group forms a sister section to the clade constituted by *O. mascula* and its allies on the one hand, and the *O. pallens* subgroup on the other. The 3 yellow-flowered species in the *O. pallens* sub-group may originate from a common ancestor that shared this character and which had previously been isolated from *O. (proto-)mascula* on the basis of the preferential selection of yellow or red flowers by pollinating insects, probably as part of facultative floral mimicry (see p. 14). Independent speciations from the *O. (proto-)mascula* are, however, also possible. Isolation mechanisms within the *O. pallens* sub-group appear to be linked to different ecological requirements; the species are rarely syntopic: montane (*O. pallens*), supra-Mediterranean (*O. provincialis*) or Mediterranean (*O. pauciflora*).

(*continued on p. 320*)

Orchis patens
DESFONTAINES

Etymology *patens*: open (a reference to the position of the lateral sepals). **Type** probably Ag (1799). **Synonyms** *O. brevicornis* VIVIANI, *O. patens* subsp. *brevicornis* (VIVIANI) ASCHERSON & GRÄBNER, *O. patens* var. *brevicornis* (VIVIANI) REICHENBACH fil.

Description 25-50 (-70)cm tall; stem purplish to brownish, at least on upper half; 3-7 (-9) basal leaves, spreading in a rosette, narrowly lanceolate, sometimes spotted pale brown, 7-20cm x 1-2.5cm; 1-3 cauline leaves, smaller, clasping; lower bracts equal to ovary; inflorescence cylindrical, rather dense, 6-30cm tall; 6-30 (-40) flowers, pink to lilac, sometimes carmine; margins of sepals and petals more intensely coloured, centre rather dark green, spotted purple inside; sepals oval, (8-) 9-11mm x 4-5mm, lateral sepals slightly concave, slightly asymmetrical, spreading to erect, with a central green patch outside; petals near equal, 6.5-8mm long, forming a loose hood with dorsal sepal; lip deeply 3-lobed, convex, pink to dark lilac, (9-) 11-14mm x (9-) 11-14mm (when spread), centre pale, spotted crimson-lilac, base pale, slightly kinked, contracted into 2 ridges that are slightly angular when viewed in profile; lateral lobes falcate, ± turned down under median lobe; median lobe longer, broadly spatulate, clearly emarginate, often toothed at the angle of incision; spur 6-8mm x 4-4.5mm (at entrance), thick, obtuse, conical, slightly descendent, forming an angle of *c*. 100° with the lip; 2n=80.

Variation Rather little variation. Well separated from *O. prisca* by the shape of the spur, from *O. spitzelii* and *O. cazorlensis* by the more open, erect lateral sepals, and from *O. ligustica* by the less crimson coloration as well as the shape and angle of the spur.

Flowering Season III-VI.

Habitat Full sun to mid-shade on dry to moist, acidic (Liguria) or alkaline substrates. Short grassland, banks, woodland edges, olive groves, open woodland of chestnut, oak or cedar, up to 1600m asl in the Atlas and up to 600m asl in Liguria.

Distribution Curiously disjunct. Liguria (Savona, Genoa, La Spezia) and the Tell Atlas (Ag Tn); never reported between these 2 regions. Rare and local, endangered in at least its Italian sites.

Countries Ag It Tn.

Photos It, Genova, 20.V.1982; 12.V.1988. P. DELFORGE.

Orchis ligustica
RUPPERT (pro hybr.)

Etymology *ligustica*: from Liguria. **Type** It, Genoa (1933). **Synonym** *O. clandestina* HAUTZINGER.

Description As *O. patens* but slender, 20-60cm tall; stem spindly, green; 3-6 basal leaves, shorter, near erect to spreading, oblong-lanceolate, acuminate, dark green, densely spotted dark purplish-brown; 1-3 cauline leaves, smaller, clasping; bracts shorter than ovary; inflorescence cylindrical, lax, short, relatively few-flowered; 10-22 flowers, reddish to crimson-lilac, usually dark, dimensions similar to those of *O. patens*; sepals and petals ± marked on inside with a rather dark green central patch, lightly spotted with purple; sepals oval-lanceolate, near pointed, lateral sepals near erect, dorsal sepal near erect or forming a loose hood with the petals, which are near equal, with reduced green; lip clearly to obscurely 3-lobed, convex, reddish to dark crimson-lilac, 12-17mm long, base not kinked, with 2 attenuated ridges framing entrance to spur, hardly angular when viewed in profile, centre pale, white to yellowish, densely spotted up to entrance of spur with small, dark purple, papillose marks; lateral lobes rounded, broad; median lobe scalloped, broadly spatulate, often indistinctly bilobed; spur robust, 8-14mm long, usually straight, obtuse, conical, crimson-lilac (as dark as lip), rarely slightly descendent, more often horizontal or angled slightly upwards. **Variation** Rather varied. Well separated by the dark spots on the leaves, colour of the flowers and shape of the spur; 2n=42.

Flowering Season V-VI.

Habitat Usually mid-shade, on moist to damp, clearly acidic (pH *c.* 4.5) substrates. Amongst moss on woodland edges and clearings, especially chestnut woods, up to 600m asl.

Distribution Endemic to Liguria. Very local and very rare, endangered by the urbanisation of the Ligurian coasts.

Countries It. **Photos** It, Genoa, 20.V.1982; 12.V.1988. P. DELFORGE.

Discussion *O. ligustica* appears to be intermediate between *O. patens* and *O. mascula*, which it resembles in its spotted leaves, flower colour, papillose lip spotting and elongated spur. Nevertheless, its hybridogenous origins are sometimes questioned. Often syntopic with *O. patens*, it occupies the moister and more acidic areas of their common habitats and is separated absolutely by its chromosome number, 2n=42 (2n=80 in *O. patens*).

Orchis scopulorum
SUMMERHAYES

Etymology *scopulorum*: from rocks. **Type** Mi (1961). **Synonym** *O. mascula* subsp. *scopulorum* (SUMMERHAYES) SUNDERMANN.

Description Slender, 30-70cm tall; stem often flexuous, upper half tinted brownish-red; 3-5 basal leaves, spreading in a rosette to near erect, unmarked, oblong to lanceolate, 9-16cm x 3-5cm; 2-5 cauline leaves, smaller, clasping, upper leaf bract-like; bracts membranous, purplish, ± equal to ovary; inflorescence conical to near cylindrical, near lax, up to 10cm tall; 8-25 flowers, large, sepals and petals lilac to crimson-pink, lip pale pink; lateral sepals oval, near pointed, spreading horizontally, tips reflexed forwards, 10-13mm x 4mm; dorsal sepal 8-10mm long, forming hood with petals, which are near equal; lip 3-lobed, broadly oval, 14-33mm x 13-25mm, spreading, margins scalloped and undulate-crisped, base and centre marked with dark purple papillose spots and streaks; lateral lobes broadly rounded; median lobe broadly spatulate, divided into 2 secondary lobes, sometimes separated by a small tooth; spur 6-8mm long, near cylindrical, straight, horizontal to directed slightly downwards.

Flowering Season V-VI. **Habitat** Full sun to mid-shade on skeletal, damp, acidic substrates (lava, basalts). Banks, cliff fissures and scree, in the rainy trade-wind zone, 1000-1800m asl. **Distribution** Endemic to Madeira. Very local but sometimes abundant in its stations. **Countries** Mi. **Photos A&C** Mi, Encumeada, 26.V.1993. D. TYTECA; **B** 27.V.2003. P. DELFORGE. **Notes** Little known, isolated. Nevertheless, clearly belongs to the *O. mascula* subgroup, in spite of its short horizontal spur. It is not possible at present to decide whether *O. scopulorum* is a relict species or has on the contrary evolved more recently in geographical isolation.

Orchis langei
K. RICHTER (pro hybr.)

Etymology Named after J.M.C. Lange, Danish botanist (1818-1898). **Type** Hs, Madrid (1890). **Synonyms** *O. mascula* subsp. *laxifloriformis* RIVAS GODAY nom. nud., *O. hispanica* A. NIESCHALK & C. NIESCHALK, *O. mascula* subsp. *hispanica* (A. NIESCHALK & C. NIESCHALK) SOÓ.

Description Slender, 25-60cm tall; stem washed red at tip; 2-6 (-10) basal leaves, spreading in a rosette or near erect, usually spotted with violet, oblong-lanceolate, 5-15cm x 1-2cm; 1-4 cauline leaves, smaller, clasping; bracts membranous, purplish, equal to ovary; inflorescence cylindrical, lax, 10-25cm tall; 10-35 flowers, rather large, lilac to dark crimson-pink, rarely pale pink; lateral sepals narrowly oval, directed forwards or spreading to near erect, 8-13mm x 3-6.5mm; dorsal sepal 7-10.5mm long, near erect or forming a hood with the petals, which are near equal; lip broadly wedge-shaped, 3-lobed, 7.5-13mm x 9-18mm, convex to abruptly folded, base pale, sometimes yellowish, unmarked, finely spotted violet or clearly marked with papillose purple dots; lateral lobes near rhomboidal, sometimes scalloped; median lobe bilobed, longer than lateral lobes, clearly kinked and sometimes crisped at base; spur 9-16mm long, cylindrical to near club-shaped, horizontal to ascendant, slightly curved; 2n=42.

Variation The lax inflorescence and the lip, kinked in the centre, are distinctive.

Flowering Season IV-VI.

Habitat Mostly mid-shade on dry to moist, slightly acidic, siliceous or schistose, more rarely calcareous, substrates. Open woodland, both deciduous and coniferous, rarely short, poor grassland, up to 1700m asl.

Distribution Centred on Spain, extending north to the French slopes of the Pyrenees and south to the Middle Atlas in Morocco. Local but often abundant in its stations.

Countries Ga Hs Ma.

Photos Hs, Cuenca, 12.VI.1988. P. DELFORGE.

Note Shows many similarities to *O. pinetorum* which may sometimes appear to be its eastern vicariant.

Orchis pinetorum
BOISSIER & KOTSCHY

Etymology *pinetorum*: from pine forests. **Type** An, eastern Cilicie (1859). **Synonym** *O. mascula* subsp. *pinetorum* (BOISSIER & KOTSCHY) E.G. CAMUS, A. CAMUS & BERGON.

Description Slender, 20-60cm tall; stem green, washed brown at the tip; 4-6 basal leaves, spreading in a rosette to near erect, unmarked, oval to lanceolate, 6-15cm x 1.5-4.5cm; 1-3 cauline leaves, smaller, clasping; bracts membranous, purplish, shorter than ovary; inflorescence near cylindrical, rather lax to dense, up to 20cm tall; 10-45 flowers, rather large, pale pink to lilac or deep crimson-pink; sepals oval-obtuse, lateral sepals deflexed, spreading to near erect, 8-13mm x 3-5mm, dorsal sepal forming a hood with the petals, which are near equal; lip broadly wedge-shaped, 3-lobed, 7-13mm x 10-18mm, flat to slightly convex, base pale, unmarked or with a few papillose purple spots; lateral lobes near rhomboidal, sometimes scalloped; median lobe flat or slightly concave, longer than lateral lobes, broadly spatulate, ± bilobed, sometimes scalloped; spur 9-15mm long, cylindrical to near club-shaped, ascendant.

Variation Distinct from *O. mascula* in its habit, weakly convex lip, and the colour and often the small size of its pale central blotch.

Flowering Season III-VI. **Habitat** Mid-shade on dry to moist, usually alkaline, substrates. Woodland edges, scrub, open woodland, up to 2400m asl.

Distribution Eastern sub-Mediterranean. Yugoslavian Macedonia to the Caucasus; limits of range poorly known due to confusion with *O. mascula*. Local but often abundant.

Countries Ae ?Al An Gr Ju Ls ?Ro Tu.

Photos An, Eskisehir, 30.V.1990. P. DELFORGE (see also p. 279).

Discussion of the *Orchis mascula* group

(continued)

Orchis mascula, with its huge range in the temperate zone, appears to be a central figure in both its group and its subgroup and is surrounded by 8 species. These are often geographically isolated (*O. scopulorum*, *O. ichnusae*), sometimes clearly vicariants (*O. langei*, *O. pinetorum*) or limited to the Mediterranean (*O. olbiensis*), supra-Mediterranean (*O. tenera*) or montane zones (*O. ovalis*). The numerous intergradations between these taxa may result from the re-establishment of sympatry.

Orchis ichnusae
(CORRIAS) J. DEVILLERS-TERSCHUREN & P. DEVILLERS

Etymology *Ichnusa:* ancient name of Sardinia.
Type Sa, Nuoro (1982). **Synonyms** *O. mascula*
subsp. *ichnusae* CORRIAS, *O. olbiensis* subsp.
ichnusae (CORRIAS) BUTTLER, *O. mascula* MORIS non L.

Description Usually spindly, rather thickset, 15-
25 (-35)cm tall; upper half of stem washed purplish-red; 3-6 basal leaves, spreading in a rosette,
near erect, unmarked, oval-lanceolate; 1-3 cauline
leaves, smaller, clasping; bracts membranous,
purplish; inflorescence rather dense, near ovoid
then near cylindrical, up to 12cm tall; (4-) 10-20
(-32) flowers, medium-sized, pink to lilac, rather
pale to rather dark, pleasantly-scented; lateral
sepals oval-lanceolate, asymmetrical, spreading
horizontally to vertically erect, tips reflexed, 9-
11mm x 3-4.5mm; dorsal sepal and petals forming a hood 6-9mm long; lip 3-lobed, slightly convex, 9.5-11mm x 10.5-13.5mm, centre extensively whitish, densely marked with dark purple
papillose dots and streaks; lateral lobes near
rhomboidal, rounded, spreading to ± turned
down; median lobe longer than lateral lobes,
bilobed, scalloped; spur 9-14mm long, 1-1.25x
length of lip, cylindrical, horizontal to ascendant.

Variation Varied. Extreme plants are sometimes
difficult to distinguish from its 2 closest relatives,
O. mascula and *O. olbiensis*; it differs from both
of these in its strong pleasant scent, slightly convex lip and shorter and more ovoid inflorescence;
furthermore, it is also distinct from *O. mascula* in
the smaller dimensions of all parts and its paler
flowers, and from *O. olbiensis* in its denser inflorescence, shorter spur and in the proportions of
the floral parts.

Flowering Season III-V.

Habitat Full sun to mid-shade on dry to moist,
calcareous substrates. Short, poor grassland,
garrigue, scrub, up to 1500m asl.

Distribution Endemic to the calcareous mountains of Sardinia where it is probably the only
representative of the *O. mascula* subgroup. Local
and rather rare.

Countries Sa.

Photos Sa, Cagliari, 14.IV.1996. P. DELFORGE.

Orchis olbiensis
REUTER ex GRENIER

Etymology *olbiensis:* from Olbia, ancient Greek colony (now Hyères, Var). **Type** Ga, Var (1859).
Synonyms *O. mascula* subsp. *olbiensis* (REUTER ex BARLA) ASCHERSON & GRÄBNER, *O. olivetorum* DÖRFLER.

Description As *O. mascula* but spindly, 10-25 (-35)cm tall; stem sometimes flexuous; 3-6 basal leaves, 5-12cm x 1.5-2.5cm, unmarked or with blackish-violet blotches or brownish streaks; 1-3 cauline leaves, clasping; inflorescence lax, often ovoid, 3-8 (-12)cm tall; 6-15 (-25) flowers, rather small, often lightly and pleasantly scented, pale, whitish, pink, red or lilac; lateral sepals near erect to vertically erect but not backing onto each other; lip 3-lobed, 7.5-13mm x 9-17mm, flat to very convex, often paler than hood and spur, margins lightly coloured, centre very pale, densely marked with red papillose spots and streaks; spur ascendant, curved upwards, 13-19mm long, 1-2x length of lip.

Variation Rather varied. Distinct from *O. mascula* in its early flowering, more slender habit, the smaller size of all floral parts and less numerous and paler flowers. The contact zone with *O. mascula* seems clearly defined in France and in Spain, the 2 species are also clearly distinct; intermediate populations in the centre of the Iberian peninsula probably belong to a separate species, *O. tenera*.

Flowering Season III-VI; early.

Habitat Full sun to mid-shade on dry, stony, calcareous, rarely slightly acidic, substrates. Short, poor grasslands, garrigue, scrub, open woodland, up to 2000m asl.

Distribution Western Mediterranean, east to Liguria, Corsica and Tunisia; it is also found slightly away from the Mediterranean coasts in France. Rather local and rather rare. **Countries** Ag Bl Co Ga Hs Lu Ma Tn. **Photos** Bl, Mallorca, 6.IV.1985; Ga, Var, 19.IV.1999. P. DELFORGE.

Key to the *Orchis mascula* subgroup

1	spur 6-8mm long, much shorter than lip .... *O. scopulorum*
1*	spur at least as long as lip 2
2	lip clearly kinked in centre...............*O. langei*
2*	lip not kinked 3
3	sepals and petals very acuminate, base of stem and leaves streaked reddish ... *O. ovalis*
3*	plants without these characters 4

(continued on p. 324)

Orchis laeta
STEINHEIL

Etymology *laeta:* pleasant. **Type** Ag (1838).
Synonyms *O. provincialis* var. *laeta* (STEINHEIL)
MAIRE & WEILLER, *O. pauciflora* subsp. *laeta*
(STEINHEIL) KREUTZ.

Description As *O. olbiensis* but 4-9 unmarked
basal leaves; bracts membranous, yellowish, ±
equal to ovary; 5-10 flowers, whitish to pale yellow; lateral sepals oval, vertically erect, often
back to back, 8.5-14mm x 4.5-7mm; dorsal sepal
7.5-11mm long, forming a loose hood with
petals; petals narrowly oval, 6.5-10mm x 4-6mm;
lip 3-lobed, 8.5-13.5mm x 11.5-17.5mm, convex
to sharply longitudinally folded, margins often reflexed, centre finely spotted purple, sometimes
slightly darker yellow than margins (but much
less intense than lip of *O. pauciflora)*; spur 17-
31mm long, cylindrical, horizontal to ascendant,
usually at least 2x as long as lip.

Flowering Season III-V.

Habitat Mid-shade to shade on moist, siliceous
substrates. Open woodland with oaks and cedars,
grassy places on the edge of woodland in the
mountains, up to 1500m asl.

Distribution Endemic to the Tell Atlas, from the
Blida region (Ag) eastwards to northwest Tunisia
(Kroumirie). Very rare and local. Gravely threat-
ened by overgrazing in Tunisia. **Countries** Ag Tn.

Watercolour Ag, Blida, 12.IV.1972. E. KLOPFEN-
STEIN. **Photos** Ag, Constantine, 1.IV.2004. G. de
Bélair.

Discussion The status of this taxon is not clearly
established; maybe it should be considered a
yellow form of *O. olbiensis*, with which intermediates are very frequent.

E.K.

Orchis tenera
(LANDWEHR) KREUTZ

Etymology *tenera:* spindly. **Type** Hs, Albacete (1977). **Synonyms** *O. mascula* var. *tenera* LANDWEHR, *O. mascula* subsp. *tenera* (LANDWEHR) DEL PRETE.

Description As *O. olbiensis* but more slender, up to 60cm tall; stem washed reddish-brown; 3-5 basal leaves, oval, obtuse, short, unmarked or with sparse brown blotches; inflorescence cylindrical, initially near lax and then lax, up to 30cm tall; flowers numerous, small, unscented, colour close to *O. mascula*, pale lilac to crimson-red, sometimes very intense; lateral sepals near erect to vertically erect, upper half often reflexed; lip 3-lobed, very small, 5-7 (-9)mm long, coloured and spotted as *O. mascula*, but paler; spur ascendant, thick, ± as long as lip; 2n=42.

Flowering Season (IV) V-VI. **Habitat** Mostly full sun on dry to moist, acidic to calcareous substrates. Short grassland and clearings in open pinewoods, 500-1800m asl. **Distribution** Poorly known. Apparently endemic to the mountains of central of Spain. Local but sometimes abundant. **Countries** Hs. **Photos** Hs, Albacete, 17.VI.1989. P. DELFORGE.

Key to the *Orchis mascula* subgroup

(continued from p. 322)

4	more than (10-) 15 flowers	5
4*	6-15 flowers	7
5	lip slightly convex, centre coloured as margins	*O. pinetorum*
5*	lip strongly convex, centre pale, spotted	6
6	lip 8-16mm long	*O. mascula*
6*	lip 5-7 (-9)mm long	*O. tenera*
7	spur 1-1.25x length of lip; flowers very sweetly scented	*O. ichnusae*
7*	spur 1.25-2x length of lip; flowers slightly scented or unscented	8
8	flowers lilac or purple	*O. olbiensis*
8*	flowers white or yellowish	9
9	leaves spotted	*O. provincialis*
9*	leaves unmarked	10
10	lip unmarked	*O. pallens*
10*	centre of lip spotted	11
11	lip bright yellow, darker than sepals	*O. pauciflora*
11*	lip as pale as sepals	*O. laeta*

Orchis mascula (L.) L.

Etymology *mascula:* male (allusion to the appearance of the subterranean parts). **Type*** Su, Gotland (1755). **Synonyms** *O. stabiana* TENORE, *O. mascula* subsp. *occidentalis* O. SCHWARZ, *O. vernalis* SALISBURY, *?O. wanjkowii* WULFF.

Description 20-60cm tall; stem washed reddish-brown; 4-8 basal leaves, spreading in a rosette to near erect, oblong-lanceolate, 5-22cm x 1.5-3.5cm, unmarked or with broad blackish-violet or brownish blotches; 2-4 cauline leaves, smaller, clasping; bracts membranous, washed violet, ± equal to ovary; inflorescence rather dense, (5-) 8-20cm tall; (10-) 15-50 flowers, crimson-red or purplish, very rarely pink or white, unscented or slightly scented, either pleasantly so or distinctly fetid; lateral sepals oval, 7-16mm long, vertically erect, touching back to back at the base, tips slightly reflexed; dorsal sepal near erect or forming a hood with petals; lip 3-lobed, 8-16mm x 8-18mm, slightly convex to sharply folded longitudinally, base white or yellowish, velvety, contracted into 2 ridges, separated sometimes by a shallow groove, centre pale, spotted with crimson tufts, margins dark, often reflexed; lateral lobes rounded at the rear, scalloped, often turned down under the lip; median lobe longer and broader than lateral lobes, divided into 2 secondary lobes, scalloped or not, sometimes separated by a small tooth; spur 11-21mm long, slightly longer than lip, near cylindrical, appearing spindly, thickened at the tip, horizontal to ascendant; 2n=42.

Variation Rather limited. *'stabiana'*: Unmarked leaves and pale flowers; *'wanjkowii'*: Spindly, few-flowered plants described from the Crimea; probably 2 variants of *O. mascula*.

Flowering Season IV-VI (-VII); rather early.

Habitat Full sun to shade on dry to damp, acidic to calcareous substrates. Short, poor grasslands, damp meadows, alpine pastures, open woodland, up to 3000m asl.

Distribution Mediterranean-Atlantic at least; due to confusion with closely related taxa, range poorly known, especially the eastern limits. From the Canaries and North Africa to north of the Arctic Circle; eastwards to at least Italy. May be replaced in central Europe by *O. ovalis* and in the Balkans and as far as Iran by *O. pinetorum*, but has recently been observed in Bulgaria and Anatolia. Widespread and sometimes abundant in the west of the range.

Countries Ag Al An Au Be Br Bu Ca Co Da Fa Ga Ge Gr He Ho Hs It Ju Lu Lx Ma No Pb Po Ro Si Su Tn.

Photos Be, Luxembourg, 13.V.1994. P. DELFORGE.

325

Orchis ovalis
F.W. SCHMIDT ex MAYER

Etymology *ovalis:* oval. **Type** Bohemia (1791).
Synonyms *O. mascula* var. *ovalis* (F.W. SCHMIDT ex MAYER) REICHENBACH vel LINDLEY, *O. signifera* VEST, *O. mascula* subsp. *signifera* (VEST) SOÓ, *O. mascula* var. *signifera* (VEST) STEUDEL & HOCHSTETTER, *O. speciosa* HOST nom. illeg., *O. mascula* var. *speciosa* W.D.J. KOCH, *O. mascula* subsp. *speciosa* (W.D.J. KOCH) HEGI, *O. mascula* var. *hostii* PATZE, MEYER & ELKAN.

Description As *O. mascula* but robust, 15-60cm tall; tip of stem washed reddish-brown, base of stem with numerous red streaks; leaves green, without broad purplish blotches but marked like the stem with numerous red streaks on both sides at the base; bracts as long as or much longer than ovary; flowers numerous, large, often pendant; sepals and petals long-acuminate, with a pointed tip, recurved upwards; lateral sepals spreading horizontally towards the front (not vertically erect or touching back to back); dorsal sepal and petals forming a bell-shaped hood; lip 3-lobed, often appearing narrow, margins undulate, often scalloped, centre frequently hardly spotted; spur straight, thick, cylindrical, ± equal to lip; 2n=42.

Flowering Season IV-VII.

Habitat As *O. mascula*, but more montane.

Distribution Poorly known due to confusion with *O. mascula*; probably eastern mid-European. In the west to the Vercors (Ga); reaches the centre of Italy (Abruzzi), Corsica and the Balkans. Local and rather rare at the periphery of the range, widespread and sometimes abundant elsewhere.

Countries Au Bu Co Cz Ga Ge ?Gr He Hu It Ju Po Rm.

Photos It, Trento, 11.VII.1987; Frosinone, 12.VI.1984. P. DELFORGE.

Discussion Reported from numerous isolated sites remote from its main range in central and eastern Europe, where it seems to replace *O. mascula* completely. Western and southern populations show a shift in a group of characters that brings them closer to *O. mascula*, and this may be evidence of broad intergradation. As a result they are sometimes considered, most probably incorrectly, as representatives of var. ***acutiflora*** KOCH, a name that in fact refers to a banal variant of *O. mascula* with briefly acuminate sepals. On the other hand, in the southeast of the range of *O. ovalis,* notably in Bulgaria, the shift is towards the characters of *O. pinetorum*. The status and distribution of *O. ovalis* needs further study.

Orchis pallens L.

Etymology *pallens:* pale. **Type*** He, Vaud (1771). **Synonym** *O. sulphurea* SIMS.

Description 15-40cm tall; 4-6 basal leaves, spreading in a rosette to erect, shiny green above, unmarked, oblong to oval, mucronate, 6-12cm x 1.5-4cm; 1-2 cauline leaves, smaller, clasping; bracts membranous, yellowish, ± as long as ovary; inflorescence dense; up to 30 flowers, pale yellow to yellowish-white, emitting a slight unpleasant scent, mostly in the evening; lateral sepals broadly oval, spreading to vertically erect, 6-9mm x 3.5-5mm; dorsal sepal 5-7.5mm long, petals near equal, together forming a hood; lip broad, 3-lobed, 7-11mm x 7-14mm, slightly convex, unmarked, yellow, slightly brighter than sepals; lateral lobes rounded, poorly developed; median lobe larger than lateral lobes, obscurely bilobed to entire; spur 7-14mm long, cylindrical, horizontal to ascendant, curved; 2n=40.

Variation Not very varied.

Flowering Season IV-VI.

Habitat Mainly mid-shade, on moist, calcareous to slightly acidic substrates. Alpine pastures, the edges of open woodland, both deciduous and coniferous, mostly in the mountains, up to 2400m asl.

Distribution Probably Balkan-Pontic, ranging east to the Crimea and Caucasus, and only found in the Atlantic zone in the Pyrenees (some reports from central Spain need confirmation; they result sometimes from confusion with *O. provincialis* and *Dactylorhiza markusii*). Rare and local.

Countries Al An Au Bu Co Cz Ga Ge Gr He Hs Hu It Ju Po Ro.

Photos Gr, Viotia, 29.IV.1994. P. DELFORGE.

Notes Despite morphological similarities, *Dactylorhiza sambucina* is not directly related to *Orchis pallens,* which is actually close to *O. mascula*. *O. pallens* lacks nectar and is pollinated, at least in the Alps, by bumblebees of the genus *Bombus* that are attracted by its scent and the resemblance of the orchid to Spring Pea (*Lathyrus vernus*), which is nectariferous. This is facultative floral mimicry (see p. 14), as *O. pallens,* which has little to offer to pollinators, is mostly pollinated in the presence of its model but is still visited by pollinators in its absence.

Orchis provincialis
BALBIS ex LAMARCK & DC.

Etymology *provincialis:* from Provence. **Type** Ga, Var (1806). **Synonyms** *O. leucostachys* GREYEBACH, *O. cyrilli* TENORE.

Description 15-35cm tall; 3-8 basal leaves in a rosette, spreading to near erect, usually strongly blotched violet, oblong-lanceolate, 5-15cm x 1.5-2.5cm; 2-3 cauline leaves, smaller, clasping; bracts membranous, yellowish, at least as long as ovary; inflorescence lax; 5-20 flowers, large, pale yellow; lateral sepals oval, asymmetrical, spreading to vertically erect, 9-14mm x 4-6mm, margins sometimes undulate; dorsal sepal 5-7.5mm long, near erect or forming a hood with the petals, which are near equal; lip broadly wedge-shaped, 3-lobed, 8-13mm x 11-18.5mm, very convex to sharply folded longitudinally, centre yellow, sometimes slightly brighter than margins, finely spotted red; lateral lobes near rhomboidal, rounded, often turned down under lip; median lobe longer than lateral lobes, distinctly kinked at base, bilobed, secondary lobes slightly divergent; spur 13-19mm long, cylindrical, horizontal to ascendant, slightly curved upwards, tip thickened; 2n=42.

Flowering Season (III-) IV-V (-VI). **Habitat** Full sun to mid-shade on moist, slightly acidic to slightly alkaline substrates. Garrigue, scrub, open woodland, both deciduous and coniferous, more rarely damp areas in the mountains, up to 1700m asl. **Distribution** (Sub-) Mediterranean, east to the Transcaucasus. Rare and local. **Countries** Ae Al An ?Bl Bu Co Cr Ga Ge Gr He Hs It Ju ?Lu Ro Sa Si ?Tu.

Photos Gr. Eyboia, 16.IV.1994; Si, Palermo, 16.IV.2000; Gr, Andros, 10.IV.1994. P. DELFORGE.

Orchis pauciflora
TENORE

Etymology *pauciflora:* few-flowered. **Type** It, Naples (1811). **Synonyms** *O. provincialis* subsp. *pauciflora* (TENORE) ARCANGELI, *O. provincialis* var. *pauciflora* (TENORE) BATTANDIER & TRABUT.

Description Thickset, 10-30cm tall; 4-9 basal leaves in a rosette, spreading to erect, unmarked, narrowly lanceolate, often slightly keeled, 4-7cm x 0.8-2cm; 1-3 cauline leaves, smaller, clasping; bracts membranous, yellowish, at least as long as ovary; inflorescence lax, sometimes dense; 2-8 (-15) large yellow flowers; sepals, petals and spur pale yellow; lateral sepals oval, spreading to near erect, 10-14.5mm x 5.5-9.5mm; dorsal sepal 7.5-11.5mm long, forming a hood with the petals, which are near equal; lip 3-lobed, (9-) 10-14.5mm x (12-) 13-19mm, convex to sharply folded longitudinally, bright yellow, base sometimes orange or bright yellowish-green, centre finely spotted with blackish-purple tufts; lateral lobes near rhomboidal, rounded, margins ± scalloped; median lobe slightly longer than lateral lobes, obscurely bilobed and toothed in the angle between the lobes; spur 15-25mm long, cylindrical, horizontal to ascendant, curved upwards; 2n=42.

Flowering Season III-IV (-V). **Habitat** Full sun to mid-shade on dry, often calcareous and stony substrates. Short, poor grasslands, garrigue, open woodland, up to 1800m asl. **Distribution** Central and eastern Mediterranean. Eastern limit of range poorly known due to confusion with *O. provincialis*; in the east, certainly extends to Thrace (Gr) and Crete. Rare and local. **Countries** Al Co Cr Gr It Ju Si.

Photos Gr, Zakynthos, 11.IV.1993; Atiki, 19.IV.1991; It, Cosenza, 8.IV.2002. P. DELFORGE.

The *Orchis militaris* group

Characteristics Flowers large; sepals and petals forming a hood; lip anthropomorphic, with narrow lateral lobes and bilobed median lobe, usually toothed in angle of incision.

Orchis anthropophora
(L.) ALLIONI

Etymology *–phora:* bearing; *anthropo-:* man (an allusion to the human shape of the lip). **Type*** Ga, ?near Paris. (1753). **Synonyms** *Ophrys anthropophora* L., *Aceras anthropophorum* (L.) W.T. AITON.

Description 10-40 (-50)cm tall; stem hairless, cylindrical; 5-10 leaves unmarked, green, slightly glaucous, clearly veined, 5-15cm x 1-4cm, oblong-lanceolate, lower leaves spreading in a rosette, median leaves erect, upper leaf bract-like; bracts pointed, green, shorter than ovary; inflorescence elongated, denser at tip, 5-20cm tall; up to 50 flowers; sepals oval, 5-8mm x 2.5-5mm, green edged with red, forming a tight hood; petals linear, pale green, concealed inside hood; lip without a spur, 3-lobed, pendent, 10-15mm long, greenish-yellow to orange, margins often darker, brownish or reddish, with 2 pale, shiny, rounded bosses at the base, forming a nectariferous cup; lateral lobes slender; median lobe longer than lateral lobes, divided into 2 strap-shaped halves, almost as long as these, often separated by a tooth; column short, obtuse; ovary sessile, twisted; 2n=42.

Flowering Season (III-) IV-VI (-VII).

Habitat Full sun to mid-shade on dry to moist, calcareous substrates. Xerophitic short grassland, garrigue, scrub, woodland edges, more rarely open woodland, up to 1600m asl.

Distribution Mediterranean-Atlantic. Widespread and rather common in the centre and west of the range, rare in the east and north. **Countries** Ae Ag An Be Bl Br Co Cr Cy Ga Ge Gr He Ho Hs It Ju Ls Lu Lx Ma Me Sa Si Tn Tu. **Photos** Lu, Lisbon, 2.IV.1990; Ga, Aisne, 9.V.1981. P. DELFORGE.

Note Since 1813 usually placed in the monospecific genus *Aceras* (= 'without a horn') due to the absence of a spur. Convergent results from different molecular studies have confirmed that '*Aceras anthropophorum*' is actually a member of the *Orchis militaris* group, and that it is probably the sister species of *O. simia*, a relationship already suggested by its morphology and the large number of hybrids formed with *O. simia* and *O. militaris* (= '× *Orchiaceras*'). A basal position within the group, as an isolated, primitive species, sister to the remainder of the species in the group, is also plausible.

Orchis galilaea
(BORNMÜLLER & SCHULZE) SCHLECHTER

Etymology *galilaea:* Galilean. **Type** Ij, Galilee (1898). **Synonyms** *O. punctulata* var. *galilaea* BORNMÜLLER & SCHULZE, *O. punctulata* subsp. *galilaea* (BORNMÜLLER & SCHULZE) SOÓ.

Description Spindly, 15-50 (-70)cm tall; 3-8 basal leaves, near erect to spreading, unmarked, pale green, shiny, lanceolate, 6-12cm x 2.5-5cm; 1-3 smaller cauline leaves; bracts membranous, coloured as flowers, 2-3mm long; inflorescence dense to near lax, 4-12cm tall, ovoid to near cylindrical, flowers opening top to bottom; 12-30 (-90) flowers, musk-scented, colour varied, bright greenish-yellow, pale yellow, white, pink, crimson or lilac; hood ovoid, long-acuminate, tight to ± lax, veined and lightly spotted purple inside, veined green outside (yellow to white flowers) or veined and spotted violet (white, pink or lilac flowers); sepals oval, 8-10mm long; petals linear, 5-8mm long, pale violet to whitish; lip pendent, deeply 3-lobed, 10-12mm x 10-12mm, centre slightly kinked, white, spotted with tufts of purple hairs, ± spreading; lateral lobes linear, sometimes slightly falcate or spatulate at tip, concolourous with hood or crimson-pink to violet (pink to lilac flowers); median lobe oblong, divided into 2 secondary lobes (similar to lateral lobes but shorter) separated by a small tooth; spur 3-4mm long, curved downwards, cylindrical, *c.* 1/3x length of ovary.

Flowering Season (I-) II-IV (-V).

Habitat Full sun to mid-shade on calcareous, often stony, dry to moist substrates. Garrigue, olive groves, scattered oak woodland with *Quercus calliprinos*, 100-1130m asl.

Distribution Endemic to the Syrio-Palestinian corridor. Very local but sometimes abundant.

Countries Ij Ls.

Photos Ij, Mt Carmel, 24.III.1992; Galilee, 23.III.1992. C.A.J. KREUTZ.

Note The flowers lack nectar and are pollinated by the social bee *Halictus (Evylaeus) marginatus* Bralle; only males are attracted by the scent of the flowers, which undoubtedly resembles the bee's pheromones. This mechanism appears to be very similar to the sexual lures of *Ophrys* but without the pollinator attempting full pseudo-copulation with the lip.

331

Orchis simia
LAMARCK

Etymology *simia:* monkey (an allusion to the shape of lip). **Type** Ga (1779). **Synonyms** *O. macra* LINDLEY, *O. militaris* subsp. *simia* (LAMARCK) BONNIER & LAYENS.

Description Often spindly, 20-40 (-60)cm tall; stem green; 2-6 basal leaves, near erect to spreading in a rosette, unmarked, whitish-green, shiny, oval to lanceolate, slightly channelled, 5-20cm x 1.5-4.5cm; 1-4 cauline leaves, smaller, clasping; bracts membranous, whitish-pink, 1-4mm long; inflorescence dense, short, flowers opening top to bottom, initially conical then ovoid to near cylindrical; 15-55 medium-sized flowers; hood ovoid acuminate, whitish to pale lilac-grey, finely spotted violet, sparsely so outside, more densely so inside where often veined violet; sepals narrowly lanceolate, 10-15mm x 3-4mm; petals linear-lanceolate, 9-12mm long; lip projecting forwards at 45°, deeply 3-lobed, 10-20mm long, centre whitish, spotted with numerous small crimson tufts, tip of lobes very dark, reddish-lilac to violet-purple; lateral lobes linear to filiform, 7-11mm x 1mm; median lobe linear at base then divided into 2 secondary lobes separated by a tooth; lateral lobes and secondary lobes near equal, curved upwards or spirally twisted and pointing in all directions; spur pale, 4-8mm long, cylindrical, obtuse, descendent, *c.* 1/2x length of ovary.

Flowering Season III-VI.

Habitat Full sun to mid-shade on dry, neutral to calcareous substrates. Short, poor grasslands, garrigue, scrub, woodland edges, open woodland, up to 1550m asl.

Distribution Mediterranean-Atlantic. North to southern England and Holland, east to Iran and Turkmenistan. Rather scattered and rare.

Countries Ae Ag Al An Be Bl Br Bu Cr Cy Ga Ge Gr He Ho Hs Hu It Ju Lx Ro ?Tn Tu.

Photos Cy, Limassol, 30.III.1989; Ga, Aisne, 9.VI.1991. P. DELFORGE.

Note In regions where *O. simia* overlaps with *O. militaris* the isolation mechanisms separating the two are sometimes less efficient, allowing some introgression between the 2 species. This can be seen in *Orchis simia* by a more robust habit, a lip with an intermediate shape and colour and a more elongated inflorescence, with the flowers at the base opening first. This situation is particularly prevalent in northeast France and makes the identification of the occasional hybrid between the two species very tricky.

Orchis taubertiana

B. Baumann & H. Baumann

Etymology Named after P. Taubert, who collected the plant in 1887. **Type** Li, Cyrenaica (2001).
Synonym *O. simia* subsp. *taubertiana* (B. Baumann & H. Baumann) Kreutz.

Description As *O. simia* but rather robust, 15-30cm tall; 4-5 basal leaves in a rosette, near spreading, margins often loosely or strongly undulate, larger, 5-10cm x 3-6cm; 2-4 cauline leaves, clasping, often reaching base of inflorescence; inflorescence similarly opening from top to bottom; 15-30 (-60) medium-sized flowers; hood acuminate, 17-20mm long, larger in proportion to lip, often marked with purple outside; sepals 17-20mm x 4.2-5.5mm; petals linear-lanceolate, 11.5-12mm long; lip (near-) horizontal, 10.5-12.5mm long, shorter than sepals, centre whitish, more abundantly spotted with small crimson tufts, tip of lobes very dark, more reddish, less rolled; secondary lobes of median lobe shorter and broader; spur pale, more elongated, 7-9mm long, *c.* 1/2-2/3x length of ovary.

Flowering Season III-IV.

Habitat Full sun to mid-shade on dry, calcareous substrates. Garrigue, scrub, woodland edges, open woodland, up to 1000m asl.

Distribution Endemic to Cyrenaica. Not very widespread and rather rare. **Countries** Li.

Photos Li, Benghazi, 15.III.2003. C.A.J. Kreutz.

Key to the *Orchis militaris* group

1	leaves with straight margins	2
1*	leaves with undulate margins	11
2	lip without a spur	*O. anthropophora*
2*	lip with a spur	3
3	flowers yellow, yellowish or creamy-white	4
3*	flowers pink, lilac or crimson	6
4	centre of lip with broad purple blotches	*O. galilaea*
4*	centre of lip finely spotted with dark-red to blackish-purple tufts	5
5	centre of lip yellow; lateral lobes as broad as base of median lobe	*O. punctulata*
5*	centre of lip creamy-white; lateral lobes narrower than base of median lobe	*O. adenocheila*
6	secondary lobes of median lobe broader than lateral lobes	7
6*	secondary lobes of median lobe filiform like lateral lobes	*O. simia*

(continued on p. 335)

333

Orchis punctulata
STEVEN ex LINDLEY

Etymology *punctulata:* spotted (an allusion to the spotted lip). **Type** Ro, Crimea (1835). **Synonyms** *O. sepulchralis* BOISSIER & HELDREICH, *O. punctulata* subsp. *sepulchralis* (BOISSIER & HELDREICH) SOÓ, *O. punctulata* var. *sepulchralis* (BOISSIER & HELDREICH) KREUTZ, *O. schelkownikowii* WORONOW, *O. punctulata* var. *schelkownikowii* (WORONOW) SOÓ.

Description Robust, 25-60 (-90)cm tall; stem thick, grooved; 4-8 (near-) erect basal leaves, unmarked, shiny, broadly lanceolate, 7-25cm x 3-6cm; 1-4 smaller cauline leaves; bracts membranous, yellowish, 1.5-4mm long; inflorescence dense to near lax, up to 40cm tall, initially ovoid, becoming long-subcylindrical; up to 100 flowers, medium-sized, weakly vanilla-scented; hood ovoid, short, greyish to greenish-yellow, unmarked outside, paler, veined and finely spotted blackish-purple inside; sepals oval to lanceolate, obtuse to shortly pointed, 8-15mm x 3.5-5mm; petals linear, concealed inside hood, 8-12mm long; lip pendent, deeply 3-lobed, 7-15mm long, yellow, sometimes greenish-yellow, centre convex, spotted with small fine blackish-purple tufts of hair; lateral lobes oblong, sometimes falcate, tip rounded; median lobe broadly spatulate, divided into 2 rounded secondary lobes of various shapes separated by a tooth; lateral and secondary lobes reflexed, sometimes ± completely washed brown; spur 3-6mm long, curved downwards, cylindrical, *c.* 1/2x length of ovary.

Variation Rather varied. '*sepulchralis*' Variant, at the most a variety, described from Anatolia; robust, with large flowers, and the lateral and secondary lobes broad and almost entirely dark brown.

Flowering Season II-V; early.

Habitat Full sun to mid-shade on dry to moist alkaline substrates. Short grassland, garrigue, abandoned cultivation, scrub, open woodland, up to 1400m asl.

Distribution Eastern Mediterranean. Occurs west to Thrace (Gr) and Rhodes (Ae), north to the Crimea (Ro) and east to Iran. Local and very rare.

Countries Ae An Cy Gr Ij Ls Ro ?Tu.

Photos Cy, Larnaca, 28.III.1989. P. DELFORGE.

Orchis adenocheila
CZERNIAKOVSKA

Etymology *-cheila:* lip; *adeno-:* [with] glands (an allusion to the lip spotting). **Type** Northwest Iran (1924). **Synonym** *O. punctulata* subsp. *adenocheila* (CZERNIAKOVSKA) SOÓ.

Description As *O. punctulata*, but on average slightly less robust, 30-60cm tall; flowers medium-sized, paler, more whitish or more greenish, with a distinct vanilla scent; hood greenish to whitish outside, veined with dark red or purple inside; sepals 10-12mm long; lip creamy-white washed green, shape recalling *O. militaris* or *O. caucasica*, with narrower and more elongated lateral lobes than those of *O. punctulata*, centre spotted with fine tufts of dark red or purple hairs; spur 4-7mm long, curved downwards.

Flowering Season IV-V; later than *O. punctulata*.

Habitat Full sun to shade on dry to moist, alkaline substrates. Short grassland, garrigue, abandoned cultivation, scrub, open or dense woods, 150-1500m asl.

Distribution Transcaucasia, Iran, Turkmenistan. Very local and very rare; the only report from Turkey (An) concerns *O. caucasica* or *O. purpurea*.

Countries Ro.

Photos Ro, Azerbaijan, 3.V.1997. D. RÜCKBRODT.

Key to the *Orchis militaris* group

(continued from p. 333)

7 secondary lobes broad, wedge-shaped 8
7* secondary lobes shaped otherwise 9

8 hood green, exterior strongly spotted brownish-purple .... *O. purpurea*
8* hood lilac, exterior spotted purple .... *O. caucasica*

9 secondary lobes rounded, formed by 2 lobules that are far shorter than lateral lobes....... 10
9* secondary lobes oblong, as lateral lobes .... *O. galilaea*

10 lip pendent, 10-15mm long .... *O. militaris*
10* lip horizontal, 16-20mm long ...... *O. stevenii*

11 lip 12-20 (-25)mm long; sepals 8-15mm long .... *O. italica*
11* lip 10.5-12.5mm long; sepals 17-20mm long. .... *O. taubertiana*

335

Orchis purpurea
HUDSON

Etymology *purpurea:* purple. **Type** Br, Kent (1762). **Synonyms** *O. fusca* JACQUIN, *O. moravica* JACQUIN, *O. maxima* K. KOCH, *O. lokiana* H. BAUMANN.

Description Robust, (25-) 30-80 (-90)cm tall; stem robust, washed purple at tip; 3-8 basal leaves, (near) erect, unmarked, glossy above, glaucous below, oblong to broadly lanceolate, 6-20cm x 2-7cm; 1-3 smaller cauline leaves; bracts membranous, pinkish, 1.5-3mm long; inflorescence broad, dense, 5-23cm tall, initially conical then long-ovoid; 25-200 large flowers; hood ovoid, short, ground colour green, densely spotted and veined dark purple outside, paler and less spotted inside; sepals oval, shortly pointed, rarely obtuse, 8-13mm x 4-6mm, lateral sepals asymmetrical; petals linear-lanceolate, sometimes near spatulate, 5-8mm long, pale violet to whitish; lip pendent to projecting slightly forwards, 3-lobed, shape varied, 9-20mm x 11-22mm, white, sometimes washed crimson-pink on margins, spotted with numerous small tufts of dark purple hairs; lateral lobes usually linear, pointed, often obliquely truncated; median lobe broad, deeply cut, toothed in the angle of incision, secondary lobes broadly wedge-shaped, margins scalloped or toothed; spur pink, 3-8mm long, curved downwards, tip bulbous, sometimes bilobed, *c.* 1/2x length of ovary.

Variation Little variation in stature, but highly polymorphic in the shape and colour of the lip. More than 30 forms, often merely individual variations, have been described. *'moravica'*: A hypochromatic form with a greenish-yellow hood and white lip spotted with yellow; *'lokiana'*: A variant with small flowers from North Africa. Plants with a lilac-washed hood are probably hybrids or, in northeast Turkey, *O. caucasica.*

Flowering Season IV-VI.

Habitat Full sun to shade on dry to moist, alkaline to neutral substrates. Short grassland, garrigue, woodland edges, open woodland, up to 1800m asl.

Distribution Probably Mediterranean-Atlantic. Eastern limits of range poorly known due to confusion with closely related taxa. Widespread but rather rare.

Countries Ag Al An Au Be Br Bu Co Cz Da Ga Ge Gr He Ho Hs Hu It Ju Lx Po Rm Ro Sa Tu.

Photos Gr, Ioannina, 8.V.1990; Hs, Navarra, 8.VI.1993. P. DELFORGE.

Orchis caucasica
REGEL

Etymology *caucasica:* from the Caucasus. **Type** Ro, Caucasus (1869). **Synonyms** *O. purpurea* subsp. *caucasica* (REGEL) B. BAUMANN *et al.*, *O. aserica* B. BAUMANN *et al.*, *O. caucasica* f. *aserica* (B. BAUMANN *et al.*) P. DELFORGE.

Description As *O. purpurea* but 35-70cm tall; stem green streaked violet or washed violet at tip; 4-8 leaves, paler green; hood with a lilac-grey to purple ground colour, spotted and veined purple outside, veined purple inside; white lip, margins often washed pale lilac, spotted with numerous tufts of red to violet hairs; spur pale lilac spotted with violet-purple.

Variation Very varied, as *O. purpurea,* in the size and shape of the lobes of the lip; distinguished by its bluer or more purplish coloration, rather than brownish-purple. *'aserica'*: A small hypochromatic morph.

Flowering Season V-VI.

Habitat Full sun to mid-shade on dry or moist, alkaline substrates. Short grassland, woodland edges, open woodland, grassy areas in hazel woods, up to 1500m asl. **Distribution** Caucasian. Northeast Anatolia, west to at least Trabzon; limits of range poorly known due to confusion with *O. purpurea*. Local and rather rare. **Countries** An Ro. **Photos** A-B An, Trabzon, 23.V.1990. P. DELFORGE; C (*'aserica'*) Aserbaidjan, Cukur Gabala. 26.IV.1997. H.-W. ZAISS.

Orchis militaris L.

Etymology *militaris:* military. **Type*** Ge, Baden-Württemberg (1753). **Synonyms** *O. rivinii* GOUAN, *O. cinerea* SCHRANK, *O. galeata* POIRET.

Description 20-45 (-65)cm tall; stem robust, washed violet at tip; 3-6 basal leaves, (near) erect, unmarked, shiny, oblong-lanceolate, pointed, 8-18cm x 2-5cm; 1-4 cauline leaves, smaller, clasping; bracts membranous, purplish, 1.5-5mm long; inflorescence initially dense and conical, then near cylindrical and near lax; 10-40 medium-sized flowers; hood ovoid acuminate, whitish to pale lilac-grey, unmarked outside, veined dark violet inside; sepals oval, long-acuminate, 10-15mm x 4-6mm; petals linear, 7-10mm x 1-2mm, pale violet, concealed inside hood; lip pendent to projecting forwards at 45°, deeply 3-lobed, as long as, or slightly longer than, hood, 10-15mm x 8-12mm, base sometimes yellowish, centre pink to pale lilac, spotted with numerous small crimson tufts, tip of lobes dark, lilac to violet-purple; lateral lobes linear, short, up to 4mm long, curved forwards; median lobe linear at base and then expanding, tip divided into 2 short lobules separated by a tooth; spur pale, 5-7mm long, cylindrical, obtuse, descendent, *c.*1/2x length of ovary.

Flowering Season IV-VI (-VII).

Habitat Mostly full sun, on dry to moist, alkaline substrates. Short, poor grassland, unimproved meadows, scrub, woodland edges, open woodland, up to 2200m asl.

Distribution Euro-Siberian. The Atlantic to Siberia; doubtfully recorded from European Turkey and the Balearics. Local and rather rare; rare in the Mediterranean region.

Countries Al Au Be ?Bl Br Bu Cz Ga Ge Gr He Ho Hs Hu It Ju Lx Pb Po Rm Ro Su ?Tu.

Photos Hs, Burgos, 6.VI.1994; Ga, Aisne, 10.VI.1991. P. DELFORGE.

Note For pollination see p. 264.

Discussion of the *Orchis militaris* group

A monophyletic group with 11 species, apparently divided into 2 subgroups, the first containing 3 allopatric species in which the order in which the flowers open is inverted (*O. simia, O. taubertiana* and *O. galilaea*); the second contains 8 species that are morphologically close and whose affinities are difficult to pin down because we lack sufficient knowledge of genotypes, pollinators, model plants and ranges. If *O. anthropophora* has been confirmed beyond doubt as belonging to the *O. militaris* group, its position is still controversial,

(continued on next page)

Orchis stevenii
REICHENBACH fil.

Etymology Named after C. von Steven, German botanist (1781-1863). **Type** Ro, Caucasus (1849).
Synonyms *O. raddeana* REGEL, *O. simia* subsp. *stevenii* (RCHB. fil.) E.G. CAMUS, *O. punctulata* subsp. *stevenii* (RCHB. fil.) SUNDERMANN, *O. militaris* subsp. *stevenii* (RCHB. fil.) B. BAUMANN *et al.*

Description As *O. militaris* but slightly more spindly, 20-50cm tall; 3-10 basal leaves 7-16cm x 1.5-4cm; inflorescence laxer, more cylindrical; 15-30 flowers, larger and slightly paler; ovoid hood more acuminate, 15-19mm long; lip (near) horizontal, more elongated and narrower, 16-20mm long, base yellowish, centre densely spotted with violet tufts; lateral lobes linear to filiform, up to 8mm long; median lobe more elongated, tip more narrowly expanded, sometimes only obscurely emarginate.

Variation Lip shape varied although always very narrow; plants with the median lobe merely spatulate and mucronate, without secondary lobes, are not rare.

Flowering Season V-VI (-VII), rather late; after *O. simia* and *O. caucasica*.

Habitat Full sun to mid-shade on dry to moist, alkaline substrates, sometimes eutrophic. Short, poor grassland, unimproved meadows, scrub, woodland edges, open conifer woods, Hazel plantations, 400-1900m asl.

Distribution Caucasian. Turkmenistan, northern Iran, Caucasus; in Anatolia the range is very fragmented, reported from the northeast (Trabzon, Tunceli) and centre (Nigde). Very rare and local.

Countries An Ro.

Photos An, Trabzon, 4.VI. 1990. P. DELFORGE.

Discussion of the *Orchis militaris* group

(continued)

as results from enzyme analysis contradict those from DNA sequences.
  Orchis punctulata (and *O. adenocheila* ?), along with *O. galilaea*, appears to be evolving towards the sexual attraction of a specific pollinator; *O. militaris* and *O. purpurea*, with their vast range, appear to be sister species that are separated by different ecological requirements but frequently hybridising when they do grow together. In the Caucasus, *O. caucasica* may have originated from one of these hybrid swarms, which then absorbed the 2 parent species; *O. stevenii* and *O. italica* are probably derived from *O. militaris*, the first by temporal isolation, the second while adapting to the most southerly areas where it is almost isolated geographically.

Orchis italica
POIRET

Etymology *italica:* from Italy. **Type** It (1798).
Synonyms *O. longicruris* LINK, *O. longicruris*
subsp. *longipenis* FONT QUER & PALAU FERRER, *O.
undulatifolia* BIVONA-BERNARDI, *O. italica* var. *purpurea* VÖTH.

Description Robust, 20-50 (-70)cm tall; stem
green, thick; 5-10 basal leaves, spreading in a
rosette, dark green, unmarked or spotted violet,
narrowly lanceolate, margins usually strongly
undulate, 5-13cm x 1.2-2.8cm; 1-4 cauline
leaves, smaller, clasping; bracts membranous,
whitish, 1-5mm long; inflorescence dense, initially short, then more elongated, conical, ovoid
or near cylindrical; flowers numerous, rather
large, hood and lip concolourous, pinkish-white,
pink, lilac, sometimes reddish or purple, rarely
white; hood ovoid, long-acuminate, sometimes
lax and/or bell-like, veined dark purplish-pink or
purple outside, spotted and veined inside; sepals
narrowly lanceolate, 8-15mm x 3-5mm; petals
oblong, shortly acuminate, 5-10mm long; lip
pendent or projecting forwards at 45°, deeply 3-
lobed, 12-20 (-25)mm long, ± densely blotched
lilac to crimson, rarely unmarked, base whitish
or yellowish; lateral lobes narrowly lanceolate,
long-acuminate; median lobe oblong, deeply divided into 2 secondary lobes separated by a
prominent tooth; lateral lobes and secondary lobes
near equal, slightly curved upwards, often flat,
slightly darker than centre of lip; spur pale, 4-
8mm long, cylindrical, rather thick, obtuse, curved
downwards, *c.* 1/2x length of ovary; 2n=42.

Variation Little variation except in flower
colour. *'purpurea'*: A hyperchromatic variant
from Sicily (see p. 25). *'longipenis'*: Lip with
long, narrow lobes; described from Mallorca (Bl)
but indistinguishable from the nominate var.

Flowering Season (I-) II-V.

Habitat Full sun to mid-shade on alkaline to
acidic, dry to moist substrates, often stony. Short,
poor grassland, open garrigue, scrub, woodland
edges, open woodland, up to 1300m asl.

Distribution Mediterranean; north to Dalmatia,
central Italy and northern Portugal. Rather local
but sometimes abundant.

Countries Ae Ag Al An Bl Cr Cy Gr Hs Ij It Ju
Li Ls Ma Me Si Tn.

Photos Cy, Limassol, 30.III. 1989; Bl, Mallorca,
2.IV.1985. P. DELFORGE.

The *Orchis tridentata* group

Characteristics Flowers usually small; sepals and petals forming a hood; lip 3-lobed; median lobe divided ± clearly into 2 lobes, rarely separated by a tooth.

Orchis lactea
POIRET

Etymology *lactea:* milky (colour of flowers). **Type** Ag (1798). **Synonyms** *Neotinea lactea* (POIRET) R.M. BATEMAN, PRIDGEON & M.W. CHASE, *O. acuminata* DESFONTAINES, *O. tenoreana* GUSSONE, *O. hanrii* JORDAN, *O. lactea* var. *hanrii* (JORDAN) E.G. CAMUS, BERGON & A. CAMUS, *O. corsica* VIVIANI, *Neotinea corsica* (VIVIANI) W. FOELSCHE.

Description Robust, (5-) 10-25cm tall; 3-8 basal leaves, near erect to spreading in a rosette, unmarked, pale green, oval-lanceolate; 1-3 cauline leaves, smaller, sheathing; bracts membranous, equal to ovary; inflorescence dense, sometimes few-flowered, ovoid to near cylindrical; flowers medium-sized (for the group); hood ovoid acuminate, white to pale pinkish, rarely dark, base green, veined green outside, spotted and veined crimson-green inside; sepals oval-lanceolate, 7-12mm long; petals narrowly lanceolate, 5.5-8mm long; lip pendent, deeply 3-lobed, 6-11mm x 6-13mm (when spread), white, sometimes slightly greenish or pinkish, spotted over the whole surface with numerous purple or violet papillose dots and streaks, centre kinked, very convex, lobes ± strongly turned down and back, sometimes tinted pink or bright crimson-lilac; lateral lobes much broadened at tip, obliquely truncated; median lobe broader and longer than lateral lobes, spatulate, near entire to bilobed, secondary lobes near toothed, rarely separated by a small tooth; spur 5-8mm long, curved downwards, cylindrical, tip broadened, sometimes bilobed, c. 1/2x length of ovary; 2n=42.

Variation *'hanrii'*: Robust variant, inflorescence elongated, rather small flowers (Photo A). *'tenoreana'*: Inflorescence short, lax; frequent alongside nominative var. **Countries** Ga It. *'corsica'*: Lateral lobes falcate, recalling *O. conica*. **Countries** Co. All these variants frequently alongside the nominative var.

Flowering Season II-IV (-V). **Habitat** Full sun to mid-shade on dry to moist, alkaline substrates. Short, poor grassland, open garrigue, scrub, olive groves, open woodland, up to 1800m asl. **Distribution** Mediterranean. Limits of range poorly known due to confusion with *O. conica* (in the west) and *O. tridentata* (Ju, An, Ls). **Countries** Ae Al ?An Bu Co Cr Ga Gr It ?Ju ?Ls ?Me Sa Si ?Tn Tu. **Photos** It, Brindisi, 30.III.1986; Cr, Iraklion, 25.II.1990. P. DELFORGE.

341

Orchis conica
WILLDENOW

Etymology *conica:* conical. **Type** Lu (1805).
Synonyms *O. tridentata* subsp. *conica* (WILLDENOW)
O. DE BOLOS & VIGO, *O. lactea* subsp. *conica* (WILLDE-
NOW) KREUTZ, *Neotinea tridentata* subsp. *conica*
(WILLDENOW) R.M. BATEMAN, PRIDGEON & M.W. CHASE, *N.
conica* (WILLDENOW) R.M. BATEMAN, *Orchis broteroana*
RIVAS GODAY & BELLOT, *O. pusilla* D. TYTECA.

Description 5-30cm tall; 3-8 basal leaves, erect to
spreading in a rosette, sheathing to clasping, unmarked, glaucous green, lanceolate, 6-10cm x 1.5-
2.5cm; 1-3 cauline leaves, bract-like; bracts membranous, whitish; inflorescence dense, initially
conical to ovoid and short, sometimes becoming
long-subglobular; flowers rather numerous, small;
hood globular, acuminate, sometimes slightly
bell-shaped, white to pale pink, base green, veined
green outside, crimson-green inside; sepals 6-
9mm x 1.5-3.5mm, lanceolate, acuminate, tips
recurved in all directions; petals linear-lanceolate,
3-5mm long; lip deeply 3-lobed, pendent to projecting forwards at 45°, 5-8mm x 5-9mm, whitish,
often paler than hood, almost unspotted to densely
but diffusely marked over the whole surface with
pale pink dots (rarely bright), centre flat to slightly
concave; lateral lobes oblong to linear, near
spatulate and toothed at tip, spreading, often
perpendicular to the lip axis; median lobe far
broader than lateral lobes, spatulate, usually entire
and simply toothed at tip, rarely emarginate or
toothed; spur pale, 3.5-5mm long, cylindrical,
curved downwards; 2n=40, 42.

Variation Rather varied. Distinct from *O. tridentata* in the green coloration of the base of the
hood and from *O. lactea* by having the lip flat to
concave in the centre, not kinked, the lobes
spreading or curved forwards.

Flowering Season II-VI; early.

Habitat Full sun to mid-shade on alkaline to
slightly acidic, dry to moist substrates. Short,
poor grassland, open garrigue, open woodland, up
to at least 800m asl. **Distribution** Western
Mediterranean. Poorly known, but apparently rare
and local. **Countries** Ag Bl Ga Hs ?It Lu Ma Me
Sa Si. **Photos** Lu, Extremadura, 3.IV.1990; Bl,
Mallorca, 11.IV.1985. P. DELFORGE.

Discussion *O. conica* seems to be closely related
to *O. tridentata,* which appears to be allopatric.
O. conica is more distant from *O. lactea*, which it
probably replaces in the Iberian peninsula, and
they may not be sympatric in Algeria, in contrast
to the situation in Palermo (Si), Mallorca (Bl), the
Corbières (Ga) and Middle Atlas (Ma). In these 4
cases, intermediate forms have been observed.
Early flowering populations of *O. tridentata* s.l.,
particularly in Italy, must perhaps be placed with
this taxon.

Orchis tridentata
SCOPOLI

Etymology *tridentata:* with 3 teeth. **Type** Ju, Slovenia (1772). **Synonyms** *Neotinea tridentata* (SCOPOLI) R.M. BATEMAN, PRIDGEON & M.W. CHASE, *O. variegata* ALLIONI, *O. tridentata* subsp. *variegata* (ALLIONI) REICHENBACH fil..

Description 15-40cm tall; 4-11 leaves, unmarked, glaucous green, lanceolate; bracts pale lilac, ± equal to ovary; inflorescence (near) ovoid, short, dense; flowers small, weakly scented; hood ovoid, acuminate, entirely lilac or crimson-pink, rarely whitish, veined purple; sepals lanceolate, 8-13mm long; lip 3-lobed, projecting forwards at 45°, 7-12mm long, the same colour as the hood but slightly paler, well spotted over the whole surface with papillose purple or violet dots, centre flat to slightly concave, sometimes yellowish; lateral lobes varied, oblong, near spatulate, tip rounded or obliquely truncated, rarely toothed; median lobe broader and longer than lateral lobes, broadly spatulate, sometimes entire, most often bilobed, secondary lobes short, broad, often near rhomboidal, rarely toothed or separated by a small tooth; spur pale, 5-10mm long, cylindrical, curved downwards, ± equal to ovary; 2n=42.

Flowering Season III-VI (VII).

Habitat Full sun to mid-shade on dry to moist, alkaline substrates. Short, poor grassland, unimproved meadows, open garrigue, mountain pastures, banks, woodland edges, open woodland, up to 1600m asl. **Distribution** Balkan-Pontic. Main range from the Pyrenees to the Caucasus, Iraq and the Caspian Sea; to the north a disjunct population from Hesse to the Oder (Ge). Widespread and rather rare in the west of the range, but rather common in Anatolia. **Countries** Ae Al An Au Bu Co Cr Cz Ga Ge Gr He Hu Ij It Ju Ls ?Me Po Rm Ro Sa Si Tu.

Photos Gr, Kefallinia, 26.IV.1993; Florina, 6.V.1990. P. DELFORGE.

Key to the *Orchis tridentata* group

1	flowers very small; hood pale outside, lip 3-5mm long .... *O. intacta*
1*	flowers without these characters 2
2	base of sepals green 3
2*	base of sepals lacking green tones 4
3	lip flat or slightly concave .... *O. conica*
3*	lip convex .... *O. lactea*
4	sepals purple to dark brown .... *O. ustulata*
4*	sepal pink, lilac or violet 5
5	lip 7-12mm long .... *O. tridentata*
5*	lip 13-20mm long .... *O. commutata*

Orchis commutata
TODARO

Etymology *commutata:* changed. **Type** Si (1842).
Synonyms *O. tridentata* subsp. *commutata*
(TODARO) NYMAN, *O. tridentata* var. *commutata*
(TODARO) RCHB. fil., *Neotinea tridentata* subsp. *com-
mutata* (TODARO) R.M. BATEMAN, PRIDGEON & M.W. CHASE,
N. commutata (TODARO) R.M. BATEMAN.

Description As *O. tridentata* but spindly and
slender, 25-50cm tall; bracts longer; inflorescence
shorter, more conical; flowers less numerous but
larger; hood very elongated; sepals 12-25mm
long, drop-shaped, long-attenuated and acuminate,
tips often recurved in all directions; petals linear;
lip 12-20mm long, 3-lobed, tip of lobes broad,
truncated, strongly toothed; median lobe obscurely bilobed; spur finer, up to 17mm long; 2n=84.

Flowering Season III-V.

Habitat As *O. tridentata*. **Countries** ?Ae Al Au
An Cr Gr He It Si.

Photos Si, Caltanissetta, 19.IV.2000. P. Delforge.
Discussion Often confused with *O. tridentata*,
the range of *O. commutata* is poorly known, today
apparently centred on Greece and extending from
Switzerland in the north to Crete in the south, and
from Anatolia to Sicily (records from North
Africa are doubtful). This region also constitutes
the centre of the range of *O. tridentata*, and the
scattered reports of *O. commutata* may appear to
represent merely a variety of *O. tridentata*, but *O.
commutata* is apparently autotetraploid (2n=84)
while *O. tridentata* is diploid (2n=42). This may
explain why no intermediates are produced when
the two taxa are syntopic and justifies their treatment as 2 distinct species. Nevertheless, it is not
certain that Greek populations should be grouped
with the Sicilian taxon.

Discussion of the *Orchis tridentata* group

A monophyletic group with 7 species that appears
to be close to the *Orchis militaris* group in
morphology and chromosome count, but this relationship is invalidated by molecular analysis. The
patchy and contradictory results given by recent
investigative techniques necessitate the continued
inclusion of the *O. tridentata* group within the
genus *Orchis,* of which it constitutes one of the
original lineages. Species from this group are
isolated by regular self-pollination (*O. intacta*), a
specific pollinator (*O. ustulata,* with its vast
distribution), by the rearrangement of the
chromosomes of *O. tridentata* (autopolyploidy: *O.
commutata*) or by geographical isolation in
refugia: the western Mediterranean (*O. conica*),
central Mediterranean (*O. lactea*) and eastern
Mediterranean (*O. tridentata*); the transitions that
have been confirmed between these 3 taxa probably result from renewed post-glaciation sympatry.

Orchis ustulata L.

Etymology *ustulata:* burnt (an allusion to the dark colour of the hood). **Type*** Su, Scania (1753). **Synonyms** *Neotinea ustulata* (L.) R.M. BATEMAN, PRIDGEON & M.W. CHASE, *Orchis parviflora* WILLDENOW, *O. ustulata* var. *aestivalis* KÜMPEL, *O. ustulata* subsp. *aestivalis* (KÜMPEL) KÜMPEL & MRKVICKA, *Neotinea ustulata* subsp. *aestivalis* (KÜMPEL) P. JACQUET & SCAPPATICCI.

Description 10-50 (-60)cm tall; 5-10 leaves, unmarked, oblong-acuminate to broadly lanceolate, 2.5-15cm x 0.5-3cm, lower 2-3 leaves spreading in a basal rosette, median leaves near erect, sheathing to clasping, upper 1-2 leaves bract-like; bracts membranous, reddish, slightly shorter than ovary; inflorescence initially dense, short and ovoid, becoming lax at the base, near cylindrical, elongating greatly after anthesis; up to 80 small flowers, slightly scented; hood tight, ovoid, short, shortly acuminate, pink to greenish washed purple inside, purple to dark blackish-brown outside, paler and greener after anthesis; sepals oval-lanceolate, 3.5-4.5mm x 1.5-2.5mm, lateral sepals asymmetrical; petals linear, near spatulate, keeled, 3-3.5mm long; lip deeply 3-lobed, pendent to slightly angled forwards, 3.5-8mm long, white, sometimes washed pink, with a few papillose purple spots, flat to slightly concave, base slightly kinked, contracted into 2 attenuated ridges framing entrance of spur; lateral lobes oblong, sometimes falcate, tip near spatulate, rounded, sometimes obliquely truncated; median lobe divided into 2 secondary lobes, similar to lateral lobes but shorter, slightly divergent, sometimes separated by a small tooth; spur greenish to crimson, cylindrical, obtuse, 1-2mm long, descendent; 2n=40, 42. **Variation** Not very varied. Distinct in the size and colour of its flowers. **'*aestivalis*':** Slender, up to 82cm tall at end of flowering season, 2n=42; probably an ecotype.

Flowering Season IV-VIII.

Habitat Full sun on alkaline to acidic, dry to moist substrates. Short grassland, mountain pastures, transitional zones in marshland, more rarely garrigue and open woodland, often montane, up to 2400m asl.

Distribution Euro-Siberian, north to the Baltic. Widespread and sometimes abundant in the mountains, rare elsewhere, very rare in the Mediterranean zone. **Countries** Al Au Be Br Bu Cz Da Ga Ge Ge Gr He †Ho Hs Hu It Ju Lx Pb Po Rm Ro Su. **Photos** Hs, León, 9.VI.1992; Gr, Imathia, 9.VI.1987. P. Delforge.

Notes An isolated species, pollinated by *Echinomyia magnicornis* (Diptera, Tachinidae, see p. 280); only regularly hybridises with *O. tridentata*; other hybrids, both intergeneric and interspecific, are extremely rare and dubious.

345

Orchis intacta
LINK

Etymology *intacta:* intact. **Type** Lu, Serra de Arrabida (1800). **Synonyms** *Neotinea intacta* (LINK) RCHB. fil., *Aceras intacta* RCHB. FIL., *A. densiflora* BOISSIER, *Satyrium maculatum* DESFONTAINES, *Neotinea maculata* (DESFONTAINES) STEARN.

Description (8-) 10-30 (-40)cm tall; stem, leaves and ovaries spotted or not; 3-6 leaves, glaucous green, basal 2-3 leaves 3-12cm x 1-4.5cm, oblong-elliptic, mucronate, spreading, cauline leaves smaller, long-sheathing; upper leaf bract-like; bracts shorter than ovary; inflorescence dense, near one-sided, 2-8cm tall; flowers numerous, very small, half-open, greenish-yellow, whitish or pinkish, sometimes crimson; hood acuminate, 3-4mm long, often spotted pink outside; sepals and petals lanceo-

late; lip directed forwards, often angled, 3-5mm long, 3-lobed; lateral lobes linear, position and length varied; median lobe toothed, sometimes bifid; spur 1-2mm long, conical, obtuse; capsules erect; 2n=40, 42.

Variation Due to of its self-pollination often forms colonies of similar plants, either with yellowish flowers and unspotted leaves, or with pinkish flowers and spotted leaves.

Flowering Season III-V (-VI); rather sporadic.

Habitat Full sun to shade on slightly alkaline to slightly acidic, dry to moist substrates, sometimes sandy. Short, poor grassland, garrigue, scrub, often conifer forests, up to 2000m asl.

Distribution Mediterranean-Atlantic. Madeira and the Canaries (except Lanzarote and Fuerteventura) to the Near East, often close to the coast; a few isolated stations, probably preglacial relicts, in southwest Ireland and on the Isle of Man (Br). Rather widespread and rather rare. **Countries** Ae Ag An Bl Br Ca Co Cr Cy Ga Gr Hb Hs Ij It Ju Ls Lu Ma ?†Me Rm Ro Sa Si Tn Tu. **Photos** Cy, Limassol, 30.III.1989; Sa, Nuoro, 12.IV.1996; Ju, Hrvatska, Hvar, 16.IV.2004. P. DELFORGE.

Note Flowers usually self-pollinating, sometimes even cleistogamous; nevertheless, pollination by tiny beetles (Malachiidae) has been reported; they climb the inflorescence and work their way into the flower buds.

Steveniella
SCHLECHTER

Etymology Dedicated to C. von Steven, German botanist (1781-1863). **Characteristics** As *Orchis coriophora* but with 2 very small ovoid root-tubers; sepals fused; lip hairless; spur bilobed at tip. Monospecific genus.

Steveniella satyrioides
(SPRENGEL) SCHLECHTER

Etymology *-eidês:* like a; *satyri-*: Satyrion, name given in antiquity to various orchids. **Type** Ro, Georgia (1826). **Synonyms** *Orchis satyrioides* STEVEN nom. illeg., *Himantoglossum satyrioides* SPRENGEL, *Peristylus satyrioides* (SPRENGEL) RCHB. fil., *Platanthera satyrioides* (SPRENGEL) RCHB. fil., *Coeloglossum satyrioides* (SPRENGEL) HARTMANN, *Stevenorchis satyrioides* (SPRENGEL) WANKOW & KRÄNZLIN, *Steveniella caucasica* GARAY nom. illeg., *Orchis prosteveniella* P. DELFORGE.

Description 15-40 (-60)cm tall, entirely purple-brown in colour; stem thick, purple to pale brown, covered with a grey bloom; 1 (-2) basal leaf, large, elliptical-subobtuse, 6-20cm x 1.5-6.5cm, near erect, spreading, purplish-green to purplish-brown; 2 cauline leaves, smaller, acuminate, clasping; bracts membranous, much shorter than, to as long as, ovary; inflorescence cylindrical, rather dense; 7-20 (-30) flowers; sepals oblong-pointed, fused almost to the tip, forming a globular hood with 3 teeth, 7-10mm long, purplish-green to violet outside, greenish inside; petals linear, 4-7mm long, green edged purple, entirely concealed inside hood; lip hairless, papillose, pendent, 3-lobed, 6-10mm long, purple to dark violet at the base, yellowish-green to olive-green on the margins, rarely entirely violet; lateral lobes reduced, triangular to rhomboidal; median lobe elongated, 4-6mm long, oval to narrowly oblong, dilated and obtuse at tip; spur 2-4mm long, thick, conical, grooved, bilobed at tip.

Flowering Season IV-V (-VI).

Habitat Full sun to mid-shade on calcareous to neutral, dry to damp substrates. Short grassland, woodland edges, hazel plantations, open deciduous and coniferous woodland, sometimes marshes in the mountains, up to 2000m asl. **Distribution** Pontic and Caucasian. Mountains along the Black Sea coasts, from the Bosphorus north to the Crimea and, in Iran, to the eastern Caspian Sea. Rare and local. **Countries** An Ro. **Photos** An, Trabzon, 29.V.1990. P. DELFORGE.

Note The affinities of *S. satyrioides* have been debated for years. Molecular analysis demonstrates that it is probably an ancestral species, sister to the genus *Himantoglossum*; this clade, in its turn, appears close to the genus *Ophrys*.

Himantoglossum

W.D.J. KOCH 1837 (nom. cons.)

Etymology *imanto-*: strap; *-glôssa*: tongue (an allusion to the long narrow lip of *H. hircinum*).

Characteristics Tall and robust – the largest European orchids; 2 large ovoid root-tubers; stem thick, hairless, whitish at base, often tinted purple or greenish-brown at tip; leaves large, numerous, lanceolate, unmarked, shiny, often withered by flowering; bracts membranous, longer than flowers, at least at base of inflorescence; inflorescence elongated; flowers numerous, large, scented, grey-ish-green, yellowish-green or ± dark violet-purple; sepals and petals bent into a ± tight hood, usually streaked or spotted purple, at least inside; petals often toothed; lip spurred, deeply 3-lobed; lateral lobes often falcate, external margins undulate-crisped; median lobe relatively short and bilobed, or ribbon-like and incised, ± deeply; centre of lip paler than margins; spur descendent, whitish, not very nectariferous; ovary contorted; pedicel very short, slightly twisted; 2n= ?30, 36, 36+B, ?38.

Discussion Euro-Mediterranean genus, monophyletic, sister to *Steveniella* and then a cluster grouping *Ophrys*, *Serapias*, *Anacamptis* and *Orchis*. Ranging from the Canaries in the west to the Transcaucasus in the east, *Himantoglossum* has 8 species, 2 hybridogenous taxa of uncertain status and 3 groups.

The first group, monospecific, is that of *H. comperianum*. It is apparently relatively primitive.

The second group is made up of 2 sister species, *H. robertianum*, which has a vast Mediterranean distribution, and *H. metlesic-sianum*, endemic to Tenerife, whose geographical isolation, apparently very ancient, seems to have resulted in a larger genetic drift than its rather minor morphological differences from *H. rober-tianum* might suggest. *H. affine*, morphologically intermediate with the next group, may actually be a member of the *H. robertianum* clade.

The third group is also monophyletic and is made up of 5 species which ± replace each other geographically. There are large areas of overlap, notably in central Europe, where intermediate forms like *Himantoglossum 'calcaratum'* appear. These 5 species have lip characteristics that have no equivalent either in the genus *Orchis* or within Serapiadinae and can be interpreted as synapo-morphys; the whole clade is thought to be the most derived group of the genus.

At the present stage, molecular analysis confirms that *H. hircinum*, *H. adriaticum* and *H. caprinum* are very closely related, more distant from other Serapiadinae than *H. robertianum*. These 3 species form a monophyletic group, sister to *H. affine*, and these 4 species in turn probably constitute a monophyletic group, sister to *H. formosum*, which, with a lip that has a short median lobe, links this group morphologi-cally to the *H. robertianum* group. *H. hircinum*, closely related to *H. adriaticum,* seems to be the most derived species in the genus, which is confirmed by its distribution, which extends fur-ther north than other *Himantoglossum*. *H. hircinum* thus appears as a recent taxon, which was able to colonise the xeric zones of Atlantic mid-Europe after the last glaciation.

Key to the genus *Himantoglossum*

1   lip with lateral lobes and secondary lobes of median lobe strongly filiform
.... *H. comperianum*
1*   lip otherwise 2

2   median lobe of lip short, bilobed 3
2*   median lobe of lip long, ribbon-like 4

3   large leaves all at base of the stem; lip tinted green .... *H. robertianum*
3*   leaves spread all along stem, lip lacking green .... *H. metlesicsianum*

4   centre of lip white, unmarked 5
4*   centre of lip white, ± clearly spotted or with tufts of purple hair 7

5   median lobe 13-17mm long ..... *H. formosum*
5*   median lobe 22-55mm long 6

6   lateral lobes 1-6mm long .... *H. affine*
6*   lateral lobes (5-) 9-15mm long
.... *H. samariense*

7   centre of lip white, with tufts of purple hair
.... 8
7*   centre of lip white, with papillose spots, strongly coloured, ± distinct ... *H. montis-tauri*

8   inflorescence dense, greenish; tip of median lobe only slightly incised .... *H. hircinum*
8*   inflorescence lax, reddish; tip of median lobe deeply incised 9

9   lateral sepals 8-11.5mm long ... *H. adriaticum*
9*   lateral sepals 13-18.5mm long .. *H. caprinum*

The *Himantoglossum comperianum* group

Characteristics External margins of lateral lobes straight; lateral lobes strongly filiform; median lobe divided into 2 strongly filiform lobules.

Himantoglossum comperianum
(STEVEN) P. DELFORGE

Etymology *Comperia:* Named after Compère, French landowner and colonist in the Crimea who collected the plant. **Type** Ro, Crimea (1829). **Synonyms** *Orchis comperiana* STEVEN, *Comperia comperiana* (STEVEN) ASCHERSON & GRÄBNER, *C. taurica* K. KOCH, *C. karduchorum* BORNMÜLLER & KRÄNZLIN.

Description 25-65cm tall; stem green, washed brownish-purple at tip, bearing numerous leaves of decreasing size, uppermost leaves sheathing; basal 2-4 leaves oblong-elliptic, 8-15cm x 2-4cm, near erect; 2-3 cauline leaves, more pointed, sheathing; bracts 1-2x length of ovary; inflorescence lax, cylindrical, up to 25cm tall; 5-20 (-30) large flowers; hood elongated, bell-like, brownish-green washed lilac outside, veined green or purple inside; sepals oval to near pointed, 5-7mm broad, dorsal sepal 11-18mm long, lateral sepals asymmetrical, 13-20mm long; petals linear, 12-14mm long, concealed inside hood, with 2-4 teeth, often extended by tiny lamellae; lip hairless, 3-lobed, spirally wound in the bud, near horizontal with pendent lobes on flowering, base wedge-shaped, 10-20mm long, pinkish-white to lilac, usually spotted lilac-pink; lateral lobes terminating in a filiform extension, median lobe ending in 2 linear filiform extensions, brownish-green, slightly twisted, 20-60mm x *c.* 1mm; spur pinkish-white, near cylindrical, curved downwards, 12-18mm long.

Variation Hypochromatic plants, very rare, have green flowers with the base of the lip white, unspotted.

Flowering Season (IV-) V-VII.

Habitat Mid-shade on dry, calcareous substrates. Open woodland of pine, cypress and deciduous trees, rarely short grassland, 400-2000m asl.

Distribution Centred on southern Anatolia: west to the Aegean (Lesbos, Samos, Kos, Rhodes), north to the Crimea, south to Lebanon and east to Iranian Kurdistan. Very local and very rare, greatly threatened in Turkey by its harvesting for salep (see p. 29).

Countries Ae An Ls Ro.

Photos An, Antalya, 30.V.1990. P. DELFORGE.

349

The *Himantoglossum robertianum* group

Characteristics External margins of lateral lobes undulate; lateral lobes short; median lobe divided into 2 short lobules.

Himantoglossum robertianum
(LOISELEUR) P. DELFORGE

Etymology Named after G.N. ROBERT, French botanist (1776-1857). **Type** Ga, Var (1807). **Synonyms** *Orchis robertiana* LOISELEUR, *Barlia robertiana* (LOISELEUR) GREUTER, *Orchis longibracteata* BIVONA-BERNARDI nom. illeg., *Aceras longibracteatum* (BIVONA-BERNARDI) REICHENBACH fil. nom. illeg., *Himantoglossum longibracteatum* (BIVONA-BERNARDI) SCHLECHTER nom. illeg., *Barlia longibracteata* (BIVONA-BERNARDI) PARLATORE nom. illeg., *Orchis fragrans* TENORE nom. illeg.

Description Robust, (20-) 25-80 (-110)cm tall; stem thick, often washed violet at tip; 5-10 leaves, fleshy, shiny green, lower leaves 8-35cm x 4-11cm, near erect, in a basal rosette, median leaves smaller, clasping, upper leaves bract-like; bracts leaf-like, washed violet, lower bracts longer than flowers; inflorescence dense, near cylindrical, 6-23 (-40)cm tall; (12-) 25-60 (-70) flowers, smelling of irises; sepals and petals forming a loose hood, reddish-violet, greenish or pinkish outside, paler, greener and spotted violet-purple inside; lateral sepals oval, concave, 10-16mm x 5-10mm, near spreading; dorsal sepal slightly smaller; petals near linear, sometimes slightly auriculate, 7-12mm x 1.5-3mm; lip 3-lobed, elongated, spirally-wound in the bud, pendent on flowering, 13-22mm long, rather convex, base compressed into 2 parallel ridges framing entrance to spur, centre pinkish-white, spotted purplish-pink, more rarely unmarked white, margins undulate-crisped, purplish-pink, brownish-violet, less often olive-green; lateral lobes falcate, shorter than median lobe; median lobe elongated, bilobed, secondary lobes obtuse, divergent; spur thick, obtuse, directed downwards, 4-7mm long; 2n=36, 38. **Variation** Not very varied. Hypochromatic plants frequent, with the hood green and the lip white with olive-green margins.

Flowering Season (XII-) I-IV (-V); early.

Habitat Full sun to mid-shade on alkaline, dry to moist substrates. Short, poor grassland, garrigue, scrub, open woodland, up to 1700m asl. **Distribution** Mediterranean: Morocco to Anatolia, extending on the Atlantic coast to northern Spain; absent from Near East. Rather widespread and rather rare. **Countries** Ae Ag Al An Bl Co Cr Cy Ga Gr Hs It Ju Lu Ma Me Sa Si Tn. **Photos** Gr, Lefkada, 5.IV.1992; Hs, Girona, 11.II.1997. P. DELFORGE.

Himantoglossum metlesicsianum
(TESCHNER) P. DELFORGE

Etymology Named after H. Metlesics, contemporary Austrian botanist. **Type** Ca, Tenerife (1982). **Basionym** *Barlia metlesicsiana* TESCHNER.

Description As *H. robertianum* but stem 40-60 (-110)cm tall; 8-12 leaves, oval-lanceolate, acuminate, slightly keeled, 7-20cm x 2-7cm, arranged all along the stem, upper 2-4 leaves bract-like; lower bracts up to 4cm long; 20-40 flowers; hood smaller, less green, with large red spots inside; lateral sepals 11-13mm x 5-7mm; petals 8-10mm x 3-4mm; lip spreading, 16-22mm long, pink, spotted or streaked purple, without any green coloration, rarely unmarked, edges slightly undulate; lateral lobes triangular-obtuse to rhomboidal; median lobe broader than long, divided into 2 short lobules, rounded to obtuse, often separated by a tooth; spur more spindly, 5-6mm long.

Flowering Season XII-II.

Habitat Full sun to mid-shade on slightly acidic lava rubble. Open garrigue, old terraces, 400-1200m asl.

Distribution Endemic to Tenerife. **Countries** Ca. **Photos** Ca, Tenerife, 17.I.1999. P. DELFORGE.

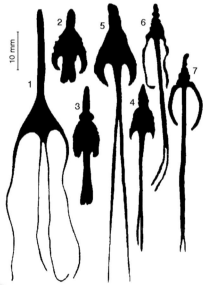

1. *H. comperianum*; **2.** *H. robertianum*; **3.** *H. formosum*; **4.** *H. affine*; **5.** *H. caprinum*; **6.** *H. adriaticum*; **7.** *H. hircinum*.

(herbar. E. NELSON and P. DELFORGE)

The *Himantoglossum hircinum* group

Characteristics Lateral lobes of lip strongly undulate-crisped, clearly shorter than median lobe; median lobe ribbon-like, ± long and incised, spirally-wound in the bud.

Himantoglossum formosum
(STEVEN) K. KOCH

Etymology *formosum:* beautiful, elegant. **Type*** Ro, Azerbaijan (1813). **Synonyms** *Orchis formosa* STEVEN, *Aceras formosum* (STEVEN) LINDLEY, *Loroglossum formosum* (STEVEN) E.G. CAMUS, BERGON & A. CAMUS, *L. hircinum* subsp. *formosum* (STEVEN) E.G. CAMUS & A. CAMUS, *Orchis mutabilis* STEVEN nom. nud.

Description Robust, 30-70cm tall; stem ± strongly washed purple at tip; 2-5 leaves in a basal rosette and 1-5 cauline leaves, yellowish-green, rather narrowly lanceolate, 7.5-17cm x 1.5-4.5cm; bracts often crimson, much longer than flowers; inflorescence rather lax, 15-30cm tall; 15-50 flowers; sepals oval-lanceolate, 9-13mm x 5-7.5mm, deep purple outside, whitish-green and ± veined purple inside, lateral sepals sometimes near spreading; petals small, rhomboidal, sometimes toothed; lip 24-30mm x 10-12.5mm, spreading near horizontally at the start of flowering and then pendent, base contracted into 2 ridges framing mouth of spur, centre narrowly whitish, unmarked, margins broadly deep purple, sometimes washed brownish in fresh flowers, becoming bright olive-green as they age, at least in basal flowers; lateral lobes falcate, much shorter than median lobe, margins strongly undulate-crisped; median lobe ribbon-like, slightly twisted, 13-17mm x 2.5-3mm at base, spatulate, tip rounded, 3.5-4.5mm wide, notched; spur fine, near cylindrical, washed purple, 7-10mm long, descendent, ± parallel to ovary.

Flowering Season V-VI.

Habitat Mostly mid-shade on dry to moist, alkaline, marly or calcareous substrates. Scrub with privet (*Ligustrum*), calcicolous oakwoods and their edges, probably up to 700m asl.

Distribution Endemic to eastern Caucasus and Transcaucasia; recently recorded from a few stations in eastern Azerbaijan; probably reaches Caspian region of northwest Iran. Very local and extremely rare. Greatly threatened due to the critically small size of the population.

Countries Ro.

Photos Ro, Azerbaijan, 5.VI.2000. C.A.J. KREUTZ.

352

Himantoglossum affine
(BOISSIER) SCHLECHTER

Etymology *affine* close, neighbour. **Type** An, Aydin (1884). **Synonym** *H. hircinum* subsp. *affine* (BOISSIER) SUNDERMANN.

Description As *H. hircinum* but 25-80 (-100)cm tall; basal leaves (8-) 10-22cm x 2.5-6cm; inflorescence very lax; (8-) 10-35 (-40) rather pale flowers; hood greenish-white, edged purple outside, veined purple inside; sepals oval-lanceolate, 4-7.5mm x 9-13mm, lateral sepals very asymmetrical, 10-15mm long; petals linear-lanceolate; centre of lip white, unmarked, hairless; lateral lobes very short, triangular-obtuse, 1-6mm long, margins undulate, brownish-green to crimson-brown; median lobe (25-) 30-50 (-55)mm long, slightly twisted, tip cut by a notch 3-15mm deep; spur sack-like, 1-3mm long.

Flowering Season V-VII.

Habitat Mid-shade on dry, calcareous substrates. Thickets, maquis, open oak- and pinewoods, up to 1500m asl.

Distribution Eastern sub-Mediterranean. Very fragmented, centred on southern Anatolia and extending from the Peloponnese (Taygete) to Iran. Very local and very rare, Greatly threatened in Anatolia due to harvesting tubers to make salep. **Countries** An ?†Cr Gr Ls. **Photos A-B** An, Diyarbakir, 27.V.1990. P. DELFORGE.

Himantoglossum samariense
CH. ALIBERTIS & A. ALIBERTIS

Etymology *samariense* ['*samariensis*']: from the gorges of Samaria. **Type** Cr, Chania (1989).

Description Apparently intermediate between *H. affine* and *H. caprinum*, with a lip showing the coloration of the former but the dimensions of the latter; 20-50cm tall; inflorescence very lax; bracts very elongated; 8-25 flowers; lip 35-52 mm long; lateral sepals 10-15mm long; centre of lip hairless, white, sometimes lightly marked purple; lateral lobes falcate, (5-) 9-15mm long, margins undulate, brownish-purple; median lobe 30-42 mm long, notch at tip 3-18mm deep; spur sack-like, 2.5-4mm long.

Flowering Season Mid V-end VI.

Habitat Mid-shade on dry, calcareous substrates. Open woodlands and their edges in the mountains. **Distribution** Known from a few stations in 3 major massifs in Crete. Extremely local and very rare. **Countries** Cr. **Photo C** (see p. 354) Cr, Chania, 1.VI.1999. C.A.J. KREUTZ.

Discussion A controversial taxon, probably hybridogenous, which may have almost completely absorbed its parent species, although these have recently been reported again from Crete.

H. affine

Himantoglossum bolleanum
(Siehe) Schlechter

Etymology Named after C.A. Bolle, German naturalist (1821-1909). **Type** An, Cilicia (1898). **Synonym** *H. montis-tauri* Kreutz & W. Lüders.

Description Intermediate between *H. affine* and *H. caprinum*; 20-90cm tall; inflorescence very lax; 8-30 flowers, weakly scented; hood greenish outside; centre of lip white, ± densely marked with red to deep purple papillose smudges; lateral lobes triangular-falcate, 7-10mm long, margins undulate, rather pale olive-green, rarely washed purple; median lobe 40-70mm long, slightly twisted, tip with a notch 6-20mm deep; spur sacklike, 3-4mm long.

Flowering Season Mid V-VI.

Habitat As *H. caprinum*, up to 1200m asl.

Distribution Known from a few sites in southern Anatolia, Lesbos (Ae) and perhaps Israel. Very rare and local. **Countries** Ae An ?Ij. **Photos A-B** An, Antalya (loc. typ.), 1.VI.1997. C.A.J. Kreutz.

Discussion A controversial taxon, hybridogenous, probably not yet stabilised, in sympatry with *H. affine* but may have almost completely absorbed *H. caprinum* in southern Anatolia and on Lesbos. Forms intermediate between *H. affine* and *H. caprinum* are rather frequent in northern Anatolia.

H. (×) samariense, ◊ p. 353

354

Himantoglossum caprinum
(M.-BIEB.) SPRENGEL

Etymology *caprinum:* [with the scent of] goat. **Type** Ro, Crimea (1819). **Synonyms** *H. hircinum* subsp. *caprinum* (M.-BIEB.) K. RICHTER, *Aceras calcaratum*, G. BECK, *Himantoglossum hircinum* var. *calcaratum* (G. BECK) SCHLECHTER, *H. calcaratum* (G. BECK) SCHLECHTER, *H. hircinum* subsp. *calcaratum* (G. BECK) SOÓ.

Description As *H. hircinum* but 25-80 (-100)cm tall; basal leaves 7-17cm x 2-3.5cm; inflorescence (near) lax; (10-) 15-40 (-50) flowers, scent fetid; flowers as *H. adriaticum* but sepals oval-lanceolate, 6-9mm broad, dorsal sepal 10-15mm long, lateral sepals very asymmetrical, 13-19mm long; petals linear to narrowly rhomboidal, 9-15mm x 2-4mm; lip with centre hairy, white blotched with purple, margins more richly coloured, reddish-brown or dark purple, very rarely green; median lobe 45-90mm long, with notch at tip 10-50mm deep; lateral lobes linear, pointed, (5-) 10-30mm long; spur thick, obtuse, 5-6.5 (-13)mm long.

10 mm

herb. E. NELSON

Variation Polytypic, very diverse, close to *H. adriaticum*. '*calcaratum*' (see silhouette) is robust, with large flowers; median lobe 50-100mm long; spur cylindrical, 8-13mm long.

Countries Ju (Serbia, Montenegro, Fyrom).

Flowering Season VI-VIII.

Habitat Full sun to midshade on dry, calcareous substrates. Short, poor grassland, banks, woodland edges, open woodland, often oak groves, up to 1500m asl.

H. 'calcaratum'

Distribution Balkan. East, in Anatolia, probably to Samsun, west perhaps to Hungary. Rare and local.

Countries Al An Bu ?†Cr Gr ?Hu Ij Ju Rm Ro Tu.

Photos Gr, Kastoria, 9.VII.1986. P. DELFORGE.

355

Himantoglossum adriaticum
H. BAUMANN

Etymology *adriaticum:* Adriatic. **Type** It, Trentin (1978). **Synonym** *H. hircinum* subsp. *adriaticum* (H. BAUMANN) SUNDERMANN.

Description As *H. hircinum* but (20-) 30-75 (-95)cm tall; basal leaves 9-16cm x 1.5-3cm; inflorescence lax; (10-) 15-40 (-50) flowers, scent fetid; hood greenish-pinkish-white, bordered purple outside, sometimes broadly so, veined purple inside; sepals oval, 4-6mm broad, dorsal sepal 7-9mm long, lateral sepals asymmetrical, 8-11.5mm long; petals linear-lanceolate, 5-7 (-8.5)mm x 1.5-2.5mm; centre of lip hairy, white spotted with purple, margins more intensely coloured, usually reddish-brown or dark purple, rarely olive-green or dark green; median lobe 35-60mm x *c.* 2mm, cut at the tip by a notch 5-18mm deep; lateral lobes linear, pointed, (5-) 10-25mm long; spur sack-like, curved, 2.5-3.5 (-5)mm long.

Flowering Season V-VII.

Habitat Full sun to mid-shade on dry, calcareous substrates. Short, poor grassland, banks, thickets, woodland edges, open woodland, up to 1600m asl.

Distribution Central sub-Mediterranean. From Slovenia, Istria (Ju) and Calabria to the south of the Italian Alps; limits of range poorly known, ?western Hungary, ?eastern Austria, ?southern Slovakia. Rare and local.

Countries ?Au ?Cz ?Hu It Ju.

Photos It, Latina, 10.VI.1984; Castrovillari, 16.VII.1989. P. DELFORGE.

Pollination of *Himantoglossum*

The flowers have little or no nectar but are sweet- or foul-scented, usually strongly so. They attract large numbers of various pollinators, above all bees, especially of the genera *Apis*, *Andrena*, *Bombus*, *Eucera*, *Osmia* and *Xylocopa*, and also Diptera, Heteroptera, Lepidoptera and Coleoptera, notably long-horned and scarab beetles.

Himantoglossum hircinum
(L.) SPRENGEL

Etymology *hircinum:* [with the scent of] goat. **Type*** Ga, Seine (Paris Bois de Boulogne) (1753). **Synonyms** *Satyrium hircinum* L., *Loroglossum hircinum* (L.) L.C.M. RICHARD, *Aceras hircinum* (L.) LINDLEY.

Description Robust, 20-90 (-110)cm tall, overall coloration yellowish-green to whitish; stem green, sometimes washed violet-purple, bearing numerous leaves of decreasing size, upper leaves sheathing; 4-6 basal leaves, often withered by flowering, elliptical-lanceolate, 6-15cm x 3-5cm; bracts grass-like, 1-2x length of ovary; inflorescence rather dense, cylindrical; (20-) 40-80 (-120) flowers, scent fetid; hood near globular, greyish-green, sometimes bordered purple outside, streaked purple inside; sepals oval, 4-6.5mm wide, dorsal sepal 7.5-10mm long, lateral sepals asymmetrical, 9.5-12.5mm long; petals linear, sometimes with 3 teeth, 7-11mm long; lip very elongated, spirally wound in the bud, spreading near horizontally on flowering, centre densely hairy, white blotched with purple, margins greenish to lilac-brown, rarely crimson, strongly undulate-crisped; median lobe linear, twisted, 30-65 x *c.* 2mm, cut at the tip by a notch 2-4 (-7)mm deep; lateral lobes linear, pointed, 5-20mm long; spur sack-like, curved, (2-) 3-6mm long; 2n=36.

Flowering Season (IV-) V-VII.

Habitat Full sun on dry, calcareous substrates. Grassy places (*Mesobrometum*), short grassland, garrigue, banks, woodland edges, rarely dunes, up to 1800m asl.

Distribution Atlantic-Mediterranean. Rather rare and local. Very local and very rare in North Africa, absent central Italy. Eastern limit of range poorly known due to confusion with other species in the genus.

Countries Ag Be Br Cz Ga Ge Gr He Ho Hs It ?Lu Lx Ma Si Tn.

Photos Hs, León, 9.VI.1992; Ga, Vienne, 17.VI.1999. P. DELFORGE.

Hybrids in the genus *Himantoglossum*

Very rarely, intergeneric hybrids have been reported between *Orchis* (*O. anthropophora, O. intacta, O. simia*) and *Himantoglossum* (*H. hircinum, H. robertianum*), but all are very dubious.

Ophrys L. 1753

Etymology *Ophirys* (from the Greek *ophis:* snake), then *Ophris* or *Ophrys:* the name given by G. BAUHIN (1560-1623) to the genus *Listera* (=*Neottia*) whose flowers, with their green hood and pendent, forked lip, recall the head and tongue of a snake. **Characteristics** 2 (-3) root-tubers, entire, ovoid to ellipsoid; bracts leaf-like; lateral sepals spreading; petals elongated, very different to sepals; lip without a spur, orientated downwards, entire or lobed, prominently hairy, hairs short, straight, in uniform layers, and a glossy, often hairless zone (= speculum), with a central symmetry, the ensemble, without any equivalent in *Orchidoidae*, resembling the body of an insect; rostellum 3-lobed, median lobe short, lamellar, separating the loculi at its base; 2 retinacles enclosed by 2 separate bursicles; ovary sessile, twisted; 2n=36, 72.

Discussion: A principally Mediterranean genus, ranging from the Canaries to the Caspian Sea and from southern Scandinavia to the northern Maghreb. The genus *Ophrys*, monophyletic, is close to the *Serapias-Orchis-Himantoglossum* assemblage (from which it derives), but is very isolated; it does not form intergeneric hybrids. It is made up of 32 groups and, in this guide, 252 closely related species. The spectacular and varied flowers mimic both the body and the scent (pheromones) of female insects and this provokes the males to attempt to mate with the flowers (pseudocopulation). This highly specialised adaptation is directed towards a few genera of bees and wasps. It has produced intense selection pressures and an exceptional adaptive radiation, probably accentuated by the small number of effective pollinations, which are rare due to the complexity of the mechanisms for attracting pollinators. In effect, the few individuals that are pollinated go on to have their genome over-represented in the following generation, and this may induce a speciation event through a 'founder effect' within the same population, a situation that is quite exceptional amongst plants.

Insect pollinators constitute without doubt the main factor in the speciation of this genus. There are no effective genetic isolation mechanisms; all *Ophrys* species can be artificially crossed and hybrids are not rare in nature, their fertility is rather commonplace as demonstrated by the high rate of supposedly hybridogenous species. Finally, a chromosome count of 2n=36 is very widespread within the genus, apart from the *O. fusca* complex where tetraploid taxa are apparently not rare.

The genus is traditionally divided into two monophyletic sister sections, separated by the position of the pollinating insect on the lip during pseudocopulation, which determines whether the head or the body pick up the pollinia. Section *Pseudophrys* Godfery, in which the abdomen picks up the pollinia (the *fusca-lutea-omegaifera* complex), and section *Euophrys* Godfery (nom. nud.), in which the pollinia are attached to the insect's head (all other species). This division of the genus was recently challenged by molecular analyses, which lumps *Pseudophrys* with *Euophrys*, but separates the *O. speculum* group and *O. tenthredinifera* group from the remainder of *Euophrys;* in this analysis the genus is thus divided into 3 sections. This phylogenetic hypo-thesis, which is neither parsimonious nor corroborated by other molecular, morphological or genetic analyses, is questionable and not followed here.

Section *Pseudophrys*, principally associated with bees Andrenidae and Colletidae, probably derives from *Orchis* s.l., as shown by a set of characteristics shared with *Orchis* and related genera: shape and position of lateral sepals (*Orchis quadripunctata...*), dorsal sepal curved down on to column (*Orchis, Serapias...*), petals hairless (*Orchis...*), elongated and narrow, margins straight (*Orchis collina, O. papilionacea...*), lip 3-lobed, with lateral lobes only slightly convex and median lobe emarginate, without appendage (*O. ustulata, O. pallens...*), totally covered with hair, even at the base (hairs of base and centre: tufted *O. coriophora, O. papilionacea, O. militaris*

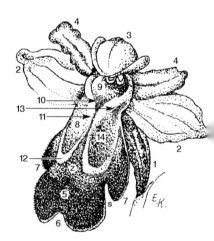

Figure 10. *Pseudophrys*: *Ophrys fusca* s.l. **1**. ovary; **2**. lateral sepal; **3**. dorsal sepal; **4**. petal; **5**. median lobe of lip; **6**. notch at tip of lip; **7**. lateral lobe of lip; **8**. speculum; **9**. stigmatic cavity; **10**. jugular brush of hairs. **11**. hairy groove bisecting speculum; **12**. subterminal crescent (2 crescents join to make a pale 'w'); **13**. basal crest; **14**. prominence; **s** Sinus; **Z** Paler zone around speculum (peri-specular zone).

group...), stigmatic cavity spherical, with a distinct stigmatic surface (*Orchis, Himantoglossum*...), column short, obtuse (*Orchis*).

In section *Euophrys*, derived from the previous section, a change in the pollinator's position on the lip has induced several modifications, probably selected because they facilitated pseudocopulation and imitated the bees' morphology: more rounded sepals, dorsal sepal often erect, column free, petals often villous (= antennae), lip velvety in centre and at tip (= abdomen), but hairless at base (= head, thorax) and on speculum (= glossy folded wings), with the margins ± completely hairy (=hairy legs), sometimes with basal swellings (= pollen sacs), frequently with an appendage (= female), tip of column often elongated and acuminate, stigmatic cavity hemispherical, cup-like, without a distinct stigmatic surface but with shiny pseudo-eyes at the sides (=insect eyes), hemispherical or elliptical and oblique, deriving from the basal ridges of the lip in *Orchis*.

Within section *Euophrys*, 6 major radiations are rather clearly defined and these have been ± confirmed by molecular analyses, although very fragmentary; 3 limited groups, isolated, probably ancient, and 3 well-developed groups, apparently closely related:

1. The *Ophrys speculum* group (sepals, shape of lip and column as *Pseudophrys*); 3 species, probably associated with bees of the family Scoliidae.

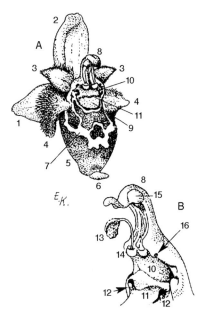

Figure 11. *Euophrys*. **A**. *O. scolopax* s.l. **B**. *O. apifera*. **1**. lateral sepal; **2**. dorsal sepal; **3**. petal; **4**. lateral lobe of lip forming a basal swelling; **5**. median lobe of lip; **6**. appendage and tip of lip; **7**. speculum; **8**. column; **9**. basal field; **10**. stigmatic cavity; **11**. ridge or sill separating stigmatic cavity from basal field; **12**. pseudo-eyes derived from internal bosses; **13**. pollinia; **14**. bursicle; **15**. loculus or theca (containing a pollinium); **16**. staminodial point.

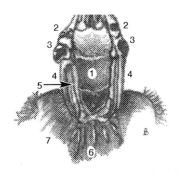

Figure 12. *Ophrys speculum*. **1**. stigmatic cavity; **2**. staminodial points; **3**. temporal bosses carrying the pseudo-eyes; **4**. external lips or swellings; **5**. internal lips or swellings (developing into pseudo-eyes in the majority of *Euophrys*); **6**. bosses on speculum; **7**. base of lip.

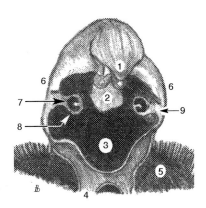

Figure 13. Stigmatic cavity of *Ophrys garganica* **1**. tip of column; **2**. specular stage (pale spot in centre of stigmatic cavity); **3**. basal field; **4**. speculum; **5**. base of lip ('shoulder'); **6**. lateral walls of stigmatic cavity; **7**. pseudo-eyes deriving from the junction of internal and external bosses (see figure 12); **8**. peri-pseudocular ring (a pale circle around the dark pseudo-eyes); **9**. pale 'bridle' connecting the pseudo-eye to the pale external face of the lateral wall of the stigmatic cavity.

2. The *Ophrys tenthredinifera* group (column as *Pseudophrys*; stigmatic cavity surrounded by internal, external, staminodial and temporal bosses, sometimes still rather marked); 9 species, principally associated with bees in the family Anthophoridae, genus *Eucera*.

3. The *Ophrys insectifera* group (position of lateral sepals, shape of petals, lip, hairiness and column as *Pseudophrys*); 3 species, adapted to 3 very different hymenopterans: 2 wasps (Sphecidae and Argidae) and a solitary bee (Andrenidae).

4. The *Ophrys fuciflora* complex (petals short, villous, often auriculate; appendage prominent, often with 3 teeth, a clean texture and inserted into a notch in the lip); 77 species in 8 groups principally associated with bees in the family Anthophoridae, genus *Eucera*.

5. The *Ophrys argolica* complex (petals rather elongated, villous, lip densely hairy on shoulders, with very short hairs elsewhere, appendage without a clean texture, prolonging the margins of the lip, which lacks a notch); 46 species forming 3 groups, principally associated with bees in the family Anthophoridae, genera *Anthophora* and *Melecta*.

6. The *Ophrys sphegodes* complex (petals elongated and hairless, margins undulate; marginal band of hairs on lip prominent and often complete; appendage triangular, ± reduced, with a clean texture, inserted into a notch); 45 species in 6 groups, mostly associated with bees in the famiies Andrenidae and Megachilidae.

The phylogenetic reconstruction of *Ophrys*, particularly *Pseudophrys*, in which numerous new species have been described, remains difficult. It has benefited in recent years, however, from significant progress in the research and definition of diagnostic characters, often subtle, allowing the distinction of lineages using the morphology of the orchids rather than their pollinators. The study of pollinators, although very informative, is actually not a great help in this respect. The attraction of the same pollinator may reveal either a common origin or result in the grouping of phylogenetically distinct but morphologically close lineages due to adaptive convergence; this is, for example, the case with *Ophrys spruneri* and *O. sipontensis*, allopatric species originating from different lineages but adapted to the same pollinator, *Xylocopa iris*.

The taxonomic prominence sometimes given to pollinators in recent years, even to the point of basing orchid systematics upon those of Hymenoptera and referring to some taxa by their pollinator, has shown its limitations. Multiple adaptations to the same pollinator are possible without damaging the orchids' specific isolation and even in cases of sympatry, interspecific barriers are maintained by differences in lip size (small *O. perpusilla*; large *O. leucadica*) or differences in flowering season, adaptations to the different waves of emergence of the same pollinator (early flowering *O. lupercalis*; late flowering *O. arnoldii*; pollinator *Andrena nigroaenea*).

The arrangement of the genus adopted here places at the heart of each species complex the group that is thought to be central, in which the characters of the ancestral species of the complex are probably still expressed: the *O. bornmuelleri* group (*O. fuciflora* complex), the *O. argolica* group (*O. argolica* complex) and the *O. lunulata* group (*O. sphegodes* complex). This arrangement has the advantage, at least sometimes, of bringing together in the guide taxa with analogous morphology that are placed in different complexes, such as *O. kotschyi* and *O. reinholdii*.

Hypochromy in the genus *Ophrys*

All *Ophrys* species may produce individuals, always spectacular, showing reduced pigmentation, with the sepals pure white or yellowish and the lip whitish with greenish-yellow patterning. Such hypochromatic plants are exceptional, except in *O. apifera*, in which although they are always rare, they may sometimes outnumber normal plants within a population, probably because of self-pollination in this species.

Hypochromatic *Ophrys fusca*. **Photo** Lu, Lisbon, 6.IV.1990. P. DELFORGE

Pollination in *Ophrys*

With the exception of *O. apifera*, which is regularly self-pollinating, all *Ophrys* are cross-pollinated and attract pollinators by mimicking the olfactory, visual and tactile signals produced mainly by female hymenopterans, provoking males to attempt to copulate with the flowers. In nature, the attraction of pollinators is highly specific, each species of *Ophrys* attracting only one species of insect, rarely 2 different species consecutively or a few very closely related species of which, theoretically, none are attracted by another species of *Ophrys* in the same section and in the same geographical area.

In the majority of hymenopterans attracted, males emerge from pupation before the females and during the daytime patrol with all senses alert in search of virgin females. These indicate their presence by marking their routes and the entrance to their nests with pheromones. These are scented secretions, produced notably by their Dufour's glands, which stimulate the males' sexual behaviour. Chemical analysis of the lip of *Ophrys* flowers show that they contain up to 100 scented chemicals, of which some are identical in composition to pheromones; these substances are located in the cuticle and hairs of the lip. There is no doubt that the main factor in the attraction and differentiation of *Ophrys* is the scent produced by the flower (which does not help human botanists!). Less specific scents, widespread amongst flowering plants, attract insects from afar; they are replaced close to the lip by a complex cocktail of less volatile substances that trigger sexual behaviour in a specific species of insect.

The importance of the visual attraction exerted by the flower sometimes appears to be significant, sometimes secondary; it is indeed very difficult to figure out what visual signal may be crucial in triggering copulatory behaviour in a bee. Visual stimuli are nevertheless obviously prominent in *Dasyscolia ciliata*, pollinator of *Ophrys speculum*; the morphological similarities between plant and insect are obvious even to our eyes. The visual similarities between the lip hairs in the *O. omegaifera* group and the body of the Anthophoridae that they attract are as striking as the black-and-white patterning of the lip in *Ophrys kotschyi* and *O. cretica*, corresponding to the black-and-white abdomen of *Melecta tuberculata*, or the analogies between the pollen sacks of bees and the conical, villous, lateral lobes of the lip in, for example, the *Ophrys scolopax* and *O. umbilicata* groups. On the other hand, in the genus *Andrena*, made up of species with very similar morphology, visual attraction appears secondary and this leads to a weak morphological differentiation between the species of *Ophrys* that attract them (the *O. sphegodes* group and *O. fusca-lutea* complex), and thus our problem with identification.

Cephalic pseudocopulation; *Eucera bidentata* on *Ophrys villosa* s.l. **Photo** Gr, Zakynthos, 13.IV.1993. P. DELFORGE The attraction exerted by the flowers on the numerous males of *Eucera* is so strong that all the flowers in the inflorescence are literally under attack, with sometimes as many as 5 insects trying to get into position at the same time on a single lip.

Abdominal pseudocopulation; *Andrena schulzi* on *Ophrys laurensis*. **Photo** Si, Catania, 22.IV.2000. P. DELFORGE. The 2 pollinia carried by the bee on its abdomen are in contact with the stigmatic surface; cross-pollination results.

On arrival on the lip, tactile stimuli, produced by its hairs, determine the orientation of the insect; the mimicry of the female's dorsal hairs is as precise as for its pheromones. On a *Pseudophrys*, the insect that alights with its head facing the column, its copulatory apparatus often already deployed, turns around immediately and slips the tip of its abdomen into the stigmatic cavity and starts intense copulatory movements; very rapidly, it makes contact with the retinacles of the pollinia which are then glued to its abdomen.

In *Euophrys*, copulatory movements often begin on arrival at the lip. The insect engages its head in the stigmatic cavity where it makes contact with the retinacles; its eyes against the pseudo-eyes of the flower, its copulatory apparatus touching the appendage of the lip or, in its absence, engaging with the terminal notch, its antennae sometimes curled around the petals which they palpate for a long time, the insect then becomes restless and flies away carrying the pollinia. A pseudocopulation may last from a few seconds to fifteen minutes.

The mode of attracting insects in *Ophrys*, veritably parasitism of the sexual behaviour of hymenopterans, gives a few clues about its evolution. It is evident that a sexual lure is easily derived from a feeding lure, where a flower without nectar mimics by smell and sight a nectariferous flower, a process itself derived from the attraction of pollinators by nectar (see pp. 12-15).

On the other hand, if olfactory signals are fundamental for the selection of sexual lures, they are not the only factors driving diversification; selection also operates on the dimensions of the flower. The study of pollinators has indeed revealed a strong correlation between the size of the pollinator and the size of the lip (or the speculum in some *Pseudophrys*) and demonstrated that what had often been considered as 2 variants, large- and small-flowered, of the same species, actually constituted 2 distinct species (*O. sphegodes*-*O. araneola*; *O. lutea*-*O. sicula*…).

Finally, flowering time and intraspecific variation are equally important. It appears that males of Hymenoptera gain experience and rapidly learn to ignore *Ophrys* flowers. Plants that began to flower before the insects emerge are at an advantage because they can offer many open flowers to inexperienced males. Nevertheless, species with a prolonged flowering season can attract males from a possible second wave of emergence or from another species with a later emergence (*O. bertolonii*, *O. lutea*…). This ability can evidently lead to a separation into 2, temporally isolated, species. For similar reasons, morphologically diverse flowers (varying in the colour of the sepals and in the shape and patterning of the lip) are at an advantage as this permits a slowing of the learning process in the pollinator and thus an increase in pollination rates for the species.

Evolution has produced in *Ophrys* very complex mechanisms of sexual lures favouring an intense radiation of the genus. Indeed, if the adaptive peaks separated by this strategy are very acute, the great number of potential pollinators offers numerous chances of selection to variations and mutations, so that the genus, without doubt of recent origin and with a limited range, comprises at least 252 species and probably many more isolated taxa that have escaped our all-too-human senses.

Hybrids in the genus *Ophrys*

Hybrids between *Ophrys* species are rather frequent; there are several thousand potential combinations of which more than 450 have already been described. *Ophrys* hybrids are not generally too difficult to identify if they originate from parents belonging to unconnected groups or with different coloration or morphology (green sepals x pink sepals for example). Hybrids between closely related species are often harder to elucidate. Locating *Ophrys* hybrids depends on a careful observation of each plant within a colony, usually large. They generally flower close to, or among, their parent. Several hybridogenous species can give an idea of the influence of each parent' on the flowers, for example *O. tardans*, *O. normanii*, *O. delphinensis* or also *O. castellana*.

Key to the genus *Ophrys*

1 base of lip hairless; stigmatic cavity with 2 glossy pseudo-eyes or blotches that resemble eyes (Section *Ophrys* L.) 2

Ophrys cilentana × *O. neglecta* = *O.* × *vanderspekiae*
P. DELFORGE. **Photo**: It, Salerno, 5.IV.2001. P. DELFORGE.

1* base of lip villous, stigmatic cavity without pseudo-eyes or black blotches ...... (Section *Pseudophrys* Godfery) (p. 364).

2 lip 3-lobed; median lobe divided into 2 secondary lobules, without an appendage in the angle between the lobules; column very short with a rounded tip..................3

2* flower otherwise 4

3 petals filiform .... *O. insectifera* group (p. 444)

3* petals short and triangular .... *O. speculum* group (p. 432)

4 petals finely velvety to villous, often short, sometimes auriculate 5

4* petals hairless, often elongated, sometimes ciliate or velvety (*O. sphegodes* complex)...... 15

5 lateral sepals uniformly-coloured; appendage with a clean texture, inserted into a notch in the lip (*O. fuciflora* complex) 6

5* lateral sepals often bicoloured; appendage of the same texture as the sides of the lip, which it prolongs (*O. argolica* complex) 20

6 column with a rounded tip, obtuse; sepals rounded ......*O. tenthredinifera* group (p. 435)

6* column with an acuminate tip 7

7 tip of column elongated, sinuous; pollinia falling onto stigma .... *O. apifera* (p. 447)

7* flowers otherwise 8

8 lip always deeply 3-lobed at base, median lobe amphoroid (broadest towards or above the equator); lateral lobe short; petals narrowly elongated, not contiguous at base........ .... *O. scolopax* group (p. 488)

8* flowers otherwise 9

9 lip deeply 3-lobed at base, median lobe sepioidal (broadest towards or below the equator) 10

9* lip otherwise 12

10 sepals often green, dorsal sepal always curved down onto column; median lobe only slightly rolled underneath; band of marginal hairs broad and dense .... *O. umbilicata* group (p. 521)

10* flowers otherwise 11

11 lip always scolopaxoid; petals separate at base .... *O. oestrifera* group (p. 494)

11* lip varied, scolopaxoid or fucifloroid, often within same population; petals elongated, usually contiguous at base .... *O. heldreichii* group (p. 514)

12 lip varied, scolopaxoid or fucifloroid, often within same population; petals elongated, usually contiguous at base .... *O. heldreichii* group (p. 514)

12* flowers otherwise 13

13 lip almost always fucifloroid; marginal band of hairs long and dense on terminal half of lip .... *O. bornmuelleri* group (p. 449)

13* marginal band of hairs attenuated or near absent on terminal half of lip 14

14 margins of terminal half of lip velvety, as centre; main flowering season IV-V (-VI) .... *O. fuciflora* group (p. 482)

14* terminal half of lip with a marginal band of hairs that is attenuated but distinct; main flowering season often late (IV-) V-VIII .... *O. tetraloniae* group (p. 469)

15 lip with central and marginal hairs ± uniform; speculum shield-shaped, located centrally or near tip of lip .... *O. bertolonii* group (p. 612)

15* lip otherwise 16

16 basal field ± dark, concolourous with centre of lip.. 17

16* pattern of coloration otherwise 18

17 stigmatic cavity without central specular stage; pseudo-eyes blackish .... *O. lunulata* group (p. 607)

17* stigmatic cavity with central specular stage (sometimes unobtrusive); pseudo-eyes often white or bluish.. *O. incubacea* group (p. 596)

18 stigmatic cavity and basal field concolourous, paler than centre of lip .... *O. sphegodes* group (p. 591)

18* pattern of coloration otherwise 19

19 stigmatic cavity heavily marked white or whitish; basal field reddish, colour different to that of centre of lip .... *O. provincialis* group (p. 588)

19* pattern of coloration otherwise .... *O. exaltata* group (p. 574)

20 stigmatic cavity with dark, glossy pseudo-eyes at sides 21

20* stigmatic cavity white, sides without dark pseudo-eyes, which are replaced by black blotches .... *O. reinholdii* group (p. 527)

21 lateral sepals slightly bicoloured; speculum central, transverse .... *O. argolica* group (p. 533)

21* lateral sepals often clearly bicoloured; speculum basal and/or central, longitudinal, often H-shaped .... *O. mammosa* group (p. 546)

Section *Pseudophrys* GODFERY 1928

Characteristics Lateral sepals greenish, highly asymmetrical, upper border almost straight, lower border rounded; dorsal sepal curved down onto column; petals oblong, (near) hairless; lip 3-lobed, entirely covered with hair, ± densely so; lateral lobes spreading, ± convex; median lobe longer than lateral lobes, emarginate, without an appendage or indentation in the angle of the lobes; speculum basal, not very shiny, formed by 2 ± narrowly juxtaposed crescents, often more sparsely hairy (sometimes near hairless); stigmatic cavity spherical, tomentose at base, anterior upper quarter open; stigmatic surface shield-shaped, visible in vault of stigmatic cavity; pseudo-eyes and staminodial points absent.

Discussion of section *Pseudophrys*

A monophyletic section, sister of *Euophrys*, comprising at least 67 essentially Mediterranean species, adapted morphologically to bees of the genus *Andrena*. *Pseudophrys* is, unquestionably, the group whose study has progressed the most over the last 15 years, with a tripling of the number of species formally described and their arrangement into 12 groups based on morphological characters, often subtle.

The reconstruction of the phylogeny of this cluster of species is undergoing a full systematic review but, hardly touched by cytological and molecular studies, naturally remains difficult. Furthermore, the definition of clearly separated monophyletic lineages is even harder due to interactions between the taxa, which seem particularly frequent. This may indicate a cyclic mode of evolution, with phases of differentiation and hybridisation (the *homogamic hybrid complexes* of Grant), and recurrent adaptations to diverse pollinators. Nevertheless, 12 groups can be distinguished provisionally: the *O. iricolor*, *O. fusca*, *O. funerea*, *O. obaesa*, *O. attaviria*, *O. blitopertha* and *O. migoutiana* groups, whose members were all considered as varieties or subspecies of *O. fusca*, the *O. lutea* group, the *O. subfusca* group, which is intermediate between *O. fusca* s.l. and *O. lutea* s.l., and finally an assemblage, probably derived, whose monophyly is perhaps not apparent, the *O. omegaifera* group, which includes 2 apparently isolated and very unusual species, *O. mirabilis* and *O. atlantica*.

Key to groups in section *Pseudophrys*

1   base of lip flat or very slight grooved 2
1*   base of lip clearly hollowed into a V-shaped groove 4

2   slight groove running from base to tip of lip, framed by fine bosses
.... *O. mirabilis* group (p. 423)
2*   lip otherwise 3

3   speculum defined at tip by a pale ω
.........................*O. omegaifera* group (p. 424)
3*   speculum blue, without pale terminal ω
.... *O. atlantica* group (p. 422)

4   external border of lateral lobe of lip forming an angle of *c.* 65° with longitudinal axis
.... *O. lutea* group (p.418)
4*   angle more acute 5

5   lip with ± broad yellow margin, with a rim of yellow hairs extending to edge; angle *c.* 45° ....
O. subfusca group (p. 407)
5*   lip otherwise; angle more acute 6

6   base of lip with a plateau whose outside edges overhang those of the unguis (see section through base of lip, next page)
............................*O. iricolor group* (p. 365)
6*   base of lip otherwise 7

7   lip with longitudinal prominences in the basal part of the speculum; speculum without hairs in the longitudinal groove
...................................*O. fusca* group (p. 370)
7*   lip otherwise 8

8   lip with weak prominences in centre of speculum's crescents; paler peri-specular zone (see fig. 10. p. 358); speculum often bisected by an increase in hairiness
...............................*O. funerea* group (p. 380)
8*   lip otherwise 9

9   lip with longitudinal prominences, a depression at base of median lobe and well-marked longitudinal groove in speculum
...................................*O. obaesa* group (p. 401)
9*   lip with neither longitudinal prominences nor almost any dividing groove in the speculum ..
.... 10

10   petals spatulate, very elongated, almost as long as sepals; hairless border of lip broad, with a regular outline, clearly delineated from hairy zone
.... *O. migoutiana* group (p. 400)
10*   flowers otherwise 11

11   lip spreading, straight, lateral lobes not turned down and under, with a regular, yellow, reflexed margin
.........................*O. blitopertha* group (p. 398)
11*   lip otherwise .... *O. attaviria* group (p. 392)

The *Ophrys iricolor* group

Characteristics Basal ridges of lip joined directly to walls of stigmatic cavi-
ty, forming an elongated
plateau whose outside edges
overhang base of unguis (see
section); speculum often
bright blue, glabrescent; lip
hairs long and regular, uni-
formly dark; hairless margin very thin or absent;
underside of lip red or tinted red in centre.

Ophrys astypalaeica
P. DELFORGE

Etymology *astypalaeica:* from Astypalea, island
in the Dodecanese (Ae), phytogeographically part
of the Cyclades (Gr). **Type** Gr, Astypalea (1997).
Synonym *O. iricolor* subsp. *astypalaeica* (P.
DELFORGE) KREUTZ.

Description As *O. iricolor* but robust and slender, 15-40cm tall, usually with large, near erect
basal leaves and 1-2 large cauline leaves, long-
clasping (Photo A); inflorescence rather dense;
(3-) 4-8 relatively small flowers; lateral sepals 8-
11.5mm x 4.5-7mm; petals oblong, 6.5-9mm x
1.8-2.7mm, green, often strongly washed dark
brown; lip 12-17mm x 9-15mm, horizontal to
near horizontal, almost as colourful as *O.
iricolor*; sometimes with a fine, greenish-yellow
hairless margin; sides of basal plateau green or
washed reddish; underside of lip always with a
large reddish centre ± broadly bordered yellowish-green; speculum bluish, less iridescent than in
O. iricolor, bisected, *c.* 7.5mm long; stigmatic
cavity whitish-green, 3-4mm wide, *c.* 1.5mm
high below the bursicles.

Flowering Season Late III-IV; at the same time
as *O. iricolor* or slightly later.

Habitat Full sun on basic, dry to moist substrates.
Garrigue with *Sarcopoterium spinosum*, up to
230m asl. **Distribution** Endemic to Astypalea.
Very rare and local.

Photos Gr, Astypalea (loc. typ.), 3.IV.1997.
P. DELFORGE.

Ophrys astypalaeica

Ophrys iricolor

365

Ophrys iricolor
DESFONTAINES

Etymology *iricolor:* colour iridescent. **Type** Between Samos (Ae) and Izmir (An) (1807). **Synonym** *O. fusca* subsp. *iricolor* (DESFONTAINES) K. RICHTER.

Description 10-25 (-35)cm tall; 1-5 large flowers; sepals green, margins reflexed, 11-18mm x 6.5-10mm, lateral sepals spreading, oval-lanceolate, asymmetrical; petals hairless, spreading, green, olive-green or brownish, sometimes washed violet, 8-12mm x 3-4mm, oblong, margins straight or slightly undulate; lip 14-23 (-26)mm x 11-20mm (when spread), (near) horizontal, 3-lobed at tip, slightly convex, dark blackish-purple, densely hairy, distinct, with purplish reflections, and a fine hairless purple border, base wedge-shaped, white, often crimson on margins, basal plateau as group, with a deep V-shaped groove, hairs white, dense and long; lateral lobes of lip rounded to near rhomboidal; median lobe shorter, obcordate; speculum basal, bilobed, bright blue marbled blackish-violet, shiny, glabrescent or sparsely hairy, hairs appressed; underside of lip entirely purple, base whitish; stigmatic cavity 3.2-5.2mm wide, 1.2-2.5mm high under the bursicles, whitish, base tomentose, formed into a 'V'.

Flowering Season III-IV (-V), rather late.

Habitat Full sun to mid-shade on dry to sometimes damp, mostly alkaline, substrates. Garrigue, scrub, open pinewoods, up to 1100m asl.

Distribution Eastern Mediterranean. North to the Bosphorus (An Tu), west to Cephalonia (Gr) and Libya. Rare and local.

Countries Ae An Cr Cy Gr Ij Li Ls Tu.

Photos A Gr, Lakonia, 15.IV.1983; **B & C** Cy, Limassol, 30.III.1989. P. DELFORGE.

Pollinator *Andrena morio* (Hymenoptera: Andrenidae).

Ophrys mesaritica

H.F. PAULUS, Ch. ALIBERTIS & A. ALIBERTIS

Etymology *mesaritica:* from the plain of Mesara (southern Cr). **Type** Cr, Iraklion (1990). **Synonyms** *O. iricolor* subsp. *mesaritica* Ch. ALIBERTIS & A. ALIBERTIS nom. nud., *O. iricolor* subsp. *mesaritica* (H.F. PAULUS, CH. ALIBERTIS & A. ALIBERTIS) KREUTZ.

Description As *O. iricolor* but 10-33cm tall; 1-5 small flowers; sepals more rounded, 10-13mm x 6-10mm, dorsal sepal sometimes orbicular; petals 6-9mm x 2-3mm; lip averages 1-3mm shorter, 12-19mm x 9-15mm (when spread), more in-
clined, near horizontal to almost pendent, often more brownish where *O. iricolor* is purplish or violet, sometimes finely edged yellow; speculum slightly greyer
and duller, often marbled with blackish-violet; underside of lip dark brownish-purple, centre sometimes whitish-green, rarely entirely green-ish, sides crimson-brown; stigmatic cavity 3.2-5.2mm wide, but shorter, 0.7-2mm high.

Flowering Season XII-II (-III), 5-8 weeks before *O. iricolor.*

Habitat As *O. iricolor* but up to 300m asl.

Distribution South-central Crete, Malta, ?Lesbos. Very rare and local. **Countries** ?Ae Cr Me. **Photos A-B** Me, Malta, 23.II.1993; **C** Cr, Iraklion, 26.II.1990. P. DELFORGE. **Note** Pollinator unknown, but not that of *O. iricolor* (*Andrena morio*, in which males are not on the wing in Crete until mid-March).

Key to the *Ophrys iricolor* group

1   underside of lip entirely purple
    .... *O. iricolor*

1*   underside of lip green or edged with green .. 2

2   very early flowering, flowering season XII-II
    .... *O. mesaritica*

2* later flowering, flowering season III-V 3

(continued on next page)

Ophrys vallesiana
J. DEVILLERS-TERSCHUREN & P. DEVILLERS

Etymology Named after V. Vallès and A.-M. Vallès-Lombard, contemporary French botanists. **Type** Tn, Djebel Amar (1994). Synonym *O. iricolor* subsp. *vallesiana* (J. DEVILLERS-TERSCHUREN & P. DEVILLERS) H.F. PAULUS & GACK.

Description As *O. iricolor* but more slender; flowers far smaller, coloration drabber; sepals 10-15mm long; petals 6-10mm long; lip 12-16mm long; finely edged yellowish; speculum greyish-blue, rather large; underside of lip purple, broadly edged green, sometimes entirely green.

Flowering Season End II-V, rather late.

Habitat As *O. iricolor*, up to 500m asl.

Distribution Northern Tunisia and Kroumirie. Very rare and local. **Countries** Ag Tn.

Photos Tn, Djebel Amar (loc. typ.), 24.II.2002; Djebel Zaghouan, 2.III.2002; Djebel Utique, 4.III.2002. P. DELFORGE.

Discussion of the *Ophrys iricolor* group

Probably a monophyletic group, with 5 species probably originating from the fragmentation of the range of an ancestral species. This was followed, for the sympatric species, by separation through an adaptation to different pollinators on the basis of floral size (large lip vs small lip: *O. iricolor* vs *O. astypalaeica*; *O. eleonorae* vs *O. vallesiana*) and temporal isolation (early flowering vs late flowering: *O. mesaritica* vs *O. iricolor*). This process was probably accompanied, in some species, by the incorporation into the genotype of elements, ± significant, from various species in the *O. fusca* group. The 2 central Mediterranean species (*O. eleonorae* and *O. vallesiana*) seem to be very closely related, linked especially by the concentric coloration of the centre of the underside of the lip – crimson bordered with yellowish-green. The structure and colour of the lip may also link the 3 eastern species into a cohesive group, of which *O. iricolor* would be the central figure; nevertheless, *O. mesaritica* is known from Crete and Malta and probably occurs on Lesbos, and this may indicate a central ancestral position for this species within the group.

Key to the *Ophrys iricolor* group

(continued from p. 367)

3   lip 16-26mm long .... *O. eleonorae*

3*   lip 12-17mm long 4

4   lip drably coloured, speculum elongated, often reaching the unguis .... *O. vallesiana*

4*   lip brightly coloured, speculum rather short, never reaching the unguis .... *O. astypalaeica*

Ophrys eleonorae

J. DEVILLERS-TERSCHUREN & P. DEVILLERS

Etymology Named after the Sardinian princess Eleanora, ruler of Arborea. **Type** Sa, Nuoro (1991). **Synonyms** *O. iricolor* subsp. *eleonorae* (J. DEVILLERS-TERSCHUREN & P. DEVILLERS) H.F. PAULUS & GACK, *O. iricolor* subsp. *eleonorae* (J. DEVILLERS-TERSCHUREN & P. DEVILLERS) H.F. PAULUS & GACK ex KREUTZ isonym., *O. fusca* f. *maxima* TERRACCIANO, *O. fusca* var. *maxima* (TERRACCIANO) E.G. & A. CAMUS, *O. iricolor* subsp. *maxima* (TERRACCIANO) H.F. PAULUS & GACK nom. illegit.

Description As *O. iricolor* but more slender, (20-) 25-50cm tall; on average 1-2 more flowers; sepals rather smaller relative to the lip; petals often paler; lip averages 2mm longer, 16-26mm long; speculum slightly duller blue, often grooved; underside of lip less intensely purple, often orange, less regularly coloured and frequently bordered yellowish-green.

Flowering Season (III-) IV-V. **Habitat** As *O. iricolor* but associated with relict Phryganas, up to 950m asl. **Distribution** Central Mediterranean. Very local and very rare.

Countries Ag Co Sa Tn. **Photos A-B** Sa, Sassari, 7.IV.1996; **C** Nuoro, 9.IV.1996; **D** Tn, Djebel Amar, 22.II.2002. P. DELFORGE.

Pollinator *Andrena morio* (Hymenoptera: Andrenidae).

369

The Ophrys fusca group

Characteristics Lip elongated (length/width ratio *c.* 1:20); external border of lateral lobe of lip making an angle of (22) 30-40 (47)° with longitudinal axis; lip with longitudinal prominences not directly joined with walls of stigmatic cavity, often prominent in base and centre of speculum, frequently accentuated by a longitudinal curve; lip densely hairy, hairs long, often irregular, generally uniformly dark or with a brighter patch at the tip of the angle formed by the 2 subterminal crescents; speculum glabrescent, usually not divided by a longitudinal groove, sometimes bisected by a narrow groove and then with hairs as speculum and not as lip; colour of lip sometimes bright, then, in parallel, a redder centre to the underside of the lip.

36°

Ophrys lojaconoi
P. DELFORGE

Etymology Named after M. Lojacono Pojero (1853-1919), Sicilian botanist. **Type** It, Foggia (1995). **Synonyms** *O. iricolor* subsp. *lojaconoi* (P. DELFORGE) KREUTZ, *O. forestieri* (REICHENBACH FIL.) LOJACONO SENSU P. DELFORGE (in 1994 guide).

Description As *O. fusca* but 20-32cm tall; inflorescence relatively dense; (1-) 3-10 medium-sized flowers; petals 1-2mm broad; lip 12-15mm x 8-11mm, horizontal, rather narrow, with 2 very well marked basal ridges, bulging; lateral lobes reduced, often short and narrow; median lobe elongated, up to 8mm long; hairs on lip straight, long, dense, blackish with purple reflections; hairs on speculum whitish, very short but nevertheless remaining dense; speculum undivided, bluish, sometimes reaching sinuses of lateral lobes; stigmatic cavity 4mm x 1.5mm.

Flowering Season II-IV, rather early.

Habitat Full sun to mid-shade on dry to moist, alkaline substrates. Abandoned cultivation, garrigue, scrub, the edge of open woodland, up to 500m asl. **Distribution** Poorly known, at least the Adriatic side of peninsula Italy (Puglia), from Mount Gargano (Foggia) south to the Brindisi region. **Countries** It.

Photos It, Foggia, 31.III.1991. P. DELFORGE.

Pollinator Probably *Andrena ocreata* (Hymenoptera: Andrenidae).

10 mm

Ophrys forestieri
(REICHENBACH fil.) LOJACONO

Etymology Named after De Forestier, French botanist who collected the plant. **Type*** Ga, Bouches-du-Rhône (1851). **Synonyms** *O. fusca* var. *forestieri* REICHENBACH fil., *O. fusca* subsp. *forestieri* (REICHENBACH fil.) KREUTZ.

Description Spindly, 9-20cm tall; inflorescence dense; 2-9 rather colourful flowers, very small for the group; petals oblong, half as long as sepals, green, often olive-green, slightly darker than sepals; lip horizontal to near horizontal, 3-lobed, 6.5-10mm x 5-8mm (when spread), slightly but

regularly transversely convex, appearing straight, with relatively prominent basal swellings, stretching longitudinally on both sides of central axis to the subterminal crescents, which they swell, often produc-

10 mm

ing a slight longitudinal curve in the lip; lateral lobes rather short, median lobe rather elongated, near quadrangular, slightly emarginate; hairs long, dense, rather tangled and dark purplish-brown, uniform in centre of lip, straighter and whitish on sides, including those on the speculum; speculum large, shiny indigo-blue, blotched darker blue, bordered at tip with 2 pale blue crescents, often forming a ⍵, undivided or finely divided by a thin prominence with dense, straight, whitish hairs (as speculum); border of lip hairless, often broad, yellow to rather bright greenish, relatively distinct, not grading into hairy zone; stigmatic cavity rarely blotched pale brown, with abundant long white hairs at base.

Flowering Season III-IV, relatively early.

Habitat Full sun to mid-shade on moist alkaline substrates. Abandoned cultivation, garrigue, probably up to 400m asl. Rare and local.

Distribution Apparently rather well represented in Bouches-du-Rhône and Var.

Countries Ga.

Photos Ga, Bouches-du-Rhône (loc. neotyp.), 4.IV.1996. P. DELFORGE.

Discussion of the *Ophrys fusca* group

A group of 10 species, probably monophyletic, and mostly only very recently recognised, in which the cladistic relationships are still obscure. One lineage emerges, however, composed of *O. bilunulata*, *O. lucifera*, *O. creticola* and *O. cressa*, closely related, isolated by floral size (*O. bilunulata*, *O. lucifera*), and by floral size and staggered flowering in the 2 Cretan species (*O. cressa, O. creticola*).

371

Ophrys caesiella
P. DELFORGE

Etymology *caesiella:* bluish-grey (an allusion to the colour of speculum). **Type** Me, Malta (2000). **Synonym** *O. fusca* subsp. *caesiella* (P. DELFORGE) KREUTZ.

Description (5-) 10-20 (-22)cm tall; inflorescence dense; (1-) 2-6 medium-sized to rather small flowers; sepals yellowish-green to whitish-green,

lateral sepals 8.5-11mm long; petals oblong to narrowly oval, 5-6mm x 1.8-2.5mm, green, sometimes olive-green, darker than sepals, margins slightly undulate; lip overall rather drab, near horizontal, 3-lobed, (9-) 10-12.5 (-13)mm x (8-) 9-11 (-12)mm (when spread) (average length/width ratio 1:17), rather convex transversely, with weak basal swellings, producing a slight longitudinal curve in the lip; external edge of lateral lobe making a rather narrow angle, *c.* 22-28°, with longitudinal axis; lateral lobes with well-marked sinus, sides turned down and under; median lobe often prominent, 2-4mm long, broadly wedge-shaped, emarginate at tip; hairs on lip long, rather untidy, dark purple, without zonation, sometimes irregularly distributed; speculum elongated, reaching and often longer than sinuses, bluish-grey, sometimes marbled with indigo, rarely with 2 crescents at tip or bisected, hairs very short, straight, regular, often sparse; border of lip narrow, hairless, with an irregular outline, yellowish to greenish; unguis of lip not very colourful; stigmatic cavity lacking any ornamentation; base and throat of stigmatic cavity with whitish hairs, generally prolonged as a slight groove to centre of speculum; underside of lip greenish-white, sometimes washed brown or purple.

Flowering Season II-III, rather early.

Habitat Full sun on dry, alkaline substrates. Abandoned cultivation, garrigue, scrub, up to 450m asl.

Distribution Currently known from southern Sicily and the Maltese archipelago. Very local but sometimes rather abundant at Malta.

Countries Me Si.

Photos Me, Malta (loc. typ.) 22.II.1993; Si, Siracusa, 16.III.2000. P. DELFORGE.

Ophrys gazella

J. Devillers-Terschuren & P. Devillers

Etymology *gazella:* gazelle. **Type** Tn, Makthar (2000). **Synonyms** *O. fusca* subsp. *gazella* (J. Devillers-Terschuren & P. Devillers) Kreutz, *O. ôafricana* G. Foelsche & W. Foelsche.

Description Small, as *O. caesiella*, few-flowered; 1-3 (-5) flowers, medium-sized to rather small; sepals 8-10mm x 4-5.5mm; petals 4.5-5.5mm x 0.7-1.3mm; lip near horizontal to pendent at 45°,

(9-) 9.8-14 (15.5)mm x 6.5-11mm (when spread) (mean length/width ratio 1:18), slightly convex transversely, almost without a longitudinal curve; base of lip narrow, with strong longitudinal prominences; external border of lateral lobe making a more open angle with longitudinal axis, 35-45°; lateral lobes with very open sinuses; hairs on lip long, rather regular, brown, without zonation, sometimes irregular in centre of lobes; speculum undivided, blue, often bright, often with 2 crescents at tip, frequently marbled bluish; border of lip narrow, hairless, yellow; underside of lip often reddish at centre.

Flowering Season (I-) II-IV, early.

Habitat Full sun on dry, alkaline substrates. Abandoned cultivation, garrigue, scrub, up to 1150m asl.

Distribution Southern Tunisia, northwest Algeria. Local and sometimes rather abundant.

Countries Ag Tn. **Photos A** Tn, Makthar (loc. typ.) 14.IV.1999. J. Devillers-Terschuren; **B** Cap Bon, El Haouira (loc. typ. for *O. africana*), 27.II.2002; **C** Sebalat Ben Amar, 23.II.2002; **D** Djebel Zaghouan, 2.III.2002. P. Delforge.

Pollinator *Andrena flavipes* (Hymenoptera: Andrenidae).

Key to the *Ophrys fusca* group

1   flowers very small, lip 6.5-10mm long, submarginal band of straight, whitish hairs, present also on outer edges of speculum ....
.... *O. forestieri*

1*   flowers and lip otherwise 2

2   lip 12-15mm long, with 2 basal ridges forming a small plateau; lateral lobes reduced .. *O. lojaconoi*

2*   flowers and lip otherwise 3

3   lip drab, 10-18mm long; base of lip often faded; hairs on lip untidy .... *O. lupercalis*

3*   lip otherwise 4

(continued on p 374.)

373

Ophrys bilunulata
RISSO

Etymology *bilunulata:* with 2 lunulae (shape of speculum). **Type*** Ga, Alpes-Maritimes (1844). **Synonyms** *O. fusca* subsp. *bilunulata* (RISSO) KREUTZ, *O. 'flavipes-fusca'* auct.

Description 15-40cm tall; inflorescence dense; 2-6 (-7) very colourful flowers, average for the group; lip near horizontal to almost pendent, 3-lobed, (8.5-) 10-15mm x (7.5-) 9-13mm (when spread) (mean length/width ratio 1:16), slightly convex

transversely, with rather well marked basal swellings and speculum producing a slight longitudinal curve in lip; external border of lateral lobe forming an angle of 35-39° with longitudinal axis; lateral lobes with well-marked sinus, often hardly turned down; median lobe prominent, broadly wedge-shaped, emarginate at tip, convex to spreading; hairs on lip long, rather regular, dark purple, uniform, sometimes with a paler diamond-shaped area between 2 crescents at tip of speculum; speculum relatively short, not reaching sinuses, shiny blue, sometimes marbled with dark violet, with 2 crescents at tip, contrasting with hairs on lip, sometimes bisected; hairless border of lip narrow, yellow, obvious, with an irregular outline, without a distinct demarcation from the hairy zone; stigmatic cavity often with a thin, transverse brownish bar; base and throat of stigmatic cavity with whitish hairs; underside of lip green, sometimes washed brown or purple at centre.

Flowering Season (III-) IV-V, rather late.

Habitat Full sun to mid-shade, sometimes full shade, on dry to moist alkaline substrates. Short grassland, garrigue, abandoned cultivation, scrub, olive groves, pinewoods, up to 1500m asl. **Distribution** Western Mediterranean. Southern Iberian peninsula to Liguria and the Balearics; rather widespread and sometimes abundant. **Countries** Bl Ga Hs It Lu.

Photos Ga, Alpes-Maritimes (loc. neotyp.), 17.IV.1999; Var, 18.IV.1999. P. DELFORGE.

Pollinator *Andrena flavipes* (Hymenoptera: Andrenidae).

Key to the *Ophrys fusca* group
(continued from previous page)

4   speculum rather elongated, reaching ± the level of the sinuses of the lateral lobes 5

4*   speculum short, not reaching the level of the sinuses 7

5   lip 15-22mm long .... *O. fusca*

5*   lip 9-13mm long 6

(continued on next page.)

Ophrys lucifera
J. DEVILLERS-TERSCHUREN & P. DEVILLERS

Etymology *-fera:* bearing; *luci-:* light. **Type** It, Grosseto (2000). **Synonyms** *O. iricolor* auct. non DESFONTAINES, *O. fusca* subsp. *lucifera* (J. DEVILLERS-TERSCHUREN & P. DEVILLERS) KREUTZ.

Description As *O. fusca* but flowers average slightly smaller, richly coloured; sepals green, 11-15mm x 5-8mm; petals 6-10mm x 1-2mm; lip (near) horizontal, elongated, (12-) 14-20mm x (8.5-) 10-14.5mm (when spread) (mean length/width ratio 1:28), very slightly convex

transversely, almost without any longitudinal curve; base of lip with strong projecting longitudinal prominences but these not producing a longitudinal curve – central and upper portions in the same plane as the base, giving the lip a straight appearance; lip hairs long, regular, blackish, without zonation, sometimes paler around sinuses of lateral lobes; speculum short, not reaching sinuses, undivided, bright blue, sometimes with 2 crescents at tip, rarely weakly bisected; border of lip narrow, hairless, yellow; stigmatic cavity demarcated by a transverse line of red to brown; underside of lip bright greenish-yellow, often red at centre.

Flowering Season III-IV. **Habitat** Full sun on dry, alkaline substrates. Abandoned cultivation, garrigue, scrub, up to 1000m asl. **Distribution** Tuscany, Sicily, the Maltese archipelago and probably also Puglia (It) and around the basin of the central Mediterranean. Very rare and local. **Countries** ?Ag It ?Ga, Me Si. **Photos** It, Grosseto (loc. typ.) 5.IV.1988; Si, Siracusa, 14.III.2000. P. DELFORGE.

Key to the *Ophrys fusca* group
(continued from previous page)

6   external border of lateral lobe of lip making an open angle, 35-45°, with longitudinal axis of lip; petals 0.7-1.3mm broad; 1-3 (-5) flowers .... *O. gazella*

6*   angle more acute, 22-35°; petals 1.8-2.5mm broad; (1-) 2-6 flowers .... *O. caesiella*

7   plant 5-15cm tall; lip 10-14mm long.............. .... *O. cressa*

7*   plant without these characters 8

(continued on p 376.)

Ophrys creticola
H.F. PAULUS

Etymology -cola: living; creti-: in Crete. **Type** Cr, Iraklion (1998). **Synonyms** O. fusca subsp. creticola (H.F. PAULUS) H. KRETZSCHMAR, O. 'Jouchtasfusca' H.F. PAULUS nom. prov.

Description Robust, 8-22cm tall; 1-6 rather large flowers; sepals green, rounded, up to 15mm x12mm; petals oblong-rounded, 6-9mm x 2.5-

3.8mm, darker than sepals, olive-green to brownish in centre, margins paler; lip massive, 3-lobed, spreading, appearing not very jagged, horizontal, regularly convex both longitudinally and transversally, 13-18 (-22)mm x 12-16.5 (-19)mm (when spread) (mean length/width ratio 1:09); base of lip with marked longitudinal prominences but these not producing a sudden longitudinal

curve (kink); lip hairs long, regular, blackish, without zonation, sometimes more reddish close to the edge and around the sinuses of the lateral lobes; speculum short, 6-8mm long, not reaching sinuses, undivided, matt bright blue, sometimes marbled with blackish-violet and with obscure crescents at tip, rarely weakly bisected; border of lip narrow, hairless, yellow; underside of lip greenish, often brownish-red at centre; stigmatic cavity very low, 2.7-4.1mm x 1-2.2mm below bursicles, usually demarcated by a marked red to brown transverse line.

Flowering Season I-III, early.

Habitat Full sun on dry, alkaline substrates. Abandoned cultivation, garrigue, scrub, up to 600m asl.

Distribution Apparently endemic to a few calcareous massifs in eastern Crete. Extremely local and very rare. **Countries** Cr. **Photos** Cr, Iraklion (loc. typ.), 25.II.1990. P. DELFORGE.

Key to the Ophrys fusca group

(continued from previous page)

8   lip massive, (12-) 14-20mm long; early flowering (I-III) .... O. creticola

8*   lip otherwise; later flowering (III-V) 9

9   flowers medium-sized; lip (8.5-) 10-15mm long, near horizontal to pendent ....
.... O. bilunulata

9*   flowers large; lip (12-) 14-20mm long, horizontal to near horizontal .... O. lucifera

Ophrys cressa
H.F. PAULUS

Etymology *cressa:* Cretan. **Type** Cr, Lassithi (1998). **Synonyms** *O. fusca* subsp. *cressa* (H.F. PAULUS) H. KRETZSCHMAR, *O.* ?'*Thripti-fusca* late' vel *O.* '*merula-fusca*' H.F. PAULUS nom. prov., *O. eptapigiensis* H.F. PAULUS, *O. fusca* subsp. *eptapigiensis* (H.F. PAULUS) KREUTZ.

Description As *O. creticola* but smaller in all parts, thickset, 5-15cm tall; 2-5 medium-sized flowers; lip less massive, 3-lobed, less spreading, near horizontal, more convex longitudinally and transversally, 10-14mm x 9-11.5mm (when spread) (mean length/width ratio 1:18); base of lip with marked longitudinal prominences producing a slight intensification of the longitudinal curve; lip hairs long, regular, 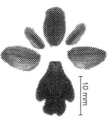 purplish-black, without zonation; speculum relatively longer but not reaching sinuses, more grooved, shiny blackish-blue, sometimes marbled and with obscure crescents at tip; border of lip often less narrow, hairless, yellow; underside of lip green; stigmatic cavity often darker green on lower half, usually demarcated by a complete transverse reddish line or 2 lateral streaks.

Flowering Season III-IV. **Habitat** Full sun to mid-shade on dry, alkaline substrates. Abandoned cultivation, garrigue, scrub, open pinewoods, up to 900m asl. **Distribution** Calcareous massifs in eastern Crete, Karpathos and Rhodes. Extremely local and very rare. **Countries** Ae Cr. **Photos A-B** Cr, Lassithi, 13.III.1990. P. DELFORGE; **C** ('*eptapigiensis*') Ae, Rhodes, 28.IV.2001. C.A.J. KREUTZ.

Pollinator Perhaps *Andrena merula* (Hymenoptera: Andrenidae).

377

Ophrys fusca
LINK

Etymology *fusca:* dark, blackish-purple. **Type*** Lu, near Lisbon (1800). **Synonym** *O.* '*Colletes-fusca*' H.F. PAULUS nom. prov.

Description 10-25 (-35)cm tall; 2-10 large flowers; sepals yellowish-green to whitish-green, margins reflexed, 11-16mm x 5.5-9mm, lateral sepals spreading, oval-lanceolate, asymmetrical, dorsal sepal oboval to elliptic, concave, curved down onto column; petals hairless, spreading, yellowish-green, olive-green or brownish, 8-12mm x 2-4mm, oblong, sometimes near spatulate, rounded at tip, margins ± undulate; lip 15-22mm x 11-17mm, (near) horizontal at base and then pendent, laterally

convex, sides turned down and under, sometimes appearing narrow; base of lip with 2 strong, projecting longitudinal prominences generally prod-ucing an accentuation (sometimes major) of the longitudinal curve (kinked), central portion of lip sloping but remaining relatively flat, tip curving downwards once more; lateral lobes triangular-rounded to near rhomboidal; median lobe prominent, obcordate, emarginate; lip hairs long, regular, blackish with purplish reflections; speculum basal, 8-13mm long, bilobed, azure-blue marbled greyish-violet, often shiny, with sparse greyish hairs, and sometimes pale crescents at tip; underside of lip predominantly green, sometimes edged yellowish, ± strongly and broadly tinted purple or brownish; stigmatic cavity 3-4mm x 2-3mm, whitish, often demarcated by a brown line, base tomentose; 2n=72.

Flowering Season (I-) III-V, probably with 2 successive waves of flowering.

Habitat Full sun to mid-shade on dry to frequently moist substrates, mostly alkaline. Short grassland, abandoned cultivation, garrigue, scrub, open woodland, up to 1100m asl.

Distribution Western Mediterranean. The Iberian peninsula, North Africa, Balearics and probably France, east to Var. Local and sometimes abundant. Most species from this and related groups have, up till now, been named as *O. fusca* (s.l.); many records should be re-examined in the light of the recent taxonomic changes.

Countries Ag Bl Ga Hs ?It Lu Ma ?Me ?Sa Tn.

Photos Lu, Lisbon (loc. neotyp.), 2.IV.1990. P. DELFORGE (see also p. 360).

Pollinator *Colletes cunicularius* (Hymenoptera: Colletidae).

378

Ophrys lupercalis

J. DEVILLERS-TERSCHUREN & P. DEVILLERS

Etymology *lupercalis:* from Lupercalia, ancient Roman festival celebrated on 15 February (an allusion to its early flowering). **Type** Ga, Aude (1994). **Synonyms** *O. fusca* auct. non LINK, *O. 'nigroaenea-fusca'* H.F. PAULUS & GACK nom. prov.

Description As *O. fusca* but 10-29cm tall; up to 10 flowers, medium-sized, coloration drabber; sepals green, 11-15mm x 4-8mm; petals 7-10mm x 1-2mm; lip near horizontal, 10-18mm x (8.5-) 10-16mm (when spread) (mean length/width ratio 1:21), only slightly transversally convex, almost without a longitudinal curve; base of lip often less colourful, with projecting longitudinal prominence but these not producing a longitudinal curve, tip slightly curved downwards; lip hairs long, blackish, without zonation, appearing untidy because the hairs are curved at the tip; speculum elongated, almost reaching the sinuses, usually undivided, coloration varied, blue, greyish, reddish or milky, often with two crescents at tip, with a central gro-ove that usually lacks lip hairs; lateral lobes separated from median lobe by well marked sinuses; border of lip narrow, hairless, yellowish, irregular, often hardly visible; underside of lip pale greenish, sometimes tinted red in centre; 2n=72.

Flowering Season (XII-) II-III (-IV), early.

Habitat Full sun to mid-shade on dry, alkaline substrates. Abandoned cultivation, garrigue, scrub, open woodland, up to 1200m asl.

Distribution Probably western Mediterranean and sub-Mediterranean. In France may extend north to Brittany. Rather local but sometimes abundant.

Countries Ag Co It Ga Hs Lu ?Ma ?Me Sa Si ?Tn.

Photos Hs, Girona, 11.II.1997; It, Cosenza, 10.IV.2002; Ga, Aude (loc. typ.), 19.II.1996. P. DELFORGE.

Pollinator *Andrena nigroaenea* (Hymenoptera: Andrenidae).

10 mm

The *Ophrys funerea* group

Characteristics See opposite.

Ophrys arnoldii
P. DELFORGE

Etymology Named after J.E. Arnold, contemporary Spanish botanist. **Type** Hs, Tarragona (1999). **Synonym** *O. attaviria* auct. non RÜCKBRODT & WENKER

Description Often robust, slender, 10-33cm tall; 2-10 flowers, rather large for the group; lateral sepals green, 11-16mm long; petals oblong, 7-11mm long, green, often washed brownish; lip near horizontal to (mostly) pendent, oboval (when spread), clearly 3-lobed, 11-18.5 (-19.5)mm x (7.5-) 8.5-13 (-15)mm (when spread), narrow and elongated (mean length/width ratio = 1:32), base wedge-shaped and sometimes slightly kinked, very rarely swollen by ridges; external border of lateral lobe of lip making an angle of 25-29° with longitudinal axis; centre of lip with faint or very faint long longitudinal prominences; lateral lobes turned down, separated from median lobe by prominent sinuses; median lobe elongated, convex, emarginate; lip hairs dense, dark, straight, rather long and relatively regular, dark reddish-brown to purplish-brown, often with poorly marked slightly paler band, visible mostly at centre of lip at end of anthesis; border of lip surrounded by a fine hairless margin, dark, rarely washed yellowish-green, rather clearly demarcated; speculum glabrescent to hairless, reddish, metallic greyish or dark mottled blue, with greyish to whitish crescents at tip, often contrasting, forming a ω, usually divided by a narrow groove that has rather long hairs (as lip), forming a continuous line connecting with the base of a prominent patch of white hairs covering the V-shaped notch; underside of lip green, sometimes washed reddish-brown; 2n=72.

Flowering Season Mid IV-VI (-VII), 6-8 weeks after *O. lupercalis*. **Habitat** Full sun to mid-shade on dry to moist, calcareous substrates. Abandoned cultivation, banks, garrigue with *Aphyllanthes monspeliensis*, up to 1350m asl.

Distribution Still poorly known. The eastern half of Spain, Balearics, Mediterranean France, east to the Rhône. Very local but sometimes abundant.

Countries Bl Ga Hs.

Photos Hs, La Rioja, 24.V.1999; Tarragona (loc. typ.), 9.VI.1989. P. DELFORGE.

Pollinator *Andrena nigroaenea* (Hymenoptera: Andrenidae).

Note Attracts the later generation of the pollinator of *Ophrys lupercalis*; hybrids with *Ophrys lupercalis* explain the appearance of characters from the *O. fusca* group in some individuals of *O. arnoldii*.

Characteristics of the *Ophrys funerea* group

Lip with longitudinal prominences, basal and on the speculum, not directly joined to the walls of the stigmatic cavity, hardly protuberant, and slightly steep, parallel to the groove bisecting the speculum and not producing a strong longitudinal curve in the lip; lip hairs dense, rather long, relatively regular, with a paler zone around the speculum (peri-specular zone), better marked at the tip than at the sides, then with a concentric darker band, covering the lobes of the lip; speculum glabrescent or irregularly ciliated, divided by a narrow longitudinal groove, with, on the basal half, white hairs analogous to those from the base of the stigmatic cavity, and, on the distal half, hairs analogous to those of the pale peri-specular zone; border of lip hairless, often narrow, irregularly demarcated; underside of lip pale green, usually without reddish tones in the centre.

Notes The pale peri-specular zone is sometimes difficult to observe, even in the field. In case of doubt, the presence (or absence) of this zone can be confirmed with a magnifying glass, viewing the spread lip against a strong light. In macrophotography, this zone shows up better with a ring-flash used alone, rather than with natural light or lateral flash. Unfortunately overexposure may also create the impression of such zones on the lip of flowers which lack them. Thus the presence of such zones on photographs of orchid lips should not on its own be taken as proof of either the presence or absence of a paler peri-specular zone.

Ophrys funerea

VIVIANI

Etymology *funerea:* funeral. **Type*** Co, Corse-du-Sud (1824). **Synonym** *O. fusca* subsp. *funerea* (VIVIANI) ARCANGELI vel NYMAN vel E.G. CAMUS, BERGON & A. CAMUS.

Description As *O. zonata* but more spindly and smaller in all parts; (5-) 10-20cm tall; (1-) 2-5 very small flowers; petals olive-green; lip elongated, (6.8-) 7.5-10.3 (-11)mm x (5.5-) 6-8 (-9)mm (when spread) (mean length/width ratio 1:24); near horizontal to pendent, transversally convex; lateral lobes rounded, sinus poorly marked, sides sometimes strongly curved down and under; median lobe less elongated, shortly obcordate; lip hairs blackish-brown with a paler brown peri-specular zone; speculum elongated, bluish to reddish, shiny, often with 2 pale crescents at tip, divided by a shallower and narrower groove, the distal part hairy (as around speculum); border of lip narrowly greenish to reddish, not obvious, with an irregular outline; base and throat of stigmatic cavity with whitish hairs, not

so dense, these extending into the central groove to the middle of the speculum; underside of lip pale green.

Flowering Season (III-) IV, earlier than *O. zonata*.

Habitat Full sun to mid-shade on dry to moist, calcareous substrates. Abandoned cultivation, garrigue, scrub, open woodland, probably up to 900m asl.

Distribution Probably endemic to Sardinia and Corsica. Extremely local and very rare.

Countries Co ?It Sa.

Photos Co, Corse-du-Nord. 5.IV.2002. É. Walravens; Corse-du-Sud (loc. neotyp.) 5.IV.1996. P. DELFORGE.

Ophrys ortuabis
M.P. GRASSO & L. MANCA

Etymology *ortuabis:* from Ortuabis, locality in Sarcidano (Sa). **Type** Sa, Nuoro (2002). **Synonym** *O. fusca* subsp. *ortuabis* (M.P. GRASSO & L. MANCA) KREUTZ.

Description Spindly, 9-16 (-20)cm tall; (1-) 2-3 (-4) small flowers; sepals yellowish-green, 8-9 (-11)mm x 5 (-7)mm; petals linear-oblong, *c.* 5mm x 1-2mm, green, sometimes washed brown; lip near horizontal, 7-10mm x 7-9mm (mean length/width ratio 1:12), flat to very slightly transversally convex, longitudinally almost flat; base and centre of lip with long longitudinal prominences, slight to rather pronounced; lateral lobes rounded to triangular with marked sinuses; median lobe wedge-shaped-rounded to obcordate, ± emarginate; lip hairs purplish-black, regular, peri-specular zone hardly visible to distinct and frequently also with a slightly paler violet-red submarginal rim; speculum relatively short, blackish-blue, bluish, sometimes marbled, shiny, often with 2 paler, bluish, blurred, broad crescents at tip, divided by a deep groove, briefly bearing on its distal half peri-specular hairs; border of lip greenish-yellow to reddish, rather broad, well-visible, with a clearly defined outline, even around the sinuses; base and throat of stigmatic cavity with dense whitish hairs, these extending into the central groove as far as or beyond the middle of the speculum; stigmatic cavity broad, sometimes marked with a transverse reddish line; underside of lip green washed orange.

Flowering Season III-mid IV, before *O. zonata.*

Habitat Full sun on dry, dolomitic substrates. Garrigue with Rosemary (*Rosmarinus officinalis*) *c.* 700m asl.

Distribution Known from a few populations in Sarcidano. Very rare and local.

Countries Sa.

Photos Sa, Nuoro, 21.III.1996. E. Gügel.

Pollinator *Andrena hypopolia* (Hymenoptera: Andrenidae).

Key to the *Ophrys funerea* group

1   lip 11-15mm long; almost as broad as long (mean L/l = 1:08) .... *O. creberrima*
1*   lip more elongated 2

2   flowers very small; lip 6-11mm long; yellow border of lip regular, even around the sinuses 3
2*   flowers otherwise 5

3   speculum reaching the sinuses .... *O. parvula*
3*   speculum short, not reaching sinuses 4
(continued on next page)

Ophrys zonata

J. DEVILLERS-TERSCHUREN & P. DEVILLERS

Etymology *zonata:* zoned (an allusion to the zone around the speculum in the lip hairs). **Type** Sa, Sassari (1994). **Synonyms** *O. fusca* subsp. *zonata* (J. DEVILLERS-TERSCHUREN & P. DEVILLERS) KREUTZ, *O. fusca* auct. non LINK, *O. funerea* auct. non VIVIANI.

Description 10-25 (-32)cm tall; up to 9 medium-sized flowers; sepals green, 9-13mm x 4.5-6.5mm; petals 7.5-8.5mm x 1-2mm, green to olive-green, sides or centre sometimes lighter; lip near horizontal to pendant, 9.7-14.5mm x (8.5-) 9.5-11.6mm (when spread) (mean length/width ratio 1:28), transversally rather convex, longitudinally slightly convex, tip curved downwards, sides slightly or,

more often, strongly curved down and under; lateral lobes rounded, sinuses poorly marked; median lobe wedge-shaped-rounded to ob-cordate, sometimes elongated; lip hairs long, brownish, rather regular, with a paler and more reddish zone, rather contrasting, all around the speculum (peri-specular zone); speculum elongated, blackish-blue, bluish, sometimes partly reddish, shiny, often with 2 paler, bluish, broad, blurred crescents at tip, divided by a deep groove with, in its distal portion, hairs as in peri-specular zone; border of lip greenish to reddish, narrow, not obvious, with an irregular outline; base and throat of stigmatic cavity with dense whitish hairs, these continuing in the central groove to middle of speculum; underside of lip pale green.

Flowering Season (III-) IV-V.

Habitat Full sun to mid-shade on dry to moist, alkaline substrates. Abandoned cultivation, garrigue, scrub, open woodlands and their edges, probably up to 1000m asl. **Distribution** Endemic to Sardinia and Corsica. Local but sometimes rather abundant on Sardinia; extremely rare and local on Corsica. **Countries** Co Sa. **Photos** Sa, Sassari, 8.IV.1996; Nuoro, 20.IV. 1996. P. DELFORGE.

Pollinator *Andrena flavipes* (Hymenoptera: Andrenidae).

Key to the *Ophrys funerea* group

(continued from previous page)

4   petals short, oblong, *c.* 5mm long .... *O. ortuabis*

4* petals more elongated, often near spatulate, 5-8mm long .... *O. perpusilla*

5   flowers medium-sized; speculum densely hairy, divided by a broad groove, hairy (as lip) almost up to the stigmatic cavity .... *O. leucadica*

5* flowers otherwise 6

(continued on p.384)

Ophrys hespera

J. DEVILLERS-TERSCHUREN & P. DEVILLERS

Etymology *hespera:* of the sunset, of the west.
Type It, Grosseto (2000).

Description As *O. funerea* but with small leaves, yellowing at onset of flowering; 2-4 flowers, very small for the group; sepals green, 8-10mm x 3.5-4.5 (-5)mm; petals more elongated, green, edged yellowish, 6-7.5mm x 1-1.5mm; lip pendant, 8-10mm x 6-8mm (when spread) (mean length/width ratio 1:31), shape more angular, more wedge-shaped; lateral lobes less rounded, triangular, sinuses more open; median lobe more elongated; lip hairs blackish, darker, with a brownish peri-specular zone, but also a fine paler zone along the hairless edge of the lip; speculum elongated, dark blue, without reddish shades, not going up onto the walls of the stigmatic cavity, sometimes longer than sinuses of lateral lobes; border of lip narrow, yellow or pale red, neater and with a more regular outline; base and throat of stigmatic cavity with whitish hairs, not so dense, extending in the central groove to the middle of the speculum; underside of lip pale green.

(herbar. J. & P. DEVILLERS-TERSCHUREN)

Flowering Season IV-V, rather late.

Habitat Full sun to mid-shade on dry, calcareous substrates. Garrigue, scrub, open woodland, up to 1200m asl. **Distribution** Still poorly known; Liguria and central Italy. Local but sometimes abundant. **Countries** It. **Photos** It, Grosseto (loc. typ.), 17.IV.2001. P. DELFORGE.

Key to the *Ophrys funerea* group

(continued from previous page)

6	flowers medium-sized; lip 12-16mm long; speculum a milky colour 7
6*	flowers otherwise 8

7	speculum often reaching or passing the sinuses .... *O. akhdarensis*
7*	speculum short, not reaching sinuses .... *O. gackiae*

8	flowers (very) small; lip 6.8-10 (-11)mm long 9
8*	flowers medium-sized to large; lip (10-) 11-20mm long 10

9	lip narrow (L/l = 1:31); speculum reaching or passing the sinuses .... *O. hespera*
9*	lip less elongated (L/l = 1:24); speculum not reaching sinuses or not passing them .... *O. funerea*

(continued on next page)

Ophrys gackiae
P. DELFORGE

Etymology Named after C. Gack, contemporary German biologist. **Type** Si, Siracusa (2004). **Synonym** *O. '(florentina-) fusca'* PAULUS & GACK nom. nud.

Description Rather spindly, not very tall, 10-20cm; 2-5 flowers, medium-sized for the group; sepals yellowish-green, near spreading, 9-11.5mm x 4.5-6mm; petals oblong, 5-6.5mm x 1-2mm, often slightly ochre; lip angled downwards at 45° to pendent, slightly convex longitudinally, 12-16mm x 9.5-13mm (mean length/width ratio = 1:26), rather narrow (external border of lateral lobe of lip making an angle of 25-32°

with longitudinal axis), deeply 3-lobed, sinuses broadly open, base faded, wedge-shaped, slightly kinked, swollen by attenuated longitudinal prominences that extend to the centre of the crescents; lip hairs rather irregular, relatively sparse, chestnut-brown, broadly zoned around speculum; margin of lip hairless, bright yellow, ± narrow, well-visible; lateral lobes triangular-rounded, rather short; median lobe relatively prominent, laterally convex, lobules reflexed; speculum milky, with fine whitish hairs, unobtrusively bisected by a rather broad but poorly marked groove, often with hairs similar to those of the peri-specular zone in the distal half, joining at the base a prominent patch of white hairs that covers the 'V'-shaped notch.

Flowering Season II-mid IV, rather early.

Habitat Full sun on dry, calcareous substrates. Abandoned cultivation, garrigue up to 700m asl.

Distribution Poorly known. Apparently endemic to the calcareous massifs of southern Sicily. Very rare and local.

Countries Si. **Photos** Si, Siracusa, 7.IV.1987; 12.III.2000. P. DELFORGE.

Pollinator Perhaps *Andrena florentina* (?and *A. thoracica*) (Hymenoptera: Andrenidae).

Key to the *Ophrys funerea* group

(continued from previous page)

10 zone around speculum hardly visible; speculum with contrastingly pale terminal crescents; late flowering .... *O. arnoldii*

10* flowers otherwise 11

11 lip 9.7-14.5mm long .... *O. zonata*

11* lip 15-20mm long .... *O. calocaerina*

Ophrys akhdarensis
(B. BAUMANN & H. BAUMANN) P. DELFORGE

Etymology *akhdarensis:* from Djebel el Akhdar (Li). **Type** Li, Cyrenaica (2001). **Basionym** *O. fusca* subsp. *akhdarensis* B. BAUMANN & H. BAUMANN.

Description Spindly, slender, 10-22cm tall; inflorescence few-flowered, placed high on stem; 2-4 medium-sized flowers; sepals yellowish-green, 9-12mm x 5-7mm, lateral sepals hardly spreading, curved forwards; petals concolourous, oblong, 6-8mm x 1.5-2.5mm, directed obliquely forwards;

lip pendent, 12-15mm x 8.8-11mm (when spread) (mean length/width ratio 1:36), transversally convex, evenly longitudinally convex, base faded, sides strongly curved down and under; external border of lateral lobe of lip making an angle of *c.* 25° with longitudinal axis; centre of lip with poorly marked, long, longitudinal prominences; lateral lobes rather reduced, wedge-shaped, appearing rounded when fresh; sinuses triangular-rounded, not very deep; median lobe obcordate, elongated, clearly emarginate; lip hairs rather long, chestnut-brown to purplish-brown, rather regular, with a distinct, pale, reddish to orange zone broadly surrounding the speculum; speculum prominent, encompassing the unguis, bluish to reddish and marbled at base, very broadly edged white or milky grey, elongated, often reaching the sinuses, bisected by a deep groove, distal half with hairs as peri-specular zone, edges with white hairs, long and straight in basal half; border of lip narrow, yellowish, not obvious, with an irregular outline.

Flowering Season Late II-IV.

Habitat Full sun on dry, alkaline substrates. Garrigue, 300-800m asl.

Distribution Cyrenaicean endemic. Very rare and local.

Countries Li.

Photos A & C Li, Benghazi, 13 & 14.III.2003. C.A.J. Kreutz; **B** 13.III.2002. E. GÜGEL.

10 mm

Ophrys calocaerina

J. DEVILLERS-TERSCHUREN & P. DEVILLERS

Etymology *calo-:* [of the] beautiful; *caerina-:* season (an allusion to the flowering season). **Type** Gr, Viotia (1994). **Synonym** *O. fusca* subsp. *calocaerina* (J. DEVILLERS-TERSCHUREN & P. DEVILLERS) KREUTZ.

Description Slender, 20-42 (-50)cm tall; up to 10 flowers, rather large; sepals green, 11-15mm x 5.5-7mm; petals 8.5-10mm x 2.5-3.5mm, olive-green, edged yellowish, directed obliquely forwards; lip pendent, elongated, 15-20mm x 13.5-16mm (when spread) (mean length/width ratio 1:42), transversally very convex, longitudinally evenly convex, base faded, sides strongly folded down and under; external border of lateral lobe of lip making an angle of (20-) 22-30° with longitudinal axis; centre of lip with poorly marked, long, longitudinal prominences; lateral lobes wedge-shaped, rather angular (when spread), appearing rounded when fresh, sinuses triangular, deep; median lobe rhomboidal, elongated; lip hairs long, chestnut-brown, rather regular, with a pale, rather distinct reddish zone broadly surrounding the speculum; speculum near hairless, elongated, formed by 2 metallic grey blotches, shiny, broadly edged reddish, with 2 paler, blue, blurred crescents at tip, not very contrasting, bisected by a deep groove, near hairless in its distal half; border of lip narrow, yellowish, not obvious, with an irregular outline; base and throat of stigmatic cavity with dense whitish hairs, these extending increasingly sparsely in the central groove to the middle of the speculum; underside of lip pale green.

Flowering Season IV-V, rather late.

Habitat Full sun on dry to moist, calcareous substrates. Abandoned cultivation, garrigue, scrub, probably up to 700m asl.

Distribution Continental Greece and the Isle of Euboea. Very local but sometimes rather abundant.

Countries Gr.

Photos Gr, Euboea, 24.IV.1994; Viotia (loc. typ.), 8.IV.1991. P. DELFORGE.

Pollinator Probably *Andrena labialis* (Hymenoptera: Andrenidae).

Ophrys perpusilla
J. DEVILLERS-TERSCHUREN & P. DEVILLERS

Etymology *perpusilla:* very small. **Type** Gr, Etolia-and-Acarnania (2004). **Synonyms** *O. fusca* subsp. *perpusilla* (J. DEVILLERS-TERSCHUREN & P. DEVILLERS) KREUTZ, *O. punctulata* auct. non RENZ, *O. funerea* auct. non VIVIANI.

Description Spindly; 2-5 small flowers; sepals green, 7-11mm long; petals oblong, sometimes near spatulate, 5-8mm x 1-2mm, olive-green, often edged yellowish; lip (near) horizontal to pendent, rather short, (7-) 8-11 (-12)mm x 6-9.5 (-10)mm (when spread) (mean length/width ratio 1:20), transversally convex, basal third slightly kinked, remainder very slightly convex longitudinally to almost flat; external border of lateral lobe of lip making an angle of 25-34° with longitudinal axis; longitudinal prominences poorly marked; lateral lobes often rather angular (when spread), sinuses deep; median lobe obcordate, sometimes spreading; lip hairs long, brown with purplish reflection, rather irregular, often with a pale perispecular zone and marked with pale streaks; speculum relatively short, dark blue, sometimes edged reddish, with 2 paler, bluish crescents at tip, densely hairy, at least on the sides of its dark blue nuclei, hairs long and purplish; bisecting groove broad and deep, distal half hairy (as lip); border of lip relatively broad and often obvious, yellowish to greenish, regular, clearly demarcated, even around the sinuses; base and throat of stigmatic cavity with dense whitish hairs.

Flowering Season IV-V, rather late.

Habitat Full sun on dry to moist, calcareous substrates. Abandoned cultivation, garrigue, scrub, woodland edges, up to 600m asl. **Distribution** Poorly known due to confusion with *O. cinereophila*. Ionian Islands, southern continental Greece, Peloponnese, Cyclades, east to at least Amorgos and Rhodes. Very rare and local.

Countries Ae Gr. **Photos** Gr, Zakynthos, 11.IV.1993; Kefallinia, 27.IV.1993. P. DELFORGE.

Note Similar plants are found elsewhere in the Mediterranean basin, notably in the Balearics; their affinities with *O. perpusilla* are not known.

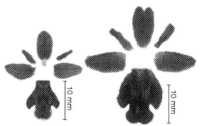

Ophrys leucadica
RENZ (pro hybr.)

Etymology *leucadica:* from [the island of] Leucade, modern Lefkada. **Type** Gr, Ionian Islands (1928). **Synonyms** *O. fusca* subsp. *leucadica* (RENZ) H. KRETZSCHMAR, *O. punctulata* RENZ (pro hybr.), *O. bilunulata* auct. non RISSO.

Description As *O. punctulata* but more robust and larger; 2-6 (-8) medium-sized flowers; lip sloping at 45° to pendent, 12-16mm x 10-13mm (when spread) (mean length/width ratio 1:22), slightly more convex both transversally and longitudinally; external margins of lateral lobes more rounded; median lobe more convex; lip hairs long, hirsute, made up of brown to greyish tufts, with a pale peri-specular zone and gaps in pigmentation; speculum rather short, bluish-grey, irregularly marbled dark blue at base and often with 2 whitish crescents at tip, densely hairy, hairs long, whitish to purplish; dividing groove very broad, with brown hairs (as lip) almost to throat of stigmatic cavity; border of lip relatively narrow, irregular, yellowish, not well demarcated.

Flowering Season III-IV, slightly before *O. perpusilla.*

Habitat Full sun to mid-shade on dry to moist, calcareous substrates. Abandoned cultivation, garrigue, scrub, olive groves, open woodland, up to 600m asl. **Distribution** Ionian Islands, southern continental Greece, Peloponnese, Aegean basin, as well as the island of Hvar (Dalmatia, Croatia). Rather widespread and sometimes abundant. **Countries** Ae An Gr Ju.

Photos A Gr, Lefkada, 4.IV.1992; B Ithaca, 19.IV.1993; C Corfu, 30.III.1992. P. DELFORGE.

Pollinator *Andrena flavipes* and perhaps *A. creberrima* (Hymenoptera: Andrenidae).

Ophrys creberrima
H.F. Paulus

Etymology *creberrima:* very frequent (specific epithet of the pollinator). **Type** Cr, Lassithi (1998). **Synonyms** *O. 'creberrima-fusca'* H.F. Paulus nom. prov., *O. fusca* subsp. *creberrima* (Renz) H. Kretzschmar, *O. bilunulata* auct. non Risso.

Description As *O. leucadica* but 12-25cm tall; 2-6 medium-sized flowers; lip pendent, very convex, both longitudinally and transversally, 11-15mm x 10-14.5mm (when spread) (mean length/width ratio 1:08); base of lip with marked longitudinal prominences, inserted without discontinuity into the strong but regular longitudinal curve; lip hairs a little more regular and with fewer gaps; speculum pale greyish, very shiny, often with 2 narrow white crescents at tip, broadly bisected by a groove that is hairy (as lip) at least for its distal half, the hairs not extending to base of stigmatic cavity; lip edged with a narrow hairless hem, rarely yellow, not obvious, sometimes lacking.

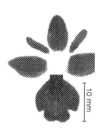

Flowering Season Mid III-V, rather late.

Habitat Full sun to mid-shade on dry, alkaline substrates. Abandoned cultivation, garrigue, scrub, open pinewoods, up to 900m asl.

Distribution Eastern Crete and the Cyclades. Very local but sometimes abundant. **Countries** Cr Gr.

Photos Cr, Lassithi, 9.IV.1982; Gr, Cyclades, 8.IV.1994. P. Delforge.

Pollinator *Andrena creberrima* (Hymenoptera: Andrenidae).

Note At the time of its description considered to be very closely related to *O. leucadica* and endemic to eastern Crete, an island where *Andrena flavipes* is absent, As *A. creberrima* apparently also pollinates *Ophrys leucadica* in the rest of the Aegean basin, the isolation of plants identifiable as *O. creberrima* in the Cyclades appears problematic. Although the morphological difference between *O. leucadica* and *O. creberrima* seem to be relatively large, the 2 taxa may be the same species.

Discussion of the *Ophrys funerea* group

This group, probably closely related to the *Ophrys fusca* and *O. attaviria* groups, is perhaps monophyletic and comprises 12 species distributed in the Mediterranean, from Iberia to at least the Aegean basin. They are united by morphological characteristics (lip prominences, bisected,

(continued on next page)

Ophrys parvula

H.F. PAULUS

Etymology *parvula:* very small. **Type** Ae, Rhodes (2001). **Synonym** *O. fusca* subsp. *parvula* (H.F. PAULUS) KREUTZ.

Description Spindly, 5.5-15.7cm tall; 1-3 (-6) very small flowers; sepals green, 7-8mm long; petals concolourous, oblong, 5-6mm long, lip (near) horizontal, rather short, 6-9mm x 6-7mm (when spread), transversally slightly convex, longitudinally very slightly convex to almost flat; longitudinal prominences rather to poorly marked; lateral lobes often spreading, rounded, sinuses narrow but deep; median lobe obcordate; lip hairs brown with purplish reflections, rather regular, often with a discrete paler peri-specular zone; speculum reaching the sinuses, dark blue to pale bluish, sometimes edged reddish, 2 paler bluish crescents at tip; bisecting groove rather broad and distinct, hairy (as lip or speculum) on distal half; border of lip yellowish to greenish, sometimes brownish, relatively broad and regular, even around sinuses, well defined, often obvious; base and throat of stigmatic cavity with dense whitish hairs; unguis often faded.

Flowering Season Mid III-IV.

Habitat Full sun on dry, calcareous substrates. Phryganas, up to 100m asl.

Distribution Endemic to southern Rhodes. Very local and rather rare. Countries Ae.

Photos Ae, Rhodes, 3 & 7.IV.1998. C.A.J. KREUTZ.

Pollinator *Andrena tomora* (Hymenoptera: Andrenidae).

Discussion of the *Ophrys funerea* group

(continued from previous page)

speculum distal peri-specular zone) which are also found to varying degrees, often more extreme, in other groups (notably the *O. obaesa* group), so that the inclusion of some species (e.g. *O. hespera, O. gackiae, O. parvula*) in the *O. funerea* group requires confirmation. Within the group, differences in size and ± large differences in flowering times have allowed speciation to occur in sympatry or parapatry within the same lineage by the repeated adaptation to different pollinators (Tyrrhenian basin *O. funerea-O. zonata*; Ionio-Aegean basin *O. perpusilla-O. leucadica*). It is likely that allopatric speciation also occurred via the adaptation of orchids of different lineages to the same pollinator (*O. zonata-O. leucadica*, adapted to pollination by *Andrena flavipes*). Information on the taxonomy and biogeography of the group is still very fragmented, rendering a more detailed cladistic analysis too speculative at present.

The *Ophrys attaviria* group

Characteristics Lip with longitudinal prominences not very prominent to almost absent; margins of unguis often with colourful fins; longitudinal convexity of lip very weak to near absent, central half often flat; speculum usually without bisecting groove, without lip hairs; lip hairs rather regular, comprising (sometimes inconsistently) a broad paler zone around the speculum, often with irregular paler blotches, then a narrow, progressively darker, concentric submarginal band; speculum shortly ciliate to near hairless; border of lip hairless, often thin, irregularly demarcated.

Ophrys thriptiensis
H.F. PAULUS

Etymology *thriptiensis:* [from mountain massif of] Thripti. **Type** Cr, Lassithi (1998). **Synonyms** *O. 'Thripti-fusca'* early' vel *O. 'bicolor-fusca'* H.F. PAULUS nom. prov., *O. fusca* subsp. *thriptiensis* (H.F. PAULUS) H. KRETZSCHMAR.

Description Spindly, 5-15cm tall; 1-3 (-5) medium-sized flowers; petals 4-8mm x 2-3mm; lip slightly convex to longitudinally flat, relatively large, 10-13 (-15)mm x 10-14mm (mean length/width ratio 1:19); speculum undivided, bluish-grey, ± dark, often marbled blackish-blue, frequently with 2 milky crescents at tip; speculum hairs greyish, short, rather dense; lip hairs dark purplish-brown, sometimes discreetly zoned; margin of lip yellowish, hairless, irregular, sometimes rather broad; lateral lobes short, turned down, sinuses not very deep; median lobe elongated, only slightly emarginate; stigmatic cavity transverse, low, sometimes marked with a lateral red spot on internal wall; underside of lip whitish-green, often washed brownish-red.

Flowering Season (I-) II-mid III, early, in 2 successive waves.

Habitat Full sun to mid-shade on dry, calcareous substrates. Mostly open pinewoods, 400-1000m asl. **Distribution** Apparently endemic to the calcareous massifs of eastern Crete; analogous plants, later flowering, have been reported from Rhodes (Ae). Very local and very rare.

Countries ?Ae Cr.

Photo Cr, Lassithi (loc. typ.), 1.III.1990. P. DELFORGE.

Pollinator Probably *Andrena bicolor* (Hymenoptera: Andrenidae).

Discussion of the *Ophrys attaviria* group

Essentially an eastern Mediterranean group, probably not natural, gathering together 6 species with characters that are often spectacular but relatively inconsistent, sometimes even within populations. The lip may, for example, be longitudinally almost flat or kinked at the base and regularly convex in the centre; the peri-specular zone may be either broad, present and very obvious or insignificant and even absent; the central part of the speculum may lack a bisecting groove carrying the lip hairs or may have all or part of this structure (e.g. *O. phaseliana*). On the other hand, knowledge of the range of variation and the distribution of the 6 species in the group is still very patchy, even if they each seem to be rather unusual.

The phylogenetic significance of this group thus still needs to be established, and several of its representatives, due to this or that character being ± constant, could be placed into neighbouring groups. Doing so would weaken its definition, however, which would not be very satisfactory.

Ophrys attaviria
D. RÜCKBRODT & WENKER

Etymology *attaviria:* [Mount] Attaviria. **Type** Ae, Rhodes (1990). **Synonym** *O. fusca* subsp. *attaviria* (D. RÜCKBRODT & WENKER) KREUTZ.

Description 15-35cm tall; 3-10 flowers, medium-sized to rather large; sepals 10-12mm x 5-7mm; petals 6-9mm x 1.5-2.5mm; lip 13-18mm x 9-13mm, almost flat longitudinally, base whitish, yellowish or ochre, centre usually with poorly marked longitudinal prominences; speculum often drab, shiny blackish-blue to sometimes reddish, marbled dark greyish-violet at base, often with 2 crescents at tip, ± clearly demarcated and contrasting, frequently divided by a slight groove, sometimes with hairs (as lip) in its distal third; speculum hairs short and dense, longer, straighter and whiter at sides; lip hairs dark purplish-brown, sometimes with broad peri-spec-ular zone, mostly lateral, but weak and hardly noticeable; lateral lobes rather short, turned down, divided by broad sinuses; median lobe elongated; border of lip reddish to greenish-yellow, ± narrow, hairless; underside of lip greenish, usually without purple or brownish tones.

Flowering Season (III-) IV-V, rather late.

Habitat Full sun to mid-shade on dry, alkaline substrates. Abandoned cultivation, garrigue, open pinewoods, up to 700m asl. **Distribution** Eastern Mediterranean. Known with certainty from Rhodes (Ae) and southwest Mediterranean Anatolia; may also occur west to the Ionian Islands (Gr) and east to Cyprus. Local and often rare. **Countries** Ae An ?Cy ?Gr.

Photo A Ae, Rhodes (holotype), 16.IV.1990; **B** An, Antalya, 26.IV.1996. D. RÜCKBRODT; **C** Ae, Rhodes, 7.IV.1998. C.A.J. KREUTZ.

Ophrys cesmeensis
(KREUTZ) P. DELFORGE

Etymology *cesmeensis:* from Çesme Peninsula (An). **Type** An, Izmir (2003). **Synonyms** *O. attaviria* subsp. *cesmeensis* KREUTZ, *O. fusca* subsp. *cesmeensis* (KREUTZ) KREUTZ.

Description Thickset, 10-22cm tall; 1-4 (-6) large flowers; sepals *c.* 12mm x 5mm; petals near spatulate, *c.* 10mm x 2.5mm; lip 14-20mm x 9-15mm, almost flat or strongly curved longitudinally but flat in the centre, base whitish, yellowish or ochre, centre usually with rather well marked longitudinal prominences; speculum near hairless, blue to blackish-blue, shiny, with 2 crescents at tip, ± clearly defined and contrasting, sometimes divided by a slight groove; speculum hairs short and dense, longer, straighter and whiter at sides; lip hairs dark purplish-brown, sometimes with a subtle peri-specular zone, with a narrow, paler submarginal band; border of lip yellowish, broad, regular, even around sinuses, obvious, rather poorly demarcated.

Flowering Season End III-IV.

Habitat Full sun to mid-shade on dry to moist, alkaline substrates. Abandoned cultivation, garrigue, open pinewoods, up to 100m asl.

Distribution Endemic to Çesme Peninsula. Very rare and local. **Countries** An. **Photos** An, Izmir, 10.IV.1997. C.A.J. KREUTZ.

Key to the *Ophrys attaviria* group

1 flowers medium-sized, lip 10-13 (-15)mm long, early flowering (I-mid III).................... ....*O. thriptiensis*
1* flowers larger, lip 11-20mm long, later flowering (III-V) 2

2 lip hairs in a uniform layer 3
2* lip hairs irregularly distributed, speckled, formed by tufts of dark hairs with the underlying yellow epidermis ± broadly visible 5

3 lip hairs chestnut-brown, often yellowish .... *O. sabulosa*
3* lip hairs dark blackish................................. 4

4 lip almost flat longitudinally, with a narrow hairless border .... *O. attaviria*
4* lip often curved longitudinally, with a broad yellow hairless border .... *O. cesmeensis*

5 flowers medium-sized; petals 5-8mm long; lip near horizontal, flowering mid III-IV .... *O. parosica*
5* flowers bigger, petals 7.5-12mm long; lip more pendent, flowering later, mid IV-V .... *O. phaseliana*

Ophrys parosica
P. DELFORGE

Etymology *parosica:* from [the island of] Paros.
Type Gr, Cyclades, Paros (1995). **Synonym** *O. fusca* subsp. *parosica* (P. DELFORGE) KREUTZ.

Description Rather small, 10-28cm tall; 2-6 flowers, medium sized for the group; petals 5-8mm x 2-3mm, oblong-rounded to narrowly oval; lip near horizontal, clearly to obscurely 3-lobed, slightly to very laterally convex, slightly kinked at base then flat longitudinally, tip curved downwards due to turneddown edges, oboval (when spread), 11-16 (-18)mm x 9-14 (-16)mm (when spread) (mean length/ width ratio 1:20), base lacking purplish tones, centre rarely swollen by longitudinal prominences; lateral lobes rather small, margins sinuous, separated from median lobe by unobtrusive sinuses; median lobe slightly emarginate to near entire; speculum undivided, greyish-blue marbled whitish, elongated, often touching hairless border of lip around sinuses, sparsely hairy with duller areas, as lip, the pale zones being, however, covered by fine whitish hairs, tip sometimes with a whitish **ω**, ± broad; lip hairs sparse, discontinuous, forming tufts of straight hairs, brown to reddish-brown, irregularly marbling the yellow epidermis with a darker, denser narrow submarginal band; lip bordered by a hairless yellow strip; underside of lip yellowish-green to green, lacking red tones.

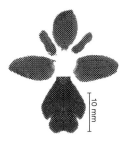

Flowering Season Mid III-IV.

Habitat Full sun on dry, calcareous substrates. Abandoned cultivation, garrigue, scrub, up to 700m asl.

Distribution Central and eastern Cyclades, perhaps eastern Aegean islands and coastal Anatolia (see, however, p. 396). Rare and local.

Countries ?Ae ?An Gr.

Photos Gr, Cyclades, Paros, 10 & 15.IV.1995. P. DELFORGE.

Ophrys phaseliana
D. RÜCKBRODT & U. RÜCKBRODT

Etymology *phaseliana:* [from the village] of Phaselis. **Type** An, Antalya (1996). **Synonym** *O. fusca* subsp. *phaseliana* (D. RÜCKBRODT & U. RÜCK-BRODT) KREUTZ.

Description As *O. parosica* but 15-40cm tall; 1-4 (-7) flowers, medium-sized to rather large for group; petals 7.5-12mm x 2.5-4mm, near spatulate; lip more pendent, more kinked at base, oboval (when spread), 13.5-18.5mm x 11.5-16.5mm (when spread), slightly more elongated (mean length/width ratio 1:25), longitudinal prominences slightly larger, shiny, but rarely swelling centre of lip; lateral lobes often better separated from median lobe by larger sinuses;

(herbar. D. & U. RÜCKBRODT)

median lobe more transversally spreading, up to 10mm broad; speculum greyish-blue to reddish, marbled whitish, less elongated, rarely touching the hairless border around sinuses, centre sometimes bisected; lip hairs discontinuous but not so sparse, forming a dense, dark submarginal band, often broader; lip bordered by a hairless yellow strip; underside of lip pale green.

Flowering Season Mid IV-V.

Habitat Full sun to mid-shade on dry to moist, alkaline substrates. Abandoned cultivation, garrigue, open woodland, banks, up to 400m asl.

Distribution Southwest Mediterranean Anatolia, from Fethiye to Antalya (Caria). The single report from Crete is dubious. Rare and local.

Countries An.

Photos An, Antalya, (loc. typ.), 14.IV.1995. D. RÜCKBRODT.

Note The range of variation of *O. parosica* and *O. phaseliana* may well overlap and the 2 taxa may be conspecific. Nevertheless, on current knowledge they seem to be allopatric and their morphology and phenology appear to be sufficiently distinct to consider them, at least provisionally, as 2 separate species.

Ophrys sabulosa
H.F. PAULUS & GACK ex P. DELFORGE

Etymology *sabulosa:* sandy or from sandy lands (the specific epithet of the pollinator). **Type** Si, Palermo (2004). **Synonyms** *O.* '*sabulosa-fusca*' H.F. PAULUS & GACK nom. nud., *O. fusca* subsp. *sabulosa* (H.F. PAULUS & GACK ex P. DELFORGE) KREUTZ, *O. fusca* auct. non LINK, *O. attaviria* auct. non D. RÜCKBRODT & WENKER.

Description Robust, up to 32cm tall; 3-8 flowers, rather large for the group; sepals yellowish-green, near spreading, 12-15mm x 7-9mm; petals oblong, 7-9.5mm x 1.5-3mm, slightly ochre; lip angled downwards at 45° to pendent, slightly convex longitudinally, 15-19mm x 13.5-16mm (mean length/width ratio = 1:22), rather massive

(external border of lateral lobe of lip making an angle of 30-36° with longitudinal axis), 3-lobed, sinuses triangular, rather narrow, base sometimes sl-ightly kinked, with a prominent groove, whitish, hairy, with weakly coloured fins and attenuated longitudinal prominences that extend into speculum; lip hairs rather regular, yellowish chestnut-brown with purplish reflection, broadly zoned around speculum, sometimes with a lighter submarginal band along border of lip; edge of lip bright yellow, hairless, ± narrow, sharply-defined, obvious; lateral lobes rounded then shortly rhomboidal, sides turned down; median lobe relatively short, laterally slightly convex; speculum milky to reddish, marbled dark bluish at centre, with regular fine whitish hairs, abruptly demarcated from those on the lip, central groove absent, at least in central third; underside of lip greenish-white.

Flowering Season III-IV, after *O. lupercalis* and *O. gackiae*.

Habitat Full sun on dry, calcareous substrates. Abandoned cultivation, garrigue, up to 1000m asl.

Distribution Probably endemic to Sicily. Rather local and rather rare.

Countries Si.

Photos Si, Palermo (loc. typ.), 16.IV.2000; Siracusa, 15.III.2000. P. DELFORGE.

Pollinator *Andrena sabulosa* (Hymenoptera: Andrenidae).

The *Ophrys blitopertha* group

Characteristics Lip elongated, spreading, straight, almost without longitudinal prominences; lip hairs rather dense, erect, slightly irregular, sometimes with a pale peri-specular zone; speculum finely hairy to near hairless, usually without a bisecting prominence; border of lip hairless, often broad, regular throughout the perimeter, rather cleanly demarcated; underside of lip yellow, sometimes washed reddish at centre.

Discussion This group comprises 2 named species, one of which is specifically pollinated by males of a small cockchafer which attempt pseudocopulation with the lip (as for male *Andrena* bees). Similar behaviour has already been observed occasionally with closely related Scarabaeidae beetles in western Europe, involving *Phyllopertha horticola* on the lips of *Ophrys fuciflora* or *O. sphegodes*. This very special feature of *O. blitopertha* may reveal a species with ancestral characters, similar to *O. migoutiana*, *O. omegaifera* s.l. and the *Pseudophrys* lineage, or be the result, only superficially very divergent, of the adaptation to a beetle instead of a bee.

Ophrys persephonae
H.F. PAULUS

Etymology Named after Persephone, queen of the underworld in Greek myth. **Type** Ae, Rhodes (2001).

Description As *O. blitopertha* but robust, 30-40cm tall; 4-5 (-9) flowers, more brightly coloured; sepals 9-11.5mm long; lip (near) horizontal, appearing a little less straight, slightly more transversally convex in centre, 9-13mm x 8-10.5mm; lip hairs denser, much darker; speculum larger, contrasting, shiny, entirely pale blue or blackish-blue, purplish, and with 2 pale blue crescents at tip ± forming a large, contrasting ω; stigmatic cavity larger, 4-5mm wide.

Flowering Season Mid III-IV.

Habitat Mid-shade on dry, alkaline substrates. Open pinewoods, up to 300m asl.

Distribution Rhodes and neighbouring regions of Anatolia. Very rare and local.

Countries Ae An.

Photos Ae, Rhodes, 20.III.2004. S. HERTEL

Key to the *Ophrys blitopertha* group

1   plant robust, flowers very colourful
    .... *O. persephonae*
1*   plant spindly, flowers drab ...... *O. blitopertha*

Ophrys blitopertha

H.F. PAULUS

Etymology *-pertha:* destroying; *blito-:* the goosefoot family (= *Chenopodium,* ancient *Blitum*) (*blitopertha* is the generic name of its phytophagous pollinator). **Type** Gr, Cyclades, Naxos (1998). **Synonyms** *O. 'Blitopertha-fusca'* H.F. PAULUS & GACK nom. prov., *O. fusca* subsp. *blitopertha* (H.F. PAULUS) N. FAURHOLDT & H.Æ. PEDERSEN.

Description Small, spindly, 6.5-15 (-20)cm tall; 1-4 (-7) medium-sized flowers; sepals whitish-green, near spreading, 7-11mm x 3-4.5mm; petals darker green to sometimes olive-green, oblong, curved forwards, 3-6mm x 0.8-1.5mm; lip (near) horizontal, with a very straight appearance, short, oboval to wedge-shaped, almost flat to sometimes reflexed longitudinally, weakly convex transversally in centre, 8-12 (-14)mm x (7.5-) 8-11 (-12)mm; (mean length/width ratio = 1:23), 3-lobed, sinuses hardly incised, only slightly open, base sometimes faded, folded into a shallow throat, yellowish-white, with a whitish to greyish jugular brush; longitudinal prominences near absent; lip hairs rather dense, erect, slightly irregular, blackish-brown with crimson to purplish reflections, becoming paler, yellowish-brown, at anthesis, sometimes with a barely perceptible paler distal peri-specular zone; lip bordered by a bright yellow (sometimes reddish), hairless margin, often broad, very obvious, very regular, parallel to the edge from base to tip of lobes, rather cleanly demarcated; lateral lobes short, shortly rhomboidal, sides spreading to reflexed; median lobe rather short, not very emarginate, spreading, sides reflexed; speculum elongated, not reaching sinuses, dark, not very contrasting and not very shiny, sometimes wrinkled, with 2 crescents at tip forming a ± narrow ω, not very contrasting, clearly separated from lip hairs, near hairless or with short, fine hairs, not very dense, central groove absent or exceptionally a slight dividing groove with hairs as peri-speculum; stigmatic cavity rather large and low; underside of lip yellow, centre sometimes washed pinkish.

Flowering Season Late III-early V, rather late.

Habitat Full sun on dry, calcareous substrates, often xeric and sandy. Abandoned cultivation, garrigue, olive groves, open pinewoods, up to 400m asl.

Distribution The eastern Aegean basin, from the central Cyclades east to southwest Anatolia (Caria) and north to Lesbos. Very rare and local.

Countries Ae An Gr.

Photos Gr, Cyclades, Naxos (loc. typ.), 25.IV.1995. P. DELFORGE.

Pollinator *Blitopertha lineolata* (Scarabaeidae: Coleoptera).

The *Ophrys migoutiana* group

Characteristics Petals broad and long, spatulate, almost as long as sepals; lip either longitudinally flat or regularly curved, longitudinal prominences almost absent; lip hairs long, regular, very dense, zoned – the paler peri-specular zone covering almost whole lip, the darker zone limited to a narrow submarginal band covering only the extremities of the lobes; speculum hairless, without a dividing prominence or hairs in the centre; hairless border of lip very broad, regular all around lip, clearly separated from hairy region; underside of lip usually green.

Discussion Only one named species, sometimes considered close to the previous group (structure of petals, indented, occasionally straight lip, broad, regular hairless border) or *O. atlantica* (elongation and structure of petals, square jugular brush, pattern of coloration), which may suggest that *O. migoutiana* occupies a position close to the common ancestor of the *O. fusca-O. atlantica* cluster.

Ophrys migoutiana
H. GAY (pro hybr.)

Etymology Named after A. Migout, French botanist, born in 1830. **Type** Ag, Algiers, Medea region (1890). **Synonym** *O. fusca* subsp. *migoutiana* (H. GAY) KREUTZ.

Description Robust, stem thick, up to 40cm tall; 3-8 flowers, rather large for the group; sepals yellowish-green, near spreading; petals often olive-green, margins undulate; lip (near) horizontal, oboval to wedge-shaped, either almost longitudinally flat from base to tip, appearing straight, or regularly longitudinally convex, 9.5-14mm x 8-11mm; (mean length/width ratio = 1:23), 3-lobed, sinuses triangular, only slightly open, base often with a transverse yellow band 1-2mm wide, a shallow yellowish-white groove, and a whitish to greyish square jugular brush; longitudinal prominences very attenuated to near absent; lip hairs dense, erect, dark brown with crimson to purplish reflections, colour progressively darker from speculum out to edge, often with a narrow dark band alongside the hairless border at tip of lobe; lip with a hairless border, lemon-yellow, greenish-yellow, sometimes purplish or brown, very regular, parallel to the edge from base to tip of lobes, clearly demarcated; lateral lobes short, shortly rhomboidal, margins turned down; median lobe rather elongated, very or slightly convex laterally, sides at tip turned down or sometimes, when lobe slightly convex, reflexed; speculum elongated, hairless, clearly demarcated, dividing groove absent, very dark, dark blackish-blue, with 2 crescents at tip forming a rather broad, angular ⍵, either dark blue and not very contrasting, or bright blue or whitish and very contrasting, often reaching tip of sinuses; stigmatic cavity rather large and low; underside of lip green, exceptionally tinted red.

Flowering Season III-IV.

Habitat Full sun to mid-shade on dry, calcareous substrates, often skeletal. Open, very xeric garrigue with *Rosmarinus officinalis*, pinewoods with *Pinus halepensis*, cypress forest with *Cupressus sempervirens*, up to 800m asl.

Distribution Calcareous massifs at the transition between the Mediterranean and Saharan regions, from Tunisia to at least central Algeria. Probably the most southerly species in the genus *Ophrys*. Local and sometimes abundant.

Countries Ag Tn.

Photos Tn, Teboursouk and Djebel Balouta, 10.IV.1993. J. DEVILLERS-TERSCHUREN.

The *Ophrys obaesa* group

Characteristics Lip with prominent basal and specular longitudinal prominences, sometimes inducing a longitudinal convexity to the whole lip, with a ± abrupt inversion of the curve in the centre; groove bisecting speculum very deep, hairy, often white on basal half, bordered by sinuous longitudinal prominences; lip hairs dense, rather long, relatively regular, forming a paler zone around the speculum, often better-marked at sides than at tip (for notes on distinguishing this zone, see p. 381), and then a darker concentric zone; speculum shortly ciliate; base of median lobe often clearly depressed near sinuses, giving the median lobe a ± globular appearance and sometimes causing its sides to overlap slightly those of lateral lobes; border of lip hairless, often thin, irregularly defined.

Ophrys fabrella
H.F. PAULUS & AYASSE ex P. DELFORGE

Etymology *fabrella:* specific epithet of the pollinator. **Type** Bl, Mallorca (2004). **Synonyms** *O. 'fabrella-fusca'* H.F. PAULUS & AYASSE nom. nud., *O. fusca* subsp. *fabrella* (H.F. PAULUS & AYASSE ex P. DELFORGE) KREUTZ, *O. funerea* auct. non VIVIANI.

Description Very slender, up to 25cm tall; 1-4 flowers, very small for the group; sepals yellowish-green, near spreading; petals green with lighter margins; lip short, oboval to near rhomboidal, 6-9.5mm x 5.5-9mm (when spread) (mean length/width ratio 1:05), (near) horizontal, transversally and longitudinally slightly convex; lateral lobes rhomboidal, with poorly marked linear sinuses; median lobe short, slightly emarginate, base sometimes depressed; lip hairs brownish with purplish reflections, with a narrow paler brown zone around distal part of speculum with whitish reflections, broader and invading all of lateral lobes; speculum short, bluish to reddish, shiny, often with 2 pale crescents at tip, divided by a narrow groove, hairy, at least distal part (hairs as peri-speculum); yellow border of lip broad, obvious, with a regular outline; base and throat of stigmatic cavity with dense whitish hairs, extending into bisecting groove, often to centre of speculum; underside of lip pale green.

Flowering Season III-mid IV.

Habitat Full sun on dry, calcareous substrates. Abandoned cultivation, garrigue, up to 400m asl.

Distribution Endemic to Balearic Islands. Rather local and rather rare. **Countries** Bl.

Photos Bl, Ibiza, 4.IV.1997. D. TYTECA.

Pollinator *Andrena fabrella* (Hymenoptera: Andrenidae).

Ophrys marmorata
G. FOELSCHE & W. FOELSCHE

Etymology *marmorata:* marbled. **Type** Co, Corsica-du-Sud (1998). **Synonyms** *O. fusca* subsp. *marmorata* (G. FOELSCHE & W. FOELSCHE) KREUTZ, *O. peraiolae* G. FOELSCHE *et al.*, *O. peraiolae* var. *rubra* G. FOELSCHE *et al.*, *O. fusca* subsp. *peraiolae* (G. FOELSCHE *et al.*) KREUTZ.

Description 12-25cm tall; 1-5 (-7) flowers rather small to medium-sized; sepals 7-11mm x 4-7mm; petals 5-7mm x 1.4-2.6mm, yellowish-green; lip pendent to angled at 45°, oboval, rather regularly laterally convex due to its turned-down edges, longitudinally flat at base, depressed at tip of speculum, then convex in upper third, 8-14mm x 7-11mm; (mean length/width ratio = 1:21), 3-lobed, hardly indented, sinuses short, triangular, not very open, base of lip faded, with a deep groove with whitish hairs edged by 2, often distinct, raised areas; longitudinal prominences rather marked; lip hairs dense, erect, dark brown with crimson to purplish reflections, often very irregular, paler and with yellow tufts around speculum, darker and more regular towards edge, forming a dark outer band covering tip of lobes; lip bordered by a yellow, exceptionally reddish, hairless margin, very regular, rather clearly defined; lateral lobes broadly rounded; median lobe not very elongated, not very to clearly emarginate; speculum rather short, irregularly demarcated, pale, milky, often marbled dark blue at base, with 2 irregular whitish crescents at tip, with a distinct dividing groove, hairy, at least distal half (hairs pale, as lip); underside of lip greenish. '*peraiolae*' A morph comprising a few plants, probably introgressed with *O. funerea*; Péraiola Cove (Co). **Photo B** loc. typ. 27.III.1999. W. FOELSCHE.

›*peraiolae*‹

Flowering Season Late II-mid IV.

Habitat Full sun on dry, calcareous substrates. Abandoned cultivation, garrigue up to 300m asl.

Distribution Calcareous massifs of southern Corsica. Very local but sometimes rather abundant.

Countries Co.

Photos A & C Co, Corsica-du-Sud (loc. typ.), 3.IV.1998. W. Foelsche; 4.IV.1996. P. Delforge.

Pollinator *Andrena wilkella* (Hymenoptera:

Ophrys sulcata

J. DEVILLERS-TERSCHUREN & P. DEVILLERS

Etymology *sulcata:* with a groove. **Type** Ga, Charente, île d'Oléron (1994). **Synonym** ?*O. fusca* subsp. *minima* BALAYER.

Description 6-20 (-24)cm tall; (3-) 4-7 rather small flowers, sometimes gathered into a short inflorescence; sepals green to whitish-green, 7-10mm x 3-6mm; petals rather elongated, erect, 5-7.5mm x 1.2-2.4mm, yellowish-green to ochre; lip pendent to angled at 45°, oboval, rather regularly convex both laterally and longitudinally, depressed at tip of speculum, (7-) 8-13 (-14)mm x 6.5-11mm; (mean length/width ratio = 1:08), 3-lobed, hardly indented, sinuses near linear, base faded, yellowish, with a broad groove bearing whitish hairs; longitudinal prominences elongated, wrinkled and marked; lip hairs dense, erect, regular, dark brown with crimson to purplish reflections, with a distinct contrasting pale purplish-brown peri-specular zone; lip surrounded by a yellow to greenish-yellow hairless border, broad near base, narrower towards tip, irregularly defined; lateral lobes rounded; median lobe rounded, slightly emarginate; speculum rather short but broad, not very contrasting, dark blue at base, sometimes greyish or reddish, with a well marked, distinct dividing groove, often white with whitish hairs extending to tip; underside of lip greenish; stigmatic cavity wall thick, border sometimes colourful; 2n=36.

Flowering Season (End IV-) V-VI, late.

Habitat Full sun on dry to damp, alkaline substrates. Abandoned cultivation, garrigue, short grassland, pastures, up to 1000m asl.

Distribution Western sub-Mediterranean. Northern Spain, southern France, north to Brittany, southern half of Italian peninsula, Istria; very rare (?absent) in the true Mediterranean zone. Local but sometimes abundant. **Countries** Ga Hs It Ju.

Photos Ga, Aude, 18.V.1999. P. DELFORGE.

Pollinators *Andrena flavipes*, *A. ovulata* and *A. wilkella* (Hymenoptera: Andrenidae).

Key to the *Ophrys obaesa* group

1	distal half of lip strongly turned down and under	*O. pallida*
1*	lip otherwise	2
2	flowers large, lip 12.5-18mm long	*O. lucana*
2*	flowers small to medium-sized, lip 6-13 (14)mm long	3

(continued on p. 405)

Ophrys lucana

P. DELFORGE, J. DEVILLERS-TERSCHUREN & P. DEVILLERS

Etymology *lucana:* from Lucana. **Type** It, Potenza (2000). **Synonym** *O. fusca* subsp. *lucana* (P. DELFORGE *ET AL.)* KREUTZ.

Description Thickset, 10-25cm tall, sometimes with 3 root-tubers; inflorescence near lax; 2-6 (-7) rather large flowers; sepals yellowish-green to whitish-green, 10-12.5mm x 4-6mm; petals rather large, oblong-rounded to near spatulate, 7-10mm x 1.6-2.5mm, edges slightly undulate, green, darker than sepals; lip frequently with a reddish tone, near horizontal then often pendent, 3-lobed, 12.5-18mm x 10-14mm (when spread) (mean length/width ratio = 1:12), transversally and longitudinally slightly convex, clearly undulating, with elongated and attenuated basal and central swellings, crescents often prominently swollen, separated by a very marked central depression; median lobe prominent, 3-5mm x 5-8mm, slightly emarginate, base depressed, centre globular; hairs on lobes straight, dark purplish-brown, not very dense, giving the lip a chestnut tone; hairs of peri-specular zone shorter and less dense, often producing (especially on sides of speculum) a subtle zonation; speculum 7-10mm long, exceptionally reaching sinuses, bluish to reddish, rarely marbled or with 2 pale crescents at tip, hairs very short, straight, regular but sparse, purplish, hairs on edges longer and white, lip clearly divided by a very broad groove, hairy (brown as lip distally, white proximally), base depressed; border of lip yellowish to greenish, hairless, distinct, with a rather regular outline, *c.* 0.5mm wide; stigmatic cavity often with 2 crimson-brown spots on walls, extended into a transverse band; underside of lip greenish-white to greenish at centre, sides often washed brown.

Flowering Season Mid V-VI.

Habitat Full sun to mid-shade on dry to moist, alkaline substrates. Short, marly grassland, abandoned cultivation, the edges of oakwoods with *Quercus cerris*, 300-1200m asl.

Distribution Peninsular Italy, from southern Campania north to Calabria. Local but sometimes very abundant.

Countries It.

Photos It, Potenza (loc. typ.), 24.V.2000. P. DELFORGE.

Pollinator *Andrena labialis* (Hymenoptera: Andrenidae).

404

Ophrys obaesa
LOJACONO

Etymology *obaesa:* swollen. **Type** Si, Palermo (1909). **Synonyms** *O. fusca* subsp. *obaesa* (LOJACONO) E.G. CAMUS & A. CAMUS, O. × *ficuzzana* H. BAUMANN & KÜNKELE, *O. caerulea* GENIEZ & MELKI.

Description As *O. lucana* but on average more spindly and smaller in all parts; inflorescence often dense, flowers grouped at tip of stem; 2-6 (-8) rather small to medium-sized flowers; sepals 7-13mm x 5-9mm; lip (near) horizontal, 9-13 (-14)mm x 7-10mm (when spread) (mean length/width ratio = 1:23), clearly undulating, with more prominent elongated basal and central swellings, separated by a marked central depression; median lobe slightly emarginate, base more clearly depressed; lip hairs straight, dark purplish-brown to chestnut, sometimes irregular, with a narrow peri-specular zone, often more obvious, even at tip of speculum; speculum shorter, not reaching sinuses, extending to sides of stigmatic cavity, divided by a broad groove, blue, often edged reddish, frequently with 2 ± contrasting crescents at tip, hairs very short, evenly purplish; border of lip hairless, very narrow, irregular; underside of lip whitish-green, often washed purple at centre.

Flowering Season Mid III-mid V.

Habitat Full sun to shade on dry to moist, alkaline substrates. Abandoned cultivation, garrigue, scrub, olive groves, pinewoods and open to dense mixed forests, up to 1100m asl. **Distribution** Endemic to Sicily. **Countries** Si. **Photos** Si, Palermo, 16 & 27.IV.2000. P. DELFORGE.

Pollinator *Andrena flavipes* (Hymenoptera: Andrenidae).

Key to the *Ophrys obaesa* group
(continued from p. 403)

3   late flowering (V-VI) .... *O. sulcata*

3*   early flowering (II-IV) 4

4   lip without yellow margin .... *O. obaesa*

4*   lip broadly edged yellow 5

5   lip 8-14mm long; coloration of lip hairs irregular, marbled .... *O. marmorata*

5*   lip 6-9.5mm long; hairs uniformly coloured ..
   .... *O. fabrella*

Discussion of the *Ophrys obaesa* group

Probably monophyletic, with 6 species combining (sometimes in an extreme manner) characteristics from closely related groups. The characteristics of the group seem to be expressed with a certain
(continued on next page)

Ophrys pallida
RAFINESQUE

Etymology *pallida:* pale. **Type** Si, Palermo (1810). **Synonym** *O. fusca* subsp. *pallida* (RAFINESQUE) E.G. CAMUS.

Description 10-30cm tall; bracts longer than ovary, concave, with whitish reflections; 2-6 small flowers; sepals white, greenish or yellowish, rarely pinkish, 17.5-10mm x 4.5-6.5mm, lateral sepals strongly curved forwards; petals oblong, 5-7mm x 2-3mm, yellowish, greenish or olive-green; lip 3-lobed, 7.5-11mm x 6-9.5mm (when spread), laterally very convex, abruptly kinked in centre, distal 2/3 strongly turned down and back, tip recurved, base yellowish, contracted into 2 protuberant longitudinal prominences, shiny, separated by a deep V-shaped throat with whitish hairs (some-times tinted purple); lateral lobes narrowly rounded; median lobe obcordate, broader than long; lip hairs dark blackish-purple, rather long, dense, regular, with purplish reflec-tions; border of lip hairless, narrow, sometimes tinted yellow, turned down and under; speculum bilobed, finely velvety, grey to bluish, shiny, with milky crescents at tip; underside of lip whitish-green; stigmatic cavity broader than tall, grooved and tomentose at base.

herb. E. NELSON

Flowering Season (II-) III-IV (-V).

Habitat Full sun to mid-shade on alkaline substrates, often skeletal and moist. Short grass-land, abandoned cultivation, garrigue, scrub, open woodland, up to 900m asl.

Distribution Endemic to Sicily. Very rare and local. **Countries** Si. **Photos** Si, Palermo, 16.IV.2000. P. DELFORGE.

Pollinator *Andrena orbitalis* (Hymenoptera: Andrenidae).

Discussion of the *Ophrys obaesa* group
(continued from previous page)

harmony in *O. sulcata, O. lucana* and *O. obaesa*, which are probably closely related; a close relationship of *O. marmorata* with this clade is plausible, despite its overall similarity with *O. bilunulata*. The 2 other species are more special and strongly diverge from each other and from the *O. obaesa* lineage; the inclusion of *O. fabrella* in the *O. obaesa* group requires confirmation, while the colour of the sepals and the very particular structure of *O. pallida* are unique within *Pseudophrys*; they may indicate an ancient origin for *O. pallida*, close to the root of *Pseudophrys*.

The *Ophrys subfusca* group

Characteristics Flowers apparently intermediate between *O. fusca* s.l. and *O. lutea* s.l.; lip 3-lobed, rather short (mean length/width ratio 1:05-1:20); external border of lateral lobe of lip making a mean angle of 45° with longitudinal axis; lateral lobes frequently turned down and under; median lobe spreading, sides often reflexed, overhanging extremities of lateral lobes; base of lip with a deep groove and 2 rounded longitudinal swellings, protruding, producing a ± marked kink and then a ± distinct depression, sometimes a break, at tip of speculum; lip hairs reaching or almost reaching margins, brown, ± dark, in centre (as far as median lobe), ± broadly yellow on sides, the 2 colours are separated by a reddish transitional zone, ± broad and obvious, with long straight whitish hairs; border of lip lacking hairless margin or with a very narrow, irregular, poorly defined hairless margin; speculum divided or not, with the same appearance and pattern as in *O. fusca* s.l.

Ophrys pectus
Mutel

Etymology *pectus:* chest (an allusion to the basal prominences on the lip). **Type** Ag, Bône (1835). **Synonym** *O. pallida* auct. non Rafinesque.

Description 10-25cm tall; 2-8 medium-sized flowers, often grouped at tip of stem; sepals broadly rounded, 7-11mm x 5-7mm; petals rather short, oblong, 4-5mm long; lip pendent, short, oboval to rhomboidal, 3-lobed, sinuses short, broadly open, 11-14mm x 9-13mm (when spread) (mean length/width ratio = 1:04), external border of lateral lobe of lip making an angle of *c.* 45° with longitudinal axis; base of lip narrow, with rounded very protuberant swellings separated by a marked groove; central depression of lip well visible, giving the impression of a break in the middle of crescents at tip of speculum; median lobe often very short, slightly emarginate; lip hairs dense, brownish, sometimes flecked, narrowly reddish then whitish to yellowish along the edges, which they reach; speculum short, shortly hairy, clearly bisected, bluish, reddish or greyish at base, with 2 broad crescents at tip, slightly hollowed, bluish to milky.

Flowering Season II-mid IV.

Habitat Full sun to mid-shade on dry, alkaline substrates. Abandoned cultivation, garrigue, scrub, up to 300m asl. **Distribution** Northeast Tunisia (Cap Bon) and Malta. Extremely local and very rare. **Countries** ?†Ag Me Tn.

Photos Tn, Cap Bon, 5.IV.1993. J. Devillers-Terschuren; Me, Malta, 24.II.1993. P. Delforge.

Tn   Me

10 mm

Tn: herb. J. & P. Devillers-Terschuren

Ophrys aspea
J. DEVILLERS-TERSCHUREN & P. DEVILLERS

Etymology *aspea:* from Aspis, Greek name for the town of Clypea, Cap Bon region. **Type** Tn, Cap Bon (2000). **Synonym** *Ophrys lutea* subsp. *aspea* (J. DEVILLERS-TERSCHUREN & P. DEVILLERS) N. FAURHOLDT.

Description As *O. subfusca* but thickset, more robust; 2-4 medium-sized flowers; sepals more elongated, 8-10mm x 4.5-6mm, greenish; petals 6-7mm x 1-2mm, yellowish; lip strongly inclined to pendent, longitudinally strongly sinuous, 9-14mm x 8-12mm (mean length/width ratio = 1:20), 3-lobed, sinuses relatively closed; base of lip faded, with a broad but not very deep throat and longitudinal very attenuated swellings; centre of lip very convex transversally, lateral lobes turned down strongly below median lobe, edges reflexed; central depression of lip marked, distal, creating a prominent transverse valley at level of sinuses; median lobe spreading, sides reflexed; lip brown, with straight, whitish, dense hairs, broadly invading lobes and encompassing tip of sinuses, usually without a diluted reddish zone; marginal hairs yellow, dense, progressively weakening towards edge of lip but still covering them; speculum short, not reaching tip of sinuses, blackish-blue, rarely with a pale ω at tip, bisecting groove absent.

Flowering Season III-IV.

Habitat Full sun on dry, sandy, calcareous substrates. Abandoned cultivation, garrigue, scrub, up to 400m asl. **Distribution** The Cap Bon promontory (NE Tn) and probably also Tripoli (Li). Extremely rare and local. **Countries** Li Tn.

Photos Tn, Cap Bon, 5 & 7.IV. 1999. J. DEVILLERS-TERSCHUREN.

Discussion of the *Ophrys subfusca* group

Perhaps monophyletic, mainly found in the southern Mediterranean zone, centred on Sicily and Kroumirie (Ag, Tn), this group comprises 11 species whose lip morphology is intermediate between those of *O. fusca* s.l. and *O. lutea* s.l. (length/width ratio; angle formed by the external border of lateral lobe with longitudinal axis), but with the characteristics combined in a variety of ways (e.g. outline of lip and colour of speculum as *O. fusca* s.l., but yellow peripheral hairs, broad hairless yellow border and yellow underside of lip as *O. lutea* s.l., or conversely outline of lip, colour of speculum and yellow underside of lip as *O. lutea* s.l., but neither peripheral yellow hairs nor hairless border).

These morphological transitions, which are very characteristic of the group, make it difficult to establish and justify its composition. Nevertheless, the incorporation of species from the *O. subfusca* group into the *O. lutea, O. obaesa* or *O. fusca*

groups would obscure the limits of those neighbouring groups and render them much less useful.

A phylogenetic reconstruction of the group is still premature; it appears to be as diverse as other groups in *Ophrys*, probably with North African, Sicilian and perhaps Aegean lineages. *O. numida* with its more extensive central Mediterranean distribution seems thus far to be the only named representative of a poorly known lineage, present also in the Tyrrhenian and Adriatic basins, and which seems to form the link with the *O. lutea* group through the expedient of *O. melena*. The definition of *O. cinereophila*, undoubtedly focused too much on the determination of its pollinator, should also be more precisely stated – its eastern morph (Ae, An, Cr eastern, Cy) is more easily integrated into the *O. subfusca* group than its western morph. The combination of characters shown by *O. pectus* places it at the intersection of the *O. obaesa* and *O. subfusca* groups, and it belongs to the latter given the proportions, outline, relief and pattern of hairs of the lip.

Key to the *Ophrys subfusca* group

1   brown hairs of centre of lip encompassing tip of sinuses .... *O. aspea*
1* brown hairs of centre of lip separated from tip of sinuses by a yellow band 2

2   lip hairs extending up to (or almost up to) edge of lip 3
2* lip with a hairless or papillose margin, ± broad, ± regular 4

3   lip 5-9 (-10)mm long .... *O. subfusca*
3* lip 11-14mm long .... *O. pectus*

4   lip 7.5-12.5mm long; brown lip hairs with an irregular outline, not very extensive; reddish intermediate zone very fragmented ....
    ....*O. battandieri*
4* lip otherwise 5

5   flowers small, lip 8-11.5mm long; blackish-brown lip hairs not very extensive; reddish intermediate zone rather broad and regular ....
    .... *O. numida*
5* flowers and lip otherwise 6

6   flowers small; lip 7-11 (-12)mm long, hairs of central lip blackish-brown, very extensive, edged with a narrow, paler zone, not obvious
    .... *O. cinereophila*
6* flowers larger, lip otherwise 7

7   hairless yellow border of lip very regular, distinct, speculum bisected .... *O. laurensis*
7* lip otherwise 8

(continued on p. 411)

Ophrys subfusca
(REICHENBACH fil.) HAUSSKNECHT

Etymology *sub-:* near; *-fusca:* [As *Ophrys*] *fusca*.
Type Ag (1851). **Synonyms** *O. lutea* var. *subfusca* REICHENBACH fil., *O. lutea* subsp. *subfusca* (REICHENBACH fil.) MURBECK, *O. murbeckii* H. FLEISCHMANN, *O. lutea* subsp. *murbeckii* (H. FLEISCHMANN) SOÓ, *O. galilaea* subsp. *murbeckii* (H. FLEISCHMANN) DEL PRETE.

Description Spindly and low; leaves large; (1-) 2-3 (-5) very small flowers, recalling those of *O. sicula*; sepals rounded, 5-8mm x 3-6mm, whitish-green; petals 3-4mm x c. 1mm, more yellowish than sepals, margins papillose; lip near horizontal, oboval-lanceolate, slightly curved longitudinally, 5-9 (-10)mm x 4.2-7.9mm (mean length/width ratio 1:20), 3-lobed, sinuses open; base of lip with a narrow throat and not very protuberant longitudinal swellings; centre of lip transversally convex, lateral lobes spreading; central depression of lip poorly marked; lip hairs brown, dense, reduced to a central spindle-shape, bordered by a diluted reddish zone, often narrow, sometimes not obvious, with long, straight, whitish hairs; marginal hairs yellow, shorter, reaching or almost reaching edge of lip; speculum not reaching tip of sinuses, without bisecting groove, blackish-blue, with 2 narrow crescents at tip, forming a bluish ⱳ, not very contrasting.

herb. P. & J. DEVILLERS-TERSCHUREN

Flowering Season III-IV.

Habitat Full sun on dry, alkaline substrates. Abandoned cultivation, garrigue, scrub, up to 1300m asl. **Distribution** Northeast Algeria, northern Tunisia. Very local but sometimes abundant. **Countries** Ag Tn.

Photo Tn, Makhtar, 14.IV.1999. J. DEVILLERS-TERSCHUREN.

Ophrys lucentina
P. DELFORGE

Etymology *lucentina:* from Alicante, ancient *Lucentum* of the Romans. **Type** Hs, Alicante (1999). **Synonyms** *O. fusca* subsp. *lucentina* (P. DELFORGE) KREUTZ, *O. dianica* M.R. LOWE *et al.*

Description Spindly, slender, 10-40cm tall; inflorescence near lax; 1-6 medium-sized flowers; lateral sepals whitish-green or yellowish-green, 9-13mm long; petals oblong, 5-7.5mm long, yellowish-green; lip horizontal to near horizontal, sometimes angled upwards, slightly convex, rather straight, clearly 3-lobed, 11.5-17mm x 10-13mm (mean length/width ratio = 1:19); external border of lateral lobe of lip making an angle of 41-47° with longitudinal axis; base of lip not or only slightly kinked, with a narrow throat and short rounded swellings; centre of speculum region clearly depressed; lateral lobes truncated, spreading to slightly turned downwards, separated from median lobe by rather prominent sinuses; median lobe spatulate, emarginate, often spreading-recurved; lip hairs dense, long and relatively irregular, dark purplish-brown around the speculum, straighter and paler in the distal zone, often becoming paler reddish-brown and irregularly yellowish; lip surrounded by a bright yellow hairless border, often broad, well demarcated from hairy central region, sometimes reflexed, especially on median lobe; speculum usually undivided, dark blue, marbled, edged with a lighter blue zone that forms a ω at tip, dark portions with very short, fine hairs, lighter areas hairless; underside of lip bright golden-yellow to greenish-yellow; 2n=?72.

Flowering Season III (-IV). **Habitat** Mostly full sun on dry, alkaline substrates, sometimes sandy and very xeric. Abandoned cultivation, garrigue, open pinewoods, up to 750m asl. **Distribution** Northern Alicante province and southern Valence province; the situation is sometimes obscured by the presence of forms intermediate with *O. bilunulata*. Similar populations have been reported from the Perpignan region and Alpes-Maritimes (Ga), as well as Malaga (Hs). Local and very rare. **Countries** Hs ?Ga. **Photos** Hs, Alicante, 20 & 27.III.1999. P. DELFORGE.

Pollinator *Andrena vulpecula* (Hymenoptera: Andrenidae).

410

Ophrys lindia
H.F. PAULUS

Etymology Named after the goddess Athena-Lindia, revered at Lindos (Rhodes). **Type** Ae, Rhodes (2001). **Synonym** *O. fusca* subsp. *lindia* (H.F. PAULUS) KREUTZ.

Description Small, thickset, robust, 9-16 (-20)cm tall; (1-) 2-4 (-8) medium-sized flowers; sepals yellowish-green, near spreading, 7.5-11mm x 5.5-9mm; petals green to yellowish-green, often with a lighter margin, curving forwards, 6.5-8mm x 1.5-2.4mm; lip near horizontal to pendent, oboval to near rhomboidal-rounded, 9-12.5mm x 7.5-10mm (when spread) (mean length/width ratio 1:20), slightly convex both transversally and longitudinally; base of lip kinked, with a narrow throat and short, rounded swellings; centre of speculum region slightly depressed; lateral lobes falcate-rounded, very convex, turned down, separated from median lobe by deep but narrow sinuses; median lobe broadly obcordate to near spatulate, emarginate, often strongly convex; lip hairs dense, long, rather dark chestnut-brown around speculum, paler in the distal zone, often becoming lighter reddish-brown and irregularly yellowish; lip surrounded by a bright yellow (sometimes reddish) papillose margin, often broad, passing around the sinuses; speculum usually undivided, dark blue to purplish-brown, usually broadly edged paler blue to white at tip, forming a large ω, with fine, short, erect, whitish hairs in dark portion but near hairless in lighter areas; stigmatic cavity rather small when compared to lip.

Flowering Season Mid III-IV.

Habitat Full sun on dry, calcareous substrates. Abandoned cultivation, garrigue, open pinewoods, up to 400m asl. **Distribution** Karpathos (Cr), Rhodes (Ae), and neighbouring regions of Anatolia. Very local and very rare. **Countries** Ae An Cr.

Photos Ae, Rhodes, 11.IV.1998; Cr, Karpathos, 18.III.2000. C.A.J. KREUTZ.

Key to the *Ophrys subfusca* group

(continued from p. 409)

8   plant thickset, 9-16 (-20)cm tall; lip 9-12.5mm long.. *O. lindia*
8*   plant more slender, (10-) 15-41cm tall; lip larger, 10-17mm long 9

9   early flowering, III (-mid IV) ... *O. lucentina*
9*   later flowering, mid IV-V 10

10   petals 6-8.5mm long; median lobe of lip elongated; sinuses open .... *O. flammeola*

10* petals 4-6mm long; median lobe short; sinuses closed .... *O. archimedea*

Ophrys cinereophila
H.F. PAULUS & GACK

Etymology *-phila:* loving; *cinereo-:* the ashy (specific epithet of pollinator). **Type** Cr, Lassithi (1998). **Synonyms** *O. 'cinereophila-fusca'* H.F. PAULUS & GACK nom. prov., *O. fusca* subsp. *cinereophila* (H.F. PAULUS & GACK) N. FAURHOLDT, *O. funerea* auct. non VIVIANI.

Description Small, sometimes slender, 7-25 (-28)cm tall; 2-8 (-11) rather small flowers; sepals whitish-green, near spreading, arching, 7-12mm x 4.5-6mm; petals yellowish, oblong, 6-8.6mm long; lip longitudinally and transversally convex, 7.5-11 (-12)mm x 5.5-10.5mm (mean length/ width ratio = 1:14), 3-lobed, sinuses open, base kinked, with a narrow throat and protruding

longitudinal swellings; external border of lateral lobe making an angle of 40-48° with longitudinal axis; centre of lip weakly to sometimes clearly depressed; lateral lobes turned down, sides flat; median lobe convex, sides sometimes slightly reflexed; lip hairs brown, dense, dark, spreading widely on lateral and median lobes, parallel to margins, even around sinuses, edged with a very narrow dilute reddish zone, sometimes hardly visible, with long, straight, whitish hairs; border of lip yellow to greenish-yellow, papillose, rather irregularly demarcated from hairy zone; speculum almost reaching tip of sinuses, blackish-blue, with 2 narrow crescents at tip, forming a bluish (0), not very contrasting, bisecting groove absent.

Flowering Season Late II-IV.

Habitat Full sun on dry to moist, calcareous substrates. Abandoned cultivation, pastures, garrigue, olive groves, open pinewoods and their edges, up to 700m asl.

Distribution Eastern Mediterranean basin, at least from the central Cyclades to northern Syria. Local and rather rare.

Countries Ae An Cr Cy Gr Ls.

Photos Cy, Larnaca, 28.III.1989; Ae, Rhodes, 10.IV.1984. P. DELFORGE.

Pollinator *Andrena cinereophila* (Hymenoptera: Andrenidae).

Note The more western reports of *O. cinereophila* (Peloponnese, Gulf of Corinth, Ionian Islands) often refer to *O. perpusilla* or a related taxon. Plants very similar to *O. cinereophila* but identified with difficulty as *O. fabrella* flower also in the Balearics.

Ophrys laurensis
GENIEZ & MELKI

Etymology *laurensis:* from Mount Lauro. **Type** Si, Mount Lauro (Catania, Siracusa) (1992). **Synonym** *O. lutea* subsp. *laurensis* (GENIEZ & MELKI) KREUTZ.

Description Robust, 5-11 (-13)cm tall, inflorescence dense, (1-) 2-4 (-5) small to medium-sized flowers; sepals whitish-green, 9-13mm long; petals yellowish-green, near spatulate, 6-10mm x 2-2.5mm, margins undulate; lip 10-15mm x 10-13mm (mean length/ width ratio = 1:15), slightly convex transversally, almost flat longitudinally, 3-lobed, sinuses broad, base of lip with prominent longitudinal swellings, inflating centre of paler crescents on speculum, separated by a broad marked groove

and limited distally by a depressed transverse fold; external border of lateral lobes making an angle of *c.* 45° with longitudinal axis; lateral lobes turned down, sides ± clearly reflexed; median lobe spreading, sides spreading to reflexed; lip hairs purplish-brown, dense, clearly demarcated, long, tangled, rarely going round the sinuses, surrounded by a submarginal rim of straight yellow hairs and long white hairs, then by a bright yellow (sometimes slightly greenish), hairless margin, *c.* 2mm broad, regular, clearly demarcated; speculum blackish-blue to brownish at centre, very shiny on swellings, sometimes with faint crescents at tip, with very short hairs, very distinct compared to lip hairs, bisected by a distinct, deep groove that is hairy (as lip) to its centre; underside of lip whitish at base, greenish-yellow at centre and broadly bordered yellow (corresponding to hairless margin above).

Flowering Season Mid IV-V.

Habitat Full sun on dry, basaltic, acidic to neutral substrates. Pastures, scrub, 650-1000m asl.

Distribution Apparently endemic to Mount Lauro. Extremely local but often abundant.

Countries Si.

Photos Si, Catania, 20.IV.2000. P. DELFORGE.

Pollinator *Andrena schulzi* (Hymenoptera: Andrenidae) (see also p. 361).

413

Ophrys flammeola
P. DELFORGE

Etymology *flammeola:* flame-coloured. **Type** Si, Caltanissetta (2000). **Synonyms** *O. fusca* subsp. *flammeola* (P. DELFORGE) KREUTZ, *O. fusca* auct. non LINK, *O. galilaea* auct. non H. FLEISCHMANN & BORNMÜLLER, *O. murbeckii* auct. non H. FLEISCHMANN, *O. subfusca* auct. non (RCHB. fil.) HAUSSKNECHT, *O. 'florentina-fusca'* H.F. PAULUS & GACK nom. nud. (pro parte).

Description Robust, 18-35 (-41)cm tall; inflorescence rather dense; 3-9 rather large flowers; sepals whitish-green, broadly oval-lanceolate, 10.5-16mm long; petals greenish-yellow, oblong, near spatulate or narrowly lanceolate, 6-8.5mm long, margins undulate; lip horizontal, narrowly to sometimes broadly oval, 11-16.5mm x (8-) 10-

14mm (mean length/width ratio = 1:20), rather convex transversally, slightly convex longitudinally and often sinuous due to a central depression, base kinked or inflated due to protruding longitudinal prominences, 3-lobed, sinuses deep and open; external border of lateral lobes making an angle of 40-47° with longitudinal median axis; lateral lobes falcate; median lobe spreading, prominent, sometimes broadly wedge-shaped, more often squared at base, then broadly obcordate at tip; hairs of central lip surrounding speculum dark brown, sometimes purplish, rather dense, long and irregular, becoming ± broadly reddish towards sides, brushing the sinuses and always extending onto median lobe, surrounded by a very narrow band of yellow hairs; border of lip ± reflexed, with a very narrow, very irregular hairless margin; speculum dark greyish-blue, glabrescent, with 2 distinct crescents at tip by end of flowering season, not reaching sinuses; stigmatic cavity rather small, base covered with thick white hairs; underside of lip yellow to greenish-yellow.

Flowering Season IV-V.

Habitat Full sun to mid-shade on dry, alkaline substrates. Abandoned cultivation, pastures, garrigue, scrub and their edges, up to 700m asl.

Distribution Sicily. Local and sometimes abundant.

Countries Si.

Photos Si, Caltanissetta (loc. typ.), 19.IV.2000. P. DELFORGE.

Ophrys archimedea
P. DELFORGE & M. WALRAVENS

Etymology Named after Archimedes (Siracusa, 287-212 A.C.), Greek scholar from Sicily. **Type.** Si, Enna (2000). **Synonyms** *O. lutea* subsp. *archimedea* (P. DELFORGE & M. WALRAVENS) KREUTZ, *O. galilaea* auct. non H. FLEISCHMANN & BORNMÜLLER, *O. murbeckii* auct. non H. FLEISCHMANN, *O. subfusca* auct. non (RCHB. fil.) HAUSSKNECHT.

Description Slender and often robust, 15-30 (-35)cm tall; inflorescence lax; 3-7 rather large flowers; sepals whitish-green, lateral sepals broadly oval-lanceolate, (9.5-) 11-14mm long; petals more intensely yellowish-green, 4-5 (-6)mm long, oblong, margins undulate; lip 10-15.5mm x 9-14mm (mean length/ width ratio = 1:11), convex transversally, slightly convex and sinuous longitudinally, 3-lobed, outline varied, narrowly to broadly oval, sinuses closed, not very deep; external border of lat-

eral lobes making an angle of 30-45° with longitudinal axis; lateral lobes rounded, slightly turned down and under, sides reflexed; median lobe reduced, spreading, reflexed; hairs of central lip brown, rather dense, rather long and regular, either clearly demarcated or progressively diluted into a more reddish zone towards margins, going round the sinuses and always extending onto median lobe, this in turn surrounded by a rather broad band of more tangled yellow hairs, sprinkled with longer, white-tipped hairs; border of lip with a narrow, irregular, hairless yellow margin; speculum basal, rather extended but without reaching sinuses, greyish to milky, near hairless, spotted at base, sometimes with a large pale ω at tip, not very contrasting; underside of lip golden-yellow.

Flowering Season IV-V.

Habitat Full sun to shade on dry to moist, alkaline substrates. Abandoned cultivation, garrigue, scrub, pinewoods, up to 900m asl.

Distribution Sicily. Local and rather rare.

Countries Si.

Photos Si, Palermo, 27.IV.2000; Enna (loc. typ.), 20.IV.2000. P. DELFORGE.

Ophrys battandieri
E.G. Camus (pro hybr.)

Etymology Named after J.A. Battandier, French botanist (1848-1922). **Type.** Ag, the Algiers region (1908). **Synonyms** *O. lutea* subsp. *battandieri* (E.G. Camus) Kreutz, *O. sicula* auct. non Tineo, *O. murbeckii* auct. non H. Fleischmann, *O.* × *gauthieri* Lievre, *O.* × *pouyannei* Maire, *O.* × *fenarolii* Ferlan.

Description Slender and often robust, 20-30 (-40)cm tall, frequently forming groups; up to 10 medium-sized to rather large flowers; sepals whitish-green, lateral sepals not very spreading; petals yellowish-green, oblong; lip angled downwards at 45°, (7.5-) 8-12.5mm x 7-11.5mm (mean length/width ratio = 1:08), transversally and longitudinally convex, 3-lobed, broadly obovoval, sinuses rather closed; base of lip kinked, yellowish, with 2 short, rounded, protruding longitudinal prominences, separated by a distinct depression, rather proximal; external border of lateral lobes making an angle of 45° with longitudinal axis; lateral lobes rounded, turned down and under, sides sometimes reflexed; median lobe reduced, spreading to slightly convex, sides reflexed; hairs of central lip pale brown, extent very varied, often restricted to a central spindle-shaped area, sometimes an irregular blotch, isolated in centre of median lobe, going round rather widely tip of sinuses, rather dense, not very regular, edged outwards with a dilute reddish zone, very fragmented, sometimes reduced to a few streaks, this in turn surrounded by a very broad band of yellow hairs, with scattered longer white-tipped hairs; lip bordered by an irregular, narrow, hairless yellow margin; speculum basal, short, pale, bluish, with a ± broad pale ω at tip, not very contrasting; underside of lip yellow.

herb. J. & P. Devillers-Terschuren

Flowering Season II-IV (-V). **Habitat** Full sun to mid-shade on dry, alkaline substrates. Abandoned cultivation, garrigue, scrub, open woodland, up to 900m asl. **Distribution** The Tell Atlas, from around Tunis to Algiers; may reach Morocco in the west. Rather widespread and sometimes abundant in the coastal massifs, rarer and more local elsewhere. **Countries** Ag ?Ma Tn. **Photos A & C** Tn, Djebel Amar, 5.III.2002. P. Delforge; **B** Djebel Lanzarine, 15.IV.1999. J. Devillers-Terschuren.

Pollinator Probably *Andrena vetula* (Hymenoptera: Andrenidae).

416

Ophrys numida

J. DEVILLERS-TERSCHUREN & P. DEVILLERS

Etymology *numida:* Numidian. **Type** Tn, Makhtar (2000). **Synonyms** *O. lutea* subsp. *numida* (J. DEVILLERS-TERSCHUREN & P. DEVILLERS) KREUTZ, *O. subfusca* auct. non (RCHB. fil.) HAUSSKNECHT, *O. melena* auct. non (RENZ) H.F. PAULUS & GACK, *O. minor* subsp. *nigrescens* MELKI & GENIEZ nom. nud.

Description Slender, robust, 10-27cm tall; (2-) 3-8 medium-sized flowers; sepals greenish-white, lateral sepals slightly spreading, 6.5-9.5mm x 4-5.5mm; petals greenish-yellow, oblong, 3.5-6mm x 0.8-1.5mm; lip horizontal to angled downwards at 45°, 8-11.5mm x 7-10.5mm (mean length/width ratio = 1:14), very slightly convex transversely, almost flat but gently sinuous longitudinally, 3-lobed, oboval, sinuses rather short and closed; lateral lobes rounded, near spreading, sides reflexed; median lobe reduced, spreading, sides clearly reflexed; hairy zone of central lip brown, spindle-shaped, reaching centre of median lobe, passing broadly around tip of sinuses, rather dense, regular, edged outwards with a dilute reddish zone, often very broad, which may almost cover lateral lobes, this in turn surrounded by a band of yellow hairs sprinkled with whitish hairs; lip bordered by a ± narrow, irregular, papillose to hairless yellow margin; speculum basal, rather elongated, dark bluish-grey, with a ± broad, pale ω at tip, not very contrasting; underside of lip yellow, washed pink in centre.

herb. J. & P. DEV-ILLERS-TERSCHUREN

Flowering Season III-V.

Habitat Full sun to mid-shade on dry, alkaline substrates. Abandoned cultivation, garrigue, scrub, up to 1300m asl.

Distribution Tell Atlas, from around Tunis to the Algiers region, and Sicily. Rare and local.

Countries Ag ?It Si Tn.

Photos A Tn, Téboursouk, 15.IV.1999. J. Devillers-Terschuren; **B** Si, Palermo, 16.IV.2000. P. Delforge.

Note In Puglia (It) (Photo C), as well as Calabria (It), Corsica and Sardinia, plants are sometimes reported (albeit with reservations) as *O. melena*, but their size, lip indentation, hairs and colour pattern seem to be very close to *O. numida*. They are probably not conspecific, however, and may be an isolated, undescribed taxon, closer to *O. numida* than *O. melena*. On Mount Gargano (It, Foggia) these flowers are pollinated by *Andrena vulpecula* (Hymenoptera: Andrenidae).

Photo C It, Foggia, 31.III.1991. P. DELFORGE.

417

The *Ophrys lutea* group

Characteristics Lip short, orbicular (length/ width ratio 0.83:1; external border of lateral lobe of lip making a mean angle of 65° with longitudinal axis); lateral lobes frquentlyspreading, sides reflexed; median lobe spreading, sides reflexed; base of lip hollowed, with 2 short, rounded, protruding longitudinal swellings, producing a ± marked kink, then a break, at level of centre of speculum; lip hairs brown, ± dark, in centre, surrounded ± broadly by yellow; lip edged with a hairless margin, ± broad.

Ophrys melena
(RENZ) H.F. PAULUS & GACK

Etymology *melena:* dark. **Type** Gr, Mount Hymette (Attica), Argolida, Corfu (1928). **Synonyms** *O. lutea* subsp. *melena* RENZ pro hybr., *O. lutea* var. *melena* (RENZ) E. NELSON nom; inval., *O. galilaea* subsp. *melena* (RENZ) DEL PRETE.

Description As *O. sicula* but slightly more robust; perianth segments 1-1.5mm longer; sepals 7.5-11mm long; petals 5.5-7.5mm long; lip near horizontal to pendent, 10-14.5mm long; central brown hairs on lip, shorter, more extensive, sprinkled laterally with white hairs, becoming progressively but often irregularly pale orange-brown toward margins, sometimes very broadly so (in centre of range), or narrowly so, the lip then ± broadly banded yellow (other regions).

Flowering Season II-V, 2-3 weeks after *O. sicula*.

Habitat As *O. lutea* but found up to 1300m asl.

Distribution Southern Balkans, north to Thessalia; similar plants are also reported from Corfu (Gr) and Lesbos (Ae). Rather rare and local.

Countries ?Ae ?Al Gr.

Photos Gr, Argolida, 17.IV.1991; Euboea, 19.IV.1994. P. DELFORGE.

Notes This taxon has been controversial for a long time. It has been treated as a melanistic variety of *O. sicula* or as an occasional hybrid between the latter and *O. fusca* s.l., but this is not supported by its morphology and stability. *O. melena* may, rather frequently, show a lip almost without a zone of dilution between the brown centre and yellow margin, and this certainly leads to mistaken identifications. For records outside Greece, see the *O. subfusca* group, previous pages.

Pollinator *Andrena transitoria* (Hymenoptera: Andrenidae).

418

Ophrys sicula
TINEO

Etymology *sicula:* from Sicily. **Type** Si, Palermo (1846). **Synonyms** *O. lutea* var. *minor* (TODARO) GUSSONE, *O. lutea* subsp. *minor* (TODARO) O. DANESCH & E. DANESCH, *O. minor* (TODARO) H.F. PAULUS & GACK, *O. galilaea* H. FLEISCHMANN & BORNMÜLLER, *O. minor* subsp. *galilaea* (H. FLEISCHMANN & BORNMÜLLER) H.F. PAULUS & GACK.

Description As *O. lutea* but more slender and spindly, 5-40cm tall; (2-) 3-8 (-11) small flowers; sepals 6-10mm x 3-7mm; petals (3-) 4.5-7mm x 1-2.5mm; lip (6-) 8-13mm x (5-) 7-12mm, more indented, horizontal or pointing upwards, rarely obliquely downwards, lip hairs often shorter, greyish, tinted violet or brown, base not kinked, with less marked longitudinal prominences, centre ± convex, often with a transverse hollow crease; speculum hairless in centre; hairy brown zone of central lip a longer and broader spindle-shape, reaching centre of median lobe; sides of lip spreading to slightly reflexed, tinted bright yellow to greenish-yellow in a (1-) 2-3mm broad strip; lateral lobes often more pointed; median lobe shorter; stigmatic cavity broader than tall. **Variation** Slight. The reduced lip hairs and habit and markings of the lip are distinct. '*galilaea*' (Photo B) An eastern variant, only slightly distinct, with a lip perhaps a little smaller relative to the stigmatic cavity.

Flowering Season (XII-) I-V, slightly earlier than *O. lutea* and *O. melena*. **Habitat** As *O. lutea* but found up to 1500m asl. **Distribution** Mediterranean, with the probable exception of the Iberian peninsula and continental France. Rather widespread and often abundant. **Countries** Ae Ag Al An Co Cr Cy Gr Ij It Ju Ls Ma Sa Si Tn Tu. **Photos** Si, Siracusa, 8.IV.1987; Gr, Cyclades, Amorgos, 29.IV.1997. P. DELFORGE.

Pollinators Several species of small bee, all belonging to the genus *Andrena: A. hesperia* (Ae Cr Gr It Ls), *A. merula* (Ae Gr Ij), and *A. taraxaci* (Cy Ls It) (Hymenoptera: Andrenidae).

Key to the *Ophrys lutea* group

1   lip 14-18mm long .... *O. lutea*
1* lip (6-) 8-14.5mm long 2

2   lip kinked at base, distal 3/4 near horizontal to pendent .... *O. phryganae*
2* lip almost flat at base, near horizontal to pointing obliquely upwards 3

3   lip bordered bright yellow or greenish in a band 2-3mm wide .... *O. sicula*
3* lip entirely orange-brown, apart from speculum .... *O. melena*

Ophrys phryganae
J. DEVILLERS-TERSCHUREN & P. DEVILLERS

Etymology *phryganae:* of phrygana. **Type** Cr, Lassithi (1991). **Synonyms** *O. lutea* subsp. *phryganae* (J. DEVILLERS-TERSCHUREN & P. DEVILLERS) MELKI, ?*O. corsica* SOLEIROL ex G. FOELSCHE & W. FOELSCHE.

Description As *O. lutea* but inflorescence laxer; flowers similar in structure (shape, convexity, coloration) but much smaller, dimensions as *O. sicula*; lip strongly kinked at the base, all except sides covered with dense, tangled hairs, slightly shorter and less dense on speculum (see Discussion); brown hairs of central lip often extending to centre of median lobe.

Flowering Season III-V.

Habitat Full sun to mid-shade on dry to moist, alkaline substrates. Mostly garrigue (phrygana) and scrub.

Distribution Poorly known, but probably central and eastern Mediterranean. Reported from southern Italy to Crete and southwest Anatolia; also Corsica (= '*corsica*' photo C, probably a synonym), Sardinia and maybe Sicily. Local and rather rare.

Countries Ae An Co Cr Gr It Ju Sa ?Si.

Photos Gr, Kefallinia, 10.IV.1992; Cyclades, Paros, 6.IV.1995. P. DELFORGE; Co, Bonifacio, 5.IV.2002. É. WALRAVENS.

Pollinators Probably *Andrena panurgimorpha* (Cr), *A. humilis* (It, Ae), *A. humilis* subsp. *cucullata* (Gr), *A. tadauchii* (Cr, Karpathos) and maybe *A. clypella* subsp. *hasitata* (Gr) (Hymenoptera: Andrenidae).

Discussion *O. phryganae* seems to replace *O. lutea* progressively in the eastern Aegean basin, and is often syntopic with the latter from Corsica

to Crete. Plants from Crete differ prominently from other populations in being hairier (strongly pubecent even on speculum). Whether the-se various populations are conspecific needs to be confirmed.

Ophrys lutea
CAVANILLES

Etymology *lutea:* yellow. **Type** Hs, Valencia (1753). **Synonym** *O. vespifera* BROTERO.

Description Robust, 10-30 (-40)cm tall; bracts longer than ovary; 1-6 (-10) large flowers; sepals greenish-yellow to greenish-white, 10-13mm x 6-10mm, dorsal sepal oboval, bent over column, lateral sepals oval, asymmetrical, concave, spreading and curving forward; petals yellowish to greenish, hairless, oblong, 6-8mm x 2-3mm, margins straight or slightly undulate, spreading or angled obliquely forwards; lip 3-lobed at tip, appearing oboval, 14-18mm x 13-19mm (when spread), pubescence long and dense, base whitish to yellowish, abruptly kinked, contracted into 2 rounded ridges with whitish to greyish hairs, separated by a deep V-shaped throat; distal 3/4 of lip near horizontal to pendent, dark centre reduced, convex, pale orange-brown to dark brown, sides spreading then reflexed, bright yellow in a strip 3-6mm wide, with a ± broad, hairless margin; lateral lobes rounded, sinuses linear; median lobe broadly obcordate, often entirely yellow; speculum bilobed, reduced, finely velvety, shiny bluish-grey, sometimes marbled brownish or whitish, sometimes pale at tip; underside of lip whitish to yellowish; stigmatic cavity taller than broad, greenish white, grooved and tomentose at base; column short, obtuse, making an acute angle with lip.

Variation Slight; the size and shape of the lip is distinctive. Conspecific populations with smaller flowers are reported from southern France and notably Sicily.

Flowering Season (II-) III-V (-VI), slightly after *O. sicula.*

Habitat Full sun to mid-shade, dry to moist, mostly alkaline substrates. Grassland, abandoned cultivation, garrigue, scrub, open woodland, up to 1800m asl.

Distribution Mediterranean-Atlantic, east to Crete and north to Charente (Ga). Rather widespread and abundant in western part of range.

Countries Ag Al Bl Co Cr Ga Gr Hs It Ju Li Lu Ma Me Sa Si Tn.

Photos Ga, Aveyron, 21.V.1983; Hs, Alicante, 25.III.1999. P. DELFORGE.

Pollinators Despite a certain morphological stability, *O. lutea* is pollinated by several species of bee, all belonging to the subgenus *Chlorandrena: Andrena cinerea* (Hs Ga Gr It Ma), *A. senecionis* (Ag Hs Ga Si) and perhaps *A. nigroolivacea* (Ag It) (Hymenoptera: Andrenidae).

The *Ophrys atlantica* group

Characteristics Petals very elongated; lip orbicular, curved into a saddle-like shape; external border of lateral lobes making a mean angle of *c.* 90° with longitudinal axis; base of lip with a very slight groove and jugular brush; speculum hairless.

Discussion Monospecific, apparently very isolated, combining in a unique way within section *Pseudophrys* the coloration of *O. iricolor*, the lip shape of *O. lutea*, the long petals of *O. migoutiana*, as well as a very unusual curvature, reminiscent of *O. bertolonii*, a characteristic obviously selected by their common pollinator. Given the lack of cytological and molecular studies, it is difficult to discuss the affinities of this curious species any further.

Ophrys atlantica
MUNBY

Etymology *atlantica:* from the Atlas. **Type** Ag, Tlemcen (1856). **Synonyms** *O. fusca* subsp. *atlantica* (MUNBY) E.G. CAMUS, *O. fusca* var. *durieui* RCHB. fil., *O. fusca* subsp. *durieui* (RCHB. fil.) SOÓ, *O. atlantica* subsp. *durieui* (RCHB. fil.) MAIRE & WEILLER.

Description 15-30cm tall; 1-4 large flowers; sepals 11-18mm long; petals hairless, spreading, green, olive-green or brownish, oblong, near spatulate, 8.5-15mm x 2-4mm, margins undulate-crisped; lip 15-22 (-25)mm x 12-22mm, near circular (when spread), (near) horizontal, very convex transversally, curved into a saddle-like shape; lateral lobes broadly rounded, turned down; median lobe very small, obcordate, narrow, very convex; base of lip slightly grooved, white then crimson or brownish, with a dense, straight

jugular brush, sometimes stained purple; lip hairs dense, regular, dark blackish-purple, bordered by a narrow, reddish, hairless margin; speculum central, hairless, transverse, bright blue, shiny; underside of lip purplish-brown, centre sometimes greenish-white.

Flowering Season III-VI.

Habitat Full sun to mid-shade, on dry to moist, alkaline substrates. Garrigue, abandoned cultivation, scrub, open woodland, up to 1500m asl. **Distribution** Maghreb (the single station from Tunisia is not confirmed) and Andalucia (Hs). Very local and often rare. **Countries** Ag Hs Ma ?†Tn.

Photos Hs, Malaga, 6.IV.1990. P. DELFORGE.

Pollinator *Chalicodoma parietina* (Hs) (Hymenoptera: Anthophoridae).

The Ophrys mirabilis group

Characteristics Lip very narrow, elongated, traversed from base to tip by a slight longitudinal groove, framed by 2 small protruding bosses (= 'longitudinal fold'), giving the lip the shape of an inverted keel; external border of lateral lobe of lip making a mean angle of 31° with longitudinal axis.

Discussion Monospecific, apparently isolated, unusual in the longitudinal prominence on the lip, unique in *Pseudophrys*. Apparently close to *O. migoutiana* and even closer to *O. dyris*, with which it shares, to a certain extent, the silhouette and coloration of the lip. A close relationship with *O. atlantica*, often mentioned, is less obvious.

Ophrys mirabilis
GENIEZ & MELKI

Etymology *mirabilis:* admirable. **Type** Si, Caltanissetta (1991). **Synonyms** *O. atlantica* sensu LOJACONO non MUNBY, *O. hayekii* H. FLEISCHMANN nom. nud., *O. fusca* subsp. *hayekii* H. FLEISCHMANN & SOÓ, *O. atlantica* subsp. *hayekii* (H. FLEISCHMANN & SOÓ) SOÓ, *O. omegaifera* subsp. *hayekii* (H. FLEISCHMANN & SOÓ) KREUTZ.

Description 15-22cm tall; 2-5 (-6) medium-sized flowers; sepals 10-15mm long, appearing narrow; petals hairless, olive-green, oblong, near spatulate,

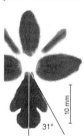

7-10mm x 1.5-2.5mm, margins undulate, crisped; lip 12-18mm x 8-10mm, 3-lobed, narrowly wedge-shaped, (near) horizontal, slightly convex, base slightly kinked; lateral lobes small, triangular-rounded; median lobe prominent, obcordate, slightly emarginate, curved at tip, sides turned down; base of lip often faded, with a slight groove concealed by a dense white jugular brush; lip hairs uniform, dense, tangled, dark blackish-purple, appearing 'frosted' due to bleaching of hair tips, lip bordered by a broad, clearly demarcated yellowish or reddish-brown hairless band; speculum extended, reaching sinuses and lateral lobes, slate-grey to reddish with long whitish hairs and sometimes a narrow, pale, angular Ω at tip; underside of lip greenish-white, sometimes edged brownish.

Flowering Season mid IV-V, rather late. **Habitat** Full sun, on dry, alkaline substrates. Garrigue, pastures, woodland edges, up to 900m asl.

Distribution Sicily (apparently extinct in its only site in Tunisia). Extremely local and often rare. **Countries** Si ?†Tn.

Photos Si, Ragusa, 23.IV.2000. P. DELFORGE.

The *Ophrys omegaifera* group

Characteristics Lip deeply 3-lobed in centre; external border of lateral lobe making a mean angle of 40°-65° with longitudinal axis; base of lip not, or only slightly grooved; lip ± kinked at base, central third flat, tip very convex; speculum with a pale, often contrasting, ⍵ at tip.

40-65°

Ophrys dyris
MAIRE

Etymology *Dyris:* name given by Pliny to the Moroccan Atlas. **Type** Ma, Great Atlas (1931). **Synonyms** *O. fusca* subsp. *dyris* (MAIRE) SOÓ, *O. atlantica* subsp. *dyris* (MAIRE) KELLER ex SOÓ, *O. omegaifera* subsp. *dyris* (MAIRE) DEL PRETE.

Description 10-35 (-50)cm tall; (1-) 3-8 flowers; lateral sepals 10-16mm x 6-8mm, oval-obtuse, green (slightly whitish), asymmetrical, spreading, dorsal sepal near equal, turned down onto column; petals hairless, green to brown, sometimes edged purple, 7.5-12mm x 2-3.5mm, oblong to narrowly spatulate; lip convex longitudinally, very convex laterally, 10-19mm x 9-16mm (when spread), (near) horizontal, brown to dark slate-grey, hairs dense, long, irregular, often with silver reflections, hairless border very narrow, greenish-yellow to reddish or brownish, not obvious due to curvature of lip; external border of lateral lobe making an angle of 31-52° (mean 40°) with longitudinal axis; lateral lobes 2-5mm x 2.5-5mm, broadly triangular-rounded; median lobe short, kidney-shaped, 5-7mm x 7-10.8mm; unguis often white, yellowish or greenish, pale at base; speculum rather glossy, pale brown to purplish or slate-grey, sometimes marbled whitish at centre, with a broad, distinct, contrasting, hairless ⍵ at tip, whitish, greyish, or sometimes bluish; stigmatic cavity 3-4mm high, 3.5-4.5mm wide, base flat or very rarely very slightly grooved, with white, straight hairs, rather long and dense; 2n=72, 90.

Flowering Season (I-) III-IV (-V).

Habitat Full sun to mid-shade, on dry to moist, alkaline substrates. Grassland, garrigue, abandoned cultivation, scrub, open woodland, up to 2000m asl.

Distribution Moroccan Atlas, Iberian peninsula, Balearic Islands. Rare and local. **Countries** Bl Hs Lu Ma.

Photos Lu, Algarve, 6.IV.1990; Hs, Barcelona, 13.IV.1990. P. DELFORGE.

Pollinator *Anthophora atroalba* (Hymenoptera: Anthophoridae).

Ophrys algarvensis
D. Tyteca, Benito Ayuso & M. Walravens

Etymology *algarvensis:* from the Algarve. **Type** Lu, Algarve (2003). **Synonym** *O. omegaifera* subsp. *algarvensis* (D. Tyteca *et al.*) Kreutz.

Description As *O. dyris* but 2-5 (-6) flowers, slightly larger; lateral sepals 13.9-16mm long; petals 9.5-12mm long; lip far less convex, 15.2-19.5mm x 11.8-15.3mm (when spread), more horizontal, brown to dark slate-grey, hairs not so long, rarely with silver reflections; hairless margin broader, clearly visible; external border of lateral lobe making an angle of 28-42° with longitudinal axis; lateral lobes smaller, 2.5-4.2mm x 1.5-4mm; median lobe more elongated, more emarginate, 6-8.5mm x 8-11mm; speculum more often brown or reddish, with a broad (**ı**) at tip, sometimes white washed reddish; base of stigmatic cavity less hairy, sometimes hairless, ± grooved.

Flowering Season Late III-IV, after *O. dyris.*

Habitat As *O. dyris*, up to 500m asl. **Distribution** Southern Iberia. Endemic to Andalucia (Hs) and the Algarve (Lu), where it seems more frequent than *O. dyris*. Local and rather rare. **Countries** Hs Lu.

Photos Lu, Algarve, 5.IV.1990; Hs, Malaga, 10.IV.1990. P. Delforge.

Discussion Like *O. vasconica* (see p. 426), *O. algarvensis* probably results from the introgression of *O. dyris* by *O. fusca* s.l., as demonstrated by the characters which distinguish it. The superficial similarity of *O. algarvensis* to *O. mirabilis* probably does not indicate a close relationship.

Discussion of the *Ophrys omegaifera* group

Probably monophyletic, this group contains 3 hybridogenous taxa (*O. algarvensis*, *O. sitiaca*, *O. vasconica*) and 5 closely allied species, principally associated with bees of the genus *Anthophora* and deriving from a common ancestor, *O.* (proto) *fusca*. The fragmentation of the ancestral range gave rise to an eastern group, composed of species that are probably very closely related and which seem to originate from the selection of new pollinators on the basis of lip size and flowering season, and a western species, *O. dyris*, geographically very isolated. The placement of *O. dyris* in this group, and thus the group's monophyly, is sometimes contested. Due, particularly, to its hairless petals, *O. dyris* may be related to *O. migoutiana* and *O. mirabilis* and not to the eastern taxa; the morphological convergence between *O. dyris* and *O. fleischmannii* may thus result from adaptation to very similar pollinators. This hypothesis implies that the evolution from a grooved throat to a flat throat could have occurred twice in *Pseudophrys*.

Ophrys vasconica
(O. DANESCH & E. DANESCH) P. DELFORGE

Etymology *vasconica:* of Gascony. **Type** Ga, Gers (1969). **Synonyms** *O. fusca* subsp. *vasconica* O. DANESCH & E. DANESCH, *O. omegaifera* subsp. *vasconica* (O. DANESCH & E. DANESCH) KREUTZ, ?*O.* × *brigittae* H. BAUMAN.

Description (8-) 12-20 (-35)cm tall; (1-) 2-6 (-12) flowers; sepals 10-14mm x 6-8mm; petals hairless, spreading, yellowish-green to brownish, 6-9mm x 1.5-3mm, oblong, margins undulate; lip 12-20mm x 13-18mm (when spread), horizontal to rather pendent, 3-lobed, slightly convex; lip 12-20mm x 13-18mm (when spread), horizontal dense, rather short, often with silver reflections, usually a fine hairless yellow border, base wedge-shaped, weakly to not at all kinked; tip of lobes pale brown or slate-grey; lateral lobes divergent, 3-5mm x 2-4mm, triangular, rounded, spreading, slightly convex; median lobe 5-11mm x 6-11mm, rather spreading, broadening and emarginate; speculum shiny, pale brown to purplish or slate-grey, often strongly marbled whitish, sometimes densely hairy, with a shiny, hairless ⍵ at tip, whitish to blue-grey, edges often blurred; base of stigmatic cavity yellowish or greenish, with short, dense, whitish hairs, ± hollowed into a 'V', often prolonged into a groove on the speculum; 2n =72, 74.

Variation Very varied. The range of variation almost overlaps with *O. dyris*, with the exception of the V-shaped throat to the stigmatic cavity, and with *O. arnoldii* at the other end of the spectrum.

Flowering Season IV-VI.

Habitat Full sun to mid-shade, on dry to moist, alkaline substrates. Grassland, garrigue, open pine and oak woodland, up to 1100m asl.

Distribution Northwestern sub-Mediterranean. Reported from the Basque country (Ga Hs) and Spanish Catalonia; probably also Mallorca (Bl). Local and rather rare.

Countries ?Bl Ga Hs

Photos A Hs, Barcelona, 13.IV.1990; **B & C:** Navarra, 9.VI.1993. P. DELFORGE.

Discussion *O. vasconica* appears to be the result of the introgression of *O. dyris* by *O. fusca* s.l., a phenomenon parallel, although here less complete, to the one which led to the formation of *O. sitiaca* in Crete. The absorption of *O. dyris* seems to be complete in France, very advanced in Mallorca, and prominent in Catalonia. *O. vasconica* is probably a species in the process of formation; polytypic and heterogeneous, the various populations have apparently not resulted from the same speciation event and perhaps only involve a single species of the *O. fusca* group. Moreover, certain late-flowering populations reported for *O. vasconica* sometimes refer to *O. arnoldii*.

Ophrys fleischmannii
HAYEK

Etymology Named after H. Fleischmann, Viennese headmaster (†1925). **Type** Cr, Chania (1926). **Synonyms** *O. funerea* subsp. *fleischmannii* Soó, *O. fusca* subsp. *fleischmannii* (Soó) Soó, *O. omegaifera* subsp. *fleischmannii* (HAYEK) DEL PRETE.

Description As *O. omegaifera* but (8-) 10-15 (-20)cm tall; (2-) 3-5 (-8) smaller flowers; lateral sepals 11-15mm x 6-9.5mm; petals brown to green, sometimes edged purple, 8-11mm x 2-3.5mm, linear to oblong, tip truncated; lip 13-17mm x 10-16mm (when spread), angled upwards, sometimes near vertical, dark slate-brown, hairs dense, long, irregular, with silver reflections; lateral lobes small, 3-5mm x 1.5-3mm, triangular-rounded; median lobe 4-8mm x 6-12mm; speculum rather shiny, sometimes brown, often dark blue with brownish reflections, rarely marbled whitish, with a broad, distinct, glossy, hairless ⍵ at tip, white, greyish or bluish; stigmatic cavity 3-4mm high, 3.5-4.5mm wide.

Flowering Season (I-) II-IV.

Habitat Full sun to mid-shade on dry, calcareous substrates. Garrigue, abandoned cultivation, olive groves, open pinewoods, up to 1200m asl.

Distribution Aegean. Crete, central Cyclades, reports from Hydra (Gr) and Attica (Gr) require confirmation. Rare and local.

Countries Cr Gr.

Photos Cr, Lassithi, 3.III.1990. P. DELFORGE.

Pollinator *Anthophora sicheli* (Hymenoptera: Anthophoridae).

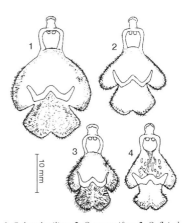

1. Ophrys basilissa. **2.** *O. omegaifera.* **3.** *O. fleischmannii.* **4.** *O. sitiaca.* (modified after GÖLZ & REINHARD).

Ophrys omegaifera
H. Fleischmann

Etymology *-fera:* bearing; *omegai-:* omega (an allusion to the crescents at the tip of the speculum). **Type** Cr, Lassithi (1925). **Synonyms** *O. lutea* subsp. *omegaifera* (H. Fleischmann) Soó; *O. fusca* subsp. *omegaifera* (H. Fleischmann) E. Nelson.

Description (8-) 12-20 (-25)cm tall; (1-) 2-3 (-5) medium-sized flowers; sepals concave, 12-17mm x 6.5-9.5mm, oval-obtuse, green (slightly whitish), lateral sepals asymmetrical, spreading, dorsal sepal near equal, bent down onto column; petals hairless or ciliate, spreading, green, sometimes brownish, 7-11mm x 2-4mm, linear to narrowly oval, tip truncated, rarely pointed, margins undulate, reddish or brownish; lip (13-) 15-21mm x 14-23mm (when spread), near horizontal or angled slightly upwards, deeply 3-lobed, base wedge-shaped and strongly kinked, tips of lobes with dense, rather long, irregular, pale brown to orange hairs; lateral lobes divergent, 4-6mm x 3-6mm, triangular-obtuse to rounded, strongly convex, turned down under lip; median lobe 5-11mm x 7-15mm, convex, rounded, broadened and emarginate; speculum slightly shiny, pale brown to orange, sometimes with blue reflections, very rarely marbled whitish, with very short, sparse hairs and a broad, distinct, glossy, hairless Ω at tip, sky blue, becoming whitish at end of flowering season; stigmatic cavity 4-5mm high, 3-5mm wide, base flat, with straight, rather long and dense white hairs.

Flowering Season II-IV.

Habitat Full sun to mid-shade on dry to moist, calcareous substrates. Grassland, garrigue, olive groves, open pinewoods, up to 1000m asl.

Distribution Aegean. Principally the Cyclades and the arc formed by Crete, Karpathos, Rhodes and southwest Anatolia; north to Chios (Ae). Local and rather rare.

Countries Ae An Cr Gr.

Photos Cr, Lassithi, 2.III.1990. P. Delforge.

Pollinators *Anthophora atroalba* subsp. *agamoides* (Cr) and *A. nigriceps* (Ae) (Hymenoptera: Anthophoridae).

Ophrys basilissa

A. ALIBERTIS & H.R. REINHARD

Etymology *basilissa:* empress (a reference to the large lip). **Type** Cr, Rethimno (1990). **Synonyms** *O. omegaifera* subsp. *basilissa* (A. ALIBERTIS & H.R. REINHARD) H. KRETZSCHMAR, *O. omegaifera* var. *basilissa* (A. ALIBERTIS & H.R. REINHARD) N. FAURHOLDT.

Description As *O. omegaifera* but (10-) 12-25 (-30)cm tall; (1-) 2-4 (-6) large flowers; lateral sepals 13-20mm x 7-11mm; petals green to dark brown, 10-14mm x 3-5mm, oblong, tip truncated; lip 17.5-28.5mm x 18-27mm (when spread), dark slate-grey, hairs dense, long, rarely with silver reflections; lateral lobes 4-6mm x 4-8mm, triangular-rounded; median lobe 6.5-10.5mm x 13-19mm; speculum slightly shiny, sometimes brown, often blue or purplish-blue, rarely marbled whitish, with a broad, distinct, shiny, hairless **(1)** at tip, white, grey or pale blue; stigmatic cavity 4.5-6mm high, 4-5.5mm wide.

Flowering Season (XII-) I-IV, 2-4 weeks before *O. omegaifera.*

Habitat Full sun, more rarely mid shade, on dry, calcareous substrates. Open garrigue, abandoned cultivation, olive groves, open pinewoods, up to 500m asl.

Distribution Southern Aegean, from Paros (central Cyclades) in the north to Patmos (Ae) in the east. Very local and rather rare. **Countries** Ae Cr Gr.

Photos Cr, Iraklio, 26.II.1990. P. DELFORGE.

Pollinator Probably *Anthophora nigrocincta* (Hymenoptera: Anthophoridae).

Key to the *Ophrys omegaifera* group

1   base of lip strongly kinked 2
1* base of lip not or only slightly kinked 5

2   lip pale brown .... *O. omegaifera*
2* lip dark, brown to slate-grey 3

3   lip 17.5-28.5mm long .... *O. basilissa*
3* lip 13-19mm long 4

4   lip angled upwards .... *O. fleischmannii*
4* lip horizontal to slightly pendent ..... *O. dyris*

5   base of lip flat .... *O. israelitica*
5* base of lip slightly grooved 6

6   flowering (I-) II-III .... *O. sitiaca*
6* flowering (late III) IV-VI 7

7   lateral sepals 14-16mm long; petals 9.5-12mm long; .... *O. algarvensis*
7* lateral sepals 10-14mm long; petals 6-9mm long .... *O. vasconica*

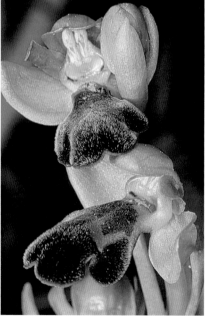

Ophrys israelitica
H. BAUMANN & KÜNKELE

Etymology *israelitica:* of the Israelites. **Type** Ij, Galilea (1988). **Synonyms** *O. omegaifera* subsp. *israelitica* (H. BAUMANN & KÜNKELE) G. MORSCHEK & K. MORSCHEK, *O. fleischmannii* auct. non HAYEK.

Description (8-) 12-17 (-23)cm tall; (2-) 3-8 flowers; sepals 9-13mm long, whitish-green to olive-green; petals hairless, spreading, greenish-yellow to reddish-brown, 7-9.5mm x 2-3.5mm, oblong, margins undulate; lip 11-16mm x 8-13mm, slightly convex, spreading, (near) horizontal, 3-lobed, base wedge-shaped, weakly kinked; lateral lobes divergent, 2-4mm x 2-4mm, triangular-rounded; median lobe obcordate, 4-8mm x 6-8mm; lip hairs dense, rather short, slate-grey with silver reflections, sometimes tinted brown or yellow, bordered by a narrow, yellow, hairless margin; speculum shiny, pale bluish-grey, rarely brownish, often marbled whitish, with very short, sparse hairs and a shiny, whitish to bluish-grey, hairless Ω at tip, sometimes rather broad, with a blurred outline; stigmatic cavity 2-3.5mm high, 3.5-4.5mm wide, base yellowish, flat, with rather short, dense white hairs.

Flowering Season (XII-) I-IV.

Habitat Full sun to mid-shade on dry to moist, alkaline to slightly acidic substrates. Garrigue, scrub, open pine and cypress woodland, up to 1300m asl.

Distribution Eastern Mediterranean, from the Cyclades to northern Israel. Local but sometimes abundant.

Countries Ae An Cy Gr Ij Ls.

Photos Cy, Larnaca, 28.III.1989. P. DELFORGE.

Note Flowers pollinated by *Andrena flavipes* (Hymenoptera: Andrenidae), the same pollinator as *Ophrys bilunulata* and *O. leucadica*; morphological analogies between the 3 species probably result from an adaptive convergence to this same pollinator.

Ophrys sitiaca

H.F. PAULUS, CH. ALIBERTIS & A. ALIBERTIS

Etymology *sitiaca:* from [region of] Sitia. **Type** Cr, Lassithi (1988). **Synonym** *O. omegaifera* subsp. *sitiaca* (H.F. PAULUS, CH. ALIBERTIS & A. ALIBERTIS) KREUTZ.

Description 7-17 (-22)cm tall; 1-3 (-6) medium-sized flowers; sepals concave, margins reflexed, 8-16mm x 5.5-10mm, oval-obtuse, green (slightly whitish); petals hairless, spreading, green, sometimes brownish, 6-11mm x 1.5-4mm, linear to oblong, rarely slightly pointed, margins undulate, red or brownish; lip (11-) 13-16 (-19)mm x 8-15.5mm (when spread), horizontal to slightly pendent, 3-lobed, base wedge-shaped, weakly kinked, tip of lobes pale brown to blackish-brown, densely hairy, hairs rather short, rarely with silver reflections; lateral lobes divergent, 3-4mm x 2-4mm, triangular, sometimes linear, rounded, strongly convex, turned down under lip; median lobe 5-7.5mm x 6-10.5mm, convex, rhomboidal, emarginate; speculum rather shiny, brownish, sometimes with blue reflections, rarely blue, often marbled whitish, with very short, sparse hairs and a broad, glossy, whitish (rarely bluish) hairless (l) at tip, with blurred margins; stigmatic cavity 3-4mm high, 3.5-4.5mm wide, base yellowish, with short, dense, white hairs, slightly hollowed into a 'V', rarely extended on to speculum as a very short, faint groove.

Variation Varied; the flowers have characters of both *O. omegaifera* and *O. fusca* s.l. There is a significant range of variation regarding the kink, shape, convexity and coloration of the lip.

Flowering Season I-III, 2-4 weeks before *O. fleischmannii.*

Habitat Full sun to mid-shade on dry to moist, calcareous substrates. Garrigue, above all open pinewoods, up to 800m asl.

Distribution Eastern Aegean. Very rare and local.

Countries Ae An Cr.

Photos Cr, Lassithi (loc. typ.), 1.III.1990. P. DELFORGE.

Pollinator *Andrena nigroaenea* subsp. *candiae* (Hymenoptera: Andrenidae).

Discussion Probably of hybrid origin, involving *O. omegaifera* and an early member of the *O. fusca* complex that may now have been absorbed; an input from *O. iricolor* is not supported by the presence of characters from that group in *O. sitiaca*. Some non-Cretan and relatively late-flowering populations may' be non-stabilised hybrid swarms, incorrectly identified as *O. sitiaca*.

431

Section *Ophrys* L. 1753

(= section *Euophrys* GODFERY 1928 nom. nud.)

Characters Lip with a hairless speculum; pseudo-eyes and staminodial points often present.

The *Ophrys speculum* group

Characters Dorsal sepal turned down onto column; petals short, villous; lip 3-lobed, densely ciliate, without appendage; median lobe divided into 2 secondary lobules; stigmatic cavity surrounded by various well-defined lips and bosses (see fig. 12, p. 359); column short, with a rounded tip. A monophyletic group, with 3 closely related species.

Ophrys speculum
LINK (nom. cons. prop.)

Etymology *speculum:* mirror. **Type*** Lu, Sétubal (1800). **Synonyms** *O. ciliata* BIVONA-BERNARDI, *O. vernixia* auct. non BROTERO, *O. vernixia* subsp. *ciliata* (BIVONA-BERNARDI) DEL PRETE, *O. vernixia* subsp. *orientalis* H.F. PAULUS, *O. ciliata* var. *orientalis* (H.F. PAULUS) KREUTZ.

Description 5-25cm tall; 2-8 flowers, relatively large; sepals oval-oblong, 7-10mm x 3-5mm, concave, green (sometimes whitish), spotted and ± broadly streaked with dark purplish-brown inside, lateral sepals spreading horizontally; petals dark purplish-brown, villous, lanceolate, 4-6mm long, curved backwards; lip with a very contracted base, blackish-brown to greenish, 12-16 (-17.5)mm long, near horizontal, 3-lobed in basal half, bordered by long, dense, dark, reddish-brown to purplish hairs, these surrounded by a hairless margin, 0.5-1.5mm wide; lateral lobes lanceolate to oval, flat, spreading obliquely sideways or forwards, sometimes erect, 0.8-1.8x as long as broad; median lobe oboval to obcordate, slightly convex, 0.6-1.1x as long as broad; speculum shiny, blue, extensive, ± broadly edged with a greenish-yellow to orange margin; basal field dark, shiny, oval to elliptic, with bosses; staminodial points very well marked; pseudo-eyes black, shiny, carried by temporal bosses. '*orientalis*' (photo B): black of basal field extending to sinuses of lateral lobes; speculum and lip hairs darker; an eastern variant.

Flowering Season (II-) III-IV (-V). **Habitat** Full sun to mid-shade on dry to moist, alkaline substrates. Short, poor grassland, banks, abandoned cultivation, garrigue, scrub, open woodland, mostly in coastal areas, up to 1200m asl.

Distribution Mediterranean. Widespread and sometimes abundant; rare in the centre of the range (It); extremely rare in France, where it flowers sporadically. **Countries** Ae Ag Al An Bl Co Cr Cy Ga Gr Hs It Li Ma Me Sa Si Tn Tu.

Photos: Hs, Malaga, 10.IV.1990; Gr, Atiki, 4.IV.1994. P. DELFORGE. **Pollinators** '*speculum*' (Photo A): *Dasyscolia ciliata* subsp. *ciliata*; '*orientalis*' (Photo B): *Dasyscolia ciliata* subsp. *araratensis* (Hymenoptera: Scoliidae).

Ophrys vernixia
BROTERO

Etymology *vernixia:* glossy. **Type*** Lu, Coïmbra (1804). **Synonyms** *O. speculum* subsp. *lusitanica* O. DANESCH & E. DANESCH, *O. lusitanica* (O. DANESCH & E. DANESCH) H.F PAULUS & GACK, *O. vernixia* subsp. *lusitanica* (O. DANESCH & E. DANESCH) H. BAUMANN & KÜNKELE, *O. ciliata* subsp. *lusitanica* (O. DANESCH & E. DANESCH) H. BAUMANN, KÜNKELE & R. LORENZ.

Description As *O. speculum* but more robust, more slender, 15-50cm tall; inflorescence (near) lax; 5-15 flowers, size as *O. speculum* but paler; lateral sepals whitish-green, less violet-tinted, sometimes unmarked; petals paler, orange or greenish; lip pendent to near horizontal, base contracted, more grooved, 3-lobed towards the middle, orange, blackish-brown or green-olive, bordered by long, pale, yellowish to russet hairs and surrounded by a hairless margin 1.5-2.5mm wide; lateral lobes linear-lanceolate, 1.5-3.5x as long as broad, divergent, very convex, kinked in middle, tip turned down and back, extending past centre of median lobe; median lobe globular, more convex, oval-oblong, 0.9-2.2x as long as broad; speculum narrower; basal field oboval to elliptic. **Variation** Slight. Hybrids occasional and forms intermediate with *O. speculum* rather rare.

Flowering Season III-V, 2-3 weeks after *O. speculum.*

Habitat Full sun to mid-shade on dry to moist, calcareous substrates. Short, poor grassland, garrigue, up to 500m asl.

Distribution Iberian. Range split into 3 areas, centred on Portugal (Extremadura, Beira Litoral and Ribatejo), the Algarve (southern Lu) and Andalucia (Jaén, Cordoue). Rare and local.

Countries Hs Lu. **Photos** Lu, Extremadura, 3.IV.1990. P. DELFORGE.

Key to the *Ophrys speculum* group

1 median lobe narrow, very convex, (1.5-) 2-4x as long as broad .... *O. regis-ferdinandii*
1* median lobe less convex, 0.6-2.2x as long as broad 2

2 petals and lip hairs pale; lateral lobes narrow, tip turned down and back ....
.... *O. vernixia*
2* petals and lip hairs dark; lateral lobes broader, flat, tip pointing forwards..........................
.... *O. speculum*

Ophrys regis-ferdinandii
(ACHTAROFF & KELLERER ex RENZ) BUTTLER

Etymology Named after Ferdinand I, King of Bulgaria (1861-1948). **Type** Λc, Rhodes (1943). **Synonyms** *O. speculum* subsp. *regis-ferdinandii-coburgii* ACHTAROFF & KELLERER nom. inval., *O. speculum* f. *regis-ferdinandii* ACHTAROFF & KELLERER ex RENZ, *O. speculum* var. *regis-ferdinandii* (RENZ) SOÓ, *O. speculum* subsp. *regis-ferdinandii* ACHTAROFF & KELLERER ex KUZMANOV, *O. vernixia* subsp. *regis-ferdinandii* (KUZMANOV) RENZ & TAUBENHEIM, *O. ciliata* subsp. *regis-ferdinandii* (RENZ) H. BAUMANN, KÜNKELE & R. LORENZ.

Description As *O. speculum* but rather spindly, 5-30cm tall; inflorescence near lax; 2-11 smaller flowers; lateral sepals strongly blotched and streaked brownish-violet; petals sometimes slightly paler, brown to purplish, tip sometimes russet; lip pendent to near horizontal, bordered by long, pale to rather dark russet-brown to purplish hairs, base greenish-brown, strongly contracted and strongly grooved; lateral lobes linear, 2-4.5x as long as broad, divergent, directed obliquely forwards and downwards, very convex, tip greenish or orange; median lobe very narrow, strongly convex, linear-oblong, 1.5-4x as long as broad, sides rolled under so strongly that hairs only visible at tip; speculum bright blue to purplish, surrounded by greenish-yellow or russet band; basal field reduced, narrow. **Variation** Very little. Hybrids occasional and forms intermediate with *O. speculum* rather rare.

Flowering Season III-IV, 2-3 weeks after *O. speculum*. **Habitat** Full sun to mid-shade on dry to moist, calcareous substrates. Short, poor grassland, garrigue, scrub, banks, open woodland, up to 400m asl. **Distribution** Eastern Aegean. Rhodes, Simi, Tilos, Samos, Chios (Ae); Kuçadaçi region and almost to Çesme (An). Rare and local.

Countries Ae An.

Photos Ae, Rhodes, 10.IV.1984. P. DELFORGE.

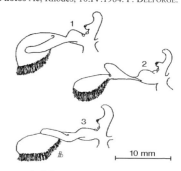

1. *Ophrys vernixia*. 2. *O. speculum*.
3. *O. regis-ferdinandii*. (after BUTTLER).

The *Ophrys tenthredinifera* group

Characters Sepals rounded; petals short, triangular, villous; submarginal band of hairs complete, thicker above appendage; stigmatic cavity cup-shaped, surrounded by well-marked internal, external, staminodial and temporal bosses; column short, obtuse.

Ophrys bombyliflora
LINK

Etymology *-flora:* flower; *bombyli-:* [with the shape] of a bee-fly (Diptera: Bombyliidae). **Type** Lu, Algarve (1800). **Synonyms** *O. tabanifera* WILLDENOW, *O. distoma* BIVONA-BERNARDI, *O. hiulca* MAURI, *O. canaliculata* VIVIANI, *O. labrofossa* BROTERO.

Description Slim, 5-20 (-35)cm tall; (2-) 3-5 root-tubers, the younger long-stalked; 1-5 small flowers; sepals bright green, rarely whitish, broadly oval, 9-12mm x 6-8mm, lateral sepals spreading, dorsal sepal turned backwards (sepals bend forwards and envelop the lip after anthesis); petals villous, broadly triangular, 3-4mm x 3-4mm, yellowish-green, base often darker, washed brown or purplish-grey; lip 8-10mm x 11-13mm (when spread), oval-rounded, brown washed green to dark bluish-grey, deeply 3-lobed at base; lateral lobes forming 2 acute conical basal swellings, villous outside, hairless at tip; median lobe globular, emarginate, with short pale grey submarginal hairs, longer above appendage, and a pale green hairless border; speculum unobtrusive, bordering basal field, shaped as a bilobed shield, pale, brownish, greyish or purplish, sometimes edged whitish; appendage triangular, fleshy, hairless, pale green, strongly bent down below lip; stigmatic cavity hemispherical, surrounded by internal, external, staminodial and temporal bosses, well differentiated (see fig. 12, p. 359); column short, tip rounded, loculus red outside.

Flowering Season II-V.

Habitat Full sun to mid-shade on dry to very damp, alkaline substrates. Short grassland, damp meadows, abandoned cultivation, garrigue, scrub, open woodland, up to 900m asl. **Distribution** Mediterranean. East to Rhodes (Ae) and western Anatolia, west to the Canaries. Widespread and sometimes found in very dense populations due to vegetative multiplication via its numerous root-tubers; very rare in France. **Countries** Ae Ag Al An Bl Ca Co Cr Ga Gr Hs It Ju Li Lu Ma Me Sa Si Tn Tu.

Photos Cr, Lassithi, 3.III.1990; Bl, Mallorca, 4.IV.1985. P. DELFORGE. **Pollinators** *Eucera orianensis* (Bl It), *E. nigrescens* subsp. *continentis* (It), *E. gracilipes* (Ca), *E. vulpes* (Gr) and *E. algira* (Cr) (Hymenoptera: Anthophoridae).

Ophrys tenthredinifera
WILLDENOW

Etymology *-fera:* bearing; *tenthredini-:* sawfly (Hymenoptera: Symphyta). **Type** Ag (1805).

Description 10-30 (-45)cm tall; leaves glaucous-green; inflorescence often lax; (1-) 3-10 rather large flowers; bracts longer than ovary; sepals narrowly oval-rounded to elliptical, spreading to turned backwards, 11-13mm x 7-10mm, whitish, pinkish, sometimes yellowish; petals co-colourous, triangular, 3-5mm x 2-4mm, often auriculate, villous, spreading to pointing obliquely upwards and forwards; lip trapezoidal (when spread), appearing as a narrow trapezium, elongated, 11-16mm long, base with poorly marked shoulders and 2 slight swellings, tip flared, distal sides slightly recurved, centre of lip with dark brown to reddish, appressed, velvety hairs, broad, complete but poorly defined submarginal rim of bright yellow to greenish-yellow hairs, sometimes brownish (as centre), tufts of hair above appendage not luxuriant; speculum small, basal, shield-shaped, brownish to purplish, bordered by a fine bluish line; appendage rather reduced, hairless, bright greenish-yellow, triangular, erect, inserted into a distinct notch; stigmatic cavity reddish to greyish-brown, demarcated at base by a ridge, bordered by 2 oblique ridges, shiny, elongated, overhanging the reddish basal field; column very short, obtuse; staminodial points often present; temporal bosses often still visible; 2n=38.

Flowering Season (I-) II-IV.

Habitat Full sun to shade on alkaline to very acidic, dry to moist substrates. Short grassland, garrigue, scrub, open woodland, up to 1800m asl.

Distribution Western Mediterranean. The Maghreb, east to Libya, the Balearics and Iberian peninsula; reaches Roussillon in the north (Ga). Rather local and often rare.

Countries Ag Bl Ga Hs Li Lu Ma ?Me Tn.

Photos Tn, Nabeul, 1.III.2002; Djebel Kechabta, 25.II.2002. P. DELFORGE.

Pollinator *Eucera nigrilabris* (Bl Ga Hs Ma) (Hymenoptera: Anthophoridae).

Ophrys tenthredinifera WILLDENOW
var. praecox RCHB. fil. ex E.G. CAMUS

Etymology *praecox:* early. **Type** Lu, Extremadura (1908). **Synonyms** *O. tenthredinifera* subvar. *praecox* RCHB. fil. ex GUIMARÃES, *O. tenthredinifera* subsp. *praecox* D. TYTECA nom. illeg., *O. tenthredinifera* subsp. *guimaraesii* D. TYTECA, *O. tenthredinifera* var. *guimaraesii* (D. TYTECA) KREUTZ comb. illeg.

436

Description As var. *tenthredinifera* but 1-4 (-5) smaller flowers; lip with shoulders and basal swellings much more reduced; appendage more reduced; stigmatic cavity redder. **Flowering Season** I-III (-IV), very early, before var. *tenthredinifera*. **Distribution** Central Portugal and maybe elsewhere in range of var. *tenthredinifera* in the Maghreb and Iberian peninsula. **Photo A** Lu, Lisbon, 2.IV.1990. P. DELFORGE.

Note The definition and validity of this taxon is still not clearly defined.

Ophrys villosa
DESFONTAINES

Etymology *villosa:* villous. **Type*** ?Ae, Chios (1807). **Synonym** *O. tenthredinifera* subsp. *villosa* (DESFONTAINES) H. BAUMANN & KÜNKELE.

Description Rather similar to *O. tenthredinifera* but flowers often smaller; sepals and petals sometimes more brightly colourful, ranging to an intense purple; petals sometimes slightly darker than sepals; lip with slightly squarer shoulders at base and distinct basal swellings; dark hairs at centre of lip, straighter, erect, surrounded by a clearly defined band of long, fine submarginal hairs, often honey-coloured, sometimes greyish-brown, whiter or frosted on outer rim, complete and uniform from shoulders to appendage, often forming a broader yellow border; hairless border to lip clearly demarcated, fine, yellow; appendage averages slightly larger; stigmatic cavity often blackish-brown or dark grey, sometimes reddish, bordered by 2 oblique ridges, shiny, elongated, dark grey or blackish; basal field red to dark reddish.

Variation *O. villosa*, in the sense presented here, is very probably heterogeneous, encompassing, with the Iberian *O. tenthredinifera* s.l., small- and large-flowered morphs, early- and late-flowering taxa and also, most probably, cryptic taxa isolated by pollinators; 4 of these taxa are detailed below.

Flowering Season (I-) II-V.

Habitat As *O. tenthredinifera*, up to 1200m asl.

Distribution Eastern Mediterranean, centred on the Aegean basin. The Balkan peninsula (probably from extreme eastern Croatia) south to Crete (perhaps also Libya) and east to Cyprus; in Anatolia east to Hatay province.

Countries Ae Al An Cr Cy Gr ?Ju ?Li.

1. *Ophrys villosa* 'central Aegean' Thickset, not very tall; flowers rather large, very colourful; sepals broadly oval; petals slightly darker than sepals; centre of lip almost blackish, marginal rim whitish-brown, buff, rarely yellow. **Flowering Season** Mid III-IV, rather late. **Distribution** Cyclades, Crete.

Photo B: Gr, Astipalaia, 3.IV.1997. P. DELFORGE.

(continued on next page)

437

2. *Ophrys villosa* 'early Cretan' Spindly; flowers rather small, lightly coloured; petals very small; marginal lip hairs whitish-yellow. **Flowering Season** II-mid III, early. **Distribution** Crete. **Pollinator** Probably *Eucera dimidiata* (Hymenoptera: Anthophoridae).

Photo A: Cr, Lassithi, 27.II.1990. P. DELFORGE.

3. *Ophrys villosa* 'very small Ionian' Very spindly; flowers very small; sepals and petals lightly coloured; lip 7-10mm x 8-11mm; marginal lip hairs rather bright yellow. **Flowering Season** Late III-mid IV. **Distribution** Ionian archipelago and neighbouring areas.

Photo B: Gr, Kefallinia, 8.IV.1990. P. DELFORGE.

4. *Ophrys villosa* 'rather small Ionian' Relatively robust; flowers rather small; sepals and petals concolourous, rather deeply-coloured, pink or lilac; lip 9-12mm x 10-15mm; marginal lip hairs rather bright greenish-yellow. **Flowering Season** Late III-IV. **Distribution** Ionian Islands and neighbouring areas. **Pollinator** *Eucera bidentata* (Hymenoptera: Anthophoridae) (see p. 361).

Photo C: Gr, Zakynthos, 13.IV.1993. P. DELFORGE.

Note: In continental Greece and the Peloponnese, plants that are rather similar but more robust, later-flowering and often with larger flowers are pollinated by *Eucera nigrilabris rufitarsis* (Gr, Amphissa) and perhaps *E. curvitarsis* (Gr, Peloponnese).

Ophrys aprilia
P. DEVILLERS & J. DEVILLERS-TERSCHUREN

Etymology *aprilia:* from April. **Type** Co, Bonifacio (2003). **Synonym** *O. tenthredinifera* subsp. *aprilia* (P. DEVILLERS & J. DEVILLERS-TERSCHUREN) KREUTZ.

Description As *O. tenthredinifera* but thickset, robust; flowers larger; lip 12.5-18mm long, broader; submarginal lip hairs denser, often entirely brownish (at centre); tuft of hairs above appendage rather prominent; stigmatic cavity black, bordered by 2 concolourous oblique ridges; basal field darker reddish-brown.

Flowering Season III-mid IV, before *O. neglecta*.
Habitat As *O. tenthredinifera*. **Distribution** Endemic to Sardinia and Corsica; local but sometimes very abundant in its stations. **Countries** Co Sa. **Photo A** Co, Bonifacio, 5.IV.1996. P. DELFORGE.

Pollinator Perhaps *Eucera nigrilabris* (Hymenoptera: Anthophoridae).

Ophrys neglecta
PARLATORE

Etymology *neglecta:* neglected, forgotten. **Type** It, ?Rome (1887). **Synonym** *O. tenthredinifera* subsp. *neglecta* (PARLATORE) E.G. CAMUS.

Description As *O. tenthredinifera* but flowers smaller; lip 9-13 (-15)mm long, globular, shoulders raised, distal sides often turned down and under; lip hairs dense, tangled, sometimes woolly; submarginal hairs denser, very different from central hairs; very prominent tuft of reddish hairs above appendage; stigmatic cavity black bordered by 2 oblique ridges, sometimes with pseudo-eyes; basal field darker reddish-brown.

Photo B & C It, Salerno, 5.IV.2001; Cosenza, 10.IV.2002. P. DELFORGE. (*continued on next page*)

Flowering Season (*O. neglecta*) III-VI, after *O. aprilia*. **Habitat** As *O. tenthredinifera*. **Distribution** Southern Italy, north to Tuscany, Corsica and Sardinia. Rather local and rather rare. **Countries** Co It Sa ?Ju. **Pollinators** Probably *Eucera clypeata* and *E. orianensis* (Hymenoptera: Anthophoridae).

Ophrys grandiflora
TENORE

Etymology *grandiflora:* with large flowers. **Type** Si, Mount Nebrodi; It, Calabria, Sila massif (1819). **Synonyms** *O. tenthredinifera* subsp. *grandiflora* (TENORE) KREUTZ, *O. tenoreana* LINDLEY.

Description As *O. tenthredinifera* but robust; bracts coloured as sepals; flowers larger; lip 13-20mm long, rounded-trapezoid (when spread), shoulders squared, basal swelling not very pronounced, distal sides generally recurved-spreading; hairs of central lip blackish-brown, dense, not very extensive; submarginal hairs very broad and dense, bright greenish-yellow; tuft of hairs above appendage very prominent, yellowish to reddish; stigmatic cavity brownish to olive-green, concolourous with basal field, bordered by 2 pseudo-eyes.

Flowering Season II-IV (-V). **Habitat** Full sun to mid-shade on alkaline to slightly acidic, dry to moist substrates. Short grassland, garrigue, scrub, open woodland, up to 1500m asl. **Distribution** Sicily (rather widespread) and southern Calabria (very rare). **Countries** It, Si. **Photos** Si, Siracusa, 12.III.2000; Ragusa, 17.III.2000. P. DELFORGE.

Pollinator Perhaps *Eucera algira* (Si) (Hymenoptera: Anthophoridae).

Key to the *Ophrys tenthredinifera* group

1   sepals bright green .... *O. bombyliflora*
1*   sepals of another colour 2

2   speculum quadrangular, broadly edged white .... *O. tardans*
2*   speculum ± bilobed, finely edged whitish or bluish, or paler border absent 3

3   prominent hirsute tuft of hairs above appendage 4
3*   hairs above appendage as those of remainder of border of lip... 7

4   lip 9-13 (-15)mm long .... *O. neglecta*
4*   lip 12.5-21mm long 5

5   late flowering, mid IV-VI .... *O. ficalhoana*
5*   early flowering, II-mid IV 6

(continued next page)

440

Ophrys ficalhoana
GUIMARÃES

Etymology *ficalhoana:* from Ficalhoa. **Type** Lu, Extremadura (1887). **Synonyms** *O. tenthredinifera* subsp. *ficalhoana* (GUIMARÃES) M.R. LOWE & D. TYTECA, *O. tenthredinifera* var. *ronda* SCHLECHTER nom. nud.

Description As *O. tenthredinifera* but robust, thickset; bracts coloured as sepals; sepals and petals concolourous, pink to lilac, rather dark; flowers larger, very colourful; lip 13-21mm x 16-23mm long, quadrangular, shoulders squared, broad, basal swellings rounded, pronounced, distal sides slightly or not recurved; hairs of central lip purplish-brown, dense, rather appressed, not very extensive; broad submarginal band of bright yellow to greenish-yellow hairs, dense, bristling, rather well defined; tuft of hairs above appendage straight, yellowish to reddish, prominent; appendage larger; stigmatic cavity blackish to olive-green or reddish, concolourous with basal field, bordered by 2 ridges that tend to become rounded into pseudo-eyes.

Flowering Season IV-VI, late.

Habitat As *O. tenthredinifera*.

Distribution Centred on the Iberian peninsula, reaching Gers in France; similar populations are reported from Algeria, Morocco and the Balearics, but whether they are conspecific with Iberian plants requires confirmation.

Countries ?Ag ?Bl Ga Hs Lu ?Ma.

Photos Hs, Cuenca, 16.VI.1988; Burgos, 13.VI.1993. P. DELFORGE.

Key to the *Ophrys tenthredinifera* group
(continued from previous page)

6 stigmatic cavity black edged with black ridges .... *O. aprilia*
6* stigmatic cavity brownish to olive-green edged with rounded pseudo-eyes................... ....*O. grandiflora*

7 lip 15-24mm long; column shortly acuminate .... *O. normanii*
7* lip 7-16mm long; column obtuse 8

8 submarginal hairs on lip very clearly demarcated from short central hairs; marginal hairs whitish or frosted, at least on shoulders of lip .... *O. villosa*
8* submarginal hairs on lip barely demarcated from short central hairs; marginal hairs without whitish reflections or frosting, even on shoulders .... *O. tenthredinifera*

Ophrys tardans
O. Danesch & E. Danesch (pro hybr.)

Etymology *tardans:* late (to flower). **Type** It, Lecce (1972). **Synonym** *O.* × *maremmae* subsp. *tardans* (O. Danesch & E. Danesch) Del Prete.

Description Intermediate between *O. neglecta* and *O. candica*, 10-40cm tall; bracts often coloured as sepals; inflorescence dense; 3-7 flowers, often large; sepals 10-15mm x 6-11mm, oval-rounded, concave, pale pink to dark purple-violet, sometimes washed green; petals triangular, often auriculate, villous, 3-4.5mm x 2.5-3mm; lip 9-15mm x 12-20mm, obcordate to trapezoid, colour as varied as *O. neglecta* and hairs similar; speculum more prominent, close to that of *O. candica*, hairless, glossy, quadrangular or shield-shaped, centre brownish-violet, often marbled white, bordered by a broad, irregular, pure white band, very often covering the basal swellings; appendage prominent, globular, triangular or sometimes obscurely 3-toothed, erect in a rather distinct notch; stigmatic cavity structured as *O. neglecta*, often blackish-purple, with oblique rounded ridges, extending forwards as a protruding ridge overhanging basal field; column short and obtuse.

Flowering Season IV-V, 2-4 weeks after *O. neglecta*, slightly before *O. candica*.

Habitat Full sun to mid-shade on dry to moist, alkaline substrates. Short, poor grassland, abandoned cultivation, garrigue, scrub, up to 400m asl.

Distribution Endemic to southern Puglia (It), principally Lecce province. Very local but sometimes rather abundant; endangered following the urbanisation of the coastline.

Countries It.

Photos It, Lecce, 26.IV.1991. P. Delforge.

Pollinator Perhaps *Eucera taurica* (Hymenoptera: Anthophoridae).

Discussion of the *Ophrys tenthredinifera* group

A Mediterranean group, probably paraphyletic, comprising 2 hybridogenous species that have a restricted distribution, *O. tardans* (= *O. neglecta* × *O. candica*) and *O. normanii* (= *O.* cf. *neglecta* × *O. chestermanii*), as well as at least 7 other species. Of these *O. bombyliflora* has a vast distribution and appears ancestral on the basis of numerous characters, notably the shape of the sepals and petals and the presence of varied lips around the stigmatic cavity, still well differentiated. Molecular analysis validates the position of *O. tenthredinifera* s.l. as sister clade to the *fuciflorae-argolicae-araniferae* assemblage, but does not confirm its proximity to *O. bombyliflora*, a very unusual species, perhaps closer to *O. speculum*.

(continued on next page)

Ophrys normanii
J.J. WOOD (pro hybr.)

Etymology Named after T. Norman, contemporary English botanist, who collected the plant. **Type** Sa, Cagliari (1983). **Synonym** *O.* × *maremmae* subsp. *normanii* (J.J. WOOD) H. BAUMANN & KÜNKELE.

Description Close to *O. tenthredinifera* s.l., with a few characters from *O. chestermanii*; 15-50cm tall; inflorescence dense; 2-7 very large flowers (larger than those of the parent species); bracts greenish, lightly coloured; sepals broadly rounded, pale pink to violet, often washed green – then 'dirty' brownish; petals darker than sepals, large, 4-6mm x 4-6mm, triangular, often auriculate, villous, turned down, margins undulate; lip 15-24mm x 14-25mm, elongated-trapezoid, very convex transversally, sides straight or slightly reflexed for distal half, centre velvety, dark blackish-brown, edges densely hairy, hairs long, sometimes greenish-yellow, more often honey-coloured or buff; speculum reduced, basal, hairless, glossy greyish, often edged whitish; appendage not very prominent, triangular to near globular, erect in a distinct notch; basal field blackish; stigmatic cavity structured as *O. neglecta*, blackish; column short, shortly acuminate.

Flowering Season IV-V, after *O. neglecta*, slightly before *O. chestermanii*.

Habitat Full sun to mid-shade on alkaline to acidic, dry to moist substrates. Abandoned cultivation, garrigue, scrub, banks, up to 400m asl.

Distribution Endemic to southwest Sardinia.

Countries Sa.

Photos Sa, Cagliari, 14.IV.1996. P. DELFORGE.

Pollinator The cuckoo bee *Bombus* (*Psithyrus*) *vestalis* (Hymenoptera: Apidae).

Discussion of the *Ophrys tenthredinifera* group

(continued from previous page)

The other members of the group form an assemblage of very closely related species in which it appears that 2 lineages can be distinguished. The first, characterised by an optically narrow lip, the tuft of hairs above the appendage reduced or absent and crest-shaped stigmatic bosses, comprises *O. tenthredinifera* and *O. villosa* and is distributed from the Iberian peninsula to Cyprus. The second, characterised by a more quadrangular lip, well developed tuft of hairs above the appendage and a tendency for the crests to form rounded pseudo-eyes, contains *O. neglecta, O. grandiflora* and *O. ficalhoana* and does not reach the eastern Mediterranean basin. *O. aprilia*, endemic to Corsica and Sardinia, seems to have characters intermediate between these two lineages, in which the number of species is probably underestimated.

The *Ophrys insectifera* group

Characters Leaves erect, not spreading in a basal rosette; petals appearing filiform due to their rolled margins, velvety; lip 3-lobed, velvety; median lobe divided into 2 lobules, without indentation at the angle of bifurcation; stigmatic cavity without lateral wall; column very short, tip rounded; pseudo-eyes placed at base of lip, apparently deriving from internal bosses, accompanied outwards by 2 less obvious shiny bosses, probably vestiges of the base of external lips.

Discussion A monophyletic group, probably comprising 3 closely related species, sub-Mediterranean, forming an isolated clade, sister to the *tenthrediniferae-fuciflorae-argolicae-araniferae* assemblage. *O. aymoninii* may be the ancestral species of the group. *O. insectifera*, more derived, has acquired the capacity to adapt to more diverse and colder habitats. It was able to follow the northwards retreat of the glaciers as far as the centre of Scandinavia and is therefore the most northerly species in the genus. The status of *O. subinsectifera* is controversial.

Ophrys aymoninii
(BREISTROFFER) BUTTLER

Etymology Named after G.G. Aymonin, contemporary French botanist. **Type** Ga, Aveyron (1981). **Basionym** *O. insectifera* subsp. *aymoninii* BREISTROFFER.

Description As *O. insectifera*, but yellower in all parts; perianth less spreading, all its divisions directed more obliquely forwards; petals pale yellowish-green, sometimes washed pale brown at the base; lip often as broad as long, 9-12mm x 8-12mm, lighter, reddish-brown, more convex, slightly globular in centre, always edged with a bright yellow band 1-2.5mm wide; central speculum bluish, column yellow.

Flowering Season V-VI.

Habitat Full sun to mid-shade on dry to moist, calcareous substrates. Short grassland, scrub, woodland edges, open woodland, 500-1000m asl.

Distribution Endemic to southern Causses, a calcareous plateau in the Massif Central (Ga). Rare and local. **Countries** Ga.

Photos Ga, Aveyron, 5.VI.1982. P. DELFORGE.

Pollinator *Andrena combinata* (Hymenoptera: Andrenidae).

Note The hypothesis of a hybrid origin for *O. aymoninii* is unfounded; based essentially on the presence of a yellow border around the lip, it is not supported by other characters from *O. lutea* or *O. araneola*, sometimes proposed as parent species.

Ophrys insectifera L.

Etymology *-fera:* bearing; *insecti-:* insect. **Type*** Su, Öland (1753). **Synonyms** *O. myodes* JACQUIN, *O. muscifera* HUDSON.

Description 15-60 (-80)cm tall; stem often flexuous, spindly, yellowish-green; 3-5 leaves, glaucous, near erect, upper 1-2 leaves erect, clasping; bracts leaf-like, equal to, or slightly longer than, ovary; inflorescence very lax, elongated; 2-15 (-20) flowers; sepals near spreading, oval-oblong, obtuse, attenuated and near hooded at tip, concave, 6-9mm x 3-4mm, whitish-green to yellowish-green; petals dark brownish-purple, velvety, spreading to directed forwards, linear, appearing almost filiform, 4-7mm long, margins rolled up; lip (8-) 9-12mm x (5-) 6-10mm, much longer than broad, pendent, 3-lobed at base, much longer than sepals, shortly pubescent, blackish-brown to purplish; lateral lobes divergent, narrow, oblong to lanceolate or obliquely truncated, sides slightly reflexed; median lobe divided into 2 triangular lobules, broadly edged paler brown or reddish, more rarely by a bright yellow strip; speculum slightly shiny, central, quadrangular to shield-shaped, hairless, bluish-grey; stigmatic cavity narrow, without lateral walls, floor flat; base of lip with 2 shiny pseudo-eyes, ± hemispherical, alongside 2 very small inconspicuous ridges; column very short, tip rounded, brownish-green, loculus red.

Flowering Season (IV-) V-VII, rather late.

Habitat Full sun to shade on calcareous to neutral, sometimes acidic, dry to damp, sometimes wet, substrates. Usually grassy banks, woodland edges and open woodland, but also short grassland, dense woods and sometimes acidic bogs, up to 2000m asl.

Distribution Mid-European. This, the most northerly *Ophrys,* reaches central Scandinavia. Widespread but rather rare.

Countries Al Au Be Bl Br Cz Da Fe Ga Ge Gr Hb He Ho Hs Hu It Ju Lx No Po Ro Rm Su.

Photos Ga, Meurthe-et-Moselle, 22.V.1988; Be, Luxembourg, 25.VI.1991. P. DELFORGE.

Pollinators The wasps *Argogorytes mystaceus* and *A. combinata* (Hymenoptera: Sphecidae).

Note Odd plants of *O. insectifera*, with the lip edged bright yellow but otherwise with all the features of the species, may appear here and there; they are, with the occasional hybrid *O. insectifera × O. araneola*, responsible for the reports of *O. aymoninii* away from Causses and *O. subinsectifera* in Catalonia. Plants with dwarf flowers and a slightly indented lip are also found throughout the whole range (= *O. insectifera* var. *parbrightlora* M. SCHULZE).

445

Ophrys subinsectifera
HERMOSILLA & SABANDO

Etymology *sub-:* near; *-insectifera:* like *[Ophrys]* *insectifera*. **Type** Hs, Navarra (1996). **Synonym** *O. insectifera* subsp. *subinsectifera* (HERMOSILLA & SABANDO) O. DE BOLOS & VIGO.

Description As *O. insectifera* but more spindly, 9.5-30 (-45)cm tall; inflorescence often denser, with small flowers; sepals more yellowish, 6-7mm x 3-4mm, petals brownish, tip often green or yellow, rarely entirely greenish, 2-4mm long; lip 6-10mm x 5-8.5mm, 3-lobed, not as flat longitudinally, often near globular at base, depressed by speculum and recurved at tip; lateral lobes much reduced to near absent, sometimes turned down; median lobe less emarginate, sides reflexed; hairs of central lip brown, surrounded by a reddish intermediate zone, ± narrow and obvious, then by a bright yellow or greenish-yellow margin, 1-1.5mm wide; speculum greyish, sometimes with brownish reflections, slightly shiny and only slightly contrasting; column very short, loculus washed red.

Flowering Season V-VI.

Habitat Full sun to mid-shade on dry to moist, alkaline substrates. Pastures, garrigue, scrub, 400-1100m asl. **Distribution** Pyrenees, from Navarra in the west to central Huesca province in the east; reports from Catalonia probably all refer to *O. insectifera* with the lip fringed yellow. Rare and local. **Countries** Hs. **Pollinator** *Sterictiphora furcata* (Hymenoptera: Argidae).

Note Flowers sometimes very small, and blooms at the same time as *O. insectifera,* which it almost always accompanies. Plants and populations of *O. insectifera* with very small flowers have been reported throughout the range (notably Br, Ge) and morphs with a yellow-edged lip are not exceptional, thus *O. subinsectifera* may appear to be a mere variant that is not isolated from *O. insectifera.* The discovery of its pollinator is an argument in favour of specific status, but this insect does not engage in pseudocopulation and it has not been demonstrated that *O. subinsectifera* does not also attract the same pollinator as *O. insectifera,* as suggested by the abundant intermediate forms usually encountered alongside these 2 taxa.

Key to the *Ophrys insectifera* group

1   petals entirely pale green, 4-7mm long, column yellow .... *O. aymoninii*

1*   petals blackish-brown, at least at base, column washed red 2

2   petals entirely blackish-brown, 4-7mm long ..
    .... *O. insectifera*

2*   petals green or yellow at tip, 2-4mm long ......
    .... *O. subinsectifera*

Photos: Hs, Navarra, 23 & 25.V.1999. P. DELFORGE.

The Ophrys apifera group

Characters Petals villous; lip with prominent submarginal hairs, interrupted by sinuses of lateral lobes; median lobe globular; appendage triangular or with 3 teeth, inserted into a notch, turned down and under; stigmatic cavity cup-shaped, base undulate; pseudo-eyes near stalked at tip of oblique, keeled ridges; column with a sinuous tip. A monospecific sister to the *O. fuciflora* complex.

Ophrys apifera
HUDSON

Etymology *-fera:* bearing; *api-:* bee. **Type** Br, England (1762). **Synonyms** *O. arachnites* MILLER, *O. aquisgranensis* KASLENBACH, *O. ripaensis* PORTA, *O. botteronii* CHODAT, *O. jurana* NEUBERGER, *O. trollii* HEGETSCHWEILER, *O. friburgensis* (FREYHOLD) NÄGELI, *O. bicolor* NÄGELI.

Description Robust, 20-50 (-70)cm tall; lower bracts greyish-green, longer than flowers; inflorescence near lax; 4-12 large flowers; sepals broadly oval-lanceolate, keeled, hooded, 11-17mm x 5-9mm, pure white to dark purple with a marked green central vein, spreading, dorsal sepal erect and then strongly turned backwards; petals directed obliquely forwards, usually very small, 1-3mm x *c.* 1mm, bright green to pinkish, very villous, triangular, sometimes auriculate, margins strongly rolled up thus appearing linear (for petals of other shapes and colours, see Variation); lip deeply 3-lobed at base, 9-14mm long (when spread), velvety, reddish-brown to blackish, submarginal hairs whitish to brownish; lateral lobes pointed, conical, short, pressed forwards, outer surface with dense, greenish-brown to whitish hairs; median lobe globular, sides bright green, strongly turned down and under; speculum varied, bluish, edged with a thick whitish to yellowish line, in the shape of a bilobed shield surrounding the reddish-brown basal field, with ± complete lines and isolated spots under basal swellings and above appendage; appendage prominent, green, 2-3mm long, strongly turned down and under lip; stigmatic cavity deep, greenish, finely barred brown, base horizontal, with a convex undulation in the centre, delineated by a ridge overhanging the basal field, bordered by 2 oblique lamellae, blotched blackish, shiny; column very well developed, making an obtuse angle with the lip, tip sinuous, 1-3mm long.

Flowering Season (III-) IV-VII; sporadic.

Habitat Full sun to shade, on dry to wet, mostly alkaline substrates, xeric to swampy short grassland, garrigue, scrub, woodland edges, open woodland, up to 1800m asl.

Distribution Euro-Mediterranean, north to temperate Europe and east to the Caucasus. Widespread and sometimes abundant.

447

Countries Ae Ag Al An Au Be Bl Br Co Cr Cy Cz Ga Ge Gr Hb He Ho Hs Hu Ij It Ju Ls Lx Ma Me Rm Ro Sa Si Tn Tu.

Photos It, Potenza, 28.V.2000; An, Izmir, 11.V.1990. P. DELFORGE.

Note An isolated species, mostly but not exclusively self-pollinating, wrongly held to be monocarpic. The pollinia, whose long caudicles wither only a few hours after the flower opens, drop from the loculi and fall onto the stigma at the slightest touch.

Variation Its regular autogamy leads to the frequent appearance, throughout the range, of hypochromatic or aberrant plants; these variants, without evolutionary significance, are often linked to normal plants by intermediates.

1. '*jurana*' (**Syn**.: *O. apifera* subsp. *jurana* Ruppert): Petals elongated, up to 7mm long, of the same colour and consistency as sepals.

    1.1. '*friburgensis*' (**Syn**.: *O. apifera* subsp. *friburgensis* (Freyhold) Soó): Lip shape and colour normal.

    1.2. '*botteronii*' (**Syn**.: *O. apifera* subsp. *botteronii* (Chodat) Schinz & Thell., *O. saraepontana* Ruppert): Lip with a normal or slightly globular shape but with broad and irregular markings. **Photo A** Ga, Drôme, 9.VI.1983. P. DELFORGE.

2. Petals short, as normal.

    2.1. '*trollii*' (**Syn**.: *O. apifera* var. *trollii* (Hegetschweiler) Rchb. fil.): Lip elongated, near triangular to oblong, long-attenuated, not turned down, tip often very pale. **Photo B** Ga, Charente, 5.VI.1981. P. DELFORGE.

    2.2. '*bicolor*' (**Syn**.: *O. mangini* Tallon): Lip shape normal, basal half slate-grey or reddish, distal half blackish-brown, speculum absent. **Photo C** It, Salerno, 29.V.2000. P. DELFORGE.

The *Ophrys bornmuelleri* group

Characters Sepals uniform, oval, dorsal sepal erect; petals villous, triangular, often short and not adjacent at base; lip mostly entire and quadrangular, velvety, marginal band of hairs complete, hairs long and dense; appendage with 3 teeth, inserted into a notch in the lip; stigmatic cavity cup-shaped, without complete lip.

Discussion of the *Ophrys bornmuelleri* group

A central and eastern Mediterranean group of 17 species which all show a primitive character, a complete (near) marginal band of hairs, almost always as long and dense on the shoulders as on the distal half of the lip. They probably all derive, directly or indirectly, from an eastern Mediterranean ancestral species, perhaps close to *O. tenthredinifera*; this proximity is sometimes expressed in a general appearance similar to, for example, *O. biancae* or *O. levantina*. The main process of speciation within the group was probably the fragmentation of an ancestral range, most likely Aegean, leading to the appearence of several subgroups: an eastern, ± isolated subgroup (*O. bornmuelleri, O. carduchorum, O. levantina, O. lyciensis*), another, more central Aegean, subgroup (*O. aeoli, O. andria, O. candica, O. episcopalis, O. helios, O. heterochila, O. lacaena, O. thesei*) and a western group (*O. annae, O. biancae, O. chestermanii, O. parvimaculata*), itself divided into the 3 species on the Tyrrhenian islands and an Italian species that is ecologically isolated (*O. parvimaculata*), which appear to be relicts. In the Aegean and eastern subgroups, the species, rather often syntopic, even in the Cyclades, have ± broadly overlapping flowering seasons. They have isolated themselves through adaptation to a new pollinator, probably on the basis of size (*O. episcopalis / O. helios*) and/or the structure and position of the lip (*O. lacaena / O. candica*; *O. bornmuelleri / O. levantina*).

The division of the group into these 3 biogeographical clusters does not, however, correspond well with their morphology: *O. annae,* for example, seems to be far closer to the eastern *O. bornmuelleri* than to *O. chestermanii* of Sardinia, which in turn very closely resembles the Cycladian *O. aeoli*. These similarities may reveal an intermediate phase in the radiation of the group, the appearance of several ancestral species occupying the whole range of the group, prior to its current fragmentation, resulting in a mosaic of sympatric or parapatric taxa, not as directly related to each other as their spatial distribution suggests.

Key to the *Ophrys bornmuelleri* group

1 speculum basal, shiny bluish, simply quadrangular, broadly edged white, sometimes marbled .... *O. candica*

1* speculum with more complex patterns 2

2 petals 1.2-3 (-3.2)mm long 3
2* petals 3-7.5mm long 10

3 basal swellings (2-) 4-7 (-10)mm long ....
.... *O. lacaena*
3* basal swellings 0-4mm long 4

4 lip (11-) 12-20mm long .... *O. episcopalis*
4* lip 7-12 (12.5)mm long 5

5 lip pale reddish-brown, often broadly edged with yellow .... *O. biancae*
5* lip darker, sometimes edged greenish or reddish 6

6 bracts much longer than flowers 7
6* bracts equal to, or shorter than, flowers 8

7 lip pendent, sides sometimes turned under.....
.... *O. carduchorum*
7* lip near horizontal, sides spreading and then reflexed forwards .... *O. bornmuelleri*

8 lip 7-9mm long, petals 1.2-2mm wide...........
.... *O. heterochila*
8* lip 8.5-12.5mm long, petals 2-3.5mm wide....
.... *O. levantina*

9 speculum with branches surrounding basal field .... *O. ziyaretiana*
9* central speculum reduced, without branches extending towards stigmatic cavity ....
.... *O. levantina*

10 stigmatic cavity and basal zone black 11
10* stigmatic cavity and basal zone paler, brown.
.... 12

11 petals (2.5) 3-5 (-6)mm long, appendage with 3-15 teeth .... *O. aeoli*
11* petals 4-6.5mm long, appendage rounded or with 3 teeth .... *O. chestermanii*

12 speculum reduced, basal or central 13
12* speculum basal, more extensive, encompassing basal swellings 15

13 sepals pink, purple, often dark, without green tones .... *O. thesei*
13* sepals washed green or whitish 14

(continued on p. 453)

Ophrys aramaeorum
P. DELFORGE

Etymology *aramaeorum:* of the Arameans. **Type** An, Diyarbakir (2000). **Synonyms** *O. holoserica* subsp. *aramaeorum* (P. DELFORGE) KREUTZ, *O. fuciflora* vel *O. holoserica* auct.

Description Slender, 25-65 (-80)cm tall; inflorescence lax, very elongated; (3-) 5-10 (-12) rather small flowers; sepals dark crimson-pink to pinkish or, less frequently, whitish, oval-lanceolate, lateral sepals 9.5-15mm x 5-8.5mm, dorsal sepal curved; petals triangular-rounded, sometimes auriculate, 1.5-3.5 (-4)mm x 1.5-3mm, rather short when compared to sepals (mean sepal length/petal length = 4:11), villous, the same colour as sepals or sometimes paler or redder; lip entire to near entire, globular, near quadrangular to trapezoid, shorter than lateral sepals, 6.5-9 (-11)mm x 8-12 (-13.5)mm (when spread), centre blackish-brown and velvety, 2 small, pointed, basal swellings, hairless on inside, sides reddish-brown, straight or spreading, with a complete band of rather long, pale buff, (near) marginal hairs, broad on basal half of lip and above appendage, narrower around lateral-distal quarters; speculum basal and central, sometimes very extensive, brownish-blue, edged pale greenish-yellow, forming a usually complete central ocellus and 2-5 lateral ocelli, ± fragmented, encompassing the basal swellings; basal field paler than centre of lip, rusty-brown; appendage greenish, well developed, with 3 teeth, pendent to directed upwards; stigmatic cavity relatively large, with a horizontal ledge marked on both sides by rounded pseudo-eyes, near stalked, shiny, blackish-green, encircled by greenish-yellow, linked to the external walls by purple bridles; staminodial points present.

Flowering Season IV-VI.

Habitat Full sun on dry to damp, calcareous substrates, often marly. Banks, short, flushed grassland and abandoned cultivation, damp pastures, open oakwoods and their edges, up to 1100m asl.

Distribution Basins of the upper Tigris and Euphrates; reaches northern Israel. Very local and rather rare.

Countries An Ls Ij.

Photos An, Siirt 18.V.1990; Diyarbakir (loc. typ.) 27.V.1990. P. DELFORGE.

Ophrys carduchorum
(RENZ & TAUBENHEIM) P.DELFORGE

Etymology *carduchorum:* belonging to the Carduques, (ancient) people inhabiting the left bank of the Tigris. **Type** An, Siirt (1980). **Basionym** *O. bornmuelleri* subsp. *carduchorum* RENZ & TAUBENHEIM.

Description As *O. bornmuelleri* but bracts much longer, up to 6cm; inflorescence very lax; flowers appearing very small; sepals whitish to greenish, sometimes washed violet, 9-11mm x 4-5mm, concave, curved forwards; petals villous, sometimes auriculate, 1.2-2mm x 1.2-2mm, greenish, often washed violet; lip pendant, entire, 6-8mm x 8-10mm (when spread), trapezoid to obcordate, more convex, looking rather square, with 2 pointed or attenuated basal swellings, sides hairless, often finely tinted greenish, dropping straight down or slightly bent under; speculum on average slightly more extensive, with 1-4 ocelli, sometimes all complete; appendage often smaller and narrower, angled downwards or forwards, inserted into a less well marked notch; stigmatic cavity averages slightly taller; column shorter, less acuminate, forming an open angle with the lip.

Variation Very similar to *O. bornmuelleri*, distinguished principally by the smaller size of the lip, its habit and convexity, as well as the position and structure of the column. May, however, form hybrid swarms with *O. bornmuelleri*, complicating the identification.

Flowering Season IV-V.

Habitat Full sun to mid-shade on dry to moist, alkaline substrates. Mostly grassy places and scrub in oakwoods, 600-1000m asl.

Distribution Northeast Anatolia, in the basin of the upper Tigris. Rare and local.

Countries An.

Photos An, Diyarbakir, 17.V.1990; Siirt, 18.V.1990. P. DELFORGE.

451

Ophrys bornmuelleri
M. Schulze

Etymology Named after J. Bornmüller, German botanist (1862-1948). **Type** Ij, Galilee (1899). **Synonyms** *O. fuciflora* subsp. *bornmuelleri* (M. Schulze) B. Willing & E. Willing, *O. holoserica* subsp. *bornmuelleri* (M. Schulze) Sundermann.

Description Slender, 15-50cm tall; bracts longer than flower; 4-15 small flowers; sepals green, whitish or pinkish, oboval, 10-13mm x 5-7mm, spreading, slightly curved forwards; petals very small, villous, obliquely erect, triangular-rounded, 1.5-2.2mm x 1.5-2.8mm, colour as sepals but darker, or sometimes lilac or olive-green; lip (near) horizontal, entire, 6-10mm x 8-12.5mm (when spread), obcordate, slightly convex, appearing trapezoid or square, centre velvety, reddish-brown to blackish, with a complete band of dense, rather long, submarginal hairs, silver-brown washed violet, with 2 pointed, conical, erect, divergent basal swellings, hairless and greenish inside; margin of lip hairless, ± broadly tinted greenish, sometimes scalloped, spreading and often reflexed forwards on distal half; speculum basal, rather reduced, bluish to purplish-grey, glossy, bordered yellowish or greenish, and forming a bilobed shield surrounding the reddish or brownish basal field, extended by lateral branches, more rarely by 2 ocelli, and, towards the tip, by 2 lines, 2 isolated dots or a central ocellus; appendage prominent, pointed, with 3 teeth or irregularly toothed, greenish-yellow, pointing forwards or upwards, inserted into a deep notch; stigmatic cavity small, transverse, dark, bordered by 2 rounded to elliptical pseudo-eyes, greenish-black, shiny; column relatively prominent, elongated, acuminate, often inclined over lip; staminodial points often present.

Variation See opposite.

Flowering Season (II-) III-V (-VI).

Habitat Full sun to mid-shade on dry to moist, alkaline substrates. Short grassland, abandoned cultivation, garrigue, scrub, open woodland, up to 1200m asl.

Distribution Near East. Cyprus and southeastern Anatolia to Iranian Kurdistan and Israel. Rather local and often rare.

Countries An Cy Ij Ls.

Photos Cy, Limassol, 31.III.1989; An, Diyarbakir, 17.V.1990. P. Delforge.

Pollinator *Eucera penicillata* (Cy) (Hymenoptera: Anthophoridae).

Ophrys bornmuelleri M. SCHULZE
var. *ziyaretiana* (KREUTZ & R. PETER) P. DELFORGE

Etymology *ziyaretiana:* from Mount Ziyaret, south of Antioch. **Type** An, Hatay (1997). **Synonyms** *O. ziyaretiana* KREUTZ & R. PETER, *O. bornmuelleri* subsp. *ziyaretiana* (KREUTZ & R. PETER) KREUTZ.

Description As *O. bornmuelleri* var. *bornmuelleri* but thickset, 15-25 (-30)cm tall; flowers slightly larger; sepals 11-14.5mm x 5.5-7.3mm; petals more elongated, 2.3-4.2mm x 1.5-3.5mm; lip pendent, entire, 8.1-10.5mm x 11.8-14.5mm (when spread), more convex transversally; band of submarginal hairs broader; sides of lip dropping straight down or slightly reflexed; basal speculum more reduced, often simply shield-shaped; appendage more robust and broader, angled downwards or upwards; column shorter, less acuminate, forming an open angle with lip.

Flowering Season III-V; slightly later than var. *bornmuelleri*.

Habitat As var. *bornmuelleri*.

Distribution The eastern part of the range of *O. bornmuelleri*, from southeast Anatolia to northern Israel. Rare and local, mostly mixed with var. *bornmuelleri* and numerous intermediates.

Countries An Ij Ls.

Photos An, Hatay, 13.IV.1996. C.A.J. KREUTZ.

Key to the *Ophrys bornmuelleri* group

(continued from p. 449)

14   lip with basal swellings (0.2-) 1-9mm long; speculum often central, without branches extending towards stigmatic cavity; early flowering, mid III-mid IV .... *O. andria*

14*   lip with basal swellings 0.5-3mm long; speculum basal, with branches surrounding basal field; later flowering, IV-V

....*O. parvimaculata*

15   sepals olive-green or purple strongly washed green; petals darker, often another colour ......
.... *O. halia*

15*   sepals and petals usually concolourous, lacking green or olive-green tones 16

16   lip 7-12mm long ....*O. annae*

16*   lip (11-) 12-17mm long 17

17   band of marginal hairs on lip very broad and thick, pale buff to brown, not thinning around lateral-distal quarters of lip .... *O. helios*

17*   band of marginal hairs on lip yellowish, often thinning around lateral-distal quarters of lip .... *O. lyciensis*

Ophrys levantina
GÖLZ & H.R. REINHARD

Etymology *levantina:* Levantine. **Type** Cy, Limassol (1985). **Synonyms** *O. bornmuelleri* f. *grandiflora* H. FLEISCHMANN & SOÓ, *O. bornmuelleri* subsp. *grandiflora* (H. FLEISCHMANN & SOÓ) RENZ & TAUBENHEIM, *O. fuciflora* subsp. *bornmuelleri* var. *grandiflora* (H. FLEISCHMANN & SOÓ) B. WILLING & E. WILLING, *O. holoserica* subsp. *bornmuelleri* var. *grandiflora* (H. FLEISCHMANN & SOÓ) LANDWEHR, *O. holoserica* subsp. *grandiflora* (H. FLEISCHMANN & SOÓ) N. FAURHOLDT, *O. pseudolevantina* M. SCHÖN-FELDER & H. SCHÖNFELDER nom. nud.

Description Often robust, 10-25 (-30)cm tall; lower bracts longer than ovary; inflorescence near lax; (2-) 3-6 (-9) flowers; sepals whitish-green, white or pinkish, often washed green at tip and pink at base, oval, 11-14.5mm x 5.5-9mm, spreading, dorsal sepal sometimes turned backwards; petals villous, erect, broadly triangular, 2-3.2mm x 2-3.5mm, often appearing auriculate, colour as sepals; lip pendent or slightly turned down and back, entire, 8.5-12.5mm x 11-17mm (when spread), obcordate, convex, globular at centre, appearing orbicular or quadrangular, velvety, reddish-brown, olive-greenish or blackish, with a complete band of dense, rather long, sub-marginal hairs, greyish-brown often washed violet, with 2 rounded to pointed conical basal swellings, near hairless and greenish inside; margin of lip hairless, pale crimson-brown, rarely tinted green, sometimes slightly scalloped, pendent, slightly turned under, rarely reflexed forwards; speculum much reduced, tending to be central and transverse, bluish to purplish-grey, glossy, often finely bordered greyish, formed by 2 contiguous diamonds, without branches surrounding basal field, sometimes fragmented and/or extended by 2 greenish blotches above the appendage; appendage relatively small, globular, ± 3-toothed, greenish-yellow, projecting forwards, inserted into a prominent notch; basal field dirty red, rather elongated; stigmatic cavity transverse, cup-shaped, with 2 rounded pseudo-eyes; staminodial points often present; column rather short, tip often short, obtuse, making a very open angle with lip. **Variation** *'pseudolevantina'*: Stem up to 70cm tall; slightly larger flowers; eastern Anatolia, probably a separate species.

Flowering Season (II-) III-IV, slightly before *O. bornmuelleri*.

Habitat Full sun to mid-shade on dry to damp, alkaline substrates. Short grassland, abandoned cultivation, garrigue, scrub, open pinewoods, up to 1400m asl. **Distribution** Eastern Mediterranean. Probably from Anatolia to Israel. Local and rather rare. **Countries** An Cy Ij Ls.

Photos Cy, Limassol, 29.III.1989. P. DELFORGE.

454

Ophrys heterochila
(RENZ & TAUBENHEIM) P. DELFORGE

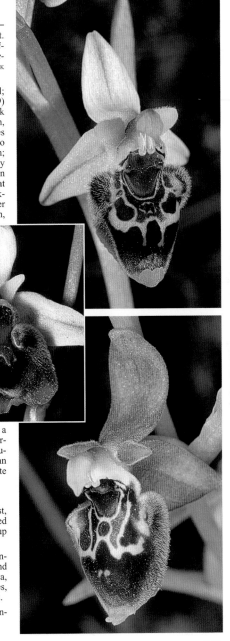

Etymology -*chila:* with a lip; *hetero-:* different.
Type An, Mugla (1980). **Synonyms** *O. holoserica* subsp. *heterochila* RENZ & TAUBENHEIM; *O. heterochila* (RENZ & TAUBENHEIM) H.F. PAULUS & GACK isonym.

Description Slender and spindly, 10-27cm tall; inflorescence rather lax, up to 12cm tall; 3-7 (-9) small flowers; sepals whitish, washed green, pink or dark lilac, oval-lanceolate, 10-12mm x 4-6mm, spreading, curved forwards then sometimes slightly turned back; petals villous, spreading to obliquely erect, triangular, 2.5-3mm x 1.2-2mm; lip pendent to near horizontal, entire or obscurely and irregularly 3-lobed, 7-9mm x 8-11mm (when spread), oboval, very convex, near globular at centre, velvety, pale reddish-brown to dark blackish-purple, with complete band of dense, rather long, submarginal hairs, brownish to whitish, with 2 small (1-2.5mm tall), divergent, ± pointed, conical basal swellings, hairless and greenish-white inside; margin of lip hairless, sometimes greenish-yellow, bent under or spreading and then slightly reflexed; speculum basal, bluish-grey to purplish-brown, glossy, edged yellowish-white, often in form of ± thickened H or X, surrounding dirty reddish basal field, sometimes extended by 2 isolated spots in centre of lip, often elaborated by a central ocellus and 2 lateral ocelli, ± complete, surrounding base of lateral lobes; appendage 1-2.5mm long, pointed, often with 3 teeth, greenish-yellow, pointing forwards to upwards, inserted into a rather weak notch; stigmatic cavity dark, bordered by 2 rounded, blackish-brown, shiny pseudo-eyes; staminodial points often present; column rather short, tip ± acuminate, making a near acute angle with lip.

Flowering Season III-V.

Habitat Full sun to mid-shade on dry to moist, calcareous substrates. Short grassland, abandoned cultivation, garrigue, scrub, open pinewoods, up to 700m asl.

Distribution Southwest Anatolia; east to Antalya, Samos and perhaps Rhodes (Ae). Rare and local. **Countries** Ae An. **Photos** An, Antalya, 30.III.1997. C.A.J. KREUTZ; Ae, Rhodes, 14.IV.1984; An, Izmir, 11.V.1990. P. DELFORGE.

Pollinator *Eucera cypria* (Hymenoptera: Anthophoridae) (Ae, Rhodes).

Ophrys halia
H.F. PAULUS

Etymology Named after the nymph Halia, mistress of Poseidon, mother of Rhodes. **Type** Ae, Rhodes (2002). **Synonym** *O. holoserica* subsp. *halia* (H.F. PAULUS) KREUTZ.

Description Rather spindly, 15-45 (-70cm)cm tall; inflorescence lax; (1-) 4-8 (-10) flowers, medium-sized for the group; sepals purplish-pink to dark purple, strongly washed green, sometimes olive-greenish, oval, lateral sepals 11-14.5mm long; petals villous and ciliate, elongated, triangular to triangular-acuminate, sometimes auriculate, obliquely erect, 4.6-6mm x 1.8-3.2mm, not adjacent at base, crimson-green to olive-green, dark, coloration sometimes different to that of sepals; lip entire, near quadrangular, centre globular, distal half often splayed by spreading sides, 10-13mm x 10.3-14.5mm (when spread), with 2 small conical swellings at base, sometimes divergent and curved, centre of lip velvety, broadly blackish-brown, ± dark, bordered rather narrowly by a complete band of marginal hairs, pale buff on shoulders, brown to pale red on distal half, sometimes ± attenuated on lateral-distal quarters; speculum central, rather varied, greyish-blue, glossy, broadly edged yellowish-green, formed by 3-4 ± complete ocelli, with distinct branches, surrounding basal field like a necklace; appendage inserted into a notch, yellowish-green, horizontal to pointing upwards, well developed, with 3 teeth; basal field red to dark brown; stigmatic cavity rather small, paler and more greyish than basal field, transverse, bordered by 2 yellowish pseudo-eyes, strongly spotted greenish-grey, upper border marked with a thin purple line; staminodial points sometimes present; column rather short, acuminate.

Flowering Season Mid IV-mid V, rather late.

Habitat Full sun on dry, often sandy, alkaline or decalcified substrates. Abandoned cultivation, garrigue, scrub, woodland edges, up to 200m asl.

Distribution Endemic to Rhodes. Very rare and local.

Countries Ae.

Photos Ae, Rhodes, 15.IV.1984. P. DELFORGE; 28.IV.2001. C.A.J. KREUTZ.

Ophrys helios
KREUTZ

Etymology Named after Helios, Greek god of the sun. **Type** Cr, Karpathos Island (2001). **Synonyms** *O. holoserica* subsp. *helios* (KREUTZ) KREUTZ, *O. karpathica* A. ALIBERTIS nom. nud., *O. 'cressa-holoserica'* H.F. PAULUS nom. nud.

Description Robust, (15-) 20-40 (-50cm)cm tall; inflorescence near lax to dense; (2-) 3-7 (-12) flowers, medium-sized for the group; sepals pink, purple, lilac, sometimes rather dark, oval, lateral sepals 11-14mm long; petals villous and ciliate, rather short, triangular, sometimes auriculate, obliquely erect, 3-5mm x 2-3mm, rarely adjacent at base, colour as sepals or slightly darker, sometimes ochre; lip entire, near quadrangular to trapezoid, sometimes splayed on distal half by spreading sides, or alternatively narrower because borders are turned down and under, 12-16mm x 13-17mm (when spread), with 2 conical swellings at base, 1.5-4mm long, rarely divergent and curved, centre of lip velvety, ± dark reddish-brown, broadly edged by a complete band of pale buff to brown marginal hairs, thick, without any attenuation in distal corners; speculum not very varied, not very extensive, greyish-blue to reddish, glossy, edged yellowish, composed of a central ocellus and 2 lateral ± complete ocelli encompassing the basal swellings, with distinct branches, surrounding the basal field like a necklace; appendage inserted in a notch, yellowish-green to reddish, horizontal to directed upwards, well developed, with 3-5 teeth; basal field dark reddish-brown to blackish; stigmatic cavity rather small, paler and more orange than basal field, transverse, demarcated by a ridge bordered by 2 shiny blackish pseudo-eyes, upper edge marked with a thin purple line; staminodial points present; column rather short, slightly acuminate.

Flowering Season Mid IV-V, rather late.

Habitat Full sun to mid-shade on dry to moist, alkaline substrates. Abandoned cultivation, garrigue, scrub, woodland edges, open pinewoods, up to 700m asl.

Distribution Karpathos Island and Crete. Local but sometimes abundant.

Countries Cr.

Photos Cr, Karpathos, 4.V.2001. C.A.J. KREUTZ.

Note This species is very likely often identified on Crete as 'small *O. episcopalis*' or as *O. fuciflora (-holoserica)* and is sometimes considered, in part, as representing the late-flowering flush of *O. episcopalis*. *O. helios* is, however, rather distinct from the latter in its smaller flower size and probably also its pollinator.

Pollinator Very probably *Eucera (Synhalonia) cressa*.

457

Ophrys episcopalis
POIRET

Etymology *episcopalis:* episcopal. **Type** Cr (1816). Synonyms *O. fuciflora* subsp. *maxima* (H. FLEISCHMANN) SOÓ, *O. holoserica* subsp. *maxima* (H. FLEISCHMANN) GREUTER, *O. maxima* (H. FLEISCHMANN) H.F. PAULUS & GACK.

Description (10-) 20-40 (-50)cm tall; (3-) 4-10 large flowers; sepals whitish, pink or dark purplish, rarely washed green, oval, 12-16mm x 6-10mm, spreading, slightly concave and curved forwards; petals small, villous, erect, triangular-rounded, 2-3.2mm x 1.5-3.5mm, colour as sepals or slightly brighter and washed ochre; lip pendent, entire, (14-) 15-20mm x 17-24mm (when spread), obcordate, ± convex, near globular at centre, appearing trapezoid or square, velvety, brown, with a complete submarginal band of dense, rather long, brownish to reddish hairs, with 2 small, conical basal swellings, ± pointed, erect, often divergent and curved, hairless and greenish inside; margin of lip hairless, pale reddish-brown, sometimes scalloped, spreading and then reflexed, ± strongly on distal half; speculum basal, sometimes reduced, glossy greyish-blue, bordered yellowish, sometimes in the form of a reddish or brown X surrounding the basal field, often extended by lateral branches, more rarely by 2 ocelli, and, towards the tip, 1-2 more ocelli, the distal of which often fragmented in centre of lip; appendage prominent, 2.5-5mm long, broad, ± pointed, with 3 teeth or toothed, greenish-yellow or reddish, angled upwards, inserted into a deep notch; stigmatic cavity small, transverse, 1.3-2mm high, sometimes slightly separated from lip, bordered by 2 rounded to elliptical, shiny, greenish-black pseudo-eyes; staminodial points often present; column rather small, ± acuminate, forming an open angle with lip.

Flowering Season Late III-IV (-V). **Habitat** Full sun to mid-shade on dry to moist, alkaline substrates. Short grassland, abandoned cultivation, garrigue, scrub, up to 1300m asl. **Distribution** Eastern Mediterranean. From Libya and Crete to Israel. Rather widespread on Crete, rare elsewhere. **Countries** Ae An Cr Ij Li. **Photos** Cr, Lassithi, 3.IV.1989. J. DEVILLERS-TERSCHUREN; An, Içel, 21.V.1997. C.A.J. KREUTZ.

Note *Eucera (Synhalonia) rufa* (Lep., 1841) [= *Tetralonia berlandi* (FONSCOLOMBE, 1846)] was at one time considered to be the usual pollinator of *Ophrys episcopalis* and *O. heldreichii* in Crete. This is apparently incorrect and the pollinator of *O. episcopalis* is currently unknown. In the light of this, the division, in Crete, of the species with large flowers into 2 taxa associated with 2 different pollinators, one early-flowering ('*O. maxima*') the other later-flowering ('*O. episcopalis*') is no longer justified (see note on previous page and p. 515).

Ophrys aeoli
P. DELFORGE

Etymology Named after Aeolus, Greek god of wind. **Type** Gr, Cyclades, Amorgos (1997). **Synonym** *O. holoserica* subsp. *aeoli* (P. DELFORGE) KREUTZ.

Description Slender, 15-32cm tall; 3-8 medium-sized flowers; sepals white, pink, dark crimson-pink, very rarely green; lateral sepals 10-16mm x 5.5-9mm, sometimes washed violet on lower half; petals triangular to triangular-rounded, often auriculate, (2.5-) 3-5 (-6)mm x 1.5-2.3mm, not adjacent at base, very villous, often intensively washed green; lip entire, near quadrangular to quadrangular, exceptionally obscurely 3-lobed, 10-15mm x 11.5-17mm (when spread), basal swellings hairless on their inner face, 0.5-3 (-5)mm long, centre of lip velvety, dark blackish-brown, often globular, sides of proximal half frequently turned down and under, those of distal half, rather broad, spreading then recurved, sometimes rolled up or undulate-crisped, paler and more reddish than centre; broad, complete marginal band of pale, blond to honey-coloured hairs; speculum basal and central, bluish-grey, bordered drab greenish-yellow or blue, in the form of a central ocellus and 2 lateral, ± complete ocelli encompassing the basal swellings, demarcating dark basal field like a necklace; appendage yellowish-green, very well developed, 3-7mm x 2.5-5.5mm, horizontal or directed upwards, very pointed, with 3-15 teeth, often arranged in 2 rows like the jaws of a trap; stigmatic cavity not narrowed at base, walls often extending the shoulders, very dark, transverse, 3-4mm broad, the vault lighter, with a transverse reddish-brown bar, external walls and upper border white; pseudo-eyes barely perceptible, green, black or pale grey, shiny; staminodial points often present; tip of column usually very acuminate.

Flowering Season IV-V, late.

Habitat Full sun on dry, alkaline substrates. Abandoned cultivation, garrigue, scrub, up to 450m asl. **Distribution** Eastern Cyclades (Amorgos and Astypalea). Very rare and local. **Countries** Gr. **Photos** (**C** holotype) Gr, Cyclades, Amorgos, 24 & 20.IV.1997. P. DELFORGE.

459

Ophrys andria
P. DELFORGE

Etymology *andria:* from Andros Island. **Type** Gr, Cyclades, Andros (1994). **Synonym**, *O. holoserica* subsp. *andria* (P. DELFORGE) N. FAURHOLDT.

Description 15-40 (-50)cm tall; lower bract up to 4cm long; (2-) 3-8 rather large flowers; sepals whitish-green, sometimes ± intensively washed pale pink or violet, 10-16mm x 5-11mm, lateral sepals spreading, dorsal sepal erect and then often bent strongly backwards; petals villous, triangular-elongated, appearing narrow, often auriculate, sometimes contiguous at base, (3-) 4-7.5mm x (2) 2.3-4mm; lip near horizontal to pendent, entire, 12-16mm x 14-20mm (when spread), quadrangular-rounded, convex, sometimes appearing near globular, centre velvety, ± dark reddish-brown, 2 pointed, conical basal swellings, sometimes near absent and rounded, (0.2-) 0.9-5 (-9)mm long, erect, sometimes slightly divergent and curved; complete submarginal band of dense, long hairs, greyish to yellowish on shoulders, brown to russet on distal half of lip; sides of lip recurved, pendent or spreading and slightly reflexed, sometimes narrowly hairless and tinged yellow on distal half; speculum central, rather varied, greyish-blue, glossy, edged whitish, broadly shield-shaped, rather often formed from 2 oblique drops, isolated or contiguous, then delineating a central ± complete ocellus, sometimes with ± distinct branches extending to stigmatic cavity, sometimes with a vague X or H shape, very short and thickened, surrounding the basal field like a necklace, extended by 1-2 pale, hairless blotches, isolated above appendage; appendage prominent, 2-4mm x 2.5-5mm, 3-5 teeth, pointed, greenish-yellow, directed forwards to upwards, inserted into a notch; basal field reddish-brown, elongated, (2-) 3-5mm high; stigmatic cavity overhanging, transverse, upper and lateral margins marked by reddish-brown lines; pseudo-eyes dark, protruding on a horizontal ridge delineating the basal field; staminodial points present; column rather short, slightly acuminate.

Flowering Season Mid III-mid IV.

Habitat Mostly full sun, on dry to moist, alkaline substrates. Banks, old terraces, abandoned cultivation, garrigue (phrygana with *Sarcopoterium spinosum*), scrub, up to 350m asl.

Distribution Northern Cyclades, apparently endemic to Andros. Very local and rather rare.

Countries Gr.

Photos (**A** holotype) Gr, Cyclades, Andros, 13 & 14.IV.1994. P. DELFORGE.

Ophrys thesei

P. DELFORGE

Etymology Named after Theseus, son of Aegeus, King of Athens. **Type** Gr, Cyclades, Naxos (1997). **Synonym** *Ophrys andria* var. *halkionis* H. KRETZSCHMAR & G. KRETZSCHMAR.

Description 14-42cm tall; 3-10 medium-sized flowers; sepals pale pink to, more often, dark crimson-pink, lateral sepals 10-15mm x 5.5-7mm; petals triangular, often auriculate, erect, 3.5-6.5mm x 1.8-3.2mm, non adjacent at base, slightly darker than sepals; lip entire, rarely obscurely 3-lobed, near quadrangular, distal half sometimes reduced due to its strong convexity and its sides bending down and underneath, 9-14mm x 11.5-16.5mm (when spread), velvety, ± dark reddish-brown, with 2 conical basal swellings, ± pointed, sometimes slender, 1-8 (-10)mm long, often divergent and curved; complete marginal band of hairs, grey-

ish to yellowish on shoulders, brown to pale russet on distal half of lip, sometimes ± attenuated on lateral-distal quarters; speculum rather varied, central, greyish-blue, sometimes reddish, glossy, edged yellowish-green, broadly shieldshaped, rather often formed by 2 oblique drops, isolated or contiguous, then delineating a central ocellus (rarely complete), sometimes with ± distinct branches extending to stigmatic cavity, rarely in the shape of a very short, thickened X or H, surrounding the basal field; appendage yellowish-green, horizontal to angled upwards, well developed, 1.5-3mm x 2-4mm, pointed, 3-5 teeth; basal field pale chestnut to dark brown, often elongated; stigmatic cavity often overhanging, transverse, bordered by 2 dark pseudo-eyes, protruding on a horizontal ridge delineating basal field, upper border marked with a purple line; staminodial points present; column rather short, slightly acuminate.

Flowering Season III-V.

Habitat Full sun on dry, alkaline or decalcified substrates. Abandoned cultivation, garrigue, scrub, up to 550m asl. **Distribution** The Cyclades. Currently known from Tinos, Naxos and Kimolos Islands. Very rare and local. **Countries** Gr. **Photos A & C** Gr, Cyclades, Naxos, 23 & 24.IV.1995; **B** Kimolos, 27.IV.1998. P. DELFORGE.

Ophrys lyciensis
H.F. PAULUS, GÜGEL, D. RÜCKBRODT & U. RÜCKBRODT

Etymology *lyciensis:* from Lycia (An). **Type** An, Antalya (2004). **Synonyms** *O. candica* subsp. *lyciensis* (H.F. PAULUS, GÜGEL, D. RÜCKBRODT & U. RÜCK-BRODT) KREUTZ, *O. minoa* sensu P. DELFORGE p.p.

Description As *O. lacaena* but robust, up to 70cm tall; inflorescence lax; sepals ± intensely pinkish, sometimes crimson, more narrowly oval-lanceolate, 13-18mm x 6-10mm, spreading; petals villous, elongated, triangular, ± auriculate, sometimes narrowly oblong, 4-5mm x 1.5-3.5mm, colour as sepals, washed darker violet at base; lip entire, 12-17mm x 14-18mm (when spread), near quadrangular to rounded, less convex or globular in centre, more elongated (optically), basal swellings averaging shorter; submarginal band of hair yellowish, complete but often attenuated on lateral-distal quarters; speculum not as varied or complex, greyish-blue, ± broadly edged yellowish-white; stigmatic cavity and basal field darker red; staminodial points present.

Flowering Season Late III-IV.

Habitat Mostly mid-shade on dry to moist, alkaline substrates. Old terraces, graveyards, the margins of scrub and open pine and oakwoods, up to 600m asl.

Distribution Southwest Anatolia, in Antalya and Mugla provinces, perhaps also further east, close to Alanya. Very rare and local.

Countries An.

Photos A-B An, Antalya, 19.IV.1997. C.A.J. KREUTZ; **C** 29.IV.1998. E. GÜGEL.

Pollinator *Eucera graeca* (Hymenoptera: Anthophoridae).

Ophrys lacaena

P. DELFORGE

Etymology *lacaena:* Lacedaemonian, nickname given by Virgil to Leda, Queen of Sparta. **Type** Gr, Laconia (2004). **Synonyms** *O. candica* subsp. *lacaena* (P. DELFORGE) KREUTZ, *O. minoa* sensu P. DELFORGE p.p.

Description Slender, relatively spindly, 20-50cm tall; bracts long, longer than flowers; inflorescence very lax, up to 30cm tall; 4-12 flowers; sepals whitish, pink or lilac, rarely washed green, oval-lanceolate, 11-16mm x 6-10mm, spreading; petals villous, obliquely erect, triangular-rounded, very small, 1.5-3mm x 1.5-3mm, slightly darker than sepals; lip pendent or near horizontal, entire to sometimes 3-lobed, 10-16mm x 10-17mm (when spread), near quadrangular to trapezoid, convex, centre near globular, velvety, reddish-brown to blackish-purple, with 2 conical basal swellings, pointed, (2-) 4-7 (-10)mm long, erect, divergent and curved, with their inner face hairless, greenish-white, often streaked brown; complete submarginal band of dense, long hairs, brown to buff; margin of lip hairless, pendent or spreading and slightly reflexed, pale reddish-brown, sometimes faintly washed greenish-yellow; speculum very varied, occupying basal half of lip, greyish-blue to violet-purple, glossy, ± broadly edged whitish, broadly shield-shaped, surrounding the restricted, reddish basal field, elaborated by 1 central ocellus and 2 lateral ocelli, sometimes marbled or in the form of a much-thickened X prolonged by 2 isolated spots; appendage rather prominent, 1.5-3mm x 1.5-3mm, pointed, with 3 teeth or toothed, greenish-yellow, directed forwards to upwards, inserted into a weak notch; stigmatic cavity small, bordered by 2 black, shiny, rounded pseudo-eyes; column rather short, rather slightly acuminate; staminodial points often present.

Flowering Season Mid IV-V.

Habitat Usually mid-shade on dry to moist, alkaline substrates. The margins of scrub and scattered oakwoods, up to 450m asl. **Distribution** Peloponnese, perhaps also in Cythera, Dodecanese and Crete. Very rare and local. **Countries** ?Ae ?Cr Gr. **Photos** Gr, Lakonia (loc. typ.),

463

Ophrys candica
W. GREUTER, MATTHÄS & RISSE

Etymology *candica:* from Candia, currently Iraklion (Cr). **Type** Cr, Chania (1985). **Synonyms** *O. fuciflora* subsp. *candica* E. NELSON, *O. candica* (E. NELSON EX SOÓ) H. BAUMANN & KÜNKELE, *O. candica* subsp. *minoa* Ch. ALIBERTIS & A. ALIBERTIS, *O. minoa* (CH. ALIBERTIS & A. ALIBERTIS) P. DELFORGE, *O. candica* var. *minoa* (CH. ALIBERTIS & A. ALIBERTIS) H.F. PAULUS *et al.*

Description 15-40cm tall; bracts longer than ovary; 2-7 (-9) flowers; sepals white to pink, sometimes purplish or crimson, oval-lanceolate, 11.5-15mm x 4.5-8.5mm, spreading; petals villous, erect, triangular, sometimes auriculate, 2-4.5mm x 1.5-3mm, rarely darker than sepals, sometimes washed violet at base; lip pendent or near horizontal, entire, 9.5-14mm x 12-16mm (when spread), near quadrangular, convex, centre near globular, velvety, reddish-brown, rarely blackish, with a complete submarginal band of dense, long hairs, brown to silver-russet or whitish, rarely slightly attenuated on distal half of lip, with 2 small, rounded to near pointed basal swellings, hairless on inner face, sometimes elongated (= '*minoa*'), margins hairless, sometimes tinted greenish-yellow, turned down and back to slightly reflexed; speculum remarkable, greyish-blue to violet-purple, glossy, sometimes finely marbled, ± quadrangular, broadly edged white or yellowish, occupying basal half of lip, surrounding the small, reddish to brown basal field, encompassing basal swellings, sometimes emarginate at tip, rarely elaborated by 1-2 lateral lines or a central ocellus; appendage rather prominent, 1-3mm long and broad, pointed, with 3 teeth or toothed, greenish-yellow, very often directed upwards, inserted into a rather distinct notch; stigmatic cavity small, bordered by 2 black, shiny, rounded pseudo-eyes; staminodial points often present; column of various sizes and shapes, ± acuminate.

Variation Distinguished by its rather varied speculum, lip shape, the presence of basal swellings, sometimes prominent, and the petals, often more elongated in Italy, perhaps due to the influence of *O. apulica*, with which it can form hybrid swarms.

Flowering Season IV-V.

Habitat Full sun to mid-shade on alkaline to sometimes acidic, dry to moist substrates. Short grassland, abandoned cultivation, garrigue, scrub, open woodland, up to 900m asl. **Distribution** Range disjunct. Southern Puglia (It), Crete, the Aegean Islands from Samos to Rhodes, southwest Anatolia; reports from Peloponnese refer to *O. lacaena*, those from Sicily to *O. calliantha*. Rare and local. **Countries** Ae An Cr It. **Photos** Ae, Rhodes, 13.IV.1984; It, Lecce, 26.IV.1991. P. DELFORGE. **Pollinator** Perhaps *Eucera ehippia* (southern It) (Hymenoptera: Anthophoridae).

Ophrys parvimaculata
(O. DANESCH & E. DANESCH) H.F. PAULUS & GACK

Etymology *parvimaculata:* with a small speculum. **Type** It, Brindisi (1975). **Synonyms** *O. fuciflora* subsp. *parvimaculata* O. DANESCH & E. DANESCH, *O. holoserica* subsp. *parvimaculata* (O. DANESCH & E. DANESCH) O. DANESCH & E. DANESCH.

Description 10-30 (-40)cm tall; lower bracts longer than ovary; 2-7 flowers; sepals green, greenish, whitish, rarely washed pink, with green central vein, oval-lanceolate, margins strongly recurved, appearing narrow, 12-15.5mm x 6.5-8.5mm, spreading, slightly curved forwards, dorsal sepal erect and then ± strongly bent backwards; petals villous and ciliate, erect, triangular-lanceolate, 4-7mm x 2-4mm, colour as sepals or sometimes yellowish; lip pendent, entire, (9-) 10-14 (-15.5)mm x 13-19mm (when spread), trapezoid to orbicular, convex to near globular, velvety, ± dark reddish-brown, with complete submarginal band of dense, rather long hairs, brownish to whitish, with 2 small, distinct basal swellings, rounded to near pointed, sometimes with their inner face hairless and greenish-white, margins of lip hairless, rarely tinted greenish, reflexed forwards or turned down and under; speculum reduced, basal, bluish to purplish-grey, glossy, finely edged whitish, in the form of a ± thickened H or X and surrounding the brownish to greenish-orange basal field like a necklace, very rarely a ± complete central ocellus; appendage rather prominent, pointed, narrow at base, often with 3 teeth, greenish-yellow, directed forwards to upwards, inserted into a distinct notch; stigmatic cavity wider than high, cup-shaped, with 2 rounded to elliptical pseudo-eyes, very pale, and sometimes with an attenuated ridge overhanging the basal field; staminodial points often present; tip of column shortly acuminate.

Flowering Season IV-V.

Habitat Usually mid-shade, on moist, alkaline substrates. Associated principally with open woodland of Downy Oak *Quercus pubescens*, rarely short grassland, garrigue, scrub, up to 600m asl.

Distribution Endemic to the southeast of peninsular Italy, principally Puglia (from Foggia to Lecce) and Basilicate. Very rare and local.

Countries It.

Photos It, Foggia, 15.IV.1986. P. DELFORGE.

Pollinator *Eucera nigrescens* (Hymenoptera: Anthophoridae).

Ophrys biancae
(TODARO) MACCHIATI

Etymology Named after the Italian botanist G. Bianca (1801-1883). **Type** Si, Mount Iblees (1842). **Synonyms** *Arachnites biancae* TODARO, *Ophrys oxyrrhynchos* subsp. *biancae* (TODARO) GALESI, CRISTAUDO & MAUGERI, *O. holoserica* subsp. *biancae* (TODARO) N. FAURHOLDT & H.Æ. PEDERSEN, *O. discors* Bianca, *O. distefani* LOJACONO.

Description 10-25cm tall; 4-10 flowers; sepals white, pink or lilac, rarely washed green or greenish-white, lanceolate, 10-14mm x 5-7mm, (near) spreading; petals villous, short, obliquely erect, triangular, 2-3mm x 1.5-2.5mm, colour as sepals or sometimes yellowish; lip pendent to near horizontal, entire, 8-12mm x 10-15mm (when spread), near quadrangular to trapezoid, velvety, reddishbrown, often broadly edged yellow, convex, with 2 small, rounded (rarely near pointed) basal swellings; complete marginal band of long, dense, hairs, whitish to yellowish on shoulders, brownish and sometimes slightly reduced on distal half of lip; margin of lip hairless, spreading then sometimes ± strongly reflexed; speculum reduced, basal, glossy bluish-grey, edged white, in the form of a ± thickened X, sometimes with lateral branches, sometimes forming a central ocellus, surrounding the dark red to blackish basal field like a necklace; appendage prominent, up to 4mm tall, pointed, triangular or with 3 teeth, greenish-yellow, directed upwards, inserted into a deep notch; stigmatic cavity dark, brownish to blackish, rather small, with 2 pseudo-eyes; staminodial points absent; tip of column often very acuminate.

Variation Rather varied. Distinguished from *O. oxyrrhynchos* by small size of flowers, its colour and complete band of marginal hairs; clearly separated from *O. tenthredinifera,* especially by structure of column and stigmatic cavity.

Flowering Season III-IV, slightly before *O. oxyrrhynchos.*

Habitat Full sun to mid-shade on dry to moist, calcareous substrates. Short grassland, abandoned cultivation, garrigue, scrub, open pinewoods, up to 700m asl. **Distribution** Endemic to Sicily. The southeast (Siracusa, Raguse, Catane) and west (Trapani, Palermo) of the island. Local and rather rare. **Countries** Si. **Photos** Si, Ragusa, 22.III.2000; Siracusa, 7.IV.1987. P. DELFORGE.

Pollinator *Eucera euroa* (Hymenoptera: Anthophoridae).

Discussion The supposed hybrid origin of *Ophrys biancae* (*O. oxyrrhynchos* × *O. tenthredinifera*) is not supported by characters from that particular combination; the Sicilian species seems closer to the origins of the *O. bornmuelleri* group. A certain influence of *O. oxyrrhynchos*, often syntopic, is nevertheless plausible.

Ophrys chestermanii
(J.J. Wood) Gölz & H.R. Reinhard

Etymology Named after D. Chesterman, contemporary English botanist. **Type** Sa, Cagliari (1982). **Synonyms** *O. holoserica* subsp. *chestermanii* J.J. Wood, *O. fuciflora* subsp. *chestermanii* (J.J. Wood) H. Blatt & V. Wirth.

Description 10-30 (-40)cm tall; lower bracts longer than flower; 2-5 (-8) large flowers; sepals whitish to pink with green central vein, narrowly oval-lanceolate, 10-18mm x (4-) 5-8mm, spreading, curved forwards; petals villous, erect, narrowly triangular-lanceolate, 4-6.5mm x 1.5-3mm, colour as sepals or greenish to yellowish, sometimes washed purple; lip pendent, entire, (11-) 12-18mm x 15-23mm (when spread), broadly quadrangular to trapezoid, slightly convex, sometimes appearing obcordate, velvety, dark, brown to blackish-purple, with complete submarginal band of dense, rather long, crimson-brown hairs, and often 2 conical or rounded basal swellings, poorly developed, 1-3mm tall, hairless and yellowish on inner face, margins of lip hairless, tinted with purple or pale greenish, spreading then sometimes reflexed forwards in distal half; speculum basal, much reduced, glossy bluish-grey, sometimes finely edged greyish, in the form of a ± thickened H, surrounding the dark basal field like a necklace, very rarely with rudimentary lateral or distal branches; appendage prominent, up to 4mm long, pointed, narrow at base, rounded to ± clearly 3-toothed, greenish-yellow, directed forwards to upwards, inserted into a deep notch; stigmatic cavity cup-shaped, dark, 4-5mm wide, with 2 black, shiny, rounded pseudo-eyes; staminodial points present; column rather elongated, tip acuminate.

Flowering Season (III-) IV-V.

Habitat Usually mid-shade on moist, calcareous or schistose substrates, often rocky. Mossy areas in *Cistus* scrub and in open oakwoods with *Quercus ilex*, up to 700m asl.

Distribution Endemic to Sardinia. Very rare and local.

Countries Sa.

Photos Sa, Cagliari, 18.IV.1996. P. Delforge.

Pollinator The cuckoo-bee *Bombus* (*Psithyrus*) *vestalis* (Hymenoptera: Apidae).

467

Ophrys annae
J. DEVILLERS-TERSCHUREN & P. DEVILLERS

Etymology Named after Anne Devillers, daughter of the authors of the description. **Type** Sa, Sassari (1992). **Synonyms** *O. fuciflora* vel *holoserica* auct., *O. holoserica* subsp. *annae* (J. DEVILLERS-TERSCHUREN & P. DEVILLERS) H. BAUMANN *et al.*, *O. fuciflora* subsp. *annae* (J. DEVILLERS-TERSCHUREN & P. DEVILLERS) ENGEL & QUENTIN.

Description Rather spindly, 15-40cm tall; inflorescence lax; 3-8 (-12) rather small flowers; sepals white, pink, rarely green, oval, 8-14mm x 4-7.5mm, spreading, concave, curved forwards, dorsal sepal sometimes turned down onto column; petals villous, erect, triangular-rounded, often auriculate, 3-5.5mm x 1-4mm, colour as sepals; lip near horizontal to pendent, entire, 7-12mm x 9-15mm, quadrangular-rounded to trapezoid, velvety, dark brown, almost flat to sometimes very convex, with small, rounded, conical, basal swellings, divergent, inner face hairless and greenish; complete submarginal band of pale reddish hairs, rather long and dense; speculum basal, glossy bluish-grey, broadly edged greenish-yellow, quadrangular or in the form of a thickened X surrounding the dark basal field like a necklace and covering basal swellings, sometimes extended by lateral branches and a ± complete distal ocellus; appendage prominent, thick, pointed, with (1-) 3-6 teeth, greenish-yellow, directed forwards, inserted into a notch; stigmatic cavity transverse, demarcated at base by a protruding ridge, and bordered by 2 oblique, elliptical pseudo-eyes, often pale green, sometimes black; staminodial points usually absent.

Flowering Season (III-) IV-V, rather late.

Habitat Full sun to shade on dry to moist, calcareous substrates. Short grassland, garrigue, open woodland, olive groves, up to 500m asl. **Distribution** Endemic to Sardinia and Corsica. Local, but sometimes found in small populations. **Countries** Co Sa. **Photos** Sa, Cagliari, 17.IV.1996; Sassari, 2.V.1996. P. DELFORGE.

Pollinator *Osmia rufa* (Hymenoptera: Megachilidae).

468

The *Ophrys tetraloniae* group

Characters Petals villous, triangular, ± elongated; lip entire to 3-lobed, then with a scolopaxoid appearance; submarginal band of hairs broad and well visible on distal half of lip and above appendage, narrower or attenuated on latero-distal quarters; late flowering.

Ophrys conradiae
MELKI & DESCHÂTRES

Etymology Named after M. Conrad, Corsican botanist (1897-1990). **Type** Co (1993). **Synonyms** *O. scolopax* subsp. *conradiae* (MELKI & DESCHÂTRES) H. BAUMANN *et al.*, *O. scolopax* subsp. *sardoa* H. BAUMANN *et al.*, *O. sardoa* (H. BAUMANN *et al.*) H.F. PAULUS.

Description As *O. santonica* but 3-10 small to medium-sized flowers; sepals mostly whitish-green, rarely pinkish or whitish, 8-12.5mm long; petals villous, triangular, auriculate, 2.8-4.5mm long (mean sepal length/petal length ± 2.61), concolourous with sepals; lip near horizontal to pendent, appearing more elongated, more clearly scolopaxoid, 3-lobed to near entire, 9-13mm × 9.5-13.5mm (when spread), very convex transversally, velvety and blackish-brown in centre, with a submarginal band of pale hairs, attenuated towards lateral-distal quarters; median lobe near cylindrical to ± amphoroid or globular, sides turned down, ± narrowly hairless, greenish; lateral lobes forming 2 ± conical basal swellings, pointed or rounded; basal field rusty-brown; speculum varied but simpler, less extensive, purplish-grey edged whitish, shield-shaped to near quadrangular, surrounding basal field, with a central or reduced ocellus; appendage transverse, more prominent, greenish-yellow, sometimes pendent; stigmatic cavity relatively smaller, narrower at base, rusty-brown; pseudo-eyes hemispherical or formed by 2 oblique ridges; upper border of stigmatic cavity sometimes finely barred dark purple. NB **'sardoa'**: Taxon artificially uniting plants with smaller, more scolopaxoid flowers, a reduced speculum and pendent appendage. It falls, however, within range of variation of *O. conradiae*, which, like all the other species in the group, is large, sometimes spectacular, with flowers that have a ± 3-lobed, ± convex lip, sometimes recalling *O. fuciflora*.

Flowering Season Mid IV-VI, rather late.

Habitat Full sun to mid-shade on dry, calcareous substrates. Banks, short grassland, abandoned cultivation, garrigue, scrub, woodland edges, up to 400m asl.

Distribution Endemic to Sardinia and Corsica. Very rare and local. **Countries** Co Sa.

Photos Sa, Nuoro, 27.IV.1990. C.A.J. KREUTZ.

469

Ophrys santonica
MATHÉ & MELKI

Etymology *santonica:* from Saintonge (Ga). **Type** Ga, Charente (1994). **Synonyms** *O. aestivalis* MATHÉ & MELKI nom. illeg., *O. scolopax* subsp. *santonica* (MATHÉ & MELKI) ENGEL & QUENTIN, *O. juliana* KERGUÉLEN, *O. philipp(e)i* auct. non GRENIER.

Description Slender, 18-59cm tall; 3-15 small flowers; sepals pink, 7-11.5mm long, dorsal sepal often curved onto column; petals villous, triangular, auriculate, 3-6mm long (average sepal length/petal length ± 2.28); lip near horizontal to pendent, 3-lobed, scolopaxoid face-on, often appearing fucifloroid when viewed in profile, 7-10mm long, very convex transversally, near cylindrical, velvety and blackish-brown at centre, with 2 conical basal swellings, pointed or rounded, often forming lateral lobes; submarginal band of hairs pale, clearly attenuated on lateral-distal quarters; sides of distal half of lip turned down to slightly reflexed, ± narrowly hairless, greenish-yellow; basal field rusty-brown; speculum varied, rather extensive, purplish-grey edged whitish, surrounding basal field, often with central ocellus; appendage transverse, greenish-yellow; stigmatic cavity large, slightly or not at all constricted at base; pseudo-eyes formed by 2 oblique ridges; staminodial points sometimes present.

Flowering Season Late V-mid VIII, sporadic, late.

Habitat Full sun to mid-shade on dry, calcareous substrates. Banks, short grassland, abandoned cultivation, garrigue, scrub, woodland edges, up to 800m asl. **Distribution** Fragmented. From western (Saintonge) to southeast France (Alpes-Maritimes). Very rare and local. **Countries** Ga.

Photos A & C Ga, Charente, 22.VI.1996; **B** Aveyron, 25.VII.1983. P. DELFORGE.

Ophrys vetula
RISSO

Etymology *vetula:* old (an allusion to the resemblance of the speculum to a 'decrepit face', see photo A). **Type*** Ga, Alpes-Maritimes (1844). **Synonyms** *O. scolopax* subsp. *vetula* (BARLA) KREUTZ, *O. scolopax* var. *atropos* BARLA, *O. atropos* (BARLA) B.D. JACKSON, *O. scolopax* auct. non CAVANILLES.

Description As *O. santonica* but 15-50cm tall; 3-9 slightly larger flowers; sepals 8-12mm long; petals 3.5-5.5mm long; lip 7.5-11mm long, more fucifloroid, median lobe splayed, not rolled under, sides slightly recurved; speculum often more extensive; marginal band of hair only slightly attenuated on lateral-distal quarters; appendage more prominent, often clearly 3-toothed; stigmatic cavity more constricted, floor often of another colour and paler than basal field.

Flowering Season V-mid VII, late.

Habitat Full sun to mid-shade on dry, calcareous substrates. Banks, grassland, abandoned cultivation, scrub, woodland edges, open pinewoods, up to 700m asl. **Distribution** Southeast France and neighbouring regions of Liguria. Very rare and local. **Countries** Ga, It.

Photos A & C Ga, Alpes-Maritimes, 16.VI.1998; **B** Var, 15.V.2001. P. DELFORGE.

Key to the *Ophrys tetraloniae* group

1	Sepals green or whitish-green (70-100% of plants)	2
1*	Sepals white, pink, purple, exceptionally green	4
2	Petals yellowish	*O. posidonia*
2*	Petals and sepals concolourous	3

(continued on next page)

471

Ophrys elatior
GUMPRECHT ex H.F. PAULUS

Etymology *elatior:* higher. **Type** Ge, Baden-Württemberg (1996). **Synonyms** *O. fuciflora* subsp. *elatior* GUMPRECHT nom. illeg., *O. holoserica* subsp. *elatior* (GUMPRECHT) GUMPRECHT nom. illeg., *O. holoserica* subsp. *elatior* (GUMPRECHT ex H.F. PAULUS) H. BAUMANN & KÜNKELE, *O. fuciflora* subsp. *elatior* (GUMPRECHT ex H.F. PAULUS) ENGEL & QUENTIN.

Description (15-) 25-80 (-92)cm tall; inflorescence very lax; (2-) 8-14 (-21) small flowers; sepals pale pink to dark violet-purple, 8-13mm long, dorsal sepal erect to often ± curved onto column; petals triangular, ± clearly auriculate, frequently red, 3-6mm x 2-4mm (mean sepal length/petal length ± 2.32); lip pendent, trapezoid to quadrangular-rounded, entire, very rarely 3-lobed, 6-11 (-12)mm x 9.5-14mm (when spread), often with pointed basal swellings, convex transversally, centre near globular, on distal half border of lip dropping straight down or slightly reflexed, centre of lip velvety brown to blackish-brown; submarginal band of hairs brown, with beige reflections on basal half, band of hairs sometimes attenuated or difficult to see on distal half; speculum blue to reddish-brown, ± broadly edged yellowish, often more complex, encompassing inner face of basal swellings; stigmatic cavity and basal field concolourous, slightly paler than centre of lip; 2n=72.

Flowering Season VII-IX, very late, 4-8 weeks after *O. fuciflora.*

Habitat Full sun to mid-shade, mostly on dry to moist, alkaline substrates. Short grassland, abandoned cultivation, scrub, open woodland, most often growing on river banks, 200-500m asl. **Distribution** The Rhine valley between Strasbourg (Ga) and Basel (He) and the Rhône basin, south to Lyon. Very local and rather rare. **Countries** Ga Ge He. **Photos** Ge, Baden-Württemberg, 27.VII.1992; Ga, Rhône, 28.VII.1999. P. DELFORGE. **Pollinator** *Eucera salicariae* (Ge) (Hymenoptera: Anthophoridae).

Key to the *Ophrys tetraloniae* group
(continued from previous page)

3 lip entire to 3-lobed, with a fucifloroid or more rarely a scolopaxoid appearance, in which case it has long, divergent basal swellings .... *O. untchjii*
3* lip clearly 3-lobed, scolopaxoid, without very elongated basal swellings .... *O. conradiae*

4 lip 11-18mm long 5
4* lip 6-11mm long 6

5 basal field reddish, entire .... *O. aegirtica*
5* basal field dark brown, often cut into 2 parts by a ramification of the speculum ...*O. dinarica*

(continued on p. 479)

Ophrys aegirtica

P. DELFORGE

Etymology *aegirtica:* from Gers. Type Ga, Gers (1996). **Synonym** *O. truncata* DULAC nom. illeg.

Description Often slender, 15-50 (-68)cm tall; lower bract up to 3.5cm long; 2-7 (-10) rather large flowers; sepals intensely purple, rarely paler, 10-17mm x 5-10mm, concave, margins recurved, lateral sepals spreading, dorsal sepal erect then often strongly bent backwards; petals villous, erect, convex, triangular-elongated, auriculate, 3.5-6mm x 2-3.5mm (mean sepal length/ petal length ± 2.80), colour as or slightly darker than sepals, sometimes washed red or green; lip near horizontal to pendent, entire to obscurely 3-lobed, (9-) 11-18mm x11-20mm (when spread), quadrangular-rounded (optically), less often trapezoid, convex, centre sometimes near globular, velvety, dark brown, usually with 2 conical basal swellings, pointed or rounded, 0.5-3mm long, their internal face hairless, pale greyish-green; submarginal band of hairs long, pale, yellowish to reddish, always clearly visible on proximal half of lip, complete on distal half in 75% of plants; sides of distal half of lip spreading or turned under then slightly reflexed, narrowly hairless, sometimes tinted yellow; basal field rusty-brown; speculum varied, basal, shaped like a very thickened H or X, purplish-grey edged whitish, surrounding basal field, sometimes with central ocellus and ± complete lateral ocelli, and with yellowish or greenish streaks and lines encompassing the basal swellings; appendage well developed, greenish-yellow, with 3 teeth, directed forwards, inserted into a notch; stigmatic cavity transverse, delineated from basal field by a ridge, bordered by 2 dark pseudo-eyes; staminodial points present.

Flowering Season V-VI, late.

Habitat Full sun to mid-shade on dry to moist, alkaline substrates. Banks, bare patches in short grassland, pastures, abandoned cultivation and garrigue, up to 400m asl.

Distribution Southern France. Lower basin of the Rhône, southwest, in the north as far as Tarn. Local and rather rare.

Countries Ga.

Photos (**B** loc. typ.) Ga, Gers, 19.VI.1996; 12.VI.1995. P. DELFORGE.

Pollinator *Eucera taurica* (Hymenoptera: Anthophoridae).

473

Ophrys linearis
(Moggridge) P. Delforge et al.

Etymology *linearis:* linear (shape of petals). **Type** Ga, Alpes-Maritimes (1869). **Synonyms** *O. insectifera* subsp. *arachnites* subvar. *linearis* Moggridge, *O. fuciflora* var. *linearis* (Moggridge) E.G. Camus, Bergon & A. Camus, *O. holosericea* var. *linearis* (Moggridge) Landwehr, *O. holoserica* subsp. *linearis* (Moggridge) Kreutz, *O. arachnites* var. *filiforme* Risso, *O. pseudoscolopax* auct. non Moggridge.

Description As *O. aegirtica* but petals elongated, often appearing linear due to rolled margins, 4.5-8mm long (sepal length/petal length = up to 1.5); lip globular at centre and sometimes very convex laterally, entire to near entire or obscurely 3-lobed, 8-12.5mm long, centre velvety, surrounded by a band of honey-coloured submarginal hairs, sometimes attenuated on lateral-distal quarters, in turn bordered by a hairless greenish-yellow or reddish-brown margin which may be up to 3mm wide; basal swellings sometime prominent, curved outwards and slightly pointed; speculum basal, usually complex and extensive, sometimes candicoid or, if simpler, recalling *O. tenthredinifera* s.l.; staminodial points usually present; tip of column acuminate, sometimes long-acuminate.

Flowering Season IV-V.

Habitat Full sun to mid-shade on dry to moist, calcareous substrates. Short grassland, pastures, abandoned cultivation, garrigue, scrub, woodland edges, up to 1100m asl. **Distribution** Southeastern France, reported in west to Ardèche and north to Drôme; probably in Tuscany as well. Local and rather rare. **Countries** Ga ?It.

Photos Ga, Bouches-du-Rhône, 23.IV.1999. P. Delforge.

Discussion of the *Ophrys tetraloniae* group

Perhaps monophyletic, principally central (sub-) Mediterranean in distribution, comprising 13 late to very late flowering species. On the basis of various characters (submarginal band of hairs ± attenuated on lateral-distal quarters, tendency to a scolopaxoid appearance), their lip structure appears intermediate between the *O. bornmuelleri*, *O. fuciflora* and *O. scolopax* groups. This assemblage appears rather coherent and may derive from an ancestral species close to the root of the whole *O. fuciflora* complex. This late-flowering taxon diversified through the attraction of new pollinators on a basis of size and geographical and temporal isolation, with the emergence of at least one very late-flowering tetraploid species, reaching the southern parts of mid-Europe via the Rhône and Rhine. Polyphyly for the group is, however, equally plausible; several species may have originated from introgression and hybridisation with various species from neighbouring groups.

Ophrys brachyotes
REICHENBACH

Etymology *-otes:* with ears, *brachy-:* short (an allusion to the small lateral lobes of the lip). **Type** It, Genoa (1830). **Synonyms** *O. fuciflora* vel *holoserica* vel *elatior* vel *serotina* auct., *O. gresivaudanica* O. GERBAUD, *O. holoserica* subsp. *gresivaudanica* (O. GERBAUD) KREUTZ.

Description Slender, 17-41 (-56)cm tall; inflorescence lax; 3-11 (-15) rather small flowers; sepals pink to purple, 9-12.5mm long; petals concolourous, villous, triangular-elongated, ± auriculate, 3-6mm long (mean sepal length/petal length ± 2.2); lip pendent, quadrangular (optically), obscurely to clearly 3-lobed, sometimes scolopaxoid, 7-13 (-14)mm x 9-15mm, near globular, velvety and reddish-brown in centre, with 2 conical basal swellings, pointed or rounded, often forming lateral lobes; submarginal band of hairs pale, attenuated on lateral-distal quarters; sides of distal half of lip turned down to slightly reflexed, ± narrowly hairless and greenish-yellow; basal field rusty-brown, ± dark; speculum basal, varied, edged whitish, surrounding basal field; appendage transverse, greenish-yellow, inserted into a slight notch; stigmatic cavity 3-4.5mm wide, lighter than basal field; pseudo-eyes formed by 2 oblique, rounded ridges; staminodial points present.

Flowering Season V-VI (-VII). **Habitat** Full sun on dry, alkaline to neutral substrates. Banks, short grassland, pastures, abandoned cultivation, scrub, woodland edges, up to 1000m asl. **Distribution** Sub-Mediterranean. Northern Italy, southeast France: the upper Rhône basin as far as Switzerland. Rather local and rather rare. **Countries** Ga He It. **Photos** It, Verona, 11.V.1988; Ga, Var, 16.V.2001; Isère (loc. typ. of *O. gresivaudanica*), 11.VI.1997. P. DELFORGE.

475

Ophrys medea

P. DEVILLERS & J. DEVILLERS-TERSCHUREN

Etymology Named after Medea, princess of Colchide. **Type** Ju, Croatia, Cres Island (2004). **Synonyms** *O. fuciflora* vel *O. holoserica* vel *O. serotina* auct.

Description Slender, up to 50cm tall; 5-11 rather small flowers, slender; sepals white to pink, 10-14mm long; petals concolourous, triangular, sometimes falcate, 2-3.5mm x 1-2mm, relatively small (mean sepal length/petal length ± 3.5); lip trapezoid to rounded-quadrangular, 8-12mm long, entire and splayed to ± clearly 3-lobed, slightly to very convex laterally, centre blackish-brown, with small, pointed basal swellings, 1-3mm long, and a very thin, hairless, yellow margin, sometimes scalloped; submarginal band of hairs often attenuated on lateral-distal quarters; speculum basal, not very extensive, with a pale edge, its branches encompassing basal swellings and demarcating a reddish to blackish basal field; stigmatic cavity slightly paler; appendage well developed, multi-toothed (see note next page).

Flowering Season V-mid VI.

Habitat Full sun to mid-shade on dry to moist, alkaline substrates. Banks, short grassland, pastures, abandoned cultivation, garrigue, scrub, woodland edges, up to 800m asl.

Distribution Sub-Mediterranean. Istria, Quarnero archipelago. Local and rather rare.

Countries Ju.

Photos A Ju, Hrvatska, Krk, 13.V.2004; **B & C** Istria, 31.V.2002. P. DELFORGE.

476

Ophrys untchjii
(M. Schulze in Ascherson & Gräbner) P. Delforge

Etymology Named after Untchj, Croatian botanist who collected the plant. **Type** Ju, Istria (1907). **Synonyms** *O. fuciflora* var. *untchjii* M. Schulze in Ascherson & Gräbner, *O. holoserica* subsp. *untchjii* (M. Schulze in Ascherson & Gräbner) Kreutz comb. inval.

Description Rather thickset, 13-30cm tall; lower bracts far longer than flowers; inflorescence near lax; 3-9 rather small flowers; sepals green (70-80% of plants), whitish-green, white or rarely pink or pale purple, broadly oval, margins recurved, 9-13 (-15)mm x 7-9mm, spreading; petals villous, erect, triangular, often auriculate, 2-6mm long, colour as sepals, sometimes a little crimson at base; lip pendent, entire to clearly 3-lobed, in that case with a scolopaxoid appearance, 9-13 (-15.5)mm x 10-14 (-16)mm, quadrangular to trapezoid (when spread), velvety, dark brown, globular in centre, convex to very rolled up transversally, slightly convex longitudinally, with near pointed basal swellings, divergent, sometimes very elongated, greenish-white on their inner face; submarginal band of hairs complete to very attenuated on lateral-distal quarters, lighter and more reddish than centre; sides of lip turned down, flat or slightly reflexed, sometimes with a very narrow hairless margin, reddish or greenish-yellow, rarely broadly greenish-yellow; speculum basal, shiny bluish-grey, edged whitish, formed into a thickened H or X shape and surrounding the basal field, with 2 lateral ocelli and often a ± complete distal ocellus; appendage prominent, thick, transverse, with 2-5 teeth, greenish-yellow, directed upwards, inserted into a notch; stigmatic cavity and basal field reddish-brown to blackish, concolourous with centre of lip; stigmatic cavity with a reduced ledge and 2 circular pseudoeyes, a whitish vault, marked with a purple transverse bar often extending onto lateral margins, upper margins also frequently underlined by a purple line; staminodial points present; external walls of stigmatic cavity white, rather contrasting.

Flowering Season Mid IV-mid VI.

Habitat Full sun to mid-shade on dry to moist, calcareous substrates. Short grassland, abandoned cultivation, garrigue, scrub, edges, up to 700m asl.

Distribution Sub-Mediterranean. Apparently Endemic to Croatia (Istria, Quarnero archipelago, hinterland of Split).

Countries Ju. Photos Ju, Istria, 28.V.2002; Krk, 12.V.2004. P. Delforge.

Pollinator Probably *Eucera clypeata* (Hymenoptera: Anthophoridae).

Note Hybrids with *O. medea* are frequent. They can be distinguished by the sepals, which are green washed purple.

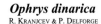

Ophrys dinarica
R. KRANJCEV & P. DELFORGE

Etymology *dinarica:* of Mount Dinara. **Type** Ju, Croatia, Lika (2004). **Synonym** *O. holoserica* subsp. *dinarica* (R. KRANJCEV & P. DELFORGE) KREUTZ.

Description Robust, 20-68cm tall; 4-10 (-12) rather large flowers; sepals oval-lanceolate, 10-12 (-15)mm x 5-7 (-8)mm, pink to dark violet, more rarely white or pale green; petals triangular, auriculate, 3.2-5.1mm x 1.5-2.9mm, villous, ciliate, darker; lip dark brown, oboval to trapezoidal, entire to rarely obscurely 3-lobed, (10-) 12-15 (16.5)mm x 10-18mm (when spread), globular and velvety in centre, very convex and sometimes rolled up longitudinally, in that case appearing scolopaxoid, with robust, divergent, near pointed basal swellings, (2-) 3-7 (-8)mm long, and a submarginal band of hairs, lighter and more russet than centre, slightly to very attenuated on lateral-distal quarters; sides of lip turned down to sometimes slightly reflexed, with a

hairless greenish-yellow margin to distal half of lip, sometimes rather broad, sometimes jagged; speculum very well developed and complex, sometimes marbled, bluish-grey to glossy reddish, broadly edged yellowish; apendage prominent, thick, transverse, with 3-7 teeth, greenish-yellow, directed upwards to horizontal; stigmatic cavity and basal field brown, often cut longitudinally into 2 parts by a ramification of speculum that reaches the macular stage or by an approximation of this; pseudo-eyes formed by 2 ridges, dark greenish, sometimes less colourful, yellowish, olive-green; staminodial points sometimes lacking.

Flowering Season Mid V-VI, late.

Habitat Full sun on dry to moist, ± neutral substrates. Short grassland, abandoned cultivation, garrigue, scrub, woodland edges, 350-800m asl. **Distribution** Sub-Mediterranean. Apparently endemic to Dalmatia (valleys in the foothills of Mount Dinara, Knin/Sinj region). **Countries** Ju. **Photos** Ju, Lika (A holotype), 27.V.2004; Dalmatinska Zagora, 26.V.2004. P. DELFORGE.

Ophrys tetraloniae
TESCHNER

Etymology *tetraloniae:* associated with bees of the genus *Tetralonia* (now usually subsumed within genus *Eucera*). **Type** Ju, Istria (1987). **Synonym** *O. holoserica* subsp. *tetraloniae* (TESCHNER) KREUTZ.

Description Rather spindly, (12-) 30-51cm tall; lower bracts longer than flowers; inflorescence lax; 3-9 rather small flowers; sepals white, pink or rarely green, oval, margins recurved, 9-10mm x 4-5mm, spreading, concave, curved forwards; petals villous, erect, triangular-rounded, 3-4.5mm x 3-4.5mm, colour as sepals (mean sepal length/petal length ± 2.5); lip near horizontal, entire, 7-11mm x 8-13mm, obcordate (when spread), velvety, dark brown, convex, basal swellings absent or small and rounded, complete submarginal band of hairs, rather short and dense, whitish on shoulders, brownish on distal half, margins of lip hairless, tinted reddish or greenish-yellow; speculum basal, glossy bluish-grey, broadly edged white, in the form of a thickened H or X surrounding the dark basal field like a necklace and covering the basal swellings, sometimes extended by distal and/or lateral branches; appendage more or less prominent, thick, pointed, with 3 teeth, greenish-yellow, directed forwards, inserted into a notch; stigmatic cavity 3-3.5mm wide, with a ledge demarcating the basal field and 2 circular pseudo-eyes; staminodial points present.

Flowering Season Mid V-VII.

Habitat Full sun to mid-shade on moist, alkaline substrates. Short grassland, pastures, scrub, 250-600m asl. **Distribution** Istria and central Dalmatia, Knin/Sinj region. **Countries** Ju.

Photos A & C Ju, Istria, 1.VI.2002. P. DELFORGE; **B** (holotype), 25.VI.1986. W. TESCHNER. **Pollinators** *Eucera fulvescens* and *E. inulae* (Hymenoptera: Anthophoridae).

Key to the *Ophrys tetraloniae* group
(continued from p. 472)

6   lip 3-lobed, clearly scolopaxoid when viewed face-on ....

6*   lip entire to 3-lobed, mostly appearing fucifloroid 7

7   flowering VII-IX .... *O. elatior*

7*   flowering IV-VI (-VII) 7

8   petals 4.5-8mm long, more than half length of sepals .... *O. linearis*

8*   petals shorter, less than half length of sepals 9

(continued on p. 481)

Ophrys posidonia
P. DELFORGE

Etymology *posidonia:* from Poseidon, Greek god of the sea, to whom is dedicated the Roman town of Pæstum, whose ancient Greek name is Posidonia. **Type** It, Salerno (2000). **Synonyms** *O. holoserica* subsp. *posidonia* (P. DELFORGE) KREUTZ, *O. elatior* vel *tetraloniae* vel *parvimaculata* auct.

Description Slender and rather spindly, 15-40 (-60)cm tall, rachis, bracts and floral buds whitish-green; inflorescence lax; 3-8 (-11) flowers small, the lowest inserted high on the stem; sepals greenish, whitish-green, whitish (30% of plants), exceptionally lightly washed pinkish, papillose on internal face, lateral sepal 7-12mm x 4-6mm; petals triangular-rounded, sometimes auriculate, 2.5-5mm x 2.5-4mm, relatively short (sepal length/petal length ± 3), very villous and ciliate, deep yellowish-green, sometimes tinted purple at base; lip entire, rarely ± clearly 3-lobed and scolopaxoid (10% of plants, photo B), rather globular, quadrangular to trapezoid-rounded (when spread), 7-10mm x 10.5-13.5mm, centre blackish-brown to reddish-brown and velvety, with 2 small, rounded basal swellings, hairless on inner face, sides straight, turned down or more rarely recurved forwards, ± broadly bright yellow to bright greenish-yellow; band of (sub-) marginal hairs usually complete, hairs long, very pale – pale yellowish on yellow portion of margins, brownish otherwise, whitish on shoulders; speculum basal, pale violet, edged pale yellowish, sometimes simply near quadrangular, often extended, fragmented and complicated with 1-2 central ocelli and ± complete lateral ocelli encompassing basal swellings; basal field coloured as centre of lip or paler, rusty-brown; appendage bright yellow, well developed, 3-5 teeth, thick, erect; stigmatic cavity concolourous with basal field, relatively small, with 2 oblique, shiny pseudo-eyes, horizontal ledge absent; staminodial points present.

Flowering Season Late V-mid VII, very late.

Habitat Full sun on dry to damp, calcareous substrates. Seepages on marly pastures and abandoned cultivation, scrub, open oakwoods and their edges, up to 1050m asl. **Distribution** Tyrrhenian, disjunct. Southern Latium, Campania (principally Cilento), northern Calabria. Local and rather rare. **Countries** It.

Photos (C loc. typ.) It, Salerno, 29 & 30.V.2000. P. DELFORGE.

480

Ophrys serotina
ROLLI ex H.F. PAULUS

Etymology *serotina:* late. **Type** It, Frosinone (2000). **Synonyms** *O. fuciflora* vel *O. holoserica* vel *O. elatior* auct., *O. holoserica* subsp. *serotina* (ROLLI EX H.F. PAULUS) KREUTZ, *O. fuciflora* subsp. *lorenae* DE MARTINO & CENTURIONE.

Description Slender, up to 40cm tall; 4-10 flowers; sepals white to dark crimson-pink, rarely greenish-white, 8-13 (-15)mm long; petals of various colours, shapes and sizes, triangular-rounded, sometimes auriculate, 2.5-5mm x 2-3.5mm (sepal length/petal length ± 2.7); lip trapezoid-rounded, (6-) 7-13 (-14.5)mm x 8-15.5mm, entire to ± clearly 3-lobed, slightly to very convex, blackish-brown to red-brown in centre, often with relatively prominent basal swellings, curved outwards and with a yellow margin; submarginal band of hairs rather attenuated on lateral-distal quarters; appendage well developed, multi-toothed; speculum rather extensive, with pale edges and 2-4 ± complete ocelli; basal field pale to dark reddish; stigmatic cavity blackish to dark greenish, 2-3mm wide, small relative to size of lip, bordered by 2 whitish to blackish-green, circular pseudo-eyes.

Flowering Season V-VI, rather late.

Habitat Full sun to mid-shade on dry to moist, alkaline substrates. Banks, short grassland, pastures, abandoned cultivation, garrigue, scrub, woodland edges, up to 1000m asl. **Distribution** Probably endemic to central peninsular Italy. Local and rather rare. **Countries** It.

Photos It, Frosinone, 23.V.2000. P. DELFORGE.

Key to the *Ophrys tetraloniae* group

(continued from p. 479)

9   petals and lip short in comparison to sepals (L sepals/L petals ± 3.5) ....*O. medea*

9*   petals and lip longer 10

10   petals as broad as long ....*O. tetraloniae*

10* petals elongated, longer than broad 11

11   stigmatic cavity 3-4.5mm wide, paler than basal field .... *O. brachyotes*

11* stigmatic cavity narrower, as dark as, or darker than, basal field ....*O. serotina*

12   median lobe strongly rolled up, sides straight or more often turned down and under .... *O. santonica*

12* median lobe slightly rolled up, sides straight or, more usually, recurved outwards ....*O. vetula*

The *Ophrys fuciflora* group

Characters Petals villous, often auriculate and then abruptly triangular; lip entire, rarely 3-lobed, margins often reflexed on distal half of lip; submarginal band of hairs attenuated to absent on distal half, except above appendage; pseudo-eyes formed by the reduction of the internal stigmatic lips; appendage prominent, with 3 teeth, inserted into a notch.

Ophrys gracilis
(BÜEL, O. DANESCH & E. DANESCH) ENGLMAIER

Etymology *gracilis:* spindly. **Type** It, Salerno (1973). **Synonyms** *O. fuciflora* subsp. *gracilis* BÜEL, O. DANESCH & E. DANESCH, *O. holoserica* subsp. *gracilis* (BÜEL, O. DANESCH & E. DANESCH) BÜEL, O. DANESCH & E. DANESCH, *O. gracilis* (BÜEL, O. DANESCH & E. DANESCH) H.F. PAULUS isonym.

Description Slender, 17-45cm tall; 4-10 (-11) rather small flowers; sepals oval-rounded, 9-13.5mm long, intense crimson-pink, rarely pure white; petals villous, relatively small, 1.2-3.4 (-4.2)mm long (mean sepal length/petal length = 3.37), triangular, concolourous with sepals or slightly darker, very divergent; lip quadrangular-rounded, rather globular, regularly convex, almost never 3-lobed or scolopaxoid, 7-11mm long, sides dropping straight down, rarely tinted yellow; lip evenly velvety and brown to the margins, slightly paler on shoulders, almost without any trace of a marginal rim; basal swellings poorly marked; appendage prominent, multi-toothed, separated from border of lip by a short stalk sometimes surmounted by a small tuft of hair; speculum in the form of a rather simple basal X, transverse, encompassing shoulders, sometimes marbled, sometimes prolonged by a central fragmentary ocellus; stigmatic cavity and basal field concolourous with centre of lip or slightly lighter and reddish; stigmatic cavity with a distinct horizontal ledge; pseudo-eyes rather unobtrusive, rounded, linked to external walls by white bridles; upper border of stigmatic cavity finely barred purple; staminodial points rather small, often absent.

Flowering Season V-VI.

Habitat Full sun to mid-shade on dry to moist, calcareous substrates. Short grassland, abandoned cultivation, scrub, open woodland and its edges, up to 1000m asl. **Distribution** Poorly known due to confusion with closely related taxa. Central peninsular Italy, from Tuscany to Basilicata, probably also southeast France, especially in Drôme. **Countries** Ga It.

Photos It, Potenza, 25.V.2000; Salerno, 30.V.2000. P. DELFORGE.

Pollinator Probably *Eucera clypeata* (Hymenoptera: Anthophoridae).

Ophrys calliantha
BARTOLO & PULVIRENTI

Etymology *calli-:* beautiful; *-antha:* flower. **Type** Si, Siracusa (1997). **Synonyms** *O. oxyrrhynchos* subsp. *calliantha* (BARTOLO & PULVIRENTI) GALESI, CRISTAUDO & MAUGERI, *O. candica* subsp. *calliantha* (BARTOLO & PULVIRENTI) KREUTZ, *O. fuciflora* vel *O. holoserica* vel *O. candica* auct.

Description As *O. oxyrrhynchos* but more slender, (15-) 20-35 (-50)cm tall; 4-8 flowers; sepals pinkish to purplish, without a green suffusion, 13-18mm x 5-7mm, dorsal sepal sometimes turned backwards; petals sometimes auriculate, 1.5-3mm x 1-3mm, colour as sepals or slightly more crimson; lip near horizontal to pendent, entire, 10-15mm x 12-16mm (when spread), trapezoid to quadrangular-rounded, reddish-brown, basal swellings small to near absent, rounded, white at least on inner face, margins of lip broadly pale brown, without orange or bright yellow, spreading then ± reflexed on distal half; speculum basal, more extensive, glossy purplish-grey, more broadly edged white (appearing less complex than in *O. oxyrrhynchos*, often recalling *O. candica*); appendage often less prominent, pointed, with 1-3 teeth, orange to reddish, rarely greenish; stigmatic cavity strongly constricted at base, appearing proportionally very small; basal field cramped, rusty-brown; staminodial points sometimes present.

Flowering Season IV-V, after *O. oxyrrhynchos*.

Habitat Full sun on dry, calcareous substrates. Garrigue, open scrub, up to 500m asl.

Distribution Sicily. Very local and often very rare. **Countries** Si. **Photos** Si, Siracusa, 24.IV.2000. P. DELFORGE.

Key to the *Ophrys fuciflora* group

1   lip 11-14mm long, always very broadly edged bright yellow; stigmatic cavity cramped, 1.4-2mm broad .... *O. lacaitae*

1* flowers otherwise 2

2   sepals purplish, pink, white, without any green tones 3

2* sepals greenish, or crimson, pinkish or whitish washed green 6

3   petals (4-) 5.5-9mm long .... *O. apulica*

3* petals 1.2-5 (-6)mm long 4

4   petals 3-5 (-6)mm long .... *O. fuciflora*

4* petals 1.2-3.4 (-4.2)mm long 5

5   lip 10-15mm long; stigmatic cavity small, very narrow .... *O. calliantha*

5* lip 7-11mm long; stigmatic cavity relatively broad .... *O. gracilis*

(continued on next page)

Ophrys lacaitae
LOJACONO

Etymology Named after C.C. Lacaita, English botanist (1853-1933). **Type** Si, 'Cozzo Croci' (1909). **Synonyms** *O. fuciflora* subsp. *lacaitae* (LOJACONO) SOO, *O. oxyrrhynchos* subsp. *lacaitae* (LOJACONO) DEL PRETE.

Description As *O. oxyrrhynchos*, but general coloration whitish-green; bracts much longer than flowers; sepals whitish-green to (sometimes) white, with 1-3 longitudinal green veins, 11.5-14mm x 5-6.5mm; petals very small, whitish, 1.5-3mm x 1.5-3mm; lip 11-14mm x 14-18.5mm, central surface very limited, near globular, velvety, pale reddish-brown to blackish-purple, with reduced, rounded basal swellings, shoulders of lip with long, dense, yellowish, whitish or orange hairs, distal half of lip hairless or almost so, margins very broadly coloured bright yellow, spreading then reflexed forwards; speculum glossy bluish-grey, ± broadly edged yellowish, in the form of an H surrounding the cramped basal field like a necklace, extended by small, lightly-coloured distal and lateral branches; appendage prominent, yellow, directed forwards; stigmatic cavity very cramped, 1.4-2mm wide, column short, acuminate, making an obtuse angle with lip.

Flowering Season III-VI, 2-4 weeks after *O. oxyrrhynchos*. **Habitat** Full sun to mid-shade on calcareous to rather acidic, dry to moist substrates. Short grassland, scrub, open woodland, up to 1200m asl. **Distribution** Malta (1 plant !), Sicily and southern Italy: Potenza, Salerno, Isernia, Latina, Foggia (Mount Gargano), also Croatia (Vis Island). Very local and often very rare. **Countries** It Ju ?†Me Si. **Photos** It, Latina, 2.VI.1984; Si, Messina, 28.IV.2000. P. DELFORGE. **Pollinator** *Eucera eucnemidea* (It) (Hymenoptera: Anthophoridae).

Key to the *Ophrys fuciflora* group
(continued from previous page)

6 petals 1.5-3.5mm long; lip appendage very pointed .... *O. oxyrrhynchos*
6* petals 3-6mm long; appendage slightly pointed .... *O. celiensis*

Discussion of the *Ophrys fuciflora* group

Perhaps monophyletic, mostly Italian (It Si) and mid-European, with 7 species belonging to the middle or end of the main flush of flowering in the genus *Ophrys* and probably deriving from a common ancestor with characters close to the root of the complex. They show a least one derived character, a significant reduction in, or even the absence of, marginal hairs on the distal half of the lip. The group may have a Sicilian origin and

(continued on p. 486)

Ophrys oxyrrhynchos
TODARO

Etymology *-rhynchos:* [with a] beak; *oxy-:* pointed (an allusion to the appendage). **Type** Si, Palermo (1840). **Synonym** *O. fuciflora* subsp. *oxyrrhynchos* (TODARO) SOO.

Description Thickset, 10-25 (-35)cm tall; 3-8 flowers; sepals green to whitish often washed purplish-pink, oval-lanceolate, margins reflexed, 11-15mm x 5-8mm, spreading, curved forwards then sometimes bent back; petals villous, ciliate, often obliquely erect, triangular, sometimes auriculate, 1.5-3.5mm x 2-3mm, yellowish, purple or as sepals; lip near horizontal, entire, 9.5-12mm x 14-18mm (when spread), trapezoid to obcordate, slightly convex and velvety in centre, reddish-brown, basal swellings often prominent but rounded, white at least on inner face, marginal band of hairs incomplete, rather long, dense and white to brownish on shoulders, then attenuating, margins broadly coloured pale brown, orange or bright yellow, hairless to finely velvety, spreading then reflexed on distal half of lip; speculum basal, glossy purplish-grey, edged white, rarely marbled, sometimes in the form of a thickened X surrounding the reddish basal field, extended by lateral anchors, or more complex, sometimes with 1-4 ± regular ocelli; appendage prominent, pointed, with 1-4 teeth, orange to greenish-yellow, directed forwards to upwards, inserted into a deep notch; stigmatic cavity dark, 2-3.5mm wide internally, with 2 rounded to elliptical pseudo-eyes; column with white external walls, tip ± acuminate, making an acute angle with lip; staminodial points sometimes present.

Variation Colour, shape and markings of lip varied. Distinguished by the colour of the sepals and the size of the lip and its prominent appendage. Nevertheless, separation from *O. calliantha, O. lacaitae* and hybrid *O. lacaitaemm* × *O. fuciflora* s.l. (*O. fuciflora, O. gracilis*...) is sometimes difficult.

Flowering Season III-V.

Habitat Full sun to mid-shade on dry to moist, calcareous substrates. Short grassland, abandoned cultivation, garrigue, scrub, open woodland, up to 800m asl.

Distribution Sicily and southern Italy; many reports from southern Italy, however, often refer to *O. celiensis* or hybrids between *O. lacaitae* and *O. gracilis,* principally. Rather local and rather rare.

Countries It †Me Si.

Photos Si, Palermo, 17.IV.2000; Caltanissetta 19.IV.2000. P. DELFORGE.

Ophrys celiensis
(O. DANESCH & E. DANESCH) P. DELFORGE

Etymology *celiensis:* from Ceglie-Messapico (Brindisi). **Type** It, Brindisi (1970). **Synonyms** *O. fuciflora* subsp. *celiensis* O. DANESCH & E. DANESCH, *O. oxyrrhynchos* subsp. *celiensis* (O. DANESCH & E. DANESCH) DEL PRETE.

Description Plant and flowers intermediate between *O. oxyrrhynchos* and *O. apulica*. As *O. oxyrrhynchos*, but 3-6 flowers; sepals pink to purplish-pink washed or tinted green; petals longer and broader, auriculate then long-triangular, 3-6mm x 2-4.5mm, base sometimes contiguous, darker than sepals, often tinted yellowish or greenish; lip pendent, entire, 9-15mm x 11-18mm (when spread), trapezoid, slightly convex, reddish-brown, often without basal swellings, margins of distal half hairless to finely velvety, very spreading then reflexed; speculum very diverse and complex; appendage less prominent, slightly pointed, often transverse and without distinct teeth; column with less contrasting external walls, tip less acuminate, forming a more open angle with lip; staminodial points present.

Flowering Season IV-V.

Habitat As *O. oxyrrhynchos*, up to 500m asl.

Distribution Apparently endemic to central Puglia, principally the region between Brindisi, Bari and Tarente; similar plants have recently been reported from Madonies (Si) (*Ophrys cephaloeditana* Falci, Giardina & Serio nom. nud.). Very local and rather rare. **Countries** It ?Si. **Photos** It, Brindisi (loc. typ.), 27.IV.1991. P. DELFORGE. **Pollinator** *Eucera graeca* (Hymenoptera: Anthophoridae).

Note Sometimes considered as *O. oxyrrhynchos-mm* × *O. apulica*, giving the superficial appearance, due to its variability, of stabilised hybrid swarms. It is not certain, however, either that *O. oxyrrhynchos* is a direct parent of *O. celiensis* or that it is a hybrid. Its numerous morphological differences from *O. apulica* and the attraction of a specific pollinator are arguments in favour of specific status for this taxon.

Discussion of the *Ophrys fuciflora* group

(continued from p. 484)

is composed of some visually very diverse species, adapted to different pollinators, themselves very diverse. *O. fuciflora*, which may seem to be the central figure in the group is one of its most recent representatives, able to colonise some of the less chilly habitats of mid-Europe. The other species, with more restricted distributions, seem to be closely related, deriving from a common ancestor with a prominent appendage and a lip with hairless margins, spreading in the distal half. In *O. lacaitae* this ancestor has been expressed in a very unusual way.

Ophrys apulica
(O. DANESCH & E. DANESCH) O. DANESCH & E. DANESCH

Etymology *apulica:* from Puglia. **Type** It, Lecce (1970). **Synonyms** *O. fuciflora* subsp. *apulica* O. DANESCH & E. DANESCH, *O. holoserica* subsp. *apulica* (O. DANESCH & E. DANESCH) BUTTLER.

Description 15-35 (-55)cm tall; 3-8 (-14) large flowers; sepals pale pink to dark purplish, oval-lanceolate, margins reflexed, 14-18.5mm x 7-10mm, spreading; petals villous, erect, triangular-lanceolate, often auriculate and contiguous, (4-) 5.5-9mm x 3-5mm, colour as sepals, sometimes edged with red; lip pendent, (near) entire, 13-18mm x 17-22mm (when spread), trapezoid to near obcordate, convex, often constricted in middle, velvety, pale brown to blackish-purple, with pointed basal swellings 1-4mm long, hairless and brownish to whitish on inner face, lip with rather long hairs, dense and whitish to russet on shoulders, then brownish and becoming thinner, margins of distal half of lip sometimes lighter, hairless to velvety, turned down and back then fully reflexed forwards; speculum basal, bluish-grey or reddish, shiny, edged whitish or yellowish, in the form of a thickened H surrounding the reddish basal field, with lateral branches, sometimes marbled, often misshapen and complex, with 1-3 central and 2-6 lateral ocelli; appendage prominent, pointed, 3-7 ± distinct teeth, greenish-yellow, directed forwards to upwards, inserted into a deep notch; stigmatic cavity dark, 3-4mm wide, with 2 black, shiny, rounded pseudo-eyes; column relatively small, acuminate, ± perpendicular to lip; staminodial points often present.

Variation Distinct from related Italian taxa by its large flowers and the length of the petals; also separated from *O. episcopalis* by the latter character, as well as the marginal lip hairs and taller stigmatic cavity.

Flowering Season (III-) IV-V.

Habitat As *O. oxyrrhynchos*, up to 900m asl.

Distribution Southern Italy, in the north from Molise and Mount Gargano (Foggia). Rather widespread and sometimes abundant in its stations. Reports from Tuscany and Umbria require confirmation, those from Hvar Island (Ju, Croatia, Dalmatia) refer to *O. pharia*, those from the Aegean Islands (Cyclades, Kos, Rhodes...) refer to *O. episcopalis*, *O. calypsus* var. *calypsus* and var. *pseudoapulica*, *O.* 'maxima' or hybrid swarms.

Countries It.

Photos It, Lecce, 25.IV.1991; Brindisi, 31.III.1986. P. DELFORGE.

Pollinator *Eucera* (*Synhalonia*) *rufa* (= *Tetralonia berlandi*) (Hymenoptera: Anthophoridae).

Ophrys fuciflora

(F.W. SCHMIDT) MOENCH

Etymology *-flora:* flowers; *fuci-:* [with a shape of a] bee. **Type*** He, Berne (1770). **Synonyms** *Orchis fuciflora* CRANTZ, *O. arachnites* SCOPOLI, *Arachnites fuciflora* F.W. SCHMIDT, *O. arachnoides* Andr., *O. holoserica* (N.L. BURM.) GREUTER (the validity of this name is controversial).

Description 10-30 (-40)cm tall; 2-10 medium-sized flowers; sepals white to dark violet-purple, exceptionally plain green, with a ± marked green central vein, 10-14.5mm x 5-9mm, spreading, concave; petals villous, ciliate, erect, triangular, often auriculate, 3-5 (-6)mm x 2-4mm, colour as, or slightly darker than, sepals; lip pendent, (near) entire, 8-13mm x 12-19mm (when spread), trapezoid to obcordate, convex, velvety, pale reddish-brown to dark blackish-purple, with basal swellings 0.5-3mm long and an incomplete marginal band of hairs, rather short, dense and whitish to brownish on shoulders, then brownish and clearly attenuated on distal half of lip, but often longer above appendage, margins sometimes finely tinted with purple or greenish-yellow, spreading then reflexed forwards, rarely turned down and under; speculum basal, bluish-grey or reddish, shiny, edged whitish or yellowish, reduced or extensive, basal design a thickened H or X surrounding the reddish or olive-greenish basal field, with lateral branches, sometimes fragmented or marbled, often elaborated by 1-2 central ocelli and 2-6 irregular lateral ocelli; appendage rather prominent, pointed, often with 3 teeth, greenish-yellow, directed forwards to upwards, inserted into a deep notch; stigmatic cavity dark, 3-4mm wide, cup-shaped and with 2 black, shiny, rounded pseudo-eyes or sometimes delineated at the base by an attenuated ridge bordered by 2 keeled, oblique crests; column rather short; staminodial points often present.

Flowering Season V-VI (-VII).

Habitat Full sun to mid-shade on dry to moist, calcareous substrates. Short grassland, abandoned cultivation, garrigue, scrub, open woodland, up to 1500m asl.

Distribution Western central-European. From Kent (southern Br) to Romania. Rather widespread and rather rare.

Countries Au Be Br Cz Ga Ge He †Ho Hu It Ju Lx Rm.

Photos Ga, Marne, 23.V.1998; Aisne, 10.VI.1991. P. DELFORGE.

Pollinators *Eucera nigrescens* (southeast Ga, Ge), *E. longicornis* (Ga, He, It) (Hymenoptera: Anthophoridae), as well as *Microdon latifrons* and *M. mutabilis* (Diptera: Syrphidae).

The *Ophrys scolopax* group

Characters Dorsal sepal erect or turned backwards; petals villous, elongated, narrowly triangular, ± auriculate, separated at base; lip 3-lobed, lateral lobes short and conical; median lobe very convex transversally, often amphoroid (greatest width ± in upper half), with a dense and complete (near) marginal band of hairs, edges usually strongly rolled up laterally; pseudo-eyes formed by the reduction of internal stigmatic lips; appendage prominent, often transverse, ± 3-toothed, inserted into a distinct notch.

Ophrys sphegifera
WILLDENOW

Etymology *-fera:* bearing; *sphegi-:* wasp. **Type** Ag (1805). **Synonyms** *O. insectifera* var. *apiformis* DESFONTAINES, *O. apiformis* (DESFONTAINES) STEUDEL, *O. scolopax* subsp. *apiformis* (DESFONTAINES) MAIRE & WEILLER, *O. fuciflora* subsp. *apiformis* (DESFONTAINES) SUNDERMANN, *O. ouritensis* GUITTONNEAU.

Description Rather spindly, (8-) 15-32cm tall; lower bracts much longer than flowers; inflorescence lax; 4-13 very small flowers, general coloration greenish; sepals green or greenish sometimes washed pinkish, oval-lanceolate, 7-11mm x 4-6.5mm; petals villous, erect, very narrowly triangular-lanceolate to almost filiform, margins rolled up, 2.5-4.5mm x 0.8-1.5mm, colour as sepals or darker; lip near horizontal to pendent, 3-lobed at base, appearing small in comparison to sepals and stigmatic cavity, 6-10mm x 6-11mm (when spread), velvety, pale reddish-brown to blackish-purple; lateral lobes tiny, conical, pointed, 1-4mm long, hairless and greenish on inner face and with long, dense, whitish-brown hairs outside; median lobe appearing narrowly amphoroid, broadest slightly below its centreline, with a complete, dense, submarginal band of hairs, rather long, silver to greenish-red, edges curved under, with a hairless, greenish-yellow margin; speculum complex and extensive, largely edged greenish-white; appendage prominent, transverse, thick, pointed, ± 3-toothed, greenish-yellow, directed forwards; stigmatic cavity rusty-brown to greenish-brown, strongly constricted at base, with a horizontal ledge delineating the basal field; staminodial points sometimes lacking; 2n=36, 38.

Flowering Season III-VI. **Habitat** Full sun to mid-shade on alkaline to acidic, dry to moist substrates. Short grassland, garrigue, olive groves, scrub, open woodland, up to 2000m asl. **Distribution** North Africa, the island of Pentalleria (Si) and the extreme south of Andalucia (Hs). **Countries** Ag Hs Ma Si Tn. **Photos** Tn, Djebel Amar, 3.III.2002. P. DELFORGE; Ag, Constantine, 5.V.1986. D. TYTECA. **Pollinator** *Eucera notata* (Ma) (Hymenoptera: Anthophoridae)

Ophrys picta
LINK

Etymology *picta:* painted. **Type** Lu, Serra de Arrábida (1800). **Synonyms** *O. scolopax* subsp. *picta* (LINK) KREUTZ, *O. corniculata* BROTERO, *O. sphegifera* vel *O. scolopax* auct.

Description As *O. sphegifera* but less spindly, 15-40cm tall; 4-12 small flowers, colour as *O. scolopax*, without a general greenish coloration; sepals white to pink or lilac, rarely dark, 7-12mm x 4-6mm; petals villous, erect, very narrowly triangular-lanceolate, rarely almost filiform, more auriculate, margins rolled up, 2.5-5mm x 1-2mm, colour as or darker than sepals, often washed violet, especially at base; lip near horizontal to pendent, not appearing as small compared to sepals and stigmatic cavity, 7-11mm x 7-11.5mm (when spread), velvety, darker, brown to blackish-purple; lateral lobes not appearing as tiny; median lobe very convex transversally, ± globular in centre, broadest at centreline, appearing narrowly ellipsoid, with a complete, dense, submarginal band of hairs, rather long and russet, slightly narrower on lateral-distal quarters; edges of median lobe turned under, with a hairless, greenish-yellow margin; speculum less complex and more distinct, usually not fragmented, shiny greyish-blue, broadly edged yellowish-white; stigmatic cavity rusty-brown, relatively prominent, not as constricted at base; 2n=36.

Flowering Season II-VI, before *O. scolopax*.

Habitat Full sun to mid-shade on dry to moist substrates, mostly alkaline and calcareous. Short grassland, abandoned cultivation, garrigue, olive groves, scrub, open woodland, up to 1200m asl.

Distribution Poorly known due to confusion with *O. scolopax* and *O. sphegifera*. The Iberian peninsula, north to the southern foothills of the central Pyrenean-Cantabrian range; reaches the Corbières in France. Rarely, in northern Tunisia, plants analogous to *O. picta* flower in pure populations on acidic soils, after, and in the absence, of *O. sphegifera*. Reports of *O. sphegifera* from Sardinia refer to *O. picta*. Rare and local.

Countries ?Ag Ga Hs Lu ?Ma Sa Tn.

Photos Lu, Serra de Arrábida, 5.IV.1990; Hs, Malaga, 9.IV.1990. P. DELFORGE.

Pollinator *Eucera barbiventris* (southern Hs) (Hymenoptera: Anthophoridae).

Discussion of the *Ophrys scolopax* group

A western group, monophyletic, with 5 species, all with a very scolopaxoid lip, probably derived from *O. proto-fuciflora*. Its species, often sympatric, are separated by flower size and flowering season, which suggests that they attract different pollinators.

Ophrys philippi
GRENIER

Etymology Named after M.Y. Philippe, French botanist (1810-1859). **Type** Ga, Var (1859). **Synonyms** *O. insectifera* subsp. *philippi* (GRENIER) MOGGRIDGE, *O. oestrifera* subsp. *philippi* (GRENIER) K. RICHTER.

Description Slender, 15-35cm tall; 4-12 flowers; sepals white to, exceptionally, pale pink, 12-14mm long; petals villous and ciliate, erect, narrowly oboval-acuminate, 5-8mm long, yellowish to greenish, pale; lip near horizontal, spindle-shaped to near cylindrical, 11-14mm long, dark brown to blackish; lateral lobes tiny, adjacent; median lobe with complete submarginal band of pale buff to reddish hairs and a hairless greenish-yellow margin; speculum very complex, fragmented, ocellate; appendage prominent, transverse, sometimes stalked and protruding; stigmatic cavity transverse, not constricted, as broad as base of lip, with an undulate floor; basal field blackish, short, sometimes bulbous; column acuminate, forming an open angle with the base of lip.

Flowering Season V (-VI).

Habitat Full sun to mid-shade on dry to moist, calcareous substrates. Banks, short grassland, garrigue, woodland edges, up to 700m asl. **Distribution** Endemic to Var (Ga). Extremely local and very rare. **Countries** Ga. **Photos** Ga, Var, 9 & 14.V.2001. P. DELFORGE. **Note** A very remarkable species, found again after a long period of absence. It may be a stabilised hybrid between *O. scolopax* s.l. and *O. apifera* f. *botteronii*, the latter evoked by some of its characters, notably shape and position of sepals, shape of petals, undulate floor of stigmatic cavity, position and structure of column and, perhaps also, a tendency towards self-pollination.

491

Ophrys scolopax
CAVANILLES

Etymology *scolopax:* woodcock. **Type** Hs, Albaida, Valence (1793). **Synonym** *O. fuciflora* subsp. *scolopax* (CAVANILLES) SUNDERMANN.

Description 10-40 (-60)cm tall; inflorescence elongated; 3-12 medium-sized flowers; sepals white, pink, lilac, violet-purple, rarely washed green or greenish, oval-lanceolate, 9-15mm x 5-9mm, spreading, slightly concave, curved; petals villous, erect, triangular-lanceolate, sometimes very narrow and elongated, often auriculate, 3.5-6mm x 1.5-3mm, colour as, or darker than, sepals; lip near horizontal to pendent, 3-lobed at base, 9-14 (-15.5)mm x 10-15mm (when spread), velvety, pale reddish-brown to dark blackish-purple; lateral lobes small, conical, pointed, 2-4 (-5)mm long, erect, slightly curved forwards, hairless and greenish on inner face, with long, dense, purplish-brown to whitish hairs outside; median lobe broadly ob-cordate (when spread), very convex transversally, ± globular in centre, amphoroid, tip sometimes attenuated, velvety; marginal hairs beige, dense, rather long, reaching the sides, ± attenuated on lateral-distal quarters, clearly visible above appendage; sides of median lobe turned under, rarely with a very narrow, yellowish to purple, hairless margin; speculum basal, bluish-grey to purple-brown, glossy, edged yellowish, greenish or whitish, varied, often in form of ± thickened H or X, surrounding blackish-brown to greenish-red basal field, sometimes prolonged by 2 isolated spots above appendage or complicated by a central ocellus and 2 lateral ocelli; appendage prominent, transverse, thick, ± pointed, ± 3-toothed, greenish-yellow, directed forwards, inserted into a notch; stigmatic cavity cup-shaped, often slightly constricted at base, dark, with 2 rounded, blackish, shiny pseudo-eyes, or sometimes with oblique, stalked ridges, vestiges of internal lips; column acuminate; staminodial points often present.

Flowering Season Mid III-VI (-VII), sometimes with several waves of flowering.

Habitat Full sun to mid-shade on dry to moist substrates, usually alkaline, sometimes acidic. Short grassland, abandoned cultivation, garrigue, scrub, open woodland, up to 1700m asl.

Distribution Poorly known due to confusion with closely related taxa. Iberian peninsula, southern France and Liguria; for Aegean basin see *O. ceto*. Rather widespread and sometimes abundant.

Countries Ga Hs It Lu.

Photos Ga, Var, 19.IV.1999; Hs, Albaida (Valencia, ± loc. typ.), 27.III.1999. P. DELFORGE.

Pollinators *Eucera interrupta* (northeast Hs) and, perhaps, *E. nigrescens* (southern Ga) (Hymenoptera: Anthophoridae).

492

Ophrys corbariensis

J. SAMUEL & J.-M. LEWIN

Etymology *corbariensis:* from Corbières (Ga).
Type Ga, Aude (2003). **Synonym** *O. vetula* auct.
non RISSO.

Description As *O. scolopax* but more robust; 3-9
large flowers, appearance varied, sepals white,
pink, lilac, purple, 12-16 (-18)mm long; petals
villous, erect, narrowly triangular, often auriculate, 3-5 (-7)mm x 2-3.5mm, colour as, or darker
than, sepals; lip near horizontal, 3-lobed at base,
13-16 (-20)mm x 13-19mm (when spread),
velvety, lighter, reddish-brown; lateral lobes
more prominent, conical, ± pointed, 3-6mm long,
erect, often divergent and curved at tip; median
lobe fuller, sometimes also more narrowly
amphoroid, sometimes very globular in centre;
speculum basal, less extensive, often prolonged
by 2 isolated distal spots; appendage more prominent, transverse, near stalked, thick, ± clearly
multi-toothed, directed forwards or sometimes
downwards; stigmatic cavity often slightly constricted at base; stigmatic cavity and basal field
concolourous, lighter, often rusty-brown; pseudo-
eyes black encircled by greenish.

Flowering Season V-VI (-VII), after *O. scolopax*.

Habitat Full sun to mid-shade on dry to moist
substrates, mostly alkaline. Short grassland,
abandoned cultivation, garrigue, scrub, open
woodland, probably up to 1700m asl.
Distribution Poorly known due to confusion
with *O. scolopax*. Central and northern Iberian
peninsula and southern France; probably also
Liguria. Rarer, more localised and less northerly
than *O. scolopax*. **Countries** Ga Hs It.

Photos Ga, Aude (Corbières), 18.V.1999; Hs,
Logroño, 9.VI.1993. P. DELFORGE.

Key to the *Ophrys scolopax* group

1	sepals and petals green or strongly tinted green in majority of plants ...... *O. sphegifera*
1*	sepals and petals white, pink, lilac, purple, generally without green tints 2
2	lateral lobes of lip tiny, located in median third of lip .... *O. philippi*
2*	lateral lobes larger, located closer to base of lip 3
3	flowers small; petals filiform; stigmatic cavity very constricted at base .... *O. picta*
3*	flowers otherwise 4
4	flowers medium-sized, lip 9-14 (-15.5)mm long; petals 3.5-6mm long .... *O. scolopax*
4*	flowers large; lip 13-16 (-20)mm long; petals 3-5 (-7)mm long .... *O. corbariensis*

493

The *Ophrys oestrifera* group

Characters Petals villous, triangular, rarely auriculate, separated at base; lip 3-lobed, lateral lobes conical, unobtrusive or very elongated; median lobe very convex transversally, often sepioid (broadest below centreline), with a narrow, often complete, (near) marginal band of dense hairs, sides usually strongly rolled up laterally; pseudo-eyes formed by the reduction of internal stigmatic lips; appendage prominent, often transverse, ± 3-toothed, inserted into a distinct notch.

Ophrys holubyana
ANDRASOVSZKY

Etymology Named after M. Holuby, Hungarian botanist (1836-1923). **Type** Hu, Konciti-Tal (1917). **Synonyms** *Ophrys fuciflora* subsp. *holubyana* (ANDRASOVSZKY) DOSTÁL, *O. holoserica* subsp. *holubyana* (ANDRASOVSZKY) KREUTZ.

Description As *O. oestrifera*, but 3-8 medium-sized to rather large flowers; sepals spreading, whitish to pinkish or pale lilac, sometimes washed green; lip shape varied, slightly to very convex, obscurely to clearly 3-lobed; lateral lobes with pointed basal swellings, 2-8mm long, sometimes filiform and recurved, hairless and greenish-white on inner face, with long, dense, whitish hairs outside; median lobe prominent, ± strongly convex, with marginal band of short, dense, russet hairs, sides slightly paler, reflexed forwards, flat or turned under. **Variation** Very varied, clearly intermediate between *O. fuciflora* and *O. oestrifera* (*bicornis*).

Flowering Season V-VI. **Habitat** As *O. fuciflora*. **Distribution** Northern Carpathians (Cz), Hungary. Reports from Istria (Ju) refer to *O. zinsmeisteri*, *O. untchjii* or other taxa in the same group. Rather rare and local. **Countries** Cz Hu. **Photos A** Hu, Pest, 16.VI.2004. P. DELFORGE; **B & C** Cz, Bílé Karpaty, 29.V.1994. C.A.J. KREUTZ.

Ophrys oestrifera
STEVEN in M.-BIEB.

Etymology *-fera:* bearing; *oestri-:* horsefly. **Type** Ro, Iberia (1808). **Synonyms** ?*O. cornuta* STEVEN IN M.-BIEB., ?*O. scolopax* subsp. *cornuta* (STEVEN) E.G. CAMUS, ?*O. fuciflora* subsp. *cornuta* (STEVEN) SUNDERMANN, ?*O. bicornis* SADLER in NENDTVICH, ?*O. scolopax* var. *bicornis* (SADLER) NYMAN, ?*O. oestrifera* subsp. *bicornis* (SADLER) KREUTZ.

Description Slender, rather spindly, up to 50cm tall; inflorescence lax to near dense; (2-) 4-9 (-14) medium-sized flowers; sepals whitish, pink, lilac or pale purple, oval-lanceolate, 9-15mm x 5-7mm long, spreading to turned backwards; petals concolourous, villous, ± triangular-rounded, ± obscurely auriculate, rather elongated, (3-) 4-6mm x 2-3mm, separated at base; lip near horizontal to pendent, (10-) 11-14 (-15)mm long, dark brown to blackish-brown, deeply 3-lobed at base; lateral lobes acuminate, parallel to weakly outspread, often angled slightly downwards, (4-) 6-8 (-9)mm long, with dense, straight, pale buff marginal hairs, outside as well as on inner face, except at base; median lobe sepioid, globular in centre, sides strongly turned under, with a complete submarginal band of pale hairs, narrower on lateral-distal quarters, bordered by a rather broad, hairless, greenish, margin; speculum basal, bluish-grey, edged yellowish, often only slightly extended and slightly complex; appendage transverse, sometimes near stalked, ± obscurely 3-toothed, directed forwards, greenish to brownish-green; stigmatic cavity and basal field concolourous, rusty-brown to blackish, lighter than, or same colour as, centre of lip; stigmatic cavity transverse, slightly constricted at base, *c.* 60% of optical width of median lobe, with a distinct ledge bordered by 2 rounded, blackish pseudo-eyes.

Flowering Season Mid IV-VI (-VII).

Habitat Full sun to shade on dry to moist, alkaline substrates. Garrigue, short grassland, scrub, open woodland, up to 2000m asl.

Distribution From southern Hungary to east of the Caspian Sea (Iran); Crimea and Georgia (Ro) in the north (see note). Rather local and sometimes abundant. **Countries** Ae An Bu Gr Hu Ju Rm Ro ?Tu. **Photos** An, Trabzon 5.VI.1990; Gr, Kastoria, 17.VI.1987. P. DELFORGE.

Note The most northerly species in the group, probably made up from at least 3 taxa that may each be separate species: '*oestrifera*', flowering mid IV-V, endemic to the Crimea (Ro); '*cornuta*' (Photo A), flowers probably slightly smaller, later flowering, V-VI (-VII), a Hyrcano-Pontic-Caucasian endemic, eastern Anatolia and Georgia to Iran; '*bicornis*', northern Balkans, from southern Hungary east to the Black Sea and northern Aegean basin (Photo B).

Ophrys rhodostephane

P. DEVILLERS & J. DEVILLERS-TERSCHUREN

Etymology *-stephane:* with a crown (= sepals); *rhodo-:* pink. **Type** Ju, Croatia, Hvar Island (2004). **Synonyms** *O. oestrifera* subsp. *rhodostephane* (P. DEVILLERS & J. DEVILLERS-TERSCHUREN) KREUTZ, *O. balcanica* Soó nom. nud., *O. oestrifera* subsp. *balcanica* SOO ex HAYEK, *O. bicornis* vel *cornuta* vel *oestrifera* auct.

Description As *O. oestrifera* but inflorescence often denser; sepals and petals more brightly coloured; sepals average slightly longer, 11-15mm long, petals more elongated, more rarely auriculate, (1.5-) 3-5.2mm long, more remote at base; lip shorter than lateral sepals; 9-13mm x 9-15mm (when spread); lateral lobes more spindly, slightly more sinuous and more outspread, often hairless on inner face; median lobe less robust, sometimes slightly globular in centre and spindle-shaped, with a submarginal band of hairs that is less constant, sometimes completely attenuated on lateral-distal quarters; hairless margin narrower, sometimes near absent, often reddish; stigmatic cavity narrower, equal to ± 50% of optical width of median lobe.

Flowering Season IV-V.

Habitat Full sun to mid-shade on dry to moist, alkaline substrates. Garrigue, abandoned cultivation, scrub, woodland edges, up to 600m asl. **Distribution** Central Dalmatia. The Dalmatian archipelago and coasts from Zadar south to Montenegro; perhaps also Mount Gargano (Foggia, It). Rather widespread but rare. **Countries** ?It Ju. **Photos** Ju, Hrvatska, Hvar, 14 & 16.IV.2004. P. DELFORGE.

Ophrys sepioides

P. DEVILLERS & J. DEVILLERS-TERSCHUREN

Etymology *-oides:* with the shape of; *sepi-:* cuttlefish. **Type** Gr, Ioannina (2004). **Synonyms** *O. cornuta* vel *oestrifera* auct. non STEVEN in M.-BIEB., *O. oestrifera* var. *grandiflora* B. WILLING & E. WILLING, *O. scolopax* subsp. *cornuta* var. *grandiflora* (B. WILLING & E. WILLING) B. BIEL comb. illeg.

Description As *O. oestrifera* but more robust, 15-50cm tall; inflorescence denser; (3-) 4-6 (-9) larger flowers; sepals and petals concolourous, pink to pale purple; sepals 12-17mm long, petals narrowly to broadly triangular-rounded, 3-5.5mm x 2.5-3.5mm, averaging 25% of sepal length; lip larger, (12-) 13-17 (-18)mm x 15-19mm (when spread), reddish-brown to blackish; lateral lobes hairless on inner face, slender, ± outspread, sinuous, 4-7mm long, often appearing small in comparison to lip; median lobe sepioid, often very globular, with a complete (near) marginal band of pale buff hairs, slightly attenuated on lateral-distal quarters; distal part of speculum sometimes marbled or fragmented; stigmatic cavity very narrow, equal to ± 36% of optical width of median lobe; appendage larger; basal field and stigmatic cavity concolourous with centre of lip; staminodial points present.

Flowering Season (End IV) V-VI (-VII), late.

Habitat Full sun to mid-shade on dry to moist, alkaline substrates. Short grassland, garrigue, abandoned cultivation, scrub, woodland edges, probably up to 1000m asl.

Distribution Sub-Mediterranean zone of north-western Greece and neighbouring regions of Albania. Rather rare and local. **Countries** Al Gr.

Photos A & B Gr, Ioannina, 20.V.1985. J. DEVILLERS-TERSCHUREN; **C** Kastoria, 17.VI.1987. P. DELFORGE.

497

Ophrys crassicornis

(RENZ) J. DEVILLERS-TERSCHUREN & P. DEVILLERS

Etymology *-cornis:* with horns (= later lobes); *crassi-:* thick. **Type** Gr, Ionian Islands, Meganisi (1928). **Synonyms** *O. cornuta* f. *crassicornis* RENZ, *O. bicornis* vel *cornuta* vel *oestrifera* auct.

Description As *O. oestrifera* but more robust; flowers large for the groups; sepals and petals concolourous; sepals on average longer, (11-) 12-16mm long, petals narrowly to broadly triangular-rounded, more remote at base, shorter, 2-4 (-5)mm x 2-3.5mm, averaging only 29% of sepal length; lip larger, 12-16 (-17.5)mm x 12-19mm (when spread); lateral lobes hairless on inner face, base robust, long-tapering, often sinuous, or alterna-tively, sometimes short and divergent, (3-) 7-11mm long; median lobe sepioid, less globular, with a complete (near) marginal band of brownish to pale buff hairs, sometimes slightly attenuated on lateral-distal quarters, with the hairless border very narrow to frequently absent; speculum often more extensive and more complex, sometimes marbled or fragmented distally; stigmatic cavity relatively narrow, equal to ± 45% of optical width of median lobe; basal field and stigmatic cavity reddish, usually lighter than lip; staminodial points present.

Flowering Season Mid III-IV, rather early.

Habitat Full sun to mid-shade on dry to moist, alkaline substrates. Garrigue, abandoned cultiva-tion, scrub, woodland edges, open pinewoods, probably up to 800m asl.

Distribution Western Greece: Ionian Islands and neighbouring areas of the mainland around the Gulf of Corinth, northwest Peloponnese. Rather rare and local. **Countries** ?Al Gr.

Photos A-B Gr, Ilia, 4.IV.1993; **C** Cephalonia, 4.IV.1991. P. DELFORGE.

Pollinator Probably *Eucera longicornis* (Hymen-optera: Anthophoridae).

Ophrys leptomera
P. DELFORGE

Etymology *leptomera:* with very thin parts. **Type** Gr, Euboea Island (2000). **Synonym** *O. oestrifera* subsp. *leptomera* (P. DELFORGE) KREUTZ.

Description As *O. oestrifera* but very slender, (25-) 35-55 (-75)cm tall, general coloration whitish-green; inflorescence very lax, up to 35cm tall; 5-9 medium-sized flowers; bracts very elongated; sepals plain green to whitish-green, sometimes washed pinkish, lateral sepals 10-13mm long; petals yellowish-green, sometimes bright, triangular, very small, 1.2-2mm x 1.2-2mm; lip 9.5-12mm long; median lobe very convex, sepioid; lateral lobes strongly tapering, sinuous, 8-12mm long, often as long as median lobe.

Flowering Season End IV-V (-VI), relatively late.

Habitat Usually mid-shade, on dry to moist, calcareous substrates. Abandoned cultivation, garrigue, open pinewoods, up to 700m asl.

Distribution Poorly known. Central Aegean; reported from Euboea Island and the central Cyclades (Paros, Naxos). Extremely rare and local. Countries Gr. **Photo** Gr, Euboea (loc. typ.), 22.IV.1994. P. DELFORGE; Euboea, 15.V.2004. C.A.J. KREUTZ.

Key to the *Ophrys oestrifera* group

1   sepals and petals green or strongly tinted green in majority of plants 2
1* sepals and petals white, pink or dark purple, usually without green tones 5

2   lateral lobes of lip tapering, 8-12mm long .... *O. leptomera*
2* lateral lobes of lip less elongated, 0.5-5mm long 3

3   lip (11-) 12-17mm long .... *O. karadenizensis*
3* lip 7.5-11 (-12)mm long 4

4   appendage very prominent; late flowering (V) .... *O. isaura*
4* appendage not very prominent; earlier flowering (III-IV) .... *O. rhodia*

5   dorsal sepal frequently or always bent onto column mid-flowering 6
5* dorsal sepal erect or turned backwards mid-flowering 8

6   rather late flowering (end IV-) V-VI 7
6* flowering III-IV .... *O. lapethica*

7   lip 7-8mm long .... *O. latakiana*
7* lip 10-14mm long .... *O. abchasica*

(continued on p. 501)

Ophrys cerastes
P. DEVILLERS & J. DEVILLERS-TERSCHUREN

Etymology *cerastes:* with horns. **Type** Gr, Ioannina (2004). **Synonyms** *O. cornuta* var. *minuscula* G. THIELE & W. THIELE, *O. cerastes* var. *minuscula* (G. THIELE & W. THIELE) P. DEVILLERS & J. DEVILLERS-TERSCHUREN, *O. cornuta* vel *oestrifera* auct.

Description As *O. oestrifera* but with 4-8 rather small to medium-sized flowers; sepals 9-14mm long, dorsal sepal often turned backwards; petals concolourous, rarely auriculate, 1.5-4.5mm x 1-2mm; lip 6.5-12mm x 7.5-15mm; lateral lobes tapering, 7-12mm long, inner face hairless, slightly sinuous and sometimes divergent; median lobe often less globular, more spindle-shaped; stigmatic cavity equal to ± 45% of optical width of median lobe. **Variation *'minuscula'*:** Flowers very small (photo C), in the lower part of the range of measurements for the species; occurs with the nominative var. and numerous intermediates, flowering at the same time.

Flowering Season IV-V.

Habitat As *O. cornutula*, but up to 1300m asl.

Distribution Aegean, east to the Ionian Islands and Epirus. Probably the most widespread and least rare of the group. **Countries** Ae An Gr. **Photos** Gr, Attiki, 9.IV.1991; Imathia, 9.V.1990; Viotia, 2.V.1997. P. DELFORGE.

Pollinator Probably *Eucera puncticollis* (Hymenoptera: Anthophoridae).

500

Ophrys cornutula
H.F. PAULUS

Etymology *cornutula:* a small [*Ophrys*] *cornuta*.
Type Ae, Rhodes (2001). **Synonyms** *O. oestrifera* subsp. *cornutula* (H.F. PAULUS) KREUTZ, *O. cornuta* vel *oestrifera* auct. non STEVEN in M.-BIEB.

Description As *O. oestrifera* but with 3-16 very small flowers; sepals whitish to purple, 9-12mm long; petals concolourous or darker, triangular-rounded, 2-4.5mm x 1.-2.5mm; lip shape varied, 6-9mm long; lateral lobes tapering, often as long as lip, inner face hairless, slightly sinuous; median lobe spindle-shaped to sepioid; speculum complex and extensive, often reaching the submarginal band of hairs above the appendage.

Flowering Season Mid III-IV, relatively early.

Habitat Full sun to mid-shade on dry to moist, calcareous substrates. Short grassland, abandoned cultivation, garrigue, old terraces, scrub, open woodland, up to 1000m asl. **Distribution** Poorly known due to confusion with related taxa. Apparently principally southern Aegean, probably from Corfu in the west. Rather local but sometimes abundant. **Countries** Ae An Gr. **Photos** Ae, Rhodes, 10 & 8.IV.1984. P. DELFORGE. **Pollinators** *Eucera punctulata* and *E. signifera* (Hymenoptera: Anthophoridae).

Key to the group *Ophrys oestrifera*

(continued from p. 499)

8	median lobe globular, very small; petals tiny, 1-1.5mm long	*O. schulzei*
8*	flowers otherwise	9
9	lip varied, median lobe sometimes slightly convex, appearing fucifloroid	*O. holubyana*
9*	lip always scolopaxoid	10
10	lateral lobes of lip ± long-tapering in the majority of plants	14
10*	lateral lobes always short	11
11	lateral sepals 11-15mm long	*O. ceto*
11*	lateral sepals 7-11mm long	12
12	early flowering, II-III	*O. dodekanensis*
12*	flowering later, IV-VI	13
13	stigmatic cavity pale	*O. minutula*
13*	stigmatic cavity blackish	*O. hygrophila*
14	sepals very colourful, 11-15mm, much longer than lip	*O. rhodostephane*
14*	flowers otherwise	15
15	stigmatic cavity very narrow, 36-41% of optical width of median lobe	16
15*	stigmatic cavity broader	17

(continued on p. 508)

501

Ophrys ceto
P. DEVILLERS, J. DEVILLERS-TERSCHUREN & P. DELFORGE

Etymology Named after the goddess Ceto, daughter of Gaia, the Earth, and Pontos, the Sea. **Type** Gr, Cyclades, Paros (2004). **Synonyms** *O. scolopax* vel *bremifera* auct.

Description Slender, rather robust, 10-35cm tall; 3-10 flowers, medium-sized to rather large, appearing superficially similar to those of *O. scolopax*; sepals pink to dark lilac, more rarely whitish or washed green, oval-lanceolate, 11-15mm x 4-6mm, spreading; petals concolourous or slightly darker, triangular-rounded, rarely auriculate, 1.5-4.5mm x 1-2mm; lip pendent, clearly 3-lobed, 10-14 (-15)mm long, very convex transversally, rarely near globular in centre,

spindle-shaped, appearing straight longitudinally, velvety, dark reddish-brown to dark blackish-purple, submarginal band of hairs often complete, sometimes very attenuated on lateral-distal quarters, rather dense, pale buff to greyish, with 2 short small basal swell-ings, ± pointed, ± divergent, 2-4mm tall, hairless and greenish-white on inner face; median lobe elongated, margins hairless, sometimes greenish-yellow, turned down and under, speculum as *O. cerastes*; basal field pale to dark reddish; appendage prominent, 3-toothed, sometimes near stalked, greenish-yellow, directed forwards to pendent; stigmatic cavity dark grey, defined by a ridge, often greatly protruding, bordered by 2 rounded pseudo-eyes.

Flowering Season IV-V.

Habitat Full sun to mid-shade on dry to moist, calcareous substrates. Short grassland, abandoned cultivation, garrigue, scrub, up to 700m asl.

Distribution Aegean, east to the Ionian Islands and Epirus. Probably the most widespread and least rare of the group. **Countries** Ae An Gr.

Photo Gr, Cyclades, Milos, 18.IV.1998; Naxos, 24.IV.1995; Paros (loc. typ.), 10.IV.1995. P. DELFORGE.

Pollinator Perhaps *Eucera euroa* and *E. plumigera* (Hymenoptera: Anthophoridae).

Ophrys rhodia
(H. Baumann & Künkele) P. Delforge

Etymology *rhodia:* from Rhodes. **Type** Ae, Rhodes (1986). **Synonyms** *O. umbilicata* subsp. *rhodia* H. Baumann & Künkele, *O. scolopax* subsp. *rhodia* (H. Baumann & Künkele) H.Æ. Pedersen & N. Faurholdt.

Description Robust, 10-36cm tall; (3-) 5-10 rather small flowers; sepals whitish-green to emerald green, very rarely pinkish, oval-elliptical, margins recurved, 10-13mm x 4.5-7mm, concave, spreading and curved forwards; petals villous, erect, triangular, often auriculate, 3-4.2mm x 3-4.2mm, colour as, or darker than, sepals, sometimes washed violet at base; lip near horizontal, 3-lobed at base, 7.5-12mm x 7.5-12mm (when spread), velvety, dark brown to blackish-purple; lateral lobes small, conical, pointed, 2-5mm long, erect, often slightly curved and divergent, hairless and greenish-white on inner face, with long, dense, purplish-brown to whitish hairs outside; median lobe obcordate (when spread), convex, globular in centre, appearing ovoid, with a dense submarginal band of rather long, greenish-red hairs, sides narrowly hairless, rarely tinted greenish, turned down and under; speculum brownish-blue, glossy, broadly edged whitish, very extensive, surrounding basal field, base of lateral lobes and sometimes even appendage, complicated by 1 (-2) central and 2-4 lateral ocelli, the distal ocelli incomplete; appendage prominent, transverse, thick, greenish-yellow, directed forwards, inserted into a large notch; stigmatic cavity cup-shaped, with a whitish macular stage, often a transverse brown bar and 2 black, shiny, rounded pseudo-eyes; basal field pale reddish-brown; upper border of stigmatic cavity with a brownish-purple line; staminodial points present; column broad at base, acuminate and sometimes sinuous at tip, ± perpendicular to lip.

Flowering Season III-IV.

Habitat Full sun to mid-shade on dry to moist, alkaline substrates. Short grassland, abandoned cultivation, garrigue, scrub, olive groves, open woodland, up to 600m asl.

Distribution Rhodes (Ae, rather widespread), Karpathos (Cr) and Cyprus (very rare); reports from Near East require confirmation.

Countries Ae Cr Cy ?Ij.

Photos Ae, Rhodes, 9.IV.1984; Cy, Larnaca, 1.IV.1989. P. Delforge.

Ophrys minutula
GÖLZ & H.R. REINHARD

Etymology *minutula:* very small. **Type** Ae, Lesbos (1989). **Synonyms** *O. scolopax* var. *minutula* (GÖLZ & H.R. REINHARD) H.Æ. PEDERSEN & N. FAURHOLDT, *O. scolopax* subsp. *minutula* (GÖLZ & H.R. REINHARD) B. BIEL, *O. oestrifera* subsp. *minutula* (GÖLZ & H.R. REINHARD) KREUTZ.

Description Spindly, 14-35cm tall; inflorescence elongated, 6-21cm high, sometimes near one-sided; (2-) 5-9 small flowers; sepals pure white to dark purplish-pink, with a green central vein, concave, oval, margins recurved, 7-11mm x 4.5-6.5mm, spreading and then (strongly) turned backwards; petals villous, erect, rather short, triangular, rarely auriculate, 2.5-4mm x 1.2-2.6mm, whitish to dark purplish-pink; lip near horizontal, 3-lobed at base, 6.5-9mm x 7-10mm (when spread), velvety, brown; lateral lobes small, conical, pointed, 1-3mm long, hairless and greenish on inner face, with dense brownish hairs outside, extremities curved outwards; median lobe convex, globular in centre, appearing elliptic, with dense marginal band of long, greenish-brown hairs, sides turned down and under; speculum rather simple, bluish-grey to purple-brown, glossy, edged yellowish, often formed into a ± thickened H or X, surrounding the reddish basal field, sometimes extended by 2 parallel lines or 2 isolated spots above the appendage and lateral branches, rarely by 2 lateral ocelli; appendage prominent, thick, pointed, 3-toothed, yellowish-green to pale reddish-brown, pendent or directed forwards, inserted into a notch; stigmatic cavity greenish to orange, pale, barred purple, separated from basal field by a rounded ridge; pseudo-eyes stalked, greenish, shiny, ± broadly ringed yellowish; column with acuminate tip, making a very open angle with lip.

Flowering Season IV-V, rather late.

Habitat Full sun to mid-shade on dry to moist, calcareous substrates. Grassy places in garrigue and olive groves, scrub, open pinewoods, up to 650m asl.

Distribution Eastern Aegean. Lesbos, Chios, Samos, Skyros, perhaps also the Izmir district and Çesme peninsula. Very rare and local.

Countries Ae ?An.

Photos Ae, Lesbos, 11 & 14.IV.1991. P. DELFORGE.

Pollinator Perhaps *Eucera albofasciata* (Hymenoptera: Anthophoridae)

Ophrys dodekanensis
H. KRETZSCHMAR & KREUTZ

Etymology *dodekanensis:* from Dodecanese (Ae). **Type** Ae, Rhodes (2001). **Synonyms** *O. oestrifera* subsp. *dodekanensis* (H. KRETZSCHMAR & KREUTZ) KREUTZ, *O. scolopax* vel *heterochila* vel *minutula* auct.

Description Small, often thickset, 7-20cm tall; rosette of basal leaves proportionally large, up to 20cm diameter; inflorescence rather dense, up to 12cm high; 3-9 very small flowers; sepals pure white to pale crimson-pink or lilac, concave, oval-lanceolate, margins recurved, 7-11mm long, lateral sepals spreading then sometimes turned backwards, dorsal sepal curved; petals villous, erect, ± triangular, rarely auriculate, very small, 1.2-2.8mm x 0.9-1.6mm, concolourous with, or often darker than, sepals, base ochre or crimson; lip pendent, strongly 3-lobed at base, 6-9mm x 6.5-10mm (when spread), velvety, blackish-brown; lateral lobes small, conical, pointed, 1-3mm long, hairless and greenish on inner face, densely hairy outside, hairs brownish to honey-coloured, extremities often curved outwards; median lobe convex, sepioid, appearing attenuated at tip face-on, with a broad, dense submarginal band of long, pale, frosted brown hairs, slightly narrower on lateral-distal quarters, and a ± fine, hairless, greenish-yellow margin; speculum rather simple but rather extensive, glossy bluish-grey, edged yellowish or whitish, with a ± complete ocellus in centre and branches encompassing the basal swellings, extending towards the appendage and to the walls of the stigmatic cavity, delineating a pale reddish basal field; appendage rather prominent, rather thick, 3-toothed, yellowish-green and directed forwards, inserted into a notch; stigmatic cavity proportionally large, pale, floor greenish to orange, back barred purple, separated from basal field by a distinct ridge; pseudo-eyes blackish, shiny, protruding, without a peri-pseudocular ring, with a pale bridle surmounted by a purple line; column rounded to acuminate at tip, making an open angle with the lip; staminodial points present.

Flowering Season Late II-III.

Habitat Usually mid-shade, on dry to moist, calcareous substrates. Abandoned cultivation, garrigue, scrub, open pinewoods, up to 700m asl.

Distribution Rhodes, perhaps also neighbouring parts of Anatolia. Rather widespread and sometimes abundant (on Rhodes).

Countries Ae ?An.

Photos Ae, Rhodes, 16.III.2000 (loc. typ.). C.A.J. KREUTZ.

505

Ophrys hygrophila
E. GÜGEL, KREUTZ, D. RÜCKBRODT & U. RÜCKBRODT

Etymology *-phila:* loving; *hygro-:* dampness.
Type An, Antalya (1997). **Synonym** *O. oestrifera* subsp. *hygrophila* (E. GÜGEL, KREUTZ, D. RÜCKBRODT & U. RÜCKBRODT) KREUTZ (Comment: It is probably this species which must be named *O. phrygia*).

Description Rather spindly, 15-25 (-30)cm tall; lower bracts longer than flowers; inflorescence near lax; 2-6 (-10) small flowers; sepels pure white to pink, rather pale, with a green central vein, marked on upper half, concave, oval-elliptical, margins reflexed, 7-11mm x 4-6mm, (strongly) bent backwards; petals villous, erect, short, triangular-rounded, often auriculate, 2.5-4mm x 1.5-2.5mm, pale to rather dark pink, sometimes washed and/or edged ochre or green; lip pendent, 3-lobed at base, 8-11mm x 8-11mm (when spread), velvety, dark, reddish-brown to blackish-purple; lateral lobes very small, conical, near pointed, hairless and shiny greenish on inner face, with dense, rather long, yellowish-brown hairs outside, extremities slightly curved downwards and outwards; median lobe prominent, convex, globular in centre, appearing elliptic or oboval, with a dense marginal band of rather long, greenish-russet hairs, narrower on lateral-distal quarters, sides turned under; speculum relatively reduced, bluish-grey to purplish-red, glossy, finely edged yellowish, often in the form of a rather thin H, surrounding blackish basal field, sometimes extended by 2 parallel lines above appendage and complicated by a central ocellus and 2 small incomplete lateral ocelli; appendage prominent, thick, sometimes pointed, entire or 3-toothed, yellowish-green, turned under lip, pendent or directed forwards, inserted into a notch; stigmatic cavity very dark, blackish, with 2 small, shiny, black crests, and a ridge overhanging basal field; column short, tip very slightly or not acuminate, making an open angle with lip.

Flowering Season V-VI, rather late.

Habitat Full sun to mid-shade, on moist to damp, alkaline substrates. Seepages in ditches, short grassland, scrub and woodland edges, moist meadows, 800-1400m asl.

Distribution Central-southern Anatolia, in Konya and Antalya provinces. Rare and local.

Countries An.

Photos An, Antalya, 30.V.1990; Konya, 29.V.1990. P. DELFORGE.

Ophrys phrygia
H. FLEISCHMANN & BORNMÜLLER

Etymology *phrygia:* from Phrygia, ancient country in Minor Asia. **Type** An, Konya (1923). (Comment: *O. phrygia* is probably the name that has to be applied to *O. hygrophila*.)

Description Slender, 25-65cm tall; bracts much longer than flowers; inflorescence very lax; 4-10 flowers; sepals white, pink, pale to rather dark, broadly oval-lanceolate, 12-16mm x 5-7mm, dorsal sepal erect and then strongly turned backwards; petals very small, villous, colour as sepals, sometimes washed ochre, pale to dark, erect, triangular-rounded to near linear, 2-3.5mm x 1-3.5mm, average 16% of sepal length; lip near horizontal, 3-lobed at base, (10-) 11-13.5 (-15)mm x (10-) 11-13.5 (-15)mm (when spread), velvety, reddish-brown to blackish; lateral lobes relatively small, conical, pointed, greenish-yellow and often hairless on inner face, with rather long hairs outside, greyish, brownish, often tinted green, extremities sometimes shortly filiform and curved outwards; median lobe prominent, convex, (very) globular in centre, appearing ovoid to sometimes hemispherical, with a dense marginal band of rather long, greenish-russet hairs, sides hairless, ± broadly tinted greenish-yellow, turned backwards or, rarely, directed backwards or slightly reflexed; speculum complex, extensive, sometimes very fragmented, bluish-grey to reddish, glossy, broadly edged yellowish, forming a bilobed shield surrounding the reddish-brown basal field, extended by an often incomplete central ocellus, 2 parallel lines and/or 2 isolated spots above the appendage as well as 2-4 (-6) ± regular small lateral ocelli; appendage prominent, thick, pointed, 3-toothed, yellowish-green, directed forwards, inserted into a notch; stigmatic cavity narrow, equal to ± 41% of optical width of median lobe, greenish to orange, broadly barred purple; pseudo-eyes, blackish, shiny, ± broadly encircled by yellow; column with acuminate tip, making an open angle with lip.

Flowering Season V-VI, rather late.

Habitat Full sun to mid-shade on dry to moist, alkaline substrates. Short grassland, scrub, open pinewoods, up to 1700m asl.

Distribution Rather poorly known due to confusion with related taxa. Southern Anatolia, principally the Antalya region, east to the Iraqi frontier. In the west, the rare reports from the Aegean islands (Ae) are doubtful. Local and rather rare.

Countries ?Ae An.

Photos An, Antalya, 30.V.1990; Içel, 16.V.1990. P. DELFORGE.

Ophrys isaura
Renz & Taubenheim

Etymology *isaura:* Isaurian, inhabitant of the northern Taurus (An). Type An, İçel (1980).

Description Slender, rather robust, 25-50cm tall; bracts longer than flowers; inflorescence lax, up to 25cm high; 6-15 small flowers; sepals whitish-green, sometimes pink or lilac, in that case washed green, oval-lanceolate, margins recurved, 11-12mm x 4-5mm, spreading to turned backwards; petals villous, triangular, 3-4mm x 2-3mm, colour as sepals or sometimes whitish, turned backwards; lip (near) horizontal, 3-lobed at base, 9-11mm long, velvety, pale reddish-brown to blackish-purple, ± broadly edged greenish-yellow; lateral lobes very small, conical, pointed, 1-2mm tall, hairless and whitish on inner face, with rather long crimson hairs outside; median lobe convex, globular in centre, appearing oboval or elliptic, surrounded by a thin band of greenish-russet hairs, sides ± strongly curved under; speculum occupying basal half of median lobe, purplish-blue to reddish, glossy, ± broadly edged whitish, surrounding the reddish basal field, complicated by 1-2 central ocelli, the distal of which is incomplete, and 2 lateral ocelli encircling base of lateral lobes; appendage very prominent, thick, pointed, triangular or 3-toothed, yellowish-green, directed forwards, inserted into a notch; stigmatic cavity dark, reddish-brown or greenish, sometimes with a lateral notch, with a ± distinct ridge at base, overhanging the basal field, and bordered by 2 vestigial internal lips, ± rounded, shiny; column with a short tip.

Flowering Season V.

Habitat Full sun to mid-shade on dry to moist, very calcareous substrates, often marly. Garrigue, mixed woodland of oak and pine, 800-1200m asl. **Distribution** Central-southern Anatolia. Known from a few stations in the region of Gülnar (İçel) and Cevizli (Antalya). Extremely local and extremely rare; threatened due to its very small populations and by cultivation of its sites. **Countries** An.

Photos An, İçel (loc. typ.), 20.V.1997; 20.V.1995. C.A.J. Kreutz.

Key to the *Ophrys oestrifera* group

(continued from p. 501)

16   petals 2-3.5mm long .... *O. phrygia*
16* petals 3-5.5mm long .... *O. sepioides*

17   basal swellings of lip hairy on inner face, almost to the base .... *O. oestrifera*
17* basal swellings hairless on inner face, almost to tip 18

(continued on next page)

Ophrys karadenizensis

M. SCHÖNFELDER & H. SCHÖNFELDER

Etymology *karadenizensis:* from Kara Deniz (the 'Black Sea' in Turkish). **Type** An, Ordu (1997). **Synonym** *O. oestrifera* subsp. *karadenizensis* (M. SCHÖNFELDER & H. SCHÖNFELDER) KREUTZ.

Description (10-) 20-35 (-49)cm tall; stem robust; inflorescence elongated, up to 25cm high; lower bracts much longer than flowers; (4-) 7-13 relatively small flowers; sepals green, whitish-green, sometimes washed violet, exceptionally white or pink without green tints, oval-lanceolate, 12-15mm x 4-6mm, spreading; petals villous, ciliate, triangular-rounded, obscurely auriculate, elongated, 5-7 (-8)mm x 1.5-2 (-3)mm, separated at base, slightly to much darker than sepals, green tinted with ochre, brownish (sepals green), purple (sepals pink) or pink (sepals white); lip inclined to pendent, (11-) 12-14 (-17)mm x 11-12 (-14)mm (when spread), dark brown to blackish-brown; lateral lobes very short, slightly pointed to rounded; median lobe elongated, ± globular in centre, sides strongly bent under; submarginal band of pale hairs, complete but narrower on lateral-distal quarters; border of lip with a narrow, greenish, hairless margin; speculum basal, bluish-grey, edged yellowish, often not very extensive, merely an X-shape branching towards the stigmatic cavity and lateral lobes, sometimes fragmented, rarely prolonged by a central ocellus; appendage transverse, obscurely 3-toothed, directed forwards, greenish to brownish-green; stigmatic cavity and basal field concolourous, rusty-brown, lighter than centre of lip; stigmatic cavity slightly constricted below pseudo-eyes, with a distinct ledge, vault greenish-white with a purple-brown transverse bar; staminodial points lacking.

Flowering Season IV-V.

Habitat Full sun to shade on dry to moist, alkaline, often calcareous, substrates. Poor and mesophytic grassland, scrub, hazel plantations, up to 600m asl. **Distribution** The centre of Pontic Anatolia; principally the provinces of Ordu and Giresun. Rather local and rather rare. **Countries** An.

Photos An, Ordu, 6 & 13.V.1997. M. SCHÖN-FELDER.

Key to the *Ophrys oestrifera* group

(continued from previous page)

18 lip 12-17.5mm long .... *O. crassicornis*
18* lip 6-12mm long 19

19 flowering season mainly mid III-mid IV; lip 6-9mm long .... *O. cornutula*
19* flowering season mid V-V; lip 6.5-12mm long .... *O. cerastes*

Ophrys abchasica
(KÜMPEL) P. DELFORGE

Etymology *abchasica:* from Abkhazia, ancient Colchide (Ro, Georgia). Type Ro, Abkhazia (1988). **Basionym** *O. oestrifera* subsp. *abchasica* KÜMPEL.

Description Robust, 25-50 (-70)cm tall; inflorescence lax, up to 30cm high; (4-) 9-17 (-21) flowers; sepals white to pink or dark purplish-red, rarely washed green, oval-oblong, 9-14mm x 4-6mm, margins recurved, dorsal sepal rather concave, often turned down onto column and longer than it, lateral sepals spreading; petals villous, white to dark crimson-pink, sometimes ochre or brownish, 3.5-6mm x 2-3.5mm, triangular; lip (near-) horizontal, 3-lobed at base, 10-14mm x 10-14mm (when spread), velvety, pale reddish-brown to blackish-purple; lateral lobes conical, 4-11mm long, extremities filiform, brownish at base, greenish-white to orange washed green on upper half, hairless on inner face, with long, dense brownish to greyish hairs outside; median lobe transversally convex, globular in centre, ± amphoroid, with a complete marginal band of greyish to brownish hairs, sides ± strongly turned down and under, hairless yellow margin absent; appendage rather small, 1-1.5mm x 1.2-1.8mm, greenish-yellow to pale crimson-brown, pointed, 3-toothed, directed forwards, inserted into a notch; stigmatic cavity pale reddish, floor greenish grey, pseudo-eyes greenish, shiny, slightly protruding, sometimes surmounted by a purple line; tip of column acuminate, 2-3mm long, often sinuous.

Flowering Season V-VI.

Habitat Full sun to mid-shade on dry to moist, usually alkaline, substrates. Short grassland, abandoned cultivation, garrigue, open woodland, up to 2000m asl. **Distribution** Caucasian. Local and rather rare. **Countries** An Ro. **Photos A & C** Ro, Azerbaijan, 5.VI.2000. C.A.J. KREUTZ; **B** An, Trabzon, 23.V.1990. P. DELFORGE.

Ophrys lapethica
GÖLZ & H.R. REINHARD

Etymology *lapethica:* from Lapethos, an ancient town in northern Cyprus, now named Lapta. **Type** Cy, Esentepe (1989). **Synonyms** *O. scolopax* subsp. *lapethica* (GÖLZ & H.R. REINHARD) G. MORSCHEK & K. MORSCHEK, *O. umbilicata* subsp. *lapethica* (GÖLZ & H.R. REINHARD) N. FAURHOLDT.

Description 12-25 (-30)cm tall; inflorescence near lax, elongated, 6-18cm tall, occupying more than half of stem; 4-9 flowers; sepals and petals pure white, pink, dark lilac or very rarely whitish-green; sepals oval-oblong, 10.5-15mm x 6-9mm, dorsal sepal concave, bent onto the column and longer than it, lateral sepals spreading; petals villous, 3-5mm x 2-4mm, triangular, rarely auriculate, concolourous with sepals or sometimes washed ochre, base darker; lip pendent to near horizontal, 3-lobed at base, 9-12mm x 9-12mm (when spread), velvety, brown to blackish-purple, dark; lateral lobes conical, reduced, attenuated, hairless and whitish to greenish on inner face, with long, dense, brownish to greyish or purplish hairs outside; median lobe obcordate to oboval (when spread), very convex longitudinally, ± globular in centre, appearing very narrow on distal half, attenuated at tip, with a complete marginal band of greyish to brownish hairs, ± attenuated and narrow on lateral-distal quarters, sides strongly turned down and rolled up, touching below lip, hairless yellow margin absent; speculum basal, reduced, rather simple, greyish-blue to purplish, glossy, rather finely edged whitish, encircling the reddish basal field, with 1 (-2) central and 2 lateral ocelli, all often incomplete, delineating in that case a thickened X or H; appendage prominent, yellowish-green, transverse, sometimes near stalked, pointed, 3-toothed, directed forwards or pendent, inserted into a notch; stigmatic cavity reddish to sometimes white barred with brown, vault whitish; pseudo-eyes rounded or in the form of small oblique ridges; staminodial points present.

Flowering Season III-IV.

Habitat Full sun to mid-shade on dry to moist, mostly alkaline substrates. Short grassland, abandoned cultivation, garrigue, olive groves, open pinewoods, up to 700m asl.

Distribution Principally Cyprus and Antalya region (An). Rather widespread and sometimes abundant in northern Cyprus; rare and local elsewhere.

Countries An Cy.

Photos Cy, Larnaca, 28.III.1989; Limassol, 30.III.1989. P. DELFORGE.

Ophrys latakiana
M. Schönfelder & H. Schönfelder.

Etymology *latakiana*: from the port town of Lattakieh (Syria). **Type** Ls, Syria, near Lattakieh (2001). **Synonym** *O. oestrifera* subsp. *latakiana* (M. Schönfelder & H. Schönfelder) Kreutz.

Description Spindly and very slender, 30-58cm tall; bracts rather longer than lower flowers; inflorescence very lax; 4-8 very small flowers, lowest flower placed very high on stem, 20-41cm above ground; sepals and petals concolourous, pink to lilac or dark purple, lateral sepals spreading, oval-lanceolate, 11-13mm x 5-6mm, dorsal sepal turned onto column; petals 2-3mm x 1-1.5mm, triangular-rounded, villous; lip deeply 3-lobed at base, 7-8mm x 8-9mm (when spread), reddish-brown to blackish-brown; lateral lobes forming 2 small basal swellings, short, near conical, near pointed, with rather long, greyish to pale buff hairs outside; median lobe amphoroid, surrounded by a thin, complete, submarginal band of greyish hairs, slightly more prominent above appendage; speculum glossy bluish, basal or extending over the whole median lobe, with a brown ocellus in centre, and, on the sides, branches that encompass the basal swellings and delineate a reddish basal field; appendage well developed, triangular, 3-toothed, yellowish-green, near horizontal or directed; stigmatic cavity rather deep, reddish-brown to greenish, delineated by a ridge bearing 2 rounded, pale greenish pseudo-eyes; staminodial points present; ovary elongated, 13-17mm long.

Flowering Season Late IV-V.

Habitat Mid-shade on moist to wet, calcareous substrates. Scrub, seepages and springs in open thermophilous pinewoods, up to 800m asl.

Distribution Hatay Province (An) and neighbouring parts of northwest Syria. Extremely rare and local, perhaps extinct in Turkey. **Countries** ?†An Ls. **Photos** Ls, Syria, Lattakieh (loc. typ.), 2.V.2000. M. Schönfelder.

Discussion of the *Ophrys oestrifera* group

Eastern, very polyspecific, perhaps monophyletic, with 20 species, always with a very scolopaxoid lip. Some have only recently been described, and there are probably still several undescribed taxa. The centre of speciation for the group is located in the north and centre of the Aegean basin, with extensions west to the Ionian plain (*O. 'bicornis'*, Hu) and Adriatic (*O. rhodostephane*), north to the Crimea (*O. oestrifera* s. str.), and east to the Caucasus and Caspian Sea (*O. abchasica*, *O. schulzei*). The Aegean species, sometimes sympatric, are separated notably by the size of the flowers and flowering season, which implies the attraction of different pollinators.

Ophrys schulzei
BORNMÜLLER & H. FLEISCHMANN

Etymology Named after M. Schulze, German botanist (1841-1915). **Type** Iraq, Kurdistan (1911). **Synonym** *O. luristanica* RENZ.

Description Slender, 15-65cm tall; bracts rather longer than lower flowers; inflorescence very lax; 4-15 small flowers; sepals spreading, large, oval-rounded, 9-11mm x 4-6mm, white to dark purplish-pink, dorsal sepal strongly turned backwards; petals tiny, 1-1.5mm x 1-2.5mm, triangular-rounded, villous at base, colour ± as sepals; lip deeply 3-lobed, reddish-brown; lateral lobes forming 2 prominent basal swellings, broad, near conical, obtuse, rounded, 4-6mm tall, hairless and sometimes whitish to greenish on inner face, exterior with rather long, white to ochre hairs; median lobe globular, relatively small, 5-7mm x 5-7mm, surrounded by a thin submarginal band of straight, whitish hairs, more prominent above appendage; speculum whitish to yellowish or shiny bluish, edged white, covering entire median lobe, with a central brown ocellus and lateral extensions towards the base, appendage and basal swellings; appendage prominent, triangular, sometimes acuminate or 3-toothed, yellowish-green, 1.5-2.5mm long, turned under lip, pendent; stigmatic cavity deep, reddish-brown, edged at base by 2 rudimentary internal lips bearing the pseudo-eyes; column acuminate, tip often sinuous, 1-2mm long.

Flowering Season IV-VI.

Habitat Full sun to mid-shade on dry to moist, calcareous substrates. Short, poor grassland, scrub, open thermophilous oakwoods, 500-1700m asl.

Distribution Southeastern Anatolia to Iran and south to Lebanon. Rare and local. **Countries** An Ls. **Photos** An, Diyarbakir, 17.V.1990. P. DELFORGE.

The *Ophrys heldreichii* group

(see pp. 514-520)

Principally southern Aegean, perhaps mono-phyletic, with 6 described species. The lip varies in the degree of indentation and convexity, from very scolopaxoid to very fucifloroid, with equally varied submarginal hairs. These different states and their intermediates are often present within the same populations, sometimes even on the same plant. Probably intermediate between the *O. bornmuelleri* and *O. oestrifera* groups, it may appear merely as the eastern equivalent of the *O. tetraloniae* group, but without the tendency towards late flowering. Well represented in the southern Aegean arc, the group is poorly represented in Anatolia but appears, along with the *O. bornmuelleri* group, to have established outliers towards the northwest, to Istria and Mount Gargano (*O. zinsmeisteri*), via the Peloponnese (*O. schlechteriana*).

The *Ophrys heldreichii* group

Characteristics As *O. oestrifera* s.l. but with large, elongated, ± auriculate petals, very often contiguous at base; lip varied, sometimes within the same population: entire and ± spreading (= fucifloroid) to deeply 3-lobed, with lateral lobes conical and median lobe very convex transversally, often amphoroid (= lip scolopaxoid).

Ophrys zinsmeisteri
A. FUCHS & ZIEGENSPECK (pro. hybr.)

Etymology Named after J.-B. Zinsmeister, Bavarian botanist (1862-1944). **Type** Ju, Croatia, Rijeka (1928). **Synonyms** *O. oestrifera* subsp. *zinsmeisteri* (A. FUCHS & ZIEGENSPECK) KREUTZ, *O. oestrifera* vel *cornuta* vel *scolopax* auct., *O. kvarneri* M.L. PERKO & KERSCHBAUMSTEINER.

Description 10-40cm tall; 2-6 rather large flowers; sepals rounded, dark purple, 11-15mm x 4-6mm; petals concolourous, villous, triangular-rounded, obscurely auriculate, 3-5.8mm x 1.5-2.2mm; lip pendent, 11-14 (-15)mm x 12-16mm (when spread), blackish-brown, 3-lobed; lateral lobes conical, 4-6mm long, near pointed; median lobe rather short, slightly convex, appearing broad, globular in centre, velvety towards margins, usually without a distinct submarginal band of hairs.

Flowering Season IV-V. **Habitat** Full sun to shade on dry, calcareous substrates. Abandoned cultivation, olive groves, oak-hornbeam woods along with *Carpinus orientalis*, up to 200m asl. **Distribution** Eastern Istria and the Quarnero archipelago; very similar plants occur on Mount Gargano (It). Very local but sometimes abundant. **Countries** ?It Ju. **Photos** Ju, Hrvatska, Krk, 11.V.2004. P. DELFORGE.

Ophrys pharia

P. DEVILLERS & J. DEVILLERS-TERSCHUREN

Etymology *pharia:* from Pharos, now the island of Hvar. Type Ju, Croatia, Hvar (2004). **Synonyms** *O. heldreichii* subsp. *pharia* (P. DEVILLERS & J. DEVILLERS-TERSCHUREN) KREUTZ, *O. holoserica* subsp. *maxima* vel *fuciflora* var. *maxima* auct.

Description Thickset, 10-25cm tall; inflorescence rather dense; 3-6 large flowers; sepals broadly lanceolate, lilac to purplish, 11-16mm long; petals concolourous or slightly darker, villous, triangular, auriculate, often contiguous at base, 3-7mm x 2.5-3.5mm; lip pendent, (10-) 12-16mm x 13-22mm (when spread), reddish-brown, entire to obscurely 3-lobed, shoulders rather squared, with conical basal swellings, 0.5-2mm long, centre transversally convex, sides turned down and under (then scolopaxoid, photo C), dropping straight down or slightly recurved (then fucifloroid, photo A), velvety up to margins, lateral-distal quarters rarely with a distinct submarginal band of hairs (if so, very short); speculum relatively limited; stigmatic cavity and basal field relatively cramped, reddish to pale rusty; pseudo-eyes greenish, rounded.

Flowering Season IV-V. **Habitat** Full sun to mid-shade on dry to moist, sandy substrates. Banks, scrub, olive groves, up to 300m asl. **Distribution** Endemic to the island of Hvar. Very local and extremely rare; threatened by agriculture.

Countries Ju. **Photos A & B** Ju, Hrvatska, Hvar (loc. typ.), 16.V.2004. P. DELFORGE; **C** 24.IV.2002. J. DEVILLERS-TERSCHUREN.

515

Ophrys schlechteriana

(Soó) J. Devillers-Terschuren & P. Devillers

Etymology Dedicated to R. Schlechter, German orchidologist (1872-1925). **Type*** Gr, Attica and Argolide (1927). **Synonyms** *Ophrys heldreichii* var. *schlechteriana* (Soó) Soó, *O. oestrifera* subsp. *schlechteriana* (Soó) Kreutz, *O. fuciflora* ?f. *pseudooestrifera* Renz.

Description As *O. heldreichii* but very robust; petals rather large, 4-6.5mm x 2-3.5mm, triangular, often contiguous at base; lip very large, 15-18mm long, strongly convex transversally; lateral lobes more elongated, over 5-10mm long, slender, sinuous or curved outwards; median lobe prominent and globular, amphoroid; appendage very well developed, horizontal, multi-toothed; stigmatic cavity transverse, contracted in upper part of lip.

Flowering Season IV-V.

Habitat As *O. heldreichii*. **Distribution** Northern limits of range poorly known due to confusion with *O. sepioides* and *O. crassicornis*; at least the eastern Peloponnese, Attica (= Attiki) and central Cyclades; local but sometimes abundant. **Countries** Gr. **Photo A** Gr, Argolida (loc. typ.), 17.IV.1991. P. Delforge.

Key to the *Ophrys heldreichii* group

1	lip clearly and deeply 3-lobed	2
1*	lip entire to obscurely 3-lobed	6
2	median lobe of lip merely velvety	*O. zinsmeisteri*
2*	median lobe with a distinct, complete submarginal band of hairs	3
3	lip 7.5-11mm long	*O. homeri*
3*	lip 11-18mm long	4
4	basal swellings of lip 2.5-10mm long	5
4*	basal swellings 1-2mm long	*O. calypsus* var. *scolopaxoides*
5	basal swellings of lip sinuous, 5-10mm long	*O. schlechteriana*
5*	basal swellings straight, 2.5-5 (-6mm) long	*O. heldreichii*
6.	centre of lip very convex transversally	7
6*	lip spreading, only slightly convex	*O. 'maxima'*
7	speculum restricted, rather simple	*O. pharia*
7*	speculum extensive, complex	8
8	lip globular, sides turned down and under	*O. calypsus*
8*	sides of lip slightly spreading to recurved	*O. calypsus* var. *pseudoapulica*

Ophrys heldreichii
SCHLECHTER

Etymology Named after Th. von Heldreich, director of the Athens Botanical Garden (1822-1902). **Type*** Cr, Chania (1923). **Synonyms** *O. scolopax* subsp. *heldreichii* (SCHLECHTER) E.G. CAMUS, *O. cornuta* subsp. *heldreichii* (SCHLECHTER) RENZ.

Description 15-50cm tall; (2-) 4-10 large flowers; sepals pinkish to dark purple, oval-lanceolate, 12.5-16mm x 6-10mm, spreading; petals villous, erect, triangular to lanceolate, rarely auriculate, very often contiguous at base, 3-6.5 (-8)mm x 2-3.5mm, colour as sepals or darker; lip near horizontal to pendent, ± clearly 3-lobed at base, 13-16mm x 15-18mm (when spread), velvety, pale reddish-brown to dark blackish-brown; lateral lobes relatively small, conical at tip, pointed, 2.5-5 (-6)mm long, straight-erect, hairless and yellowish on inner face, exterior with long, dense, russet to whitish hairs; median lobe obcordate (when spread), very convex transversally, very globular in centre, amphoroid; marginal band of hairs dense, long, yellowish-russet, complete but attenuated in lateral-distal quarters; sides usually lacking a hairless rim, strongly turned down, frequently touching below the lip; speculum blue to purplish-red, glossy, ± broadly and irregularly edged whitish or yellowish, quadrangular, extensive, surrounding the pale reddish-brown basal field, with a central ocellus and 2 lateral ocelli, sometimes fragmented or marbled; appendage very prominent, 2.5-5mm long, thick, with 3-9 teeth, greenish-yellow to, more rarely, brownish-red, pendent to pointing forwards, inserted into a prominent notch; stigmatic cavity relatively small, brownish, paler than basal field, transverse, 5-6mm wide, low, only slightly separated from lip, with 2 shiny blackish-brown pseudo-eyes and a horizontal ledge delimiting the basal field; staminodial points present.

Flowering Season III-IV (-V).

Habitat Mostly full sun on dry to moist, alkaline substrates. Short, poor grassland, garrigue, abandoned cultivation, old terraces, scrub, up to 1200m asl. **Distribution** Southern Aegean. Perhaps endemic to Crete, where widespread and rather abundant. **Countries** ?Ae ?An Cr ?Gr. **Photos A & C** Cr, Lassithi, 4.III.1990; **B** 4.IV.1982. P. DELFORGE.

Pollinator *Eucera rufa* (Hymenoptera: Anthophoridae).

Ophrys calypsus
HIRTH & SPAETH

Etymology Named after the nymph Calypso. **Type** Ae, Lepsoi Island (1994). **Synonyms** *O. heldreichii* var. *calypsus* (HIRTH & SPAETH) P. DELFORGE, *O. heldreichii* subsp. *calypsus* (HIRTH & SPAETH) KREUTZ.

Description Not very tall, rather spindly, 9-27cm tall; (1-) 2-5 rather large flowers; sepals pale pink to dark purple, 10-17.5mm x 6-11mm, petals concolourous, 5-8.4mm x 2.5-3.5mm, often contiguous at base; lip near entire to ± obscurely 3-lobed, varying within the same population (see var. below), 10.5-15 (-16)mm x 12-18mm (when spread), globular in centre, appearing oval or near quadrangular, sides turned down and under, with rather short basal swellings, 2-5mm long; submarginal band of hairs dense and long at base and above appendage, complete to very attenuated on lateral-distal quarters; speculum often extensive, complex, broadly edged ivory-white, sometimes fragmented and marbled or candicoid; appendage well developed, rather short, horizontal, 3-toothed; stigmatic cavity transverse, often contracted in upper part of lip.

Flowering Season Mid III-IV.

Habitat As *O. heldreichii*.

Distribution Eastern Aegean. Rather widespread and rather abundant.

Countries Ae An Gr. **Photos** Gr, Cyclades, Paros, 13.IV.1995; Amorgos, 21.IV.1997. P. DELFORGE.

Pollinator *Eucera dalmatica* (Hymenoptera: Anthophoridae).

Ophrys calypsus
var. *scolopaxoides* (P. DELFORGE) P. DELFORGE

Etymology *scolopaxoides:* similar to [*Ophrys*] *scolopax*. **Type** Gr, Cyclades, Paros (1995). **Basionym** *O. heldreichii* var. *scolopaxoides* P. DELFORGE.

Description As *O. calypsus* var. *calypsus*, but more spindly, size falling in lower part of range for the species; inflorescence often denser; flowers relatively small, recalling slightly those of *O. ceto*; petals smaller, less elongated, often contiguous at base; lip smaller, 11-14mm long; lateral lobes shorter, 1-2mm long, tip rarely sinuous or recurved; median lobe less prominent, less or only slightly globular, sides strongly bent down and under.

Distribution Mostly centre of range, with var. *calypsus* and intermediate forms; limits of distribution poorly known due to confusion with *O. ceto*. **Photo A** (p. 519) Gr, Cyclades, Paros (loc. typ.), 9.IV.1995. P. DELFORGE.

Ophrys calypsus
var. *pseudoapulica* (P. Delforge) P. Delforge

Etymology *pseudoapulica:* false [*Ophrys*] *apulica*.
Type Gr, Cyclades, Antiparos (1995). **Synonyms**
O. heldreichii var. *pseudoapulica* P. Delforge, *O. heldreichii* subsp. *pseudoapulica* (P. Delforge)
Kreutz, *O. apulica* auct. non (O. Danesch & E. Danesch) O.
Danesch & E. Danesch, *O. episcopalis* auct. non Poiret.
Description As *O. calypsus* var. *calypsus*, but
flowers recalling those of *O. apulica* or *O.* '*maxima*'; petals large, triangular, often contiguous at
base; lip near entire, large to very large, sometimes
appearing trapezoid, up to 16mm long, convex in
centre, sides spreading, ± recurved.
Distribution Mostly centre and east of range
(Cyclades, Rhodes). **Photo B** Gr, Cyclades, Antiparos (loc. typ.), 12.IV.1995. P. Delforge.

Ophrys '*maxima*'

Etymology *maxima:* very large; this taxon lacks a valid
name (*O. maxima* is a synonym of *O. episcopalis*).
Synonyms *O. apulica* auct., *O. episcopalis* auct.
Description As *O. calypsus* var. *pseudoapulica*,
but sepals and petals ± concolourous, pink to intensely purple; petals broadly triangular-rounded,
size varied, 3-8mm x 3-5mm, averaging 4.33mm
long, averaging slightly shorter than those of *O.
apulica*, longer than those of *O. episcopalis*; lip entire, trapezoid to broadly oboval (when spread),
large to very large, up to 18mm long, slightly convex, sides spreading, recurved forwards; band of
marginal hairs attenuated on distal half; speculum
not very extensive.
Flowering Season III-V. **Habitat** As *O. heldreichii*.
Distribution Eastern Aegean. Known with certainty
from Rhodes (Ae), perhaps extends east to Syria.
Rather rare and local. **Countries** Ae ?An ?Cr ?Ls.
Photo C Ae, Rhodos, 9.IV.1984. P. Delforge.

Ophrys homeri
HIRTH & SPAETH

Etymology Named after Homer, poet of ancient Greece. **Type** Ae, Chios (1997). **Synonym** *O. holoserica* subsp. *homeri* (HIRTH & SPAETH) KREUTZ.

Description Rather spindly, (12-) 15-36 (-42)cm tall; 2-10 flowers; sepals dark pink to pinkish, lanceolate, lateral sepals 8.7-14.5mm x 4.1-9mm, dorsal sepal usually curved over onto column; petals triangular, sometimes auriculate, 4.3-6.4mm x 1.5-3.3mm (mean sepal length/petal length = 2.30), villous, colour as sepals, sometimes contiguous at base; lip near entire to 3-lobed, globular, trapezoid-rounded, 7.5-11mm x 9-13.5mm (when spread), reddish-brown and velvety in centre, with 2 basal swellings, pointed to rounded, ± divergent, hairless on inner face, sides reddish-brown to broadly yellowish, straight, with ± narrow hairless margin; submarginal band of hairs complete, pale whitish-brown, broad on basal half of lip, narrower distally; speculum basal and central, brownish-blue, rather broadly edged greenish-yellow, forming a central ocellus, usually complete, and ± fragmentary lateral ocelli encompassing the basal swellings; basal field rather angular, rusty-brown, slightly paler than centre of lip; appendage greenish-yellow, rather well developed, with 1-5 teeth, ascendant; stigmatic cavity relatively large, often with a greyish specular stage, upper border barred brownish-purple; pseudo-eyes rounded, shiny, blackish-green, encircled by greenish-yellow; staminodial points present.

Flowering Season IV-V, rather late.

Habitat Full sun to mid-shade on dry, alkaline substrates. Abandoned cultivation, garrigue, scrub, open pinewoods, up to 700m asl.

Distribution Eastern Aegean. Chios, Kos, Lesbos and Mugla Province (An). Rare and local. **Countries** Ae An. **Photos** Ae, Chios, 21.V.1991. H. SPAETH; Lesbos, 25.IV.1999. C.A.J. Kreutz; 18.IV.1998. A. JOUKOFF.

The *Ophrys umbilicata* group

Characteristics Dorsal sepal almost always bent over onto column; petals triangular, villous, margins straight; lip 3-lobed at base, velvety, with prominent marginal hairs; lateral lobes conical; median lobe convex; speculum extensive, with ocelli; appendage ± clearly 3-toothed, inserted into notch in lip; stigmatic cavity cup-shaped; pseudo-eyes and staminodial points present.

Discussion An eastern Mediterranean group, probably monophyletic, within the *O. fuciflora* complex. The 6 species show a primitive character (the dorsal sepal being consistently bent forwards), which gives them the appearance, along with indented lip, prominent marginal hairs and often rudimentary appendage, of a collection of archaic taxa, closely related to the *O. bornmuelleri* group; they probably differentiated via sympatric speciation through recurrent adaptations to new pollinators.

Ophrys attica
(BOISSIER & ORPHANIDES) B.D. JACKSON

Etymology *attica:* from Attica. **Type** Gr, Attica (1859). **Synonyms** *O. arachnites* var. *attica* BOISSIER & ORPHANIDES, *O. carmeli* subsp. *attica* (BOISSIER & ORPHANIDES) RENZ, *O. umbilicata* subsp. *attica* (BOISSIER & ORPHANIDES) J.J. WOOD, *O. scolopax* subsp. *attica* (BOISSIER & ORPHANIDES) E. NELSON p.p.

Description As *O. umbilicata* but up to 35cm tall; inflorescence denser, near cylindrical, up to 6cm in diameter; 3-12 flowers; sepals green, very rarely whitish or pinkish, dorsal sepal on average more elongated, exceeding the column by a greater margin; petals and median lobe of lip slightly more elongated; lateral lobes with parallel or convergent tips, more rarely divergent.

Flowering Season III-V.

Habitat As *O. umbilicata*, but up to 800m asl.

Distribution Poorly known due to confusion with related taxa. Southern Albania to, probably, western Anatolia. Rather rare and scattered.

Countries Ae An Gr.

Photos Gr, Cephalonia, 4.IV.1991; Attica, 9.IV.1991. P. DELFORGE.

Pollinator *Eucera seminuda* (Hymenoptera: Anthophoridae).

Discussion Although no clear-cut morphological character seems to distinguish *Ophrys attica* from *O. umbilicata*, which has led to the frequent refusal to separate the 2 taxa, it seems that they are isolated due to their different pollinators. Nevertheless, the situation within the (vast?) contact zone needs to be investigated further.

Ophrys umbilicata
DESFONTAINES

Etymology *umbilicata:* with an umbilicus (= navel, an allusion to the central ocellus of the speculum). **Type** Ae, Chios or Samos Island (1807). **Synonyms** *O. carmeli* H. FLEISCHMANN & BORNMÜLLER, *O. dinsmorei* Schlechter, *O. easternis* (RENZ) SOÓ.

Description 10-25 (-40)cm tall; inflorescence lax, up to 5cm in diameter; 2-7 (-10) flowers; sepals whitish to pinkish or, less often, whitish-green, oval-oblong, 8-15mm x 4-8mm, margins reflexed, dorsal sepal concave, bent down onto the column and just slightly longer than it, lateral sepals spreading; petals coloured as sepals but darker, villous, 3.5-6.5mm x 2-4mm, triangular, often auriculate; lip near horizontal, 3-lobed at base, 7-12.5mm x 8.5-15mm (when spread), velvety, pale to dark reddish-brown; lateral lobes conical, pointed, directed forwards, tips often divergent or curved outwards, inner face hairless and whitish, exterior with long, dense, brownish to greyish hairs; median lobe subobcordate to oboval (when spread), convex, globular in centre, appearing ovoid to spherical, with greyish to brownish marginal hairs, sides turned down and under, yellow margin absent; speculum extensive, covering almost entire median lobe, varied, greyish-blue to reddish, glossy, ± broadly edged whitish or yellowish, surrounding the reddish to blackish-brown basal field, with 1-3 central ocelli, the distal of which is incomplete, and 2 lateral ocelli, surrounding base of lateral lobes; appendage yellowish-green, transverse, thick, sometimes pointed or 3-toothed, directed forwards, inserted into a weak notch; base of stigmatic cavity reddish to blackish-brown, upper third whitish, finely barred brown; pseudo-eyes dark greenish-brown, sometimes reduced; staminodial points present.

Flowering Season (I-) II-IV.

Habitat Full sun to mid-shade on dry to moist, calcareous substrates, rarely sandstone. Short grassland, abandoned cultivation, garrigue, scrub, open woodland, up to 1200m asl.

Distribution Eastern Mediterranean. Limits of range poorly known due to confusion with related taxa. Aegean basin to south of Iran. Rather local but sometimes abundant.

Countries Ae An Cy ?Gr Ij Ls.

Photos Ae, Lesbos, 10.IV.1991; Cy, Paphos, 5.IV.1989. P. DELFORGE.

Pollinators *Eucera galilaea* (Ij), *E. spatulata* (Ae, Lesbos) and *E. gaullei* (Cy) (Hymenoptera: Anthophoridae).

Ophrys bucephala
GÖLZ & H.R. REINHARD

Etymology *bucephala:* [shaped like] a bull's head. **Type** Ae, Lesbos (1990). **Synonym** *O. umbilicata* subsp. *bucephala* (GÖLZ & H.R. REINHARD) B. BIEL.

Description Thickset, 10-25cm tall; inflorescence dense; 2-7 large flowers; sepals green, sometimes whitish-green or washed violet, oval-oblong, sometimes pointed, 12-17.5mm x 6-9mm, margins reflexed, dorsal sepal concave, bent onto column and often rather longer than it, lateral sepals spreading; petals villous, green, 5-8mm x 2.5-5mm, triangular, sometimes auriculate and washed violet at base; lip near horizontal, 3-lobed at base, 12-15.5mm x 15-19mm, oboval (when spread), velvety, pale to dark reddish-brown; lateral lobes conical, pointed, directed forwards or recurved upwards, inner face brownish, hairless and often whitish, exterior with long, dense, brownish to whitish hairs; median lobe trapezoid to obcordate (when spread), very convex, globular in centre, appearing narrow, sides turned down and under, marginal hairs, greyish to brownish, rather short; speculum basal and central, covering entire median lobe, varied, metallic blue, broadly edged whitish or yellowish, surrounding the reddish basal field, with 1-2 central ocelli, the distal of which is sometimes incomplete, and 2 lateral ocelli, surrounding base of lateral lobes; appendage yellowish-green, prominent, transverse, slightly pointed, obscurely 3-toothed, often directed forwards, inserted into broad notch in lip; stigmatic cavity reddish, as tall as broad, relatively small; pseudo-eyes dark greenish-brown, sometimes reduced; staminodial points present.

Variation Slight. Distinguished by the large flowers and relatively cramped stigmatic cavity. Forms intermediate with *O. umbilicata* and *O. attica* have been reported.

Flowering Season IV.

Habitat Full sun to mid-shade on dry to moist, calcareous substrates. Short, poor grassland, abandoned cultivation, garrigue, scrub, olive groves, open woodland, up to 500m asl.

Distribution Northern Aegean. Principally Lesbos, northwest Anatolia and European Turkey. Rare and local.

Countries Ae An Tu.

Photos Ae, Lesbos, 11.IV.1991. P. DELFORGE.

Pollinator *Eucera curvitarsis* (Hymenoptera: Anthophoridae).

523

Ophrys flavomarginata
(RENZ) H. BAUMANN & KÜNKELE

Etymology *flavomarginata:* with a yellow margin.
Type Cy, Nicosie (1929). **Synonyms** *O. attica* f.
flavomarginata RENZ, *O. fuciflora* f. *flavomarginata*
(RENZ) HAYEK, *O. umbilicata* subsp. *flavomarginata*
(RENZ) N. FAURHOLDT.

Description 15-30cm tall; (2-) 4-11 (-13) medium-sized flowers; sepals green, sometimes
whitish-green or yellowish, oval, 11-14.5mm x
5.5-8.5mm, margins recurved, dorsal sepal concave, ± bent onto column, lateral sepals spreading; petals villous, green to olive-green, 4-7mm x
2.5-5mm, triangular, sometimes auriculate and
washed lilac at base; lip 3-lobed at base, 9-14mm
x 11.5-16mm, oboval (when spread), pendent,
velvety, pale to dark reddish-brown; lateral lobes
conical, ± pointed, directed forwards, brownish to
greenish, inner face hairless and sometimes
whitish, exterior with long, dense, greyish hairs;
median lobe obcordate (when spread), convex,
hardly globular in centre, with a marginal band of
greyish to brownish hairs, rarely attenuated on
distal half, sides sometimes reflexed, with a
greenish-yellow to orange-brown hairless margin
1-4mm wide; speculum varied, basal and central,
covering up to 3/4 of lip, greyish-blue or
purplish, glossy, ± broadly edged whitish or
yellowish, broadly trapezoid, surrounding the
basal field, with 1-2 central ocelli, the distal of
which is often incomplete, and 2 lateral ocelli,
encompassing base of lateral lobes; appendage
greenish-yellow, prominent, transverse, roll-
shaped and obscurely 3-toothed, sometimes
pointed or clearly 3-toothed, inserted into broad
notch in lip; basal field reddish; stigmatic cavity
slightly taller than broad, reddish; pseudo-eyes
dark greenish-brown, often reduced; staminodial
points present.

Variation Varied. Distinguished from *O. umbilicata* by its early flowering and larger flowers,
with the sepals always green and median lobe
less convex. There are, nevertheless, populations
intermediate between the 2 species.

Flowering Season II-IV, slightly earlier than *O.
umbilicata.*

Habitat Full sun to mid-shade on dry to moist,
calcareous substrates. Short grassland, abandoned
cultivation, garrigue, scrub, up to 600m asl.

Distribution The Near East. Cyprus (rather scattered and rare) and Israel (very local and very rare).

Countries Cy Ij.

Photos Cy, Larnaca, 28.III.1989. P. DELFORGE.

Pollinator *Eucera dimidiata* (Hymenoptera: Anthophoridae) – also the pollinator of *O. villosa*, an
early-flowering Cretan taxon (see p. 438) absent
from the range of *O. flavomarginata.*

Ophrys khuzestanica
(RENZ & TAUBENHEIM) P. DELFORGE

Etymology *khuzestanica:* from Khuzistan. **Type** Iran, Khuzistan (1983). **Basionym** *O. umbilicata* subsp. *khuzestanica* RENZ & TAUBENHEIM.

Description As *O. umbilicata* but slender, 20-60cm tall; inflorescence lax, diameter up to 4cm; (5-) 7-12 rather small flowers; sepals green, whitish-green, sometimes pinkish, oval-elliptical, dorsal sepal erect to curved forwards onto column; petals 2-4.5mm x 2-4.5mm, often auriculate; lip 7-10.5mm long, pale reddish-brown to dark blackish-purple; hairs of lateral lobes sometimes purplish; median lobe globular in centre but less convex, sides often tinted greenish-yellow, turned down and back rather than underneath; appendage more pointed, narrower, 3-toothed, directed forwards or upwards, inserted into a deep notch.

Variation Rather varied. May appear as an intermediate between the *O. umbilicata* group and *O. bornmuelleri,* which may have introgressed it.

Flowering Season III-V.

Habitat As *O. umbilicata* but 400-2100m asl.

Distribution Near East. Southeast Anatolia to Iran. Rare and local.

Countries An.

Photos An, Diyarbakir, 17.V.1990. P. DELFORGE.

Key to the *Ophrys umbilicata* group

1   median lobe of lip slightly convex, sides sometimes reflexed, with a greenish-yellow margin 1-4mm wide; appendage thick, transverse .... *O. flavomarginata*
1*   lip otherwise 2

2   lip 11.5-15.5mm long 3
2*   lip 7.5-12.5mm long 4

3   lip blackish, pseudo-eyes glossy white with a black dot .... *O. kotschyi*
3*   lip brown to dark greenish-brown, pseudo-eyes dark greenish-brown .... *O. bucephala*

4   margins of lip greenish-yellow, appendage narrow, pointed .... *O. khuzestanica*
4*   lip otherwise 5

5.   sepals mainly green .... *O. attica*
5*   sepals mainly whitish to pink
    .... *O. umbilicata*

Ophrys kotschyi

H. FLEISCHMANN & SOÓ

Etymology Named after Th. Kotschy, Austrian botanist (1813-1866). **Type** Cy, Larnaca (1928). **Synonyms** *O. cypria* RENZ, *O. sintenisii* subsp. *kotschyi* (H. FLEISCHMANN & SOÓ) SOÓ.

Description Thickset, (8-) 12-35cm tall; inflorescence dense, 5-14cm tall; 3-10 large flowers; sepals whitish-green, base whitish to pinkish, rarely entirely white, pink or pale ochre, oval-lanceolate, 12.5-16mm x 6-8.5mm, margins recurved, dorsal sepal concave, bent onto column (50% of flowers) or erect, lateral sepals spreading; petals villous, olive-greenish, white or pink, washed green, rarely bright purple, 5.5-8mm x 2-4.5mm, triangular, rather elongated, sometimes auriculate, erect or recurved backwards; lip pendent to near horizontal, 3-lobed at base, 11.5-15mm x 14-17mm (when spread), velvety, dark blackish-purple; lateral lobes convex, conical to rounded, tip obtuse, inner face hairless, whitish to violet-purple, exterior with long, dense, whitish, greyish or purplish hairs; median lobe prominent, obcordate (when spread), very convex, sometimes globular in centre, appearing (narrowly) ovoid to amphoroid, with a complete, rather short, marginal band of greyish hairs, sides turned down and under, lacking a yellow hairless margin; speculum varied, very extensive, sometimes covering entire median lobe, glossy slate-grey, ± broadly edged white, very complex, often fragmented, surrounding blackish basal field, with 2-3 central ocelli and 4-10 lateral ocelli, mostly irregular and incomplete; appendage yellowish-green to purplish-brown, relatively small, thick, pointed, directed forward or pendent, inserted into a notch; stigmatic cavity constricted at base, blackish with a whitish to pale bluish-grey specular stage or transverse bar; pseudo-eyes glossy white with a black dot; staminodial points present, blackish.

Flowering Season III-IV.

Habitat Full sun to mid-shade on dry to moist, calcareous substrates, sometimes sandstone. Short grassland, abandoned cultivation, garrigue, open pinewoods, up to 1000m asl.

Distribution Endemic to Cyprus. Rather local and rather rare.

Countries Cy.

Photos Cy, Larnaca, 1.IV.1989. P. DELFORGE.

Pollinator *Melecta tuberculata* (Hymenoptera: Anthophoridae), which is also the pollinator of *Ophrys cretica* (Cr, Gr). The similarities between the 2 species, members of 2 rather distantly related groups, may result from convergence in their adaptation to the same pollinator.

The *Ophrys reinholdii* group

Characteristics Lateral sepals often bicoloured; petals triangular, villous; lip 3-lobed at base; lateral lobes with dense, long hairs; median lobe dark, velvety, with a continuous submarginal band of hairs and hairless border; appendage triangular or 3-toothed, extending margins of lip; stigmatic cavity cup-shaped, white, barred or blotched with black, without black pseudo-eyes; staminodial and temporal bosses distinct, the former often marked with a broad dark blotch; internal lips near absent; vestiges of external lips in the form of small, shiny, white ridges. A monophyletic, eastern Mediterranean group, with 5 species replacing each other geographically and/or reproductively isolated by their pollinators, and one hybridogenous species.

Ophrys reinholdii
SPRUNER ex H. FLEISCHMANN

Etymology Named after Reinhold, an Athens doctor (1802-1880). **Type** Gr, Attica and Corfu (1907). **Synonym** *O. mimnolea* O. SCHWARZ.

Description 20-60cm tall; 2-8 (-10) flowers; sepals faded pink to purple, often washed green, rarely white or green, oval-lanceolate, 12-16 (-19)mm x 4-7.5 (-9)mm, lateral sepals spreading, sometimes tinted violet; petals villous, pale olive-pink to dark purplish-brown, sometimes green, 4-8 (-11)mm x 1.5-2.5 (-4)mm, narrowly triangular, sometimes auriculate, spreading or turned backwards, margins straight; lip deeply 3-lobed at base, 10-15mm x 12-19mm (when spread); lateral lobes conical, pale brown to blackish-purple, exterior with long, dense, whitish to greyish hairs; median lobe much larger than lateral lobes, broadly wedge-shaped to oboval, velvety, very dark, bordered by fine silver hairs and then a paler, reddish to olive-green hairless margin; speculum varied, central, white or slate-grey, broadly edged white, made up of 2 oblique spatulate drops, isolated or contiguous; appendage prominent, often thick, triangular or 3-toothed, pendent or erect, greenish to reddish; stigmatic cavity broad, whitish, transversally barred black.

Flowering Season III-VI.

Habitat Full sun to shade on alkaline to slightly acidic, dry to moist, substrates. Short grassland, garrigue, scrub, open to dense woodland, up to 1300m asl.

Distribution Eastern Mediterranean, from Macedonia (Ju) to southwest Anatolia. Rather scattered and rather rare. **Countries** Ae Al An Gr Ju. **Photos** Gr, Imathia, 9.VI.1987; Lakonia, 20.IV.1992. P. DELFORGE.

Pollinators *Eupavolvskia obscura* and perhaps *E. funeraria* (Hymenoptera: Anthophoridae).

Ophrys straussii
H. FLEISCHMANN & BORNMÜLLER

Etymology Named after Strauss, Austrian botanist (1850-1922). **Type** Iran, Kerind (1923). **Synonyms** *O. reinholdii* subsp. *straussii* (H. FLEISCHMANN & BORNMÜLLER) E. NELSON, *O. reinholdii* subsp. *leucotenia* RENZ & TAUBENHEIM, *O. straussii* var. *leucotenia* (RENZ & TAUBENHEIM) R. PETER.

Description As *O. reinholdii* but petals narrower; lateral lobes of lip more rounded; median lobe more convex, appearing obovoid; speculum often reduced and more centrally placed, comprising 2 parallel, contiguous drops, sometimes linked by a ± broad transverse line; appendage reduced; tip of column more acuminate.

Flowering Season IV-VI.

Habitat As *O. reinholdii*, but up to 2100m asl.

Distribution From Rhodes (Ae) to Iranian Kurdistan. Rather rare and local. **Countries** Ae An. **Photos A & B** An, Çevisli, 19.V.1997. C.A.J. KREUTZ; Içel, 15.V.1990. P. DELFORGE. **Discussion** A controversial taxon, intergrading broadly with *O. reinholdii* within the Aegean basin and in Anatolia; often considered a subspecies of the latter. **Variation** *'leucotenia'*: Variant with sepals pale, lateral lobes of lip white, speculum large; reported from 6 stations. **Photo C** An, Antalya (loc. typ.), 13.V.1991. P. DELFORGE.

Ophrys antiochiana
H. Baumann & Künkele (pro hybr.)

Etymology *antiochiana:* from Antioch (=Antakya). **Type** An, Hatay (=Antakya) (1986). **Synonym** *O. straussii* subsp. *antiochiana* (H. Baumann & Künkele) Kreutz.

Description Appears intermediate between *O. straussii* and *O. amanensis*. As *O. straussii* but stem 20-40cm tall; 3-6 relatively large flowers; sepals 14-17.5mm x 6.5-8.5mm, spreading, pale pink to dark purple, sometimes irregularly spotted; petals 6-10.5mm long, slightly darker than sepals, pink to dark purple, ± strongly tinted orange or brown; lip near entire to 3-lobed, 11-16mm long, velvety, blackish-brown to blackish-purple, shoulders rounded; lateral lobes not obvious and parallel to median lobe, or obvious and very rounded, with a marginal band of slightly longer, paler hairs with silver reflections; median lobe near trapezoid to ellipsoid, velvety, with hairless reddish margin, sides straight or turned under; appendage reduced; speculum reduced, central, sometimes ± H-shaped; floor of stigmatic cavity blackish, with white to bluish specular stage, vault white, ± clearly barred by a transverse brown line; sides of stigmatic cavity often with rudimentary bluish pseudo-eyes; blotches of staminodial bosses reduced; tip of column acuminate.

Flowering Season IV-V.

Habitat Full sun to mid-shade on moist calcareous substrates. Short, poor grassland, abandoned cultivation, the margins of scrub and woodland, 500-900m asl. **Distribution** Apparently endemic to the centre of southern Anatolia, principally the south of the Antakya region and neighbouring parts of Syria. Very rare and local. **Countries** An Ls.

Photos An, Çevisli, 19.V.1997. C.A.J. Kreutz.

Key to the *Ophrys reinholdii* group

1	lip very narrow; lateral lobes conical, tiny, 1-2.5mm high	*O. cilicica*
1*	lip broader; lateral lobes larger, and conical or rounded	2
2	speculum extensive, starting at stigmatic cavity and reaching or almost reaching appendage	3
2*	speculum reduced, central	4
3	stigmatic cavity large (height 0.2-0.4 x length of lip), constricted at base, lateral margins curved	*O. cretica*
3*	stigmatic cavity small (height 0.08-0.2 x length of lip), not constricted at base, lateral margins straight	*O. ariadnae*

(continued on p. 532)

529

Ophrys cilicica
SCHLECHTER

Etymology *cilicica:* from Cilicia. **Type** An, Adana (1923). **Synonyms** *O. mammosa* subsp. *boissieri* (SOÓ) SOÓ, *O. kurdistanica* RENZ, *O. kurdica* D. RÜCKBRODT & U. RÜCKBRODT, *O. kurdica* subsp. *kurdistanica* (RENZ) SOÓ.

Description Slender and spindly, 15-40 (-60)cm tall; inflorescence lax; 3-12 flowers; sepals green, sometimes whitish, often washed pinkish or violet, 9-13mm x 3.5-5mm, narrowly oval-lanceolate, curved forwards, margins recurved, dorsal sepal erect or bent onto column, lateral sepals spreading, longer than lip; petals linear-lanceolate, 4-7mm x 1-2mm, villous, crimson-pink washed green to brownish, margins straight; lip deeply 3-lobed at base, 10-12mm x 6-9mm (when spread), appearing very narrow; lateral lobes conical, short, directed forwards, pointed, 1-2.5mm high, yellowish-green, green or purplish-brown, inner face hairless, exterior with dense greyish hairs; median lobe elongated, narrowly obovoid, broadest in distal half, very convex, blackish-brown to reddish, sides pale brown to greenish-yellow turned down and under; speculum central, white or greyish broadly edged whitish, sometimes reduced to 2 small parallel drop-shapes, more often extensive, formed by 2-4 vertical bars sometimes reaching stigmatic cavity, linked by 1-4 transverse bars, horizontal or oblique, forming ± distinct anchor-shapes and ocelli; appendage triangular, pointed, yellowish, pointing downwards, extending sides of lip; stigmatic cavity small, without pseudo-eyes, vault whitish, transversally barred brown; red staminodial blotches often present; staminodial points sometimes present.

Variation Narrow petals and lip very distinctive.

Flowering Season IV-V.

Habitat Full sun to mid-shade on dry to moist, alkaline substrates. Short grassland, scrub, open woodland, 500-1400m asl.

Distribution Endemic to southern Anatolia. Reported from a few stations from Antalya Province east to Siirt Province; reaches the Syrian border in the south. Very rare and local.

Countries An Ls.

Photos An, Diyarbakir, 17.V.1990. P. DELFORGE.

Note The flowers may be pollinated by a wasp of the genus *Argogorytes* (Hymenoptera: Sphecidae), which would explain the morphological convergence between *Ophrys cilicica* and *O. insectifera*; the latter is not closely related but also attracts pollinators of the genus *Argogorytes*.

Ophrys cretica

(VIERHAPPER) E. NELSON

Etymology *cretica:* from Crete. **Type** Cr, Lassithi (1916). **Synonyms** *O. spruneri* subsp. *cretica* (VIERHAPPER) RENZ, *O. kotschyi* subsp. *cretica* (VIERHAPPER) SUNDERMANN, *O. cretica* subsp. *beloniae* G. KRETZSCHMAR & H. KRETZSCHMAR, *O. cretica* subsp. *bicornuta* H. KRETZSCHMAR & R. JAHN.

Description 10-40cm tall; bracts longer than ovary; inflorescence dense to near lax; 2-10 flowers; sepals green, pink or white, 11-15mm x 5-7.5mm, oval-lanceolate, margins strongly recurved, dorsal sepal erect or slightly curved forwards, lateral sepals spreading, ± strongly tinted purple on lower half; petals narrowly triangular, (4-) 6-9mm x 1.5-3mm, villous, green washed pink, olive-green, ochre or violet-purple, erect to turned down and back; lip deeply 3-lobed at base, 10-14mm x 10-14mm (when spread), dark brown to blackish-purple; lateral lobes very convex, divergent, forming 2 rounded cones, rather short or very long (see Variation), with long, dense, whitish to greyish hairs; median lobe prominent, convex, appearing ovoid, velvety in centre, sides turned down and under, with fine greyish hairs and then a paler hairless margin; speculum prominent, slate-grey, broadly edged white, covering entire median lobe, formed by 2 (-4) vertical bars, slightly sinuous, ± parallel, linked transversally, at least at level of basal field, then H-shaped, often with appendices and anchors demarcating 1-3 fragmentary ocelli; appendage pendent, often large, triangular or 3-toothed, greenish to reddish, extending margins of lip; stigmatic cavity rounded, constricted at level of basal field, relatively large, height equal to 0.2-0.4x length of lip, whitish, blotched or barred transversally black, without black pseudo-eyes. **Variation** Comprises 2 variants with the same pollinator: the first with an elongated median lobe and poorly developed lateral lobes (**Photo A**), the second (= *'bicornuta'*, **Photo B**) with a shorter median lobe and horn-like lateral lobes; these 2 forms coexist in Crete and the Cyclades; intermediates are frequent.

Flowering Season III-IV (-V).

Habitat Full sun to mid-shade on dry to moist, calcareous substrates. Short grassland, abandoned cultivation, garrigue, scrub, up to 1200m asl.

Distribution Southern Aegean. Laconie, Cyclades, eastern Crete, Rhodes (Ae); other reports probably refer to *O. ariadnae*. Local but sometimes rather abundant.

Countries Ae Cr Gr.

Photos Gr, Cyclades, Paros, 13.IV.1995; Cr, Lassithi, 4.IV.1982. P. DELFORGE.

Pollinator *Melecta tuberculata* (Hymenoptera: Anthophoridae) (see *O. kotschyi* p. 526).

Ophrys ariadnae
H.F. PAULUS

Etymology Named after Ariadne, daughter of King Minos. **Type** Cr, Lassithi (1994). **Synonyms** *O. cretica* subsp. *ariadnae* (H.F. PAULUS) H. KRETZSCHMAR, *O. kotschyi* subsp. *ariadnae* (H.F. PAULUS) N. FAURHOLDT, *O. cretica* subsp. *karpathensis* E. NELSON, *O. cretica* subsp. *naxia* E. NELSON, *O. karpathensis* (E. NELSON) H.F. PAULUS & GACK nom. illeg.

Description As *O. cretica* but 10-30 (-40)cm tall; 2-8 (-12) flowers; lateral sepals green, less often and less strongly tinted violet on lower half; lip larger, 12-16mm long; lateral lobes rounded, only slightly or not at all divergent, not forming pointed cones; median lobe more elongated, wider at tip, appearing obovoid, sides not so strongly turned down; speculum often more complex and more extensive, pattern at base forming a thickened H, marked with 1-3 central ocelli, sometimes fragmented, extended by anchors, extensions and 2 vertical bars underlining lateral lobes and delineating 2 ocelli; appendage shorter, triangular; stigmatic cavity cup-shaped, lateral margins straight, not constricted at level of basal field, smaller, height equal to 0.08-0.2x length of lip, white, less marked with black. **Variation** Varied in patterning. Distinct from *O. cretica* in its small stigmatic cavity and early flowering; forms intermediate between the two species can make identification difficult at some sites.

Flowering Season II-IV (-V), slightly before *O. cretica*.

Habitat As *O. cretica*.

Distribution Eastern Crete, Karpathos, Cyclades, Egine (Gr). Local and rather rare.

Countries Cr Gr.

Photos Cr, Iraklion, 27.II.1990. P. DELFORGE.

Pollinator *Melecta albifrons* subsp. *albovaria* (Hymenoptera: Anthophoridae).

Key to the *Ophrys reinholdii* group

(continued from p. 529)

4   speculum formed by 2 oblique drop shapes .... *O. reinholdii*

4*   speculum formed by 2 parallel drop shapes, sometimes joined by a transverse line or, more rarely, H-shaped 5

5   hairs on shoulders of lip brown with silver reflections; lateral walls of stigmatic cavity often with rudimentary bluish pseudo-eyes.... .... *O. antiochiana*

5*   hairs on shoulders of lip white; lateral walls of stigmatic cavity without bluish pseudo-eyes .... *O. straussii*

The *Ophrys argolica* group

Characteristics Petals rather large, villous, ±
narrowly oval to sometimes falcate, margins not
or only slightly undulate; lip velvety in centre
with a complete submarginal band of hairs,
whitish and ± prominent on shoulders; speculum
central, transverse, often reduced; appendage
prolonging sides of lip; stigmatic cavity often low
and transverse, slightly or not at all constricted at
base, with a specular stage and 2 small, rounded
pseudo-eyes, located at junction of internal and
external lips.

Ophrys crabronifera
MAURI

Etymology *-fera:* bearing; *crabroni-:* hornet.
Type* It, Rome (1820). **Synonyms** *O. exaltata*
auct. non TENORE, *O. fuciflora* subsp. *exaltata* auct., *O.
argolica* subsp. *crabronifera* (MAURI) N. FAURHOLDT.

Description 20-65cm tall; 3-8 (-12) flowers;
sepals whitish to pink or dark lilac, sometimes
greenish washed violet or green, spreading or
turned backwards, oval-lanceolate, 12-17mm x 6-
8.5mm; petals villous, oval-lanceolate, 4-10mm x
2.5-4.5mm, spreading, whitish to dark purple or
olive-brown, margins sometimes tinted yellowish
or ochre; lip entire, orbicular to obcordate (when
spread), very convex to globular, appearing ±
ovoid, broadest in centre, 11-15mm x 13-19mm
(when spread), velvety and reddish-brown in centre, lighter and sometimes olive-green or greenish
at base, surrounded by a submarginal band of
long, dense, ochre, hairs, whitish on shoulders,
sometimes attenuated on lateral-distal quarters,
then with a narrow greenish-yellow hairless margin, turned down and under or sometimes spreading or reflexed; speculum glossy grey, central,
much reduced, often formed by 2 small isolated
lozenges, more rarely by 2 contiguous oblique
drop-shapes, delineating a central ocellus; appendage ± prominent, greenish-yellow,
triangular to 3-toothed, directed forwards or pendent; stigmatic cavity olive-greenish, low, transverse, 4-6mm wide at base, margins divergent,
often extending shoulders of lip; pseudo-eyes
glossy greenish-brown, poorly marked, sometimes absent; staminodial points rarely present.

Flowering Season III-V.

Habitat Full sun to shade on dry to moist,
alkaline substrates. Short grassland, garrigue,
open woodland near coasts, up to 600m asl.

Distribution Endemic to Italy, probably from
Livourne south to Rome; reaches Marches
(Urbino) in the east. Rare and local. **Countries** It.
Photos It, Livorno, 13.IV.2000. P. DELFORGE.

Pollinator *Anthophora plumipes* (Hymenoptera:
Anthophoridae).

Ophrys pollinensis
E. NELSON ex J. DEVILLERS-TERSCHUREN & P. DEVILLERS

Etymology *pollinensis:* [from Mount] Pollino, a massif lying within the confines of Basilicate and Calabria. **Type** It, Salerno (2000). **Synonyms** *O. fuciflora* subsp. *pollinensis* E. NELSON nom. inval., *O. holosericea* subsp. *pollinensis* E. NELSON ex O. DANESCH & E. DANESCH nom. inval., *O. holosericea* subsp. *pollinensis* (E. NELSON) LANDWEHR COMB. INVAL., *O. argolica* subsp. *pollinensis* (E. NELSON ex J. DEVILLERS-TERSCHUREN & P. DEVILLERS) KREUTZ.

Description As *O. crabronifera* but often less slender, 12-50cm tall, sometimes forming groups of stems; inflorescence denser; 3-8 (-12) flowers, of a similar size but appearance more varied; sepals pale pink to dark purple, very often washed green; petals villous, oval-lanceolate, sometimes falcate or auriculate at base, 6-8mm x 2-4mm, spreading, colour often more saturated than sepals, or different, sometimes ochre, olive-green or brownish; lip entire, orbicular to near trapezoid (when spread), velvety and reddish-brown in centre, surrounded by a reddish-brown submarginal band of hairs; speculum more extensive and more complex, almost always with extensions reaching base of stigmatic cavity and delineating basal field; stigmatic cavity less transverse, narrower at base; pseudo-eyes glossy blackish, better marked; staminodial points often present.

Flowering Season IV-V.

Habitat As *O. crabronifera*, up to 1000m asl. **Distribution** Italian endemic, centred on the Cilento massif (Campanie), Mount Alburni (Naples) south to northern Calabria; extends east to Potenza province (Basilicate). Local and sometimes abundant. **Countries** It. **Photos A & B** It, Salerno, 1.IV.2002. P. DELFORGE; **C** 14.IV.2000. J. DEVILLERS-TERSCHUREN. **Note** Intermediate between *O. biscutella* and *O. crabronifera*, and has apparently been introgressed by *O. fuciflora* s.l., as indicated by the sometimes auricule petals, shape and colour of the lip, complexity of the speculum and structure of the appendage and stigmatic cavity.

Ophrys morisii
(MARTELLI) SOÓ

Etymology Named after G.G. Moris, Italian botanist (1796-1869). **Type** Sa, (1896). **Synonyms** *O. aranifera* var. *morisii* MARTELLI, *O. exaltata* subsp. *morisii* (MARTELLI) DEL PRETE, *O. argolica* subsp. *morisii* (MARTELLI) KREUTZ.

Description (10-) 15-40 (-50)cm tall; 3-10 flowers; sepals white to ± dark pink, sometimes greenish, rarely green, 10.5-15mm x 5.5-8.5mm, oval-lanceolate; petals 5.5-10mm x 2-4.5mm, oblong-lanceolate, obtuse, centre pink, reddish or greenish, rarely whitish or yellowish, clearly more richly coloured than sepals, margins darker than centre, pink, ochre, olive-green, purple or brownish, ± strongly undulate and ciliate, rarely straight; lip entire to obscurely 3-lobed, rusty-red to dark brown, oboval to near trapezoid, rounded, globular in centre, often very convex transversally at tip, 10-16mm x 13-22mm (when spread), with a submarginal band of dense brown hairs (denser and longer on basal half); speculum very varied, glossy grey, edged white, made up of 2 rectangular to trapezoid central segments, ± clearly forming a H or X and surrounding the basal field like a necklace, sometimes reduced to an inverse horseshoe or to 2 small isolated lozenges; appendage prominent, yellowish, triangular or 3-toothed, directed forwards or downwards; stigmatic cavity as broad as tall, ± constricted at base; pseudo-eyes shiny blackish, rounded; staminodial points sometimes present.

Flowering Season (II-) III-V, after *O. panormitana* var. *praecox*.

Habitat Full sun to mid-shade on alkaline to slightly acidic, dry to moist, substrates, often stony. Short, poor grassland, garrigue, banks, scrub, open woodland, up to 1400m asl.

Distribution Endemic to Corsica and Sardinia. Local but sometimes abundant.

Countries Co Sa.

Photos Sa, Nuoro, 10 & 12.IV.1996. P. DELFORGE.

Note Close to *O. crabronifera* but seems to have been strongly introgressed by a representative of the *O. exaltata* group, which may have been completely absorbed.

Pollinator *Anthophora sicheli* (Hymenoptera: Anthophoridae).

Ophrys biscutella
O. DANESCH & E. DANESCH

Etymology *biscutella:* with 2 shields (a reference to the shape of the speculum). **Type** It, Foggia (1970). **Synonyms** *O. argolica* subsp. *biscutella* (O. DANESCH & E. DANESCH) KREUTZ, *O. exaltata* subsp. *sundermannii* SOó, *O. crabronifera* subsp. *sundermannii* (SOó) DEL PRETE.

Description 10-50cm tall; 2-8 (-10) flowers; sepals white to dark violet-purple, rarely greenish, spreading then strongly turned back, oval-lanceolate, 13-18mm x 6-9mm; petals villous, triangular-rounded to narrowly lanceolate, 6-11mm x 2-4.5mm, pale pinkish to dark purple, sometimes edged yellowish or red; lip entire, orbicular, slightly convex, appearing trapezoid, 12-15mm x 15-20mm, broadest in upper third, blackish-brown to dark reddish, scarcely paler at base, velvety in centre, submarginal band of hairs long, dense and whitish on shoulders, shorter elsewhere; speculum central, glossy bluish-grey, sometimes edged white, made up of 2 small transverse lozenges, often contiguous, sometimes with extensions demarcating a central ocellus or, rarely, extending to the stigmatic cavity and delineating a basal field; appendage small, pointed, greenish-yellow, pendent or directed forwards; stigmatic cavity entirely greyish or with a broad specular stage, small, low, 3-4mm wide and rather clearly constricted at base; pseudo-eyes black, shiny.

Flowering Season IV-V.

Habitat Full sun to mid-shade on dry to moist, mostly alkaline substrates, sometimes schistose. Short grassland, garrigue, scrub, open woodland, up to 1300m asl.

Distribution Adriatic. Puglia (It). Local but sometimes abundant. **Countries** It. **Photos** It, Foggia, 9.IV.1986. P. DELFORGE.

Pollinator *Anthophora retusa* (Hymenoptera: Anthophoridae).

Discussion of the *Ophrys argolica* group

Probably monophyletic, from the central and eastern Mediterranean, and comprising 13 species, this group is distinguished principally by the structure of the petals (villous, large, narrowly oval, with straight margins), and by the pseudo-eyes, which appear to be located at the junction of the internal and external lips. Other characters, which appear to give the group coherence, are not exclusive to it; for example, white hairs on the shoulders of the lip (*O. reinholdii, O. straussii*), speculum central, bi-scutellate (*O. reinholdii, O. ferrum-equinum, O. andria*). An adaptation to pollinators of the genus *Anthophora*, sometimes invoked to define the group, does not constitute an absolute guide, as *Ophrys lesbis* attracts an *Andrena* sp.

(continued on next page)

Ophrys icariensis
HIRTH & SPAETH

Etymology *icariensis:* [from the island of] Ikaria.
Type Ae, Ikaria (1990). **Synonym** *O. argolica*
subsp. *icariensis* (HIRTH & SPAETH) KREUTZ.

Description Sometimes spindly, (11-) 15-23
(-35)cm tall; inflorescence elongated, up to 17cm
tall; 2-8 rather small flowers; sepals dark purplish-
pink, rarely pale, oval, 9-16mm x 4.5-9mm, spreading; petals villous, erect, triangular-rounded, often
elongated, (4-) 5-7 (-8)mm x 1.2-3.5mm, colour as
sepals or slightly brighter, sometimes finely edged
ochre or purple; lip entire or obscurely 3-lobed, 10-
13mm x 8-16mm (when spread), obcordate, convex, appearing trapezoid or quadrangular, velvety,
reddish-brown to deep blackish, often with 2 small,
conical, basal swellings, ± pointed, 0.5-2mm high,
sometimes hairless and greenish on inner face;
complete (sometimes broad) submarginal band of
dense, rather long hairs, brownish to russet on
shoulders, sometimes attenuated on distal half of
lip; border of lip hairless, reddish-brown,
sometimes scalloped, pendent, slightly reflexed or
turned down; speculum basal and central, rather
extensive, greyish-blue to reddish, glossy, finely
edged pale greyish, often in the form of an X or
incomplete H, demarcating a reddish-brown to
blackish basal field, frequently prolonged by lateral
or distal extensions, sometimes fragmented or
reduced to 2 vertical, ± parallel lines; appendage
rather small, *c.* 1mm long, 2mm wide, pointed,
entire or obscurely 3-toothed, reddish-brown, rarely
greenish-yellow, directed forwards, inserted into a
rather weak notch; stigmatic cavity slightly
constricted at base, floor blackish, specular stage
sometimes absent; pseudo-eyes rounded, black,
shiny, partially encircled by yellowish and
surmounted by a purple line; staminodial points
often lacking; column with an acuminate tip.

Flowering Season III-IV.

Habitat Mostly full sun on dry to moist, calcareous substrates. Grassy areas in garrigue and scrub,
up to 400m asl.

Distribution Ikaria and northeast Naxos
(Cyclades). Very rare and local. **Countries** Ae Gr.

Photos Ae, Ikaria, 26.III.1989. H. SPAETH; Gr,
Cyclades, Naxos, 5.IV.1996. A. JOUKOFF.

Discussion of the *Ophrys argolica* group

(continued from previous page)

Difficulties in defining this group also arise from
the inclusion of a significant number of species that
are thought to be hybridogenous or ± strongly introgressed by taxa from other groups, all of which
help to obscure its morphological coherence.

(continued on next page)

Ophrys delphinensis
O. DANESCH & E. DANESCH (pro hybr.)

Etymology *delphinensis:* from Delphi (Phocide, Gr) (latinisation rather unorthodox). **Type** Gr, Achaïe (1963).

Description 20-40cm tall; inflorescence lax; 3-10 flowers; sepals ± dark purplish-pink, oval-lanceolate, 12-16mm x 6-9mm, margins recurved, dorsal sepal erect, lateral sepals spreading to slightly turned back; petals villous, triangular, 4.5-7mm x 2-4mm, purplish-pink to purple, often darker than sepals; lip 3-lobed in basal half, oval, 10-12.5mm x 11-16mm (when spread), reddish-brown to blackish-purple; lateral lobes rounded, sometimes forming basal swellings, near pointed and densely covered with long white hairs; median lobe convex, velvety in centre, sides with fine silver hairs, turned down and under; speculum varied, glossy metallic blue, edged white, central, reduced, made up of 2 small blotches, isolated or joined at the top or bottom, sometimes more extensive with a central ocellus and extensions towards the stigmatic cavity or lateral lobes; appendage prominent, 3-toothed, greenish-yellow to reddish, pendent or directed forwards, sometimes extending margins of lip. **Variation** Often significant due to its recent hybrid origin (*O. argolicamm* × *O. oestrifera* s.l.). Distinct, however, in its clearly 3-lobed, convex lip with the white hairs characteristic of *O. argolica.*

Flowering Season IV-V.

Habitat Full sun to shade on dry to moist, alkaline substrates. Short grassland, seepages in garrigue and scrub, open woodland, up to 1100m asl.

Distribution Principally around the Gulf of Corinth, from Etolie to the Isle of Euboea and from Achaïe to Corinth. Local and rather rare.

Countries Gr. **Photos** Gr, Euboea, 24.IV.1994; Ahaïa, 22.IV.1991. P. DELFORGE.

Pollinator *Anthophora plagiata* (Hymenoptera: Anthophoridae).

Discussion of the *Ophrys argolica* group

(continued from previous page)

This is the case for *O. delphinensis, O. pollinensis* and probably *O. icariensis* (characters from the *O. fuciflora* complex), *O. morisii* (characters from the *O. exaltata* group) or even *O. lesbis* and *O. lycia*, both appearing superficially similar to *O. ferrum-equinum* (*O. mammosa* group). *O. argolica* and its allies probably lie close to the common ancestor of the *O. reinholdii* and *O. mammosa* groups; they probably derived from an ancestral species from the Aegean, whose most unique characters are now expressed by *O. argolica* and *O. crabronifera.*

Ophrys argolica

H. FLEISCHMANN

Etymology *argolica:* from Argos, (ancient) town of Peloponnese. **Type** Gr, Argolida (1919). **Synonym** *O. ferrum-equinum* subsp. *argolica* (H. FLEISCHMANN) SOÓ.

Description 15-50cm tall; bracts longer than flowers; (2-) 3-9 (-11) flowers; sepals pale pink to dark violet-purple, oval, spreading, 10 16mm x 5-8mm, lateral sepals sometimes slightly tinted purple on lower half; petals pale pink to dark purple, villous, narrowly to rather broadly oval or lanceolate, sometimes slightly falcate, 5-9mm x 2.5-4mm; lip entire or sometimes weakly 3-lobed, orbicular to oboval, 9-15mm x 12-16.5mm (when spread), slightly convex to, rarely, rather convex, orange to reddish-brown, pale to dark, velvety in centre, shoulders with long, dense, very white hairs, sides of lip with a narrow submarginal band of whitish to purplish-brown hairs; speculum glossy bluish-grey, edged whitish, central, often made up of 2 isolated or contiguous drops, if latter joined at top or bottom, sometimes delineating a central ocellus, rarely with extensions framing the basal field; appendage ± prominent, broadly triangular or 3-toothed, greenish-yellow to reddish, pendent or directed forwards, extending margins of lip; stigmatic cavity low, transverse, almost without a basal constriction, barely separated from lip, brownish, floor sometimes with a pale bluish specular stage; pseudo-eyes shiny black; staminodial points often present.

Flowering Season III-IV.

Habitat Full sun to shade on dry to moist, alkaline substrates. Short grassland, garrigue, scrub, open woodland, up to 1000m asl.

Distribution Endemic to southern Greece (Gulf of Corinth, Peloponnese). Rather local and often rare.

Countries Gr.

Photos Gr, Argolida, 16.IV.1991; Lakonia, 18.IV.1991. P. DELFORGE.

Note Flowers pollinated by *Anthophora plagiata* (Hymenoptera: Anthophoridae), as *Ophrys delphinensis*, which is probably in the process of absorbing *O. argolica* around the Gulf of Corinth; the 2 species are nevertheless rarely syntopic.

Ophrys aegaea
KALTEISEN & H.R. REINHARD

Etymology *aegaea:* from Aegeus. **Type** Cr, Karpathos Island (1987). **Synonym** *O. argolica* subsp. *aegaea* (KALTEISEN & H.R. REINHARD) H.Æ. PEDERSEN & N. FAURHOLDT.

Description (7.5-) 10-20 (-30)cm tall; (2-) 3-5 (-7) flowers; sepals whitish to pale purplish-red, narrowly oval-elliptical, spreading, 12-16mm x 6-8.5mm, lateral sepals sometimes slightly tinted violet on lower half; petals purplish-brown to olive-green, rather dark, villous, narrowly oval, 7-10.5mm x 2.5-4mm; lip entire, orbicular to broadly trapezoid-rounded, 11-14mm x 16-20mm (when spread), rarely slightly bulging, convex, reddish-brown, centre lighter, orange-red, velvety, sides spreading then ± reflexed, with a dense sub-marginal band of hairs, greyish to pale brownish on basal half, shorter and sometimes purplish on distal half; speculum glossy grey or greyish-blue, central, reduced, comprising 2 small lozenges, isolated or contiguous; appendage very small, tri-angular, pendent or directed forwards, prolonging sides of lip; stigmatic cavity broad, slightly constricted at base, whitish, transversally barred brown; pseudo-eyes dark glossy brown, some-times whitish; staminodial points rarely present.

Flowering Season III-IV.

Habitat Full sun to mid-shade on dry to moist, alkaline substrates. Grassy places in garrigue, abandoned cultivation, plantations of carob trees and olive groves, up to 700m asl. **Distribution** Karpathos Island and the southern Cyclades. Local and rather rare. **Countries** Cr Gr. **Photos** Cr, Karpathos, 20.III.2000. C.A.J. KREUTZ.

Pollinator *Anthophora orientalis* (Hymenoptera: Anthophoridae).

Key to the *Ophrys argolica* group

1   petals bright greenish-yellow ..... *O. climacis*
1* petals of another colour 2

2   lip clearly 3-lobed at base; lateral lobes rounded, sometimes conical, with long, very white hairs .... *O. delphinensis*
2* lip entire or ± obscurely 3-lobed; lateral lobes not as above 3

3   speculum in the shape of an H or X, ± com-plete, with 2 extensions to the walls of the stigmatic cavity, delineating a basal field 4
3* speculum central, reduced, usually without extensions delineating a basal field 7

4   plant spindly; lip often with small pointed basal swellings .... *O. icariensis*
4* plant robust; lip without basal swellings 5

(continued on next page)

Ophrys elegans
(RENZ) H. BAUMANN & KÜNKELE

Etymology *elegans:* elegant. **Type** Cy, Agios Nikolaos (1929). **Synonyms** *O. gottfriediana* subsp. *elegans* RENZ, *O. argolica* subsp. *elegans* (RENZ) E. NELSON.

Description As *O. argolica* but more spindly, few-flowered, 7-20 (30)cm tall; 1-4 flowers; sepals pale pink, oval-lanceolate, margins strongly recurved, spreading then rapidly turning strongly backwards; petals narrowly oval-lanceolate, erect then turned backwards, pink to purple, slightly darker than sepals; lip 3-lobed in distal half, very convex to globular in centre, appearing slender at tip, hairs on shoulders not so long or dense; appendage much smaller, sometimes near absent, triangular; stigmatic cavity strongly constricted under pseudo-eyes, clearly separated from lip, floor blackish-brown, specular stage only slightly contrasting, vault white, transversally barred brown; pseudo-eyes blackish, shiny, often protruding.

Flowering Season II-IV, early.

Habitat Full sun to mid-shade on dry to moist, often acidic, substrates. Garrigue, scrub, open pinewoods, up to 1400m asl.

Distribution Endemic to Cyprus; reports from Anatolia refer to related taxa. Rare and local.
Countries Cy. **Photos** Cy, Larnaca, 28.III.1989. P. DELFORGE.

Pollinator *Anthophora erschowi* (Hymenoptera: Anthophoridae).

Key to the *Ophrys argolica* group

(continued from previous page)

5   floor of stigmatic cavity blackish, with a contrastingly pale specular stage, very narrow; pseudo-eyes yellowish, spotted darker in centre .... *O. lycia*

5* floor of stigmatic cavity brownish, with a pale specular stage, hardly contrasting, broad; pseudo-eyes blackish 6

6   petals rather short, sometimes auriculate, 6-8mm long, 2-4mm wide, margins coloured as centre .... *O. pollinensis*

6* petals rather elongated, never auriculate, 5.5-10mm long, 2-4.5mm wide, margins darker than centre .... *O. morisii*

7   stigmatic cavity constricted at base 8

7* stigmatic cavity not constricted or flared at base 11

8   lip 3-lobed..9

8* lip entire... 10

(continued on next page)

Ophrys lucis
(Kalteisen & H.R. Reinhard) H.F. Paulus & Gack

Etymology *lucis:* with light. **Type** Ae, Rhodes (1987). **Synonyms** *O. aegaea* subsp. *lucis* Kalteisen & H.R. Reinhard, *O. argolica* subsp. *lucis* (Kalteisen & H.R. Reinhard) H.Æ. Pedersen & N. Faurholdt.

Description (7-) 10-20 (-30)cm tall; 2-4 flowers; sepals whitish to dark purplish-pink, sometimes blotched violet, rarely slightly greenish, narrowly oval-elliptical, spreading, 11-15mm x 6-8.5mm, margins reflexed; petals darker than sepals, purplish-pink to ochre or carmine-brown, villous, narrowly oval, sometimes slightly auriculate or falcate, 6.5-9.5mm x 2.5-4mm, edges straight to slightly undulate; lip 3-lobed, orbicular to broadly trapezoid, 11-13mm x 14-19mm (when spread), slightly to rather convex, greenish-brown to olive-green, sometimes orange, pale to dark, bordered ± broadly by a greenish-yellow hairless margin; lateral lobes convex, rounded, rarely bulging, with relatively sparse, greyish to brownish hairs; median lobe convex, velvety in centre, edged by a weak band of purplish-brown hairs; speculum glossy greyish-blue, central, rather reduced, composed of 2 isolated or contiguous drops, forming a horseshoe or a shield-shape with a central ocellus; appendage rather small, triangular, pendent to near horizontal, extending sides of lip; stigmatic cavity rather broad, slightly constricted at base, dark greenish-brown, floor with a pale specular stage, vault whitish, with a brown transverse bar; pseudo-eyes shiny blackish-brown; staminodial points almost always present.

Flowering Season III-IV.

Habitat Full sun to mid-shade on dry to moist, alkaline substrates. Grassy places in garrigue, abandoned cultivation, open woodland of pine and cypress, up to 1000m asl.

Distribution Rhodes, Tilos and Nisyros (Ae), southwestern half of Anatolia, east to Içel. Rare and local. **Countries** Ae An. **Photos** Ae, Rhodes, 21.III.2000. C.A.J. Kreutz; 13.IV.1984. P. Delforge.

Pollinator *Anthophora* cf. *mucida* (Hymenoptera: Anthophoridae).

Key to the *Ophrys argolica* group

(continued from previous page)

9   sepals and petals turned backwards; lip very globular, 3-lobed at tip .... *O. elegans*

9*   sepals and petals spreading; lip 3-lobed at base .... *O. lucis*

10   pseudo-eyes black .... *O. biscutella*

10* pseudo-eyes brownish to whitish ... *O. aegaea*

(continued on next page)

Ophrys lesbis
GÖLZ & H.R. REINHARD

Etymology *lesbis:* daughter of Lesbos. **Type** Ae, Lesbos (1989). **Synonym** *O. argolica* subsp. *lesbis* (GÖLZ & H.R. REINHARD) H.Æ. PEDERSEN & N. FAURHOLDT.

Description Thickset, (8.5-) 10-28 (-40)cm tall; (1-) 2-6 (-12) flowers; sepals whitish to pink or lilac, sometimes reddish, oval-lanceolate, 13-18mm x 7-10mm, lateral sepals sometimes blotched or washed purple on lower half; petals whitish to reddish or ochre, pale to dark, villous, ± elongated, narrowly oval-lanceolate to sometimes triangular, 7.5-11mm x 3.5-5.5mm; lip entire, trapezoid-rounded, wedge-shaped at base, 13-16mm x 13.5-20mm (when spread), rather slightly convex, sometimes slightly bulging, pale to dark reddish-brown, velvety, lighter and orange to olive-green in centre, shoulders with dense, rather short, whitish to brown hairs; speculum red or blue, sometimes purplish, glossy, often edged whitish or marbled, central, size and shape varied, often forming a horseshoe, sometimes divided into 2 ± symmetrical blotches; appendage relatively prominent to near absent, pale to dark brown, pointed, extending sides of lip; stigmatic cavity transverse, with thick walls, slightly constricted at base, floor brown to blackish with a lighter specular stage; pseudo-eyes rounded, rather large, shiny, ± dark brown in centre, encircled by grey, surmounted by a brown eyebrow sometimes barring the entire vault of the stigmatic cavity; staminodial points sometimes present.

Flowering Season III-IV.

Habitat Full sun to mid-shade on dry to moist, alkaline substrates. Short grassland, grassy places in garrigue, scrub, open oak woodland, up to 320m asl. **Distribution** Eastern Aegean. Lesbos and Samos (Ae) and southwest Anatolia (mainly the Bodrum peninsula); reports further east in Anatolia refer to related taxa. Very local and very rare. **Countries** Ae An. **Photos** An, Mugla, 7.IV.1997; 12.III.1998. C.A.J. KREUTZ.

Pollinator *Andrena curiosa* (Hymenoptera: Andrenidae).

Key to the *Ophrys argolica* group

(continued from previous page)

11   pseudo-eyes large, rounded, brown, ± broadly
      encircled with greyish .... *O. lesbis*

11*   pseudo-eyes small to near absent, black or
      greenish-brown, without a pale peripheral
      circle 12

12   pseudo-eyes black; hairs on shoulders of lip
      very white and contrasting .... *O. argolica*

12*   pseudo-eyes greenish-brown, unobtrusive to
      near absent; hairs on shoulders ochre, slightly
      contrasting .... *O. crabronifera*

Ophrys climacis
HEIMEIER & PERSCHKE

Etymology *climacis:* from Klimax, ancient name for Mount Beyler Dagi. **Type** An, Antalya (1998).

Description 16-35 (-40)cm tall; inflorescence near lax; 4-6 flowers; sepals whitish-green, pale olive-green, rarely white, lateral sepals sometimes washed purple on lower half, oval-lanceolate, spreading, 11.5-15mm x 5-7.5mm, dorsal sepal often curved and bent forwards; petals greenish-yellow, often bright, villous, very narrowly oval-lanceolate, sometimes falcate, 7-10.5mm x 2-3.2mm, margins ± undulate; lip 3-lobed to near entire, orbicular to broadly trapezoid, 13-16mm x 15-19mm (when spread), slightly convex, chestnut-brown to dark blackish-brown, rather broadly bordered by a yellow hairless margin; lateral lobes near spreading, rounded, without basal swellings, with rather dense greyish to pale-buff hairs; median lobe velvety in centre, with a very attenuated submarginal band of brown hairs; speculum shiny greyish-blue, edged whitish, central, very reduced, comprising 2 isolated or contiguous drops, forming a horseshoe or a shield-shape with a central ocellus; appendage rather small to near absent, triangular to 3-toothed, pendent to near horizontal, extending sides of lip; stigmatic cavity rather broad, often rather clearly constricted at base, floor dark brown, with a pale specular stage, narrow, vault whitish, sometimes with a transverse brown bar; pseudo-eyes glossy blackish, often with a pale surround; staminodial points present, sometimes extended.

Flowering Season (Mid II-) III-IV (-mid V), rather early.

Habitat Mid-shade on dry to moist, alkaline substrates. Open woodland with pines and cypresses, sometimes banks, up to 1200m asl.

Distribution Known from a few stations in the Antalya region. Very local and extremely rare.

Countries An.

Photos An, Antalya (loc. typ.), 8.III.1998. C.A.J. KREUTZ.

Ophrys lycia
RENZ & TAUBENHEIM

Etymology *lycia:* from Lycia (An). **Type** An, Antalya (1980).

Description Robust, 15-40 (-60)cm tall; inflorescence dense to near lax; 2-6 (-10) large flowers; sepals oblong-lanceolate, spreading, 13-18mm x 4-7mm, pale pink to dark lilac, lateral sepals sometimes blotched purple; petals papillose to velvety, narrowly oval-lanceolate, 7-9mm x 2-3.5mm, colour as sepals or washed yellowish; lip entire, oboval to narrowly trapezoid-rounded, 13-18mm x 13-18mm, without basal swellings or almost so, slightly convex, centre pale reddish-brown to dark brown, sometimes greenish-brown, velvety; submarginal band of hairs whitish on basal half, brownish, shorter and sometimes very attenuated on distal half; sides with a ± narrow hairless margin, orange to sometimes bright yellow; speculum basal and central, glossy bluish-grey, edged whitish, like a ± thickened H, elaborated by indentations, sometimes with a central ocellus, reaching base of stigmatic cavity and delineating basal field; appendage very small or lacking, extending sides of lip; basal field blackish, edged pale brown; stigmatic cavity constricted at base, floor blackish, with a pale specular stage, very narrow, vault yellowish, with a transverse brownish-purple bar; pseudo-eyes rounded, rather large, shiny, yellowish, spotted ± broadly in centre with brown or black; staminodial points sometimes present.

Flowering Season III-IV.

Habitat Full sun on moist, calcareous substrates. Short grassland, garrigue, the margins of scrub, 400-600m asl.

Distribution Known from a few stations in the west of Antalya Province. Extremely rare and local.

Countries An.

Photos An, Antalya, 9.IV.1998. C.A.J. KREUTZ.

Discussion of the *Ophrys argolica* group

In the western assemblage, *O. morisii* and *O. pollinensis* seem to be recent hybridogenous taxa, as do *O. delphinensis* and *O. icariensis* in the Aegean basin. The eastern species, apparently influenced by *O. mammosa* s.l. (in particular *O. ferrum-equinum*), may in fact represent a relict, ancestral lineage, close to the common ancestor of the two groups, rather than recently stabilised hybrid swarms.

545

The *Ophrys mammosa* group

Characteristics Lateral sepals ± clearly bicoloured; petals elongated, villous to finely velvety, rarely hairless; lip with a reduced marginal band of hairs, visible primarily on shoulders, clearly attenuated distally; micro-hairs of lip give a uniformly velvety appearance to centre and distal half; pattern of base of speculum often H-shaped or forming 2 ± parallel vertical lines, joined to walls of stigmatic cavity; appendage with the same texture as sides of lip, usually not inserted into a notch but imperceptibly extending sides; stigmatic cavity cup-shaped, rounded, ± strongly constricted at base, with a pale specular stage; pseudo-eyes present, colour varied, located at junction of internal and external lips.

Ophrys ferrum-equinum
DESFONTAINES

Etymology *ferrum-equinum:* horseshoe (an allusion to the shape of the speculum). **Type** Ae (Samos) or An (Izmir) (1807). **Synonyms** *O. ferrum-equinum* var. *anafiensis* B. BIEL, *O. ferrum-equinum* var. *minor* B. BIEL.

Description Often thickset, 10-30cm tall; inflorescence dense to near lax; (2-) 3-8 (-10) flowers; sepals oval, spreading, 12-17mm x 5-9mm, pink to lilac, pale to dark, rarely white or greenish, lateral sepals sometimes slightly tinted violet on lower half; petals pale pink to dark purple, hairless to velvety, narrowly triangular to lanceolate, 6-11mm x 2.5-4mm, margins straight or undulate; lip entire or rarely weakly 3-lobed, orbicular, 11-17mm x 12.5-19mm (when spread), without basal swellings, dark, blackish-brown to reddish, slightly convex to rather convex and velvety in centre, margins rarely tinted with yellow, sometimes reflexed, with a submarginal band of greyish to purplish-brown hairs, pale and clearly visible on shoulders; speculum glossy bluish-grey, rarely edged whitish, situated on distal half, often comprising 2 bars or isolated drops, longitudinal, parallel, sometimes contiguous, then forming a horseshoe; appendage small to near absent, triangular, greenish, pendent to near horizontal, extending sides of lip; stigmatic cavity black, broad, slightly constricted at base, with a pale blue specular stage; pseudo-eyes blackish to pale blue with a greyish central spot, a whitish bridle and black to dark purple eyebrow.

Photos Gr, Cyclades, Andros, 16.IV.1994; Thesprotia, 2.IV.1991. P. DELFORGE.

Pollinator *Chalicodoma parietina* (Hymenoptera: Anthophoridae).

Flowering Season III-V.

Habitat Full sun to shade on dry to moist, alkaline substrates. Short grassland, garrigue, scrub, open woodland, up to 1100m asl.

Distribution Eastern Mediterranean. Southern Albania to southern Anatolia; probably absent from Cephalonia (Gr), where replaced by *O. gottfriediana*, and perhaps from Crete (present however on Karpathos (Cr)). Rather scattered and often rare.

Countries Ae Al An Cr Gr.

Variation Varied, and sometimes confused with *O. argolica* or incorrectly placed within its group. Numerous taxa have been described but all fall within the range of variation of the nominative var. and often flower with it.

'labiosa' (*O. labiosa* KREUTZ, *O. ferrum-equinum* subsp. *labiosa* (KREUTZ) KREUTZ): Centre of distal half of lip very convex transversally, margins spreading-reflexed. **Distribution** Ae An. **Photo A** Ae, Lesbos, 15.IV.1991. P. DELFORGE.

'subtriloba' (*Ophrys ferrum-equinum* f. *subtriloba* Hayek): Sepals sometimes washed green, lip 3-lobed; lobes rounded, median lobe not narrowed at tip. Often reported as *O. gottfriediana* outside the Ionian Islands, principally in the central Aegean basin. **Photo B** Gr, Cyclades, Amorgos, 18.IV.1997. P. DELFORGE.

'parnassica' (*Ophrys mammosa* f. *parnassica* Vierhapper): Sepals washed green to green, lip (near) entire, without basal swellings; speculum often extending towards stigmatic cavity. **Distribution** Throughout the range, with the other forms; rather frequent in the Cyclades. **Photo C** Gr, Cyclades, Astypalaia, 3.IV.1997. P. DELFORGE.

Ophrys gottfriediana
Renz

Etymology Named after Gottfried Keller, Swiss botanist (1873-1945). **Type** Gr, Cephalonia (1928). **Synonyms** *O. spruneri* subsp. *gottfriediana* (Renz) Soó, *O. ferrum-equinum* subsp. *gottfriediana* (Renz) E. Nelson, *O. ferrum-equinum* var. *gottfriediana* (Renz) B. Biel.

Description As *O. ferrum-equinum* but sepals often olive-green, if not pink to lilac or pure white, lateral sepals frequently bicoloured; petals elongated, with straight margins, pink, purple or dark purplish (if sepals pink) or green, olive-green or brown (if sepals green); lip entire or 3-lobed, appearing heart-shaped, tip strongly convex, slender, sides ± strongly turned under; speculum may be reduced to 2 tiny central lozenges. **Variation** Distinct from *O. ferrum-equinum* in the convexity of the lip; isolated plants with these characters, found within populations of *O. ferrum-equinum*, are probably the source of reports of *O. gottfriediana* from the Peloponnese and Aegean islands as (see *O. ferrum-equinum* f. *subtriloba*, previous page).

Flowering Season IV.

Habitat As *O. ferrum-equinum*, up to 700m asl. **Distribution** Ionian. Pure populations occur on Cephalonia (= Kefallinia), Ithaca and Zante; also present on other Ionian islands and probably also Epirus. Rather local but sometimes abundant. **Countries** Gr.

Photos Gr, Cephalonia, 3.IV.1991. P. Delforge.

Key to the *Ophrys mammosa* group

1	lip with a speculum	2
1*	lip entirely cherry-red, apparently without a speculum	*O. helenae*
2	speculum central, no extension towards stigmatic cavity	3
2*	speculum with extensions reaching stigmatic cavity	4
3	distal half of lip slightly convex transversally, sides often reflexed forwards	*O. ferrum-equinum*
3*	distal half of lip very convex, sides strongly turned under	*O. gottfriediana*
4	lip with an almost complete submarginal band of hairs	5
4*	lip velvety on distal half	6
5	basal field greenish, much paler than centre of lip	*O. montenegrina*
5*	basal field concolourous with centre of lip	*O. negadensis*

(continued on p. 550)

Ophrys spruneri
NYMAN

Etymology Named after W. von Spruner, Bavarian botanist (1805-1874). **Type** Gr, Aegina island (1855). **Synonyms** *O. hiulca* SPRUNER ex RCHB. fil., *O. ferrum-equinum* subsp. *spruneri* (NYMAN) E.G. CAMUS, *O. sphegodes* subsp. *spruneri* (NYMAN) E. NELSON nom. inval.

Description 15-40 (-50)cm tall; 2-8 flowers; sepals oval, spreading, curved forwards, 10-16.5mm x 5-6.5mm, whitish to dark purplish-pink, sometimes greenish-white, lateral sepals usually bicoloured, tinted violet-purple on lower half; petals often dark, pinkish to purple or ochre-brown, hairless to velvety, narrowly triangular to lanceolate, 7-12mm x 2-4mm, margins sometimes undulate; lip ± deeply 3-lobed, orbicular to broadly elliptic, 12-17mm x 12-19mm (when spread), dark, blackish-purple to brownish, bordered by a thin, hairless, paler brownish-purple margin; lateral lobes convex, sometimes forming rounded basal swellings, with rather short, purplish-grey to rather pale brownish hairs; median lobe ± strongly convex, finely velvety, sides with a submarginal band of short hairs, turned under or reflexed; speculum glossy azure-blue, edged pale blue, often forming 2 parallel longitudinal lines from basal field to distal 1/4 of lip, sometimes linked by 1-2 transverse bars, forming an H or delineating a central ocellus; appendage small or absent, greenish to crimson-brown, pendent to near horizontal, prolonging margins of lip; stigmatic cavity black, slightly constricted at base, with a pale blue to whitish specular stage; pseudo-eyes blackish to pale blue with a greyish central spot, whitish to pink bridle and black to dark purple eyebrow.

Variation Bright colours, dark, 3-lobed lip, the black contrasting with the azure-blue speculum and pink sepals, distinctive. Other characters rather varied. Range of variation significant, to near *O. ferrum-equinum* and *O. mammosa*.

Flowering Season II-IV (-V).

Habitat Full sun to mid-shade on dry to moist, alkaline substrates. Short grassland, garrigue, scrub, open woodland, up to 900m asl.

Distribution Endemic to Greece. Epirus and Macedonia south to Crete; reaches the Ionian islands in the west and Ikaria and Chios (Ae) in the east. Reports from Anatolia refer principally to *O. amanensis*; those from Cyprus *O. elegans*. Rather widespread and sometimes rather abundant.

Countries Ae Cr Gr.

Photos Gr, Zakynthos, 8.IV.1993; Fokis, 6.IV.1991. P. DELFORGE.

Pollinator *Xylocopa iris* (Hymenoptera: Anthophoridae).

Key to the *Ophrys mammosa* group
(continued from p. 548)

6   basal field pale brown, orange or rusty, lighter than centre of lip 7
6*   basal field blackish to pale brown, concolourous with centre of lip 10

7   early flowering, I-III (-IV) 8
7*   late flowering, (IV-) V-VI 9

8   pseudo-eyes dull, greenish .... *O. herae*
8*   pseudo-eyes shiny, centre blackish
                 .... *O. alasiatica*

9   plant robust; lateral sepals 12-18mm long......
              .... *O. caucasica*
9*   plant spindly; lateral sepals 9-12mm long......
              .... *O. grammica*

10   pseudo-eyes pale, linked to the specular stage on the floor of the stigmatic cavity 11
10* pseudo-eyes dark or pale but not linked to specular stage 12

11   lateral sepals dark, olive-green, ± bicoloured.
            .... *O. leucophthalma*
11* lateral sepals pale, uniform or faintly blotched reddish .... *O. aesculapii*

12   tip of column rather elongated, tending to curve upwards 13
12* tip of column short, straight 19

13   tip of column very elongated, (1.5-) 2-4mm long 14
13* tip of column slightly elongated, 0.8-1.5 (-2)mm long .... *O. cyclocheila*

14   main flowering season II-IV 15
14* main flowering season V-VI 17

15   lip 8-11mm long .... *O. hittitica*
15* lip 12-19mm long 16

16   lip globular in centre, optically oval...............
              .... *O. transhyrcana*
16* lip very convex transversally on distal half, appearing 3-lobed .... *O. morio*

17   lip 9-12mm long .... *O. iceliensis*
17* lip 12-18mm long 18

18   petals 5-7mm long .... *O. antalyensis*
18* petals 7-14mm long .... *O. amanensis*

19   lip with a wedge-shaped elongated base ....
                              ....*O. gortynia*
19* lip with a rounded base 20

(continued on next page)

Ophrys sphaciotica
H. FLEISCHMANN

Etymology *sphaciotica:* from the Sphakia region.
Type Cr, Chania (1925). **Synonyms** *O. grigoriana* G. KRETZSCHMAR & H. KRETZSCHMAR, *O. spruneri* subsp. *grigoriana* (G. KRETZSCHMAR & H. KRETZSCHMAR) H. KRETZSCHMAR.

Description As *O. spruneri* but robust, 15-35cm tall; flowers less numerous, 3-6, but larger, lip (18-) 20-30 (-35)mm long, 19-32mm wide.

Flowering Season III-V.

Habitat As *O. spruneri*, 100-600m asl.

Distribution Southern Crete; here and there in the Cretan range of *O. spruneri* and often with it. Very rare and local.

Countries Cr.

Photos Cr, Lassithi, 13.III.1990. P. DELFORGE.

Discussion A controversial taxon. Slightly later-flowering than *O. spruneri* and frequently producing intermediates with it. The very large lip, which is probably not adapted to the pollinator of *O. spruneri*, and the existence of a few pure populations, add weight to the argument in favour of a specific rank for this taxon, but this status requires confirmation.

Ophrys hystera
KREUTZ & R. PETER

Etymology *hystera:* late. **Type** Gr, Imathia (1985). **Synonym** *O. mammosa* subsp. *serotina* B. WILLING & E. WILLING.

Description As *O. mammosa* but very robust; 2-6 (-10) large flowers, sometimes very colourful; lip entire or 3-lobed, (14-) 16-20mm long, with rounded or angular basal swellings, 3-7.5mm high, and often with a bright yellow border; distal half of lip or median lobe often very convex trans-versally, tip thus attenuated; speculum glossy, pale blue or slate-grey, edged white; stigmatic cavity slightly constricted at base, floor blackish, with a bluish specular stage in the centre, white at sides, ± contrasting; pseudo-eyes white to bluish, with a greyish central spot, linked to external walls of stigmatic cavity by a pale bridle.

Flowering Season V-VI, 4-5 weeks after *O. mammosa*.

Habitat As *O. mammosa*, up to 1100m asl.

Distribution Greece. Northern Peloponnese and Etolia-and-Acarnania to Macedonia; reports from Cyprus and Anatolia are errors.

Countries ?Al Gr.

Photos Gr, Imathia (loc. typ.), 7.VI.1987; Kozani, 9.VI.1987. P. DELFORGE.

Key to the *Ophrys mammosa* group

(continued from previous page)

20 lip 7-12mm long, edged yellow; speculum complex, extensive, often with 1-3 central ocelli .... *O. hebes*
20* lip otherwise; speculum simpler, H-shape or 2 longitudinal parallel lines 21

21 main flowering season II-IV 22
21* main flowering season V-VI 25

22 lip 6-11mm long .... *O. cretensis*
22* lip (10-) 11-30mm long 23

23 lip 18-35mm long .... *O. sphaciotica*
23* lip (10-) 11-17mm long 24

24 dorsal sepal pink .... *O. spruneri*
24* dorsal sepal green .... *O. mammosa*

25 lip 7-10 (-11)mm long .... *O. epirotica*
25* lip 10-20mm long 26

26 lip 10-14mm long .... *O. macedonica*
26* lip (14-) 16-20mm long .... *O. hystera*

Ophrys leucophthalma
J. DEVILLERS-TERSCHUREN & P. DEVILLERS

Etymology *leucophthalma:* with white [pseudo] eyes. **Type** Gr, Preveza (1994). **Synonym** *O. mammosa* subsp. *leucophthalma* (J. DEVILLERS-TERSCHUREN & P. DEVILLERS) KREUTZ.

Description As *O. mammosa* but few-flowered, 15-30cm tall; sepals olive-green, lateral sepals strongly tinted purple on lower half; petals triangular-rounded; lip dark, orbicular, (9-) 10-12mm long, with marked basal swellings, rounded, sometimes white and hairless on inner face, exterior with straight whitish hairs; speculum pale blue or slate-grey, broadly edged white, sometimes entirely white; stigmatic cavity slightly constricted at base, floor blackish, with a white specular stage, very broad, usually extending to pseudo-eyes, vault white; pseudo-eyes white on outer face, bluish on internal face, broadly linked to the very white external walls of the stigmatic cavity.

Flowering Season V-VI, late.

Habitat As *O. mammosa*, up to 700m asl.

Distribution Poorly known due to confusion with closely related taxa. Northern continental Greece, northwestern Anatolia, at least to Bolu. Rare and local.

Countries An Gr.

Photos Gr, Ioannina, 7.V.1990; An, Bolu, 31.V.1990. P. DELFORGE.

Discussion of the *Ophrys mammosa* group

Monophyletic, eastern Mediterranean, with 27 species. None of its members is directly related to *O. sphegodes* s.l., with the exception of *O. negadensis* and *O. montenegrina*, which form the morphological and geographical transition between the *O. mammosa* group and the *O. sphegodes* complex. The few superficial similarities between the two assemblages (notably a basically H-shaped speculum, the shape of the petals and structure of the stigmatic cavity) probably result from convergent evolution prompted by a frequent adaptation to bees of the genus *Andrena*. The *Ophrys mammosa* group forms a vast cluster united by lip structure and coloration that is close to *O. ferrum-equinum* and, beyond, to *O. argolica* and *O. reinholdii*, often associated with a dark or blackish tone to the basal field and lip, and white to pale blue speculum, pseudo-eyes and specular stage. Most species in this group were traditionally treated as subspecies of *O. sphegodes*, while around a dozen have only recently been described, and so the elucidation of relationships within the group is difficult. It is nevertheless possible to distinguish:

(continued on next page)

Ophrys gortynia
(H. BAUMANN & KÜNKELE) H.F. PAULUS

Etymology *gortynia:* ancient site in Crete. **Type** Cr, Iraklion (1986). **Basionym** *O. sphegodes* subsp. *gortynia* H. BAUMANN & KÜNKELE.

Description Slender, 15-35cm tall; bracts longer than ovary; inflorescence lax; 3-10 flowers; sepals spreading, oval-lanceolate, 8-11mm x 4-6mm, whitish-green, rarely slightly tinted violet on lower half; petals yellowish-green, often blotched purple, hairless to velvety, erect, lanceolate, 6-8mm x 2.5-4mm, margins ± undulate; lip entire, oboval, base wedge-shaped, appearing narrow, (8-) 9-14mm x 9-14mm, velvety, dark, brown to blackish-purple, sometimes finely edged yellow on distal half, rather convex transversally, with 2 basal swellings, attenuated to ± near pointed, marginal band of hairs short and greyish on shoulders, very attenuated on sides; speculum basal and central, glossy bluish-grey, sometimes narrowly edged whitish, comprising 2 parallel longitudinal lines, sometimes slightly sinuous, often linked transversally, forming an H; appendage very small to absent, yellowish, prolonging margins of lip; basal field dark blackish-brown; stigmatic cavity rounded, dark, reddish-brown to blackish, slightly constricted at base, floor with a specular stage but often only slightly distinct and slightly contrasting; pseudo-eyes whitish, shiny, ± broadly spotted blackish in centre, with a white external bridle.

Flowering Season Late III-V, rather late, after *O. mammosa.*

Habitat Full sun to mid-shade on dry to moist, calcareous substrates. Short grassland, garrigue, scrub, up to 600m asl.

Distribution Central Aegean. Crete, Cyclades and perhaps Peloponnese. **Countries** Cr Gr.

Photos Gr, Cyclades, Milos, 8.IV.1998; Tinos, 7.IV.1994. P. DELFORGE.

Discussion of the *Ophrys mammosa* group

(continued from previous page)

1. An Aegean subgroup (*O. ferrum-equinum* and its derivatives with the tip of the lip transversally convex, *O. gottfriediana*), which seems to have an ancient origin, close to the common ancestor of the *O. argolica* and *O. mammosa* groups.

2. A principally Mediterranean-Pontic subgroup, characterised notably by a shortly acuminate column, of which *O. mammosa,* with its vast distribution, seems to be the central figure. The other species in this assemblage appear to be very close to it and may derive individually from it, principally by processes of sympatric or parapatric speciation:

(continued on p. 557)

553

Ophrys mammosa
DESFONTAINES

Etymology *mammosa:* full-breasted (an allusion to the basal swellings). **Type** Ae (Samos) or An (Izmir) (1807). **Synonyms** *O. sphegodes* subsp. *mammosa* (DESFONTAINES) SOÓ, *O. aranifera* var. *taurica* AGGEENKO, *O. sphegodes* subsp. *taurica* (AGGEENKO) SOÓ, *O. taurica* (AGGEENKO) NEVSKI.

Description Robust, (15-) 20-60 (-70)cm tall; inflorescence lax; (2-) 5-12 (-18) flowers; sepals oval-lanceolate, spreading, 10-17mm x 4-8mm, olive-green, sometimes whitish-green washed pink, lateral sepals usually bicoloured, tinted violet or purple on lower half, rarely all 3 sepals entirely tinted violet; petals yellowish-green, ochre, olive-green or purple, hairless to velvety, narrowly triangular to lanceolate, 7-12mm x 2-4.5mm, margins straight to undulate; lip entire or, rarely, obscurely 3-lobed, orbicular to broadly oboval, 12-17mm x 10-20mm (when spread), velvety, dark, reddish-brown to blackish-purple, bordered by a thin, paler (brownish, purple, rarely yellow), hairless margin, convex, with a submarginal band of short, straight hairs, greyish on shoulders, very attenuated at sides, and 2 large, rounded basal swellings, attenuated to protuberant and near pointed, often hairless on inner face; speculum basal and central, glossy, grey, bluish-grey or lilac, sometimes finely edged whitish, comprising 2 parallel longitudinal lines, or an H surrounding the blackish basal field; appendage small to absent, triangular, greenish-yellow to crimson-brown, pendent to near horizontal, prolonging margins of lip; stigmatic cavity blackish, constricted at base, with a bluish specular stage, often only slightly contrasting; pseudo-eyes whitish to pale blue with a greyish central spot, whitish bridle and sometimes a purple eyebrow; column shortly acuminate, making an open angle with lip, tip 0.5-1.5 (-2)mm long. **Variation** '*taurica*': Morph from Crimea (Ro), with lip entire and prominent basal swellings; falls within range of variation of *O. mammosa*.

Flowering Season III-IV (-V).

Habitat Full sun to mid-shade on dry to moist, usually alkaline, substrates. Short grassland, garrigue, scrub, open woodland, up to 1400m asl.

Distribution Eastern Mediterranean. From Montenegro probably east to Israel and north to Bulgaria. Rather widespread and sometimes abundant.

Countries Ae Al An Bu Cr Cy Gr Ij Ju Ro Tu.

Photos Gr, Cyclades, Milos, 5.IV.1998; Thesprotia, 2.IV.1991. P. DELFORGE.

Pollinator *Andrena fuscosa* (Hymenoptera: Andrenidae) (Cr Gr ?Ij).

Ophrys alasiatica
KREUTZ, SEGERS & H. WALRAVEN

Etymology *alasiatica:* from Alasia, the name for Cyprus in ancient Egypt. **Type** Cy, Larnaca (2002). **Synonyms** *O. sintenisii* auct. non H. FLEIS-CHMANN & BORNMÜLLER, *O. sphegodes* auct. non MILLER, ?*O. sphegodes* subsp. *sintenisii* (H. FLEISCHMANN & BORNMÜLLER) E. NELSON p.p., *O. aesculapii* auct. non RENZ, *O. aesculapiiformis* G. MORSCHEK & K. MORSCHEK nom. nud., *O. cypricola* H.F. PAULUS nom. nud.

Description As *O. mammosa* but rather spindly, 20-60cm tall; sepals spreading, oval-lanceolate, margins slightly to strongly recurved, 10-16mm x 4-7mm, rather pale, whitish-green to pink, lateral sepals uniform or, frequently, irregularly tinted purple on lower half; petals 6-11mm long, often darker than sepals; lip entire to clearly 3-lobed, orbicular to oboval, 10-16mm long, velvety, pale or-ange-brown to blackish-brown, slightly to strongly convex, with str-aight whitish hairs on shoulders, and, at the base, 2 atten-uated to rather prominent and rounded swellings; speculum glossy bluish-grey, often edged whitish; sides of lip reflexed or turned under, frequently coloured pale purple or yel-low, sometimes broadly so on distal half; basal field

slightly paler than centre of lip, pale chestnut-brown to greenish-rusty; stigmatic cavity slightly paler again, floor with a bluish-grey specular stage, often only slightly contrasting; pseudo-eyes rounded, blackish at least in centre, shiny, with a rather broad and pale (or narrow and crimson) bridle. **Variation** Very varied in size of flo-ral parts and colour and shape of lip, sometimes superficially resembling *O. aesculapii* (photo A).

Flowering Season III-mid IV, *c.* 2 weeks before *O. mammosa.*

Habitat As *O. morio.*

Distribution Endemic to Cyprus. Widespread and sometimes abundant. **Countries** Cy.

Photos A & B Cy, Larnaca, 28.III.1989; **C** 29.III.1989. P. DELFORGE.

Pollinator *Andrena bimaculata* (Hymenoptera: Andrenidae).

Ophrys morio
H.F. PAULUS & KREUTZ

Etymology *morio:* clown, the specific epithet of the pollinator. **Type** Cy, Larnaca (2004). **Synonyms** *O. transhyrcana* subsp. *morio* (H.F. Paulus & Kreutz) Kreutz, *O. transhyrcana* auct. non CZERNAKOWSKA.

Description As *O. mammosa* but robust, 25-70cm tall; sepals green, sometimes washed pinkish, margins often strongly recurved, rolled up, thus appearing narrower, dorsal sepal sometimes appearing oblong, lateral sepals ± strongly tinted red or purple on lower half; petals average slightly more narrowly elongated, 8.2-11.5mm x 2.5-3.4mm; lip 13.6-19mm long, shape varied, entire to obscurely (less often deeply) 3-lobed, basal swellings more rounded longitudinally, but very convex transversally; median lobe or distal half of lip usually very convex transversally, sometimes appearing conical or very attenuated, sides turned under; sides of lip sometimes with a thin hairless margin, yellowish to dark reddish; stigmatic cavity relatively smaller, sometimes strongly constricted at base, basal field thus elongated, pale to dark reddish-brown; pseudo-eyes often darker; upper half of column often parallel to centre of lip, tip elongated, (1.5-) 2-3.9mm long, tend to curve upwards.

Variation Varied, distinct in elongated perianth segments, shape of lip and stigmatic cavity and, particularly, position and shape of column. May produce intermediates or hybrid swarms with *O. mammosa* and *O. alasiatica*, making identification tricky.

Flowering Season II-III (mid IV), *c.* 3-4 weeks before *O. mammosa.*

Habitat Full sun to mid-shade on dry to moist, calcareous substrates. Short grassland, garrigue, scrub, open pinewoods, up to 700m asl.

Distribution Cyprus, probably also southern Anatolia (from Antalya). Rather widespread and sometimes abundant on Cyprus.

Countries ?An Cy.

Photos Cy, Larnaca, 28.III.1989; Paphos, 5.IV.1989. P. DELFORGE.

Pollinator *Andrena morio* (Hymenoptera: Andrenidae).

Ophrys antalyensis
KREUTZ & SECKEL

Etymology *antalyensis:* from Antalya. **Type** An, Antalya (1998). **Synonym** *O. amanensis* subsp. *antalyensis* (KREUTZ & SECKEL) KREUTZ.

Description As *O. amanensis* but spindly, 20-35cm tall; inflorescence lax; 4-6 (-10) flowers, smaller, sometimes very colourful; sepals 10-12mm long, greenish-white or pale pink to lilac, lateral sepals usually bicoloured, crimson on lower half; petals 5-7mm long; lip near entire to clearly 3-lobed, 12-15mm long, with prominent basal swellings, rounded to angular, and sometimes a yellowish border; distal half of lip or median lobe slightly to very convex transversally; speculum glossy, pale blue or slate-grey, edged white; stigmatic cavity slightly constricted at base, floor blackish, with a bluish specular stage, only slightly contrasting; pseudo-eyes white to bluish with a greyish central spot, sometimes entirely blackish-grey, often poorly marked.

Flowering Season V-VI, well after *O. mammosa* and *O. transhyrcana.*

Habitat Full sun to mid-shade on dry to moist, calcareous substrates. Short, poor grassland, abandoned cultivation, scrub, open pine and oak woods, up to 800m asl.

Distribution Mediterranean Anatolia. Antalya province and neighbouring areas. Very rare and local. **Countries** An.

Photos (A holotype) An, Antalya, 18.V.1997. C.A.J. KREUTZ.

Discussion of the *Ophrys mammosa* group

(continued from p. 553)

selection of an allele within a continuum by a specific pollinator (sepals pink: *O. spruneri*), temporal isolation and/or spatial isoation with adaptation to a new pollinator (*O. leucophthalma*, *O. hystera*, *O. gortynia*, *O. alasiatica*) or reorganisation of the genome by auto-polyploidy (?*O. sphaciotica*).

3. Close to the *O. mammosa* subgroup there is a peripheral assemblage in the Balkans, with 4 closely related species, endowed with pale green sepals, often uniform, and often a broad yellow border to the lip: *O. aesculapii*, *O. hebes*, *O. epirotica* and *O. macedonica*. Specialists of supra-Mediterranean environments, they may have a common ancestor with a Balkan distribution, separating earlier from *O. (proto-)mammosa* and undergoing speciation after the fragmentation of its range by temporal isolation coincident with an adaptation to different pollinators and environments. *O. helenae*, a very unusual species, may well also be related to this subgroup.

(continued on p. 560)

559

Ophrys amanensis
(E. Nelson ex Renz & Taubenheim) P. Delforge

Etymology *amanensis:* from Mount Amanus, now Nur Daglari, northern Antitaurus. **Type** An, Adana (1983). **Synonyms** *O. sphegodes* subsp. *amanensis* E. Nelson nom. inval., *O. transhyrcana* subsp. *amanensis* E. Nelson ex Renz & Taubenheim.

Description 30-50 (-60)cm tall; 4-7 (-12) large flowers; sepals oval-lanceolate, spreading, 13-19mm x 5-9mm, pinkish to pale purple, rarely whitish or greenish, lateral sepals tinted purple or violet on lower half; petals slightly darker than dorsal sepal, pale pink to purple, sometimes greenish or ochre, hairless to velvety, triangular-lanceolate to oblong, 7-14mm x 2-5.5mm, margins straight to undulate, sometimes coloured yellow; lip near entire to (usually) 3-lobed, orbicular to oval, 12-18mm x 10-20mm (when spread), velvety, dark, dark brown to blackish-purple, rather to very convex, crisped in centre, submarginal band of hairs short and purplish-brown to greyish on shoulders, very attenuated at sides, and with 2 rounded basal swellings, only slightly developed and slightly protuberant; lateral lobes rounded; speculum basal and central, glossy, purplish-blue, edged bluish, comprising 2 parallel longitudinal lines, often linked by 1-2 transverse bars, delineating a central ocellus or forming a ± thickened H and rarely with lateral extensions; appendage small to absent, triangular, greenish-yellow to crimson-brown, prolonging margins of lip; stigmatic cavity blackish, slightly constricted at base, with a bluish specular stage, often only slightly contrasting; pseudo-eyes bluish to blackish, circular, with a dark purple bridle; upper half of column often parallel to centre of lip, tip elongated, (1.5-) 2-3.5mm long, often tending to curve upwards.

Flowering Season V-VI, rather late.

Habitat As *O. mammosa*, up to 900m asl.

Distribution Apparently endemic to the foothills of the Taurus and Antitaurus, from Içel to Hatay (An). Local and often rare.

Countries An.

Photos An, Mersin Yenikoÿ. 21.V.1997. C.A.J. Kreutz.

Ophrys iceliensis
KREUTZ

Etymology *iceliensis:* from İçel. **Type** An, İçel (2000). **Synonym** *O. amanensis* subsp. *iceliensis* (KREUTZ) KREUTZ.

Description Spindly, 25-45cm tall; inflorescence lax; 6-12 medium-sized flowers; sepals 7-13mm long, greenish-white, pale green or olive-green, lateral sepals usually bicoloured, purple on lower half; petals triangular-rounded to oblong, 3-7mm x 1-3mm, yellowish-green, pale pink or reddish, sometimes irregularly spotted red; lip entire or ± clearly 3-lobed, often slightly convex, 9-12mm long, sometimes with rudimentary rounded basal swellings, velvety, blackish-brown, with a submarginal band of very short, straight greyish hairs on shoulders; speculum glossy, pale blue or slate-grey, edged greyish, in the shape of a ± complete H, delineating a dark and often very short basal field; side of lip narrowly reddish; stigmatic cavity slightly constricted at base, floor blackish, with a whitish to bluish specular stage, often only slightly contrasting; pseudo-eyes blackish surrounded by pale circles, surmounted by a broad dark purple eyebrow; tip of column acuminate, (1.5-) 2-3.2mm long, tending to curve upwards.

Flowering Season V-VI, after *O. mammosa* and *O. morio*, slightly later than *O. amanensis*.

Habitat Full sun to mid-shade on dry to moist, calcareous substrates. Grassy areas in open pinewoods, 600-900m asl.

Distribution Mediterranean Anatolia; İçel province. Very rare and local.

Countries An.

Photos A & C An, İçel, 15.V.1990. P. DELFORGE. **B** 21.V.1995. C.A.J. KREUTZ.

Discussion Still poorly known and controversial. May appear to be a mere form of *O. amanensis* with small flowers, or a grouping of hybrid swarms between *O. amanensis* and *O. morio*.

Ophrys hittitica
KREUTZ & R. PETER

Etymology *hittitica:* from Hittits. **Type** An, Antakya (Hatay) (1997).

Description Spindly, (14.5-) 18-29 (-34)cm tall; 3-7 small flowers; sepals 13-15.5 (-17)mm long, oval-lanceolate, pink, greenish-white, pale green or olive-green, lateral sepals ± bicoloured, ± crimson on lower half; petals triangular-rounded to oblong, 6.4-9mm x 2-3.5mm, narrowly lanceolate to oblong, yellowish-green, pale pink or ochre in centre, margins ± undulate, broadly coloured yellow or ochre; lip obscurely to clearly 3-lobed, very convex transversally, 8-11mm x 10.5-13mm (when spread), velvety, brown (often reddish), with a submarginal band of very short, straight, greyish hairs on shoulders, sometimes with rudimentary rounded basal swellings; median lobe appearing slender at tip; speculum glossy, bluish, edged greyish, in the form of a ± complete H, often reaching pseudo-eyes and delineating a basal field (sometimes very short) concolourous with lip; sides of lip turned under; stigmatic cavity slightly to clearly constricted at base, floor brownish, with a whitish to bluish specular stage, rather contrasting; pseudo-eyes greyish to greenish, encircled by white, surmounted by a broad dark purple eyebrow; tip of column sometimes acuminate, 1.5-3.5mm long, tending to curve upwards.

Flowering Season III-IV (-V), rather early.

Habitat Full sun to mid-shade on dry to moist, calcareous substrates. Grassy places in garrigue, scrub and open pinewoods, up to 700m asl.

Distribution Mediterranean Anatolia; Adana and Hatay provinces. Very rare and local.

Countries An.

Photos An, Hatay (loc. typ.), 1.IV.1997. C.A.J. KREUTZ.

Discussion of the *Ophrys mammosa* group

(continued from p. 557)

4. A pattern of pale coloration (basal field greenish-orange, often paler than centre of lip) could define a lineage grouping together *O. grammica*, *O. herae*, *O. cretensis* and *O. caucasica*.

5. An eastern subgroup, centred on eastern Anatolia and the Caucasus, appearing to group 6 species around *O. transhyrcana* (*O. morio*, *O. antalyensis*, *O. amanensis*, *O. hittitica*, *O. iceliensis*, *O. cyclocheila*), united notably by an elongated, recurved tip to the column. This assemblage is as diverse as the *O. mammosa* subgroup and the processes of speciation are probably similar.

Ophrys transhyrcana
CZERNAKOWSKA

Etymology *trans-:* beyond; *-hyrcana:* Hyrcania (ancient province, south of Caspian Sea). **Type** Ro, Turkmenia (1923). **Synonyms** *O. araneifera* subsp. *transhyrcana* (Czernakowska) Soó, *O. sphegodes* subsp. *transhyrcana* (CZERNAKOWSKA) BUTTLER, *O. sintenisii* H. FLEISCHMANN & BORNMÜLLER, *O. sphegodes* subsp. *sintenisii* (H. FLEISCHMANN & BORNMÜLLER) E. NELSON pro parte, *O. transhyrcana* subsp. *sintenisi* (H. FLEISCHMANN & BORNMÜLLER) KREUTZ, *O. adonidis* A. CAMUS & GOMBAULT.

Description As *O. mammosa* but robust, 20-50 (-60)cm tall; inflorescence lax, occupying up to 2/3 of stem; (4-) 8-20 flowers; sepals 12-17mm x 4-8mm; petals finely velvety, 7-11mm x 2-3mm; lip entire or, often, obscurely to clearly 3-lobed, orbicular (when spread), 12-16mm x 11-18mm (when spread), dark brown to blackish-brown, very convex, globular in centre, optically oval, sides turned under, bordered by a thin, paler, hairless margin (brownish, purple, rarely yellow), base with 2 rounded swellings, often poorly marked, attenuated, rarely hairless on inner face; speculum simple, dark blue, edged pale blue, comprising 2 parallel longitudinal lines, or a π surrounding the blackish basal field; appendage small, narrowly triangular, greenish-yellow, pendent; stigmatic cavity blackish, broad, slightly constricted at base, floor with a ± dark bluish specular stage, sometimes contrasting; pseudo-eyes whitish to pale blue with a greyish to black central spot; column long-acuminate, forming a rather closed angle with lip, tip 2-3.5mm long, tending to curve upwards.

Flowering Season III-IV (-V), rather early.

Habitat Full sun to mid-shade on dry to moist, calcareous substrates. Short grassland, garrigue, scrub, open woodland, up to 2300m asl.

Distribution Eastern Mediterranean and Transcaucasus. From eastern Anatolia (from Antakya) to Israel and the eastern Caspian Sea; more westerly reports from Anatolia probably refer to *O. morio* or *O. icelensis*. Rather widespread and sometimes abundant.

Countries An Ij Ls Ro.

Photos An, Antakya, 1.IV.1997; Ij, Galilee, 31.III.1992. C.A.J. KREUTZ.

Pollinator Probably *Andrena fuscosa* (Hymenoptera: Andrenidae) (Ij).

Ophrys cyclocheila
(AVERYANOV) P. DELFORGE

Etymology *-cheila:* lip; *cyclo-:* circular. **Type** Ro, Azerbaijan, Baku (1994). **Synonyms** *O. cyclocheila* NEVSKI nom. nud., *O. caucasica* subsp. *cyclocheila* AVERYANOV, *O. mammosa* subsp. *cyclocheila* (AVERYANOV) B. BAUMANN *et al.*, *O. ferrum-equinum* auct.

Description As *O. mammosa* but sepals and petals often coloured as *O. caucasica*; sepals 9.5-15mm x 4-6mm; petals 6-9mm x 2-3.5mm; lip entire to obscurely 3-lobed, orbicular, 9-14mm x 8.5-14.5mm (when spread), reddish to blackish-brown, globular, rather square at base, sometimes with 2 rounded basal swellings, often poorly marked and attenuated; speculum simple, with a ± complete H shape, delineating a basal field concolourous with centre of lip or darker; appendage small; stigmatic cavity rounded, floor sometimes with a whitish specular stage; pseudo-eyes whitish to pale blue, with a small greenish to black central spot and surmounted by a dark purple line; column rather long-acuminate, forming a rather closed angle with lip, tip 0.8-1.5 (-2)mm long, tending to curve upwards.

Flowering Season IV-V.

Habitat Full sun to mid-shade on calcareous substrates, sometimes sandstone, often moist. Short grassland, meadows, grassy places in garrigue, scrub and open forests, up to 1300m asl.

Distribution Eastern Caucasus, probably east to Iran. Very local and rather rare. **Countries** Ro.

Photos A & B Ro, Azerbaijan, 24 & 25.IV.1997. H.-W. ZAISS; **C** 25.IV.1997. E. GÜGEL.

Ophrys caucasica
WORONOW ex GROSSHEIM

Etymology *caucasica:* from the Caucasus. **Type** Ro, Abkhazie (1928). **Synonyms** *O. sphegodes* subsp. *caucasica* (WORONOW EX GROSSHEIM) SOÓ, *O. mammosa* subsp. *caucasica* (WORONOW EX GROSSHEIM) SOÓ.

Description Often robust, 20-40 (-50cm) tall; 3-10 flowers; sepals oval to lanceolate, spreading, margins recurved, 12-18mm x 4-8mm, whitish-green, lateral sepals uniform or weakly tinted or blotched violet on lower half; petals slightly darker than sepals, yellowish-green, olive-green, ochre or greenish-pink, sometimes spotted red, hairless to velvety, ± narrowly triangular, 6-12mm x 2-5mm, margins undulate; lip entire or 3-lobed, orbicular to oval-elongate, 11-18mm x 10-20mm (when spread), velvety, often rather pale, reddish-brown to orange, sometimes blackish-purple, slightly to very convex transversally, marginal hairs short and greyish on shoulders, very attenuated on margins, with 2 rounded basal swellings, indistinct to prominent, often slightly divergent; lateral lobes rounded; border of median lobe often yellow; speculum basal and central, glossy bluish-grey, edged whitish, basic design a ± thickened, sinuous H, sometimes complex or fragmented, often extending to pseudo-eyes; appendage rather prominent, triangular, greenish-yellow, prolonging margins of lip; colour of basal field and stigmatic cavity varied, brown or olive-green to orange, lighter than centre of lip; floor of stigmatic cavity sometimes undulate, central hollow with a small greyish specular stage, only slightly contrasting; vault of stigmatic cavity whitish to pale greenish, separated from floor by a horizontal purple line; pseudo-eyes shiny, often large, protuberant, ± pale greenish-brown, sometimes spotted in centre; upper half of column often parallel to centre of lip, tip elongated, (1-) 2-3.5mm long.

Variation Varied. The only representative of its group in north-east Anatolia, distinguished by its colour pattern.

Flowering Season IV-VI.

Habitat Full sun to mid-shade on dry to sometimes moist, alkaline substrates. Short grassland, scrub, hazel plantations, open woodland, up to 900m asl.

Distribution Caucasian. The coastal massifs of north-east Anatolia, from Trabzon in the west, probably to the Caspian Sea. Local but sometimes abundant.

Countries An Ro.

Photos An, Trabzon, 23.V.1990. P. DELFORGE.

Ophrys herae
HIRTH & SPAETH

Etymology Named after the ancient Greek goddess Hera. **Type** Ae, Samos (1992). **Synonyms** *O. sphegodes* subsp. *herae* (HIRTH & SPAETH) KREUTZ, *O. sphegodes* auct. non MILLER, *O.* × *pseudomammosa* auct. non RENZ, *O. janrenzii* HIRTH.

Description As *O. mammosa* but slender, often less robust, (15-) 20-50 (-60)cm tall; 2-12 flowers, often medium-sized; sepals oval, margins recurved, 9-15mm x 3.5-7mm, rather pale, whitish-green to pinkish, dorsal sepal erect or, sometimes, curved forwards, lateral sepals spreading, uniform or sometimes ± strongly washed violet on lower half; petals often darker than sepals, yellowish-green, ochre, olive-green, brownish or purplish, finely velvety, lanceolate, sometimes auriculate, 4.5-10mm x 1.5-3.5mm; lip entire or, rarely, obscurely 3-lobed, (near) orbicular to trapezoid, 9-14mm x 10-16mm (when spread), ± strongly convex transversally, blackish-brown, reddish or olive-greenish, sometimes finely edged yellow, with 2 small basal swellings, rounded to near pointed; lip hairs, speculum and column as those of *O. mammosa*; appendage absent or prominent and triangular-pointed, sometimes inserted into a weak notch; stigmatic cavity and basal field pale, olive-green to orange washed green; floor of stigmatic cavity with a greyish specular stage, only slightly contrasting, vault whitish, often separated by a purple bar; pseudo-eyes greenish, shiny, rather drab, often with a pale surround.

Flowering Season I-III (-IV), early, before most other species in its group, before or at the same time as *Himantoglossum robertianum*.

Habitat As *O. mammosa*, but more often on acidic substrates and up to 800m asl.

Distribution Limits of range poorly known due to confusion with related taxa. Certainly Greece (from the Ionian islands to the Aegean islands and Crete) and Cyprus; probably also southern Albania; reports from Anatolia most often refer to *O. grammica*. Rare and local.

Countries Ae ?Al Cr Cy Gr.

Photos Cr, Iraklion, 25.II.1990; Gr, Kerkyra, 30.III.1992. P. DELFORGE.

Pollinator *Andrena nigroaenea* subsp. *candiae* (Hymenoptera: Andrenidae).

Discussion The superficial similarity of *Ophrys herae* to *O. sphegodes* probably results from convergence due to adaptation to very closely related pollinators.

Ophrys grammica

(B. WILLING & E. WILLING)
J. DEVILLERS-TERSCHUREN & P. DEVILLERS

Etymology *grammica:* from Mount Grammos (on the border of Greece and Albania). **Type** Gr, Kastoria (1985). **Synonyms** *O. mammosa* subsp. *grammica* B. WILLING & E. WILLING, *O. sphegodes* subsp. *grammica* (B. WILLING & E. WILLING) KREUTZ, *O. mammosa* subsp. *oodicheila* (RENZ) A. RIECHELMANN.

Description Rather spindly, 20-35cm tall; 2-11 small flowers; sepals oval-lanceolate, 9-12mm x 5-7mm, rather pale, olive-green to whitish-green washed lilac, dorsal sepal erect or curved forwards, lateral sepals spreading, uniform or sometimes slightly tinted violet on lower half; petals green to ochre-brown, hairless to velvety, narrowly triangular to lanceolate, 5-8mm x 1.5-3mm, margins sometimes finely edged red; lip entire or, rarely, obscurely 3-lobed, orbicular to near oboval, 9-13mm x 9-13mm (when spread), convex, centre velvety, reddish-brown, olive-green, yellowish-brown, rather pale, with rather dense marginal hairs on basal half, greyish on shoulders, short on distal half, with 2 small rounded basal swellings, margins paler, rarely reflexed, yellow or sometimes orange washed green; speculum basal and central, shiny, greyish, rarely edged white, often a simple H surrounding basal field; appendage very small to absent, greenish, prolonging margins of lip; stigmatic cavity and basal field pale, olive-green to orange washed green; floor of stigmatic cavity with a greyish specular stage, only slightly contrasting; pseudo-eyes greenish, shiny, rather drab.

Variation Probably rather slight. Distinguished from related species and from *O. mammosa* by the small flowers and their overall dirty greenish colour.

Flowering Season (Late III-) IV-VI, rather late, at the same time as *Orchis tridentata* in the mountains.

Habitat Full sun to shade on dry to moist, alkaline to slightly acidic substrates (notably sandstone, serpentines), often skeletal. The eroded areas on slopes and short grassland, scrub, open woodland, probably up to 1200m asl.

Distribution Western Greece. The mountains of southern Macedonia (Kastoria, Grevena), and northern Epirus (Ioannina), Ionian islands (Corfu) and perhaps Albania. Rare and local.

Countries ?Al Gr.

Photos Gr, Kastoria, 6.V.1990. P. DELFORGE.

Ophrys cretensis
(H. Baumann & Künkele) H.F. Paulus

Etymology *cretensis:* from Crete. **Type** Cr, Lassithi (1986). **Synonyms** *O. sphegodes* subsp. *cretensis* H. Baumann & Künkele, *O. araneola* subsp. *cretensis* (H. Baumann & Künkele) Kreutz.

Description Slender and rather spindly, (15-) 20-50cm tall; bracts much longer than flowers; inflorescence lax; (2-) 6-11 small flowers; sepals oval-lanceolate, 8-11mm x 4-5mm, whitish-green, sometimes washed pink, dorsal sepal erect to bent forwards, lateral sepals spreading, uniform or weakly tinted violet-purple on lower half; petals slightly darker than sepals, yellowish-green, green, olive-green or purplish-brownish, near hairless to velvety, erect, narrowly lanceolate, 5-9mm x 1.5-3mm, margins undulate, sometimes slightly tinted red; lip entire, orbicular to near oboval, 6-9mm x 7-10mm (when spread), velvety, reddish-brown to blackish-purple, sometimes finely bordered yellow on distal half, convex, marginal hairs short and greyish on shoulders, very attenuated at sides, and with 2 distinct to indistinct basal swellings, rounded to near pointed, almost hairless on inner face; speculum basal and central, extensive, glossy bluish-grey, sometimes finely edged white, basic design an H, sometimes thickened, complicated by a central ocellus or ± strongly fragmented, surrounding the basal field and reaching pseudo-eyes; appendage very small to absent, yellowish, prolonging margins of lip; stigmatic cavity and basal field reddish-brown to blackish-purple, concolourous with lip; floor of stigmatic cavity with a pale greyish specular stage, rather contrasting, vault whitish, often separated by a purple bar; pseudo-eyes greenish, shiny, rather drab, often with a pale surround.

Variation Distinguished from *O. gortynia* by its early flowering and more rounded base to the lip.

Flowering Season II-mid IV, rather early, slightly after *O. herae*, well before *O. gortynia*.

Habitat Full sun to mid-shade on dry to moist, calcareous substrates. Short grassland, garrigue, scrub, olive groves and open woodland, up to 600m asl.

Distribution Southern Aegean. The Cyclades (Paros, Amorgos...), Crete and, probably, Karpathos. Local and rather rare.

Countries Cr.

Photos Cr, Lassithi, 3.III.1990; Rethimnon, 28.II.1990. P. Delforge.

Pollinator *Andrena vachali* subsp. *creticola* (Hymenoptera: Andrenidae).

566

Ophrys macedonica
(H. FLEISCHMANN ex SOÓ)
J. DEVILLERS-TERSCHUREN & P. DEVILLERS

Etymology *macedonica:* from Macedonia. **Type** Gr, Kozani (1929). **Synonyms** *O. aranifera.* *macedonica* H. FLEISCHMANN nom. nud., *O. aranifera* subsp. × *macedonica* H. FLEISCHMANN ex SOÓ, *O. macedonica* (H. FLEISCHMANN ex SOÓ) SOÓ nom. inval., *O. mammosa* subsp. *macedonica* (H. FLEISCHMANN ex SOÓ) KREUTZ, *O. sphegodes* auct.

Description As *O. mammosa* but more spindly, flowers smaller; sepals spreading, oval-lanceolate, 10-12mm x 4-6mm, rather pale, whitish-green, lateral sepals often uniform; petals 5-9mm long, often slightly darker than sepals; lip entire or obscurely 3-lobed, orbicular to oboval, 10-14mm long, velvety, purplish-brown to blackish-brown, slightly convex, basal half flat or with 2 attenuated rounded swellings, and, on shoulders, short, straight, whitish hairs; speculum glossy bluish-grey, edged white, H-shaped with the branches often connected to pseudo-eyes; sides of lip spreading; basal field concolourous with centre of lip; stigmatic cavity dark brown to a slightly greenish rusty-brown, floor with a bluish-grey specular stage, only slightly contrasting, vault greenish to whitish, sometimes with a dark brown transverse bar; pseudo-eyes rounded, greyish to bluish, spotted blackish, shiny, with a pale bridle.

Flowering Season Late IV-VI, late.

Habitat As *O. mammosa*.

Distribution Poorly known due to confusion with related species and with *O. sphegodes*; probably the northwest of continental Greece and neighbouring regions. Very rare and local.

Countries ?Al Gr ?Ju.

Photos Gr, Grevena, 7.V.1990; Kastoria, 14.VI.1987. P. DELFORGE.

Discussion Controversial, close to *O. mammosa*, often incorrectly treated as an occasional hybrid between *O. mammosa* s.l. and *O. sphegodes*, or placed with *O. sphegodes*, even though it lacks its diagnostic characters.

567

Ophrys helenae
RENZ

Etymology Named after Helene Renz, mother of the author of its description. **Type** Gr, Corfu (1928). **Synonyms** *O. aranifera* subsp. *helenae* (RENZ) Soó, *O. sphegodes* subsp. *helenae* (RENZ) Soó, *O. mammosa* subsp. *helenae* (RENZ) Soó.

Description Robust and slender, 15-40cm tall; inflorescence dense to near lax; 2-8 flowers; sepals oval, 10-16mm x 5-8mm, rather pale, whitish-green or yellowish, dorsal sepal sometimes curved forwards, lateral sepals spreading, sometimes washed pale violet; petals pale green to ochre, hairless to velvety, narrowly triangular, sometimes auriculate, 6-13mm x 2-4mm, margins straight to undulate; lip entire, orbicular to broadly oboval, 11-18mm x 15-24mm (when spread), globular, usually without basal swellings, cherry-red to pale reddish-brown, velvety, submarginal band of hairs very attenuated and sometimes ochre (short and whitish on shoulders), bordered by a thin, paler, sometimes yellow, hairless margin; speculum lacking or concealed under the micro-hairs, sometimes visible, but then reduced to 2 unobtrusive bluish streaks at base of stigmatic cavity; appendage very small to absent, triangular, greenish-yellow to crimson-brown, prolonging margins of lip; basal field sometimes slightly darker than centre of lip; stigmatic cavity concolourous with basal field, lacking a distinct specular stage, relatively small, slightly constricted at base; pseudo-eyes reduced, whitish, hardly visible; column short.

Variation Morphologically very stable, very unusual and very distinct.

Flowering Season (III-) IV-V (-VI).

Habitat Full sun to mid-shade on dry to moist, alkaline substrates. Short grassland, garrigue, scrub, open woodland, up to 1000m asl.

Distribution Northwest Greece, southern Albania; from Corfu and Cephalonia east to Thessalia, south to the Gulf of Corinth and north to Kastoria; centre of range in Epirus. Also reported from a station in the Peloponnese (Ilia). Rather local but sometimes abundant.

Countries Al Gr.

Photos Gr, Cephalonia, 28.IV.1993; Ioannina, 7.V.1990. P. DELFORGE.

Pollinator Probably *Eucera longicornis* (Hymenoptera: Anthophoridae).

Ophrys epirotica

(RENZ) J. DEVILLERS-TERSCHUREN & P. DEVILLERS

Etymology *epirotica:* from Epirus (Gr). **Type** Gr, Thesprotia (1928). **Synonyms** *O. aranifera* f. *epirotica* RENZ, *O. sphegodes* subsp. *epirotica* (RENZ) GÖLZ & H.R. REINHARD, *O. epirotica* (RENZ) H.F. PAULUS isonym.

Description Spindly, 10-35cm tall, inflorescence lax; 3-7 rather small flowers; sepals yellowish-green to, mainly, whitish-green, 7-10mm x 3.5-5mm, dorsal sepal erect or curved forwards, lateral sepals spreading, uniform or, rarely, slightly tinted purple on lower half; petals yellowish-green to olive-green, slightly darker than sepals, velvety, ± narrowly lanceolate, 5.5-8.5mm x 1.8-3mm, sometimes turned back, edges loosely undulate; lip entire, orbicular, globular, sometimes appearing near heart-shaped and obscurely 3-lobed due to its greater convexity distally, 7-10 (-11)mm x 8-11mm (when spread), with very short micro-hairs, dark reddish-brown to blackish, not bulging or with small, rounded basal swellings, sides ± narrowly coloured yellow (Photo A) or brownish, sometimes hardly visible due to convexity of lip (Photo B); speculum elongated, narrow, blue, sometimes without paler edges, forming a π shape and delineating a small basal field or, more often, 2 longitudinal lines extending from stigmatic cavity to near tip of lip, without a clearly demarcated basal field; appendage small to absent, yellowish, prolonging margins of lip; stigmatic cavity only slightly constricted at base, floor coloured as lip, with a rather contrasting, pale, bluish to whitish specular stage; pseudo-eyes bluish, broadly encircled by white or very pale bluish, often surmounted by a dark purple eyebrow.

Flowering Season V-VI, late.

Habitat Full sun to mid-shade on dry to moist, alkaline substrates. Short grassland, abandoned cultivation, garrigue, scrub, open woodland, probably up to 500m asl.

Distribution Poorly known due to confusion with *O. negadensis.* Albania and neighbouring areas of Greece. Very rare and local.

Countries Al Gr.

Photos Gr, Ioannina, 13.VI.1990; Thesprotia, 9.V.1990; P. DELFORGE

569

Ophrys aesculapii
RENZ

Etymology Named after the Greek god Asclepius.
Type Gr, Argolide (1928). **Synonyms** *O. renzii*
(Soó) Soó, *O. aesculapii* subsp. *pseudoaranifera*
RENZ, *O. sphegodes* subsp. *aesculapii* (RENZ) Soó.

Description 15-40cm tall, sometimes forming
groups of stems; inflorescence often dense; 3-14
flowers; sepals pale, whitish-green to yellowish
or olive-green, oval-lanceolate, 9-14mm x 3.5-
5.5mm, dorsal sepal erect or curved forwards,
lateral sepals spreading, uniform or sometimes
tinted or blotched brownish-red on lower half;
petals barely more colourful than sepals, yellowish-green to olive-green, sometimes washed pink
at base, hairless to velvety, narrowly lanceolate,
5-8.5mm x 2-3.5mm, margins straight or undulate; lip entire or, rarely, obscurely 3-lobed,
orbicular to broadly oboval, (8-) 9-12mm x 10-
14mm (when spread), slightly convex, with much
reduced or imperceptible basal swellings, centre
sometimes near globular, velvety, reddish-brown
to blackish, sides tinted with yellow or orange for
1.5-3mm, submarginal band of hairs short and
whitish on shoulders, very attenuated on distal
half; speculum basal and central, bluish-grey or
purplish, glossy, edged white, rather simple,
forming a sinuous H, extending almost to pseudo-
eyes, sometimes thickened or with a central
ocellus; appendage small, triangular, yellowish,
prolonging margins of lip; basal field concolourous with centre of lip; stigmatic cavity
small, narrow, with a contrasting whitish specular
stage, very broad, often reaching pseudo-eyes;
pseudo-eyes greenish-white, sometimes with
black central spot and linked to external walls by
a broad whitish bridle.

Variation *'pseudoaranifera'*: (Photo B) Few-
flowered variant; lip 8-10mm long, with yellow
margins narrower or absent; speculum broader;
occurs here and there with nominative var.

Flowering Season III-V.

Habitat Full sun to shade on dry to moist,
alkaline substrates, in sub-Mediterranean regions
with low rainfall (< 600mm/yr). Short grassland,
abandoned cultivation, garrigue, scrub, open
woodland, up to 1000m asl.

Distribution Endemic to the eastern half of the
Peloponnese and northern half of Greece, up to
Magnesia and on the Isle of Euboea. Rather local
and rather rare.

Countries Gr.

Photos Gr, Viotia, 8.IV. 1991; Fokis, 7.IV.1991.
P. DELFORGE.

Pollinator *Andrena paucisquama* (Hymenoptera:
Andrenidae).

Ophrys hebes
(KALOPISSIS) B. WILLING & E. WILLING

Etymology Named after Hebes Kouyeas, Athens professor. **Type** Gr, Taygete (Peloponnese) (1975). **Basionym** *O. sphegodes* subsp. *hebes* KALOPISSIS.

Description Rather spindly, 10-30 (-40)cm tall, overall colour rather whitish; bracts whitish-green; (2-) 3-7 (-12) small flowers; sepals whitish-green to pinkish, oval, spreading, margins recurved, 10-15mm x 4.5-6.5mm, dorsal sepal sometimes bent onto column, lateral sepals uniform or, frequently, tinted or blotched pale violet on lower half; petals green, often ochre and more colourful than sepals, velvety, narrowly triangular to lanceolate, 5-11mm x 1.5-3mm, margins undulate; lip pendent, entire or ± clearly 3-lobed, oval, 7-12mm x 9-15mm (when spread), sometimes slightly bulging, centre velvety, convex to globular, pale reddish-brown to blackish-purple, margins flat to reflexed forwards, broadly tinted greenish-yellow or pale brown, band of short, greyish hairs on shoulders, becoming very attenuated on distal half; speculum basal and central, prominent, varied, glossy reddish-grey, finely edged white, rarely H-shaped, often complex or fragmented, with (1-) 2-3 central ocelli; appendage small, triangular, greenish-yellow, prolonging margins of lip or sometimes inserted into a weak notch; basal field concolourous with centre of lip; floor of stigmatic cavity with a small greyish specular stage; pseudo-eyes shiny, whitish, sometimes spotted in centre, surmounted by a red eyebrow; column sometimes acuminate and inclined somewhat towards lip.

Variation Varied. Distinguished by its overall pale coloration, small lip and complex speculum. Plants from the north of the range are sometimes difficult to distinguish from some spindly morphs of *O. negadensis* or *O. aesculapii*.

Flowering Season III-V.

Habitat Full sun to shade on moist, calcareous substrates. Open woodland of oaks, less often conifers, frequently north-facing, rarely short grassland, up to 1700m asl.

Distribution Balkans. Montenegro to the central Peloponnese. Very local but sometimes abundant.

Countries Al Gr Ju.

Photos Gr, Arkadia, 17.IV.1991. P. DELFORGE.

Pollinator *Andrena symphiti* (Hymenoptera: Andrenidae).

Ophrys negadensis
G. THIELE & W. THIELE

Etymology *negadensis:* from Negades (Gr). **Type** Gr, Ioannina (2001). **Synonym** *O. hebes* var. *negadensis* (G. THIELE & W. THIELE) KREUTZ, *O. epirotica* auct. *O. zeusii* HIRTH, *O. sphegodes* subsp. *zeusii* (HIRTH) KREUTZ.

Description (15-) 17-40 (-64)cm tall, 4-8 (-12) flowers; sepals yellowish-green to whitish-green, 8-13mm x 3.5-6.5mm, dorsal sepal erect or curved forwards, lateral sepals spreading, uniform or sometimes slightly tinted purple on lower half; petals yellowish-green to ochre, darker than sepals, velvety, ± narrowly lanceolate to triangular, 6-11.5mm x 1.8-4mm, margins undulate; lip obscurely to deeply 3-lobed, broadly rhomboidal to near oval, (8-) 10-13mm x 10-15mm (when spread), velvety, not bulging or with rounded basal swellings, ± prominent, sometimes very protruding, slightly to very convex laterally, pale reddish-brown to blackish-brown, sides ± broadly coloured yellow, submarginal band of hairs whitish on shoulders, extending to distal half, where narrower and often attenuated in lateral-distal quarters, more prominent above appendage; speculum elongated, reddish-brown to purplish-grey, glossy, finely edged whitish, with a rather simple H shape, almost reaching tip of lip; appendage small to absent, yellowish, prolonging margins of lip; basal field rusty-brown to dark blackish-brown, concolourous with centre of lip; stigmatic cavity constricted at base, floor with a ± pale, ± contrasting specular stage; pseudo-eyes black to greenish, shiny, ± broadly encircled by white, often surmounted by a dark purple eyebrow.

Flowering Season Late IV-mid VI.

Habitat Full sun to shade on dry to moist, alkaline substrates, mostly in sub-Mediterranean regions with significant rainfall (> 1000mm/yr). Short grassland, abandoned cultivation, garrigue, scrub, woodland edges, open woodland, 300-1300m asl.

Distribution Albania and the western half of northern Greece, to Phocide in the east (reports from Peloponnese probably refer to *O. hebes*). Rather local and rather rare.

Countries Al Gr.

Photos Gr, Imathia, 7.VI.1987; Ioannina, 8.V.1990. P. DELFORGE.

Discussion Shows at the same time characters of the *O. mammosa* group (sepals sometimes bicolored, velvety petals, structure of appendage) and the *O. sphegodes* complex (marginal band of hairs on lip often complete). Forms, with *O. montenegrina* (but with a different combination of characters), the transition between the two assemblages in their contact zone, within the basins of the western and eastern Mediterranean.

Ophrys montenegrina

(H. BAUMANN & KÜNKELE) J. DEVILLERS-TERSCHUREN & P. DEVILLERS

Etymology *montenegrina:* from Montenegro.
Type Ju, Montenegro (1988). **Basionym** O. sphegodes subsp. *montenegrina* H. BAUMANN & KÜNKELE.

Description Slender, 20-60cm tall; lower bracts
longer than flowers; 2-16 large flowers; sepals
oval-lanceolate, 11-13 (-18)mm x 3.5-7mm,
rather pale, whitish-green, lateral sepals sometimes slightly tinted purple on lower half; petals
yellowish-green to carmine, hairless, oval-lanceolate, 8-9 (-12)mm x 3-4mm, edges slightly
undulate, sometimes finely edged red; lip entire
to orbicular or 3-lobed, 12.5-15 (-20)mm x 13-
16mm (when spread), convex, sometimes with 2
small rounded basal swellings, reddish-brown,
centre velvety, submarginal band of hairs brownish, rather dense on basal half, short to rather
dense on distal half, sometimes almost complete,
edges with a thin, pale, yellow or carmine margin; speculum basal and central, shiny, blue,
edged whitish, with a simple H shape or ±
complex and surrounding the very pale basal
field, which is rusty to orange washed green, contrasting with centre of lip; appendage absent or
very small, then greenish, prolonging margins of
lip or sometimes inserted into a weak notch;
stigmatic cavity rounded, colour as basal field,
floor with a greyish to whitish specular stage;
pseudo-eyes shiny, often large, protruding, ± pale
greenish-brown, sometimes spotted in centre,
encircled by white; upper edge of stigmatic
cavity often with a purple line.

Flowering Season III-IV, early.

Habitat Full sun on dry to moist, acidic to calcareous substrates. Cypress woodland (with *Cupressus
sempervirens*), grassy places in garrigue, up to
400m asl. Not far from the coast.

Distribution Endemic to the coast of Montenegro
and the Dubrovnik riviera (Croatia); may reach
Albania. Reports from Corfu (Gr) are erroneous.
Rather local but sometimes rather abundant in its
stations.

Countries ?Al Ju.

Photos Ju, Hrvatska, Dubrovnik, 28 & 29.III.2004.
P. DELFORGE.

Discussion A stabilised hybridogenous species,
showing simultaneously characters from the *O.
mammosa* group (sepals sometimes bicoloured,
shape and velvety hairs of lip, structure of
appendage, if present) and from the *O. sphegodes*
complex (hairless petals, marginal band of hairs
on lip sometimes complete, appendage sometimes inserted into a notch); in the contact zone of
the 2 groups. *O. montenegrina* is the dominant
species in the first wave of flowering *Ophrys*
between Dubrovnik and the Albanian border.

The *Ophrys exaltata* group

Characteristics Plant slender; sepals uniform; petals hairless to sometimes velvety and ciliate, elongated; lip with a complete submarginal band of hairs; appendage with a clean texture, not prominent to absent, inserted into a ± deep notch; stigmatic cavity and basal field concolourous with centre of lip; pseudo-eyes large, circular, formed by internal bosses, drab, greyish to greenish, encircled by yellow or green, linked to the external walls by a pale bridle; external walls of stigmatic cavity drab, hardly contrasting.

Key to the *Ophrys exaltata* group

1*	lip (9-) 10-15mm long	2
1	lip 5-9 (-10)mm long	10
2	petals hairless	3
2*	petals velvety and/or finely ciliate	7
3	sepals always green; lip entire; main flowering period IV-V	*O. tarquinia*
3*	plant otherwise	4
4	lip often 3-lobed; speculum with a simple H shape; pseudo-eyes greyish, broadly edged green, or entirely greenish; early flowering, mostly II-III	*O. panormitana*
4*	plant otherwise	5
5	sepals always green; lip trapezoid, angular at base, with distinct basal swellings	*O. classica*
5*	flower otherwise	6
6	lateral sepals often forming an obtuse angle with dorsal sepal; lip very convex transversally; main flowering period mid III-IV	*O. exaltata*
6*	lateral sepals perpendicular to dorsal sepal; lip sometimes only slightly convex transversally; main flowering period II-III	*O. arachnitiformis*
7	sepals usually white or pink; petals 6-11mm long	8
7*	sepals always green or whitish-green	11
8	petals often auriculate; appendage often 3-toothed; staminodial points always present	*O. montis-leonis*
8*	flower otherwise	9
9	lip dark brown to blackish-brown	*O. cilentana*
9*	lip olive-brown to reddish-brown	*O. archipelagi*

10	inflorescence dense; submarginal band of hairs on lip pinkish-grey	*O. incantata*
10*	inflorescence lax; submarginal band of hairs reddish-brown	*O. argentaria*
11	petals 9-13mm long	*O. cephalonica*
11*	petals 6-8mm long	*O. liburnica*

Discussion of the *Ophrys exaltata* group

Due to the occurrence of 'arachniform' plants (sepals pink, petal margins vividly coloured) in many species in the *O. sphegodes* complex, the majority of species in the group have often been considered as forms or variants of *O. sphegodes*, lacking evolutionary significance. The acknowledgement that most of these taxa deserved specific status certainly constituted real progress in the understanding of the *O. sphegodes* complex; it nevertheless produced problems in the definition of one group. This group, in fact, necessarily included species that sometimes or always have green sepals and petals (e.g. *O. cephalonica* and *O. arachnitiformis* itself), whereas species with the sepals always pink and the petals very colourful, like *O. sipontensis*, were excluded. Moreover, such a grouping, based on such an obviously inconstant character, obliged one to treat as closely related species which, like *O. aveyronensis*, diverged significantly in important characters (structure and ornamentation of stigmatic cavity, colour of basal field, petal width...). These contradictions led to serious doubts about the monophyly of a group defined in this way. Taking into account the latter characters, rather than sepal colour, the *O. sphegodes* complex can be resolved into groups that are probably more natural, whilst revealing species in the domain of *O. arachnitiformis*, which were still confused with *O. sphegodes* due to their green sepals. On this basis, the *Ophrys exaltata* group is central Mediterranean, probably monophyletic, with 12 species that can most probably be divided into 3 subgroups:

1. The first subgroup, essentially Tyrrhenian, is composed of morphologically very similar species sharing characters originating exclusively from the *O. sphegodes* complex. They replace each other geographically from Catalonia to Sicily (*O. arachnitiformis*: Catalonia, southern France, northern Liguria; *O. tarquinia*: Tuscany; *O. classica*: coastal south Tuscany to Campania; *O. exaltata*: Calabria-Sicily; *O. panormitana*: var. *praecox* Corsica-Sardinia). In Tuscany, species from the group with large or medium-sized flowers co-exist with a small-flowered species, *O. argentaria*, which has a specific pollinator; in Sicily, 2 species from the lineage with large flowers also coexist, separated by their different pollinators: *O. panormitana* and *O. exaltata*.

(continued on next page)

Ophrys cephalonica

(B. BAUMANN & H. BAUMANN) J. DEVILLERS-TERSCHUREN & P. DEVILLERS

Etymology *cephalonica:* from Cephalonia [island]. **Type** Gr, Cephalonia (1984). **Synonyms** *O. sphegodes* subsp. *cephalonica* B. BAUMANN & H. BAUMANN, *O. exaltata* subsp. *cephalonica* (B. BAUMANN & H. BAUMANN) SOCA.

Description Often slender and robust, 15-50 (-70)cm tall; inflorescence near lax, elongated, up to 30cm tall; (2-) 3-12 (-17) flowers; sepals whitish-green to pale green, lanceolate, 11-15mm x 5-7mm, lateral sepals rarely slightly washed violet on lower half; petals yellowish-green to bright olive-green, oblong to narrowly triangular, 9-13mm x 2-4mm, margins undulate, often finely ciliate, sometimes darker than centre; lip entire, (near) orbicular to obcordate, 12-15mm x 7-10mm (12-16mm when spread), appearing obscurely 3-lobed, sometimes with unobtrusive or distinct basal swellings, base narrowed, very convex in centre, sides turned down and back, greenish-brown, with a complete, dense band of rather long, ochre to sometimes purplish marginal hairs; speculum central, often extensive, forming a ± branched H, greyish, often finely edged white; appendage bright yellowish-green, triangular, *c.* 0.5mm long, erect, inserted into a prominent notch; stigmatic cavity constricted at base, olive-green, often streaked, floor with ± contrasting specular stage; pseudo-eyes large, oval, blackish-brown and shiny in centre, broadly and almost completely encircled by yellowish-green, inclined obliquely, surmounted by a red eyebrow; staminodial points often present.

Flowering Season III-IV, rather early.

Habitat Full sun to shade on dry to moist, alkaline substrates. Short, poor grassland, garrigue, scrub, banks, open woodland, mostly of cypress, up to 500m asl. **Distribution** Ionian. The Ionian islands and coastal regions of Epirus (Thesprotia) and Etolia-and-Acarnania; apparently absent from Levkas and Zante. Local and rather rare. **Countries** Gr.

Photos Gr, Cephalonia, 4 & 5.IV.1991. P. DELFORGE.

***

Discussion of the *Ophrys exaltata* group

(continued from previous page)

2. The second subgroup, Adriatic, comprises 2 species. Often sympatric, they also have characters that essentially originate from the *O. sphegodes* complex: *O. incantata* has small flowers, *O. liburnica,* medium-sized flowers. *O. cephalonica*, the most easterly species in both the group and whole complex, may have belonged to this lineage, but has been introgressed by *O. mammosa* s.l.

3. An intermediate subgroup, Adriatic-Tyrrhenian, with species sharing characters from *O. argolica* s.l. and/or *O. fuciflora* s.l. which replace

(continued on p. 581)

Ophrys liburnica
P. DEVILLERS & J. DEVILLERS-TERSCHUREN

Etymology *liburnica:* from Liburnia (region of ancient northern Adriatic). **Type** Ju, Croatia, Cres Island (2004). **Synonym** *O. sphegodes* auct.

Description Slender, 20-45cm tall; 2-7 medium-sized flowers; sepals 10-14mm x 4-7mm, oval-elongate, whitish-green, lateral sepals often washed pale purple towards tip; petals 6-8mm x 2-4mm, oblong, velvety and sometimes ciliate, margins undulate-crisped, darker than sepals, green, often washed ochre or brown; lip entire, quadrangular, reddish-brown to blackish-brown, 9-12mm x 10-12.5mm (when spread), with distinct basal swellings, rounded to near pointed, very convex transversally, sides straight, hairless, tinted yellow; complete submarginal band of hairs, dense and pale buff on shoulders, brownish and not obvious on distal half of lip; speculum greyish-blue, finely edged white or blue, rather simple, forming a rather fine H or π, sometimes with central ocellus; appendage yellowish, very small, inserted into a deep notch; basal field concolourous with centre of lip or darker; stigmatic cavity concolourous, rounded, floor with an irregular pale specular stage, sometimes contrasting; pseudo-eyes greyish to greenish, rather large and protruding, linked to external walls by a narrow pale bridle; external walls of stigmatic cavity whitish, hardly contrasting; staminodial points sometimes present.

Flowering Season III-mid IV, rather early.

Habitat Full sun to mid-shade on dry to moist, alkaline substrates. Grassy places, abandoned cultivation, garrigue, scrub, banks, woodland edges, up to 500m asl. **Distribution** Adriatic Croatia. Rather scattered and rather rare. **Countries** Ju. **Photos** Ju, Hrvatska, Zadar, 22.III.2004; Peljesak, 31.III.2004; Hvar, 16.IV.2004. P. DELFORGE.

Ophrys incantata

P. Devillers & J. Devillers-Terschuren

Etymology *incantata:* enchanted. **Type** Ju, Croatia, Dalmatia (2004). **Synonyms** *O. araneola* auct. non Rchb., *O. tommasinii* auct. non Visiani.

Description Habit rather robust, 15-30cm tall, general coloration yellowish. Inflorescence dense; 3-7 small flowers; sepals whitish-green, oval-lanceolate, 7-10mm long; petals darker, more yellow, broadly lanceolate, 6-8mm x 2-3.5mm, margins undulate; lip brown, 6.5-9.5mm x 7-10.5mm, entire, orbicular, slightly and regularly convex, sometimes with very small basal swellings; sub-marginal band of hairs pinkish grey, paler, very narrow and attenuated on lateral-distal quarters; broad yellow border to lip; speculum greyish to bluish, glossy, edged yellow, forming a ± complex thickened H, with branches reaching pseudo-eyes, sometimes even stigmatic cavity; appendage very small; stigmatic cavity and basal field concolourous with centre of lip; pseudo-eyes relatively prominent, black to greyish, broadly encircled by yellow, sometimes linked to specular stage; staminodial points lacking.

Flowering Season III-IV; the first wave of small-flowed *Ophrys* 'sphegodes' s.l.' in Croatia.

Habitat Full sun to mid-shade on dry to moist, alkaline to neutral substrates. Short grassland, garrigue, road verges, the edges of pine and oak-hornbeam woods, up to 400m asl. **Distribution** Adriatic Croatia. Very local but sometimes occurring in large populations. **Countries** Ju.

Photos A & B Ju, Hrvatska, Dalmatinska Zagora, Primosten (loc. typ.), 26.III.2004; **C** Dubrovnik, 30.III.2004. P. Delforge.

Ophrys archipelagi
GÖLZ & H.R. REINHARD

Etymology *archipelagi:* from the (Dalmatian) archipelago. **Type** Ju, Croatia, Korçula Island (1986). **Synonyms** *O. exaltata* subsp. *archipelagi* (GÖLZ & H.R. REINHARD) DEL PRETE, *O. arachnitiformis* subsp. *archipelagi* (GÖLZ & H.R. REINHARD) KREUTZ, *O. arachnitiformis* auct. non GRENIER & PHILIPPE, *O. mateolana* MEDAGLI, D'EMERICO, BIANCO & RUGGIERO, *O. exaltata* subsp. *mateolana* (MEDAGLI, D'EMERICO, BIANCO & RUGGIERO) H.F. PAULUS & GACK.

Description Robust and slender, (20-) 24-40 (-55)cm tall; inflorescence near lax; bracts greenish-white, the lower slightly longer than flowers; (3-) 4-8 (-10) rather large flowers; sepals yellowish-green to whitish (50%), or white to pale pink, 10.5-17mm x 5.5-9mm, lanceolate, spreading, slightly curved forwards; petals 6-11mm x 2.5-4.5mm, oblong to lanceolate, obtuse, centre pale, slightly darker than sepals, green or greenish-yellow, or whitish, white or pink, rarely red, margins undulate and ± clearly ciliate, darker than centre, broadly coloured green, yellow, ochre or red; lip entire, transversally convex, olive to reddish-brown, sometimes edged yellow or pale green, oval, obcordate or slightly trapezoid, 9-14mm x 11-19mm (when spread), band of marginal hairs short and greyish, sometimes with weak, obtuse, basal swellings; speculum central, prominent, glossy greyish-blue edged white, forming a broad, thickened H or X, complicated by ocelli and indentations, often fragmented; appendage yellowish-green, rather small, triangular, pointed, directed upwards, forwards or downwards, inserted into a distinct notch; stigmatic cavity constricted at base with a broad specular stage, sometimes reaching pseudo-eyes; pseudo-eyes greyish, ± protuberant, rarely with a complete pale surround; staminodial points sometimes present.

Flowering Season III-IV, early.

Habitat Full sun to mid-shade on dry to moist, calcareous substrates. Short, poor grassland, garrigue, banks, scrub, open woodland, up to 680m asl.

Distribution Disjunct Adriatic. Korçula Island (Croatia) and southeast Italy (Foggia, Matera and Bari). Very local and rather rare.

Countries It Ju.

Photos It, Foggia, 31.III.1991; 7.IV.1986. P. DELFORGE.

Pollinator *Colletes cunicularius* (Hymenoptera: Colletidae).

Ophrys cilentana
J. DEVILLERS-TERSCHUREN & P. DEVILLERS

Etymology *cilentana:* [from the massif] of Cilento.
Type It, Salerno (2000). **Synonym** *O. arachniti-formis* subsp. *cilentana* (J. DEVILLERS-TERSCHUREN & P. DEVILLERS) KREUTZ.

Description 20-40cm tall; 3-12 medium-sized flowers; sepals 11-15mm x 4-7mm, oval-elongate, white to pinkish, less often greenish or green, spreading; petals 7-9mm long, narrowly lanceolate, sometimes with micro-hairs and ciliate, margins undulate-crisped, green, slightly darker than sepals (if sepals green) or centre pale, white to pinkish (if sepals white to pink), margins sometimes darker, yellow to ochre; lip entire, trapezoid or ovoid to rhomboidal, 10-14 (-16)mm x 11-16mm (when spread), ± strongly convex transversally, dark brown to dark blackish-brown, sometimes with rudimentary basal swellings, margins greenish-yellow, ± reflexed; submarginal band of hairs dense, crimson, sometimes attenuated on lateral-distal quarters; speculum varied and complex, forming a thickened H or X, fragmented, with ± distinct ocelli, reddish to bluish, glossy, edged white; appendage yellowish, rather small, triangular, directed downwards, inserted into a distinct notch; stigmatic cavity constricted at base, usually with a distinct, sometimes contrasting, pale specular stage; pseudo-eyes black to greyish, broadly encircled with white, linked to external walls by a pale bridle; staminodial points sometimes present. **Variation** Very varied, with numerous poorly marked plants, weakly coloured with a small lip and simple speculum.

Flowering Season III-IV.

Habitat Full sun to mid-shade on dry to moist, alkaline to acidic substrates. Short, poor grassland, garrigue, abandoned cultivation, scrub, up to 700m asl. **Distribution** Tyrrhenian. The northern Bay of Naples to Mount Pollino; centred on Cilento. **Countries** It. **Pollinator** *Andrena florentina* (Hymenoptera: Andrenidae).

Photos A-B: It, Salerno, 5.IV.2001; 1.IV.2002. P. DELFORGE; C: 14.IV.2000. J. DEVILLERS-TERSCHUREN.

579

Ophrys montis-leonis

O. DANESCH & E. DANESCH (pro hybr.)

Etymology *montis-leonis:* from Mount Leoni. **Type** It, Grosseto (1972). **Synonyms** *O. exaltata* subsp. *montis-leonis* (O. DANESCH & E. DANESCH) SOCA comb. illeg., *O. arachnitiformis* auct. non GRENIER & PHILIPPE, *O. exaltata* auct. non TENORE, *O. tyrrhena* GÖLZ & H.R. REINHARD, *O. exaltata* subsp. *tyrrhena* (GÖLZ & H.R. REINHARD) DEL PRETE.

Description (15-) 20-35 (-40)cm tall; bracts longer than ovary; (2-) 4-8 relatively large flowers; sepals 11-17mm x 5-8mm, oval, white to crimson-pink or dark purplish, rarely greenish or green, spreading, often curved forwards; petals 7-10mm x 2.5-4.5mm, oblong to lanceolate or triangular, often auriculate, centre pale, white to purplish-pink, sometimes olive-greenish, margins darker, yellow, ochre, olive-green, pink, purple or brownish, straight to strongly undulate, often ciliate, sometimes slightly pubescent; lip entire or sometimes 3-lobed, trapezoid or rhomboidal, more rarely ovoid, 10-14mm x 11-17mm (when spread), pale reddish-brown to dark blackish-brown or olive-green, ± strongly convex transversally, sometimes with small pointed basal swellings, hairless on inner face, sides sometimes spreading or reflexed; sub-marginal band of hairs dense, brown to greyish; speculum varied and often complex, forming a thick H with ± distinct ocelli, purplish-grey or crimson-pink, shiny, edged white, often broadly so; appendage yellowish, prominent to very small, triangular or 3-toothed, directed upwards, forwards or downwards, inserted into a rather distinct notch; stigmatic cavity constricted at base, rarely with a specular stage; pseudo-eyes black; staminodial points present. **Variation** Varied, showing a range of variation fluctuating between *O. exaltata* (petals long, hairless, with undulate margins, lip rounded, appendage much reduced) to *O. fuciflora* (petals short, triangular, auriculate, ciliate; lip trapezoid with small pointed basal swellings; appendage prominently 3-toothed).

Flowering Season III-V.

Habitat Full sun to shade on dry to moist, alkaline to acidic substrates. Short, poor grassland, garrigue, but mostly scrub and open woodland, up to 500m asl. **Distribution** Endemic to the Tyrrhenian coast, where reported from the provinces of Genoa, Livorno, Siena, Grosseto, Latina and Frosinone. Local and rather rare. **Countries** It. **Photos** It, Livorno 13.IV.2000; Grosseto (loc. typ.), 14.IV.2000. P. DELFORGE.

Pollinator *Colletes cunicularius* (Hymenoptera: Colletidae).

Discussion Very probably of hybrid origin, involving *O. fuciflora* (and *O. crabronifera*?) and a species from the *O. exaltata* group with coloured sepals that has probably been completely absorbed.

Ophrys classica

J. DEVILLERS-TERSCHUREN & P. DEVILLERS

Etymology *classica:* of the fleet, naval (a reference to the location of its stations, on the Tyrrhenian coasts and at the port of Ostie). **Type** It, Grosseto (2000). **Synonym** *O. sphegodes* auct. non MILLER.

Description Robust and slender, 25-50cm tall; 4-10 rather large flowers; sepals 11-14mm x 5-8mm, oval-elongate, bright green to whitish-green, spreading; petals 7-10mm long, oblong to narrowly lanceolate, hairless, margins undulate-crisped, green, slightly darker than sepals, often washed ochre or brown, margins often yellow; lip entire, trapezoid, rather square at base, 10-13mm x 11-14mm (when spread), usually with distinct basal swellings, rounded to near pointed, dark brown to dark blackish-brown, ± strongly convex transversally, margins ± reflexed, hairless, often broadly tinted yellow; submarginal band of hairs dense, blackish-purple, often attenuated on lateral-distal quarters; speculum relatively simple, forming a thickened H or X, sometimes with a central ocellus, drab greyish-blue, finely edged whitish or bluish; appendage yellowish, very small, inserted into a deep notch; stigmatic cavity constricted at base, dark, usually with a relatively narrow, pale specular stage, sometimes contrasting; pseudo-eyes black to greyish or greenish, rather small, rather broadly to sometimes incompletely encircled by whitish, linked to external walls by a narrow pale bridle; external walls of stigmatic cavity rather contrasting; staminodial points lacking.

Flowering Season III-IV, rather early, before *O. argentaria.*

Habitat Full sun to mid-shade on dry to moist, alkaline substrates. Short, poor grassland, garrigue, abandoned cultivation, scrub, up to 600m asl.

Distribution Central Tyrrhenian. Currently known from Mount Argentario (Grosseto, Tuscany) to the Rome area; probably reaches the Gulf of Gaete in the south, not far from the coast. Rare and local.

Countries It.

Photos It, Grosseto (loc. typ.), 4.IV.1988; 12.III.2000. P. DELFORGE.

Discussion of the *Ophrys exaltata* group

(continued from p. 575)

each other geographically in peninsular Italy (*O. archipelagi*: Adriatic; *O. cilentana:* Campania; *O. montis-leonis:* Tuscany). They represent either recent hybridogenous species or, contrariwise, ancestral species, close to the common ancestor of the 3 complexes.

Ophrys argentaria

J. DEVILLERS-TERSCHUREN & P. DEVILLERS

Etymology *argentaria:* silver, from Mount Argentario. **Type** It, Grosseto (1991). **Synonyms** *O. sphegodes* subsp. *litigiosa* var. *argentaria* (J. DEVILLERS-TERSCHUREN & P. DEVILLERS) N. FAURHOLDT, *O. araneola* subsp. *argentaria* (J. DEVILLERS-TERSCHUREN & P. DEVILLERS) KREUTZ, *O. araneola* auct. non RCHB.

Description Often spindly, 15-30cm tall; inflorescence lax; 3-10 small flowers; sepals whitish-green, oval-lanceolate, 8-12mm long; petals darker, often washed brown, hairless to slightly velvety, shape varied, narrowly oblong to broadly lanceolate, sometimes falcate, 5-8mm x 2-4mm, margins undulate, ± broadly yellowish; lip 5-10mm x 6-12mm, entire, near orbicular, brown, slightly to very convex transversally, sometimes with small basal swellings; submarginal band of hairs paler reddish-brown, sometimes narrower and attenuated on lateral-distal quarters; sides of lip often spreading or slightly reflexed, with a pale brown to yellow hairless margin, ± narrow and visible; speculum greyish to bluish, only slightly glossy, edged white, usually forming a ± complex, thickened H, ± fragmented and marbled, complicated by extensions, anchors and ocelli, sometimes reaching pseudo-eyes; appendage very small, inserted into a prominent notch; basal field concolourous with centre of lip or slightly lighter and more reddish; stigmatic cavity with a broad specular stage, greyish edged whitish, often reaching pseudo-eyes, with a ± complete horizontal purple bar; pseudo-eyes relatively prominent, irregularly tinted grey to sometimes entirely greenish-yellow, surrounded by a ± complete whitish circle, with a whitish bridle and often surmounted by a red eyebrow.

Flowering Season III-IV (-V).

Habitat Full sun to mid-shade on dry to moist, alkaline to slightly acidic substrates, sometimes sandy. Short grassland, garrigue, road verges, the edges of pine and oakwoods, up to 600m asl.

Distribution Tyrrhenian. From Golfo di Spezia south to Latium. Very local but sometimes found in large populations.

Countries It.

Photos It, Grosseto (loc. typ.), 14.IV.2000. P. DELFORGE.

Pollinator *Andrena fulvata* (Hymenoptera: Andrenidae).

582

Ophrys tarquinia
P. DELFORGE

Etymology *tarquinia:* the Tarquins, Etruscan kings. **Type** It, Livorno (2000). **Synonyms** *O. sphegodes* subsp. *tarquinia* (P. DELFORGE) KREUTZ, *O. sphegodes* auct. non MILLER.

Description Slender, often robust, sometimes up to 55cm tall; basal leaves glossy bluish-grey; stem rather thick, whitish-green; bracts much longer than flowers; inflorescence near lax, sometimes spiral, with (2-) 5-11 relatively large flowers; sepals whitish-green, pale yellowish-green, sometimes very slightly washed pink, 10-15mm long, oval-lanceolate, dorsal sepal curved, appearing narrow due to its strongly rolled-up margins; petals hairless, narrowly oblong to, less often, broadly lanceolate or near elliptical, 8.5-12.5mm x 2.5-4mm, darker than sepals and not concolourous, yellowish-green, amber, olive-green or greenish-brown, margins strongly undulate-crisped and frequently tinted red or dark brown; lip usually without basal swellings, strongly convex laterally, appearing very narrow, actually obovoid and entire to near 3-lobed, (9-) 11-16mm x 10-17mm (when spread), finely velvety and brown in centre, with a rather broad, slightly paler submarginal band of long, straight, reddish-brown hairs, and a thin hairless yellow-ish-brown to yellow border; speculum basal, sometimes very extensive and fragmented, forming a very thickened X or H, sometimes with ocelli in the centre, glossy bluish-grey or simply grey, edged whitish, extending outwards from the peripseudo-ocular circles; appendage very small, triangular, greenish-yellow, inserted into a deep notch; basal field and stigmatic cavity concolourous with centre of lip; stigmatic cavity relatively small, with a distinct but often frag-mented specular stage, crossed by a horizontal purple line; pseudo-eyes prominent, irregularly tinted grey, surrounded by a whitish circle; exter-nal walls of stigmatic cavity rather white.

Flowering Season IV-V, slightly before *O. argentaria.*

Habitat Full sun to mid-shade on dry to moist, alkaline to mostly acidic substrates. Road banks, abandoned cultivation, short grassland, damp meadows, seepages in scrub, woodland edges, up to 900m asl.

Distribution Principally Tuscany; generally away from the coast. Local but sometimes abundant.

Countries It.

Photos It, Livorno (loc.typ.), 14.IV.2000. P. DELFORGE.

Pollinator *Andrena tibialis* (Hymenoptera: Andrenidae).

583

Ophrys exaltata
TENORE

Etymology *exaltata:* high. **Type*** It, Calabria, Sila massif; Si, Messina (1819). **Synonyms** *O. araneifera* subsp. *exaltata* (TENORE) E.G. CAMUS, *O. sphegodes* subsp. *sicula* E. NELSON, *O. trinacrica* DEL PRETE.

Description Slender and robust, (20-) 30-50 (-60)cm tall; stem thick; inflorescence dense to near lax, sometimes up to 32cm tall; 4-15 (-18) flowers; sepals white to pale pink or purplish, sometimes rather dark, sometimes greenish-white or pale yellowish-green, rarely bright green, with a prominent green vein, oval-lanceolate, 10-15mm x 5.5-9mm, margins often strongly recurved (thus appearing narrow), spreading, lateral sepals sometimes forming a very obtuse angle with dorsal sepal; petals hairless, narrowly lanceolate to oblong, spreading, sometimes curved forwards or backwards, 7-11.5mm x 2-3.5mm, centre pinkish, reddish or greenish-yellow, darker than sepals, often with a green longitudinal vein, margins straight or undulate, brightly and broadly coloured yellowish-green, ochre, orange or red, darker or as dark as centre; lip ± dark reddish-brown, entire or, rarely, obscurely 3-lobed, ovoid to orbicular, 9-15mm x 10-16mm (when spread), very convex transversally, appearing small and narrow, often with attenuated basal swellings, with a dense submarginal band of long, pale brown (sometimes greyish) hairs and a hairless border, sometimes narrowly tinted yellow; speculum basal, bluish-grey to reddish, glossy, often edged white, usually rather simple, forming an H or X, sometimes fragmented, very reduced or with a central ocellus; appendage very small, inserted into a deep notch; basal field and stigmatic cavity concolourous with centre of lip; stigmatic cavity relatively small, with a broad, slightly contrasting, distinct specular stage; pseudo-eyes large, irregularly tinted grey, surrounded by a narrow whitish circle, and with a white bridle.

Flowering Season Mid III-IV.

Habitat Full sun to mid-shade on dry to moist, alkaline to acidic substrates. Short grassland, garrigue, scrub, open woodlands and their edges; often disturbed sites – road verges, banks, stabilised rock-falls, abandoned cultivation, up to 800m asl.

Distribution Endemic to Calabria and Sicily. Local and rather rare.

Countries It Si.

Photos It, Cosenza, 5.IV.1987; Si, Palermo, 11.IV.1987. P. DELFORGE.

Pollinator *Colletes cunicularius* subsp. *infuscatus* (Hymenoptera: Colletidae).

Ophrys panormitana
(Todaro) Soó

Etymology *panormitana:* from the region of Palermo (ancient Panhormus). **Type** Si, (1842). **Synonyms** *Arachnites fuciflora* var. *panormitana* Todaro, *Ophrys spruneri* subsp. *panormitana* (Todaro) Soó, *O. sphegodes* subsp. *panormitana* (Todaro) Kreutz.

Description Slender, (15-) 20-40 (-55)cm tall; inflorescence rather dense to lax; 3-7 (-11) flowers; sepals white to pale pink, whitish-green, sometimes bright green, with a prominent longitudinal green vein, oval-lanceolate, 10-15mm x 5-8mm, margins recurved; petals hairless, oblong to ± narrowly lanceolate, sometimes near falcate, 7-11mm x 2-4mm, centre whitish, pink, reddish or yellowish, slightly darker than sepals, margins ± undulate, darker than centre, brightly and ± broadly coloured yellow, yellowish-green, ochre, orange or red; lip reddish-brown to blackish-brown, entire or ± deeply 3-lobed, oval to near orbicular or quadrangular-rounded, 11-15mm x 10-18mm (when spread), slightly to very convex transversally, often with rudimentary, barely distinct basal swellings; submarginal band of hairs paler, reddish-brown; sides of lip often turned down and under with a ± narrow, pale brown to yellow hairless edge; speculum basal, usually forming a simple, ± thickened H, glossy blue to reddish, often finely edged white or greyish, sometimes extending to pseudo-eyes; appendage very small, inserted into a prominent notch; basal field and stigmatic cavity concolourous with centre of lip or slightly paler; stigmatic cavity with a broad specular stage, often reaching the pseudo-eyes, crossed horizontally by a ± complete purple line; pseudo-eyes prominent, irregularly tinted grey to sometimes entirely greenish, surrounded by a whitish circle, with a white bridle and often surmounted by a red eyebrow; external walls of stigmatic cavity rather white.

Variation See over.

Flowering Season (I-) II-III (-IV), early, before *O. exaltata.*

Habitat Full sun to mid-shade on dry to moist, alkaline substrates. Short grassland, garrigue, scrub, open woodland; often disturbed sites – road verges, banks, abandoned cultivation, up to 900m asl.

Distribution Endemic to Sicily (but see overleaf). Local but sometimes abundant.

Countries Si.

Photos Si, Siracusa, 13 & 15.III.2000. P. Delforge.

Pollinators *Andrena thoracica* and *A. sabulosa* (Hymenoptera: Andrenidae).

Ophrys panormitana (TODARO) SOÓ
var. *praecox* (CORRIAS) P. DELFORGE

Etymology *praecox:* early. **Type** Sa, Sassari (1983). **Synonyms** *O. sphegodes* subsp. *praecox* CORRIAS, *O. praecox* (CORRIAS) J. DEVILLERS-TERSCHUREN & P. DEVILLERS, *O. panormitana* subsp. *praecox* (CORRIAS) H.F. PAULUS & GACK.

Description As *O. panormitana* var. *panormitana* but basal field rarely slightly paler than centre of lip; specular stage of stigmatic cavity sometimes absent, sometimes more contrasting; pseudo-eyes more often green.

Flowering Season (End I-) II-IV (-V), early.

Habitat Full sun to mid-shade on dry to moist, alkaline to acidic substrates. Garrigue, scrub, often disturbed sites – road verges, banks, abandoned cultivation, up to 400m asl.

Distribution Endemic to Corsica and Sardinia. Very local and rather rare.

Countries Co Sa.

Photos Sa, Sassari, 7.IV.1996. P. DELFORGE.

Pollinators *Andrena thoracica* and perhaps *A. nigroaenea* (Hymenoptera: Andrenidae).

Ophrys arachnitiformis
GRENIER & PHILIPPE

Etymology *-formis:* shape [of]; *arachniti-:* spider. **Type** Ga, Var (1859). **Synonyms** *O. aranifera* var. *specularia* RCHB. fil., *O. specularia* (RCHB. fil.) LOJACONO, *O. aranifera* var. *nicaeensis* BARLA, *O. nicaeensis* (BARLA) RUPPERT, *O. sphegodes* subsp. *arachnitiformis* (GRENIER & PHILIPPE) SUNDERMANN, *O. exaltata* subsp. *arachnitiformis* (GRENIER & PHILIPPE) DEL PRETE, *O. insectifera* subsp. *integra* MOGGRIDGE & RCHB. fil., *O. sphegodes* subsp. *integra* (MOGGRIDGE & RCHB. fil.) H. BAUMANN & KÜNKELE, *O. integra* (MOGGRIDGE & RCHB. fil.) PAULUS & GACK comb. inval., *O. gallica* H. VAN LOOKEN, *O. exaltata* subsp. *marzuola* GENIEZ, MELKI &.SOCA, *O. arachnitiformis* subsp. *occidentalis* SCAPPATICCI.

Description Slender, 15-30 (-40)cm tall; (2-) 4-7 (-10) flowers; sepals usually pale, whitish to pink, or whitish-green, lanceolate, 10-15mm x 4-7.5mm, lateral sepals spreading, frequently making an angle of more than 90° with dorsal sepal; petals hairless, oblong-lanceolate, often pointed, 6-11mm x 2-4mm, centre darker than sepals, margins ± broadly brightly coloured; lip dark brown, entire to rarely obscurely 3-lobed, ovoid, 8.5-13mm x 10-15mm (when spread), ± convex transversally, appearing narrow, often with rounded basal swellings, with a marginal band of brown hairs and sometimes an unobtrusive hairless yellowish border that is turned down and under; speculum very varied, greyish to purplish, glossy, sometimes marbled or edged whitish, central, often forming a simple H, sometimes fragmented, thickened or shield-shaped; appendage lacking or much reduced, inserted into a distinct notch; stigmatic cavity rather small, constricted at base, dark, with a narrow, ± contrasting specular stage; pseudo-eyes rather large, greyish, often with a pale surround, and with a poorly marked bridle.

Variation Very varied, sometimes even within the same population: '*specularia*', often spindly, flowers rather small; speculum shield-shaped, ± central (Photo B); '*nicaeensis*' (Photo D), robust, few-flowered; flowers large, richly coloured; lip entire, dark; speculum very extensive, forming a complex H; '*marzuola*' = '*occidentalis*' (Photo C), a variant with green sepals.

Flowering Season (I-) II-IV (-V), early.

Habitat Full sun to mid-shade on dry to moist, alkaline substrates. Short, poor grassland, garrigue, scrub, up to 800m asl. **Distribution** From Catalonia (Hs) to Provence (Ga) and the northern Ligurian coast (It); also reported from Pyrénées-Atlantique. Local but sometimes abundant. **Countries** Ga Hs It.

Photos A, B, D Ga, Bouches-du-Rhône, 14.III.1999; **C** Hs, Girona, 22.II.1998. P. DELFORGE.

Pollinators *Andrena sabulosa* subsp. *trimmerana* (Hymenoptera: Andrenidae), *Osmia aurentula* (Hymenoptera: Megachilidae) and *Colletes cunicularius* (Hymenoptera: Colletidae).

587

The *Ophrys provincialis* group

Characteristics Sepals uniform; petals hairless, broad; lip with a complete submarginal band of hairs; speculum broadly edged whitish; appendage with a clean texture, reduced to absent, inserted into a ± deep notch; stigmatic cavity and basal field reddish, colour not as centre of lip; stigmatic cavity broadly barred bright white, often with 2 white lines surrounding the pseudo-eyes and linked to external walls by a pale bridle.

Discussion A group of 3 species, unusual in the reddish colour of the basal field and in the specific combination (a little like hybrids) of characters from the *O. exaltata* group (colour pattern, lip structure…) and from the *O. incubacea* group (enlargement of petals…).

Key to the *Ophrys provincialis* group

1   flowering very late, mid VI-VII
.... *O. argensonensis*
1*   flowering mainly IV-V 2

2   lip 10-13.5mm long .... *O. provincialis*
2*   lip 6-10mm long .... *O. quadriloba*

Ophrys argensonensis
GUÉRIN & MERLET

Etymology *argensonensis:* [from the massif of] Argenson. **Type** Ga, Charente-Maritime (1998). **Synonyms** *O. sphegodes* subsp. *argensonensis* (GUÉRIN & MERLET) KREUTZ, *O. araneola* auct. non RCHB.

Description As *O. provincialis*, but spindly, 15-32 (-39)cm tall; 3-11 small flowers; sepals 7-9mm long; petals darker, often washed or broadly edged ochre or red, narrowly to broadly lanceolate, sometimes near orbicular, 6-8mm x 2-4.5mm; lip 7-10mm x 8-11mm, entire, near orbicular, near globular, sometimes with small basal swellings; submarginal band of hairs lighter reddish-brown, long and straight; speculum reddish to bluish, slightly glossy, edged white, forming a rather simple thickened H or X, extending to pseudo-eyes; basal field not concolourous with centre of lip, slightly lighter or reddish.

Flowering Season Mid VI-mid VII, late.

Habitat Full sun to mid-shade on dry, marly-calcareous substrates. Short, xeric grassland, up to 200m asl.

Distribution Poitou-Charentes. Extremely rare and local.

Countries Ga.

Photos Ga, Charente-Maritime (loc. typ.), 18.VI.1999. P. DELFORGE.

Ophrys provincialis
(H. BAUMANN & KÜNKELE) H.F. PAULUS

Etymology *provincialis:* from Provence. **Type** Ga, Alpes-Maritimes (1988). **Synonyms** *O. sphegodes* subsp. *provincialis* E. NELSON nom. inval., *O. sphegodes* subsp. *provincialis* H. BAUMANN & KÜNKELE.

Description Rather robust, 20-43cm tall; inflorescence lax; (3-) 4-8 (-10) flowers; sepals whitish-green, sometimes washed pinkish, 10-13mm x 4-6mm, oval-lanceolate, spreading; petals 6-8mm x 2.5-4mm, hairless or slightly velvety, lanceolate to broadly oval, pale whitish-green to intense olive-green, margins almost straight to, more often, undulate-crisped; lip entire or obscurely 3-lobed, orbicular to ovoid, 10-13.5mm x 12-17mm (when spread), relatively pale reddish-brown to dark brown, transversally convex to near globular, sometimes with 2 obtuse basal swellings, centre velvety; submarginal band of hairs long, straight and dense, greyish-brown, crimson or ochre, slightly shorter on distal half; narrow hairless margin to lip, not obvious, paler, reddish, rarely yellowish; speculum extensive, bluish, grey or reddish, glossy, broadly edged white, forming a very thickened H or X, sometimes broadly shield-shaped, often with a central ocellus and extensions towards the shoulders and pseudo-eyes; basal field rather pale red, not concolourous with centre of lip; appendage rather small but distinct, greenish-yellow, entire, inserted into a prominent notch; stigmatic cavity reddish to greyish-brown, with 2 (very) broad, contrasting transverse white bars, underlining and surmounting the pseudo-eyes and linking them to the very broad, white specular stage; pseudo-eyes obliquely tinted greyish in centre.

Flowering Season (III-) IV-V, 2-4 weeks after *O. arachnitiformis.*

Habitat Full sun to mid-shade on dry to moist alkaline substrates. Short, poor grassland, garrigue, terraces, scrub, open woodland, up to 800 asl.

Distribution Poorly known due to confusion with related taxa. Coastal regions of southern France, from Hérault to Alpes-Maritimes, probably also northern Liguria. Local and rather rare.

Countries Ga ?It.

Photos Ga, Alpes-Maritimes (loc. typ.), 14.V.1988; Var, 20.IV.1999. P. DELFORGE.

Pollinator *Anthophora atriceps* (Hymenoptera: Anthophoridae).

Ophrys quadriloba
(REICHENBACH fil.) E.G. CAMUS

Etymology *quadriloba:* with 4 lobes. **Type** Ga, Alpes-Maritimes (1851). **Synonyms** *O. aranifera* var. *quadriloba* RCHB. fil., *O. sphegodes* subsp. *quadriloba* (RCHB. fil.) KREUTZ, *O. araneola* auct. non RCHB., *O. sphegodes* s.l. x *O. lutea* auct., *O. riojana* HERMOSILLA.

Description Spindly, 15-40cm tall; 5-14 small flowers; sepals 6-8mm long, green to whitish-green, sometimes washed pink; petals darker, often tinted or broadly edged greenish-yellow or ochre, broadly triangular-lanceolate, sometimes auriculate, 5-7mm x 3-4mm, margins undulate; lip 6-10mm x 8-11mm (when spread), near orbicular, near entire or ± deeply 3-lobed; submarginal band of long, straight hairs, lighter reddish-brown, often attenuated on lateral-distal quarters; border of lip hairless, ± broadly coloured yellow or orange; speculum bluish-grey, glossy, broadly edged whitish, extensive, forming a very complex H, ocellated, fragmented, extending to pseudo-eyes; basal field much reduced, often of a different colour to that of centre of lip, a little lighter or more reddish; stigmatic cavity often marked as in *O. provincialis*, but less invaded with white, specular stage less extensive; staminodial points sometimes present.

Flowering Season Late IV-V.

Habitat Mostly full sun, on dry to moist, alkaline substrates. Short grassland, abandoned cultivation, banks, from 300-800m asl.

Distribution Poorly known. Currently mostly the upper Èbre basin; similar plants or populations also exist in Catalonia (see Discussion). Local and rather rare. **Countries** ?†Ga Hs.

Photos (**A** loc. typ. of *O. riojana*) Hs, La Rioja, 20.V.1999; Alava, 22.V.1999. P. DELFORGE.

Discussion An unusual taxon, often considered to be a hybrid of *O. sphegodes* with *O. lutea*, but apparently formed by hybrid swarms between various species of the *O. sphegodes* complex which almost always grow alongside it: *O. virescens, O. sphegodes, O. passionis, O. arachnitiformis, O. provincialis* (Ga) or *O. castellana* (Hs). In these conditions, the demarcation of this taxon and its status are hard to define. The 2 photos show one of the very spectacular forms of this taxon, whose colour pattern, speculum and stigmatic cavity recall *O. provincialis*, which in turn probably has a hybrid origin between some taxa in the complex. Be that as it may, *O. quadriloba*, which may be a species in the process of being absorbed, is currently rather well represented in the upper Ebro basin. Similar plants have been observed in Catalonia and Corbières (Ga). Two populations, which may belong to this taxon, recorded since 1970 in Alpes-Maritimes (Ga), appear to be extinct.

The *Ophrys sphegodes* group

Characteristics Sepals uniform; petals usually hairless, margins undulate; lip with a complete submarginal band of hairs, often narrower on lateral-distal quarters; speculum usually forming a simple H, only slightly contrasting; appendage with a clean texture, reduced to absent, inserted into a distinct, ± deep notch; stigmatic cavity and basal field rather drab, brown (often greenish), not concolourous with centre of lip and also paler.

Ophrys massiliensis
VIGLIONE & VÉLA

Etymology *massiliensis:* from Massilia, now Marseille. **Type** Ga, Bouches-du-Rhône (1999). **Synonym** *O. sphegodes* subsp. *massiliensis* (VIGLIONE & VÉLA) KREUTZ.

Description As *O. sphegodes*, but more spindly, up to 35cm tall, general coloration whitish-green; 3-10 flowers; sepals whitish-green to green; petals darker, narrower, often ochre; lip more convex transversally, usually with prominent basal swellings; submarginal band of hairs pale purple to greyish; border of lip less broadly tinted yellow, often reddish; speculum forming an H, greyish to blue, unobtrusively edged whitish, more complex, more extensive, frequently with extensions encompassing inner face of basal swellings; basal field slightly lighter than centre of lip; stigmatic cavity less constricted at base, floor with a distinct whitish specular stage, sometimes linked to peripseudo-ocular circles; pseudo-eyes more contrasting, iridescent greenish-grey, sometimes ± completely encircled with pale greyish, and with a distinct bridle.

Flowering Season (XII-) I-III, very early.

Habitat Usually mid-shade on moist calcareous substrates. Frost-free coasts, stabilised rock-falls, north-facing slopes, open pinewoods, up to 500m asl.

Distribution Principally calcareous coastal hills, from Bouches-du-Rhône east to the Menton region and extreme northern Liguria. Very rare and local.

Countries Ga It.

Photos Ga, Bouches-du-Rhône (loc. typ.), 14.III.1999. P. DELFORGE

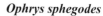

Ophrys sphegodes
MILLER

Etymology *-eidês:* similar to; *spheg-:* a wasp.
Type* Br, England (1768). **Synonyms** *O. aranifera* HUDSON, *O. crucigera* JACQUIN, *O. fucifera* CURTIS, *O. galeopsidea* LAG. ex COLM.

Description (15-) 25-40 (-60)cm tall; inflorescence lax; (3-) 5-9 (-12) flowers rapidly fading after anthesis; sepals broadly oval-lanceolate, 8-14mm x 3-6mm, bright green, whitish-green, yellowish or olive-green, rarely white or pink; petals 4-8 (-10)mm x 2.5-4 (-5)mm, spreading, hairless, of various shape, oblong, lanceolate, oval, sometimes oboval or falcate, greenish-yellow to olive-green or brownish, rarely pink, margins ± strongly undulate, sometimes straight, petals when green often edged red; lip entire or rarely 3-lobed, 10-16mm x 9-18mm (when spread), blackish to pale reddish-brown, with a brownish submarginal band of hairs, sometimes reaching shorter on distal half, and bordered by a hairless margin, often narrow, lighter, sometimes yellow, often turned down, sometimes reflexed, centre velvety, convex, with basal swellings absent or ± well marked; speculum greyish to bluish, glossy, sometimes finely edged whitish, often simply forming a ± thickened H and only slightly developed; appendage small to lacking, inserted into a distinct notch; stigmatic cavity and basal field rather reduced, coloration dirty, reddish-brown or pale olive-green, paler than centre of lip; stigmatic cavity rounded, constricted at base, floor with a greyish specular stage, only slightly contrasting; pseudo-eyes iridescent greenish-grey, sometimes encircled with pale greenish; external walls of stigmatic cavity drab, tinted green, ochre or reddish, slightly contrasting; 2n=36, 37.

Flowering Season (III-) IV-V (-VI), rather early.

Habitat Full sun to mid-shade on dry to moist, alkaline substrates. Short grassland, meadows, sometimes marshy, garrigue, scrub, open woodland, up to 1300m asl. **Distribution** Probably western European, rather northerly. Southern limits of range poorly known due to confusion with related or unrelated taxa; reaches the supra-Mediterranean zone in southern Spain and extends north to southern England, Belgian Lorraine and central Germany and east to Corfu (Gr). Rather widespread but only slightly abundant. **Countries** Al Au Be Br Cz Ga Ge Gr He Hs It Ju Lx.

Photos A & C Br, Kent, 7.V.1994; **B** Ga, Vaucluse, 12.V.2001. P. DELFORGE.

Pollinators *Andrena nigroaenea* (Br Ga It), *A. barbilabris* (Ga), *A. cineraria* (Ga) and *A. limata* (Ge) (Hymenoptera: Andrenidae).

Ophrys ausonia

P. DEVILLERS, J. DEVILLERS-TERSCHUREN & P. DELFORGE

Etymology *ausonia:* from Ausones, via poetic licence, Italy. **Type** It, Latina (2004). **Synonyms** *O. araneola* auct. non RCHB., *O. tommasinii* auct. non VISIANI.

Description Slender, (15-) 20-50cm tall; inflorescence lax; (2-) 4-9 (-11) small flowers; sepals spreading, whitish-green, 9-12mm x 4-6mm, oval-lanceolate; petals broadly oblong-rounded, 6-9mm x 2.5-4.5mm, hairless, yellowish-green, slightly darker than sepals, edges slightly undulate; lip relatively small compared to sepals and petals, (5.5-) 7-9mm x (6-) 7.5-10mm (when spread), entire, orbicular to obcordate, without basal swellings, transversely angularly convex, centre rather flat, velvety, brown (often rather pale), submarginal band of hairs dense and rather long, pinkish-grey, rather narrow on distal half; border of lip hairless, straight, broadly edged bright yellow or greenish-yellow; speculum basal, drab, greyish to bluish, edged bluish, not very extensive, often forming a ± thickened π; appendage small, distinct, triangular, inserted into a deep notch; basal field and stigmatic cavity olive-green, clearly lighter than centre of lip; stigmatic cavity strongly constricted at base, with a broad bluish to whitish specular stage; pseudo-eyes greenish grey, pale, circular, only slightly contrasting; rather distinct, protruding external bosses often present (photo A).

Flowering Season Mid V-VI, late.

Habitat Full sun to shade on dry to moist, alkaline substrates. Short grassland, garrigue, road verges, open woodland, up to 700m asl.

Distribution Central peninsular Italy. Very local but sometimes abundant in its stations.

Countries It.

Photos It, Latina (loc. typ.), 1.VI.2000. P. DELFORGE.

Key to the *Ophrys sphegodes* group

1	lip 10-16mm long	2
1*	lip 5-10mm long	4

2	main flowering season III-V.........................	3
2*	flowering late, VI-VII	*O. majellensis*

3   lip very dark, broadly edged by dense, straight blackish-purple hairs, not attenuated on distal half; basal field much lighter than lip *O. brutia*

3*	lip otherwise	*O. sphegodes*

4	flowering very early, XII-III ...	*O. massiliensis*
4*	flowering late, mid V-VI	*O. ausonia*

Ophrys majellensis
(DAISS) P. DELFORGE

Etymology *majellensis:* [from the massif of] Maiella. **Type** It, Abruzzo or Molise (1997). **Synonyms** *O. sphegodes* subsp. *majellensis* DAISS, *O. passionis* subsp. *majellensis* (DAISS) ROMOLINI & SOCA, *O. garganica* subsp. *majellensis* (DAISS) KREUTZ.

Description As *O. sphegodes*, but very slender, 30-70 (-90)cm tall; inflorescence few-flowered, lax; 3-7 rather large flowers; sepals green, whitish-green to pinkish, sometimes reddish; petals darker, often ochre, brown; lip (10-) 13-20mm long, dark brown to blackish, often with basal swellings; speculum forming an H, dark greyish, unobtrusively edged pale grey, more complex, more extensive, frequently with extensions encompassing the inner face of basal swellings; basal field lighter than centre of lip; stigmatic cavity broad, strongly constricted at base, floor with a distinct yellowish specular stage; pseudo-eyes greyish to blackish, more contrasting, sometimes encircled, ± completely, with pale greyish, with a distinct white bridle, surmounted by a purple line; external walls of stigmatic cavity whitish, often contrasting.

Flowering Season VI-VII, very late.

Habitat Mostly full sun on moist, calcareous substrates. Short grassland and scrub in hills and mountains, up to 1300m asl.

Distribution Central Italy, from southern Tuscany to northern Campania; a few reports from south-west France refer to *O. passionis* or hybrids with the latter. Very rare and local. **Countries** It. **Photos** It, Caserta, 12.VI.1984; Frosinone, 2.VI.2000. P. DELFORGE.

Discussion of the *Ophrys sphegodes* group

Probably monophyletic, with 5 central Mediterranean species clearly belonging to the complex, having a drab stigmatic cavity and the basal field clearly paler than the centre of the lip. *O. brutia* and, to a lesser extent, *O. majellensis*, the most southerly species in the group, are also those that have the most primitive characters, approaching *O. incubacea* and, beyond that, the root of the complex constituted by *O. lunulata* and its allies. *O. sphegodes*, with a more northerly distribution, is probably the most derived species and since the last glaciation has successfully colonised mid-Europe and its Atlantic seaboard as far as southern England. *O. massiliensis* is a highly specialised and very early-flowering form from the Mediterranean coast of France. *O. ausonia*, with its apparently very restricted distribution on the Adriatic slope of the central Apennines, is probably a relict species, as apparently indicated by a primitive structure, the frequent presence of protruding external bosses on the margins of the stigmatic cavity.

Ophrys brutia
P. DELFORGE

Etymology *brutia:* from Brut(t)ium (modern Calabria). **Type** It, Reggio de Calabria (2003). **Synonyms** *O. incubacea* subsp. *brutia* (P. DELFORGE) KREUTZ, *O. sphegodes* auct. non MILLER.

Description As *O. sphegodes* but flowers slightly smaller; sepals 7-12mm x 3-6mm, whitish-green; petals 5-7mm x 2.5-3.5mm, sometimes velvety or ciliate, lanceolate-obtuse, centre concolourous with sepals, margins brighter green or ochre, undulate, sometimes straight, petals green, often edged red; lip dark, entire, 10-14mm x 11-15mm (when spread), structure, hairs and speculum as *O. incubacea* but basal swellings less well marked, basal field and stigmatic cavity reddish to olive-green, contrastingly paler than centre of lip; stigmatic cavity strongly constricted at base, with a ± broad yellowish specular stage, only slightly contrasting; pseudo-eyes rounded, black to greenish in centre, ± broadly encircled by yellowish or whitish, often surmounted by a red eyebrow linked by a bridle to the contrastingly white external walls of stigmatic cavity.

Flowering Season Mid III-IV, rather early.

Habitat Full sun to mid-shade on dry to moist, often marly, alkaline substrates. Short grassland, garrigue, abandoned cultivation, scrub, woodland edges, up to 500m asl. **Distribution** Probably endemic to Calabria. Rather local and rather rare. **Countries** It.

Photos It, Reggio di Calabria (loc. typ.), 6.IV.2002; Cosenza, 11.IV.2002; Catanzaro, 13.IV.2002. P. DELFORGE.

595

The *Ophrys incubacea* group

Characteristics Flowers often brightly coloured; petals tending to be broad; lip often dark, with a complete submarginal band of hairs; stigmatic cavity and basal field dark, blackish or reddish, concolourous with centre of lip; specular stage present, often very contrasting; pseudo-eyes blackish, pale blue or white; external walls of stigmatic cavity frequently contrasting.

Ophrys incubacea
BIANCA

Etymology *incubacea:* with a small size. **Type** Si, Iblées (1842). **Synonyms** *O. atrata* LINDLEY nom. illeg., *O. aranifera* subsp. *atrata* ARCANGELI, *O. aranifera* subsp. *incubacea* (BIANCA) Soó, *O. sooi* H. FLEISCHMANN pro hybr., *O. incubacea* var. *dianensis* PERAZZA & DORO.

Description 20-40 (-60)cm tall; 3-8 flowers; sepals green (slightly whitish), very rarely pinkish, spreading, oval-lanceolate, 10-15.5mm x 4-7.5mm; petals green to brown, sometimes pink (= '*sooi*', '*dianensis*'), darker than sepals, narrowly to broadly lanceolate, 6-9.5mm x 2.5-5mm, hairless, margins ± strongly undulate, sometimes tinted red; lip (9-) 10-14mm x 10-14.5mm, entire or obscurely 3-lobed, orbicular to obcordate, directed obliquely forwards, dark brown to blackish, centre velvety, transversally convex, margins turned down, with prominent triangular basal swellings up to 4mm high, hairless on inner face; submarginal band of hairs long, straight and dense, brown to blackish-purple; speculum central, rather simple, forming an H, blue or grey, glossy, rarely edged whitish; appendage much reduced to absent, inserted into a deep notch; basal field and stigmatic cavity concolourous with centre of lip, contrasting with their whitish edges; stigmatic cavity strongly constricted at base, floor with a strongly contrasting white or pale bluish specular stage, sometimes reaching pseudo-eyes; pseudo-eyes circular, spotted black or blue in centre, edged pale blue and then white; external walls of stigmatic cavity contrastingly white; 2n=36-38;

Flowering Season III-V.

Habitat Full sun to mid-shade on dry to moist, alkaline substrates. Short grassland, meadows, garrigue, scrub, open woodland, up to 1300m asl.

Distribution Western and central Mediterranean. Southern Portugal to northern Albania; reports from Corfu (Gr) are no longer confirmed. Rather widespread and sometimes abundant. **Countries** Al Bl Co Ga Hs It Ju Lu Sa Si. **Photos** Si, Palermo, 18.IV.2000; Lu, Extremadura, 5.IV.1990. P. DELFORGE.

Pollinator *Andrena morio* (Hymenoptera: Andrenidae).

Ophrys passionis
SENNEN

Etymology *passionis:* from the Passion (an allusion to Easter). **Type** Hs, Barcelona (1926). **Synonyms** *O. sphegodes* subsp. *passionis* (SENNEN) SANZ & NUET, *O. sphegodes* var. *garganicoides* BALAYER, *O. passionis* SENNEN ex J. DEVILLERS-TERSCHUREN & P. DEVILLERS nom. illeg., *O. garganica* subsp. *passionis* (SENNEN ex J. DEVILLERS-TERSCHUREN & P. DEVILLERS) H.F. PAULUS & GACK comb. inval.

Description 20-40 (-50)cm tall; inflorescence (near) lax; (3-) 5-10 rather large flowers; sepals green, pale green, rarely white or pinkish, spreading, oval to lanceolate, 8-13 (-15.5)mm x 4-7mm; petals green, pink or purple, darker than sepals, narrowly to broadly lanceolate, 6-9mm x 2-3.5 (-4.5)mm (larger petals: var. *garganica*), hairless, shape varied, margins ± strongly undulate, often tinted red or purple; lip (9-) 10-13.5mm x 12-15mm, entire or 3-lobed, orbicular to near heart-shaped, globular, transversely angularly convex at base, centre rather flat, margins sometimes spreading or reflexed, often slightly bulging, dark blackish-purple, velvety in centre, with a dense submarginal band of blackish-purple hairs, slightly shorter on distal half, bordered by a fine paler hairless margin, purple, orange, sometimes yellowish; speculum rather extensive, glossy grey, formed by 2 broad lines, vertical or in a broad rectangle with a central ocellus and lateral triangular extensions, covering basal swellings; appendage much reduced or absent, inserted into a distinct notch; basal field and stigmatic cavity very dark, contrasting rather with their pallid margins; floor of stigmatic cavity with a narrow, rather unobtrusive specular stage, sometimes contrasting; pseudo-eyes black, glossy, with a narrow, not very bright ocular bridle, often surmounted by a purple line; 2n=20. 36.

Flowering Season (III-) IV-VI, with at least 2 successive waves of flowering.

Habitat Full sun to mid-shade on dry to moist, alkaline substrates, mostly calcareous. Short, poor grassland, meadows, abandoned cultivation, banks, terraces, garrigue, scrub, open woodland, up to 1300m asl.

Distribution Var. *passionis:* the western part of the range, from La Sierra de la Demanda and Catalonia (Hs) east to Alpes-Maritimes (Ga) and north to Morbihan (Ga); also rather frequent in peninsular Italy and perhaps Sicily, often with var. *garganica*. Local and rather rare.

Countries Ga Hs It ?Si.

Photos Hs, Tarragona, 13.IV.1990; Burgos, 17.VI.1994. P. DELFORGE (see also p. 24).

Pollinator *Andrena carbonaria* (Hymenoptera: Andrenidae).

597

1 petals ciliate, sometimes auriculate 2
1* petals hairless, never auriculate 3

2 flowers small, petals 2-4mm broad
   .... *O. castellana*
2* flowers medium-sized, petals 4-5.5mm broad
   .... *O. aveyronensis*

3 specular stage white, highly visible and contrasting with dark floor of stigmatic cavity ..4
3* specular stage drab, not obvious 6

4 sepals usually green, lip with prominent
   basal swellings .... *O. incubacea*
4* sepals white to pink, lip with basal swellings
   not prominent or absent 5

5 petals entirely dark pink to dusky red or
   brown .... *O. sipontensis*
5* petals bicoloured, centre whitish, margins
   darker, yellow or orange .... *O. splendida*

6 lip (9-) 10-13.5mm long .... *O. passionis*
6* lip 5-10 (-10.5)mm long 7

7 inflorescence lax, lip only slightly convex,
   without basal swellings, blackish, not rapidly
   turning green after anthesis; late flowering
   (V-VI at low altitudes) .... *O. illyrica*
7* plant otherwise 8

8 lip chestnut-brown to yellowish-brown, often
   with rounded basal swellings; stigmatic cavity greenish-grey, paler than basal field; pseudo-eyes greenish-grey, iridescent, rather
   large .... *O. tommasinii*
8* flowers otherwise 9

9 early flowering (III at low altitudes); lip entire, broadly edged yellow, smaller than dorsal sepal .... *O. araneola*
9* late flowering (IV-V at low altitudes); lip
   sometimes 3-lobed, with or without yellow
   border, larger than dorsal sepal ... *O. virescens*

Discussion of the *Ophrys incubacea* group

A group of 10 species, perhaps monophyletic,
often with contrasting colours and petals that
tend to widen. Two, *O. aveyronensis* and *O.
castellana*, have integrated into their genotype
material from the *O. fuciflora* complex. In its
coloration and hairs, *O. incubacea* seems related
to the *O. lunulata* group, itself close to the root
of the complex. *O. sipontensis* and *O. passionis*
most probably form a clade. *O. splendida* appears to be a rather unique species, whose affinities remain obscure.

(continued on p. 602)

Ophrys passionis SENNEN
var. *garganica*
(E. NELSON ex O. DANESCH & E. DANESCH) P. DELFORGE

Etymology *garganica:* from Mount Gargano (It,
Foggia). **Type** It, Foggia (1975). **Synonyms** *O.
sphegodes* subsp. *garganica* E. NELSON nom. inval.,
O. garganica E. NELSON ex O. DANESCH & E. DANESCH,
O. incubacea subsp. *garganica* (E. NELSON ex O.
DANESCH & E. DANESCH) GALESI, CRISTAUDO & MAUGERI.

Description As *O. passionis* var. *passionis* but
sepals always green; petals usually large and
broad, 8-11mm x 3.5-6mm, hairless, shape
varied, broadly oblong to orbicular, sometimes
broadly falcate, olive-green to dark crimson-
brown, margins ± strongly undulate, sometimes
darker than centre; lip slightly larger, 11-15mm x
13-17mm (when spread); floor of stigmatic cavity
with a larger specular stage; pseudo-eyes with a
narrow ocular-bridle that is brighter.

Flowering Season, Habitat As var. *passionis*,
but up to 1100m asl.

Distribution Mostly Italian; from Tuscany and
Puglia to Calabria, also Sicily and Sardinia.
Rather scattered and rather rare, but sometimes
found in large populations.

Countries ?Ga It Sa Si.

Photo Si, Ragusa, 22.III.2000. P. DELFORGE.

Pollinator *Andrena carbonaria* (Hymenoptera:
Andrenidae).

Ophrys sipontensis
R. LORENZ & GEMBARDT

Etymology *sipontensis:* from Siponto, a village at the foot of Mount Gargano (It, Foggia). **Type** It, Foggia (1987). **Synonyms** *O. sphegodes* subsp. *sipontensis* GUMPRECHT nom. inval., *O. sipontensis* GUMPRECHT ex O. DANESCH & E. DANESCH nom. inval., *O. garganica* subsp. *sipontensis* (GUMPRECHT) DEL PRETE nom. inval., *O. garganica* subsp. *sipontensis* (R. LORENZ & GEMBARDT) KREUTZ.

Description Often robust, (15-) 20-50 (-60)cm tall; inflorescence lax; (2-) 3-8 large flowers; sepals whitish to purplish-pink, 10-15mm x 4-7.5mm, lanceolate, spreading; petals 7-13mm x 3-7mm, hairless, shape varied, broadly oblong to oval-lanceolate, very colourful, pink to garnet-red, often washed brown or ochre, with a central vein and undulate-crisped margins; lip entire, oval to near rhomboidal, blackish-brown to black, ± convex, rather squared at base, sometimes obscurely bulging, 10-15mm x 10-17mm (when spread), centre velvety, margins turned down, with dense, long, blackish-purple or dark brownish hairs, slightly shorter on distal half; speculum central, formed by 2 thick, parallel, vertical lines, often linked at level of basal field, thus ± forming an H complicated by appendages and hooks, sometimes fragmented, bright glossy blue, rarely greyish or purple, often edged by a narrow pale line; appendage very small to absent, entire, inserted into a deep notch; basal field and stigmatic cavity blackish, contrasting with their paled margins; floor of stigmatic cavity with a rather broad, contrasting specular stage, whitish to bluish; pseudo-eyes blue, with a very narrow, bright ocular bridle, often surmounted by a purple line, sometimes diffuse.

Flowering Season III-IV (-V).

Habitat Full sun to mid-shade on dry to moist, calcareous substrates. Short, poor grassland, meadows, abandoned cultivation, garrigue, up to 700m asl.

Distribution Endemic to Mount Gargano, principally the southern foothills and Siponto plain. Very local and rather rare.

Countries It.

Photos It, Foggia, 6.IV.1986; 31.III. 1991. P. DELFORGE.

Discussion *O. sipontensis* is probably a vicariant of *O. garganica* with colourful sepals, adapted to a specific pollinator, *Xylocopa iris* (Hymenoptera: Anthophoridae), which is also the pollinator of *Ophrys spruneri* in Greece. The striking morphological convergence between flowers of these 2 species may indicate that visual attraction plays a prominent role in the search for female mates in this bee.

Ophrys virescens
PHILIPPE ex GRENIER

Etymology *virescens:* turning green. **Type** Ga, Var (1859). **Synonyms** *O. aranifera* subsp. *litigiosa* var. *virescens* (PHILIPPE ex GRENIER) E.G. CAMUS, *O. araneola* subsp. *virescens* (PHILIPPE ex GRENIER) KREUTZ, *O. araneoloides* H.F. PAULUS nom. nud.

Description As *O. araneola* but more leafy and more robust with fewer flowers; flowers appear darker; sepals whitish-green to bright green, sometimes pinkish; petals darker and tending to be larger; lip proportionally larger relative to sepals, 7.5-10mm long, darker, more convex, sometimes obscurely 3-lobed; submarginal band of hairs brownish to blackish; sides of lip less broadly tinted yellow, often reddish; speculum H-shaped, more complex and more extensive, greyish to blue, often edged paler, sometimes marbled; stigmatic cavity less constricted at base; bridles linking pseudo-eyes to external walls neater.

Flowering Season IV-VI, relatively late, after *O. sphegodes*, well after *O. arachnitiformis*.

Habitat Full sun to mid-shade on dry to moist, alkaline substrates. Short grassland, garrigue, road verges, open woodland, probably up to 800m asl.

Distribution Poorly known due to confusion with related taxa. Less northerly than *O. araneola*, probably the Mediterranean and supra-Mediterranean regions of France and northern Spain and perhaps also Tuscany. Similar but slightly earlier-flowering plants also occur on Mount Gargano (It, Foggia).

Countries Ga Hs ?It.

Photos A & C Ga, Bouches-du-Rhône, 23.IV.1999; 13.V.2001; **B** Hs, Burgos, 12.VI.1993. P. DELFORGE.

Ophrys araneola
REICHENBACH

Etymology *araneola:* small spider. **Type** He, Wallis (1831). **Synonyms** *O. aranifera* subsp. *araneola* (RCHB.) K. RICHTER, *O. pseudospeculum* var. *araneola* (RCHB.) MUTEL, *O. sphecodes* var. *araneola* (RCHB.) SCHINZ & THELL., *O. litigiosa* E.G. CAMUS, *O. sphegodes* subsp. *litigiosa* (E.G. CAMUS) BÉCHERER.

Description Rather robust, (15-) 20-35 (-45)cm tall; inflorescence dense to near lax; (2-) 4-10 (-15) small flowers; sepals spreading, yellowish-green, 8-12mm x 4-6mm, lanceolate; petals broadly oblong-lanceolate, 4-8mm x 2-4mm, hairless, yellowish-green, slightly darker than sepals, margins ± strongly undulate; lip small in proportion to sepals and petals, (5-) 6.5-9mm x (6-) 7.5-10mm (when spread), entire or rarely obscurely 3-lobed, orbicular to obcordate, without basal swellings, slightly convex, centre velvety, reddish-brown to blackish, quickly fading after anthesis, submarginal band of hairs dense and rather long, reddish-brown to ochre, external rim sometimes yellow; border of lip hairless, sometimes reflexed, broadly bright yellow or greenish-yellow; speculum basal, only slightly glossy, greyish, rarely edged whitish, surrounding a very small basal field, often forming a ± thickened (rather than an H), not very extensive, sometimes near quadrangular; appendage small to near absent, triangular, inserted into a deep notch; basal field and stigmatic cavity concolourous with lip or slightly lighter; stigmatic cavity strongly constricted at base, specular stage absent or brownish, hardly visible; pseudo-eyes blackish, circular, only slightly contrasting, with a greenish bridle sometimes underlined by a thin purple line.

Note Plants with pink sepals and petals are rather frequent in Corbières (Ga) and probably refer to *O. virescens.*

Flowering Season III-V, early, before *O. sphegodes* and *O. virescens*, ± the same time as *O. arachnitiformis* in Mediterranean France.

Habitat Full sun to mid-shade on dry to moist, alkaline substrates. Short grassland, garrigue, road verges, open woodland, up to 1300m asl.

Distribution Centred on France, almost reaches Belgium in the north; limits of range poorly known due to confusion with related taxa.

Countries Ga Ge He Hs It.

Photos Ga, Hérault, 29.III.1999; Drôme, 29.V.1981. P. DELFORGE.

Pollinator *Andrena lathyri* (Hymenoptera: Andrenidae).

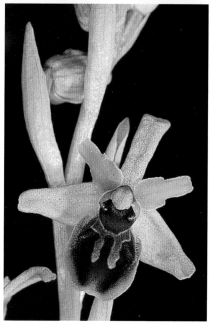

Ophrys tommasinii
VISIANI

Etymology Named after M.G.S. de Tommasini, Austrian-Hungarian botanist (1794-1879). **Type** Ju, Croatia, Losinj Island (1851). **Synonyms** *O. aranifera* var. *tommasinii* RCHB. fil vel (VISIANI) SCHLOSSER & FARKAS-VUKOTINOVIC, *O. aranifera* subsp. *tommasinii* (VISIANI) E.G. CAMUS, *O. sphecodes* subsp. *tommasinii* (VISIANI) SOÓ, *O. araneola* subsp. *tommasinii* (VISIANI) KREUTZ.

Description As *O. araneola* but slender, 15-40cm tall; inflorescence rather dense; (2-) 4-11 small flowers; sepals spreading, whitish-green, 8-12mm x 4-6.5mm, lanceolate; petals narrowly lanceolate, 6-8.6mm x 2-4mm; lip 7.5-10.5mm x 9.5-11mm (when spread), entire, convex, chestnut-brown to yellowish-brown, fading rather quickly after anthesis, base rather squared, often with rounded basal swellings, distal half attenuated; submarginal band of hairs broad, reddish-brown to pinkish-grey, sometimes yellowish, border of lip hairless, yellow or reddish, sometimes absent; speculum basal, rather drab, dark greyish, edged whitish, often forming a ± thickened, sometimes with a central ocellus; basal field cramped, concolourous with lip; stigmatic cavity paler, greenish-grey, with a blurred bluish to whitish specular stage, not obvious; pseudo-eyes greenish-grey, iridescent, rather large, globular.

Flowering Season IV-early V, the second wave of small-flowered *Ophrys* 'sphegodes s.l.' in Croatia.

Habitat As *O. illyrica*. **Distribution** As *O. illyrica* but less localised and sometimes abundant. **Countries** Ju. **Photos** Ju, Hrvatska, Istria, 25.IV.2003; Krk, 23.IV.2003. P. DELFORGE.

Discussion of the *Ophrys incubacea* group

(continued from p. 598)

Within the group were placed *O. araneola* and 3 other species with small flowers, which were, until very recently, confused with it: *O. virescens*, *O. tommasinii* and *O. illyrica*. *O. araneola* is a very remarkable species that remains difficult to place in the phylogeny of the *O. sphegodes* complex. The recognition of *O. virescens*, *O. tommasinii* and *O. illyrica*, whose characters demonstrate more clearly that they belong to the *O. incubacea* group, may indicate that they form, together with *O. araneola*, a subgroup within the *O. incubacea* group, divided into 2 geographically isolated pairs: the Istrio-Dalmatian endemics *O. tommasinii* and *O. illyrica*, and *O. araneola* and *O. virescens*, whose range is centred on France. The 2 species in each pair are isolated by at least their staggered flowering seasons. Nevertheless, the hypothesis of an origin from other species in the group, via distinct speciation events on the basis of lip size, may not be entirely excluded.

Ophrys illyrica
S. Hertel & K. Hertel

Etymology *illyrica:* from Illyria. **Type** Ju, Croatia, Cres Island (2002). **Synonym** *O. araneola* subsp. *illyrica* (S. Hertel & K. Hertel) Kreutz.

Description As *O. araneola* but slender, 15-40cm tall; inflorescence very lax; (2-) 4-10 small flowers; sepals spreading, greenish, 9-12mm x 4-6mm, lanceolate; petals broadly lanceolate, 7-9mm x 3-5mm; lip 8-10.5mm x 9-12mm (when spread), entire to obscurely 3-lobed, very slightly convex, dark brown to blackish, not rapidly fading after anthesis; submarginal band of hairs narrow, blackish-brown to pinkish-grey, border of lip hairless, rather narrowly coloured bright yellow or reddish; speculum basal, only slightly glossy, dark bluish, often edged whitish, often forming a ± thickened π and sometimes branched or fragmented; basal field and stigmatic cavity concolourous with lip; stigmatic cavity strongly constricted at base, bluish specular stage clearly visible; pseudo-eyes blackish, contrastingly encircled pale bluish and with a whitish bridle sometimes underlined by a thin purple line.

Flowering Season (End IV-) V-mid VI, late; the third and last wave of small-flowered *Ophrys* '*sphegodes* s.l.' in Croatia.

Habitat Full sun to mid-shade on dry to moist, alkaline substrates. Short grassland, garrigue, road verges, open woodland, up to 300m asl.

Distribution Istria and the Quarnero archipelago (Ju). Very rare and local. **Countries** Ju.

Photos Ju, Hrvatska, Cres, 29 & 31.V.2004; Istria, 28.IV.2003. P. Delforge.

Ophrys splendida
GÖLZ & H.R. REINHARD

Etymology *splendida:* splendid. **Type** Ga, Bouches-du-Rhône (1980). **Synonyms** *O. exaltata* subsp. *splendida* (GÖLZ & H.R. REINHARD) SOCA, *Ophrys arachnitiformis* auct. non GRENIER & PHILIPPE.

Description Rather spindly, 10-25 (-35)cm tall; inflorescence near lax; (2-) 4-6 (-8) rather small flowers; sepals white, pink or crimson, exceptionally green, 10-15mm x 5-8mm, lanceolate, spreading, curved forwards; petals 6-10mm x 3-5mm, hairless, broadly triangular, elliptical or near orbicular, centre white, pink or yellowish, as pale as, or paler than, sepals, margins ± strongly undulate, broadly coloured yellow, greenish-yellow, orange or red, darker than centre; lip (near) entire, convex, reddish-brown to blackish-brown, oval-rounded, sometimes ± clearly bulging, (8-) 9.5-12mm x 10-14mm (when spread), with a submarginal band of brown to ochre or greyish hairs, margins hairless, often broadly coloured greenish-yellow; speculum varied, basal to central, glossy greyish-blue edged white, forming a π or H, ± thickened and with ocelli and branches, sometimes shield-shaped; appendage yellowish-green, small to absent, entire, triangular, directed forwards or downwards, inserted into a distinct notch; basal field and stigmatic cavity concolourous with centre of lip, contrasting with the pallid margins; floor of stigmatic cavity with a rather broad and contrasting greenish specular stage, often reaching the pseudo-eyes; pseudo-eyes circular, black to greyish, encircled by white or green, with a broad, bright bridle.

Flowering Season Mid IV-V (-VI), 3-6 weeks after *O. arachnitiformis*.

Habitat Full sun to mid-shade on dry to moist, calcareous substrates. Short, poor grassland, grassy places in garrigue and scrub, open woodland, up to 600m asl.

Distribution Endemic to Provence: Bouches-du-Rhône, Var, Alpes-Maritimes. Local and rather uncommon. **Countries** Ga.

Photos A & B Ga, Alpes-Maritimes, 19.IV.1999; C?16.V.2001. P. DELFORGE.

Pollinator *Andrena squalida* (Hymenoptera: Andrenidae).

Ophrys aveyronensis
(J.J. WOOD) P. DELFORGE

Etymology *aveyronensis:* from Aveyron. **Type** Ga, Aveyron (1983). **Synonyms** *O. sphegodes* subsp. *aveyronensis* J.J. WOOD, *O. aveyronensis* (J.J. WOOD) H. BAUMANN & KÜNKELE isonym.

Description Often robust, (10-) 20-40cm tall; (3-) 5-8 (-12) large flowers; sepals pale to dark pink, rarely creamy-white, exceptionally greenish, 10-16mm x 6-8mm, lanceolate, spreading; petals broadly triangular, lanceolate, elliptical or near orbicular, 7-10mm x 4-5.5mm, centre whitish, pink or reddish, sometimes paler than sepals, margins undulate, often ciliate, broadly coloured yellow, ochre, orange or red (of another colour and darker than centre); lip entire or 3-lobed, (9-) 11-15mm x 12-18mm (when spread), slightly to very convex transversally, orbicular to near rhomboidal, sometimes with small, ± prominent, pointed basal swellings, pale brown with a submarginal band of dense, long, pale brown hairs, margins hairless, sometimes yellow, turned down and under or, often, reflexed and undulate; speculum very varied, central, greyish-blue or glossy reddish, edged whitish, sometimes forming a ± distinct, thickened H, more often shield-shaped or even shapeless, very fragmented or marbled; appendage yellowish-green, not very prominent to lacking, entire, triangular, directed downwards, inserted into a distinct notch; basal field and stigmatic cavity concolourous with centre of lip; floor of stigmatic cavity with a rather broad specular stage, often slightly contrasting, frequently reaching peripseudo-ocular circles; pseudo-eyes circular to oblique and keeled, black to greyish, often protuberant, ± encircled by white, with a broad, bright ocular bridle, often surmounted by a purple line.

Flowering Season V-VI, late.

Habitat Full sun to mid-shade on dry to moist, calcareous to neutral substrates. Short, poor grassland, hay meadows, scrub, scattered oak woods, 400-800m asl.

Distribution Endemic to the southern foothills of the Massif Central, mainly Causse du Larzac (Ga). Reports from northern Spain refer to non-stabilised hybrids between other taxa in the complex. Very local and rather rare. **Countries** Ga.

Photos Ga, Aveyron, 22.V.1983; 13.V.2002. P. DELFORGE.

Pollinator *Andrena hattorfiana* (Hymenoptera: Andrenidae).

605

Ophrys castellana
J. DEVILLERS-TERSCHUREN & P. DEVILLERS

Etymology *castellana:* from Castile. **Type** Hs, Cuenca (1988). **Synonym** *O. exaltata* subsp. *castellana* (J. DEVILLERS-TERSCHUREN & P. DEVILLERS) SOCA.

Description Spindly, 12-20 (-25)cm tall; (2-) 3-8 (-10) small flowers; sepals white to pale pink, rarely whitish-green to yellowish, 7-13mm x 3-5mm, lanceolate; petals 5-9mm x 2-4mm, oblong, narrowly lanceolate to oval, often auriculate and pubescent, centre white to pale pink, rarely yellowish or greenish, margins straight to slightly undulate, strongly ciliate, ± broadly coloured yellow, orange, reddish or bright green, darker than centre; lip entire or 3-lobed, convex, pale brown to blackish, ovoid, sometimes with rounded or pointed basal swellings, 7-11 (-13)mm x 9-13mm (when spread), submarginal band of hairs pale brown, denser on shoulders and basal half, margins hairless, turned down and under or slightly reflexed and undulate, sometimes tinted yellow on distal half; speculum central, extensive, often complex, glossy greyish-blue, edged creamy-white, forming a thickened H, extended by lateral branches; appendage yellowish-green, very small to well developed, entire, triangular, directed downwards, inserted into a distinct notch; basal field and stigmatic cavity concolourous with centre of lip, contrasting with their pallid margins; stigmatic cavity strongly constricted at base, floor with a varied specular stage, often contrastingly whitish; pseudo-eyes circular, black to greyish, encircled with whitish or greenish, with a broad bright bridle, often surmounted by a purple line.

Flowering Season (IV-) V-VI, late, 2-4 weeks after *O. sphegodes*.

Habitat Full sun to shade on damp to wet, alkaline to slightly acidic substrates. Marshy or water meadows, moist ditches, seepages on slopes and in open woodland, 650-1400m asl.

Distribution Endemic to the Spanish mountains, from Navarra south to Andalucia (Jaén). Local and often rare; threatened by the cultivation of damp areas.

Countries Hs.

Photos Hs, Cuenca, (loc. typ.) 2.VI.1988; La Rioja, 9.VI.1993. P. DELFORGE.

The *Ophrys lunulata* group

Characteristics Sepals uniform; petals uniform, elongated, often pubescent and ciliate; lip convex, with a prominent marginal band of hairs, paler than centre; speculum central, often reduced; appendage well developed, inserted into a notch; stigmatic cavity without a specular stage, very dark, concolourous with lip. A mono- or paraphyletic group with 5 species in the guide.

Ophrys promontorii
O. DANESCH & E. DANESCH

Etymology *promontorii:* of promontory (of Mount Gargano). **Type** It, Foggia (1971).

Description 10-20 (-40)cm tall; 2-7 (-12) flowers; sepals bright green to yellowish-green, sometimes washed pink or brown, spreading, oval-lanceolate, 11.5-17mm x 4-6mm; petals often very large, yellowish-green, bright green, olive-green or reddish-brown, darker than sepals, long-triangular to broadly lanceolate or elliptical, (6-) 8-12mm x (3-) 4-6mm, hairless to pubescent, margins ± strongly undulate and ciliate; lip 9.5-15mm x 10-15mm (when spread), entire, orbicular to near obcordate, convex, appearing narrowly oval, dark brown to blackish-purple, velvety in centre, often with prominent basal swellings (hairless on inner face), sides turned down and under, marginal hairs long and dense, brown to blackish-purple; speculum central, small, rather simple, blue or grey, glossy, sometimes edged whitish, sometimes shield-shaped or lacking, more often forming a very incomplete H or X, sometimes reduced to 2-4 lines or isolated streaks; appendage small, distinct, greenish-yellow, sometimes reddish, triangular, inserted into a distinct notch; stigmatic cavity rounded, slightly pinched below pseudo-eyes, blackish, specular stage absent; pseudo-eyes sometimes only poorly marked. **Variation** A morphologically stable species that is sometimes considered, probably incorrectly, to be of hybrid origin (see Discussion, p. 561)

Flowering Season IV-V (-VI); rather late.

Habitat Full sun to mid-shade on dry to moist, alkaline substrates. Short grassland, meadows, garrigue, scrub, open woodland, up to 1300m asl.

Distribution Central peninsular Italy. Abruzzi (L'Aquila, Chieti, Pescara); Puglia (Foggia, Bari, Brindisi); Latium (Frosinone, Latina). Rather rare and local; most frequent at Mount Gargano (Foggia). **Countries** It.

Photos It, Frosinone, 23.V.2000; Foggia, 10.IV.1986. P. DELFORGE.

Pollinator *Osmia mustelina* (Hymenoptera: Mega-chilidae).

Ophrys panattensis
SCRUGLI, PESSEI & COGONI (pro hybr.)

Etymology *panattensis:* from Panatta (near Opinki, Nuoro, Sa, the origin of the type). **Type** Sa, Nuoro (1992).

Description Slender, 20-50cm tall; inflorescence near lax; (4-) 6-12 relatively large flowers; sepals whitish to rather dark purplish-pink, spreading, broadly oval-lanceolate, margins recurved, 13-16mm long, lateral sepals often directed obliquely downwards, dorsal sepal erect, curved forwards; petals concolourous with sepals, erect, linear-oblong to narrowly lanceolate, 6-8.5mm x 2-3mm, shortly ciliate, margins straight or undulate, sometimes darker or tinted green; lip pendent, 11-18mm x 11-20mm (when spread), near entire to deeply 3-lobed, oboval to obcordate (when spread), slightly to very convex longitudinally, thus appearing oblong, often with distinct basal swellings, centre velvety, dark reddish-brown to blackish, marginal hairs long and dense, greyish to orange or crimson, lighter than centre of lip, then a ± broad, yellowish, hairless outer margin (the yellow may sometimes invade part of the lip), sides turned down and under or reflexed; speculum central to basal, not very extensive, bluish-grey, sometimes edged whitish, glossy, forming a horseshoe, reduced to 2-4 isolated drop-marks or ± forming an H or X; appendage greenish-yellow, broad, triangular, sometimes 3-toothed, often prominent, protruding, inserted into a distinct notch; basal field blackish; stigmatic cavity similar, small, narrow, bordered by 2 prominent shiny black pseudo-eyes, specular stage absent.

Variation Very varied, principally because the lip may be very convex and 3-lobed or entire and spreading; the first state is very close to *O. lunulata* and even recalls *O. scolopax*, the second, notably, *O. morisii*; between these two extremes exist numerous intermediates. The sepals and petals are more constant.

Flowering Season IV-V.

Habitat Full sun to mid-shade, on dry to moist substrates, mostly alkaline. Short grassland, garrigue, scrub, up to 800m asl.

Distribution Currently known from calcareous massifs in the province of Nuoro; reported in the past from Sassari (as *Ophrys lunulata*). Local but sometimes abundant.

Countries Sa.

Photos Sa, Nuoro. 11 & 29.IV.1996. P. DELFORGE.

Pollinator *Osmia rufa* subsp. *rufa* (Hymenoptera: Megachilidae).

Ophrys lunulata
PARLATORE

Etymology *lunulata:* with lunula. **Type** Si, Palermo (1838). **Synonyms** *O. aranifera* subsp. *lunulata* (PARLATORE) E.G. CAMUS, *O. sphegodes* subsp. *lunulata* (PARLATORE) SUNDERMANN.

Description 10-40cm tall; bracts longer than flowers; inflorescence (near) lax; (4-) 6-10 rather large flowers; sepals whitish, pink, reddish or lilac, pale to dark, spreading, oval-lanceolate, margins recurved, 11-16mm x 4.5-7mm, lateral sepals often directed obliquely downwards, dorsal sepal erect, hooded, curved forwards; petals concolourous with sepals, erect, linear-lanceolate, 8-11mm x 2-3mm, hairless or shortly ciliate, margins straight; lip pendent, 10-14mm x 13-18mm (when spread), 3-lobed, oboval to obcordate, very convex longitudinally, appearing oblong, not or slightly bulging, pale reddish-brown to more often deep blackish, velvety in centre, submarginal band of hairs orange, long and dense, then a ± broad yellowish hairless margin; sides turned under then, sometimes, reflexed; speculum central, not very extensive, bluish-grey to reddish, glossy, often forming a horseshoe, reduced to 2 isolated drop-marks or sometimes ± H-shaped; appendage greenish-yellow, broad, often transverse, sometimes triangular, pendent or erect, inserted into a distinct notch; basal field blackish; stigmatic cavity similar, small, narrow, bordered by 2 prominent, shiny, black pseudo-eyes, specular stage absent; tip of column sometimes acuminate and sinuous.

Variation An unusual species, only slightly varied. Easily distinguished by the sepal colour, elongated petals and relatively large size of the lip, as well as its shape and colour, strongly convex transversely, along with the dense submarginal band of pale hairs, yellow border and reduced central speculum.

Flowering Season III-IV (-V).

Habitat Full sun to mid-shade on dry to moist substrates, mostly alkaline. Short grassland, meadows, garrigue, scrub, open woodland, up to 1000m asl.

Distribution Sicily and the Eolian Islands; other reports (Malta, Sardinia, Elba, Calabria) very probably refer respectively to *O. melitensis*, *O. panattensis* and *O. tarentina*. Local and rather rare

Countries Si.

Photos Si, Siracusa, 22.III.2000. P. DELFORGE.

Pollinator *Osmia kohli* (Hymenoptera: Megachilidae).

Ophrys melitensis
(SALKOWSKI) J. DEVILLERS-TERSCHUREN & P. DEVILLERS

Etymology *melitensis:* of Malta. **Type** Me (1992). **Basionym** *Ophrys sphegodes* subsp. *melitensis* SALKOWSKI.

Description Thickset, (7-) 10-20cm tall; 2-6 flowers; sepals whitish-green, rarely pale pink or whitish, spreading, oval-lanceolate, obtuse, 10-13mm x 4.5-6mm, margins recurved, lateral sepals sometimes tinted purple on lower half; petals yellowish-green, most often tinted purple or chestnut, sometimes dark, rarely white or pink, 7-9mm x 2-4mm, hairless, oblong to narrowly lanceolate, margins undulate, sometimes strongly so, weakly ciliate; lip 12-16mm x 9-13mm, entire, not or only slightly bulging, oboval, brown to dark blackish, velvety in centre, transversally convex, sides turned under or sometimes spreading, marginal hairs long and dense, orange to dark brown, lighter than centre of lip; speculum basal to central, poorly developed, reddish grey to glossy bluish, forming a horseshoe, 2 contiguous drops or a small H; appendage small, triangular, pointed, inserted into a deep notch; basal field dark brownish to blackish; stigmatic cavity concolourous, sometimes with a weak specular stage; pseudo-eyes blackish, shiny, sometimes faded.

Flowering Season III-early IV.

Habitat Full sun on dry, calcareous substrates. Short, rocky grassland, up to 60m asl.

Distribution Endemic to the Maltese archipelago (Malta and Gozo). Very local and very rare; sometimes with a single individual at a site. **Countries** Me.

Photo Me, Malta, 4.III.1995. J.-M. HERVOUET.

Pollinator *Chalicodoma sicula* (Hymenoptera: Megachilidae).

Discussion of the *Ophrys lunulata* group

A mono- or paraphyletic group from the central Mediterranean (the southern half of peninsular Italy, Sardinia, Sicily, the Maltese archipelago), made up of species that replace each other geographically. Within the *O. sphegodes* complex, they simultaneously possess characters that approach the *O. bertolonii* group (petals elongated, lip very convex, with very prominent marginal hairs, speculum rather central), and the *O. incubacea* group (e.g. stigmatic cavity with pale external border and blackish interior), and have their own characters (pseudo-eyes shiny black and rather large, without a bridle, specular stage absent, marginal hairs paler than centre of lip), as well as characters recalling the *O. fuciflora* complex (petals ciliate, appendage prominent, sometimes 3-toothed…). *O. promontorii* was sometimes considered to be a species of recent hybrid origin between *O. garganica*, *O. incubacea* and *O. tarentina*; *O. panattensis* was described as a hybrid between *O. morisii* and *O. scolopax*. Although morphologically very diverse, the species in this group are stable and appear to have an ancient origin, close to the common ancestor of the *O. incubacea* and *O. bertolonii* groups and even the *O. fuciflora* and *O. sphegodes* complexes, rather than originating from various recent hybridisations.

Key to the *Ophrys lunulata* group

1   petals linear-lanceolate, margins straight ....*O. lunulata*

1*   petals broader, margins wavy 2

2   sepals whitish to dark purplish-pink ....*O. panattensis*

2*   sepals usually green, rarely whitish or pinkish 3

3   lip without basal swellings, marginal hairs orange to pale brown...................*O. tarentina*

3*   lip usually bulging, marginal hairs blackish-purple...4

4   petals (3-) 4-6mm wide, often broadly lanceolate or elliptical....................*O. promontorii*

4*   petals narrow, 2-4mm wide ....*O. melitensis*

Ophrys tarentina
GÖLZ & H.R. REINHARD

Etymology *tarentina:* from Tarente. **Type** It, Tarente (1982).

Description Rather robust, (10-) 15-35 (-48)cm tall; 3-8 (-10) flowers; sepals green, sometimes slightly yellowish or whitish, rarely pale pink, spreading, oval-lanceolate, obtuse, 10-14.5mm x 4.5-7mm; petals yellowish-green, sometimes ochre, rarely with pale pink centre and yellow margins, 8-11mm x 2.5-4.5mm, hairless, oblong to narrowly lanceolate, margins almost straight to wavy, rarely strongly so; lip 10.5-15mm x 13-17mm (spreading), entire or obscurely 3-lobed, not or only very slightly bulging, oboval to obcordate, directed obliquely forwards, pale reddish-brown to dark blackish-brown, velvety in centre, transversally convex, sides turned under, submarginal band of hairs long and dense, orange to purplish-brown, rather pale, margin hairless, greenish-yellow; speculum central, poorly developed, glossy grey, sometimes forming a horseshoe or 2 contiguous drops, most often a ± fragmented and incomplete H or a X; appendage much reduced to lacking, triangular, pointed, inserted into a deep notch; basal field blackish; stigmatic cavity blackish, sometimes with a rudimentary specular stage, relatively little constricted below pseudo-eyes.

Variation Rather slight. Distinctive in the relatively large lip, its shape (strongly transversely convex), as well as the dense, pale marginal hairs and reduced central speculum.

Flowering Season III-IV.

Habitat Full sun to mid-shade on dry to moist, calcareous substrates. Short grassland, meadows, garrigue, scrub, olive groves, open woodland, up to 600m asl.

Distribution Southern peninsular Italy; reported from the provinces of Cosenza, Matera, Tarente and Brindisi, as well as Calabria. Local but sometimes abundant.

Countries It.

Photos It, Taranto, 3.IV.1986. P. DELFORGE (see also Photo A, p. 25).

Discussion Pollinated by *Osmia tricornis* (Hymenoptera: Megachilidae). *Ophrys tarentina* is the member of the *O. lunulata* group that is morphologically closest to the later-flowering *O. bertolonii.* They often forms large hybrid swarms that flower at the end of April and these may pose an identification problem when the parent species are poorly represented.

The *Ophrys bertolonii* group

Characteristics Lip convex, ± clearly curved into a saddle shape, marginal and central hairs dark, concolourous; speculum shield-shaped, distal to central; stigmatic cavity and basal field dark; specular stage whitish, usually well marked; tends to have lateral walls of stigmatic cavity hollowed-out. Flowers pollinated by bees of the genus *Chalicodoma*.

Discussion A monophyletic group, centred on Italy, reaching Ibiza (Bl) in the west and Corfu (Gr) in the east, with 10 species arranged into 3 subgroups:

1. Monophyletic, with 2 sister species, not influenced by *O. sphegodes* s.l.: *O. aurelia*, which appears to be the central figure and which shows all the characters of the group, and *O. bertolonii*, which represents a supplementary derived stage as shown by a stigmatic cavity that is unique within the genus and which, combined with the strong curvature of its lip, is particularly well adapted to its pollinators and constitutes without doubt an isolating character.

2. Comprising 5 species, *O. balearica*, *O. catalaunica*, *O. saratoi*, *O. drumana* and *O. benacensis,* which apparently result from introgressions of *O. (proto-)aurelia* by taxa from the *O. sphegodes* complex when it expanded north and west and penetrated the supra-Mediterranean montane zones. These 5 species represent stabilisations at different stages in this progression with a crystallisation around particular characters in each case. They each occupy well defined ranges, often not in contact with other taxa in the group.

3. Comprising 3 recently stabilised hybridogenous species, *O. bertoloniiformis*, *O. explanata* and *O. flavicans*, whose parent species are *O. bertolonii* and early taxa from the *O. sphegodes* complex. Each occupies a small, restricted coastal region where they are in sympatry with their parent species. The *O. lunulata* group and then the *O. incubacea* group are the closest to the *O. bertolonii* group, as shown by morphology, especially the analogies between *O. aurelia* and *O. tarentina*, the large number of introgressions and the relative abundance of hybrids between syntopic taxa from the 2 groups.

In Italy and northwest Croatia, hybrid swarms of *O. bertolonii* with *O. incubacea*, *O. tarentina*, *O. promontorii* or *O. lunulata*, as well as between *O. benacensis* and *O. incubacea,* are not rare.

Key to the *Ophrys bertolonii* group

1 stigmatic cavity taller than broad, deeply incised laterally ....*O. bertolonii*

1* stigmatic cavity broader than tall, not or only slightly incised laterally................................2

2 sepals frequently green or washed green (90%) ....*O. bertoloniiformis*

2* sepals violet, pink or white...........................3

3 lip (13-) 14-21mm long, appearing broadest at tip..4

3* lip 8-16mm long, appearing broadest in centre or at base 6

4 speculum placed towards tip of lip, rather simple 5

4* speculum central, with ocelli, indentations or branches ....*O. benacensis*

5 large lip, often entire, basal field elongated ... .*O. aurelia*

5* lip often 3-lobed (80%), basal field rather short..*O. balearica*

6 few-flowered, averaging 3-4 blooms but may be up to 7 (-9); lip as long as dorsal sepal or longer..7

6* flowers more numerous, averaging 6 but may be up to 10 (-13); lip shorter than dorsal sepal..*O. drumana*

7 lip 8.7-11.5mm long, with yellow hairs ....*O. flavicans*

7* lip (10-) 11-16mm long, with reddish to blackish hairs..8

8 early flowering, mainly end III-early IV ....*O. explanata*

8* later flowering, mainly end IV-V 9

9 petals sometimes broad, centre often pale, margins differently and brightly coloured; appendage very small to absent, inserted into a weak notch; stigmatic cavity rounded when viewed from the front ....*O. catalaunica*

9* petals often narrow, rarely arachnitiform; appendage rather prominent, inserted into a distinct notch; stigmatic cavity (near) quadrangular when viewed from the front .... *O. saratoi*

Ophrys bertolonii
MORETTI

Etymology Named after A. Bertoloni, Italian botanist (1775-1869). **Type*** It, Genoa; Si, Palermo (1823). **Synonym** *O. romolinii* SOCA

Description Slightly less robust than *O. aurelia*, 10-30 (-35)cm tall; inflorescence lax; 2-7 (-8) flowers; sepals slightly concave, 13-18mm x 5-8mm, oval-lanceolate to elliptical-obtuse, pink, white, rarely greenish, with a well-marked green central vein, dorsal sepal elongated, erect, lateral sepals spreading; petals linear to oblong, acuminate, frequently slightly curved forwards, 8-12mm x 2-4.5mm, often intensely coloured, violet or |purplish-pink, darker than sepals, margins flat and finely ciliate; lip 13-19mm long (on average 2.5mm shorter than *O. aurelia*), entire or rarely slightly 3-lobed, without basal swellings, very convex transversally, regularly and clearly curved into a saddle-shape, densely covered with blackish-brown hairs, slightly redder and longer on margins; speculum near tip, shield-shaped, rather large, usually simple, sometimes ocellated; appendage rather voluminous, often rounded, inserted into a prominent notch; stigmatic cavity taller than broad, strongly constricted above pseudo-eyes, at the insertion of the column, without lateral walls, thus on a side view showing as a deep, acutely-angled notch; pseudo-eyes protruding at the extremities of a horizontal projection; specular stage white to pale blue; basal field descendent, thickening under pseudo-eyes; column elongated, acuminate. **Variation** Slight. Distinguished by the structure of the stigmatic cavity; populations from southern peninsular Italy often have whitish-green sepals (Photo B).

Flowering Season (III-) IV-VI.

Habitat Full sun on dry to moist, calcareous substrates. Garrigue, clearings, grassy places in the hills, up to 1450m asl.

Distribution Central Mediterranean. From the plain of the Pô to Sicily, from Istria to Montenegro, reaches Greece on Corfu. Rather widespread and rather common but usually scattered in its stations.

Countries Gr It Ju Si.

Photos Si, Palermo, 13.IV.1987; It, Lecce, 26.IV.1991. P. DELFORGE.

Pollinators The curvature of the lip and the stigmatic cavity, unique within the genus, result from an adaptation to 2 bees, *Chalicodoma parietina* and *C. pyrenaica*, which have the characteristic of arching the abdomen to copulate. The former emerges rather early and is widely distributed in the Mediterranean basin, the latter is more local and emerges later, at the end of May; this explains the long flowering season of *O. bertolonii*.

Ophrys aurelia
P. DELFORGE, J. DEVILLERS-TERSCHUREN & P. DEVILLERS

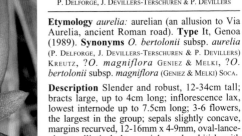

Etymology *aurelia:* aurelian (an allusion to Via Aurelia, ancient Roman road). **Type** It, Genoa (1989). **Synonyms** *O. bertolonii* subsp. *aurelia* (P. DELFORGE, J. DEVILLERS-TERSCHUREN & P. DEVILLERS) KREUTZ, ?*O. magniflora* GENIEZ & MELKI, ?*O. bertolonii* subsp. *magniflora* (GENIEZ & MELKI) SOCA.

Description Slender and robust, 12-34cm tall; bracts large, up to 4cm long; inflorescence lax, lowest internode up to 7.5cm long; 3-6 flowers, the largest in the group; sepals slightly concave, margins recurved, 12-16mm x 4-9mm, oval-lanceolate to elliptical-obtuse, pink, rarely whitish, with 3 longitudinal green veins, dorsal sepal elongated, erect, ± curved forwards, lateral sepals asymmetrical, spreading; petals 8-11mm x 2-4 (-5)mm, usually linear-lanceolate, less often a little triangular or auriculate at base, flat, purplish-pink, slightly darker than sepals, margins rarely weakly undulate or ciliate, finely tinted orange or garnet-red; lip 15-21mm long, entire or slightly 3-lobed, 1.2-1.5x length of dorsal sepal, entirely covered with blackish-brown hairs, short but dense, longer and more reddish on margins, slightly to strongly curved into a saddle-shape, slightly convex, appearing sturdy and broad, especially at tip, with marked shoulders; speculum rather large, distal, shield-shaped, sometimes ocellated, or forming a horseshoe or divided into 2 drop-shapes, glossy bluish-grey, sometimes edged white; appendage prominent, triangular, erect, inserted into a deep notch; stigmatic cavity broader than tall, not notched laterally, not pinched under pseudo-eyes; specular stage pale; basal field rectangular, elongated, overhanging lip.

Flowering Season III-IV (-V), slightly earlier than *O. bertolonii* and *O. saratoi.*

Habitat Full sun on dry, calcareous substrates, sometimes very basic (pH up to 9.5). Garrigue, old terraces, up to 700m asl.

Distribution Limits of range remain poorly known. Probably endemic to coastal massifs from the Golfe du Lion, Bouches-du-Rhône (Ga) to the Portofino peninsula (It); may reach Corbières (Ga, Aude) in the west (= ?'*magniflora*', see p. 617). In the east, the contact zone with *O. bertolonii* is poorly known; it is located within the quadrilateral made by Pisa, Florence, Parma and Genoa, where pure *O. bertolonii* seems to be extremely rare. Very rare and local.

Countries Ga It.

Photos It, Genoa (loc. typ.), 12.V.1988; Ga, Bouches-du-Rhône. 4.IV.1996. P. DELFORGE.

Pollinators *Chalicodoma parietina* and *C. pyrenaica* (Hymenoptera: Megachilidae).

Ophrys benacensis

(REISIGL) O. DANESCH, E. DANESCH & EHRENDORFER

Etymology *benacencis:* from Lake Garda (It). **Type** It, Trento (1972). **Synonyms** *O. bertoloniiformis* subsp. *benacensis* REISIGL, *O. bertolonii* subsp. *benacensis* (REISIGL) P. DELFORGE, *O. saratoi* subsp. *benacensis* (REISIGL) DEL PRETE, *O. pseudobertolonii* auct. non MURR.

Description Robust and rather slender, 10-30 (-45)cm tall; inflorescence near lax; 2-4 (-7) flowers; sepals 10.5-17mm x 4-7.5mm, oval-lanceolate, pink, lilac, white, rarely green; petals 7-12mm x 2.5-4 (-5.5)mm, shape varied, linear to lanceolate, sometimes slightly auriculate, margins hairless, flat to slightly undulate, pink to garnet-red, rarely brownish, darker than sepals; lip (13-) 15-20mm long, usually entire, rarely 3-lobed, appearing oval, sometimes with weak basal swellings, longitudinally flat, rather convex, often constricted in the centre and thus spreading in the distal half, densely covered with hairs, brownish-black in centre, longer and browner on margins; speculum greyish-blue or reddish-brown, glossy, large, central, diverse, sometimes simple, shield-shaped, often indented, fragmented, complicated by ocelli, rarely by branches extending to base of lip (1% plants); appendage rather reduced, directed forwards, inserted into a notch; stigmatic cavity broader than tall, rarely rounded, often rather quadrangular and not constricted under pseudo-eyes, rarely laterally incised; specular stage distinctly white to poorly marked.

Variation Distinct from *O. aurelia* notably in the shape of the petals (margins not as straight), with the lip broadest below the tip and longer relative to the dorsal sepal, the speculum more central and more complex, and the basal field not so elongated.

Flowering Season (III-) IV-V (-VI).

Habitat Full sun on dry to moist, calcareous substrates. Short grassland, old terraces, olive groves, from 200-850m asl.

Distribution Endemic to l'Insubrie, in the northern Pô valley between Côme and Belluno. Very local and rarely abundant; threatened by the development of tourism around the great Italian lakes.

Countries It.

Photos It, Verona, 11.V.1988. P. DELFORGE.

Discussion The flowers may be pollinated by *Chalicodoma parietina* (Hymenoptera: Megachilidae). Considered when first described to be a paleo-hybrid between *O. bertolonii* and *O. sphegodes* s.l., but more probably has *O. aurelia* as its parent. Odd plants with brownish sepals and brown petals are most probably often hybrids with *O. sphegodes* or *O. incubacea*.

615

Ophrys balearica
P. DELFORGE

Etymology *balearica:* from the Balearics. **Type** Bl, Mallorca (1990). **Synonyms** *O. bertolonii* subsp. *balearica* (P. DELFORGE) L SAEZ & ROSSELLO, *O. bertolonii* subsp. *balearica* (P. DELFORGE) SOCA isonym., *O. bertolonii* f. *triloba* RENZ nom. nudum.

Description Robust and slender, 10-35cm tall; inflorescence lax; 3-7 flowers, rather large for the group; sepals rather elongated, pink, rarely white, 11-16mm x 4-7mm, oval-lanceolate to elliptical-obtuse, dorsal sepal erect, lateral sepals rather frequently bicoloured, lower half often blotched violet, spreading broadly, at right angles to dorsal sepal; petals erect, 6-10mm x 2-4mm, narrowly oblong to triangular, sometimes slightly lanceolate, purplish-pink to red, usually darker than sepals, margins slightly undulate; lip 14-19mm long, very often 3-lobed (80% of plants), sometimes with slight basal swellings, flat, rarely slightly curved, often strongly convex transversally, mostly at level of median lobe, entirely and densely covered with short purplish-black hairs, longer and more reddish on margins; speculum most often placed towards tip, glossy grey, rarely edged whitish, rather small, simple, shield-shaped, sometimes divided into segments forming 2 drop-shapes or a horseshoe; appendage rather large, erect, triangular to globular, inserted into a prominent notch; stigmatic cavity not notched laterally, not deep, rarely constricted below pseudo-eyes, frequently extending basal field such that it appears far broader than tall; specular stage distinct, whitish; pseudo-eyes sometimes rather distinctly projecting forwards; column medium-sized, acuminate.

Variation Rather slight. Nevertheless, some extreme plants with an entire lip and pale petals may superficially resemble *O. catalaunica*; they are distinguished from it by their more elongated petals, larger (on average) and more elongated lip, and their speculum, which is smaller, simpler, placed more towards the tip of the lip and rarely edged white.

Flowering Season (III-) IV-VI.

Habitat Full sun on dry to moist, calcareous substrates. Garrigue, pinewoods, abandoned terraces, up to 450m asl.

Distribution Endemic to the Balearics; known from Mallorca, Minorca, Ibiza and Formentera. Local and rather rare.

Countries Bl.

Photos Bl, Mallorca, 4.IV.1985; 10.IV.1985 (loc. typ.). P. DELFORGE.

Pollinator *Chalicodoma sicula* (Hymenoptera: Megachilidae).

Ophrys catalaunica
O. DANESCH & E. DANESCH

Etymology *catalaunica:* from Catalonia. **Type** Hs, Gerona (1972). **Synonyms** *O. pseudobertolonii* subsp. *catalaunica* (O. DANESCH & E. DANESCH) H. BAUMANN & KÜNKELE, *O. bertolonii* subsp. *catalaunica* (O. DANESCH & E. DANESCH) SOCA, *O. benacensis* var. *catalaunica* (O. DANESCH & E. DANESCH) D. TYTECA & B. TYTECA, *?O. magniflora* GENIEZ & MELKI, *?O. bertolonii* subsp. *magniflora* (GENIEZ & MELKI) SOCA, *O. bertolonii* var. *ferrequinoides* BALAYER, *O. bertolonii* var. *bertoloniiformis* BALAYER.

Description Robust and often slender, 12-25 (-35)cm tall; inflorescence near lax; 3-7 (-9) flowers; sepals (9-) 10-14mm x 4-7mm, oval-elongate, white to pink, usually pale; petals 5.5-10mm x 2.5-5.5mm, shape varied, narrowly triangular to broadly lanceolate, centre pink, margins straight or ± undulate, often distinct from centre and darker, red, ochre, olive-green or a mixture of these; lip (9-) 10-16mm long, entire, rarely slightly 3-lobed or slightly bulging, rounded, longitudinally flat, rather convex, greatest apparent width in centre, covered with black hairs, uniformly distributed or sometimes low and black in centre, longer and dark red on margins; speculum greyish-blue, glossy, often edged pale grey, rarely reddish, varied, relatively rather large and often central, sometimes shield-shaped and rather simple, more rarely forming a horseshoe, rather frequently complex (especially in Spanish populations), with indentations, ocelli and branches sometimes forming a thickened H; stigmatic cavity usually strongly rounded and rather constricted at the level of the basal field, below the pseudo-eyes; specular stage poorly marked; appendage reduced and triangular, frequently absent, not inserted into a prominent notch.
Variation Very varied. More polymorphic and with bicoloured petals in the more peripheral Spanish populations. '*magniflora*': Large-flowered plants that appear sporadically in French populations; these probably represent the closest phenotype to the ancestral *O. (proto-)aurelia* in the hybridogenous species *O. catalaunica* or in *O. aurelia* itself.

Flowering Season IV-V (-VI), 2-4 weeks after *O. aurelia*.

Habitat Full sun on dry to moist, alkaline substrates. Short grassland, garrigue, woodland edges and pinewoods in supra-Mediterranean hills, often on calcareous sandstones, 200-1100m asl.

Distribution Catalan. Spanish Catalonia and in France from Aude to Hérault (Minervois). Local and not common.

Countries Ga Hs.

Photos Hs, Barcelona, 14.IV.1990. P. DELFORGE

Ophrys saratoi
E.G. Camus (pro hybr.)

Etymology Named after C. Sarato, a botanist from Nice (1830-1893). **Type** Ga, Alpes-Maritimes (1893). **Synonyms** *O. bertolonii* subsp. *saratoi* (E.G. Camus) Soca, *O. grassensis* Jauvy ex Steudel nom. nud., *O. bertolonii* var. *aranifero-Bertoloni* Barla & Sarato.

Description Thickset with a spindly stem, 9-24cm tall; inflorescence near lax; 2-5 (-6) flowers; sepals pale to rather dark, pink, lilac, rarely white, oval-elongate, 10-15mm x 4-7.5mm, appearing narrow; petals 7-10mm x 2.5-4mm, oblong to triangular-elongated, slightly darker than sepals, pink, sometimes red, margins often emphasised with ochre or dark red, rarely flat, frequently undulate-crisped, strongly so in 50% of plants; lip 13-16mm long, as long as, or slightly longer than, dorsal sepal, entire or slightly 3-lobed, rarely clearly 3-lobed, sometimes with rudimentary or weak basal swellings, longitudinally flat (30% of plants) or slightly curved, appearing broadest at base, covered rather uniformly with hair, giving a regular, velvety, brownish-black appearance; speculum shield-shaped and rather large, glossy, grey, rarely red, sometimes edged pale grey, usually rather central, simple, rarely with ocelli or branches; appendage green, rounded triangular, well visible, obliquely erect in a prominent notch; stigmatic cavity broader than tall, rather quadrangular when viewed from the front, almost always without a constriction below the pseudo-eyes, may show a very slight notch in the lateral walls when viewed in profile (40% of plants); specular stage distinct, whitish. **Variation** Distinguished from *O. aurelia* by its smaller floral parts and lip shape, from *O. drumana* by its thickset habit, fewer flowers and larger floral parts. Plants with brownish-green sepals and broad petals are probably hybrids with *O. incubacea* s.l.

Flowering Season (IV-) V (-VI), 2-5 weeks after *O. aurelia*.

Habitat Full sun on rather moist, calcareous substrates; often on seepages. Garrigue and old terraces in the supra-Mediterranean hills, 200-900m asl.

Distribution Endemic to the calcareous French Pre-Alps, close to the Mediterranean, from Bouches-du-Rhône to the Italian border; extends along the Rhône corridor to Ardèche and southern Drôme. Rare and local.

Countries Ga.

Photos Ga, Alpes-Maritimes, 14.V.1988. P. Delforge.

Pollinator *Chalicodoma albonotata* (Hymenoptera: Megachilidae).

Ophrys drumana

P. DELFORGE

Etymology *drumana:* from Drôme. **Type** Ga, Drôme (1988). **Synonym** *O. bertolonii* subsp. *drumana* (P. DELFORGE) KREUTZ.

Description Slender and rather spindly, 10-32 (-35)cm tall; inflorescence near lax; (2-) 4-10 (-13) flowers, smallest in group; sepals pink, pale lilac, rarely white, 10-14mm x 3.5-6mm, margins recurved, appearing oblong-obtuse; petals erect, 6-9mm x 2-3.5mm, shape varied, oblong-acuminate to near oval, pink or purplish, usually darker than sepals, margins often undulate-crisped, frequently tinted greenish-yellow, orange or dark red; lip 8-13mm long, shorter than dorsal sepal, entire (75% of plants) or ± clearly 3-lobed, very convex transversally, optical appearance oblong and narrow, with greatest apparent width over entire central portion, longitudinally flat to very slightly convex, even at end of flowering, covered with low hairs that give a velvety red-brown appearance, hairs longer and lighter on margins, sometimes with weak to accentuated basal swellings (independent of presence of lateral lobes); speculum proportionally large, central, shield-shaped, complicated by ocelli and indentations, with branches extending to stigmatic cavity (60% of plants), bluish-grey, glossy, rarely reddish, edged with a grey line; appendage small, triangular, sometimes imperceptible, inserted into a weak notch; stigmatic cavity rounded, broader than tall, not laterally notched, pinched below pseudo-eyes; specular stage present but poorly marked; column very short but acuminate.

Variation Distinct in its small, often numerous, flowers and small, unbent lip with a complex speculum.

Flowering Season V-VI.

Habitat Full sun to mid-shade on dry to moist, calcareous substrates. Short grassland, banks, clearings in thermophilous oakwoods, in the hills and mountains of the sub-Mediterranean zone, 250-1100m asl.

Distribution The calcareous Pre-Alps of Drôme (southern foothills of Vercors), with a few stations in central Côtes du Rhône (Ardèche), the Pre-Alps of Digne (Alpes-de-Haute-Provence) and perhaps also the northern slopes of Sainte-Victoire and Val de Durance (Bouches-du-Rhône). The potential contact zone with *Ophrys saratoi* is poorly known. Local but sometimes abundant in its stations.

Countries Ga.

Photos Ga, Drôme (loc. typ.), 5.V.1988; 9.VI.1984. P. DELFORGE.

Pollinator Probably *Chalicodoma albonotata* (Hymenoptera: Megachilidae).

Ophrys bertoloniiformis
O. DANESCH & E. DANESCH

Etymology *-formis:* with the shape of [*Ophrys*] *bertolonii.* **Type** It, Foggia (1971). **Synonyms** *O. bertolonii* subsp. *bertoloniiformis* (O. DANESCH & E. DANESCH) SUNDERMANN, *O. pseudobertolonii* subsp. *bertoloniiformis* (O. DANESCH & E. DANESCH) H. BAUMANN & KÜNKELE, *O. saratoi* auct. non E.G. CAMUS.

Description Thickset and robust, 10-21cm tall; inflorescence near lax; 2-4 (-5) flowers; sepals usually green or greenish, rarely pink or white (10% of plants), 9-14mm x 4-7mm, oval-lanceolate, margins recurved; petals 6-11mm x 2-5mm, shape varied, oblong to, more often, triangular-obtuse, relatively short, darker than sepals, green, olive-green, brownish-pink, rarely reddish-pink, margins sometimes slightly undulate; lip 12-14.5mm long, entire, short, rather slightly convex, appearing oval, broadest at base or centre, flat to slightly curved, rarely with weak rounded basal swellings, densely covered with blackish hairs, only just longer and browner on margins; speculum glossy greyish-blue, rather large, central or placed a little towards the tip, usually simple, shield-shaped, rarely with an ocellus, indentations or branches; appendage green, triangular, well visible, inserted into a rather weak notch; stigmatic cavity rather varied, broader than tall, rounded, sometimes pinched below pseudo-eyes, sometimes with a rudimentary lateral notch; specular stage distinct, whitish.

Variation Rather varied, mostly in its stigmatic cavity and speculum. Clearly distinct from *O. bertolonii* as its stigmatic cavity lacks hollow walls. Odd plants with slightly brownish sepals and a rather notched stigmatic cavity are probably hybrids with *O. bertolonii.*

Flowering Season (III-) IV (-V), 2-3 weeks before *O. bertolonii.*

Habitat Full sun on dry to moist, calcareous substrates. Short grassland, garrigue, olive groves, banks, up to 850m asl.

Distribution Endemic to Mount Gargano (Foggia), where it is more frequent than *O. bertolonii.* Very local and often not common, with *c.* 120 known stations.

Countries It.

Photos It, Foggia, 6.IV.1986. P. DELFORGE.

Pollinator *Chalicodoma benoisti* (Hymenoptera: Megachilidae).

Ophrys explanata
(Lojacono) P. Delforge

Etymology *explanata:* distinct. **Type** Si, Palermo (1909). **Synonyms** *O. bertolonii* var. *explanata* Lojacono, *O. bertolonii* subsp. *explanata* (Lojacono) Soca.

Description Thickset, 10-19 (-22)cm tall; inflorescence near lax to rather dense; 2-5 (-7) flowers; sepals 11-15mm x 5-9mm, pink, lilac (sometimes rather dark), rarely white, oval-lanceolate, margins slightly recurved; petals 6-10mm x 3-5.5mm, shape varied, oblong to triangular-obtuse, pink to reddish or lilac, as dark as or darker than sepals, margins hairless or clearly ciliate, flat to slightly undulate; lip 11-15mm long, entire, rather convex, thus appearing rather elongated and narrow, looks broadest towards base, very slightly and evenly curved, densely covered with blackish hairs, slightly longer and browner on margins; speculum glossy greyish-blue, often edged whitish, sometimes reddish-brown, large, placed at the tip or a little more central, varied, usually simply shield-shaped, rarely indented or slightly branched towards basal field; appendage green, rounded triangular, erect, well visible, inserted into a rather prominent notch; stigmatic cavity always broader than tall but frequently slightly notched laterally, thus projecting the pseudo-eyes on a small protuberance; specular stage distinct, whitish.

Variation Rather varied, especially in the shape of the petals and stigmatic cavity, which show a strong influence from *O. bertolonii*. The latter has larger flowers, a stigmatic cavity that is taller than broad and clearly notched and a more markedly curved lip.

Flowering Season III-IV, 2-3 weeks before *O. bertolonii.*

Habitat Full sun on dry to moist, calcareous substrates. Short grassland and garrigue, up to 800m asl.

Distribution Endemic to Sicily, in the Palermo region and the southern calcareous massifs. Very rare and local. Populations of *O. explanata* are probably underestimated due to confusion with *O. bertolonii.*

Countries Si.

Photos Si, Palermo, 10.IV.1987; Caltanissetta, 17.III.2000. P. Delforge.

Discussion Pollinated by *Chalicodoma sicula* (Hymenoptera: Megachilidae). A species with a hybridogenous origin between *O. ?panormitana* (earlier flowering) and *O. bertolonii. O. explanata* sometimes grows in sites where its presumed parents are absent and forms few intermediates with *O. bertolonii.*

621

Ophrys flavicans
VISIANI

Etymology *flavicans:* turning yellow. **Type** Ju, Dalmatia (1842). **Synonyms** *O. bertolonii* subsp. *flavicans* (VISIANI) K. RICHTER, *O. bertolonii* var. *dalmatica* MURR, *O. dalmatica* (MURR) Soó (pro hybr.).

Description Spindly, (10-) 15-29cm tall; inflorescence lax; 3-5 flowers; sepals 8-11.5mm x 1.9-4mm, oval-elongate, pale to dark, pink to lilac, rarely washed green; petals 6-8mm x 2.2-3.5mm, oblong, tip attenuated or triangular, pink to dark reddish-brown, margins straight to slightly undulate, usually darker than, and distinct from centre, red, olive-green or brownish; lip 8.7-11.5mm long, usually entire, rounded, longitudinally flat or with a slight, saddle-like curve at tip, transversally rather convex, appearing broadest in centre, densely hairy, initially pale to dark reddish-brown, then strongly yellowish and becoming pale reddish-brown in centre, yellowish on margins; speculum greyish-blue, glossy, sometimes purplish, edged pale grey, relatively small, often central, sometimes apical, rather simple, shield-shaped or, more rarely, forming a horseshoe; appendage reduced, triangular, inserted into a prominent notch; stigmatic cavity broader than tall, rather flat, sometimes rounded and slightly notched, slightly pinched below pseudo-eyes; specular stage distinct, whitish.

Variation Slight. Distinctive in its small flowers and the hairs on the lip fading to yellowish as soon as the flower is pollinated or withers (Photo A).

Flowering Season III-mid IV, early, before *O. bertolonii*.

Habitat Full sun on dry to moist, alkaline substrates. Short grassland and garrigue, up to 200m asl.

Distribution Endemic to Dalmatia. Very local and very rare.

Countries Ju.

Photos Ju, Hrvatska, Dalmatinska Zagora, Primosten, 26 & 21.III.2004. P. DELFORGE.

Discussion Often considered to be the occasional hybrid between *O. bertolonii* and *O. sphegodes* s.l. or *O. tenthredinifera* s.l. *O. flavicans* does indeed appear to have a hybrid origin involving the first two species, but has succeeded in establishing sympatry with them and in occupying habitats where they are absent. The isolating mechanisms permitting this independence are its early-flowering and its adaptation to a specific pollinator, probably as well as slightly different ecological requirements.

Pollinator *Chalicodoma manicata* (Hymenoptera: Megachilidae).

Appendices
Further reading

Numerous publications have been produced on European orchids. It is, therefore, not possible to give an exhaustive bibliography here and it is preferable to cite a few classic studies. A bibliography of publications mentioning European orchids in their title, although incomplete, has been compiled, and lists more than 11, 000 references:

WILLING, B. & WILLING, E. 1977 Bibliographie über die Orchideen Europas und der Mittelmeerländer 1744-1976. 325pp, *Willdenovia* Beiheft **11**, Berlin.

WILLING, B. & WILLING, E. 1985 Bibliographie über die Orchideen Europas und der Mittelmeerländer - 1. Supplement 280pp, *Englera* **5**, Berlin.

WILLING, E. 2004 Bibliographie über die Orchideen Europas und der Mittelmeerländer - 2. Supplement. *J. Eur. Orch.* **36**: 3-400.

General systematics

BATEMAN, R.M., HOLLINGSWORTH, P.M., PRESTON, J., YI-BO, L., PRIDGEON, A.L., & CHASE, M.W. 2003 Molecular philogenetics and evolution of Orchidinae and selected Habenariinae (Orchidaceae). *Biol. J. Linn. Soc.* **142**: 1-40.

DRESSLER, R.L. 1993 *Phylogeny and Classification of the Orchid Family.* 314pp, Dioscorides Press, Portland, Oregon.

FREUDENSTEIN, J.V. & RASMUSSEN, F.N. 1999 What does morphology tell us about Orchid relationships? - A cladistic analysis. *Amer. J. Bot.* **86**: 225-248.

GRANT, V. 1981 *Speciation.* 2nd ed. Columbia University Press, New York.

JUDD, W.S., Campbell, C.S., Kellogg, E.A. & Stevens, P. 2002 *Botanique systématique - Une perspective phylogenetic.* 467pp, De Boeck Université, Paris & Bruxelles.

MAYR, E. 1981 *La biologie de l'évolution.* 175pp, Hermann, Paris.

SOLTIS, D.E., SOLTIS, S.P. & DOYLE, J.J. [eds] 1998 *Molecular Systematics of Plants.* 2nd ed. Kluwer, Amsterdam.

VERMEULEN, P. 1966 The system of the Orchidales. *Acta Bot. Neerl.* **14**: 224-253.

WILEY, E.O. 1981 *Phylogenetics: The Theory and Practice of Phylogenetic Systematics.* 439pp, John Wiley & Sons, New York.

Orchids of Europe: Some classics

BAUMANN, H. & KÜNKELE, S. 1989 Die Gattung *Serapias* L. – eine taxonomische Übersicht. *Mitt. Bl. Arbeitskr. Heim. Orch. Baden-Württ.* **21**: 701-946.

BOURNÉRIAS, M. [ed.] 1998 *Les Orchidées de France, Belgique and Luxembourg.* 416pp, Biotope, coll. Parthénope, Paris.

BUTTLER, K.P. 1991 *Field Guide to Orchids of Britain and Europe.* 288pp, The Crowood Press, Swindon.

CAMUS, E.G. & CAMUS, A. 1921-1929 *Iconographie des Orchidées d'Europe and du basin Mediterranean.* 133 pl., 559+72pp. Lechevalier, Paris.

DANESCH, O. & DANESCH, E. 1969 *Orchideen Europas. Südeuropa.* 256pp, Hallwag, Bern und Stuttgart.

DAVIES, P., DAVIES, J. & HUXLEY, A. 1988 *Wild Orchids of Britain and Europe.* 256pp, The Hogarth Press, London.

DEVILLERS, P. & DEVILLERS-TERSCHUREN, J. 1994 Essai d'analyse systématique du genus *Ophrys*. *Natural belges* **75** (Orchid. 7 suppl.): 273-400.

GODFERY, M.J. 1933 *Monograph and Iconograph of Native British Orchidaceae.* 259pp, Cambridge University Press, Cambridge.

KELLER, G., SCHLECHTER, R. & VON SOÓ, R. 1930-1940 *Monographie und Iconographie der Orchideen Europas und des Mittelmeergebietes.* Bd. **2-5** 472pp + 640 pl. *Fedde Repert.*, Sonderbeih. Nachdruk 1972, Königstein.

KLOPFENSTEIN, E. 1994 *West European Orchids.* 5x12pl. National Botanic Garden of Belgium, Meise.

KULLENBERG, B. 1961 Studies in *Ophrys* pollination. *Zool. Bidr. Uppsala* **34**: 1-340.

LANDWEHR, J. 1982 *Les orchidées sauvages de France et d'Europe.* (2 vol.) 587pp, Piantanida, Lausanne.

MOSSBERG, B. & NILSSON, S. 1987 *Orkidéer: Europas vildväxande arter.* 253pp, Walhström & Widstrand, Stockholm.

NELSON, E. 1962 *Gestaltwandel und Artbildung erörtert am Beispiel der Orchidaceen Europas und der Mittelmeerländer, insbesondere der Gattung* Ophrys *mit einer Monographie und Ikonographie der Gattung* Ophrys. 250pp + 58 pl. + 8 maps. E. Nelson, Chernex, Montreux.

PAULUS, H.F. & GACK, C. 1990 Pollinators as prepollinating isolation factors: evolution and speciation in *Ophrys* (Orchidaceae). *Israel J. Bot.* **39**: 43-79.

PEREZ CHISCANO, J.L., GIL LLANO, J.R. & DURAN OLIVA, F. 1991 *Orquideas de Extremadura.* 223pp, Fondo Natural, s.l., Avila.

PROCHAZKA, F. & VELISEK, V. 1984 *Orchideje nasi prirody.* 281pp, Cesk. Ak. Ved, Praha.

REICHENBACH, H.G. fil. 1851 *Icones Floræ Germanicæ and Helveticæ simul Pedemontanæ, Lombardoveneticæ, Istriacæ, Dalmaticæ, Hungaricæ, Transsylvanicæ, Borussicæ, Danicæ, Belgicæ, Hollandicæ, Alsaticæ ergo Mediæ Europæ.* Vol. xiii-xiv 194pp. + 170pl. F. Hofmeister, Lipsiæ.

RENZ, J. 1943 *Orchidaceae.* Pp. 809-845 in Rechinger, K.H. *Flora Aegaea. Denkschr. Akad. Wiss. Wien* **105**.

ROBATSCH, K. 1998 Die Gattung *Epipactis* und ihre systematische Stellung innerhalb der Unterfamilie Neottioidae, im Lichte entwicklungsgeschichtlicher Untersuchungen. *Jahresber. Naturwiss. Ver. Wuppertal* **51**: 43-100.

SUMMERHAYES, V.S. 1968 *Wild Orchids of Britain.* 2nd ed. 366p. + 48p + xxii pl. Collins, London.

SUNDERMANN, H. 1980 *Europäische und mediterrane Orchideen - Eine Bestimmungsflora* 3. Aufl., 279pp. Brücke-Verlag Kurt Schmersow, Hildesheim.

Glossary

Editor's note. The glossary has been updated to include as many unfamiliar words as possible whilst removing some that seem to require no explanation in an English-language context. As a literal translation of some of the author's definitions would be unhelpful, the glossaries of standard British Floras have been consulted to provide suitable alternatives.

Note. 'Ant.' = antonym, the term in the glossary with the opposite meaning. Many technical terms are illustrated in the introduction to the genera *Epipactis, Dactylorhiza, Serapias, Orchis* and *Ophrys*.

Acidic: a substrate with a higher hydrogen ion concentration than pure water (pH<7). Ant.: alkaline.

Acidophile: a plant growing preferentially on acidic substrates. Ant.: calcicole.

Actinomorphic: having radial symmetry; can be cut vertically through the axis in any of 2 or more planes so that the two halves are mirror images.

Acuminate: tapering to a slender point.

Albinism: a complete lack of pigmentation, including the leaves. See also: hypochromy.

Albino: a plant which completely lacks pigment.

Alkaline: a substrate with a lower hydrogen ion concentration than pure water (pH>7); usually due to the presence of calcium ions. Ant: acidic.

Allele: one of the possible forms of a gene.

Allogamy: fertilisation of a flower by pollen from another plant of the same species (ie cross-fertilisation). Ant.: autogamy. When the pollen comes from a flower from the same inflorescence, it is termed geitonogamy (which is equivalent to autogamy); if it comes from the flower of another individual, it is termed xenogamy; whenever the pollen is brought by an insect, it is termed entomogamy.

Allopatric: species occupying geographic ranges that do not overlap. Ant.: sympatric.

Allopolyploidy: polyploidy (qv) resulting from fertilisation between parents of two different species (to produce a diploid chromosome set) being followed by a doubling of chromosome number. The parental chromosome numbers do not have to be identical and this can result in a new species being formed. Cf. autopolyploidy.

Alternate: leaves inserted singly at different levels on the stem, usually on ± opposite sides.

Amphoroid: shaped like an amphora (an ancient, narrow-necked, two-handled jar).

Anemophilous: : wind-pollinated.

Aneuploidy: lacking or having an additional chromosome or chromosomes (but not a complete set) or having one or more visibly altered chromosomes.

Anther: the pollen-bearing part of a stamen, usu-

ally terminal on a filament; in *Epipactis*, refers to the terminal part of the column.

Anthesis: the period from flower opening to fruit set; in this guide refers specifically to the moment that pollen arrives on the stigmatic surface.

Anthocyanins: blue or red pigments in plants.

Anthoxanthins: yellow pigments in plants.

Aphyllous: without leaves.

Apical: at the tip. Ant.: basal.

Apochromy: colour abnormality. See also albinism, hyperchromy and hypochromy.

Apomixis: a method of asexual reproduction in some vascular plants.

Appendage: a small structure joined to another organ.

Appressed: lying flat against another organ.

Arachnitiform: covered with soft, fine hairs.

Articulate: a lip with 2 sections (the hypochile and epichile), connected by an articulation or constriction.

Ascendant: horizontal and then directed upwards. Ant.: descendant

Association: a collection of plant species in a natural environment.

Asymmetric: lacking symmetry.

Attenuated: progressively decreasing in size.

Auriculate: with 2 projections shaped like ear-lobes.

Autogamy: fertilisation by pollen from the same plant, either from the same flower or from a different flower on the same plant (geitonogamy) (ie. self- fertilisation) Ant.: allogamy, xenogamy.

Autopolyploidy: polyploidy (qv) resulting from an inherited doubling of chromosome number arising in an individual plant; can result in a new species being formed. Cf. allopolyploidy.

Autotrophic: an organism that is able to manufacture complex compounds from simple inorganic substances; plants achieve this through photosynthesis. Ant.: heterotrophic.

Basal: located at the base of an organ. Ant.: apical. Of a leaf, placed at the base of a stem. Ant.: cauline.

Basal field: in *Ophrys*, the basal part of the lip, sometimes distinctively coloured or surrounded by a pale line.

Basionym: the first name published in association with a type, forming the foundation of a new nomenclatural combination.

Bi–: prefix meaning 2.

Bifid: divided into 2 parts, usually deeply so, to the centre.

Bilateral symmetry: can be cut in only one plane to produce halves which are mirror images of each other.

Biotope: physicochemical characteristics of an environment in which a species or a plant association grows; a habitat.

Bract: a small leaf or scale located at the base of a flower stalk.

Bulbil: propagule arising on the margins of the leaves or rhizome of some plants which can produce a new plant once it is detached.

Bursicle: the pouch-like membranous envelopes surrounding the viscidia of the pollinia that prevents them from drying out.

Calcareous: a substrate rich in calcium ions and therefore alkaline.

Calcicole: a plant or group of plants growing preferentially on alkaline substrates.

Campanulate: bell-shaped.

Candicoid: with a speculum resembling that of *Ophrys candica*.

Capsule: dry, many-seeded dehiscent fruit formed by an ovary with several sealed carpels and opening via longitudinal slits to disperse the seeds.

Carpel: in angiosperms, a unit of the female part of the flower consisting of ovary, style and stigma; the carpels of a flower collectively form the gynoecium or pistil.

Caryological: relating to the number of chromosomes.

Caryotype: images of a set of chromosomes arranged into homologous pairs.

Caudicle: stalk of the pollinium.

Cauline: a leaf inserted on the stem. Ant.: basal.

Ciliate: edged with small erect hairs, arranged in rows.

Cleistogamy: self-pollination in the bud, the flower remaining closed.

Clinandrium: the small cavity located on top of the column in some orchids, holding the pollinia. See also *Epipactis*, p. 47.

Cline: the gradual change in frequency of variants of a species over geographical distance.

Clone: group of individuals that are genetically identical, produced from a single individual by vegetative reproduction.

Column (technically **gynostegium**): in orchids, the organ originating from the fusion of the male floral parts and the style.

Complex: a collection of closely related species which can be distinguished only with difficulty.

Concolorous: with the same colour.

Connivent: two or more structures separated at the base but with their tips close or overlapping, without being joined.

Convenience: in taxonomy, species placed together but which probably have different evolutionary origins, that is, a polyphyletic group (qv).

Convergence: similarity between 2 species belonging to unrelated groups but subject to similar selective processes, for example the adaptation of several species of *Ophrys* to the same pollinator despite having evolved separately.

Cordate: heart-shaped.

Cotyledon: an organ within a seed which may emerge to form the first leaf of the seedling.

Crenate: edged with obtuse or rounded teeth.

Cross-pollination: transfer of pollen from one plant to another of the same species.

Cryptic: a species that cannot be distinguished from another morphologically.

Cultivar: a man-made taxon unknown in the wild.

Cuneiform: wedge-shaped, with the thin end at the base.

Decalcified: with calcium compounds (usually calcium carbonate) removed.

Dehiscent: opening naturally at maturity to shed seeds; of an anther, the release of pollen.

Dentate: edged with teeth (small triangular pointed projections).

Denticle: A small, isolated tooth.

Denticulate: edged with (very) small teeth or denticles.

Derived: referring to any state or feature that has evolved from another; a relative term, like primitive.

Descendant: initially horizontal, then pointing downwards. See also: ascendant.

Dicotyledons: a member of the class Dicotyledonae, with 2 embryonic seed leaves. See also monocoyledons.

Digitate: divided like the fingers on a hand.

Diploid: of a nucleus, having two complete sets of chromosomes (2n); the normal state for vegetative cells in plants.

Distal: distant from the base or point of insertion of an organ. Ant.: basal.

Dorsal: relating to the side of an organ that is directed away from the axis (i.e. the back); in this guide used especially for the median sepal to distinguish it from the lateral sepals.

Draw-down zone: area of ground covered at high water levels (usually in the winter) and exposed on drying.

Ecology: the relationship between a plant and its environment, both physical and biological.

Ecotone: the transition zone between 2 different habitats.

Ecotype: a subdivision of a species, usually a simple variant, based on morphological differences shown in a specific habitat.

Edaphic: the relationships between plants and the physical and chemical properties of the substrate.

Elliptic: elongated and similarly rounded at both ends.

Emarginate: with a notched tip or edge. See: Incised.

Endemic: limited to a certain region.

Endophyte: any living organism developing inside a plant.

Enrichment: long-term modification of a substrate by the addition of mineral or organic substances.

Entire: with a regular shape, neither divided nor incised or with teeth.

Entomogamy: the transfer of pollen by an insect.

Epichile: distal part of the lip in some orchid species, separated from the basal part (hypochile) by a rigid or articulated joint.

Epiphytic: a plant growing on another plant without contact with the soil, the host plant being used only as a support.

Eutrophic: rich in plant nutrients. Ant.: oligotrophic.

Eutrophication: excessive enrichment of a habitat with plant nutrients.

Ex: follows an author's name when a second author formally describes a taxon but credits the identification to the first.

Facultative: able to exist under more than one set of environmental conditions.

Falcate: sickle-shaped.

Filiform: thread-like.

Flexuous: wavy.

Free: not joined to another organ.

Garrigue: in this guide, an open plant community, characteristic of the Mediterranean region, formed by low shrubs (<1 m), growing on acid or alkaline substrates.

Geitonogamy: fertilisation by pollen from a different flower on the same plant; genetically equivalent to self-fertilisation (autogamy).

Geophyte: a plant with its perennating buds placed underground.

Genotype: set of potentialities of an individual, determined by its genes. The expression of these genes, modified by the organism's environment, results in its phenotype (qv).

Glabrous: hairless.

Glabrescent: becoming hairless with age.

Glands: tiny globular bodies containing oil or other liquids.

Glandular: furnished with glands.

Globular: almost spherical.

Gynostegium: technical term fo column (qv).

Hood: in some orchids, the part of the flower made up from the 3 sepals and 2 petals when they all curve forwards over the column.

Herbaceous: not woody, dying down each year. Ant.: ligneous.

Heterosis: superiority of individuals with heterozygous genes compared with those with homozygous genes for one or more characters; responsible for hybrid vigour.

Heterotrophic: a plant that uses complex organic compounds to manufacture its own organic constituents rather than rely on photosynthesis. Ant.: autotrophic. See also myco-heterotrophic.

Heterozygote: with reference to specific genes, having two different alleles in the genotype. Ant.: homozygote.

Heterozygous: describing a heterozygote.

Holotype: the unique specimen or drawing named in the formal scientific description of a taxon. See also lectotype.

Homozygote: with reference to specific genes, having two identical alleles in the genotype Ant.: heterozygote.

Homozygous: describing a homozygote.

Hyaline: thin and translucent.

Hybrid: a plant produced by the crossing of 2 individuals belonging to different taxa.

Hybridogenous: a fertile taxon originating from a hybridisation event, usually ancient.

Hygrophilous: growing in damp to wet habitats.

Hyperchromy: a colour anomaly characterised by the very strong expression of blue and red pigments in the flowers and sometimes also the leaves. Ant.: hypochromy, albinism.

Hypochile: the basal part of the lip in some orchids. See also: epichile.

Hypochromy: colour anomaly originating from a ± strong reduction of blue and red pigments in the flowers and sometimes also the leaves, giving the flowers or the whole plant an unusually pale tint. Ant.: hyperchromy.

Incised: cut, the incisions deeper than broad.

Incurved: curved inwards.

Inferior: when the ovary is placed entirely below the perianth. Ant.: superior.

Internode: a section of the stem between the insertion point of 2 adjacent leaves.

Introgression: progressive acquisition, by a population or a taxon, of genetic characters from another taxon, by natural recurrent crosses.

Labellum: see lip.

Lip (technically **Labellum**): in Orchidaceae, the specialised central petal, differing from the 2 other petals.

Lamella: thin plate or scale.

Lanceolate: narrowly spear-shaped, 3-4x as long as broad and attenuating into a point.

Lax: loose.

Lectotype: the specimen or drawing selected to be the nomenclatural type of a taxon when a unique type was not specified in the original scientific description or the holotype has been lost. See also: holotype.

Lamina: the flat portion of a leaf (leaf blade).

Linear: narrow, with near-parallel borders.

Lingulate: tongue-shaped.

Lobe: broad, ± rounded division, not cut beyond the centre of an organ.

Lobulus: secondary lobe on a main lobe.

Loculus: housing of the pollinia (also called theca).

Median: central or dorsal.

Membranous: thin and translucent.

Meristem: plant tissue with actively dividing or potentially actively dividing, undifferentiated cells, found in the tips of roots and shoots and at some other locations.

Mesotrophic: a habitat that is moderately rich in plant nutrients. Ant.: eutrophic, oligotrophic.

Mesophytic: growing in an area that receives an average supply of water.

Monocarpic: a plant that flowers only once and then dies after producing seeds.

Monocotyledons: members of the class Monocotyledonae, with a single embryonic seed leaf; includes grasses, lilies, palms and orchids. See also: dicotyledons.

Monophyletic: a natural taxonomic group, with all the descendants from a common ancestor, to the exclusion of any other taxon. Ant.: polyphyletic, paraphyletic, group of convenience.

Monopodial: a stem in which growth is continued from year to year by the same terminal growing point.

Monotypic: a taxonomic group with only one representative.

Morph: an informal category grouping together individuals distinguished by morphological characters.

Mucro: a short, bristle-like point.

Mucronate: terminating in a short, bristle-like straight point (a mucro).

Mycorrhiza: a symbiotic association between the mycelium of a fungus and the roots of a plant.

Myco-heterotrophic: receiving some or all of its nutrition through association with a fungus.

Mycotrophic: synonym for myco-heterotrophic (see above).

Nectar: a sweet liquid.

Nectariferous: nectar-bearing.

Neotype: a new type specimen designated for a taxon the type specimen of which has been lost or destroyed.

Neutral: a substrate which is neither acidic nor alkaline so has a pH close to 7.

Node: the point on a stem where a leaf arises.

Ob–: prefix, used to reverse the meaning of a term (e.g. oboval = an oval that is broadest at the top).

Oblong: clearly longer than broad, with ± parallel sides.

Obtuse: ± rounded at the tip.

Ocellus (plural **ocelli**): an eye-like marking.

Oligotrophic: an habitat that is poor in plant nutrients. Ant.: eutrophic.

Optical width: The *apparent* width of a three-dimensional object (usually used for objects as seen through a lens of microscope).

Opposite: 2 organs arising laterally at one node on opposite sides of the the stem.

Orbicular: circular.

Ovary: thick basal part of the female reproductive organ containing the ovules; in Orchidaceae it becomes the capsule at maturity.

Oval: used for a ± flat object that is egg-shaped, with the broad end towards the base.

Ovoid: used for a 3-dimensional object that is egg-shaped.

Palmate: arranged like a spread hand, the fingers representing the divisions.

Palynology: the study of pollen, especially fossil pollen.

Papilla: a tiny, cylindrical or conical, nipple-like projection; papillae are grouped into small tufts on the lip of some orchids.

Papillose: with papillae.

Paraphyletic: a taxonomic group that does not contain *all* the descendants of a common ancestor. For example, the genus *Orchis* is paraphyletic because it does not include the genus *Ophrys*, which has very probably evolved from this latter.

Parasite: an organism that lives in or on a host organism of a different species and is nutritionally dependent on its host.

Pendant: hanging, directed downwards from the point of attachment.

Pedicel: flower stalk.

Perianth: the floral leaves, including the calyx (sepals) and the corolla (petals); in orchids, the lip, which is a specialised petal, is part of the perianth.

Peri-specular zone: See fig. 10, p. 358.

Petal: one of the segments of the inner whorl of the perianth; there are 3 petals in the Orchidaceae, 2 lateral petals and 1 differentiated petal, (the lip).

Petaloid: petal-like.

Petiole: the stalk of a leaf.

Petiolate: with a petiole. Ant.: sessile.

Phenology: the study of the growth period, flowering time and fructification of a species.

Phenotype: the characters observable in an organism.

Pheromone: a chemical substance secreted by an animal that influences the behaviour of other individuals of the same species.

Phrygana: shrubby vegetation, found primarily in

the Aegean, characterised by low, rounded, ball-shaped bushes.

Phylogeny: the evolutionary history of an organism or group of organisms.

Phytophagous: of insects, feeding on plants.

Pioneer: a species or a group of plants that is able to colonise a virgin habitat, devoid of plants.

Pollinium (plural **Pollinia**): regularly shaped mass of pollen formed by a large number of grains adhering; the pollinia can be transported in one piece by insects.

Pollination: transfer of pollen on to the stigma of a flower.

Polymorphic: with two or more genetically determined variations.

Polyphyletic: placing together taxa that do not all share the same common ancestor. Ant.: monophyletic.

Polyploid: cells with more than two complete sets of chromosomes; organisms with polyploid cells.

Polytypic: a taxon containing several distinct types (several species for a genus, several varieties or variants for a species). Ant.: monotypic.

Postzygotic: events occurring after fertilisation of the female sex cell.

Prezygotic: events occurring before fertilisation of the female sex cell.

Primitive: a relative term used in the sense of ancestral. A feature that is primitive for one group may be an advanced, or derived, feature in another group. A primitive feature is not necessarily a simple one.

Proeminent: overgrowing neighbouring structures.

Protocorm: first stage in orchid growth after germination, before its differentiation into a foliar bud and a radicle.

Proximal: adjacent to the base or point of insertion of an organ. Ant.: distal.

Pruinose: coated with a powdery or waxy bloom that can be removed by rubbing. Also known as 'bloom'.

Pseudobulb: a thickening at the base of the stem, resembling a bulb but not bulb-like in internal structure.

Puberulous: covered with very short hairs, thin and not very obvious.

Pubescent: covered with short, thin hairs, not very dense, resembling down.

Raceme: unbranched inflorescence made up of flowers the stalks of which are inserted at different levels along an elongated axis.

Rachis: the axis of the inflorescence.

Radicular: of, or pertaining to, the roots.

Recurved: curved backwards.

Reflexed: curved upwards.

Relict: a formerly widespread species that persisted through a cataclysm (e.g. a glaciation) thanks to a very local and stable habitat area.

Reniform: kidney-shaped.

Resupinate: rotated through 180°.

Reticulate: a surface or an organ covered with net-like lines (see *Goodyera repens*).

Retinacle: an alternative name for viscidium; the viscous or sticky discoid part of the rostellum, fixed to the pollinia or to their stalks, functioning to attach the pollinia to a pollinator.

Revolute: rolled downwards.

Rhizome: elongated subterranean stem, giving rise to aerial stems and adventitious roots.

Rhomboidal: lozenge-shaped.

Rim: band of submarginal hairs, sometimes contrastily coloured, on the lips of some *Ophrys*.

Ripicolous: growing on the margins of rivers.

Root-tuber (often simply '**tuber**'): subterranean thickening of a root or a stem, used as nutritive store and with buds that will produce new leafy stems.

Rosette: a group of spreading leaves, arranged in a circle, often at the base of the stem.

Rostellum: in orchids, part of the column, sometimes shaped like a beak, sometimes ± completely covered with a sticky substance (see also viscidium); structurally, the rostellum is a modified sterile stamen.

Saprophytic: feeding on decomposing organic matter.

Scale: a small, membranous structure, analogous to a leaf or bract.

Scolopaxoid: recalling *Ophrys scolopax*.

Scrub: in this guide, plant associations with woody shrubs *c.* 1-4m tall, mostly closed and difficult to penetrate, but not dense throughout, growing on acid or alkaline substrates.

Scutellum: a small, shield-shaped structure, hence scutellate.

Scutiform: shield-shaped.

Self-pollination: transfer of pollen from the stamen to a stigma in the same flower or another flower on the same plant (= autogamy).

Sepal: the outer sections of the perianth; in orchids there are 3 sepals, the dorsal or upper sepal and two symmetrical lateral sepals.

Sepaloid: sepal-like.

Sessile: stalkless; without a petiole (leaf) or pedicel (flower).

Sheathing: a leaf, the lamina (leaf blade) of which surrounds the stem, at least at the base.

Shoulder: enlargement of the base of the lip in some species of *Ophrys*.

Siliceous: containing silica.

Spatulate: flat and paddle- or spoon-shaped at the tip.

Speciation: processes of species formation.

Specular stage: see fig 13.

Spike: inflorescence formed with sessile flowers inserted at different levels along an elongated axis.

Spirally: in a spiral. A spirally-arranged inflorescence (e.g. in *Spiranthes spiralis*) has each successive flower inserted at less than 180° to the one below and thus twists around the axis like a spiral staircase.

Spur: tubular projection located at the base and behind the lip in some orchids.

Stamen: the male reproductive male organ in flowering plants, comprising a filament and an anther, the latter containing the pollen.

Staminode: a rudimentary stamen, often aborted, without pollen and thus sterile; shape very varied depending on the species.

Staminodial (point): a small dark blotch or spot terminating the staminode and visible on the upper border of the stigmatic cavity, principally in some members of the genus *Ophrys*.

Station: a site, variable in extent, where a species occurs.

Sterile: not producing seeds; by extension, a male organ that does not produce pollen or a female organ that does not produce ovules.

Stigma (or **stigmatic surface**): extremity, often glandular, of the style, on which the pollen is deposited; forms part of the column in orchids.

Stolon: spindly stem, prostrate, often subterranean, which can root at its tip, giving rise to a new plant.

Stoloniferous: with stolons, bearing stolons.

Style: structure connecting the ovary to the stigma.

Sub–: prefix meaning near.

Substrate: superficial part of the soil on which plants grow.

Subulate: awl-shaped, being narrow, more or less flattened and ending in a very acute point.

Symbiosis: mutually beneficial association between two organisms of different species.

Sympatric: species occurring in the same area or whose ranges overlap. Ant.: allopatric.

Syntopic: organisms occurring at the same stations.

Sympodial: a form of growth in which the growing point of a stem either terminates in an inflorescence or dies each year, growth being continued by a new lateral growing point. Ant.: monopodial.

Synapomorphy: a character which is shared by all basal members of a clade and is derived from their common ancestor.

Taxon (plural **Taxa**): a systematic unit at any rank, although most used for ranks below that of genus, complex, group, species, subspecies…

Taxonomy: the science of the classification of living organisms into hierarchical groups.

Tepal: a perianth segment, usually used when the sepals and petals are similar.

Tetrad: group of 4 pollen grains originating by meiosis from a pollen mother cell.

Theca: a pocket or pouch containing 1-2 pollinia.

Thermophilous: thriving in warm conditions.

Throat: the entrance to the spur or stigmatic cavity at the base of the lip.

Tomentose: covered with a thick, cottony down, formed by soft, intertwined hairs, like felt.

Trifoliate: divided into 3 lobes by 2 incisions.

Triploid: cells with three sets of chromosomes (3n); also applied to organisms, all cells of which are in this state.

Truncated: abruptly cut transversally.

Undulate: a surface alternately convex and concave, mostly at the edges. Ant.: flat (surface), straight (border).

Unguis: the slender base of a petal, often the lip.

Velvety: covered with very small, dense hairs, similar to velvet.

Viscidium: in orchids the viscous or sticky discoid part of the rostellum, fixed to the pollinia or to their stalks, functioning to attach the pollinia to a pollinator, usually an insect; also known as the retinacle.

Villous: covered with rather long, flexible hairs.

Veined: with visible veins.

Vicariants: allopatric taxa originating from the same ancestral species.

Xeric: dry.

Xenogamy: another term for allogamy (cross-fertilisation). Ant: autogamy.

Xerophitic: adapted to dry habitats.

Zygomorphic: having a single plane of symmetry.

Index of scientific names

639